TAX PLANNING

WITH PRECEDENTS

Socrates: The Tyrant hopes, does he not, that the taxes his subjects have to pay will impoverish them, so that they will be compelled to give their minds to earning their daily bread, and not to conspiring against him.

Glaucon: Why, obviously.

Plato, Republic, VIII, 567

And it is not so becoming to the dignity of a king to reign over beggars, as to reign over rich and happy subjects.

Sir Thomas More, Utopia

POTTER AND MONROE: TAX PLANNING

Fourth Edition

Cumulative Supplements to this book will be published from time to time and if you purchased it direct from the publishers you will be advised when Supplements are issued.

If you did not purchase the main work direct from the publishers and would still like to be notified when Supplements are published, please fill in and return this card.

N.B.—This card need only be returned in cases where the book has not been purchased direct from the publishers

BLOCK CAPITALS PLEASE

Name ....

Address ....

....

Date ....

Name of Bookseller ....

PRINTED PAPER

SWEET & MAXWELL LTD.

11 New Fetter Lane

London E.C.4

TAX PLANNING

WITH

PRECEDENTS

BY

D. C. POTTER, LL.B.
of the Middle Temple and Lincoln's Inn,
Barrister-at-Law

H. H. MONROE, M.A.
One of Her Majesty's Counsel,
of the Middle Temple and the Northern Circuit

AND

STEWART BATES, M.A.
of the Middle Temple and the Northern Circuit,
Barrister-at-Law

FOURTH EDITION

LONDON
SWEET & MAXWELL
1963

AUSTRALIA
The Law Book Co. of Australasia Pty Ltd
Sydney : Melbourne : Brisbane

CANADA AND U.S.A.
The Carswell Company Ltd.
Toronto

INDIA
N M. Tripathi Private Ltd.
Bombay

ISRAEL
Steimatzky's Agency Ltd.
Tel Aviv

NEW ZEALAND
Sweet & Maxwell (N.Z.) Ltd.
Wellington

PAKISTAN
Pakistan Law House
Karachi

Published in 1963 by
Sweet & Maxwell Limited of
11 New Fetter Lane London
and printed in Great Britain
by The Eastern Press Limited
of London and Reading

PREFACE

THE function of the present edition, as of previous editions, of *Tax Planning*, is to illustrate the possibilities : to show what can be done and suggest ways of doing it. But this book is not a collection of ready-made schemes to be picked off the peg and used in any circumstances, and those who regard it as that ignore its inevitable limitations and the waywardness of its subject-matter. All tax problems merit individual attention, and most are solved only by a compromise between conflicting requirements. It cannot be too strongly emphasised that simply to copy a precedent from *Tax Planning* is no substitute for a detailed consideration of all the circumstances of the problem.

Since the third edition was published in 1959, Parliament has created a great deal of new revenue law. Dividend stripping and similar activities have been restricted, the " golden handshake " has been reduced to mere alloy, post-cessation receipts of trades and professions—with one exception—have been brought into charge, property dealers have been swathed in some well-nigh incomprehensible enactments, short-term capital gains have been brought into charge to tax, Schedule A has been condemned to death and replaced by a new Case VIII of Schedule D which applies to premiums as well as rents, income tax and surtax have been reduced, and, with less publicity, profits tax has been increased. Stamp duty has been substantially reduced. As for estate duty, the five-year period has been modified, immovables overseas have lost their position as an avoidance device, and the exemption relating to gifts made in consideration of marriage has been restricted. All this has necessitated, not a rewriting of *Tax Planning*, but a careful scrutiny, to see that the new hazards are clearly charted. In addition, the editors have added a short chapter on insurance, which is now resorted to more often than formerly in making arrangements to reduce estate duty liability, and have added a section on the Variation of Trusts Act, 1958. The opportunity has also been taken to consider the numerous suggestions that have been made by readers, and amend or add

v

to the text accordingly. The editors wish to record their gratitude
to all those who have made suggestions: it is largely due to them
that the fourth edition contains much more information than the
first.

When *Tax Planning* first appeared, some critics averred that
it offended against decency by stripping the veil of mystery from
its subject-matter. The authors remain unrepentant. Law should
be reasonably intelligible: if it is shrouded in impenetrable
authorities, or secreted in the interstices of procedure, it lacks the
qualities of clarity and universal application that are at the present
time more than ever necessary. The complexity of fiscal legislation
and the seemingly insuperable problem of drafting a Finance Act
that is both clear and comprehensive impose on those who give
advice on this subject a particular duty to be clear and decisive,
and to resist the temptation to utter incantations that barely make
sense even to the initiated. Where so much is inevitably obscure
there can be no justification for an artificially maintained fog which
it would baffle a twentieth-century Dickens to dispel.

There is another result of the growing complexity of successive
Finance Acts, to which attention may be directed. When those
who administer are no less uncertain than those who advise,
departmental practice becomes as important as the law, and, to
adopt the language of Coke (4 Inst. 41), the " uncertain and crooked
cord of discretion " displaces the " golden and straight mete wand
of the law." It is sometimes suggested that those who seek to
guide others through the jungle of fiscal law and practice perform
an anti-social function. May not the fault lie with those who
frame the laws? The authors repeat the suggestion made in their
Preface to the third edition of *Tax Planning*, that the machinery
for framing, debating and enacting tax legislation is in need of
overhaul.

It is possible that in the near future our tax system will be
reformed. If such reform results in simplification of the law affecting covenants, settlements and other documents relating to income
and property, then, provided such simplification is accompanied
by a lowering of rates and a fairer distribution of the burden, the
authors will not complain, even though much of what this book
contains will be made obsolete. But a parent is frequently reluctant

to mutilate his own child. Should there be a further edition of this book, the promised reform having in the meantime been carried through, major rewriting of the text is likely to be required. It is better that this work be entrusted to editors who will not be inhibited by lingering parental fondness. The original authors jointly lay down their pen for the last time, asserting once more that the defects of this work so far have been their own, the merits largely attributable to the numerous kind suggestions and criticisms of friends and colleagues.

H. H. M.
D. C. P.

September 1963.

EXTRACT FROM
THE PREFACE TO THE FIRST EDITION

"No man in this country is under the smallest obligation, moral or other, so to arrange his legal relations to his business or to his property as to enable the Inland Revenue to put the largest possible shovel into his stores. The Inland Revenue is not slow—and quite rightly—to take every advantage which is open to it under the taxing statutes for the purpose of depleting the taxpayer's pocket. And the taxpayer is, in like manner, entitled to be astute to prevent, so far as he honestly can, the depletion of his means by the Inland Revenue." (*Per* Lord Clyde, Lord President of the Court of Session, in *Ayrshire Pullman Motor Services and D. M. Ritchie* v. *I. R. C.* (1920) 14 Tax Cas. 754, 763-4.)

THIS book has a twofold purpose. It is intended first to provide the legal draftsman with a supplementary precedent book for use where considerations of tax or estate duty arise outside the scope of the standard works on conveyancing precedents. Secondly, it is hoped that the book will be of value to a wider class of reader: to all who are called upon to deal with the disposition or management of property which bears a heavy burden of tax and estate duty and wish, before taking specialist advice, to understand the principles concerned and to visualise the type of disposition likely to be advantageous. In order to preserve the book's practical nature, the text has been built round the precedents. It is not merely a precedent book, however, and the policy has been to provide at the beginning of each chapter an account of the tax problems arising out of the particular topic. It is hoped that thereby the book will be of use to all who deal with matters of taxation.

There are some forty precedents, grouped in eight chapters. So far as possible, complete precedents are given, even at the cost of some repetition. On the other hand, this book is not intended to supplant the existing books of conveyancing precedents, but to be complementary to them. The editor of conveyancing precedents is bound to have regard primarily to established conveyancing practice; he cannot attempt to deal fully with tax and estate duty, because revenue law changes so rapidly, and because also a precedent dealing with tax inevitably requires greater adaptation to individual circumstances than the ordinary precedents. There has of recent years been a growing realisation that the precedents in common use are out of date as far as tax law is concerned: this book reflects that realisation.

Equally important is the other purpose of this book: to describe the principles involved in what may for the want of a better name be called "tax planning," in such a way that the reader may comprehend them without previously having a specialised knowledge of this field. For this reason, footnotes have, so far as possible, been reduced to the minimum, and the text and the precedents have set one against the other so that theory and practice are to some extent balanced. It is hoped that thereby the book may be read through without the reader being hindered by the interposition of the precedents.

By the expression "tax planning" nothing more sinister is meant than that a man should make an intelligent appreciation of the incidence of tax and should take it into account as a relevant factor in planning what dispositions he will make of his property as between himself and the members of his family.   Too often prejudice is substituted for reason in the discussion of this topic.   There was a time when the onus of justifying taxation rested on the State.   All taxation was an evil only to be tolerated on the grounds of extreme necessity and subject to certain stringent conditions as to its imposition.   Today, when the unhappy notion that the State knows best is the basis of much of what passes for thought in the political world—by no means confined to those who subscribe to the notion in its extreme forms—it seems to be widely accepted that the onus of proving a claim for exemption from or a reduction of tax rests on the subject.   From this premise it is but a short step to the view that any attempt which a man makes to reduce the burden of tax, regardless of the character of the method he adopts, is an anti-social act deserving unqualified condemnation.

It is submitted that if we are to be taxed according to law—if John Hampden's protest is not to have been in vain—the introduction of pseudo-moral judgments into the administration of fiscal measures is to be deprecated.   While private property is recognised, we must also recognise a man's right to dispose of his own as he will within the limits allowed by law.   If one lawful course involves the payment of more tax and another less, the choice between them raises no moral issue.   What the law permits cannot, in a branch of the law to which equity is a stranger, be reprehensible.

Envy, hatred and malice are seldom reliable guides in framing or administering law, least of all fiscal law.   Let indignation be reserved for, and indeed lavished upon, those guilty of fraud or dishonesty, who seek to cloak the true character of their transactions or who create a fictitious form in order to avoid the liability attaching to the disposition which they have in reality effected.   For the rest, for every disposition lawfully made, whatever its implications for the tax gatherer, there should be neither praise nor blame; only that "indifference" which the compilers of the Book of Common Prayer recognised as an essential requisite of the sound administration of our laws.

Political issues are not in point in a work of this kind.   Whether our fiscal legislation reflects any coherent political or social policy is open to doubt.   But haphazard though the operation of the rules may be, there is a slight bias in favour of spreading wealth within the family. Problems of tax planning should normally be approached by regarding the family rather than the individual as the taxpaying entity, and on this basis, as some of the precedents contained in this book show, a saving of tax and duty may often be effected.   To suggest possible lines of approach is the purpose of this book rather than to provide ready-made solutions.   Individual requirements are infinite; it is the practitioner's function to satisfy them.   The true function of a book of this kind can only be to illustrate the possibilities.

One other basic principle must be stated clearly: a familiar rule that is, however, frequently forgotten. A man cannot eat his cake and have it. Moreover, it is not the function of his lawyer to devise a scheme whereby this fact of life is falsified. If a man disposes of his property for another's benefit, certain tax results may follow; but the results cannot be achieved unless the disposition is in the first place effected not as a fiction but as a fact.

CONTENTS

1. DEEDS OF COVENANT   1

Nature and effect of deeds of covenant—Statutory restrictions on covenants
—Suggestions of Royal Commission—Recovery of tax paid—Annual payments
—Income tax of the covenantor—Surtax of the covenantor—Income tax of the
covenantee—Surtax of the covenantee—Possible disadvantage—The amount
covenanted—Change of rate of income tax—Failure to deduct tax—" Tax-free "
payments under deeds of covenant—Calculation of refund to trustees under
the " *Re Pettit* " principle—Expressions meaning " free of tax "—Payments free
of surtax—Pre-war deeds or wills—Covenants and estate duty—Stamp duty on
covenants—What can be done by a covenant.

4. Discretionary Trusts   181

Requirements for a discretionary trust—The class of beneficiaries—Powers and trusts for a wide class—Infant children of the settlor as beneficiaries—The settlor or his wife as beneficiaries : Income tax—The settlor's wife as beneficiary : estate duty—Separated wives—Administration of discretionary trusts—Insurance by the trustees of the settlement—Private companies—Estate duty on shares in controlled company—Controlled companies : reduction of duties —Money owed by company to settlor—Exempt private companies—Control and director control.

5. Marriage Settlements   225

Estate duty—Persons within the marriage consideration—Death before the settlement is finally constituted—Tax on marriage settlements—Stamp duty.

6. INSURANCE POLICIES   245

Income tax—Estate duty—Gifts of policies—Section 34 of the Finance Act,
1959—Policies as separate estates: non-aggregation—Conversion of existing
policies—Annuity and policy combined—Insurance against estate duty.

7. VARIATION OF EXISTING SETTLEMENTS   264

The surrender of a life interest in possession to the remainderman—The
surrender of a reversionary life interest—The disclaimer of a life interest—The
release of an annuity—Advancements—Partition of the trust fund between
the life-tenant and remaindermen—The sale of a reversion to the life-tenant—
Applications to the court—Variation of Trusts Act, 1958—Partition with the
approval of the court—Tenant for life past age of childbearing—Accountability of trustees—Other transactions with existing settlements.

10. WILLS 448

Burden of estate duty—" Free of duty " provisions—Annuities—Life
interest bequeathed to widow—Supplementing the widow's life interest—Payment
of estate duty by widow—Property settled by will.

APPENDIX

TABLE OF CASES

TABLE OF STATUTES

CHAPTER 1

DEEDS OF COVENANT

Nature and effect of Deeds of Covenant

A Deed of Covenant in the sense in which the term is used in this chapter is a deed whereby a person binds himself to make periodical payments to another. A deed is used because it provides a means by which a promise may be made legally binding upon the promisor even though made voluntarily. The special force of a deed, that it makes a bare promise binding in law, is traditionally allied to certain stringent requirements as to form: the promise must be in writing, signed, sealed and delivered by the promisor. Today the former solemnity of parchment adorned with green silk and verified by the crest of the covenantor embossed in red wax to the accompaniment of the ritualistic utterance, " I deliver this as my Act and Deed," is usually lacking. The covenant is often a printed form, scarcely larger than a bank-note. The seal is usually a printed mark. The solemn words are left unsaid.

The effect of a deed of covenant is to transfer part of the covenantor's income to the covenantee. The annual sum covenanted to be paid is taken from the top slice of the covenantor's income for tax purposes and is added to the income of the covenantee. The covenantor's total income will be reduced by the amount he covenants to pay, so that he will save income tax and surtax—if he pays surtax—on that amount, and may also enjoy a consequential reduction of the rate of surtax payable on the balance of his income. The covenantee will be able to obtain, in accordance with his personal circumstances, the benefit of the personal reliefs and allowances in respect of the income which he receives under the covenant, assuming that the total reliefs to which he is entitled have not already been given to him in respect of his other income. Such an arrangement is open to abuse and the legislature has accordingly laid down certain limits within which covenants may be effectively operated for tax purposes. The purpose of this chapter is to discuss and illustrate the form of various deeds of covenant which can be effective under the existing law as a means of saving tax.

An authoritative statement on covenants as transfers of income is to be found in the Final Report of the Royal Commission on the Taxation of Profits and Income, the relevant passage from which is set out in the Appendix at the end of this book. The extent to which deeds of covenant are made use of is shown by the fact that in any one year the total amount subject to deeds of covenant (other than deeds of covenant in favour of charities) is about £30 million before deduction of tax. The loss to the revenue in taxation is between £15 and £20

1

million of which rather more than a third is income tax and the rest
surtax: see *Hansard*, H. of C., May 19, 1960, Vol. 623, Col. 152.

Statutory restrictions on covenants

The principal tax advantage to be derived from a deed of covenant
is that the covenantor's taxable income will be reduced and the
beneficiary under the covenant will receive income on which he will pay
tax, if at all, at a lower rate than the rate of tax which would have been
payable by the covenantor. The restrictions imposed by the statute are
designed to ensure that this advantage will accrue only to those taxpayers
who genuinely intend to make a gift of part of their incomes, and not
to those who contrive to cloak other transactions in the form of a
covenant.

(i) *The period of payment*

The first restriction is concerned with the time during which
payments under a deed of covenant are to last. Under section 392
of the Income Tax Act, 1952, income payable under a covenant "for
a period which cannot exceed six years" is to be treated for tax purposes
as the income of the covenantor, if living, and not as the income of the
beneficiary. To ensure their effectiveness covenants are usually drafted
to last for seven years; hence the common expression "a seven-year
covenant."

But it cannot be over-emphasised that it is the period during which
income is to be paid under the covenant, and not the period of the
covenant itself, which is material for the purposes of section 392. In
computing the period during which income is payable under a covenant
regard must be had to the dates on which the first payment due under
the deed and the last payment are payable; to avoid the section the
period between these two dates must not be a period which is bound
to be less than six years. Particular care must be taken in drafting
a deed of covenant if the date selected from which the period of seven
years is to run is a date earlier than the date of the execution of the
deed: see *I.R.C.* v. *St. Luke's Hostel Trustees* (1930) 15 Tax Cas. 682.
In such a case the first payment due under the deed cannot be payable
before the deed is executed while the last payment may be due six years
and one day after a date prior to the execution of the deed. Thus,
though the deed may provide for seven payments in all to be made,
the period separating the first from the last payment may be less than
six years. Even the experienced may be excused if in such circumstances
they play for safety and make such covenants eight- rather than seven-
year covenants. As to the effect of a covenant to make payments each
year during a period, see *I. R. C.* v. *Hobhouse* [1956] 1 W.L.R. 1393; 36
Tax Cas. 648, and *cf. I. R. C.* v. *Verdon-Roe* (1962) 41 A.T.C. 342.

So long as the payments could have extended over more than six
years when the covenant was made, it makes no difference that in the

events which happen the duration of the covenant is very much less than six years: see *I. R. C.* v. *Black* [1940] 4 All E.R. 445; 23 Tax Cas. 715. If, therefore, a deed of covenant provides for payments to be made:

" during joint lives or the period of seven years whichever shall be the shorter,"

income payable under the covenant will not become the covenantor's income and the tax advantage will not be lost if in fact the period is terminated by the death of either party. Nor will this be the result if the period is terminated before the expiry of six years by the mutual consent of the parties. Provided that the deed of covenant does not in terms provide for its own revocation (a point to be dealt with in paragraph (ii) below), the possibility of its revocation by mutual consent will produce no adverse tax result while the covenant remains in force.

If a deed of covenant provides for the payment of a large sum initially and smaller annual payments subsequently, the large initial payment must be regarded separately as a payment for one year only and will therefore be caught by the section : see *D'Ambrumenil* v. *I. R. C.* [1940] 1 K.B. 850; 23 Tax Cas. 440.[1] But the mere fluctuation of the annual sum payable from year to year will not cause the section to operate if the amount is fixed by reference to a constant formula, for example a constant fraction of the covenantor's income : see *D'Ambrumenil's* case and *Black's* case, *supra*; or similarly, if it is a constant fraction of the covenantee's other income.

(ii) *Revocable covenants*

The second restriction is contained in section 404 (1) of the Income Tax Act, 1952, which provides that " if and so long as the terms of any settlement are such that—

(a) any person has or may have power, whether immediately or in the future, and whether with or without the consent of any other person, to revoke or otherwise determine the settlement or any provision thereof and, in the event of the exercise of the power, the settlor or the wife or husband of the settlor will or may cease to be liable to make any annual payments payable by virtue or in consequence of the settlement ; or

(b) the settlor or the wife or husband of the settlor may, whether immediately or in the future, cease, on the payment of a penalty, to be liable to make any annual payments payable by virtue or in consequence of any provision of the settlement,

any sums payable by the settlor or the wife or husband of the settlor by virtue or in consequence of that provision of the settlement in any year of assessment shall be treated for all the purposes of this Act as

---

[1] *Cf. I. R. C.* v. *Mallaby-Deeley* [1938] 3 All E.R. 463; 23 Tax Cas. 153. In the Court of Appeal (55 T.L.R. 293; 23 Tax Cas. 163) the sums payable were held to be instalments of capital and not " annual payments " at all. And *cf. I. R. C.* v. *Prince-Smith* [1943] 1 All E.R. 434; 25 Tax Cas. 84.

the income of the settlor for that year and not as the income of any
other person." By virtue of section 21 (1) of the Finance Act, 1958,
section 404 (1) of the Income Tax Act, 1952, extends to a case where any
person has power to diminish the amount of the covenanted sum.

Section 404 (1) has been quoted in full to illustrate two features
common to most of the statutory provisions affecting the tax position
under deeds of covenant. The word "settlement" which runs
throughout the relevant legislation is given a wide meaning; it includes
"any disposition, trust, covenant, agreement or arrangement." [2]
For the purpose of applying the statutory provisions, therefore, a deed
of covenant falls within the definition of "settlement" as will most
other arrangements for the payment of annual sums designed to produce
the same tax results as a deed of covenant.

The second point illustrated by section 404 is that in considering
the operation of deeds of covenant the identity of husband and wife for
tax purposes must be remembered. The relevant sections carry the
identity even further than the ordinary tax rules.

The effect of section 404 as amended is that any express power to
revoke the covenant or to diminish the amount payable under the
covenant will deprive it of its effectiveness as a method of saving tax.
The proviso to section 404 (1) makes the section inoperative if the
power of revocation cannot be exercised within six years from the time
when the first annual payment under the covenant becomes payable;
the section will, however, operate as soon as the power can be exercised
after the six years.

To cause section 404 (1) to operate the power of revocation must be
a power to revoke or determine contained in the deed of covenant. The
power which covenantor and beneficiary together have of mutually
revoking the deed of covenant is not, therefore, within the scope of the
section. Nor is the power of shareholders to wind up a company within
the scope of the section where a member of the company has covenanted
to make annual payments equal to the dividends received by him in
respect of his shares : see *I. R. C.* v. *Wolfson* [1949] 1 All E.R. 865;
31 Tax Cas. 141. The determination of the "settlement" in such
circumstances would not be by virtue of any power of revocation contained in the terms of the "settlement."

Where the operation of section 404 (1) is suspended in accordance
with the proviso because the power of revocation is not exercisable
within six years from the date of the covenant, the time during which
the power to revoke the covenant is not exercisable cannot be extended
retrospectively : see *Taylor* v. *I. R. C.* [1945] 1 All E.R. 698; 27
Tax Cas. 93. To satisfy the proviso the restriction on the exercise of
the power of revocation must be contained in the same "settlement"

---

[2] See s. 411 (2) and *cf. Thomas* v. *Marshall* [1953] A.C. 543; 34 Tax Cas. 178;
Yates v. *Starkey* [1951] Ch. 465; 32 Tax Cas. 38; and *Hood-Barrs* v. *I. R. C.*
[1946] 2 All E.R. 768; 27 Tax Cas. 385.

as the original power, whether the " settlement " consists of one or
several documents. In this connection reference may also be made to
I. R. C. v. *Nicolson* [1953] 1 W.L.R. 809; 34 Tax Cas. 354, in which
it was held that a deed of release which attempted to extend the period
of restriction on revocation operated as a new settlement.[3]

(iii) *Discretionary covenants*

Until the passing of the Finance Act, 1958, it was often advantageous
to execute a deed of covenant in favour of trustees who were directed by
the deed to apply the income by distributing it among a discretionary
class of persons, of whom the spouse of the covenantor could be one.
Now, by virtue of section 22 of the Finance Act, 1958, a covenant is
ineffective for tax purposes if the spouse of the covenantor (or the
covenantor himself) is a possible recipient of income thereunder. This
section applies even if the spouse is living apart from the covenantor.
And, generally, there is no tax advantage in including unmarried, infant
children of the covenantor among the discretionary class of persons. Any
payments made to such children would be treated as the income of the
covenantor for tax purposes.[4] Apart from these limitations discretionary covenants may be effective instruments of tax saving although
the Royal Commission on the Taxation of Profits and Income thought
that this should no longer be so.[5]

(iv) *Accumulated payments*

Another type of covenant which is rendered ineffective as a method
of saving tax is a covenant which provides for the making of annual
payments to be accumulated. Under section 407 of the Income Tax
Act, 1952, sums paid by a " settlor " (*i.e.*, by definition, a covenantor),
which would otherwise be allowable in any year as a deduction in computing his total income for surtax purposes, are not to be so allowed if
they exceed the amount of income arising under the " settlement "
in that year and distributed so as to form part of some other taxpayer's
income. A covenant to pay annual sums to trustees upon trust to
accumulate the sums paid will therefore be ineffective as a method of
saving tax.

What is meant by income being " distributed " in this context is
defined in section 411 (3). Sums are distributed if paid " to any persons
. . . in such manner that they fall to be treated . . . as the income of
those persons." The precise scope of these words is obscure; but it is
submitted that sums applied for the benefit of a beneficiary would be
" distributed." Thus sums would be applied for the benefit of a
beneficiary if they were used to purchase in the name of the beneficiary
National Savings Certificates or to pay premiums on a life assurance

---

[3] Contrast *F. C. Scott* v. *I. R. C.* (1957) 37 Tax Cas. 486.
[4] See s. 397 of the I. T. A., 1952, as amended.
[5] Final Report, Cmd. 9474, para. 156: see *post*, p. 487.

policy effected for the benefit of the beneficiary and being his absolute property.

It is considered that a distinction must be drawn between those covenants where the trustees have no discretion as to the amounts of income to be allotted to each beneficiary, and those where they have such a discretion. In the former type of covenant, the trustees are a mere conduit pipe for the transfer of income from the covenantor to the beneficiary: the income is income of the beneficiary for tax purposes as soon as it is paid to the trustees, and even if they retain it, there is no room for the application of section 407. But in the latter type of covenant, the income does not become income of a particular beneficiary until the trustees have irrevocably exercised their discretion in his favour: see Cornwell v. Barry (1955) 36 Tax Cas. 268. Therefore in this type of case care should be exercised by the trustees to ensure that all sums payable to them in any year of assessment are paid out in that year to the beneficiaries.[6] It is understood the distinction just mentioned is in accordance with the practice of the Revenue.[7]

Moreover under section 407 (2) any sums paid to a company connected with the " settlement " are to be treated as if paid to the trustees of the " settlement." This means that any device involving the settlement of shares in a private company in conjunction with a covenant to make annual payments to the company and the accumulation by the company of the sums so paid will be as ineffective in saving tax as a straightforward covenant to make payments to trustees upon trust to accumulate the sums paid.

(v) Covenant for child of covenantor

Section 397 of the Income Tax Act, 1952 (formerly section 21 of the Finance Act, 1936), which as amended by section 20 of the Finance Act, 1958, provides that any income paid in pursuance of a covenant to or for the benefit of a child of the covenantor who at the time of the payment is an infant and unmarried shall be treated as the covenantor's and not the child's income for tax purposes. It follows that no tax advantage will be gained by a parent covenanting to pay sums to or for the benefit of his child until after the child's twenty-first birthday or marriage.

Formerly, if a parent entered into a seven-year covenant in favour of his child in the year of assessment in which the child was born, the sum payable in the first year (if paid not later than April 5) was a good deduction for tax purposes from the parent's income and was treated as the infant child's income for that year; but the six subsequent annual payments were treated for tax purposes as the parent's income.

[6] Delay may also have the result that any claim on behalf of the infant beneficiary to recover from the Revenue tax deducted by the covenantor will fail: cf. Cornwell v. Barry (1955) 36 Tax Cas. 268.
[7] See a note by Mr. D. C. Potter in [1957] British Tax Review 281.

The effect of section 20 (2) of the Finance Act, 1958, is that payment made by a parent under a covenant in the year in which his child is born and applied for the child's benefit, no less than the payments made in the six subsequent years, will be treated as the parent's income for tax purposes. But payments under a covenant to a child who has attained twenty-one will be the child's and not the parent's income notwithstanding that the child was at the commencement of the fiscal year an infant and unmarried. It is no longer necessary to wait until April 5 following the child's twenty-first birthday before the parent can with advantage make covenanted payments to his child.

Any provision whereby the annual payments under a covenant are to be accumulated for the child's ultimate benefit is rendered ineffective as a means of saving tax by section 407 of the Income Tax Act, 1952.

In this context " child " includes a stepchild, an adopted child and an illegitimate child: see section 403. It has been held that the child of a former marriage of the wife of the settlor is a stepchild notwithstanding that the child's father is alive: *I. R. C.* v. *Russell* (1955) 36 Tax Cas. 83. If, notwithstanding section 397, a parent covenants to make annual payments to or for the benefit of his infant child, the normal rules regarding the deduction of tax will apply, but no repayment claim in respect of reliefs and allowances can be made on the child's behalf. Since for tax purposes the child will be treated as having no income from this source, no question of restriction of the parent's claim for child allowance under section 212 will arise because of the covenant: note subsection (4) of section 212.

(vi) *Special surtax provisions*

Under section 415 of the Income Tax Act, 1952, unless sums payable under a deed of covenant are payable to an individual for his own use or applicable for the benefit of a named individual or individuals, or for the benefit of the child or children of a named individual, they will not be admissible as deductions in computing the covenantor's income for surtax purposes. It is also provided by the section that the beneficiary must not be in the service of or accustomed to act as the solicitor or agent of the covenantor.

Section 415 has therefore two principal effects in relation to deeds of covenant. First, it is not possible for a surtax payer to make a deed of covenant in favour of his solicitor or servant so that the sums paid under the deed will be deductible in computing his liability for surtax.[8] Secondly, so far as saving surtax goes, covenants in favour of charities are no longer valid as a means of making contributions to charities at the expense of the Revenue; previously a surtax payer liable to tax at the top rate could apply part of his income in making charitable contributions

[8] This provision is intended to nullify the effect of the decision in *I. R. C.* v. *Duke of Westminster* [1936] A.C. 1; 19 Tax Cas. 490.

at little real cost to himself although the charity receiving the contributions would obtain the gross amount of the covenanted payments. A covenant in favour of a charity still yields a benefit so far as income tax is concerned : the payer makes a gross payment less income tax at the standard rate and the charity can recover from the Revenue the tax so deducted, thus obtaining the full benefit of the gross payment.[9] Provided that the covenantor has sufficient taxed income out of which to make the annual payments due under the covenant, section 169 will apply and the only cost to the covenantor will be the net amount of the covenant.

(vii) *Covenants for dependent relatives of the covenantor*

A covenant in favour of a relative may be used in a proper case in order to effect a saving of tax. An important provision is, however, contained in section 216 of the Income Tax Act, 1952, which gives relief to the extent of tax at the standard rate on £75 in respect of a relative incapacitated by old age or infirmity from maintaining himself or herself and maintained by the taxpayer at his own expense, or in respect of his wife's widowed mother if so maintained, whether she is incapacitated or not.[10] If the relative or mother-in-law has a total income (whether by virtue of a covenant or otherwise) exceeding £180 a year, the taxpayer's relief is scaled down, and if the total income exceeds £255 a year, the relief is lost.[11] The amount to be stated in a covenant in favour of a person so maintained therefore requires careful consideration.

Suggestions of Royal Commission

In their Final Report the Royal Commission on the Taxation of Profits and Income [12] expressed dissatisfaction that the control over covenants for annual payments to relatives of the covenantor only extended to covenants in favour of an unmarried child under twenty-one, and not to other relatives of the covenantor. The Report points out that " the very circumstances of the family connection make it possible for abuses of the system to grow up and for covenants which satisfy all the legal requirements of a transfer of income to conceal private understandings by virtue of which the benefit of the income never really leaves, or is somehow returned to, the covenantor." [13] To meet any such abuses the Commission recommended a procedural, not a substantive, change. If the covenantee is a child, grandchild or other member of the covenantor's family, the covenantor should be required by statute to produce annually a formal declaration made by himself and the recipient

---

9 Exemption from tax on annual payments received is available to charities under s. 447, Income Tax Act, 1952.
10 See s. 216 of the Income Tax Act, 1952, as amended by s. 18 (1) of the Finance Act, 1960.
11 Finance Act, 1961, s. 15; Finance Act, 1963, s. 12 (4).
12 Cmd. 9474. See *post*, p. 487.
13 *Ibid.*, para. 158.

of the covenanted payments to the effect that there exists no agreement or understanding, whether or not regarded as having legal force, by virtue of which the benefit of any part of the payments is returned, directly or indirectly, to the covenantor or any other person designated by him.[14]

By reason of the provisions of section 22 of the Finance Act, 1958, discretionary covenants under which the spouse of the covenantor is a member of the discretionary class are ineffective for tax purposes even where the discretion is not exercised in favour of the spouse. And discretionary covenants for relatives, not including the spouse of the covenantor, may attract the attention of the legislature in the future. The Commission stated that a discretionary covenant failed to secure something which in their opinion was implicit in the idea of a genuine transfer of income when effected by annual payments under covenant, namely, that the income in question became the regular income of someone else for a commensurate period.[15] In paragraph 157 the Commission recommended that " a statutory provision should be added to the code for the purpose of rendering covenants of this kind nugatory for tax purposes."

Recovery of tax paid

One feature common to all the sections of the Income Tax Act which cause annual payments made under deeds of covenant to be treated as the covenantor's income for tax purposes, other than section 415, may be noted. If by virtue of one of the relevant statutory provisions covenanted payments are so treated, the covenantor has a right to recover from the person or persons to whom the payments are made the amount of the additional tax which he is required to pay.[16] If, for example, a parent makes a covenant in favour of trustees for his infant child and the sums paid under the covenant are treated as the parent's and not the child's income by virtue of section 397, the parent will be entitled to recover from the trustees the difference between the tax he is actually called upon to pay and what he would have paid if the covenant had been effective in reducing his income for tax purposes.

An important point in relation to deeds of covenant which are intended to save tax should be observed. To obtain the benefit of a covenant there must be actual payment of the covenanted sum; a payment made on the understanding that the recipient will hand the sum back to the covenantor is no payment and no deduction will be allowed: see *Albert Lee* v. *I. R. C.* [1943] 2 All E.R. 672; 25 Tax Cas. 485.[17] And if no actual payment is made in pursuance of the covenant but an equivalent amount or more

---

[14] *Ibid.*, para. 161.

[15] *Ibid.*, para. 156.

[16] See ss. 394, 400 and 406.

[17] Contrast *Russell* v. *I. R. C.* [1944] 2 All E.R. 192; 26 Tax Cas. 242, where it was found that the sums handed back to the covenantor were to be taken care of by him for the covenantees.

is applied for the beneficiary's maintenance by the covenantor, no deduction will be allowed: see *I. R. C.* v. *Compton* (1946) 27 Tax Cas. 350.[18]

In their Final Report the Royal Commission thought that where a covenantor made a covenant in favour of a member of his family he should be required by statute to produce formal declarations by himself and the recipient of the payments to the effect that there existed no agreement or understanding by virtue of which the benefit or any part of the payments was returned, directly or indirectly, to the covenantor or any other person designated by him.[19] As yet there is no such provision in the Statute Book. But the Board of Inland Revenue have instructed Inspectors of Taxes to call for declarations as part of the evidence required to support a claim for tax relief that there are no conditions or counter-stipulations in regard to payments under any deed of covenant whether or not the beneficiary is a member of the covenantor's family.[20]

Annual payments

Under Case III of Schedule D, which is contained in section 123 of the Income Tax Act, 1952, tax is charged in respect of " any annuity, or other annual payment, whether such payment is payable within or out of the United Kingdom, either as a charge on any property of the person paying the same by virtue of any deed or will or otherwise, or as a reservation out of it, or as a personal debt or obligation by virtue of any contract, or whether the same is received and payable half-yearly or at any shorter or more distant periods." Thus, Case III imposes the charge to tax upon annual payments made under a deed of covenant.

There is, however, no definition or exposition in the Income Tax Acts of " annual payment "; it has been left to the courts to put some limitation on the broad sense of the words. Examples of what are not " annual payments " in the relevant sense were given by Scrutton L.J. in *Earl Howe* v. *I. R. C.* [1919] 2 K.B. 336 at p. 352; 7 Tax Cas. 289 at p. 303. First, sums paid annually by a man who contracts with a garage for a period of years for the hire and upkeep of a car. Similarly, sums paid annually by a man who contracts with his butcher to supply all his meat each year for an annual sum. These annual sums would not be wholly taxed as annual payments under Case III of Schedule D in the hands of the payees. They would be trading receipts of the payees and only those parts of them which were profits would be taxed under Case I of Schedule D.

The distinction lies between the class of payment which the Income Tax Acts regard as " pure income profit " of the recipient, on which he suffers tax without any set-off, and which the payer is entitled to treat virtually as an assignment of part of his income, and the class of

18 And *cf. Waley-Cohen* v. *I. R. C.* (1945) 26 Tax Cas. 471.
19 Cmd. 9474. See *post*, p. 487.
20 Hansard, 1959, H. of C., Vol. 610, col. 148.

annual payment which by its very quality and nature cannot be treated as a pure income profit of the recipient, but forms an element to be taken into account in discovering what the profits of the recipient are.[21]

In *I. R. C.* v. *City of London (as Conservators of Epping Forest),*[22] referring to the payments made annually by the city corporation to the conservators, Lord Reid put the distinction in the following words:

" It is, I think, clear that the sums payable by the City have all the necessary characteristics of annual payments, taking ' annual ' in the sense in which that word is generally used in the Income Tax Act; but it is equally clear that by no means all payments which have those characteristics fall within the scope of Case III [or, Lord Reid might have added, sections 169 and 170]. There is no qualification or limitation of the words ' annual payment ' expressed in the rules applicable to Case III, but a limitation must be implied so as to exclude certain kinds of annual payments. The Act must be read as a whole and construed so as to produce, so far as possible, a coherent scheme; and it is settled that Case III does not apply to payments which are in reality trading receipts in the hands of the recipients although such payments take the form of annual payments. One reason is that income tax is a tax on income, and trading receipts are not income: a trader's income from his trade can only be determined after he has deducted his expenditure from his receipts, and it cannot be supposed that sums which are not income are to be taxable under Case III. . . . "

Lord Reid went on to suggest that trading receipts are generally received in return for something done or provided by the payee for the payer. It now appears from the decision of the House of Lords in *British Commonwealth International Newsfilm Agency Limited* v. *Mahany* [1963] 1 W.L.R. 69 that annual sums paid to a trader may be trading receipts and, therefore, not annual payments, even if nothing is done or provided by the payee for the payer. The relevant question appears to be whether, in all the facts of the case, the payments are received by the payee as trading receipts; and that they may be received as trading receipts if they are intended to supplement the trading receipts of the payee, even though there are no conditions or counter-stipulations in favour of the payer.[23]

Although it is clearly not the sole or exclusive test, if there are conditions or counter-stipulations in favour of a payer in a deed of covenant, the sums paid under the deed will not be annual payments in the relevant sense. Thus payments made under deeds of covenant

[21] See *per* Lord Normand in *I. R. C.* v. *City of London (as Epping Forest Conservators)* [1953] 1 W.L.R. 652 at p. 659; 34 Tax Cas. 293 at p. 320; citing Lord Greene in *Re Hanbury*, 20 A.T.C. 333 at pp. 334–335. And *cf. I. R. C.* v. *National Book League* [1957] Ch. 488; 37 Tax Cas. 455; and *West Hertfordshire Main Drainage Authority* v. *I. R.C.* (1963) 42 A.T.C. 102.

[22] [1953] 1 W.L.R. at p. 667; 34 Tax Cas. at p. 326.

[23] See *per* Lord Evershed M.R. in *British Commonwealth International Newsfilm Agency, Ltd.* v. *Mahany* [1962] 1 W.L.R. 560 at p. 567.

by way of subscription to the National Book League were held not to
be annual payments because of the privileges which were conferred by
the League upon the members who paid their subscriptions in this way.[24]
The payments were not " pure income profit " in the League's hands.
It follows from this that the short answer to the question which is
sometimes asked, can school fees or a club subscription be paid under
a deed of covenant so as to give the payee the tax advantages which
a deed of covenant gives in other cases, is " No."

Subject to the statutory restrictions dealt with above, there may be
circumstances in which some at least of the tax advantages of a deed of
covenant may be obtained, notwithstanding that the motive which
induces the payer to execute the deed is the hope or expectation of
receiving some advantage.   The hoped-for advantage may be received
from the payee.[25] Or it may be some commercial advantage which is
aimed at.   For example, the payments made by I.C.I. under deed of
covenant in favour of children of overseas employees who were being
educated in this country were made to obtain a commercial advantage:
I.C.I. was not actuated by benevolence.[26] But the advantage was
simply the motive, not the consideration, for the payments.   There
were no conditions or counter-stipulations under the deed of covenant
in favour of I.C.I., and the payments under the deed were, therefore,
annual payments in the relevant sense.   But where the arrangement is
one whereby the payer can demand services or facilities as of right in
return for his covenant, the position will be open to challenge by the
Revenue on the ground that the covenanted payment is not an " annual
payment."

" Annual payments " must also be distinguished from payments which
are taken by the recipient as instalments of capital.   The latter are not
taxed as income in the hands of the recipient, and cannot be deducted
from the income of the payer for tax purposes.   While the distinction is
in practice often difficult to draw, it rarely arises in connection with
voluntary covenants: it is more common in cases where a person buys
a capital asset in return for a series of payments and claims relief in
respect of the payments on the ground that they are annual payments,
albeit given in return for a capital asset.   Further consideration of this
topic will be undertaken in a later chapter of this book.[27]

---

[24] See *I. R. C.* v. *National Book League* [1957] Ch. 488; 37 Tax Cas. 455 and *cf.*
Taw and Torridge Festival Society, Ltd. v. *I. R. C.* (1959) 38 Tax Cas. 603.

[25] See *Duke of Westminster* v. *I. R. C.* [1936] A.C. 1; 19 Tax Cas. 490. The Duke's
covenants would no longer save surtax having regard to s. 415 of the Income Tax Act,
1952. See also *I. R. C.* v. *National Book League* [1957] Ch. 488.

[26] See *Barclays Bank, Ltd.* v. *Naylor* [1961] 1 Ch. 7; 39 Tax Cas. 256.

[27] See *post*, pp. 30, 329. For the distinction between a deed of covenant which provides
for a capital payment by instalments (which are not allowable as a deduction from
income for tax purposes) and a deed of covenant to make income payments, see
Mallaby-Deeley v. *I. R. C.* (1938) 23 Tax Cas. 153. And *cf. Dott* v. *Brown* [1936]
1 All E.R. 543 at p. 548, *Ramsay* v. *I. R. C.* (1935) 20 Tax Cas. 79 and *Vestey* v.
I. R. C. [1962] Ch. 861; 40 Tax Cas. 112.

" Annual " in this context does not mean occurring once a year: the payments will be none the less " annual " if the deed provides that they are to be made at weekly or monthly intervals. " The authorities lay it down that where an agreement provides . . . for the payment of a sum in periods of less than a year which may continue for more than a year, that payment is an annuity." [28]

Income tax of the covenantor

The covenants contained in the precedents set out below are all covenants to make " annual payments " which will be " pure income profit" in the covenantee's hands. The annual payments will, therefore, be within the scope of Case III of Schedule D, and the income tax, though not the surtax, will be collected by deduction at the source in accordance with sections 169 and 170 of the Income Tax Act, 1952, the former General Rules 19 and 21. It was held by the House of Lords in *I. R. C.* v. *Whitworth Park Coal Co. Ltd.* [1961] A.C. 31; 38 Tax Cas. 531, that Rule 21 did not apply to payments by the Crown out of moneys provided by Parliament. This position was reversed with retrospective effect by the provisions in section 39 of the Finance Act, 1960. These provisions enable all public offices and departments of the Crown to deduct tax on making payments from which tax would be deducted if such payments were made by an ordinary taxpayer. The provisions for assessment, charge, deduction and payment of income tax are made to apply to government departments but in such a way that the departments will not be liable for any tax which would ultimately be borne by the Crown.

A comprehensive summary of the operation of those rules is to be found in the speech of Viscount Simon L.C. in *Allchin* v. *Coulthard* [1943] A.C. 607 at pp. 618–619; 25 Tax Cas. 445 at p. 460:

" The three heads under which the existing scheme of collection of income tax embodied in rules 19 and 21 may be stated are as follows :

(a) A person liable to pay any yearly interest of money, annuity or any other annual payment to a recipient is not entitled to deduct this payment in arriving at his profits or gains to be assessed and charged with income tax. If the amount is payable and paid out of his profits or gains, he is assessed on a sum which includes such payments, while the recipient is not directly assessed in respect of the amount at all. Consequently, the Crown gets from the payer both the tax at the standard rate which would otherwise be due from the recipient of the annual payment and the tax due from himself in respect of what is left of his profits and gains after the payment is made.

(b) If the annual payment is payable and paid out of his profits and gains, the payer is *entitled* to deduct from the payment he makes

[28] *Per* Slessor L.J. in *Taylor* v. *Taylor* [1938] 1 K.B. 320 at p. 335. And *cf. Re Janes' Settlement, Wasmuth* v. *Janes* [1918] 2 Ch. 54; *Smith* v. *Smith* [1923] P. 191; *Clack* v. *Clack* [1935] 2 K.B. 109.

to the recipient income tax at the current rate, and the recipient is bound to allow the deduction upon receipt of the residue and to treat the payer as acquitted of liability to him in respect of the amount thus deducted. By this means, the payer recoups himself for the tax which he has paid or will pay on the annual payment.

(c) If and in so far as the annual payment is not payable and paid out of profits or gains brought into charge, the person making the payment is *bound* to deduct from it income tax at the current rate and to account to the Crown for the amount deducted. In effect, the payer in such a case acts as collector for the Crown of the tax due from the recipient. The requirement that the recipient must allow the deduction and treat the payer as acquitted of liability in respect of this amount is not repeated in rule 21 [section 170], but must be implied."

When therefore a covenantor covenants to make annual payments to a beneficiary, even if nothing is said in the covenant regarding the deduction of tax, the covenantor will have discharged his obligation to the beneficiary under the deed if he pays the covenanted sum less income tax at the standard rate in accordance with sections 169 and 170 of the Income Tax Act, 1952. If the covenantor has sufficient taxed income for the year of assessment in which the payment is due, *i.e.*, equal to, or in excess of, the gross payment, section 169 (rule 19) will apply and he is entitled to retain for his own benefit the tax deducted. But if the covenantor has insufficient taxed income in any particular year of assessment, section 170 (rule 21) will apply to the excess of the annual payment over his total income. In these circumstances the covenantor is obliged, not merely entitled, to deduct standard rate tax in making the payment, and to deliver an account of the payment to the Commissioners of Inland Revenue who shall assess and charge him on the payment.

To determine whether section 169 or section 170 applies the test is whether the total income of the payer, as measured for income tax, (*e.g.*, gross taxed dividends, direct assessments under Schedules A, B, D and E, including earned income dealt with under P.A.Y.E.) suffices to " cover " the gross amount of the annual payment under the deed of covenant. In practice, an adjustment of the covenantor's income tax may be due, owing to the loss of the allowance of earned income, personal, and reduced rate reliefs against assessments [29]; but this does not affect the principle set out above.

Tax is set off against tax. If the covenantor has paid or is liable to pay tax at the standard rate on a part of his income equal to the amount which he pays away under the covenant, he may retain the sum representing standard rate income tax which he has deducted from the annual payment. The beneficiary bears the burden of the income tax on the annual payment, which by virtue of the covenant becomes his

[29] See Income Tax Act, 1952, s. 221; *post*, p. 15.

income, by having had it deducted at source. The covenantor in effect only pays tax on what is left of his income after making the annual payment, since, although he is assessed to income tax as if he had not executed the covenant (apart from the possible loss of his reliefs), he is compensated for the income tax he pays on the covenant by deducting, and retaining, standard rate tax on the gross amount he has covenanted to pay.

If the covenantor has no taxed or taxable income, deduction of tax is mandatory and he must pay the whole of what he deducts from the annual payment to the Revenue. And if he is only liable to tax on that part of his income which he pays over to the beneficiary under the covenant at a rate which is less than the standard rate, he must out of the tax deducted from the annual payment make good to the Revenue the difference between the tax payable on the annual payment at the highest effective rate applicable to him and tax on the payment at the standard rate: Income Tax Act, 1952, s. 221.

In drafting deeds of covenant which provide for the payment of gross annual amounts which are intended to be paid under deduction of tax, it may remove a possible source of doubt for those who are unfamiliar with the detailed working of section 169 if the words " less income tax at the standard rate for the time being in force " are expressly added when stating the amount payable under the deed.

Difficulties sometimes arise when payment is made in arrear. Under section 169, the payer is entitled to deduct income tax at the standard rate of tax in force at the date when the payment was *due*, and under section 170, that in force at the *date of payment*. These will coincide when the annual payment is made at the due date. Section 169 will apply to the payment of arrears where there was taxed income in the year when the payment became due, at least when it is not demonstrable that the payment has been made out of some fund other than taxed income: cf. *Re Sebright* [1944] 1 Ch. 287. And under concession 22 of the extra-statutory concessions of the Board of Inland Revenue,[30] tax will not be required to be accounted for under section 170 to the extent that, in the year of assessment in which the annual payment was due (though not then paid) there was sufficient taxed income out of which the payment could have been made, even though in the year of actual payment there is no taxed income.[30]

Surtax of the covenantor

The covenantor will effect a reduction in his surtax liability by executing a deed of covenant which satisfies the conditions contained in

---

[30] See the appendix relating to extra-statutory concessions in the 103rd Report of the Commissioners of Inland Revenue for the year ended March 31, 1960: Cmnd. 1258 of 1960. None of the concessions published in the Board's 103rd and 104th Reports was cancelled during 1961: see the 105th Report, Cmnd. 1906. The " concession " may, in fact, be no more than a statement of the law.

the Income Tax Acts.[31] Sections 169 and 170 of the Income Tax Act, 1952, have no application to surtax, which is computed on principles different in certain respects from those applicable to income tax. The rate of surtax varies with, and the surtax is chargeable on, the " total income " of the taxpayer. In computing his total income for surtax purposes the taxpayer is entitled to deduct from the gross income he enjoys those annual payments which he himself makes under deduction of tax.[32]

Income tax of the covenantee

The covenantee who has received the annual payment less tax at the standard rate may be entitled to recover from the Revenue some or all of the tax deducted by the covenantor, if he has not already claimed the whole of the personal reliefs and allowances to which he is entitled against the tax payable on some other part of his income. The Revenue are, of course, entitled to proof that the payment has been made and the tax deducted. Therefore, if a claim for recovery of tax is to be made the covenantee should obtain from the covenantor a completed Tax Deduction Certificate on the appropriate form of the R 185 series, which can be obtained from any tax office. There is no statutory authority for the use of any particular form, but the use of a standard form simplifies the procedure. By sending the Tax Deduction Certificate to his inspector of taxes, together with a return of income, the recipient of the net covenanted sum will be able to recover any repayment from the inspector.

EXAMPLE :

A covenantor with a total unearned income of £10,000 gross per annum pays by deed of covenant an amount of £10 per week to his son aged 21 who has no other income except a University scholarship.

Tax position.

		£	s.	d.
(1) *Covenantor*				
Total covenanted sums ... ... =		520	0	0
Less income tax @ 7s. 9d. ... ... =		201	10	0
Total net payments made ... ... =		318	10	0
Saving of surtax (assuming payments represent " top slice ")—				
£520 @ 7s. 6d. ... ... =		195	0	0
Therefore net cost =		£123	10	0
(2) *Covenantee*				
Repayment-claim (assuming that he is unmarried).				
Personal relief £200 @ 7s. 9d. ... ... =		77	10	0
Reduced rate relief,				
£100 @ 3s. 9d. (7s. 9d. − 4s.) ... ... =		18	15	0
£220 @ 1s. 9d. (7s. 9d. − 6s.) ... ... =		19	5	0
Amount reclaimable =		£115	10	0

(The scholarship income is exempt.)

---

[31] *Cf. ante,* p. 2.
[32] See *per* Scrutton L.J. in *Earl Howe* v. *I. R. C.* [1919] 2 K.B. 336 at p. 352; 2 Tax Cas. 289 at p. 303; and *cf.* Schedule 24, Income Tax Act, 1952, " Declarations and Statements of Total Income."

Total amount received by son—

						£	s.	d.
(a) Net under deed of covenant ...	...	...	...	...	=	318	10	0
(b) By repayment claims ...	...	...	...	...	=	115	10	0

(which, if desired, may be made periodically)

£434 0 0

(3) Net saving of tax, £434 − £123 10s. ... ... = £310 10 0

There would be no further saving of income tax by increasing the amount, as the son would become liable at the standard rate. But a saving of surtax could still be obtained as the son does not become liable until his income reaches £2,000 per annum, and then at a lower rate than his father.

Surtax of the covenantee

Should it happen that the covenantee's income, including the sums covenanted to be paid to him, is sufficiently great to be chargeable to surtax, he will include the gross amount of the covenanted sums in his total income, in the same way that he will include dividends in respect of which tax at the standard rate has been deducted at source.

Possible disadvantage

It can happen that in certain circumstances a covenantor may increase his liability to income tax by covenanting to make payments which he previously made out of his taxed income without having bound himself to do so. This will only occur when the covenantor is not liable to pay the full standard rate of income tax on a part of his income sufficient to cover the gross amount of the covenanted sum. A covenantor who has a total income for tax purposes of £2,000 a year, all of it earned, will be obliged, if he executes a covenant for, say, £100 gross a year, in effect to lose the earned income allowance on that amount of his income (see Income Tax Act, 1952, s. 221). This is a point which is sometimes overlooked by taxpayers who respond to appeals to pay a donation by a seven-year deed of covenant. For an illustration of the working of this rule reference may be made to *Lewin* v. *Aller* [1954] 1 W.L.R. 1063; 35 Tax Cas. 483.

The amount covenanted

Where a covenant is made in favour of another person's child—say, where a grandparent covenants in favour of his infant grandchild—attention must be paid to the possible effect of the covenant on the " child allowance " claimed by the child's parents. Section 212 of the Income Tax Act, 1952, which deals with child allowances, provides by subsection (4), as amended by section 12 of the Finance Act, 1963, that " no relief " shall be allowed under this section in respect of any child who is entitled in his own right to an income exceeding £115 a year."

Therefore, if the gross amount covenanted is £115 a year or less and the child has no other income, the parents can still claim the child allowance. If the gross amount is £116 a year, the parents will, until the year of assessment 1964–65, lose the whole of the child allowance, although repayment may be made on behalf of the child in respect of the child's personal reliefs.

This harsh result is modified by the provisions in section 13 of the Finance Act, 1963, in respect of the year 1964–65 and subsequent years of assessment.

The new provisions introduce marginal relief in respect of child allowance, where the child's income exceeds £115. The child allowance is reduced by the amount by which the child's income exceeds £115.[33] A child's own earnings constitute income in his own right for this purpose: see section 212 of the Income Tax Act, 1952, and *Williams* v. *Doulton* (1948) 28 Tax Cas. 522.

Change of rate of income tax

A troublesome problem may arise if, during the currency of a deed of covenant, the standard rate of tax is changed. The covenantor—unless he has agreed to pay a " tax-free " sum—may find that he should deduct more, or less, by way of income tax in making payments under his covenant. The Finance Act which provides for the change in the standard rate usually receives the Royal Assent towards the end of July, which is almost four months after the commencement of the year of assessment in which the new standard rate is to operate. By virtue of the Provisional Collection of Taxes Act, 1913, the covenantor is not obliged to await the Royal Assent, but may adjust the deduction which he makes, as soon as the budget resolutions are passed by the Commons, which is usually about the middle of April. Even so, a covenantor may perhaps deduct the wrong amount in respect of payments made in April or the succeeding three months. If he has made too small a deduction, the standard rate having been increased, his remedy is to balance this by a subsequent over-deduction: if, however, there is no subsequent payment from which to make the over-deduction, he may recover the amount under-deducted as a debt from the covenantee.[35]

If the standard rate is reduced, occasioning an over-deduction, the covenantor is still liable to pay the excess deducted and his covenant has not been performed unless he does so.[35]

Failure to deduct tax

The failure on the part of the covenantor to deduct standard rate income tax in making the payments under a seven-year covenant does not affect the surtax position, but may have an unexpected result as

---

[33] Accordingly, marginal relief will be available up to £230 in the case of a child under the age of eleven years, up to £245 in the case of a child aged between eleven and sixteen years and up to £260 in the case of a child over sixteen years.

[35] Income Tax Act, 1952, ss. 491, 492.

regards income tax. If the covenantor fails to deduct the tax which he may retain under section 169 of the Income Tax Act, 1952, he is himself nevertheless obliged to pay income tax on his own income, and moreover has no right of action against the covenantee to recover the amount that should have been retained, since it is money paid under a mistake of law: *Re Hatch* [1919] 1 Ch. 351; *Ord* v. *Ord* [1923] 2 K.B. 432. But if the annual sum is paid in instalments, it may be that an earlier instalment paid without deduction of tax may be adjusted by an extra retention out of some later instalment of the same year: *Taylor* v. *Taylor* [1938] 1 K.B. 320.

Deductions which are directed to be made by section 170 are on a different footing. When the covenantor fails to deduct, the Revenue may demand from him the amount that he should have deducted, or alternatively may proceed against the covenantee by assessing him on the gross amount paid: see *Grosvenor Place Estates Ltd.* v. *Roberts* [1961] Ch. 148; 39 Tax Cas. 433.[36] And even if the Revenue recover from the covenantor, he has no right of action against the covenantee to recover any sums that should have been deducted on payment.

" Tax-free " payments under deeds of covenant

It may happen that a covenantor wishes to express the amount which he is to pay to the beneficiary as a " tax-free " sum. Instead of stating an annual sum from which tax will be deducted on payment, he may wish to deal with the matter by stating the net sum which he is prepared to hand over or, alternatively, the net sum which he wishes the beneficiary to have after the beneficiary's liability to tax has been taken into account. Section 506 of the Income Tax Act, 1952 (formerly General Rule 23 of the Income Tax Act, 1918), however, provides first that a person who refuses to allow a deduction of tax authorised by the Act to be made out of any payment is to forfeit the sum of £50, and secondly, that every agreement for payment of interest, rent or other annual payment in full without allowing such deduction is void. It follows that a covenantor cannot in terms covenant to pay an annual sum " free of tax "; if he attempts to do so, the covenant will take effect as an undertaking to pay the stated sum less tax.

Section 506 (2) does not apply to wills or to court orders since they are not agreements.[37] A testator can, therefore, validly direct the payment of an annuity to be made " tax-free " or " free of tax ": see *I. R. C.* v. *Cook* [1946] A.C. 1; 26 Tax Cas. 489. And the court has

---

[36] For a time it was thought that s. 26 of the Finance Act, 1927, which was passed to deal with the position in *Re Lang Propellor, Ltd.* [1927] 1 Ch. 120, had deprived the Crown of the right to go against the covenantee. The thought, however, was not accepted by, for example, Upjohn J. who in *Stokes* v. *Bennett* [1953] Ch. 566 at p. 576; 34 Tax Cas. 337 at p. 343 held that the decision in *Glamorgan Quarter Sessions* v. *Wilson* (1910) 5 Tax Cas. 537 which allowed the Crown the right to go against the covenantee was still good law.

[37] In the absence of authority it is safer to assume that a covenant is an " agreement " even if the covenantee is not party to it.

power to make orders for the payment of maintenance " free of tax " :
see *Burroughs* v. *Abbott* [1922] 1 Ch. 86.[38]

In the case of a deed of covenant the difficulty created by section 506
can be avoided by using in place of the expression " free of tax " some
such expression as:

" such a sum as after the deduction of income tax will leave "
the specified sum which it is desired to pay free of tax.

An alternative form of words which it is always advisable to use in
practice, unless there are particular reasons to the contrary is:

" such a sum as after deduction of income tax at the standard rate
will leave "
the specified sum.

The different results achieved by the alternative forms of words were
described by Sir Wilfrid Greene M.R. (as he then was) in *Re Maclennan,
Few* v. *Byrne* [1939] Ch. 750, at p. 755:

" In the simple case of a covenant to pay an annuity with nothing
more, the payer is not concerned with the tax liability of the recipient
save in the sense that he is entitled to deduct in making the payment
tax at the standard rate, and the recipient is then at liberty to claim
relief from the Revenue and keep whatever sum he may recover. But
the language of any particular provision may alter that state of affairs.
In order to avoid the difficulty and inconveniences caused by the
provision in rule 23, sub-rule (2) [now section 506 (2) of the Income Tax
Act, 1952], which prohibits agreements for payment of annual payments
in full without allowing deductions, the well-known device has been used in
the case of documents *inter vivos* of providing for payment of such a sum
as after deduction of income tax at the standard rate will leave a clear
sum of the stated amount. Such a covenant is, in truth, nothing more
nor less than a covenant to pay a gross sum; it is only a covenant to pay
a gross sum that is permissible in view of rule 23, sub-rule (2). The only
difference between such a case and the case of a covenant to pay a
named sum is that the gross sum can only be ascertained by taking into
account the factor stated; it is really a covenant to pay £x and the value
of x has to be ascertained by taking the net figure which is mentioned
in the covenant and applying the standard rate of tax at the relevant
time, and by that method the actual gross sum is ascertained. In such a
case where the language used is what I have described, the directions
given for the purpose of ascertaining what that gross sum is to be, make
quite clear what are the factors to be taken into account in arriving at
it; and the tax factor which is to be taken into account in such a case
is the standard rate of tax and nothing else. But it is clear that a
covenantor, if he is so minded, may go a step further, and by appropriate
language may provide that the sum of £x shall be arrived at by taking
into account not merely the factor of the standard rate of income tax,

---

[38] For the present practice of the Divorce Division, see *post*, p. 61.

but that factor adjusted by bringing into account also any recoveries which the payee, as a person entitled to relief, may be able to claim. If language of that character has been used, effect must be given to it. The real question in the present case is whether or not in arriving at the figure of a gross sum of £x which this document is contemplating, the reliefs to which the payee is entitled are to be brought in as a figure in ascertaining the amount of £x."

The first alternative form of words referred to above would be appropriate for the covenantor who wishes to go the step further referred to by the Master of the Rolls in the passage cited. And on taking this step the rule in Re Pettit, Le Fevre v. Pettit [1922] 2 Ch. 765, will become applicable. That case concerned an annuity given by will " free of tax." The question for the court was this: where the annuitant's personal circumstances were such that the annuitant was not liable to tax at the full standard rate deducted by the trustees from the notional gross annuity on payment, and the annuitant accordingly recovered from the Revenue the tax deducted in excess of the amount properly payable by him, was the annuitant entitled to retain the amount so recovered, or was he accountable to the will trustees for some part of it? The court held that the annuitant must account to the trustees for such proportion of the amount recovered by him as the annuity bore to the total income of the annuitant from all sources.[39]

It follows, therefore, that where a covenant is to pay " such a sum as after payment of income tax will leave £x," or some other form of words is used which makes it clear that the beneficiary is to receive no less and no more than the stated amount, the beneficiary must account to the covenantor for a due proportion of the reliefs he is entitled to obtain by way of repayment of tax calculated with reference to his total income.

A further complication produced by the rule in Re Pettit concerns the nature of such refunds made by the covenantee. The practice at the moment is to treat such sums as not liable to tax in the hands of the covenantor, although they may be treated as part of the covenantor's income for the purpose of ascertaining his reliefs and allowances.[40] It could be argued that the repayments are annual sums, so that the covenantee should deduct tax under section 169 or 170 of the Income Tax Act, 1952; indeed, this argument is used by the Revenue authorities if the covenant itself provides expressly for such repayments. Whichever view is taken leads to almost inextricable complexity.[41] The

---

[39] In Re Kingcome, Hickley v. Kingcome [1936] Ch. 566, the matter was carried a stage further when it was held that an annuitant, entitled under a will to a tax-free annuity to which the rule in P ttit's case applied, was a trustee of his statutory right to recover for the benefit of the testator's estate the tax overpaid in respect of his annuity and was bound at the request of the trustees to sign a proper application form for that purpose.

[40] Similarly the refunds are treated as part of the net taxed income of a trust for the year of receipt.

[41] The problem is dealt with in an article in Vol. 18 of The Conveyancer and Property Lawyer, p. 218, written by Mr. D. R. Stanford. The complexity is illustrated by I. R. C. v. Duncanson (1949) 31 Tax Cas. 257.

better course is to avoid a *Re Pettit* covenant whenever possible, and to
employ the formula " to pay such a sum as after deduction of income tax
at the standard rate will leave " the specified amount. This formula
shows the net sum which the covenantor actually has to pay. Even if
the standard rate of tax is changed while the covenant is running, the
amount payable does not vary. It may therefore be paid by a Banker's
Standing Order without inconvenience. There is no great difficulty in
" grossing up " the net covenanted sum for the purpose of calculating
the covenantor's surtax and the covenantee's income tax repayment
claim.

Calculation of refund to trustees under the " Re Pettit " principle [42]

In the actual decision in *Re Pettit* it was held that as the
total income had borne deduction of income tax at the then standard
rate of 5s., the amount repaid should be refunded to the trustees
according to the proportion which the *net* amount of the annuity bore
to the *net* total income. The practice has been altered since the decision
in *I. R. C.* v. *Cook* [1946] A.C. 1; 26 Tax Cas. 489, in which it was
held that the income tax measure of the annuitant's income whose only
income was £100 per annum " tax free " was not £100 and any tax
liability personal to the annuitant, but the *gross* amount which after
deduction of income tax at the standard rate produced the " tax free "
annuity. Thus, when the annuitant has no other income, the whole of
the repayment (which is calculated on this basis of measuring the income)
is to be refunded. If the annuitant has other income, the amount of the
personal reliefs, excluding earned income relief, calculated as though
the total income had been received less income tax at the standard rate,
should be apportioned in the proportion of the *gross* amount of the
annuity to the total *gross* income. The reliefs should also include any
repayment due to claiming relief for a business loss against other income
under section 341 of the Income Tax Act, 1952,[43] and a proportion of
the personal reliefs which a married woman may claim by making application for separate assessment,[44] and in practice any other reliefs except
such as are expressed to be allowable only against other income, *e.g.*,
maintenance relief under section 101 of the Income Tax Act, 1952.

EXAMPLE :
    (1) Single Annuitant having the following income :

		£	s.	d.
(i) " Tax free " annuity of £110 (this, with tax at 7s. 9d. in the £ is equal to a gross annuity of £(80 ÷ 49 × 110) = £179 4s. 10d. say in round figures ... ... =		180	0	0
(ii) Other income, taxed dividends ... ... =		300	0	0
		£480	0	0

----

[42] The problem is dealt with in an article in [1960] B.T.R. 155 by Mr. D. C. Potter.
[43] See *Re Lyons* [1952] Ch. 129.
[44] See *Re Batley* [1952] 1 All E.R. 1036.

						£	s.	d.
Repayment:								
Personal allowance, £200 @ 7s. 9d.	...	...	...	=		77	10	0
Reduced rate relief, £100 @ 3s. 9d.	...	...	...	=		18	15	0
„ „ „ £179 @ 1s. 9d.	...	...	...	=		15	13	3

£111 18 3

Refund due to trustees, 180 ÷ 480 × £111 18s. 3d. ... ... = £41 19 4

(2) If the annuitant's other income had included income received in full, the calculation of the refund should be made by reference to the allowances and reliefs due and not by reference to the actual repayment because this would be diminished if some of the reliefs had been given in the assessment before charging to tax. Earned income relief is deducted from earned income in calculating the figure of total income.

Expressions meaning " free of tax "

Various expressions used by testators or covenantors wishing to give tax-free annuities have been considered by the courts, the problem in each case being to determine whether as a matter of construction the rule in *Pettit's* case did or did not apply. According to the authorities the question of construction is in substance whether the reference to income tax is a reference to the standard rate of income tax merely as an arithmetical factor in the calculation of the gross amount of the annuity given by the deed or will, or whether the provision as to income tax indemnifies the annuitant against that part of the annuitant's income tax which is properly referable to the annuity. If construed in the former sense, the actual income tax ultimately suffered by the recipient of the annuity does not enter into the picture; tax at the standard rate is deducted from the gross amount resulting from the calculation and the annuitant receives £x in cash and the income tax referable to the gross amount is paid, as it were, for his account. If construed in the latter sense, complete effect cannot be given to the covenant or bequest by payment to the annuitant. The provisions of the Income Tax Acts compel the paying hand, in order that £x may reach the hand of the annuitant, in the first instance to make an overpayment (for the tax attributable to the gross amount resulting in £x is a payment for the account of the annuitant). The position is then adjusted by the annuitant claiming his reliefs and allowances and handing back the due proportion.[45]

A gift of " such an annuity as after deducting therefrom income tax at the current rate for the time being would amount to the clear yearly sum of £350 " has been held to fall within the first category, the reference to " income tax at the current rate " being merely a reference to income tax at the standard rate as an arithmetical factor in computing the gross sum payable: see *Re Jones* [1933] Ch. 842. A gift of "such an annual sum as would after deduction of income tax but not surtax leave

---

[45] See *per* Uthwatt J. in *Re Williams, Midland Bank Executor and Trustee Co., Ltd. v. Williams* [1945] 1 Ch. 320.

in her hands the sum of £500 clear of all deductions for income tax but not surtax " has been held to fall within the second category : see *Re Maclennan, Few* v. *Byrne* [1939] Ch. 750. So also has a gift of " such a sum in every year as after deduction of income tax for the time being payable in respect thereof will leave a clear sum of £350 " : see *Re Tatham, National Bank, Ltd., and Mathews* v. *Mackenzie* [1945] 1 Ch. 34.

Payments free of surtax

If the covenantor wishes to indemnify the beneficiary against surtax in addition to income tax, a specific direction to that effect should be given or a general reference should be made to taxes in such terms that the covenantor's intention is clear. In the same way if the indemnity is not to include surtax and the possibility of surtax being payable by the beneficiary is likely to arise, words should be added to make this intention clear.[46] In *Re Bates, Selmes* v. *Bates* [1925] Ch. 157, a testamentary gift of " such a sum in every year as after deduction of the income tax for the time being payable in respect thereof will leave a clear sum of £2,000 " was held not to include surtax.[47] In *Re Horlick's Settlement Trusts, College* v. *Horlick* [1938] 4 All E.R. 602, a reference to income tax at the standard rate and " every other tax on income for the time being in force " was held to include surtax.

Pre-war deeds or wills

In the case of a provision contained in a deed or will for payment of an annual sum or annuity free of income tax (whether or not including surtax) which was made before September 3, 1939, section 486 of the Income Tax Act, 1952, as amended by section 16 of the Finance Act, 1960, will apply. It was held by the Court of Appeal in *Re Westminster's Deed of Appointment* [1959] Ch. 265, that a rentcharge appointed on February 19, 1930, by the Duke of Westminster in favour of his intended wife, to commence on his death, was a provision made for the purposes of section 486 before September 3, 1939, so that the section applied, notwithstanding that the Duke did not die until 1953.

The effect of section 486 is that the gross amount will not be the net sum grossed up at the current standard rate, but the " appropriate proportion." This means in relation to years of assessment from 1960–61 onwards the proportion which the difference between twenty shillings in the pound and the standard rate of income tax for the year bears to fourteen shillings and sixpence in the pound. For example, if the standard rate is 7s. 9d., the appropriate proportion is $\frac{49}{58}$. In the case of wills, the effective date is the date of death (*Berkeley* v. *Berkeley* [1946] A.C. 555). The refund, if any, due under the *Re Pettit* decision, will be similarly reduced to the " appropriate proportion " of the refund

---

[46] See *Re Skinner, Milbourne* v. *Skinner* [1942] 1 Ch. 82.
[47] *Cf. Re Crawshay* [1915] W.N. 412.

which would have been due to the trustees if the 1938–39 rates of reliefs were still in force. (Thus two calculations are necessary: (1) the refund on the basis of the 1938–39 reliefs, and (2) the " appropriate proportion " of this sum for the current year.)

Covenants and estate duty

On the death of a covenantor, the covenant usually comes to an end. Sometimes however a covenant is framed to continue after the death of the covenantor, and if so, it must be observed that the amount of the outstanding payments is not allowed as a deductible debt in assessing the aggregate value of the estate for estate duty purposes.

The question may arise whether payments made by the deceased in the five years preceding his death may be property deemed to pass on his death under section 2 (1) (c) of the Finance Act, 1894. In practice, although it seems that such payments must be caught by section 2 (1) (c), the exemption contained in section 59 (2) of the Finance (1909–10) Act, 1910, in respect of gifts which are proved to the satisfaction of the Commissioners both to have been part of the normal expenditure of the deceased and also to have been reasonable having regard to the amount of his income or to the circumstances, would appear to be applicable to almost all payments made under covenants. Mention is also required of the exemption in the same section relating to gifts in consideration of marriage and it is considered that this would extend to a covenant made with a person on the occasion of his or her marriage. There is also exemption under section 33 (1) and (2) of the Finance Act, 1949, and it is considered that this will apply where the total amount of the gross payments in the five years preceding death does not exceed five hundred pounds.

On the death of a covenantee there will be no charge to estate duty in respect of the cesser of the payments unless they were charged on a particular piece of property or unless the covenant was made with two persons jointly and the survivor, in which case the actuarial value of the covenant will pass on the death of the first covenantee to die: see *Re Payton* [1951] Ch. 1081, and *cf. Re Norfolk (Duke)* [1950] Ch. 25. This may be avoided by drafting the covenant as two distinct covenants, as was in fact done in the *Payton* case.

Stamp duty on covenants

Stamp duty is payable under the heading in the Schedule of the Stamp Act, 1891: " BOND, COVENANT, or INSTRUMENT of any kind whatsoever. . . . Being the only or principal or primary security for any annuity (except upon the original creation thereof by way of sale or security, and except a superannuation annuity), or for any sum or sums of money at stated periods, not being interest for any principal sum secured by a duly stamped instrument, nor rent reserved by a lease or tack."

There are under this heading two distinct scales of duty:

(1) " For a definite and certain period, so that the total amount to be ultimately payable can be ascertained. . . . The same *ad valorem* duty as a bond or covenant for such total amount, *i.e.*, roughly 2s. 6d. for every £100.[48]

(2) " For the term of life or any other indefinite period : For every £5, and also for any fractional part of £5, of the annuity or sum periodically payable, 2s. 6d."

From these two clauses the stamp to be affixed to any " seven-year covenant " is to be assessed.

Thus, for example, a covenant to pay a gross sum of £120 a year for seven years will come under the first provision. The total amount payable being £120 × 7 = £840, the stamp, at 2s. 6d. per cent., will be £1 2s. 6d.

The same stamp will be payable if the covenant is to pay £10 a month for seven years.

Where, however, the covenant is to pay a gross sum of £120 each year for an indefinite period, such as the joint lives of the covenantor and convenantee, the second clause will apply. The rate will be 2s. 6d. on every £5, giving a stamp of £3.

If the same covenant were expressed to be £120 a year payable by monthly payments of £10 each, or by quarterly payments of £30, or to be quarterly payments of £30, it would still be an " annuity " and the annual sum would still be taken, giving the same result: *Lewis and Lewis* v. *I. R. C.* [1898] 2 Q.B. 290.

A saving may however be made, where the total period is indefinite, by covenanting for a weekly or monthly sum: see *Hennell* v. *I. R. C.* [1933] 1 K.B. 415. Thus a covenant for a monthly sum of £10 for the duration of the joint lives of the covenantor and covenantee would be stamped 10s.

Where the duty on a covenant for an indefinite period is greater than the duty which would be payable for a fixed period of twenty years, it is conceded that no greater duty will be demanded than that which would be payable on a covenant for twenty years.

A troublesome problem arises where the covenant is expressed as a tax-free sum—either a sum " after deduction of tax " or a sum " after deduction of tax at the standard rate." *Ad valorem* duty is

---

[48] The following scale shows the amounts accurately:

				£	s.	d.
Not exceeding £10	..	..	.. .. ..	0	0	3
Exceeding £10 and not exceeding £25	..	.. ..	0	0	8
,, £25 ,,	£50	..	.. ..	0	1	3
,, £50 ,,	£100	..	.. ..	0	2	6
,, £100 ,,	£150	..	.. ..	0	3	9
,, £150 ,,	£200	..	.. ..	0	5	0
,, £200 ,,	£250	..	.. ..	0	6	3
,, £250 ,,	£300	..	.. ..	0	7	6
,, £300, for every £100 and also for any fractional part of £100 of the amount secured	..	0	2	6

nonetheless chargeable, even though the gross sum covenanted is, in all but the first year, uncertain, and may vary from year to year. The duty is in practice understood to be charged on the sum appearing on the face of the covenant, and no further duty is levied in respect of the further amount in fact due under the covenant. Therefore a saving of stamp duty may sometimes be made by covenanting to pay a sum after deduction of tax. It seems, however, that the Revenue must be able to demand a minimum stamp of 10s., since the document is a deed. Moreover, the amount payable in the first year, for which the rates of tax are known, is ascertainable, and so *ad valorem* duty will be charged thereon at the rate of 2s. 6d. for every £100 of the amount payable in the first year.

Where the covenant is to pay a fixed sum " for seven years or for life," there is some doubt whether this is a payment for a definite or for an indefinite period. In strictness these covenants would appear to be liable to *ad valorem* duty at the rate of 2s. 6d. per £5 of the sum periodically payable. Where, however, duty at this rate exceeds the duty assessed on the total sum contingently payable during the covenant period the Revenue practice is understood to be to charge the lower duty. This must be regarded as a concession on the part of the Revenue, which may be withdrawn when the doubt is finally dispelled by judicial pronouncement.

What can be done by a covenant

It is proposed now to mention the particular circumstances in which a covenant may be found useful, classifying them according to the relationship of the parties.

(i) *Husband and wife*

As a general rule a husband cannot make any saving of tax by covenanting with his wife, since her income, if she is living with her husband, is deemed for income tax purposes to be that of her husband. To this rule there is an exception, provided for by section 361 of the Income Tax Act, 1952, that a wife is not living with her husband if they are separated under a court order or a deed of separation. It often happens, however, that a husband and wife are living apart, usually where one party has deserted the other, and one or other of them, in order not to spoil the chances of eventually getting a divorce, refuses to agree to a deed of separation. In such a situation a covenant may be of use. Where the parties, although not separated under an order or an agreement, are " in fact separated in such circumstances that the separation is likely to be permanent " section 361 provides that they are assessed as two, not one, persons, and so a seven-year covenant by the husband may provide considerable tax relief. Even so, the covenant must not offend against section 21 of the Finance Act, 1958, by being reducible in amount, or against section 22 by being merely discretionary.[49]

[49] See *ante*, p. 5, and note the concluding words of s. 21 (4) of the Finance Act, 1958.

(ii) *Parent and child*

As a general rule the effect of section 397 of the Income Tax Act, 1952, as amended by section 20 (2) of the Finance Act, 1958, is that a parent cannot make use of a seven-year covenant in favour of his infant children so as to reduce his tax liability. There may, however, be an advantage where a non-resident parent makes a covenant in favour of his child who is resident out of income which is subject to United Kingdom tax. By virtue of subsection (4) of section 397 the provisions of the section do not apply when the covenantor is not chargeable to United Kingdom income tax as a resident in the United Kingdom.

(iii) *Children of another person*

In practice, the seven-year covenant is often most useful where it is made by the covenantor in favour of infants who are not his own children. In a proper case it is possible to make a considerable saving of income tax and surtax by use of a covenant.

For example, let it be supposed that a bachelor with an unearned income of over £4,000 is in the habit of helping his married brother who has three infant children, and usually spends about £200 a year on such help. The £200 is paid by the bachelor out of income which has borne standard rate income tax at 7s. 9d. in the £ and also surtax at the rate of 4s. 6d. in the £, and in the hands of the married brother is not subject to tax at all. Now let the bachelor execute a covenant with trustees in favour of his nephews and nieces, by which he is to pay £200 a year. He will save on his own surtax to the extent of 200 × 4s. 6d., *i.e.*, £45. Further, in making the payment he will only hand over £200 minus 200 × 7s. 9d., *i.e.*, £122 10s. Thus he will have discharged his covenant to pay £200 by paying £122 10s. only, and will also save £45 in surtax: a net outgoing of only £77 10s., compared with the £200 he used to pay. The trustees will receive £122 10s., representing income which has already borne tax at 7s. 9d. in the £. They will, let it be supposed, apportion this equally among the three children, and, as each child has no other income and is entitled to a personal relief of £200, thus not being chargeable with any tax, the trustees must claim repayment to themselves by the Revenue of the tax deducted at source by the bachelor. They should obtain £77 10s., thus making the £122 10s., which they have, up to £200.

Where the covenantees are trustees for an infant child or infant children they should use the income for the maintenance, education and benefit of the children in accordance with section 31 of the Trustee Act, 1925. The word " benefit " is widely construed, and it is conceived to be permissible for the trustees to use the money to pay for the holidays or board and lodging of the children or to give them reasonable pocket money. If income is applied for the maintenance, education and benefit of an infant, it is his income for tax purposes.[50]

---

[50] See *Drummond* v. *Collins* [1915] A.C. 1011; 6 Tax Cas. 525.

The amount to which an infant is entitled under a covenant requires particular consideration. This aspect has already been dealt with.[51]

If the parent of the children whom it is desired to benefit by means of the covenant is the solicitor or employee of the covenantor, some care is required in drafting the covenant, to see that the children are named individually and not referred to as the children of the solicitor or employee.[52]

(iv) Pensions to retired employees

Where the owner of a business desires to pay a voluntary pension to a retired employee, or to the widow or child or any relative or dependant of a deceased employee, it is usually not necessary or advisable to use a covenant. The pension can normally be set off against the gross profits of the business for the purposes of ascertaining the net taxable profits. And the recipient, who is taxed under Schedule E, is entitled to earned income relief. The same rules apply where it is not the original employer who pays the pension, but his successor.

But suppose the employer executes a seven-year covenant? On its strict wording, section 376 of the Income Tax Act, 1952, can, it seems, extend to annuities secured by covenants, and if it does, it is not wholly clear that the payer would be able to get relief from income tax or surtax.[53] It is considered that the better view is that an employer who executes a seven-year covenant to provide for a retired employee or his child, widow or dependant is entitled to treat the covenant as one for annual payments within the meaning of section 169, and to retain standard rate tax at source, thus treating the annuity in the same way as if the recipient were not an employee, or child, widow or dependant of an employee, at all. The recipient is, moreover, entitled to earned income relief. It is understood that at present this view is acted upon by the Revenue. It seems that the only relevant authorities are *Duncan's Executors* v. *Farmer*[54] and *Kemp* v. *Evans*.[55]

(v) Retired partners

It is often possible to provide for a retired partner, or the widow or dependants of a retired partner, by means of covenanted annuities payable by the continuing partners. These may be for a fixed period less than seven years, if they are given " for valuable and sufficient consideration " and so fall outside the scope of section 392 of the Income Tax Act, 1952. The provision of a pension for the widow of a partner may have the additional attraction that it may bear a low rate of estate duty as an estate by itself[56]; or may be completely free of duty.[57]

---

[51] *Ante*, p. 17.   [52] See Income Tax Act, 1952, s. 415 (1) (c).
[53] See *ibid.*, ss. 169, 524 (3).
[54] (1909) 5 Tax Cas. 417.
[55] (1935) 20 Tax Cas. 14. See also *Stedeford* v. *Beloe* [1932] A.C. 388; 16 Tax Cas. 505.
[56] See *Re Payton* [1951] Ch. 1081, where this point was conceded.
[57] See *Re Miller's Agreement* [1947] Ch. 615. See *post*, p. 322.

(vi) *Purchase of assets*

In practice, a covenant to make annual payments is rarely used in the purchase of assets, probably because circumstances seldom arise where the seller is willing to accept annual payments, but partly also because it is not always possible to ensure with certainty that the covenanted payments, if for a fixed period, are annual payments and not instalments of capital.[58] Nor, on the other hand, is it always possible to ensure with certainty that the contrary position has been achieved: see *Vestey* v. *I. R. C.* [1962] 2 W.L.R. 221; 40 Tax Cas. 112. The mere fact that what is being purchased is a capital asset does not determine the character of the payments. The reported cases, such as *Mackintosh* v. *I. R. C.,*[59] *Ramsay* v. *I. R. C.,*[60] *I. R. C.* v. *Ledgard,*[61] *I. R. C.* v. *Hogarth,*[62] have for the most part been concerned with shares in partnership businesses.[63]

(vii) *Charities*

Many covenants are executed in favour of charities. This is so notwithstanding the fact that since 1946 the covenantor has been able to save no surtax: relief from income tax is available to the charity. Thus the net sum paid by the covenantor represents in the hands of the charity that sum plus the tax recoverable. In a proper case, seven-year covenants can greatly increase the income of a charity; but, in addition to the problems which normally arise with covenants, certain particular points require mention.

Over-enthusiastic promoters are fond of getting all their subscribers, even those of modest means, to execute covenants. The result, in the case of a subscriber who pays tax under P.A.Y.E. and does not pay tax at the full standard rate on any part of his income, may be an additional assessment to tax. This assessment has its origin in the loss of reliefs (reduced rate, earned income, etc.) on the gross amount of the covenanted sum. In practice, it may be better, where an invitation is being sent out in a printed brochure, to say that only those subscribers should consider executing a covenant who are in the fortunate position of paying over £100 a year in income tax. As a rule of thumb, this may serve to exclude those who fall far short of the standard rate on any part of their income.

Another point is that a business man is often able to include the subscription he pays to a trade charity in his accounts as money wholly and exclusively expended for the purposes of the trade, and thus in

---

[58] See *I. R. C.* v. *Hogarth*, 1941 S.C. 1; 23 Tax Cas. 491 at p. 498, *per* Lord Normand.
[59] (1928) 14 Tax Cas. 15.
[60] (1935) 20 Tax Cas. 79.
[61] (1937) 21 Tax Cas. 129.
[62] 1941 S.C. 1; 23 Tax Cas. 491.
[63] See *post*, p. 329.

effect to get relief in respect of surtax as well as income tax. If he executes a seven-year covenant, he cannot have it both ways, and the subscription will be disallowed as a deduction under section 137 (*l*) of the Income Tax Act, 1952.

Again, the payments to be made under the covenant must be "annual payments" within the meaning of section 169 of the Income Tax Act, 1952. If the charity agrees to make some return to its subscribers so that they are able as of right to demand certain facilities or services, the Revenue will be able to refuse the charity's repayment claim on the ground that the payments are not "annual payments" at all.[64] In practice, it may often be advisable to fix a subscription, in return for the payment of which the subscriber is entitled to the facilities the charity is able to offer, and in addition to ask for donations, the giving of which confers no further privileges on the subscriber. If this is done, the donations alone may then be paid by means of covenant. Where, however, the charity desires that the whole payment which its subscriber makes shall be an annual payment, so that the tax advantages of a covenant may be enjoyed, it may be possible to take advantage of a narrow distinction the application of which may in practice prove unacceptable to the Revenue in particular cases. If there is no binding arrangement by which the charity provides facilities or services to its subscribers, it is suggested that the subscription may be paid under covenant as an annual payment, notwithstanding that the motive of the subscriber is the well-founded expectation of receiving facilities or services. This distinction appears to follow from the decision in *Duke of Westminster* v. *I. R. C.*[65]

Where the purpose of a charity is the support of persons of small means, an alternative to the usual seven-year covenant may perhaps be found which enables its supporters to make a saving of surtax as well as income tax. It is suggested that a list of the persons in fact assisted may be scheduled to a trust deed, and the supporters invited to covenant with those trustees for the benefit of the persons scheduled. While this type of arrangement may be successful in a proper case, it may, as a result of the recommendations made by the Royal Commission on the Taxation of Profits and Income in their Final Report (Cmd. 9474), soon receive the attention of the legislature.

---

64 See *I. R. C.* v. *National Book League* [1957] Ch. 488.
65 [1936] A.C. 1. See also *Barclays Bank, Ltd.* v. *Naylor* [1961] 1 Ch. 7; 39 Tax Cas. 256.

PRECEDENT No. 1

Covenant for the Payment of an Annual Sum to an Adult

Covenant
with adult.

I, —— of ——, HEREBY COVENANT with —— of ——
(hereinafter called " the Covenantee ") that for a period
of seven years from the date hereof or during the residue
of my life, whichever period shall be shorter, I will pay
annually to the Covenantee during his life the sum of
—— pounds (£——) [the first payment to be made on
the —— day of —— next].

IN WITNESS whereof I have hereunto set my hand and
seal this —— day of —— 19—.

SIGNED SEALED AND DELIVERED by
the above-named COVENANTOR
in the presence of ——

This form of covenant is suitable for use by a covenantor who
wishes to benefit an adult other than a person who is in the service of
the covenantor or is his solicitor or is accustomed to act as his agent.
(See above, p. 7.) It is considered that this covenant will be effective if
made direct with an infant, although in practice, where the infant is of
tender years, it will in almost every case be more practical to make the
covenant with trustees who will apply the sums paid to them for the
benefit of the infant. Where a covenant is made direct with an infant,
the covenantor can only discharge his obligation to pay by applying the
sums for the maintenance or benefit of the infant in accordance with
section 31 of the Trustee Act, 1925: in practice, if the infant is in his
teens, payment of reasonable sums to him direct is unlikely to be
questioned as a proper exercise of the discretions under section 31.

Section 169 or 170 of the Income Tax Act, 1952, will apply and the
gross sum mentioned in the covenant will be payable subject to the deduction of tax at the standard rate. (See above, p. 13.)

The sum payable under the covenant will be a deduction from
the covenantor's total income when his liability for surtax is computed.
(See above, p. 15.) And the beneficiary will be entitled to claim
repayment of all or part of the tax deducted if he has not already been
given credit for his personal reliefs and allowances against the tax
due on some other part of his income. (See above, p. 16.)

The words in square brackets may be omitted if it is desired not to
tie the parties down to any fixed day of payment. If they are omitted
it is possible that the Revenue will contend that the payment in each
year is not due until the expiration of that year, so that, if the covenantor dies before the seven years have expired, the payment for the
year of the covenant's currency during which the covenantor died, if in

fact made before the covenantor's death, will be treated as a voluntary payment, not as an annual payment made in pursuance of the covenant.

If covenantor and beneficiary live for more than seven years from the date of the covenant the obligation to make annual payments under the covenant will last for at least six years and one day; it is not bound to come to an end in less than six years. Section 392 of the Income Tax Act, 1952, will not, therefore, operate to make the covenanted payments the covenantor's income for tax purposes. (See above, p. 2.) It is not essential, but usual, that the lives chosen should be those of the covenantor and of the covenantee.

Precedent No. 2

Covenant for the Payment of Monthly Sums to Trustees for the Benefit of Infant Grandchildren

Parties.

THIS DEED OF COVENANT is made the —— day of —— 19— BETWEEN —— of —— (hereinafter called " the Grantor ") of the one part and —— of —— and —— of —— (hereinafter called " the Trustees ") of the other part ;

WHEREAS :

Grandchildren of covenantor.

(A) The Grantor has two grandsons the sons of his daughter —— namely —— who was born on the —— day of —— 19— and —— who was born on the —— day of —— 19— (hereinafter together called " the Beneficiaries ") ;

(B) The Grantor is desirous of making such provision for the Beneficiaries as is hereinafter contained ;

NOW THIS DEED WITNESSETH as follows :

Covenant to pay annual sum.

1. FOR effectuating the said desire the Grantor hereby covenants with the Trustees that the Grantor will during his life or for a period of seven years from the date hereof whichever shall be the shorter as long as any one of the Beneficiaries is living pay to the Trustees on the Tenth day of every month such a sum as after the deduction of income tax at the standard rate for the time being in force shall be equal to the sum of —— pounds (£——) the first of such payments to be made on the Tenth day of —— next.

Trusts for beneficiaries.

2. THE Trustees shall stand possessed of each such monthly sum upon trust to apply the same as soon as it is paid to them for or towards the maintenance education support or otherwise for the benefit of the Beneficiaries or either of them in such manner in all respects as the Trustees shall in their absolute discretion without being liable to account think fit.

Payment direct to beneficiary.

3. FROM and after the attainment by either of the Beneficiaries of the age of sixteen years the Trustees may apply any part or parts of the said monthly sum for or towards such maintenance education support or otherwise as aforesaid by paying the same to such Beneficiary and the receipt of such Beneficiary shall be a complete discharge to the Trustees and the Trustees shall not be answerable for the application of any sum so paid.

IN WITNESS whereof the said parties hereto have hereunto set their respective hands and seals the day and year first above written.

SIGNED SEALED AND DELIVERED by

the above named —— ——,

etc., etc.

By reason of section 397 of the Income Tax Act, 1952, a covenant by a parent for the benefit of his infant children offers no tax advantage; the covenanted sums will remain the parent's for tax purposes. (See above, p. 6.) But a covenant by a grandparent or by an uncle or godparent or other well-disposed friend or relative offers a substantial advantage.[66] The covenanted sum will be a deduction in computing the payer's total income for surtax purposes and tax can be reclaimed on the infant's behalf in respect of his personal reliefs and allowances. Further, the parent would still be entitled to claim child allowance provided that the child's total income accruing to him under the covenant and otherwise does not exceed the statutory limit, at present £115 a year.[67] Under a covenant in this form any sums applied by the trustees for either of the grandchildren become the income of the grandchild for whose benefit they are applied: see *Drummond* v. *Collins* [1915]

---

[66] Mutual covenants, *e.g.*, "I will covenant to pay your son £100 a year if you will do the same for mine," and whether or not expressly so stated, will not achieve this result: see *I. R. C.* v. *Clarkson-Webb* [1933] 1 K.B. 507; 17 Tax Cas. 451. And a tripartite, or multiple, "back-scratching" arrangement will produce no different result. A covenant by John to pay £60 a year for Geoffrey's son if Geoffrey pays £60 a year for George's son, and George pays £60 a year for John's son, will still be a "settlement" by John under which income is paid to his own son—and similarly in the case of Geoffrey and George.

[67] See Finance Act, 1963, s. 12 (3).

A.C. 1011; 6 Tax Cas. 525, and *cf. Johnstone* v. *Chamberlain* (1933) 17 Tax Cas. 706.

This covenant provides for the payment of a net sum. The reference to the standard rate of income tax is merely a reference to the standard rate as an arithmetical factor in computing the gross sum payable under the covenant. The sum which can be deducted by the payer in computing his or her total income will, therefore, be the specified sum " grossed up " at the standard rate. For example, if the standard rate of tax is 8s. 6d., the amount payable will represent 11s. 6d. of each £1 of the gross amount; therefore the " grossed up figure " will be $20 \div 11\frac{1}{2}$ or $\frac{40}{23}$ of the net sum. Thus the gross amount will vary with the standard rate of income tax. The rule in *Pettit's Case* [1922] 2 Ch. 765, will not apply and any tax recovered under a repayment claim made on behalf of a beneficiary will belong to the beneficiary. (See above, p. 16.) In practice referring to a net sum in the present form is likely to be more convenient to the covenantor than reference to a gross sum, since the amount he will actually pay over will remain constant during the currency of the covenant, notwithstanding any changes that may occur in the standard rate of tax.

An incidental advantage to be derived from making the covenanted sums payable monthly is that stamp duty will be calculated by reference to the monthly sum (and not by reference to the full amount payable over the year) as being the " sum periodically payable ": see *Hennell* v. *I. R. C.* [1933] 1 K.B. 415, and *ante*, p. 26.

The trustees under a covenant in this form must make a point of applying all income received by them for the benefit of the beneficiaries within the year of assessment in which they receive it. Otherwise section 407 of the Income Tax Act, 1952, which is discussed at p. 5, *ante*, may operate so as to nullify the effect of the deed. Thus if the covenanted date of payment in each month is earlier than the 6th, some inconvenience may arise in respect of the payment for the month of April, since the Trustees may find difficulty in applying that payment for the benefit of the beneficiaries before April 5.

It should be noted that under a covenant in this form it would be a proper application of income by the Trustees for the benefit of an infant beneficiary to purchase, for example, savings certificates in the beneficiary's name [68] or to pay premiums on an " educational policy." In the latter case care must be taken to ensure that the policy, if it takes the form of a policy on the life of the infant beneficiary's parent, is irrevocably held upon trust for the beneficiary absolutely. If the policy is merely one which the parent has effected in his own name, payment of the premiums by the Trustees will not be an application for the beneficiary's benefit.

---

[68] *Cf. Re Vestey's Settlement* [1951] Ch. 209; *Re Wills' Will Trusts* [1958] 3 W.L.R. 101.

Precedent No. 3

Covenant in Favour of a Discretionary Class

Parties.
THIS DEED OF COVENANT is made the —— day of —— 19— BETWEEN —— (hereinafter called " the Grantor ") of the one part and —— (hereinafter called " the Trustees ") of the other part ;

WHEREAS the Grantor is desirous of making such provision as is hereinafter contained for the individuals hereinafter described as Beneficiaries ;

NOW THIS DEED WITNESSETH as follows :

Class defined.
1. IN this Deed the expression " the Beneficiaries " means and includes the individuals named in the Schedule hereto the child or children whether now in being or born hereafter of any of the individuals so named and such other individual or individuals and the child or children of any of them as the Grantor may from time to time nominate by deed or deeds supplemental to this Deed but so that neither the Grantor nor any wife of his shall be capable of being beneficiaries.

Covenant.
2. THE Grantor hereby covenants with the Trustees that he will pay to the Trustees in each year of assessment during his life or during the period of seven years from the date hereof whichever period shall be the shorter as long as any one of the beneficiaries is living the annual sum of —— pounds (£——) to be held upon the trust hereinafter declared concerning the same such sum to be paid free of all deductions except income tax at the standard rate for the time being in force on the —— day of —— in every year the first of such payments to be made on the execution hereof.

Trusts for class.
3. THE Trustees shall stand possessed of the said annual sum hereinbefore covenanted to be paid by the Grantor UPON TRUST to pay or apply the same as and when received by them to or for the maintenance education or otherwise for the benefit of all or any to the exclusion of the others or other of the Beneficiaries for the time being in existence in such shares and in such manner in all respects as the Trustees in their discretion may think fit with power to the Trustees to pay any sum to any parent or guardian of any of the Beneficiaries for the time being an infant for the

maintenance education or benefit of such infant without being responsible for the application thereof by such parent or guardian and in the exercise of their discretion as aforesaid the Trustees may have regard to but without being bound by the wishes of the Grantor as expressed to them from time to time in writing.

Persons
excepted.

4. NOTWITHSTANDING the foregoing provisions of this Deed nothing hereinbefore contained shall authorise the Trustees to pay or apply any sum to or for the maintenance education or otherwise for the benefit of any individual who is at the date of such payment in the service of the Grantor or accustomed to act as the solicitor or agent of the Grantor.

New
trustees.

5. THE power of appointing new trustees shall be vested in the Grantor.

IN WITNESS, ETC.

[THE SCHEDULE]

Whether as a strict matter of law the trustees of a covenant such as this have a duty to enforce the covenant against the covenantor may be open to question: see *Re Kay's Settlement, Broadbent* v. *Macnab* [1939] Ch. 329. The argument in that case appears to be that, as equity will not assist a volunteer, the trustees, even if willing, should not be directed to enforce the covenant, for this would only be an indirect way of assisting the volunteer—the beneficiary under the covenant.[69] The provision sometimes found in deeds of covenant that the trustees are to be under no obligation to enforce the covenant thus appears possibly to be superfluous. Such a provision is in any event considered to be undesirable since it suggests that the covenantor may not intend to meet his obligations in full under the covenant. From the tax point of view it is essential that the covenant can be presented as creating a firm obligation; whether that obligation can be enforced is not, it is submitted, so far as tax is concerned, material.

The circumstances in which a covenant in this, or some similar, form may be appropriate will vary. By way of example a wealthy parent may wish to benefit a child on the occasion of the child's marriage. Subsequently grandchildren may be born for whose benefit sums can be applied under the discretionary trust. The net tax advantage to be gained if this is done may well exceed the advantage which would have accrued under a simple covenant in favour of the covenantor's child.

[69] In a closely reasoned article in 76 L.Q.R., Mr. O. W. Elliott concludes that *Re Kay's Settlement* was wrongly decided.

It is essential that the spouse of the covenantor should not be a member of the discretionary class. A covenant under which the covenantor's spouse is a potential recipient of income is by virtue of the provisions of section 22 of the Finance Act, 1958, ineffective for tax purposes, even though the discretion is not in fact exercised in favour of the spouse.

The sum payable under this covenant is expressed as a gross sum and, by way of reminder, express reference is made to the deduction of income tax at the standard rate on payment. (See above, p. 14.) Also by way of reminder, clause 4 expressly excludes from the discretionary class persons within the prohibited category under section 415 (1) of the Income Tax Act, 1952. (See above, p. 7.)

The children whose issue are to be objects of the discretion will have to be named individually in the Schedule: see section 415 (1) (c) of the Income Tax Act, 1952.

It would seem to be the case that there is no objection to including the children of some person in the covenantor's service as potential recipients of income provided that they are named and not simply described as the children of their parent. Applications of income for the benefit of such named children will, it is submitted, be payments " to an individual for his own use " within the meaning of subsection (1) (a) of section 415 and that individual will not be in the service of the settlor. Of course, an employer who makes covenants in favour of his employees' children as an alternative to paying the employees increased wages may find himself involved in an argument with the Revenue on the question whether or not the covenant is a covenant to make annual payments at all.

This is the kind of covenant commented upon unfavourably in the Report of the Royal Commission on the Taxation of Profits and Income. (See above, p. 5.) It should perhaps therefore be avoided by those with a nervous disposition towards future trends in legislation. Those who take the robust view that retrospective legislation cannot happen here, may still have a use for it.[70] A warning must however be added, that the execution of a supplemental deed under clause 1 of this precedent may possibly be regarded as a fresh settlement which would in some circumstances be rendered ineffective under the provisions of section 392 of the Income Tax Act, 1952: cf. I. R. C. v. Nicolson [1953] 1 W.L.R. 809; 34 Tax Cas. 354.

---

[70] It is to be noted that ss. 21 and 22 of the Finance Act, 1958, apply to settlements whether made before or after the Act but the sections offer, or purport to offer, a locus poenitentiae in respect of settlements made before the Act.

PRECEDENT No. 4

Covenant in Favour of a Charity

Parties.

THIS DEED OF COVENANT is made the —— day of —— 19— BETWEEN —— of —— (hereinafter called " the Subscriber ") of the one part and —— (hereinafter called " the Charity ") of the other part ;

Recital.

WHEREAS the Subscriber is desirous of binding himself to support the Charity and its work by entering into the covenant hereinafter contained ;

NOW THIS DEED WITNESSETH as follows :

Covenant for seven years.

THE Subscriber hereby covenants with the Charity that he will during the term of seven years from the —— day of —— 19— or during his lifetime (whichever is the shorter period) pay to the funds of the Charity annually out of his taxed income such a sum as will after deduction of income tax at the standard rate for the time being in force leave a sum of —— pounds (£——) the first annual payment to be made on the —— day of —— 19— and subsequent annual payments to be made on the —— day of —— in each subsequent year.

IN WITNESS, ETC.

The advantage to be derived from a deed of covenant in favour of a charity is limited by section 415 of the Income Tax Act, 1952. No deduction from the payer's surtaxable income will be made in respect of the sum payable under the covenant; the gross sum will be included in his total income for surtax purposes. Nevertheless a saving of income tax may be made. If the payer has sufficient taxed income out of which to make the covenanted payment, then, by giving the net sum out of his own pocket he can benefit the charity to the extent of the gross sum. (See above, p. 30.) The payer hands over the net sum and the charity can recover from the Revenue the amount of the tax deducted from the gross sum, if it establishes its claim to exemption under section 447 of the Income Tax Act, 1952.

The words " out of his taxed income " or similar words are frequently found in this type of covenant. Whether they add anything to the effect of the covenant seems doubtful. At least they serve as a reminder that it is assumed that the payer will have sufficient taxed income to cause section 169 and not section 170 of the Income Tax Act, 1952, to operate. (See above, pp. 13 et seq.)

In fixing the date on which the first annual payment under this covenant is to be made care must be taken to ensure that the period

between the first and last payments under the covenant *can* exceed six
years: see *I. R. C.* v. *St. Luke's Hostel Trustees* (1930) 15 Tax Cas.
682, and see above, p. 2.   This will be effected if the date in line 2
of the operative clause is the same as the date in line 8.

For the exemption of tax to apply, the charity should be one in the
United Kingdom: *Camille and Henry Dreyfus International Foundation
Inc.* v. *I. R. C.* [1956] A.C. 39; 36 Tax Cas. 126.

If a covenant in favour of a charity is to have the effects here
described, there must be no suggestion that the charity is to provide a
quo for the subscriber's *quid*: *I. R. C.* v. *National Book League* [1957]
Ch. 488; 37 Tax Cas. 455.

The practice has grown in recent years whereby charities invite
their subscribers to execute covenants similar to the above and the subscribers do so, under the impression that they thereby almost double
their subscription without cost to themselves.   This is not always so.
Under sections 169 and 170 of the Income Tax Act, 1952 (the old rules 19
and 21) the taxpayer in effect deducts from his payments to the charity
tax at the standard rate and accounts for this to the Revenue authorities.
Where the taxpayer has income on which he pays tax at the standard
rate, the effect is that he pays no more tax once he has executed the
covenant, than before.   But if his reliefs and allowances are such that
he pays the standard rate on no part of his income, he will find that
he has to account to the Revenue for the difference between tax at
the highest rate which he pays and tax at the standard rate on the gross
sum covenanted: Income Tax Act, 1952, s. 221.   In other words, the
taxpayer gets no reliefs or allowances on the gross sum in the covenant.
If his unearned income is less than the covenanted sum the covenantor
will lose the earned income relief on the payment made out of earned
income.

It is considered that the above precedent can be adapted to meet the
circumstance that the covenantor wishes to select the charities which are
to benefit from time to time.   It is suggested that the charities should
be listed in a Schedule, and the covenant made with trustees, who should
be directed to apply the income among such of the scheduled charities
as they select, subject to the requirement that they conform to the
directions of the covenantor expressed to them in writing.

PRECEDENT No. 5

Release of Existing Covenant with Substitution of New Covenant for Payment of Monthly Sum to an Adult

Parties.

THIS DEED OF COVENANT is made the —— day of —— 19— BETWEEN —— (hereinafter called " the Grantor ") of the one part and —— (hereinafter called " the Beneficiary ") of the other part ;

WHEREAS :

Recitals: Former covenant.

(A) By a Deed of Covenant made the —— day of —— 19— between the Grantor of the one part and the Beneficiary of the other part (hereinafter called " the original covenant ") the Grantor covenanted to pay to the Beneficiary during the term of seven years from the —— day of —— 19— or during his lifetime whichever should be the shorter period the monthly sum therein mentioned ;

Payment acknowledged.

(B) The Grantor as the Beneficiary hereby acknowledges has duly paid to the Beneficiary all the monthly sums which have become due under the original covenant down to and including the date of these presents ;

New covenant.

(C) The Grantor is desirous of substituting for the original covenant the covenant hereinafter contained ;

Agreement to release

(D) In consideration of the covenant by the Grantor hereinafter contained the Beneficiary has agreed to release the Grantor from all future obligations under the original covenant in manner hereinafter appearing ;

Release.

NOW THIS DEED WITNESSETH as follows :

1. IN consideration of the covenant by the Grantor hereinafter contained the Beneficiary hereby releases the Grantor from all future obligations arising under the original covenant and from all actions proceedings claims and demands whatsoever for or upon account of or in respect of the original covenant or the moneys therein mentioned or any part thereof.

Covenant.   2. IN pursuance of the desire hereinbefore recited the Grantor hereby covenants with the Beneficiary that he will during the term of seven years from the date hereof or during their joint lives whichever is the shorter period pay to the Beneficiary on the first day of every month such a sum as after deduction of income tax at the standard rate for the time being in force shall be equal to the sum of —— pounds (£——) the first such monthly payment to be made on the first day of —— next.

    IN WITNESS, ETC.

Circumstances may arise in which a covenantor may wish to vary or extend a covenant with the approval and consent of the covenantee. By way of example, the original covenant may have been drafted so that the rule in *Pettit's Case* [1922] 2 Ch. 765 applied (see above, p. 2) and the parties may wish to eliminate the necessity of the covenantee accounting to the covenantor for a proportion of his or her personal reliefs and allowances.

Under this covenant a net sum is payable and the rule in *Pettit's* case (*supra*) will not apply.

The date inserted in the last line of clause 2 must be such that the period between the first and last payments under the covenant *can* exceed six years. (*Cf.* p. 2, above.) A fresh period of at least seven years must run from the commencement of the substituted covenant.

The stamp duty advantage to be derived from monthly payments is referred to on p. 26, above.

PRECEDENT No. 6

Supplemental Covenant Extending Period of Existing Covenant

Parties.   THIS DEED OF COVENANT is made the —— day of —— 19— BETWEEN —— of —— (hereinafter called " the Grantor ") of the one part and —— of —— and —— of —— (hereinafter called " the Trustees ") of the other part and is SUPPLEMENTAL to a Deed of Covenant (hereinafter called " the Principal Deed ") dated the

Principal deed. —— day of —— 19— whereby the Grantor covenanted to pay to the Trustees during the period of seven years from the —— day of —— 19— or during the life of the Grantor whichever should be the shorter period the annual sum of £—— to be held upon the trusts set out in the Principal Deed ;

WHEREAS the Grantor desires to extend the duration of the Principal Deed for —— further years and for that purpose to amend the terms of the Principal Deed;

Covenant to extend principal deed. NOW THIS DEED WITNESSETH that the Principal Deed shall be amended by the substitution of the word " —— " for the word " seven " wherever the same occurs therein and shall have effect accordingly as if such substitution had been made before the execution of the Principal Deed.

IN WITNESS, ETC.

It may happen that a seven-year covenant fails to achieve its object because the seven-year period is expressed to commence at a date earlier than the date of execution of the covenant itself so that the total span from the date of execution to the last payment under the covenant cannot exceed six years: see section 392 of the Income Tax Act, 1952, and *I. R. C.* v. *St. Luke's Hostel Trustees* (1930) 15 Tax Cas. 682.

Where this happens, it may be possible to release the existing covenant and to create a fresh obligation by a new covenant. This may not, however, always be advisable; the covenantees may be trustees not having any clear power to release an existing covenant. In such a case it may be simpler to amend the defective deed by a supplemental deed as in the above precedent.

The new period during which the covenanted sums are to be payable must be such that the span between the execution of the supplemental deed and the last payment under the amended arrangement can exceed six years. It is not sufficient to amend the principal deed so that it will run for more than six years from its execution: see *Taylor* v. *I. R. C.* (1946) 27 Tax Cas. 93; *I. R. C.* v. *Nicolson* [1953] 1 W.L.R. 809.

The stamp on a deed in the form of the above precedent should be 10s.

PRECEDENT No. 7

Covenant for Payment of a Net Annual Sum to an Adult

Parties. THIS DEED OF COVENANT made the —— day of —— 19— BETWEEN —— of —— (hereinafter called " the Grantor ") of the one part and —— of —— (hereinafter called " the Annuitant ") of the other part;

WITNESSETH as follows :

Covenant to pay clear annual sum.

THE Grantor hereby covenants with the Annuitant that the Grantor will pay to the Annuitant for the period of eight years from the 6th day of April last or during the joint lives of the Grantor and the Annuitant whichever period shall be the shorter such a yearly sum as after deduction of income tax for the time being payable in respect thereof will leave in the hands of the Annuitant the clear yearly sum of —— pounds (£——) to commence from the said 6th day of April last and to be payable by equal half-yearly instalments in advance on the 6th day of April and on the 6th day of October in each year the payments due on the 6th day of April and the 6th day of October last to be made by the Grantor to the Annuitant immediately on the execution hereof.

IN WITNESS, ETC.

This covenant may be used where the covenantor wishes to pay the covenantee a net sum and no more. The covenantor in effect indemnifies the covenantee against the tax actually payable by the covenantee on the sums received under the covenant. Tax at the full standard rate must be deducted on payment but the rule in *Pettit's Case* [1922] 2 Ch. 765 will apply and the covenantee must account to the covenantor for a part of any such tax subsequently recovered from the Revenue. The measure of the part for which the covenantee must account to the covenantor is the proportion which the gross sum payable under the covenant bears to the covenantee's total income as measured for income tax.

The covenant is drafted so that the covenantor may execute the covenant towards the end of a year of assessment, but still create an effective charge against his income for that year. To ensure that the period during which the payments under the deed will be due will be a period which can exceed six years, reference is made to an eight-year period in place of the usual seven-year period. If, for example, the covenant is executed on March 31, 1963, the first payment due under the covenant will be made on that date and the last (assuming that grantor and annuitant so long live) on October 6, 1969, a period exceeding six years. Had the period referred to in line four of the operative clause been a period of seven years, the first payment would have been due on March 31, 1963, and the last on October 6, 1968, a period less than six years, so that the covenant would be ineffective for tax purposes. (*Cf.* *I. R. C.* v. *St. Luke's Hostel Trustees* (1930) 15 Tax Cas. 682, and see above, p. 2.)

The annuity should not be secured on any part of the covenantor's income or capital because of the risk of estate duty becoming payable on the death of the annuitant. For the same reason there should only be one annuitant, not two entitled in succession to the same annuity, as estate duty would be payable on the death of the first annuitant.

PRECEDENT No. 8

Covenant for Payment of a Fraction of the Covenantor's Income

Parties.
THIS DEED OF COVENANT made the —— day of —— 19— BETWEEN —— of —— (hereinafter called " the Grantor ") of the one part and —— of —— (hereinafter called " the Grantee ") of the other part;

WITNESSETH as follows :

Covenant to pay one-quarter of annual income.
1. THE Grantor hereby covenants with the Grantee that during their joint lives he will in every year of assessment pay to the Grantee an annual sum (subject to deduction of income tax at the standard rate for the time being in force) equal to a one-fourth part of his income as defined in clause 2 hereof.

Definition of income.
2. THE expression " income " in relation to any year of assessment means the total income of the Grantor for that year as computed for the purposes of the Income Tax Acts but so that the sum payable under this Deed or any sum payable under any other deed executed after the date hereof shall be left out of account in computing such total income for the purposes of this Deed.

IN WITNESS, ETC.

Although the sum payable under this covenant may fluctuate from year to year the covenanted sum will, none the less, be income which is payable to or applicable for the benefit of some other person for a period which *can* exceed six years. Section 392 of the Income Tax Act, 1952, will accordingly not operate so as to make the sums payable under the covenant the covenantor's income for tax purposes. (See *I. R. C.* v. *Black*, 23 Tax Cas. 715; [1940] 4 All E.R. 445 and *cf. D'Ambrumenil* v. *I. R. C.* [1940] 1 K.B. 850; 23 Tax Cas. 440, and see above, p. 3.)

Section 404 of the Income Tax Act, 1952, makes ineffective a covenant if and so long as its terms are such that any person has or may have power to revoke or otherwise determine the covenant. By virtue of section 21 of the Finance Act, 1958, a power to diminish the amount of any payments which the covenantor is liable to make is to be treated as a power to revoke or determine the covenant. It is not, however, considered that the possible reduction of the covenantor's total income, for example, by the covenantor giving away a substantial block of shares previously held by him, represents the exercise of such a power as is mentioned in section 404 or section 21. To fall within the provisions of these sections the power to revoke or diminish must be found within the settlement, that is in the express terms of the covenant: see *I. R. C.* v. *Wolfson* [1949] 1 All E.R. 865; 31 Tax Cas. 141.

Express reference is made to the deduction of tax at the standard rate from the amount payable under the covenant. The reference is not essential but serves as a reminder that the payment must be made under deduction of tax.

In a complex case it may be prudent to add a clause to the effect that the amount of the grantor's income will be certified by an accountant selected by him and that the accountant's certificate will be binding on all concerned. For example :—

Accountant's certificate.

" 3. THE amount of the Grantor's total income in any year of assessment computed in accordance with the last preceding clause hereof shall be certified by a qualified Accountant to be nominated by the Grantor and the certificate of such Accountant shall be binding upon the parties hereto for all the purposes of this Deed."

There can be other variations of the amount payable, *e.g.*, the excess of the covenantor's income over a stated amount in any year of assessment, and it is also possible to define the term by reference to such years of assessment as those in which the covenantor's income exceeds a stated amount.

PRECEDENT No. 9

Protected Covenant in Favour of an Adult Beneficiary

Parties.

THIS DEED OF COVENANT is made the —— day of —— 19— BETWEEN —— (hereinafter called " the Covenantor ") of the one part and —— (hereinafter called " the Beneficiary ") of the other part ;

WHEREAS the Covenantor is desirous of making such provision for the maintenance and benefit of the Beneficiary as is hereinafter contained ;

Covenant
to pay
annuity until
bankruptcy.

NOW THIS DEED WITNESSETH that in pursuance of the said desire the Covenantor hereby covenants with the Beneficiary that he will until the death of either of them or until the expiration of the term of seven years from the date hereof or until the Beneficiary shall become bankrupt or shall assign or charge his interest hereunder or any part thereof (whichever shall first occur) pay to the Beneficiary for his use and benefit on the —— day of every month the sum of —— pounds (£——) less income tax at the standard rate for the time being in force the first such monthly payment to be made on the —— day of —— next.

IN WITNESS, ETC.

The purpose of this covenant is to give an interest limited to determine upon bankruptcy. If there were a power to revoke the covenant reserved to the covenantor, either generally or on the bankruptcy of the covenantee, income payable under the deed would be treated by reason of section 404 of the Income Tax Act, 1952, as that of the covenantor, and any tax advantage which might otherwise be derived from the covenant would be lost. (See above, p. 3.)

It is considered to be the most cautious method of drafting an interest which will not pass to the beneficiary's trustee in bankruptcy, to create an interest which will come to an end on bankruptcy, rather than an absolute interest which by a later clause of the deed is expressed to be defeated upon the bankuptcy of the beneficiary. It is possible that a clause in defeasance will be interpreted as being merely *in terrorem* and therefore void (see *Bird* v. *Johnson*, 18 Jur. 976).

PRECEDENT No. 10

Deed of Covenant for the Benefit of an Infant for the Maximum Amount for the Time being Allowed without Depriving the Infant's Parents of the Child Allowance

(*Drafted by James H. George, LL.B., Solicitor*) [71]

Stamp duty under the heading Bond Covenant is chargeable on an amount equal to the child allowance in the year in which the covenant is executed at the rate of 2s. 6d. per £100. But for subsequent years the

[71] The authors desire to express their thanks to Mr. George and to the editor of *The Conveyancer and Property Lawyer* for permission to use this and the following precedent, which appeared in Vol. 17, at pp. 521, 523.

child allowance is uncertain. In respect of the future payments under the covenant, the Stamp Office claim 10s. fixed deed duty, making the total duty payable 15s.

The covenant, to be effective so as to permit the covenantor to treat the payments as a deduction for income and surtax purposes, must not be for a period which cannot exceed six years from the date of the first payment to the date of the last payment (Income Tax Act, 1952, s. 392; *I. R. C.* v. *St. Luke's Hostel Trustees* (1930) 15 Tax Cas. 682), nor in favour of a child of the covenantor (Income Tax Act, 1952, s. 397). It could be by a grandparent, uncle or stranger-in-blood.

Where a child has an income of its own in excess of a certain amount, at present £115, the parent loses the whole or part of the child allowance.[72] The precedent enables the maximum advantage to be derived without prejudicing the child allowance if the statutory maximum income permitted to the child should be reduced. The danger and disadvantages of specifying a particular figure are that if the statutory maximum is reduced the child allowance may be lost, that if the statutory maximum is increased a supplemental deed or deeds will be necessary to take advantage of the increase and that *ad valorem* duty is payable.

The fact that Parliament may by reducing the child allowance diminish the amount which the covenantor is required to pay under a Deed of Covenant in this form is not considered to bring the covenant within the scope of section 21 of the Finance Act, 1958. It is understood that at least one Inspector of Taxes has advanced the contrary view. But in this particular respect the Finance Act, 1958, has made no significant change in the law. If Parliament abolished the income limit so that the child allowance was lost if a child had any income at all, nothing would be payable under the covenant. But it cannot seriously be suggested, it is submitted, that the covenant is therefore one the terms of which are such that any person has power to revoke or determine the covenant within the meaning of section 404 of the Income Tax Act, 1952. Any power to revoke, determine or diminish must be found in the terms of the settlement: *cf. I. R. C.* v. *Wolfson* [1949] 1 All E.R. 865; 31 Tax Cas. 141.

Parties.   THIS DEED is made the —— day of —— 19— BETWEEN A B of *etc.* (hereinafter called " the Grantor ") of the one part and C D of *etc. [father of the child]* (hereinafter called " the Trustee ") of the other part; WHEREAS the Grantor is desirous of making such provision as is hereinafter contained for the benefit of [*child*] (hereinafter called "the Beneficiary") who is the son [daughter] of the Trustee and who was born on the —— day of —— 19—.

---

[72] Finance Act, 1963, s. 12 (3), and s. 13. See also p. 18, *ante*.

NOW THIS DEED WITNESSETH as follows:

Covenant. 1. In pursuance of such desire as aforesaid and in consideration of the natural love and affection of the Grantor for the Beneficiary the Grantor hereby covenants with the Trustee that the Grantor will pay to the Trustee during every year ending on the 5th day of April happening during the period mentioned in Clause 3 hereof such a sum (if any) as with the other income [if any] of the Beneficiary in his [her] own right (without taking into account any income which is by statute not to be taken into account in calculating the amount mentioned in Clause 4 hereof) will make up the Beneficiary's income for every such year to the amount mentioned in Clause 4 hereof without any deduction whatsoever (except for income tax) the first of such payments to be made in respect of the year ending on the 5th day of April 1959 on or before the 1st day of April, 1959.

Trust for beneficiary. 2. The Trustee shall stand possessed of all sums (if any) payable under Clause 1 hereof as and when received by the Trustee UPON TRUST to apply the same for or towards the maintenance upbringing education or otherwise howsoever for the benefit of the Beneficiary as the Trustee shall in his absolute discretion think fit.

A power to accumulate income should not be inserted for two reasons: first, any sums not distributed are not allowable as deductions in computing the total income of the settlor for the purposes of surtax (Income Tax Act, 1952, s. 407); and secondly, any income arising from accumulations would automatically reduce the amount payable under the deed *pro tanto*. If it is not desired to spend the income it can be invested, *e.g.*, by purchasing in the name of the child National Savings Certificates or by paying premiums on a life assurance policy for the child's benefit.

Period of covenant. 3. The period referred to in Clause 1 hereof is the period commencing on the date of this deed and terminating on whichever shall first occur of the following events namely the death of the Grantor the death of the Beneficiary and the attaining by the Beneficiary of the age of 16 years.

Amount. 4. The amount referred to in Clause 1 hereof is the sum which by virtue of section 212 (4) of the Income Tax Act 1952 as amended or re-enacted or any similar statutory provision for the time being in force in respect of the relevant year is the maximum amount of income to which a child may be entitled in his own right without the loss by his parent of the right to the income tax allowance commonly known as the child allowance or any part thereof.

Investment clause.

5. Any moneys requiring investment hereunder may be laid out in or upon the acquisition or security of any property of whatsoever nature and wheresoever situate including in particular (but without prejudice to the generality of the foregoing words) insurance policies for the benefit of the Beneficiary whether on the life of the Beneficiary or the Trustee or any other person.

IN WITNESS, ETC.

PRECEDENT No. 11

Supplemental Deed of Covenant for the Benefit of Infants to Increase Annual Amounts already Covenanted for to the Maximum for the Time being Allowed without Depriving the Infants' Parents of any part of the Child Allowance

(*Drafted by James H. George, LL.B., Solicitor*)

Parties.

THIS DEED is made the —— day of —— 19— BETWEEN A B of *etc.* (hereinafter called " the Grantor ") of the one part and C D of *etc.* [*father of the child*] (hereinafter called " the Trustee ") of the other part

Recital of first deed.

WHEREAS by a Deed (hereinafter called " the First Deed ") dated the —— day of —— 19— and made between the Grantor of the one part and the Trustee of the other part the Grantor covenanted to pay to the Trustee on the first days of April and October in every year during the period therein mentioned the sum of twenty-four pounds without any deduction (except for income tax) and it was provided that such periodical sums should be held upon the trusts therein mentioned for the benefit of [*child*] (hereinafter called " Arthur ") who is the son of the Trustee and was born on the —— day of —— 19—.

Recital of second deed.

AND WHEREAS by a Deed (hereinafter called " the Second Deed ") dated the —— day of —— 19— and made between the Grantor of the one part and the

Trustee of the other part the Grantor covenanted to pay to the Trustee on the first days of April and October in every year during the period therein mentioned the sum of twenty-four pounds without any deduction (except for income tax) and it was provided that such periodical sums should be held upon the trusts therein mentioned for the benefit of [child] (hereinafter called " Merelina ") who is the daughter of the Trustee and was born on the —— day of —— 19—.

AND WHEREAS the Grantor is desirous of making such further provision as is hereinafter contained for the benefit of Arthur and Merelina respectively.

NOW THIS DEED WITNESSETH as follows :

Covenant
supplemental
to first deed.

1. In pursuance of such desire as aforesaid and in consideration of the natural love and affection of the Grantor for Arthur the Grantor hereby covenants with the Trustee that the Grantor will pay to the Trustee during every year ending on the 5th day of April happening during the period mentioned in Clause 5 hereof such a sum (if any) as with the payments covenanted to be made under the First Deed and with the other income (if any) of Arthur in his own right (without taking into account any income which is by statute not to be taken into account in calculating the amount mentioned in Clause 7 hereof) will make up Arthur's income for every such year to the amount mentioned in Clause 7 hereof without any deduction whatsoever (except for income tax) the first of such payments to be made in respect of the year ending on the 5th day of April 19—.

Covenant
supplemental
to second
deed.

2. In further pursuance of such desire as aforesaid and in consideration of the natural love and affection of the Grantor for Merelina the Grantor hereby covenants with the Trustee that the Grantor will pay to the Trustee during every year ending on the 5th day of April happening during the period mentioned in Clause 5 hereof such a sum (if any) as with the payments covenanted to be made under the Second Deed and with the other income (if any) of Merelina in her own right (without taking into account any income which is by statute not to be taken into account in calculating the amount mentioned in Clause 7 hereof) will make up Merelina's income for every such year to the amount mentioned in

Clause 7 hereof without any deduction whatsoever (except for income tax) the first of such payments to be made in respect of the year ending on the 5th day of April 19—.

Trusts for first beneficiary. 3. The Trustee shall stand possessed of all sums (if any) payable under Clause 1 hereof as and when received by the Trustee UPON TRUST to apply the same for or towards the maintenance upbringing education or otherwise howsoever for the benefit of Arthur as the Trustee shall in his absolute discretion think fit.

Trusts for second beneficiary. 4. The Trustee shall stand possessed of all sums (if any) payable under Clause 2 hereof as and when received by the Trustee UPON TRUST to apply the same for or towards the maintenance upbringing education or otherwise howsoever for the benefit of Merelina as the Trustee shall in his absolute discretion think fit.

Period of first covenant. 5. The period referred to in Clause 1 hereof is the period commencing on the date of this deed and terminating on whichever shall first occur of the following events namely the death of the Grantor the death of Arthur and the attaining by Arthur of the age of 16 years.

Period of second covenant. 6. The period referred to in Clause 2 hereof is the period commencing on the date of this deed and terminating on whichever shall first occur of the following events namely the death of the Grantor the death of Merelina and the attaining by Merelina of the age of 16 years.

If the covenant period is to be one which can exceed six years so as to satisfy section 392 of the Income Tax Act, 1952, both Arthur and Merelina will have to be less than 10 years of age on the date of execution of the supplemental deed.

Amount. 7. The amount referred to in Clauses 1 and 2 hereof is the sum which by virtue of section 212 (4) of the Income Tax Act 1952 as amended or re-enacted or any similar statutory provision for the time being in force in respect of the relevant year is the maximum amount of income to which a child may be entitled in his or her own right without the loss by his or her parent of the right to the income tax allowance commonly known as the child allowance or any part thereof.

Investment
clause.

8. Any moneys requiring investment hereunder may be laid out in or upon the acquisition or security of any property of whatsoever nature and wheresoever situate including in particular (but without prejudice to the generality of the foregoing words) insurance policies for the benefit of Arthur or Merelina (as the case may be) whether on the life of Arthur or Merelina or the Trustee or any other person.

IN WITNESS, ETC.

───────────

CHAPTER 2

SEPARATION DEEDS

WHEN a marriage comes to grief and the parties separate, by agreement
or as a result of a divorce or judicial separation or otherwise, important
tax considerations arise. The object of this chapter is to offer guidance
on those tax considerations to solicitors who have to negotiate deeds of
separation or agreed orders for maintenance.

Assessment of married persons

Generally a married woman's income is deemed for income tax
purposes to be the income of her husband and not her income.[1] However, either spouse may, even while they are living together, apply for
separate assessment, although the effect of this is not to alter the total
amount of tax payable by the two spouses together. It is expressly
provided by section 358 of the Income Tax Act, 1952, that the same
reliefs and allowances shall apply as if there was no separate assessment,
and the same section also specifies the allocation of the reliefs and allowances between the husband and wife. The only effect of a claim for
" separate assessment " is that each spouse is liable for his or her own tax.

On the other hand, if a husband and wife are separated under an
order of the court or by a deed of separation, or are in fact permanently
separated, they are assessed as two separate individuals.[2]

Each is therefore treated as a single person, and in consequence, if
both have incomes, the total tax payable by them is usually much less
than if they were living together.

Separation Deed

A separation deed is void unless followed immediately by actual
separation: Bindley v. Mulloney, L.R. 7 Eq. 343; and if the parties
subsequently resume cohabitation, it ceases to have effect: Nicol v. Nicol,
31 Ch.D. 524; on resuming cohabitation, however, the parties may
expressly agree that some provisions of the separation deed are to remain
in force. Where a separation deed contains provisions to benefit the
children of the marriage, those provisions may remain valid, even when,
by reason of resumed cohabitation, the clauses affecting the husband and
wife become void: Re Spark [1904] 1 Ch. 451.

---

[1] Income Tax Act, 1952, s. 354. It is a nice point whether this principle has the
effect of making " tax " deducted from a wife's income and subsequently recovered
under a repayment claim the property of her husband. Can he keep the tax recovered,
or must he account to his wife for it if it represents tax deducted from her income?
The point may be material if the husband dies. For estate duty purposes the Revenue
consider that the tax recovered belongs to the husband: see Dymond, 13th ed., p. 574.

[2] Income Tax Act, 1952, s. 361 (1). For cases where one spouse is resident outside, or
absent from, the United Kingdom, see s. 361 (2).

Generally, a separation deed includes financial provision for the wife, sometimes by a settlement of capital, more usually by a covenant by the husband to pay an annuity. The degree of care required in drafting such an annuity in order to achieve a saving of tax has been accentuated by the provisions of the Finance Act, 1958.

Section 21 (1) of the Finance Act, 1958, extends the meaning of " a power to revoke or otherwise determine a settlement or any provision thereof " in section 404 (1) of the Income Tax Act, 1952, so as to include any power to diminish the amount of any payments which are or may be payable under the settlement. The result is that where there is a power to diminish the amount payable under a settlement, the sums payable thereunder are, in accordance with the provisions of section 404 of the Income Tax Act, 1952, treated as the income of the settlor and not as the income of any other person. As a provision to vary the amount payable under a separation deed, either by addition or diminution, has been commonly used in order to provide in advance for any future changes in the fortunes of the parties to the deed, section 21 clearly introduces a new and awkward hazard in the negotiation of separation deeds. Thus, if a husband covenants to pay £500 per annum to his wife subject to a provision that in the event of the husband's income being reduced to less than £1,500 the husband may reduce the sum payable to the wife by one-third of the difference between his reduced income and £1,500, section 21 will operate to make the whole of the sums paid to the wife income of the husband. If the adjustment were automatic it might be argued that section 21 did not apply since the settlement conferred no " power " to diminish the sum payable. The alternative solution is simply to provide that the husband's obligations under the deed shall only continue until there is a significant change in his circumstances.

It should be noticed, however, that in the case of a settlement made *before* 16th April, 1958, and entered into in connection with any judicial separation or any agreement between spouses to live apart or in connection with the dissolution or annulment of a marriage, the income payable under the settlement will not be treated as the income of the settlor even if section 21 (1) of the Finance Act, 1958, would otherwise apply to the settlement: see subsection (4) of section 21.

Section 22 of the Finance Act, 1958, which provides that where there is a power in a settlement to pay or apply income to or for the benefit of the settlor or any wife or husband of the settlor the income arising under the settlement shall be treated as the income of the settlor for tax purposes, only applies to settlements where the power in question is discretionary. Section 22 will not therefore have any adverse effect on the usual type of separation deed under which the annuity is payable to the wife direct and is not subject to any discretionary power.

If the above-mentioned provisions are satisfied, the effect of the covenant will be to make the sum covenanted the income of the wife for tax purposes. The effect is virtually the same as under a "seven year covenant," [3] and is briefly, that the husband, instead of paying over the whole of the gross sum covenanted, is entitled to deduct and to retain thereout a sum representing tax at the standard rate provided the sum is paid out of income charged to tax.

At present rates he retains somewhat less than half the gross amount. The standard rate is that of the year of assessment in which the payment is due: see section 169 of the Income Tax Act, 1952. Where, however, the sum covenanted is not payable or wholly payable out of income brought into charge to tax the standard rate applicable is that in force at the time of payment: see section 170 of the Income Tax Act, 1952. And in the latter case the husband is required to account to the commissioners of Inland Revenue for the tax deducted from so much of the payment as is made otherwise than out of income brought into charge to tax.

The wife, receiving a sum on which tax has in effect already been paid at the standard rate, is entitled (provided her income from other sources is not so great as to exhaust her reliefs and allowances) to reclaim from the Revenue a sum representing her reliefs and allowances on the gross amount appearing in the deed. This sum she may keep. And provided the husband makes the payment out of income charged to tax he keeps the sum which he deducted on making the payment, and thereby recoups himself for the tax on that amount of his own income which corresponds to the gross amount payable under the deed. For the purposes of assessing his reliefs and allowances under Part VIII of the Income Tax Act, 1952, the gross sum covenanted is deducted from his own income,[4] so that those reliefs may be reduced; if so, he will be obliged to account to the Revenue for the difference between the standard rate of tax on the gross sum covenanted and the rate he actually paid on the highest part of his income, out of which he in fact paid the sums to his wife.[5] This may involve restriction of earned income relief.

The treatment of surtax in relation to a separation deed is different. The gross amount payable out of the husband's income is deductible in arriving at the "total income" of the husband for surtax purposes: *Eadie* v. *I. R. C.* [1924] 2 K.B. 198; 9 Tax Cas. 1; and is included in the wife's "total income" for the purposes of her surtax. The husband is not entitled to deduct any surtax when making the payment, in the absence of express agreement.

Tax-free provision for the wife

The husband and wife frequently prefer to arrange for a "tax-free" payment. Thus, for example, where the wife has no other income, the

---

[3] See *ante*, p. 1.
[4] Income Tax Act, 1952, s. 221.
[5] *Ibid.*, ss. 169, 170.

husband may wish to give her so much spendable income, in order that, whatever tax is payable, she has just that amount, no more, no less. This result may be achieved, as regards income tax, but may be complex in operation.[6]

Section 506 (2) of the Income Tax Act, 1952, provides that " every agreement for payment of interest, rent or other annual payment in full without allowing any such deduction (*i.e.*, a deduction under sections 169, 170, *inter alia*) shall be void." Consequently an agreement to pay " £100 a year free of tax " means a gross annuity of £100: the words " free of tax " are without effect. Even if both the husband and the wife intended that the deed should provide what it plainly says, *i.e.*, a grossed-up £100, the court will not rectify it, since the mistake was not as to the parties' intentions, but as to the effect of tax law: *Whiteside* v. *Whiteside* [1950] Ch. 65.

In order to give his wife a tax-free sum, the husband should agree to pay " such a sum as after deduction of the tax payable in respect thereof shall leave a clear sum of £x." He will then hand over £x, having in effect retained tax at the standard rate on a grossed-up £x.[7] The wife will make a repayment claim in respect of reliefs and allowances on a grossed-up £x and will hand over the sums so obtained, or an appropriate proportion, to her husband: *Re Pettit* [1922] 2 Ch. 765; *Re Maclennan* [1939] Ch. 750.[8] Some practitioners in drafting separation deeds include an express covenant by the wife to claim her reliefs and pay them back, but this is not necessary, since the law imposes a trust on the wife to claim her reliefs and to hand back the proper proportion: *Re Kingcome* [1936] Ch. 566.

It was decided in *I. R. C.* v. *Duncanson* [1949] 2 All E.R. 846, that as the annuitant in a case of the kind in question is merely a bare trustee of the reliefs reclaimable from the Revenue, the amount which is required to be handed over to the payer under the rule in *Re Pettit* is never the annuitant's own income. Therefore, the amount should be excluded from the annuitant's income for surtax purposes. The actual decision was that the net refund grossed up at the standard rate should be deducted from the gross amount of the annuitant's income. It is advisable not to insert in a deed an obligation on the wife to make a refund of any tax reliefs to the husband, since a possible interpretation is that this would constitute an " annual payment " from which income tax is deductible, and retainable against the husband.

A " *Re Pettit* " annuity is in practice more common in separation deeds than in other forms of provision, the probable reason being that it provides an invariable tax-free sum at minimum cost to the husband. Even if the wife has another source of income the amount she gets from

---

[6] See *Re Maclennan* [1939] Ch. 750, 755, *per* Sir Wilfrid Greene M.R., *ante*, p. 20.
[7] See *Hutton* v. *Hutton* (*No. 2*) (1961) 40 A.T.C. 239.
[8] See *ante*, pp. 19, 20 *et seq.*, where these rules are fully explained.

the separation deed will not vary : she will then account to her husband
for the proportion of the total reliefs and allowances ascribable to the
sum payable under the separation deed.

The rule in *Re Pettit* does not apply if the covenant is to pay a stated
proportion of the husband's income, *e.g.*, one-third. Reference should
be made to *Re Batley* (*No.* 2) [1952] Ch. 781, where the covenant was to
pay a " free of tax " annuity of £416 per annum, or one-third of the
husband's income after payment of tax, if less, and the latter was in fact
payable.

A second form of tax-free provision provides for the payment of
" such a sum as shall after deduction of tax at the standard rate leave
£x." This is really a covenant to pay a grossed-up £x: the husband
retains tax at the standard rate, and pays over £x to his wife, who may
keep any repayments she may be able to obtain. This form is much
more convenient than the " *Re Pettit* " form for the purpose of
accounting, and is as economical of tax.

The annuity given by a separation deed may be given free of surtax,
or free of surtax up to certain limits. The phrase " such sum as after
deduction of income tax " (whether with or without the additional words
" at the standard rate ") does not give an annuity free of surtax. The
reason is not that income tax is distinct from surtax, for surtax is
simply a further instalment of income tax,[9] but that the word
" deduction " in itself shows that surtax, which is never deducted by
the payer, could not have been intended: *Re Bates* [1925] Ch. 157.
Where a sum free of surtax is intended, some phrase should be used like
" such sum as after deduction of tax and after payment of surtax . . ."
The wife will then be entitled to payment of a sum, in addition to the
amount appearing in the deed, to cover that proportion of her surtax
which is ascribable to the gross amount covenanted. Calculations of
some complexity are involved, and for that reason, and also because of
the very large sums which could become payable, it is wiser to leave the
wife to bear her own surtax.

Maintenance orders: maintenance of a wife

Maintenance of a wife by the husband may be ordered by the court
on the ground of wilful neglect to maintain without instituting a matrimonial cause: Matrimonial Causes Act, 1950, s. 23. And maintenance
may be ordered by the court either upon or after pronouncing a decree of
divorce or nullity: Matrimonial Causes Act, 1950, s. 19 (3), as amended [10]
by the Matrimonial Causes (Property and Maintenance) Act, 1958, s. 1.
Permanent alimony may be ordered on or after a decree for judicial
separation: Matrimonial Causes Act, 1950, s. 20 (2), as amended by the

---

[9] Income Tax Act, 1952, s. 229.
[10] No application for leave is necessary where maintenance and/or secured provision is
subsequently sought by a wife even although no prayer for such relief was included
in the pleadings to the action: *Hodge* v. *Hodge* [1963] 2 W.L.R. 297.

Matrimonial Causes (Property and Maintenance) Act, 1958, s. 1. Often the amount ordered is arrived at by negotiation, and then included by consent in the court's order. Consequently the effect of taxation on maintenance must be borne in mind in negotiating the settlement of a maintenance or alimony claim.

In drawing up an order the words "free of tax" may properly be used. The reason for this is that section 506 (2) of the Income Tax Act, 1952, which makes void an agreement for payment in full without deduction of tax, does not extend to court orders: *Spilsbury* v. *Spofforth* [1937] 4 All E.R. 487; 21 Tax Cas. 247; although it does apply to an agreement made to give effect to such an order: *Blount* v. *Blount* [1916] 1 K.B. 230; *Burroughs* v. *Abbott* [1922] 1 Ch. 86. The difficulties which may arise from tax-free orders have, however, come to be appreciated; and it is now the usual practice of the court to order a sum "less tax," *i.e.*, a gross sum.[11]

Where a gross sum is ordered, the husband is entitled to deduct tax under section 169 or 170 of the Income Tax Act, 1952, and the wife may claim and keep any repayments of tax to which she becomes entitled. There is, however, a statutory exception: where "small maintenance payments" as defined in section 205 of the Income Tax Act, 1952, as amended by section 42 (5) of the Finance Act, 1957, and section 40 of the Finance Act, 1960, are ordered, the payments must be made under deduction of tax; but in computing his income, the payer is entitled to deduct the gross sums paid to the wife, and she is assessable to tax thereon on the basis of the amounts received: Income Tax Act, 1952, s. 206. This simplified procedure can only apply where "small maintenance" is ordered by a court (usually of summary jurisdiction) not exceeding the weekly amounts set out in section 205 (3) of the Income Tax Act, 1952, as amended by section 40 of the Finance Act, 1960. Under these provisions the maximum amounts are £7 10s. 0d. in respect of a wife and £2 10s. 0d. in respect of a child. The amount contained in Matrimonial Proceedings (Magistrates' Courts) Act, 1960, is £7 10s. 0d. In the case of maintenance made for the benefit of a wife under section 5 of the Summary Jurisdiction (Married Women) Act, 1895, as amended, the amount is £5. There is, of course, no saving of tax in making "small maintenance" payments: the procedure is merely intended to simplify matters for the taxpayer, especially for the wife.

Where an order is made of a sum "free of tax" it means, in effect, the "grossed-up" amount of the sum stated. The husband must pay the sum stated to the wife and account for the tax on the grossed-up sum. The wife may make a claim for repayment in respect of her reliefs and allowances: *Spilsbury* v. *Spofforth* [1937] 4 All E.R. 487; 21 Tax Cas. 247; *Spencer* v. *Robson* (1946) 27 Tax Cas. 198; *Jefferson* v. *Jefferson* [1956] P. 136. In both *Spencer* v. *Robson* and *Jefferson*

---

[11] See *Wallis* v. *Wallis* [1941] P. 69.

v. *Jefferson*, the latter of which was a decision of the Court of Appeal upon a " small maintenance payment," the court took the view that the wife could keep the amount she recovered from the Revenue on her repayment claim. If this view is correct, the *Re Pettit* rule, which makes the wife accountable for an appropriate proportion of the reliefs and allowances, would seem to be excluded from orders of the Divorce Division. There is no logical basis for such exclusion.

The provisions relating to deduction of tax from annual payments under a deed, are applicable only if the deed or other instrument under which the amounts are payable is governed by the law of the United Kingdom. Thus, in *Keiner* v. *Keiner* (1952) 34 Tax Cas. 346, it was held that a husband was not entitled to deduct income tax on paying arrears due under a deed which was made in New Jersey, U.S.A., and governed by the law of that state.[12] When, however, maintenance was payable to a wife under an order of the High Court in England of £22 per month free of tax, and the husband subsequently became resident abroad, the wife was not assessable to tax (under Sched. D, Case III) on the net sums received by her under the order: *Stokes* v. *Bennett* (1953) 34 Tax Cas. 337. The basis of the decision was that the amounts received by the wife should be regarded as the net sums after deduction of income tax, without reference, so far as the wife was concerned, to the question of whether the husband had accounted to the Revenue for the tax. In principle the husband should have accounted to the Revenue for the tax which he had deducted, for, as a matter of construction, it seems clear that section 170 of the Income Tax Act, 1952, is no less applicable to a person resident abroad than to one resident in the United Kingdom.[13]

Where alimony or small maintenance payments are made by a non-resident person under a United Kingdom court order or agreement to a person resident in the United Kingdom, relief by way of credit is allowed if (a) the payments are made out of income charged to tax in the overseas country; (b) United Kingdom tax if deducted from the payments is duly accounted for and (c) the payee effectively bears the overseas tax.[14]

In a case where maintenance payments are made under an order of a foreign court by a non-resident husband out of income charged to tax in the husband's country of residence, the wife would normally be entitled to relief by way of credit either under the provisions of a double taxation agreement or under the provisions relating to unilateral relief.[15]

[12] See also *Bingham* v. *I. R. C.* [1956] Ch. 95; 36 Tax Cas. 254.
[13] *Cf.* Upjohn J. in *Stokes* v. *Bennett* (1953) 34 Tax Cas. 337, at p. 344, and Hill J. in *Shearn* v. *Shearn* (1930) 46 T.L.R. 652, at p. 654.
[14] See the extra-statutory concession originally published in the One Hundred and Second Report of the Commissioners of Inland Revenue (Cmnd. 922); British Tax Encyclopedia, § 14–005.
[15] Income Tax Act, 1952, s. 348 and the Seventeenth Schedule.

Maintenance of children

Where the parents are separated or divorced, the " child allowance " is divided between them in such proportions as they may agree, and in default of agreement in proportion to the amount or value of the provision made by them respectively for the child's maintenance and education, excluding, however, payments deductible in assessing the parent's total income: Income Tax Act, 1952, s. 213; and *cf. Aitken* v. *Aitken and I. R. C.* (1955) 36 Tax Cas. 342. Prior to the passing of the Finance Act, 1940, both parents could claim the full allowance. A similar apportionment applies where a person is employed or maintained to look after the children: section 218 (4).

Section 26 of the Matrimonial Causes Act, 1950, gives the court power by subsection (1) to " make such provision as appears just with respect to the custody, maintenance and education of the children of the marriage." Subsection (3) gives the court power to order " secured maintenance " for the children. Rather troublesome questions arise regarding the tax liability of the parents when an order is made.

Where, as is usually the case, the father is ordered to pay annual sums to maintain the children, the court may order the payments to be made to the wife, who has the custody of the children, in trust for the children. Although it is questionable whether the court has power to create a trust under section 26 (1), it has in the past made such orders, and their effect on tax liability was considered in the case of *Yates* v. *Starkey* [1951] Ch. 465; 32 Tax Cas. 38.[16] It was held that such an order is a " settlement " as defined by section 403 of the Income Tax Act, 1952, so that the gross sums paid are deemed to remain the income of the father under section 397.

Alternatively the court may order payment by the father to the child or for his benefit directly, without any trust, and in this case it is accepted by the Revenue that there is no " settlement," [17] so that section 397 does not apply and the payments made under the order are treated as the income of the child for tax purposes. Whether the first or second type of order is the more beneficial order from the tax point of view depends on the facts of each particular case.

Take the case, for example, of a father who is a surtax payer and who is ordered to pay £100 a year to his child who is aged five and has no other income. If the first type of order is made, the father gets no relief from tax in respect of the £100, as it is deemed to be his income, not the child's. But, provided his wife makes no claim in respect of the child allowance, the father will be entitled to the child allowance which, until the child is eleven years old, affords relief from income tax and

---

[16] See also *Stevens* v. *Tirard* [1940] 1 K.B. 204; 23 Tax Cas. 321, where the payments were held to be the income of the wife and not that of the children.

[17] The matter has been the subject of a published correspondence between the Solicitor to the Board of Inland Revenue and the Senior Registrar of the Divorce Registry: see *Law Notes*, January 1953.

surtax on £115: see section 212 (1) of the Income Tax Act, 1952, as amended by section 2 (5) of the Finance Act, 1955, and section 12 (3) of the Finance Act, 1963. But if the second type of order is made, the father does get relief in respect of income tax and surtax in respect of the £100: in effect he reduces his taxable income by £100. And at the same time, assuming his wife does not make any claim in respect of the child allowance, he will be entitled to the child allowance since his child is not entitled to an income exceeding £115: see section 212 (4) of the Income Tax Act, 1952, as amended by section 12 (3) of the Finance Act, 1963. Thus in this case the second type of order is preferable.

On the same facts as the above case, except that the father is ordered to pay £200 a year to his child, the position is as follows. Under the first type of order the father gets no relief from tax in respect of the £200, which is deemed to be his income. He still gets his child allowance as his child has no income of its own. This gives relief from income tax and surtax on £115. Under the second type of order the father does get relief from income tax and surtax in respect of the £200, in effect reducing his taxable income by that amount. Further, with effect from the year of assessment 1964–65, he will still be entitled to £30 of the child allowance.[17a]

An order directing the husband to pay the sums to the child direct will not affect the liability to tax of the wife, except insofar as, by giving to the child an income of its own, it precludes the wife from claiming child allowance. Where the payments are made to the wife, who undertakes the maintenance of the children, she is entitled to claim child allowance (subject to any allocation to the husband) but must include the payments as her own income; cf. Stevens v. Tirard [1940] 1 K.B. 204; 23 Tax Cas. 321; Spencer v. Robson (1946) 27 Tax Cas. 198.

As an alternative, the court may make an order for a child's maintenance which is a " small maintenance payment " under section 205 of the Income Tax Act, 1952, as amended. The limit in amount is £2 10s. 0d. weekly, up to a maximum age of the child of twenty-one years. The amount is payable gross and forms a deduction from the income of the person making the payment. If there is any liability to tax on the recipient, the sums so received are assessable under Sched. D, Case III, for the year in which due.

Secured maintenance

Under sections 19 (1) and 26 (3) of the Matrimonial Causes Act, 1950, the court may order that the husband secure such gross sum or annual sum in favour of the wife or children as the court shall think fit; by section 26 (3) the wife may also be ordered to secure a gross or annual sum in

[17a] Finance Act, 1963, s. 13.

favour of the children. These enactments clearly refer to the setting apart of substantial property, or to the taking of a guarantee; the former is clearly within the meaning of the word " settlement " in sections 403 and 411 of the Income Tax Act, 1952. Therefore the provisions of Part XVIII of the Income Tax Act, 1952, require to be borne in mind in considering the terms of such an order; in particular, section 397 will invariably apply to income paid to a child out of provision made by either parent, with the result that the income will be deemed, for tax purposes, to be income of the parent.

In practice it may be found more beneficial, instead of providing secured maintenance in the traditional way, to obtain an order of the court for payment of an annual sum by the father to the child without direct security, so that, according to the practice mentioned above,[18] the payments are not caught by section 397 of the Income Tax Act, 1952: then to provide the security by a separate settlement. This settlement should provide that the fund settled is subject to an overriding charge to pay any sums payable under the order that have not been discharged promptly. Surplus income could be paid to the settlor.

If a husband dies within a short period after settling a capital sum pursuant to an order of the court, or after paying or settling a substantial sum so that the payment or settlement has been referred to in an order made by the court with the parties' agreement, a question may arise whether for estate duty purposes the payment or settlement must be treated as a gift. The position is obscure and must depend on the precise circumstances found in any particular case. At least it can be argued that a sum paid with a view to discharging an obligation which would otherwise be enforced by the court, albeit in another form, could not be said to be a disposition purporting to operate as an immediate gift *inter vivos*.

Jurisdiction of court

Section 2 of the Maintenance Agreements Act, 1957, provides that if an agreement between spouses for the purposes of their living apart includes a provision purporting to restrict any right to apply to a court for an order containing financial arrangements, that provision shall be void, but that any other financial arrangements contained in the agreement are not thereby rendered void or unenforceable. The effect of the section is to avoid the severe consequences of the decision in *Bennett* v. *Bennett* [1952] 1 K.B. 249, where it was held that a wife could not bring an action for arrears of payments under a deed which contained covenants by the wife which purported to oust the jurisdiction of the Divorce Court.

---

[18] See *ante*, p. 61.

PRECEDENT No. 12

Deed of Separation Providing a Tax-free Income for the Wife, Terminable Upon any Considerable Change in the Husband's Means. Provision of a House as Residence for the Wife

The following precedent is intended to meet the case where the husband's means are likely to increase in the future, and the wife is unwilling to tie herself down to a fixed sum which may in a few years be out of proportion to what the husband may be able to afford. Upon the termination of this deed, the parties will be free to negotiate a fresh agreement, although the wife may, if she chooses, apply to the court for maintenance.

The stamp required will be 10s. on the agreement to separate and provide the house, and *ad valorem* on the sum covenanted to be paid at the rate applicable to a bond, *i.e.*, 2s. 6d. per £5 covenanted. A saving may be made by agreeing to pay the annuity by reference to a weekly or monthly sum; but a quarterly or half-yearly sum will bear the same stamp as on the amount payable annually.[19]

Parties.

THIS DEED OF SEPARATION is made the —— day of —— 19— BETWEEN —— of —— (hereinafter called " the husband ") of the one part and —— of —— (hereinafter called " the wife ") of the other part;

Agreement to separate.

WHEREAS unhappy differences have arisen between the husband and the wife in consequence whereof they have agreed to live separate and apart from each other and to enter into the agreement hereinafter contained;

NOW THIS DEED WITNESSETH and it is hereby mutually agreed and declared by and between the parties hereto as follows :

Separation.

1. THE wife may and shall henceforth during the life of the husband live separate and apart from him as if she were unmarried and shall be free from his marital control.

2. NEITHER the husband nor the wife shall molest annoy or interfere with the other or any member of their respective families or any of their respective friends and neither shall they the husband or the wife institute any proceedings for a restitution of conjugal rights.

Payments to wife.

3 (a). FROM and after the date hereof and until the happening of the first to occur of the events specified in sub-clause (b) of this Clause the husband shall pay or

[19] See *ante*, p. 26.

cause to be paid to the wife on the first day in every
month such a sum as after deduction of the income tax
for the time being payable in respect thereof will leave
a clear sum of [thirty-five pounds] the first of such payments to be made on the first day of —— next.

This clause is designed to give the wife a " spendable income " of the
sum stated. The rule in *Re Pettit* [20] applies, so that the wife will be
liable to pay back to the husband a due proportion of her reliefs and
allowances (except earned income relief, if any); this will be so, even
if her other income is so great that no actual repayment of tax will
be made to her. If it is intended that the wife should retain any repayments she may receive, the following form of words should be employed :

such a sum as after deduction of income tax at the
standard rate for the time being will leave a clear sum
of . . .

If it should be desired to free the sum from surtax, the words " free of
surtax " may be employed, but it is generally inadvisable to give a sum
free of surtax.

Since the husband covenants to make payments direct to the wife and
there is no discretionary element in the " settlement," section 22 of the
Finance Act, 1958, will not apply to this Deed.

Termination
of payments.
(b) The events referred to in sub-clause (a) of this
Clause are the following events namely :

    (i) the death of the husband ;

    (ii) the death of the wife ;

    (iii) an increase or decrease in excess of [two
          hundred and fifty pounds] in the husband's
          gross yearly income in any year of assessment ;

    (iv) the making of an order by the court consequent
          upon an application under any of the provisions
          of sections nineteen to twenty-nine inclusive of
          the Matrimonial Causes Act, 1950, or in any
          other proceedings of a similar nature whereby
          the husband is ordered to pay or secure to the
          wife or any other person any sum whether a
          lump sum or a periodical sum for the main-
          tenance of the wife or to execute any deed or
          other document to provide for such maintenance
          or whereby any settlement is varied in such a

[20] [1922] 2 Ch. 765, *ante*, p. 21.

manner as to be less advantageous to the
husband; or

(v) if the husband and the wife shall at any future
time resume cohabitation or if their marriage be
dissolved or annulled or if they be judicially
separated or if the wife be unchaste;

The fact that the husband and wife have power, by resuming cohabitation, to put an end to this deed, does not mean that they have " power to revoke or otherwise determine the settlement " so as to bring the deed within the provisions regarding revocable settlements contained in section 404 of the Income Tax Act, 1952. The House of Lords has decided that, in order to be within the section, the power must be found in the terms of the settlement: *I. R. C.* v. *Wolfson* [1949] 1 All E.R. 865; 31 Tax Cas. 166.

Section 21 of the Finance Act, 1958, which makes a power to diminish the amount payable under a covenant equivalent to a power to revoke or determine the covenant, is inapplicable for the same reason, namely that there is no power contained in the settlement to diminish the covenanted payment. It is possible to draft a covenant which provides for an automatic adjustment of the husband's obligation in accordance with any fluctuation in his income but the task of steering between the Scylla of section 404 and the Charybdis of section 21 is likely to daunt all but the most confident draftsmen.

and for the purposes of this sub-clause the husband's
gross yearly income shall in any year of assessment be
deemed to be equal to the husband's total income for
that year as computed for income tax purposes before
deduction of the payments made under this Deed except
that there shall be left out of account any interest or
annual payment payable by the husband under or by
virtue of any disposition made after the date hereof
otherwise than in favour of the wife and the husband's
gross yearly income shall be deemed to have increased or
decreased as the case may be in any fiscal year in which
it is more or less than [two thousand pounds] and such
increase or decrease shall be deemed to be an event
occurring on the last day of such year of assessment.

It is somewhat exceptional to provide for cesser of the agreement upon a change in the husband's income, but this precedent may be adapted to the case where the maintenance will increase in the event of an increase in the husband's earnings.

Repayments
of tax.

4 (a). THE wife hereby acknowledges that she is a trustee for the husband of her statutory right to recover from the Commissioners of Inland Revenue any tax deducted from the payments made to her hereunder in excess of the tax ultimately found to be properly payable in respect thereof, or of the proportion of her personal reliefs applicable to the said payments.

This clause is instead of the covenant to repay, which often appears in separation deeds. The objection to such a covenant is that there is a danger that the repayments will be chargeable to tax under Case III of Schedule D. This clause is in fact not strictly necessary, since it only repeats what is the settled rule of equity laid down in *Re Kingcome* [1936] Ch. 566; it serves nevertheless as a reminder.

If the alternative form of annuity, providing a sum with tax deducted at the standard rate, is used, this clause should be omitted.

(b) The husband hereby covenants with the wife that he will at his own expense make such arrangements as may be convenient to the wife for a solicitor accountant or other properly qualified person to act as the agent of the wife for the purpose of recovering the said tax and paying the same to the husband and the wife hereby covenants with the husband that she will furnish all such information as may reasonably be required to enable such recovery to be made.

This is an unusual provision which will not be required where the wife already employs her own solicitors or accountants. It may possibly be open to the reproach that the wife has not been separately advised; but in practice a husband and wife do sometimes execute a deed of separation without employing separate advisers, and the intention of the clause is that the arrangements made by the husband shall merely cover the making of the wife's repayment claim.

Wife to
support
herself.

5. SUBJECT to the terms of Clause 6 hereof the wife shall out of the provision made for her by these presents and out of her separate estate or otherwise in all respects support and maintain herself and pay and discharge all the debts, engagements and liabilities which she may incur or enter into and shall indemnify the husband his heirs executors and administrators therefrom and from all actions proceedings costs damages expenses claims demands and liabilities on account thereof.

House for
wife's
residence.
6 (a). FROM and after the date hereof and until the happening of the first to occur of the events specified in sub-clause (b) of Clause 3 the husband shall permit the wife to reside in the house known as —— or in such other house as the husband shall purchase or take in accordance with the provisions of sub-clause (c) or (d) of this Clause.

(b) The husband shall pay the following outgoings in respect of the said house or such other house as aforesaid so long as the wife shall continue to reside therein, namely :

(i) any mortgage interest [and instalments of capital] charged on the house as the same become due;

(ii) all rates payable in respect of the house;

(iii) the premiums on any policy of insurance effected on the house exclusive of any part thereof payable for the insurance of the contents;

(iv) any tithe rentcharge or similar charge payable in respect of the house; and

(v) the cost of any repairs carried out on the house or any part thereof provided that the husband shall not be required to pay

(1) for any alterations improvements or additions made to the house or

(2) for any item of repair of which the cost shall exceed five pounds unless the same shall first have been approved by the husband.

(c) If at any time the wife shall so request the husband shall sell the said house known as —— (hereinafter referred to as " the old house ") and shall apply the net proceeds of sale in the purchase of a new house selected by the wife provided that the purchase price of any such new house together with all costs stamp duties agent's fees and other similar expenses incurred in connection with the sale of the old house and the purchase of such new house as aforesaid shall not exceed the sale price of the old house.

(d) Alternatively if at any time the wife shall so request the husband shall sell the old house and shall take and pay the rent of another house selected by the

wife provided that the rent of such other house together
with all outgoings payable by the husband as tenant
other than such outgoings as are referred to in sub-clause
(b) of this Clause shall not exceed the monthly sum of
—— pounds.

Furniture
and fittings.

7. THE husband hereby acknowledges that the
furniture fittings and effects now in the old house are
the property of the wife and the husband hereby assigns
to the wife all such interest as he may have in the same.

Costs.

8. THE husband hereby agrees to pay the costs of and
incidental to these presents.

IN WITNESS whereof the parties hereto have hereunto
set their hands and seals the day and year first above
written.

———————

PRECEDENT No. 13

**Maintenance Deed under which Husband covenants to pay weekly sums
to Wife living apart from Husband. Not a Deed of Separation.**

Where there is an agreement between a husband and a wife to live
apart, either party is estopped from alleging that he or she had not
consented to the separation and is therefore not able to claim desertion
as a ground for divorce: cf., for example, *Smith* v. *Smith* [1945] 2 All
E.R. 452. In order to preserve the parties' rights it may be advantageous
to have a deed simply providing for the maintenance of the wife in place
of a separation deed. A deed in the form contained in this Precedent
would not in itself prevent either of the parties to the deed from
establishing desertion as a ground for divorce.

Stamp duty under the heading " Bond Covenant " will be payable at
the rate of 2s. 6d. per £5 of the amount periodically payable under the
Deed.

Parties.

THIS MAINTENANCE DEED made the —— day of
—— BETWEEN —— (hereinafter called " the Husband ")
of the one part and —— (hereinafter called " the Wife ")
of the other part ;

Witnesseth.

WITNESSETH and the Husband and the Wife
hereby covenant with each other as follows :

Net weekly
payments.

1. THE Husband shall during the joint lives of the
Husband and the Wife pay or cause to be paid to the
Wife until their marriage shall be dissolved or they shall

be judicially separated such a weekly sum as after the deduction of income tax at the standard rate for the time being in force shall leave £—— the first payment hereunder to be made on the —— day of —— next.

Where a husband and a wife are separated in such circumstances that the separation is likely to be permanent, the income of the wife is not treated as the income of the husband for tax purposes: see section 361 of the Income Tax Act, 1952. Accordingly, in appropriate circumstances, the sum payable under the Deed by the husband to his wife is treated as the wife's income for tax purposes. And even if the wife is required under the provisions of the Deed to maintain children of the marriage out of the sums paid to her, the sums paid to her are nonetheless her income, not the income of the children. The children have no title to the income: see, for example, *Stevens* v. *Tirard* [1940] 1 K.B. 204; 23 Tax Cas. 321. It follows, therefore, that section 397 of the Income Tax Act, 1952, is not applicable so as to make any income applied for the maintenance of the children income of the husband for tax purposes.

Wife to maintain herself [and children].

2. THE Wife shall out of the said weekly sum or otherwise support and maintain herself [and maintain and educate such of the children of the Husband and the Wife as shall be under the age of 21 years] and shall indemnify the Husband against all debts and liabilities incurred by her [and against all liability whatsoever in respect of the said children] and from all actions proceedings costs damages expenses claims and demands whatsoever in respect of such debts or liabilities or any of them.

Custody and control.

3. THE Wife shall [so long as she shall remain chaste] have the custody and control of the said children and the Husband shall at all convenient and reasonable times have access to and communication with the said children.

IN WITNESS, ETC.

PRECEDENT No. 14

Deed of Security whereby Investments are Charged with the Due Payment of Maintenance Ordered to be Paid by a Divorced Husband to a Child of the Marriage

As stated earlier in this chapter it may sometimes be more convenient for a husband, whom it is sought to make liable for the maintenance of a child of a marriage that has ended in divorce, to be ordered to make payment direct to the child. As a general rule, however, where the court orders the husband to set aside a fund as security under section 26 (3) of the Matrimonial Causes Act, 1950, the advantage gained by the order for direct payment is lost, since the creation of the security under the Order is caught by section 397 of the Income Tax Act, 1952.

This precedent is designed as a means of providing security and yet retaining the advantage of an order for direct payment. It is supposed that the court makes an Order for maintenance under section 26 (1), the husband consenting, and that the security consists in the right of the child, through the trustees, to turn to the settled fund for payment, whenever the husband omits to make a payment under the Order.

The income of the settled fund is treated as income of the husband, whether it is paid to him or to the child. It is in the interests of the parties that recourse should not be had to the fund except where this is unavoidable.

Parties.   THIS DEED OF SECURITY is made the —— day of —— 19— BETWEEN —— of —— (hereinafter called " the Husband ") of the one part and —— of —— and —— of —— (hereinafter called " the Trustees " which expression where the context demands includes the survivor of them or other the trustee or trustees for the time being of these presents) :

WHEREAS :

Order of Divorce Division.   (A) By an Order made the —— day of —— 19— in the proceedings in the Divorce Division of the High Court of which the title and reference to the record are —— v. —— 19— No. —— the Husband having undertaken to execute these presents (of which a draft had prior to such Order being made been approved on behalf of the parties to the said proceedings) was ordered to pay to or for the benefit of —— —— (hereinafter called " the Child ") who is a child of the Husband and of —— —— (hereinafter called " the Wife ") the sum of £—— in each month the first such payment to be made on the 1st day of —— 19— until the Child attains the age of —— years or dies ;

Investments.   (B) In order to provide security for the due payment of the said monthly sums the Settlor has transferred into the joint names of the Trustees the investments mentioned in the Schedule hereto ;

Witnesseth.   NOW THIS DEED WITNESSETH and it is hereby declared as follows :

Trust to convert.

1. THE Trustees shall stand possessed of the investments mentioned in the Schedule hereto Upon Trust that the Trustees shall either permit the same to remain as invested or shall with the consent of the Husband during his life and subject thereto at their discretion sell call in or convert into money all or any of the said investments and shall with the like consent and at the like discretion invest the money arising thereby in the names or under the control of the Trustees in any of the investments hereinafter or by law authorised with power from time to time with the like consent and at the like discretion to change such investments for others of a like nature.

Trust to pay maintenance in default.

2. THE Trustees shall stand possessed of the investments mentioned in the Schedule hereto and the investments and property for the time being representing the same (hereinafter called " the Charged Fund ") Upon Trust that if after the termination of any month the Husband shall for any reason have omitted to pay the sum of £—— ordered to be paid by him as hereinbefore recited in respect of that month or any part of such sum the Trustees (after having been notified in writing by the Wife or the Child or by any person acting on behalf of either of them of such omission and after having demanded from the Husband immediate proof of such payment having been made and having failed to elicit such proof) shall pay or apply so much of the income or capital of the Charged Fund to or for the benefit of the child and in such manner as will ensure that the net income of the child will be no less than if the payment under the Order had been made and so that any payment so made shall be received in full or partial satisfaction as the case may be of the said sum of £—— ordered to be paid as aforesaid.

Surtax paid by husband.

3. IN respect of any such payment made out of the Charged Fund as aforesaid the Husband will not seek to recover from the Child or the Trustees any surtax payable by him and sections 400 (1) (a) and 406 (3) (a) of the Income Tax Act, 1952, shall not be applicable.

Gift over.

4. SUBJECT to the foregoing trusts the Trustees shall stand possessed of the Trust Fund Upon Trust for the Husband absolutely.

Investment.   5. MONEYS, etc. [*set out any power of investment which it may be desired to confer upon the Trustees*].

New trustees.   6. THE power of appointing new trustees of these presents shall be exercised by the Wife.

IN WITNESS, etc.

THE SCHEDULE
[*Investments constituting the Charged Fund*]

CHAPTER 3

FAMILY SETTLEMENTS

SUCCEEDING generations of conveyancers have directed their attention to meeting the particular requirements of succeeding generations of men of property. The strict family settlement of realty has given way to the more modern personalty settlement or common form marriage settlement, as landed acres have fallen to stocks and shares in the estimation of men of wealth. Precedent books are no less records of social changes than of changes in the law. In the mid-twentieth century a profound social change is being brought about by the incidence of taxation at a level and of a complexity unequalled amongst civilised peoples since the days of Rome's decline. Inevitably the attention of conveyancers at the present time has been directed to the problem of preserving from the inroads of the tax collector such part of a family's fortune (whether inherited or earned during the lifetime of the family's present head) as may lawfully be preserved, by a redistribution of property amongst the members of the family.

The man of property sometimes wishes to save estate duty, sometimes income tax and surtax, but usually all three. As will be seen, it is possible by means of a settlement to effect considerable savings of estate duty, income tax and surtax, but only if numerous stringent conditions are observed. The thread which runs through most of these conditions is that in settlements, as in life, a man cannot eat his cake and have it. The man of property may not retain an interest in property which he distributes among his family during his life if the distribution is to be effective for tax and estate duty purposes.

Generally speaking, the tax-paying unit is the individual, or to a limited degree the individual and his wife. So also for estate duty purposes, duty is levied by reference to the circumstances of the deceased individual and not by reference to the circumstances of those entitled to his property at his death. If the property is retained in the hands of the head of the family until his death, a high rate of tax and death duty is likely to be incurred, and the whole family will suffer a financial loss. If, however, the property vested in the head of the family is regarded as the property of the family, it is a normal step for him to spread his property over the whole family during his life, and if this is done the tax and duty imposed upon the property will thereby be reduced. The law is so complex, however, that it is not always advantageous to give property to children or other members of the family. There are circumstances in which property disposed of to other members of a family will none the less be treated for tax and estate duty purposes

74

as still belonging to the head of the family. A family settlement is therefore only of use as a means of reducing the burden of tax and estate duty for the family as a whole if it so removes property from the head of the family that liability to income tax, surtax and estate duty will no longer be incurred as if the property had remained vested beneficially in the settlor.

One consequence of spreading the property vested in the head of the family among the younger members may be that those members may find themselves, at the early age of twenty-one, able to dispose of considerable amounts of capital. The temptation to dissipation or to improvident marriage must surely be as great today, though perhaps more sturdily resisted, than in the eighteenth century, when the young members of wealthy families had expectations rather than free estate. The remedy often adopted is to advise the young man or woman of property to execute a settlement providing for his or her future issue. Advice sometimes turns into moral pressure.

Care must be taken that the moral pressure does not amount to undue influence. The young settlor should have the benefit of independent legal advice with a full explanation of the nature of the settlement. Undue influence, which renders the settlement voidable, may exist even when the person exercising the influence has no idea of personal gain and is acting quite honestly.[1]

Selection of trustees

The first problem confronting the prospective settlor is the selection of trustees. In theory, any individual or body corporate is capable of being a trustee. The practical choice, however, usually lies between appointing not less than two nor more than four adult individuals, or appointing a body corporate which qualifies as a " trust corporation " to act alone or jointly with one or more individuals. It is sometimes said that in choosing individuals to act as trustees the intending settlor should try to appoint one lawyer, one accountant, one stockbroker and one member of the family; he would thereby have advice on every topic which can arise in administering the trust. A trustee must act gratuitously, and, unless the trust deed states otherwise, is not allowed more than his out-of-pocket expenses. This rule is inconvenient if a solicitor-trustee or other professional trustee does professional work for the trust, since he is unable to charge his usual costs; but in practice almost every well-drawn trust deed contains a " professional charging clause." Apart from the professional charging clause, it is not usual to provide for remuneration of individuals acting as trustees. However, where complicated trusts have to be administered, a trustee who is not a solicitor or accountant may sometimes be burdened with a great deal

---

[1] See *Dutton* v. *Thompson* (1883) 23 Ch.D. 278; *Bullock* v. *Lloyds Bank* [1955] Ch. 317.

of work, and in exceptional circumstances therefore—as where a considerable estate is settled upon discretionary trusts for the benefit of a large number of persons—it may be thought proper to provide in the trust deed for remuneration.[2]

The custom is quite widespread of appointing, instead of personal trustees, a single " Trust Corporation." This is a body corporate which is permitted by statute to act as a sole trustee where otherwise two or more trustees are required. All the larger banks and most of the small private banks, are, or have subsidiaries that are, trust corporations ready to act as trustees, provided a clause is included in the trust deed permitting the trust corporation to charge remuneration.

The advantages of a bank as trustee are well advertised, and it is possible to obtain a booklet from any branch or bank setting out the terms upon which the bank is willing to act. The chief advantages are that the bank never dies and never absconds, and that in order to qualify as a trust corporation a body corporate is required to have a very substantial paid-up capital. In many cases, however—and more particularly where the trustees may be required in the exercise of their discretion to adjudicate between different branches of the family—if reliable friends can be found who are willing to act, the settlor should be advised at least to consider whether he will not appoint them as trustees. Many prospective settlors could do worse than to invite their solicitor and accountant to act. In some cases it will be advantageous to appoint an individual trustee jointly with a trust corporation, such as a bank.

It is possible to appoint as trustee a body corporate that is not a trust corporation. Firms of solicitors or accountants, for example, could form unlimited companies or companies limited by guarantee or having large uncalled capital to act as trustees jointly with individual members of the firm. This is not, however, an arrangement often found in practice.

Having obtained suitable trustees the settlor must transfer the trust fund into the names of the trustees and have the trust deed executed.[3] It is not essential to have securities in the joint names of the trustees. If the instrument recites that the securities may be held " under the control of " the trustees, the trustees are enabled, if it is convenient, to have the securities registered in the name of a third party, such as the nominee company of a bank, as nominee for themselves. If this is done there will be no need for transfers when new trustees are appointed. Moreover, owing to the technical requirements affecting the transfer of American and Canadian stocks, it is often convenient and economical to have such stocks registered in a recognised " marking name " which is good delivery on the London Stock Exchange. Nearly all British bankers are " marking names."

---

[2] See *post*, p. 212.
[3] The first-named trustee should not be a person whose exercise of voting powers may have unfortunate tax repercussions, *e.g.*, for profits tax purposes; see *I. R. C.* v. *Silverts* [1951] Ch. 521; 29 Tax Cas. 491.

It may sometimes be convenient to appoint a corporate trustee as custodian trustee and individuals as the managing trustees.

The settlor as trustee

Care must be taken that the settlement is irrevocable. Some draftsmen prefer to include an express provision that the settlement is irrevocable, but this is not absolutely necessary, since a settlement is irrevocable, once it is fully constituted, unless the contrary is expressed.[4] More important, however, is the requirement that as a general rule the settlor, and his wife or any future wife, should be entirely excluded from the property given, and should retain no benefit therefrom by contract or otherwise, and from this requirement arises the further question whether the settlor should himself be one of the trustees.

Prima facie, sections 1 and 2 (1) of the Finance Act, 1894, include in "property passing on death," on which estate duty is charged, property of which the deceased was only a trustee, and, in the absence of other provisions, it is arguable that a trust would be ineffective as a means of saving estate duty if the settlor himself acted as trustee. However, section 2 (3) of the same Act has the effect of excluding from "property passing on death" property held by the deceased as trustee for another person under a disposition made by the deceased more than five years before his death. This exemption only applies where possession and enjoyment of the property was bona fide assumed by the beneficiary immediately upon the creation of the trust and thenceforth retained to the entire exclusion of the deceased or of any benefit to him by contract or otherwise.

One consideration to be taken into account, therefore, is whether the fact that a settlor is himself a trustee means that he is not excluded from possession and enjoyment of the settled property or amounts to a "benefit reserved" for estate duty purposes. The general rule may be stated that the fact that the settlor is a trustee will not of itself leave him with possession and enjoyment of the settled property or constitute the reservation of a benefit. Admittedly it may be argued that, if the trustees have power, as they normally do, to invest in a wide range of investments, they could exercise this power in such a way as to benefit themselves: this argument is invalid, however, since it does not take sufficient notice of the principle that a trustee's administrative powers are fiduciary, so that he must select investments not for the purpose of benefiting himself, but with a view to the benefit of the beneficiaries under the trust.[5]

On the other hand, a well-drawn trust deed often contains a professional charging clause, which in effect enables a trustee to enjoy part of the income of the trust funds by way of remuneration for his professional or business services to the trust. The question arises

---

[4] *Boughton* v. *Boughton* (1739) 1 Atk. 625.
[5] See *Vestey's Executors* v. *I. R. C.* [1949] 1 All E.R. 1108, 1132; 31 Tax Cas. 1.

whether such a clause constitutes a benefit reserved, where the settlor is a trustee. This has never been determined by the courts, although it has been held [6] that a clause expressly conferring remuneration upon a trustee for acting as trustee does amount to a benefit reserved. In view of this, the more cautious policy, where the settlor is a trustee and there is a charging clause, is to exclude him expressly from benefiting from the clause, and in addition or alternatively to include a separate provision in the settlement excluding him from any benefit thereunder.

A similar consideration arises out of section 404 of the Income Tax Act, 1952, as amended by section 21 of the Finance Act, 1958, and out of section 22 of the Finance Act, 1958. The question is whether a professional charging clause may be interpreted as a power to " diminish the property comprised in the settlement " or to " diminish the amount of any payments which are or may be payable under the settlement or any provision thereof to any person other than the settlor . . ." within the meaning of section 21 (2) of the Finance Act, 1958, or as a power " to secure the payment or application to or for the benefit of the settlor or the wife or husband of the settlor of the whole or any part of that income or property " which may at any time arise under or be comprised in the settlement within the meaning of section 22 (1) (b) of the Finance Act, 1958. If the answer to either question is in the affirmative, it follows that a professional charging clause where the settlor is trustee may have the effect of causing the whole income of the settled funds to be treated for tax purposes as income of the settlor. Here again, the more cautious policy, where the settlor is a trustee and there is a charging clause, is to exclude him expressly from benefiting under the clause, and in addition or alternatively to include in the trust instrument a separate provision excluding him from any benefit thereunder.

A further consideration which may require to be taken into account arises where the settlement confers on the trustees a power to advance capital to a beneficiary who has a contingent interest therein,[7] or a power to resettle capital for the benefit of one or more of a class of beneficiaries, or a similar power. If a settlor as trustee exercises or joins in exercising such a power in favour of a " relative " of his, it could be argued that section 44 (1) of the Finance Act, 1940, as amended by section 46 of the Finance Act, 1950 (which makes every disposition in favour of a relative a " gift " for estate duty purposes), applies, so that estate duty on the sum advanced would be payable in the event of the settlor dying within five years of exercising the power.[8] If a settlor wishes to be a trustee, he should keep in mind the advisability of his retiring before any such power is exercised. Alternatively, the trust

---

[6] Cf. Oakes v. Commissioner of Stamp Duties of New South Wales [1954] A.C. 57.
[7] See Trustee Act, 1925, s. 32.
[8] See also Finance Act, 1940, s. 58 (4). In practice, however, duty may not be claimed: see Dymond on Death Duties, 13th ed., p. 199.

instrument should contain a provision that he is not to join in the exercise of any such power.

It may be advisable not to include the settlor among the trustees if questions concerning controlled or family companies may arise: for example, if the settled property is likely to include shares in a company which is controlled by the settlor, that is to say, a company to which section 46 or 55 of the Finance Act, 1940, as amended by sections 29, 30 and 31 of the Finance Act, 1954, may apply on the settlor's death. By the operation of sections 55 (5) and 58 (5) of the Finance Act, 1940, a settlor may still have " control " even though he has transferred the shares that gave him a voting majority to a trust of which he is trustee.[9] Moreover, where the settlor is also a director in the company whose shares are settled, attention must be given to the question of " director-control " for the purposes of profits tax [10] and pension schemes.

Where shares in a controlled investment company are settled, account must be taken of section 260 of the Income Tax Act, 1952, particularly subsection (3) (b). That section has been held to cover the possibility of a breach of trust by the settlor.[10a]

Settlor's spouse as trustee

Until the passing of the Finance Act, 1958, there was no objection in general to the appointment of the spouse of the settlor as a trustee. The question, however, now arises whether, if there is a professional charging clause or a clause enabling the trustees to retain remuneration for acting as trustees, and there is no provision excluding the spouse of the settlor, the Revenue could not argue that the settlement came within sections 21 (2) and 22 (1) (b) of the Finance Act, 1958, which have been referred to above on page 78, with the result that the whole income of the trust fund would be deemed for tax purposes to be income of the settlor. It may be thought that this argument is too exotic even for an inspector of taxes, particularly if the spouse of the settlor has no professional qualification and thus is unlikely to benefit from a professional charging clause: nevertheless, the more cautious policy is to include a provision excluding the spouse or any future spouse of the settlor from the charging clause, and in addition or alternatively, a provision excluding her or him from any benefit under the settlement.

Power to appoint and remove trustees

Usually a settlor desires to retain the right to appoint any future trustees during his lifetime. The retaining of such a right is in itself, not objectionable. However, if the settlement contains a professional charging clause or a clause for the remuneration of the trustees, the

---

[9] See Barclays Bank, Ltd. v. I. R. C. [1961] A.C. 509 (Shipside's case).
[10] See I. R. C. v. J. Bibby and Sons, Ltd. [1945] 1 All E.R. 667.
[10a] See I. R. C. v. L. B. (Holdings), Ltd. [1946] 1 All E.R. 598; 28 Tax Cas. 1 and see also Halbur Trust v. I. R. C., Burlah Trust v. I. R. C. (1953) 35 Tax Cas. 162.

question arises whether the fact that the settlor can appoint himself a trustee and thus possibly obtain part of the income of the trust fund, gives rise to any disadvantage as regards tax or estate duty. It is considered that, as regards estate duty, the inclusion of the usual professional charging clause together with a power for the settlor to appoint himself a trustee would not amount to a benefit reserved. As regards tax, however, the question arises whether section 404 of the Income Tax Act, 1952, as amended by section 21 of the Finance Act, 1958, and section 22 of the latter Act do not apply to the settlement in much the same way as has been suggested above in the discussion of the question whether the settlor can be himself one of the trustees. No certain answer is possible, but the more cautious policy is to take one or more of three courses: either to provide that the settlor cannot appoint himself a trustee, or to provide that the professional charging clauses do not apply to the settlor or any wife of his, or to include in the settlement an overriding clause which states that no power in the settlement is capable of being exercised so as to confer any benefit on the settlor or any wife of the settlor.

Another clause which the settlor may wish to see included is one which confers upon him the right to remove trustees. There seems to be little authority on the efficacy of such a power, and presumably the question could only arise if a trustee removed under such a power refused to surrender the trust property; the court would then have to decide whether the exercise of the power automatically disbars the trustee from acting, or whether the court itself has the final word, whether he be removed or not. Section 36 (2) of the Trustee Act, 1925, is some authority for saying that a power to remove trustees is effective. The real objection to including such a power is that the settlor, having a power to appoint and remove trustees in his discretion, is, in fact though not in name, a trustee. It is difficult to be more definite than this: in practice such a power is best avoided, unless there are particular reasons for including it.

If such a power is included, it should be made clear to the settlor that it must be exercised in the interests of the beneficiaries, not of the settlor or any other person. Thus if a settlor purported to remove a trustee because the settlor had quarrelled with him, or no longer employed him in a professional capacity, the validity of the settlor's act would be open to question, and the trustee would be placed in an invidious position, from which he could only be released by an application to the court.

Estate duty on gifts and settlements

It is proposed to deal first with the question of estate duty on the death of a settlor who has executed a family settlement, and then to deal with the questions of income tax and surtax which the draftsman should bear in mind, and lastly to indicate what stamp duty is likely to be payable.

It is often said that the owner of property must, in order to avoid estate duty on his death, give away his property and live for another five years. That is broadly true—except that there are certain reliefs if the donor survives at least two, but less than five years, and moreover if the gift is to a charity, he need live only one year, while if it is a wedding gift, he need not even live for a day after the wedding—but the requirements of the law are more stringent than that statement implies.

Generally speaking the object of an out-and-out gift, or a settlement, in relation to estate duty, is to take the property outside the scope of section 2 (1) (c) of the Finance Act, 1894. The relevant part of that enactment is in the following terms :

" 2.—(1) Property passing on the death of the deceased shall be deemed to include the property following, that is to say :— . . .

(c) Property which would be required on the death of the deceased to be included in an account under section 38 of the Customs and Inland Revenue Act, 1881, as amended by section 11 of the Customs and Inland Revenue Act, 1889, if those sections were herein enacted and extended to real property as well as personal property, and the words ' voluntary ' and ' voluntarily ' and a reference to a ' volunteer ' were omitted therefrom; . . . "

The Customs and Inland Revenue Act, 1881, provided for the payment of stamp duty on accounts of personal property, and section 38 (2) (as amended), in so far as it is relevant, provides as follows:

" (2) The personal or movable property to be included in an account shall be property of the following descriptions, viz. :—

(a) Any property taken as a *donatio mortis causa* made by any person dying on or after the 1st day of June, 1881, or taken under a voluntary disposition, made by any person so dying, purporting to operate as an immediate gift *inter vivos* whether by way of transfer, delivery, declaration of trust or otherwise, which shall not have been bona fide made [five years [11]] before the death of the deceased.

(b) . . . [12]

(c) Any property passing under any past or future voluntary settlement made by any person dying on or after such day by deed or any other instrument not taking effect as a will, whereby an interest in such property for life or any other period determinable by reference to death is reserved either expressly or by

[11] The original statute had " three months." This was later increased to twelve months, then to three years, and then to five years: finally Finance Act, 1960, s. 64, introduced the reliefs mentioned on p. 83.
[12] Clause (b) deals with property transferred to a donee jointly with the donor.

implication to the settlor, or whereby the settlor may have reserved to himself the right, by the exercise of any power, to restore to himself, or to reclaim the absolute interest in such property."

The scope of that enactment was extended by section 11 of the Customs and Inland Revenue Act, 1889, as follows:—

" (1) . . . The description of property marked (a) shall . . . include property taken under any gift, whenever made, of which property bona fide possession and enjoyment shall not have been assumed by the donee immediately upon the gift and thenceforward retained, to the entire exclusion of the donor, or of any benefit to him by contract or otherwise: . . .

" The description of property marked (c) shall be construed as if the expression ' voluntary settlement ' included any trust, whether expressed in writing or otherwise, in favour of a volunteer, and, if contained in a deed or other instrument effecting the settlement, whether such deed or other instrument was made for valuable consideration or not as between the settlor and any other person, and as if the expression ' such property,' wherever the same occurs, included the proceeds of sale thereof: . . . "

From these provisions it is clear that a settlement made by a person in his lifetime will not succeed in removing the property settled from the ambit of the charge to estate duty unless a number of requirements are satisfied. The most important of these may be summarised as follows:

(1) There must be no interest for life reserved to the settlor;
(2) There must be no power of revocation by which the settlor may regain the property [13];
(3) The settlement must be executed at least five years before the settlor's death;
(4) Bona fide possession and enjoyment must be assumed by the donee immediately upon the gift and thenceforward retained to the entire exclusion of the donor.
(5) The donor must be excluded from any benefit by contract or otherwise whether obtained directly or by virtue of any associated operations of which the gift is one.

Some explanation is required of each of these requirements and particularly of the last.

(i) Reservation of an interest for life

It is clear that a settlement will be ineffective to save duty if an interest in even a small part thereof is reserved to the settlor during his life. Thus a settlement of a landed estate out of which the settlor reserves to himself a right to occupy a cottage or fish a stream during his life will be ineffective to save estate duty, unless the settlor pays full consideration in money or money's worth for his right: see Finance Act, 1959, s. 35 (2). The same rule is not necessarily applicable if the interest

---

[13] See, however, p. 122, *post*.

has, as a separate transaction prior to the settlement, been created in favour of the settlor. The creation of an interest in favour of the settlor may well be an operation associated with the gift; but the creation of the interest in these circumstances is unlikely to be regarded as a benefit obtained by the settlor within the meaning of section 35 (3) of the Finance Act, 1959. The settlor would not obtain any benefit: he would simply retain the benefit of an interest which he had not given away. But it is clear that the " interest " does not have to be enforceable in order to render the settlement ineffective for estate duty purposes: thus, a settlement upon a discretionary class of whom the settlor is one is to be regarded as a gift with an interest reserved, even though the settlor may get nothing unless the trustees exercise their discretion in his favour.[13a]

(ii) *A power of revocation*

Section 38 (2) (c) of the Customs and Inland Revenue Act, 1881, would appear to refer only to a settlement where the power to revoke is reserved to the settlor alone; in consequence it appears—although this has not been decided by the courts, so far as is known—that a power of revocation reserved to the settlor and another person jointly is not caught by this enactment. In practice, however, it would be unwise to include such a power in any settlement, since the Revenue might well argue that the settlor has not been excluded from the property given, so that the settlement would be caught by section 11 of the Customs and Inland Revenue Act, 1889. Whether this argument would meet with success is not clear.

(iii) *The five-year period*

The statutory period was extended from three to five years by section 47 of the Finance Act, 1946. Section 64 of the Finance Act, 1960, has however introduced a graduation of the charge. Where death takes place in the third, fourth or last year of the five-year period, the principal value of the property passing is reduced for estate duty purposes:

    (a) by fifteen per cent., if the death takes place in the third year;

    (b) by thirty per cent., if the death takes place in the fourth year; and

    (c) by sixty per cent., if the death takes place in the fifth year.

In case of gifts and settlements for charitable purposes the period is only one year and no reductions are obtainable.

A point sometimes overlooked is that the statutory period begins to run, not from the date when the deed of settlement is executed, still less from the date appearing on its face; but from the date upon which the trust property is vested in the trustees upon the trusts of the settlement, that is to say, when the trust is completely constituted.

(iv) *Exclusion of the settlor*

The statutory requirement under section 38 (2) (c) of the Customs and Inland Revenue Act is really twofold: possession and enjoyment

---

[13a] See *Att.-Gen.* v. *Farrell* [1931] 1 K.B. 81.

must be assumed and retained by the donee to the exclusion of the donor, and this exclusion must be continuous until the donor's death; furthermore, the donor must be excluded from any benefit by contract or otherwise. Thus, if a house were the subject-matter of a settlement, and the settlor in fact continued to live therein after the gift in the same way as before, or returned to live in the house even for a short period at a later date, it would appear that enjoyment would not have been assumed by the donee to the exclusion of the donor.[14] It would be different if the donor, owning two distinct rights over the same house, namely, a term of years and a reversion (assuming that it is possible to vest these two interests in him without causing a merger), kept the lease and settled the reversion.[15] It was pointed out in the judgment of the Privy Council in *Chick* v. *Commissioner of Stamp Duties* [1958] A.C. 435, at p. 446, that it must often be a matter of fine distinction, what is the subject-matter of a gift. If the gift is of a property shorn of certain of the rights which appertain to complete ownership—as of a freehold reversion out of which the donor has carved and retained a leasehold term which entitles him to continue in actual occupation—the donor cannot be said not to be excluded from possession and enjoyment of that which he has given. The leasehold interest would, of course, constitute an asset of the donor's free estate.

It may be deduced from the foregoing that if a donor wishes to make a gift of, say, a house, so as to reduce the burden of estate duty, but wishes to go on living in the house during his life, he may be advised first to create a term of years for a period roughly equal to his own expectation of life,[16] and then to make a gift of the freehold reversion. This is true. Parliament has, however, recently provided a simpler alternative: section 35 (2) of the Finance Act, 1959, provides that in case of property being an interest in land, or being chattels, retention or assumption by the donor of actual occupation of the land or actual enjoyment of an incorporeal right over the land, or actual possession of the chattels, shall be disregarded if for full consideration in money or money's worth. The donor may therefore remain in possession, paying a full economic rent.

Where the donee is an infant he may assume possession of the property given, because, through the medium of trustees, he is put into such bona fide beneficial possession and enjoyment of the property comprised in the gift as the nature of the gift and the circumstances permit.[17] Furthermore, what is given is not the whole property which is vested in the trustees to hold upon the trusts of the settlement; it is only the equitable interest under the settlement which the settlement confers on the beneficiary. Therefore an ultimate gift in favour of the

---

[14] See *Chick* v. *Commissioner of Stamp Duties* [1958] A.C. 435.
[15] See *Munro* v. *Commissioner of Stamp Duties* [1934] A.C. 61.
[16] Regard must be given to the decision in *Rye* v. *Rye* [1962] A.C. 496.
[17] *Commissioner for Stamp Duties, N. S. W.* v. *Perpetual Trustee Co.* [1943] A.C. 425, 440.

settlor is not enjoyment of, a benefit reserved out of, the property given, but is simply property not forming part of the gift. Similarly, payments made to the settlor in a fiduciary capacity, for example, for the maintenance of his children, the beneficiaries under the trust, are not a " benefit " to the settlor.[18]

(v) *Benefit reserved by contract or otherwise*

It has long been settled that the words " or otherwise " in the phrase " any benefit to him by contract or otherwise " are to be read as *ejusdem generis* with " by contract," and therefore that the benefit reserved must, in order to give rise to liability for duty, be secured by some legally enforceable arrangement as opposed to being merely casual or eleemosynary.[19] It is however, not entirely clear from the wording of the Act how bona fide possession can be said to be assumed by a donee, when the donee is an infant who is not entitled to any interest at all until he attains the age of twenty-one, except to the extent to which income or capital may be applied for his maintenance and advancement under discretionary powers. Nor is it entirely clear from the Act how the settlor can be said to be excluded from any benefit, if a gift over is reserved to him (whether expressly or by implication) in the event of the beneficiary failing to attain a vested interest. These two points may, however, for all practical purposes, be regarded as finally settled by the decision in *St. Aubyn* v. *Att.-Gen.* [1952] A.C. 15.

In that case a valuable summary of the effect of the enactment was given by Lord Radcliffe [20]:

" A man may have an arrangement which gives him contractual benefits that affect an estate and may subsequently make a gift of his interest in that estate; if he does, the donee has possession and enjoyment of what is given, to the entire exclusion of the donor or of any benefit to him. That is the *Munro* case.[21] Shares may be made the subject of a trust for another person, the maker of the trust having the right under it to be one of the trustees, to retain in his control the voting-power in respect of the shares and to take an ultimate resulting interest; yet that benefit does not bring the property within the mischief of a similar provision. That is *Commissioner of Stamp Duties for New South Wales* v. *Perpetual Trustee Co., Ltd.*[22] No more is possession and enjoyment of a gift compromised if a man vests property in trustees upon trust to provide out of it certain limited benefits for a donee, but subject thereto upon trust for himself. That is *Re Cochrane.*[23] All these decisions proceed upon a common principle, namely, that it is the possession and enjoyment of the actual property given that has to be

---

[18] *Oakes* v. *Commissioner of Stamp Duties, N. S. W.* [1954] A.C. 57.
[19] *Att.-Gen.* v. *Seccombe* [1911] 2 K.B. 688, 701; *Att.-Gen.* v. *St. Aubyn* [1950] 2 K.B. 429, 449, 450.
[20] [1952] A.C. 49.
[21] *Munro* v. *Commissioner of Stamp Duties* [1934] A.C. 61.
[22] [1943] A.C. 425.
[23] [1905] 2 I.R. 626; [1906] 2 I.R. 200.

taken account of, and that if that property is, as it may be, a limited equitable interest or an equitable interest distinct from another such interest which is not given, or an interest in property subject to an interest that is retained, it is of no consequence for this purpose that the retained interest remains in the beneficial enjoyment of the person who provides the gift."

Although Lord Radcliffe was dealing with a case under section 43 of the Finance Act, 1940, the principles involved were the same as those involved in construing section 2 (1) (c) of the Finance Act, 1894.

It follows from the foregoing that in the great majority of family settlements, the question of " benefit reserved " need not, so far as liability to estate duty is concerned, trouble the draftsman, except in relation to the question of trustee remuneration. Nevertheless it may be relevant to mention the decision of the House of Lords in *Earl Grey* v. *Att.-Gen.* [1900] A.C. 124, since it affords an illustration of a case where it was held that there had been a benefit reserved. In that case the donor gave real and personal estate to Lord Grey, subject to an annual rentcharge issuing out of the realty, and Lord Grey covenanted to pay the rentcharge and all the funeral and testamentary expenses of the donor and all his debts to the exhaustion of all the property real and personal of the donor. The Lord Chancellor, the Earl of Halsbury, gave a short judgment, saying it was absolutely clear that there was a benefit reserved, but, to the misfortune of subsequent generations of litigants, not indicating the reason why it was clear, or what a " benefit reserved by contract or otherwise " meant. It has been left to later decisions to reach the conclusion that the benefit reserved in that case was the covenant which the donor received and which left him the effective master of all he had given, and that the reservation of the rentcharge in itself was not such a benefit.[24] It seems, therefore, that a collateral benefit directly referable to the gift or settlement will be such a " benefit reserved " as will give rise to liability on the settlor's death even after the statutory five years have elapsed.

Section 35 (3) of the Finance Act, 1959, provides that a benefit obtained by virtue of any " associated operations " (as defined by section 59 of the Finance Act, 1940) of which the gift is one shall be treated as a benefit to the donor by contract or otherwise. Having regard to the decisions in *Att.-Gen.* v. *Worrall* [1895] 1 Q.B. 99 and *Earl Grey* v. *Att.-Gen.* [1900] A.C. 124, it is doubtful whether section 35 (3) effects any substantial change in the law. It may, however, introduce a measure of confusion since the determination of what is and what is not an " associated operation " depends on a definition of remarkable width and complexity.

It is not always easy to distinguish a gift with a benefit reserved from a sale; for example, where the owner of shares transfers them to another person in return for a covenant to make annual payments to the

[24] *Re Cochrane* [1906] 2 I.R. 200; *St. Aubyn* v. *Att.-Gen.* [1952] A.C. 15, 50.

transferor during his life. In practice the distinction is unlikely to arise in regard to family settlements except on rare occasions. Section 44 of the Finance Act, 1940, as amended by section 46 of the Finance Act, 1950, in effect deems all dispositions in favour of relatives to be gifts, except in so far as made for consideration in money or money's worth: and an annuity for the life of the donor is expressly stated not to be money's worth.

Examples of a benefit reserved

It may be of use if examples are given of transactions which it is considered are benefits reserved, or are so doubtful that the draftsman should as a general rule avoid them.

One example which may be overlooked in practice is where two persons jointly make a settlement for the benefit of a third, in which there is a gift over to the donors, or to one of them; in such a case each donor retains the chance of obtaining a greater benefit than the amount which he has put into the settlement.

Another case is where a grandparent makes a settlement on his infant grandchildren, thus reducing his income, and is compensated by a deed of covenant executed by the father of the grandchildren in favour of the grandparent. Although the covenant does not appear to reserve anything out of what is given, since the covenantor does not take what is given, the decision in *Att.-Gen.* v. *Worrall* [1895] 1 Q.B. 99 makes it reasonably clear that this is a benefit reserved, and the position is now put beyond doubt by the provisions in section 35 (3) of the Finance Act, 1959.

Another case is where a settlor retains some legal right to live in or occupy the whole or part of land which is the subject of a gift and does not give full consideration in money or money's worth.[25]

A situation which sometimes arises is where the settlor declares himself a trustee, perhaps of shares in a company of which he is the principal shareholder, in favour of infants, and then for all practical purposes disregards the settlement, treats the company's money as his own, and uses the votes to vote himself a large salary as managing director of an amount which could not be justified on commercial grounds. It is reasonable to suppose that the Revenue will insist, with a fair expectation of success if the matter were litigated, that the settlor has not been excluded from possession and enjoyment of the property which is the subject-matter of the gift, or has reserved a benefit by associated operations.

Another case is where the settlor acts as a trustee of the settlement and a power for trustees to retain remuneration from income is included

[25] See *Revenue Commissioners* v. *O'Donohoe* [1936] Ir.R. 342; and *cf. H.M. Adv.* v. *M'Taggart Stewart* (1906) 43 S.L.R. 465; *Att.-Gen.* v. *Seccombe* [1911] 2 K.B. 688, 703; *Re Taylor*, 1958, 13 D.L.R. (2d) 470, noted in [1958] B.T.R. 426. See also Finance Act, 1959, s. 35 (2).

in the trust deed.[26] It is not certain whether a power for a professional trustee to charge, or for a director-trustee to retain fees secured by the exercise of votes attached to the trust shares, is a benefit reserved, but the more cautious course may be to exclude the settlor from the possibility of benefiting under such clauses.

Moreover, the reservation of a benefit may have serious consequences on the payment of income tax. This topic is dealt with later in the present chapter.[27]

It may be noted that, if a settlor is entitled to an ultimate reversion under a settlement, estate duty will be payable on the reversion, for what it is worth, at his death.[28]

Beneficial interest arising on settlor's death

So far, the argument has been concerned with estate duty liability under section 2 (1) (c) of the Finance Act, 1894, which is the chief enactment imposing liability to estate duty on gifts made by the deceased. However, in addition the draftsman must ensure that there will be no charge to duty on the death of the settlor under section 2 (1) (d) of the Finance Act, 1894. This enactment provides that property passing on the death of the deceased shall be deemed to include:

" (d) Any annuity or other interest purchased or provided by the deceased, either by himself alone or in concert or by arrangement with any other person, to the extent of the beneficial interest accruing or arising by survivorship or otherwise on the death of the deceased."

The charge to duty thus created has been enlarged by section 28 of the Finance Act, 1934, which provides that the extent of the beneficial interest shall be ascertained " without regard to any interest in expectancy the beneficiary may have had therein before the death."

Every settlement constitutes an interest provided by the deceased within the meaning of section 2 (1) (d). It is therefore necessary to draft a settlement so as to ensure that there is no " beneficial interest arising on the death of the deceased." It may be thought that this is a task of no great difficulty, because the steps taken to avoid section 2 (1) (c), particularly the exclusion of the settlor from any benefit, must of necessity ensure that there can be no beneficial interest arising on the death of the settlor. However, it has been decided by the House of Lords in *Adamson* v. *Att.-Gen.* [1933] A.C. 257 that there is a charge under section 2 (1) (d) if the interest provided by the settlor is materially changed at his death from being an interest liable to be divested and contingent into an interest absolute and indefeasible: see also *Parker* v. *Lord Advocate* [1960] A.C. 608.

---

26 *Oakes* v. *Commissioner of Stamp Duties, N. S. W.* [1954] A.C. 57. See p. 72, ante.
27 *Post*, p. 103.
28 See *post*, p. 127.

There are two rules which the draftsman would do well to observe regarding section 2 (1) (d). First, no power of appointment or of revoking the existing trusts and declaring new trusts, or of advancing capital to any beneficiary, or any similar power, should be limited so as to terminate upon the death of the settlor. For example, a settlement should not confer upon either the settlor or any other person a power, exercisable during the lifetime of the settlor, to resettle the share of any beneficiary. On the other hand, there is no objection to conferring such a power on the settlor during his life, provided that after his death the power is transmitted to some other person or persons and does not terminate or change in quality. Moreover, there is no objection to conferring upon the settlor during his lifetime the power of consenting or refusing to consent to the exercise of a power by some other person or persons, for example, the trustees, of a power of declaring fresh trusts, if that power continues as well after as before the death of the settlor.

Secondly, it is advisable, where a settlement is made upon a class of existing and future children of the settlor, to provide that all children shall be excluded who are born after the attainment of the age of twenty-one years by the first child of the settlor to attain that age. Such future-born children may indeed be excluded by the rule in *Andrews* v. *Partington* (1791) 3 Bro.C.C. 60, even where they are not expressly excluded by the terms of the settlement. It is considered that if, when the first child attains the age of twenty-one years and thus acquires a vested interest in income or capital, that interest is liable to be divested in part on the birth of a further child to the settlor, the Crown could argue, in the event of the settlor dying after the first child attains the age of twenty-one years, that the death of the settlor removes the possibility of further children being born and thus also removes the possibility of the interest of the adult child being partly defeated. The decision in *Adamson* v. *Att.-Gen.* lends some support for such a claim, although the case is not on all fours with that decision, because the settlement there considered included an overriding power of appointment conferred upon the settlor during his life. Nevertheless, it is considered that the safest course, in the normal case, is to exclude any child born after the first child attains the age of twenty-one years.

It is sometimes argued that the draftsman should observe an even more strict rule: that he should exclude all future-born children, or at least all born more than two years after the date of the settlement. It is considered however that this argument carries little weight. If the settlor dies before any of the children has attained the age of twenty-one years, his death admittedly closes the class of beneficiaries, but it does not thereby remove the possibility of the defeasance of any vested interest; it simply constitutes one of several events which define the quantum of each child's expectant interest, and this expectant interest remains, after the death as before it, a future contingent interest.

Since the decision of the House of Lords in *Westminster Bank* v.

I. R. C., Wrightson v. *I. R. C.* [1958] A.C. 210, it has been plain that
the scope of section 2 (1) (d) is limited. It does not not apply to
interests which vest before the death even though the property in which
the interests subsist yields no income until the date of the death.
Section 2 (1) (d) tends to be in point where under the trusts of a settlement the persons who are to take interests in particular property can
only be identified at the date of death. Consequently it provides
something in the nature of a trap for the unwary, since it will not always
be immediately apparent that the identity of the persons entitled can
only be discovered with certainty following the death.

Estate duty on accumulations

So far the discussion has dealt with sections 2 (1) (c) and 2 (1) (d) of
the Finance Act, 1894, which extend liability to estate duty to gifts.
There often arises, however, a rather more difficult question where
income is accumulated under the settlement. If accumulations cease on
the death of any person, or after a period fixed by reference to such
death, such as twenty-one years thereafter, there may be a claim for duty
on property which is deemed to pass.

Moreover, regard must be had to section 164 of the Law of Property
Act, 1925, which takes the place of the Accumulations Act, 1800, known
as the Thellusson Act. This makes void any power [29] or direction to
accumulate in so far as it exceeds one of the following periods: —

(a) the life of the grantor or settlor; or

(b) a term of 21 years from the death of the grantor, settlor or
    testator; or

(c) the duration of the minority or respective minorities of any person
    or persons living or *en ventre sa mère* at the death of the grantor,
    settlor or testator; or

(d) the duration of the minority or respective minorities only of any
    person or persons who under the limitations of the instrument
    directing the accumulations would, for the time being, if of full
    age, be entitled to the income directed to be accumulated.

(i) *Choice of accumulation periods*

Where a settlement *inter vivos* does not successfully define any valid
period, the first, the life of the grantor, is usually taken,[30] so that a
charge to estate duty may arise on the death of the settlor. The task of
the draftsman must be, therefore, to ensure that accumulations, where
they occur, are for either of the last two permitted periods. There is one
exception to this general rule which may be disposed of here. It may
be advisable in a proper case to direct the accumulation of income for

[29] *Re Robb* [1953] Ch. 459.
[30] *Re Bourne's Settlement Trusts* [1946] 1 All E.R. 411.

the period of two years from the execution of the settlement; such a direction will be interpreted as an accumulation for the life of the settlor or two years, whichever is the shorter, and in view of the fact that estate duty will be payable without reduction in any event on the death of the settlor within two years, all that is lost by an accumulation for those two years is the additional estate duty payable by reason of the fact that the accumulations also pass, as well as the capital of the settled funds.

(ii) *Accumulation during minority*

A settlement on a named infant, or on an ascertained class of infants, who attain vested interests at the age of twenty-one, with a direction or a power to accumulate during the respective minorities of the beneficiaries, is acceptable, since the accumulations are valid under section 164 (1) (d) of the Law of Property Act, 1925. It is considered that accumulations may validly be made, even where the interest to which the infant becomes entitled at the age of twenty-one is an interest in income only, either for the life of the infant or some shorter period, and even where the interest of the infant is liable to be defeated by the exercise of a power of appointing fresh trusts. Thus even where a settlor does not wish his children to acquire free capital at the age of twenty-one years, or even to acquire an assured income at that age, it is still possible to draft a settlement that provides for accumulation of income during the minorities of the children.

(iii) *Accumulation for the settlor's life*

The draftsman's aim is, as a general rule, so to draft his accumulation provisions that the first period, the life of the grantor or settlor, is not the relevant period. Although that is a reliable general rule, circumstances may arise where it is desired for some reason that accumulations should continue for a time, and the life of the settlor is the only permitted period which is available by which to limit the accumulations. To what extent therefore may accumulations be directed for the life of the settlor, without running the risk of incurring estate duty? The answer lies in the proposition that if, both before and after the death, the same beneficiaries are entitled to the property, and for the same interests, there is no passing. Thus if a settlor gives an immediate vested interest to a beneficiary, and provides that the income and capital are not to be paid to the beneficiary yet, but the income is to be accumulated during the settlor's lifetime, all that happens on the death of the settlor is that the accumulations stop; the same beneficiary was entitled to them before the death as after and if he was adult and *sui juris* could have put an end to the accumulations at any time; consequently no estate duty is payable under section 1 of the Act of 1894,[31] or under section 2 (1) (d), since there is no removal of any possibility

[31] *Adamson* v. *Att.-Gen.* [1933] A.C. 257.

of defeasance. It will be appreciated, therefore, that accumulation for
the life of the settlor is in certain circumstances a practical possibility.
The limits of the possibility are, however, narrow: how narrow, may be
seen from the decision of the Court of Appeal in *Re Hodson's Settlement*
[1939] Ch. 343. In practice accumulation for the life of the settlor is
best avoided.

It appears from the decision in *Hodson* that a settlement which gives
a vested life interest to A for life, remainder to B absolutely, with a
direction to accumulate income during the settlor's life, will cause a
passing of the fund on the settlor's death. The reasoning behind this
decision is that immediately before the settlor's death the income of the
fund was being rolled up for the benefit of B, the person ultimately
entitled to capital, whereas after the death it became payable to A alone.

Enough has been said to demonstrate that, as a general rule, a settlement on adults cannot easily be drafted so that accumulations may be
made, while a settlement on infants should give property of which either
the capital or an interest in income will vest on the infants' reaching
majority, and that accumulations should be directed, or left to be
implied by section 31 of the Trustee Act, 1925, only during the infancy
of the beneficiaries.

(iv) *Accumulation after attainment of majority*

It was formerly common to draft a settlement under which the
beneficiaries were infant children of the settlor in such a way that they
did not become entitled to interests in capital under the trusts until
they attained the age of twenty-two years. This was done in order to
avoid the provisions of section 397 of the Income Tax Act, 1952; and
some draftsmen were accustomed also to direct that the accumulation
of income should continue until the twenty-second birthday of the
infant concerned. Section 397 of the Income Tax Act, 1952, having
now been amended by section 20 of the Finance Act, 1958, there is no
reason whatever why the age of twenty-two should be preferred to that
of twenty-one, except in the unlikely event of the settlor not wanting
the child to have capital until the age of twenty-two. Problems concerning estate duty in case of a direction to accumulate to the age of
twenty-two years are thus unlikely to arise.

Those who wish to provide for the accumulation of income for a
period extending beyond a beneficiary's minority may like to consider
the scope given to the draftsman under the law of Northern Ireland
where neither the Thellusson Act of 1800 nor section 164 of the Law of
Property Act, 1925, applies.[32]

(v) *Portions trusts*

Accumulation of income may be directed for any period that is within
the perpetuity rule, provided that its purpose is to raise a portion for

---

[32] For an example of a Northern Ireland settlement providing for extended accumulation
see *I. R. C.* v. *Allan*, 9 Tax Cas. 234.

any child, children or remoter issue of the settlor, or for any child, children or remoter issue of any person who takes a beneficial interest under the settlement: Law of Property Act, 1925, s. 164 (2) (ii). The use of a portions trust may, in a proper case, enable a settlor to provide for accumulation of a settled fund even where his children, the beneficiaries, are already adult. There is no clear dividing line between what is and what is not a portion (see Beech v. Lord St. Vincent (1850) 3 De G.J. & S. 678; Barrington v. Liddell (1852) 2 De G.M. & G. 480; Re Stephens [1904] 1 Ch. 322; Re Elliott [1918] 2 Ch. 150), but in the typical case the capital is settled upon the eldest child, upon certain contingencies, while the whole or part of the income is skimmed off each year into a separate fund, held for the benefit of the other children or their issue upon certain contingencies.

(vi) *Life insurance*

Where part of the income of a trust fund is being applied to the payment of premiums on the life insurance of a beneficiary there is in effect an accumulation. And this " accumulation " may continue for a period outside any of the four periods permitted by section 164 of the Law of Property Act, 1925: *Bassil* v. *Lister* (1851) 9 Hare 177; *Re Vaughan* [1883] W.N. 89. An express power to apply income in the payment of the premiums may be included among the powers of the trustees.[33]

Estate duty on the death of a beneficiary

If a fund is settled in the normal way on an infant beneficiary so that he obtains income or capital on attaining twenty-one, but until then has only a contingent interest, no duty is payable if the beneficiary dies under twenty-one: section 5 (3) of the Finance Act, 1894. It seems clear also that the exemption applies even if the child in fact enjoyed the income under a power of maintenance, whether expressed in the settlement or implied therein by virtue of section 31 of the Trustee Act, 1925: *Att.-Gen.* v. *Power* [1906] 2 Ir.R. 272; see also *Lord Advocate* v. *Muir's Trustees*, 21 A.T.C. 204.

If, however, the beneficiary's interest in capital is made contingent on his attaining some age greater than twenty-one, and section 31 applies, estate duty will be payable if he dies after attaining twenty-one but before attaining a vested interest: *Re Jones* [1947] Ch. 48. When the beneficiary attains twenty-one he will be entitled to the income of the settled fund under the provision of section 31 (1) of the Trustee Act, 1925, so that, even if he dies before attaining a vested interest, estate duty will be payable on his death under section 1 or section 2 (1) (b) of the Finance Act, 1894.

It follows that, as regards estate duty, there is an advantage in giving an interest in capital contingent on attaining twenty-one or some greater age, rather than a vested interest.

---

[33] See *ante*, p. 50; *post*, pp. 167, 210.

The property passing

If the settlor dies within the five-year period, or if the provisions of the settlement are such that, even if he survives the five-year period, estate duty is payable on his death in respect of the settled property, the question arises, what property passes for estate duty purposes? Section 7 (5) of the Finance Act, 1894, makes it clear that the property passing is to be valued as at the date of the death of the settlor, but does not indicate whether it is the property originally given which has to be valued, or the property representing the settled funds at the death of the settlor, or some other property.

Formerly the fundamental rule, finally established in *Sneddon* v. *Lord Advocate* [1954] A.C. 257, was that what passed was the property taken under the original gift, that is, the investments comprised in the settlement at the date it was set up. These were to be valued at the date of the settlor's death, regardless of what was then in the settlement. This rule gave rise to many anomalies, however. Thus, if the property originally taken was no longer in existence at the death of the settlor it could not pass: *Strathcona* v. *I. R. C.*, 1929 S.C. 800. If the gift was a gift of a valuable racehorse and the horse predeceased its donor, there was nothing to value at the date of death, only a dead horse. This particular anomaly was made much use of, and the device became known in some circles as the " disappearing trick." Short-dated securities which would shortly " disappear " were at a premium. Less publicity was given to cases where the rule worked injustice on the subject, as where the property originally taken consisted of money, which the trustees proceeded to invest in trustee securities, the value of which then fell so disastrously that the whole trust fund was barely adequate to pay the duty charged upon it. As was pointed out in the previous editions of this book, the law produced hardship and uncertainty.

The situation has been changed by section 38 of the Finance Act, 1957, which in no less than eighteen subsections of tortuous complexity amends the fundamental rule. The dead racehorse is a dead letter. But the new section has produced fresh problems, which are admittedly less numerous than those which previously existed, and provides fewer opportunities for the avoidance of estate duty in cases where the settlor or donor fails to survive the five-year period.

The general rule as to settlements is now stated in section 38 (8) of the Finance Act, 1957.[34] Broadly, it is that the property passing is the property comprised in the settlement at the time of the settlor's death.

The rule as regards gifts which are not settled is contained in section 38 (1) of the same Act, and makes a distinction between those gifts

---

[34] Where there is a disposition or determination of an interest limited to cease on death within the meaning of s. 43 of the Finance Act, 1940, the rule is contained in subs. (12) of s. 38 of the Finance Act, 1957, and is that the claim for duty is to be based on the property comprised at the time of the death in the settlement in which the interest subsisted. This reverses the rule stated in *Iveagh* v. *I. R. C.* [1954] Ch. 364.

which are sums of money in sterling or any other currency, and those which are not. In the former case, it is the sum of money which passes; in the latter, the rule is, broadly, that, if the donee sells the thing given for its market value, the price obtained is what passes on the death of the donor, while if the donee himself makes a gift of the thing given to him, or sells at an undervalue, its value at the date of the gift or sale at an undervalue is taken as the value for estate duty purposes. Again, if the donee exchanges the thing given for something else of equal value, that thing taken in exchange is treated as the property passing on the death.

Bonus shares require special mention. The rule before the Finance Act, 1957, became law was established as to gifts which were not settled by *Att.-Gen.* v. *Oldham* [1940] 2 K.B. 485 and as to gifts which were settled by *Sneddon* v. *Lord Advocate* [1954] A.C. 257, overruling *Re Payne* [1940] Ch. 576: in either case the subject-matter of the disposition was the shares originally taken under the gift or settlement, and it was this which was deemed to pass for estate duty purposes, to the exclusion of any bonus shares which might have been issued to the donee or trustees subsequent to the making of the gift or settlement. This meant that bonus shares could escape the charge to estate duty even if the donor or settlor failed to survive the statutory five-year period.

One of the objects of section 38 of the Finance Act, 1957, is clearly to bring such bonus shares back into charge to duty. As regards gifts which are not settled, subsection (4) of section 38 clearly achieves this object. It provides that where the donee of shares is, as the holder thereof, issued with shares or granted any right to acquire shares, the shares so issued or the right so granted is to be treated as having been comprised in the gift in addition to the shares actually given. As regards settled gifts, however, it is arguable that the section has failed to achieve its object. Subsection (8) is the relevant subsection. This provides that where the property given is settled by the gift, subsection (4) shall not apply, but that the enactments as to estate duty in respect of gifts shall apply as if the property comprised in the gift had consisted of the property comprised in the settlement at the time of the donor's death. Had the subsection stopped there, it would be reasonably clear that bonus shares issued to the trustees as holders of shares originally settled would be taken into charge to estate duty. But it goes on to use the following words: " . . . except in so far as that property neither is nor represents nor is derived from property originally comprised in the gift." It is arguable that this exception covers bonus shares. This argument would be based on the reference to bonus shares in subsection (4), which subsection (8) expressly excludes from applying to settled shares, and on the terminology used in subsection (4) to describe a bonus issue which contains no suggestion that a bonus issue is " derived from " the share

to the holder of which it is issued.[35] Notwithstanding this argument,
it is understood that the official view is that bonus shares do form part
of the property comprised in the gift and that duty will accordingly be
claimed in respect of them.[36]

It is not intended to set out the relevant enactments here verbatim
and any paraphrase may be misleading: nevertheless a few examples,
in each of which it is assumed that the settlor dies within five years from
the date of the settlement or gift, may show how the rule is thought to
operate in practice: —

(1) The trustees of a settlement of investments have sold investments and reinvested the proceeds in realty. Here what passes is the
trust fund at the time of the settlor's death, including the realty.

(2) The trustees of a settlement of investments on the infant son of
the settlor have accumulated the whole income and invested it in purchasing from the settlor shares in a private company. The price paid
for the shares has been the fair market value. Otherwise the trustees
have kept the shares originally settled. Here it is the shares originally
settled which pass. The shares bought from the settlor representing
accumulated income are not liable for estate duty: Finance Act, 1957,
s. 38 (14); and see section 44 of the Finance Act, 1940, as amended by
section 46 of the Finance Act, 1950.

(3) A sum of money is settled, which the trustees proceed to invest
in buying freeholds from the settlor at the proper market price, namely,
£10,000. The trustees borrow the sum of £3,000 on mortgage from an
independent lender, and spend this sum in improving the freeholds, so
as to increase their market value to £18,000. On the settlor's death the
freeholds pass and are valued at £18,000, although the amount of the
mortgage is deductible, under section 7 (1) of the Finance Act, 1894.

(4) A freehold property worth £10,000 is settled. In exercise of a
power of advancement the trustees transfer the freehold to the principal
beneficiary. He borrows £3,000 and improves the freehold so as to
increase its market value to £18,000. What passes on the settlor's death
is the freehold, valued as at the date of the advancement, i.e., £10,000.
It seems that, even if the £3,000 has been secured by a mortgage, it
cannot be deducted from the £10,000; the proviso to section 38 (8) of
the Finance Act, 1957, which deals with property taken out of settlement, overrides section 7 (1) of the Finance Act, 1894, which allows a
valuation to be made subject to a deduction for incumbrances.

(5) Preference shares valued at 15s. each are settled. The trustees
appoint them to a beneficiary as his absolute property. The company
then, as part of a reorganisation of its capital, changes the shares into
ordinary shares. At the settlor's death the ordinary shares are valued

---

[35] Examples of the sort of share, other than bonus shares, which may be covered by the
words " represents " and " derived from " in subs. (8) are referred to in *Re Kuypers*
[1925] 1 Ch. 244, where a specific gift of shares was held not to include additional
shares issued under a scheme of reorganisation.
[36] See Hanson's *Death Duties*, 10th ed., Sixth Cumulative Supplement, p. 106.

at £3 each. Apparently for the purposes of estate duty the ordinary shares pass, but they are valued at the value which the preference shares had at the date of the appointment, that is, 15s.: see the proviso to section 38 (8) of the Finance Act, 1957.

(6) A sum of money is settled which the trustees immediately invest in buying shares from the settlor in a company of which he has voting control. On the death of the settlor these shares pass and will be valued on an assets basis under section 55 of the Finance Act, 1940.

(7) A sum of money is given to a donee. He immediately invests it in subscribing for shares in a private company in which the settlor has voting control. The amount subscribed is the fair market value. Probably, on the death of the donor, the sum of money is what passes, not the shares: see *Potter* v. *I. R. C.*, 37 A.T.C. 58, and section 38 (1) of the Finance Act, 1957.[37]

(8) Shares are given to a donee, having a market value of £1 each. The donee in turn either sells or gives the shares to a member of his family, the market value still being £1 a share. On the death of the donor the shares are valued at £1, this being their value at the time when the donee divested himself of them, and no account is taken of later changes in value: Finance Act, 1957, s. 38 (2).

Valuation of shares in a family company

An interesting problem arises on the valuation of property settled, where the trust fund consists of property which has no " market price " in the popularly accepted meaning of the phrase. This situation often arises when shares in a family company are settled. Two methods of valuation are provided: the open market price basis and the " assets " basis, being a valuation of the shares by reference to the value of the company's net assets.

The open market price is the basis of valuation provided for by section 7 (5) of the Finance Act, 1894. The difficulty of applying this to a private company arises from the fact that the right to transfer shares in a private company must be restricted, and in practice is often restricted to such an extent that a minority interest in the shares is practically unmarketable. Frequently the directors have an absolute discretion to refuse to register any person as a member, or may compel members wishing to sell their shares to do so to other members at a valuation. The rule is that shares of this type must be valued on the footing that the purchaser would be registered, but once registered, would hold his shares subject to the same restrictions on transfer as affected the shares in the hands of the deceased: *Att.-Gen.* v. *Jameson* [1904] 2 Ir.R. 644; *I. R. C.* v. *Crossman*

---

[37] Even if it was the shares, and not the money, which passed, it is likely that it would be maintained that the shares were aggregable with the rest of the deceased's estate, notwithstanding that the shares only came into existence after the payment of the money and it might therefore be thought that the deceased never had an interest in the shares: see Dymond's *Death Duties*, 13th ed., p. 433.

[1937] A.C. 26; *Holt* v. *I. R. C.* [1953] 1 W.L.R. 1488.[38]   In principle, this value will be no more than the price which an outsider would be willing to pay.   But in the absence of any cheap and effective appeal procedure (such as that available under the Income Tax Acts to the tax-payer) executors will frequently find themselves in practice obliged to accept a valuation which though less than an assets valuation is in excess of any price which they can in fact obtain.

The " assets " value is applied where the shares passing or deemed to pass on the death of the settlor are (to put the matter shortly) shares in a company of which he either had control or in which he held a majority interest at any time in the five years preceding his death.   The continued application of this method of valuation, which was introduced by sections 46 to 58 of the Finance Act, 1940, has, notwithstanding con-siderable modifications introduced by sections 29 and 30 of the Finance Act, 1954, and section 66 of the Finance Act, 1960, given rise to much criticism, which in the view of the editors might often be more usefully directed at the high rates of duty than at the method of valuation.

It is not intended here to give any further account of the two methods, or to explain how a company may be prevented from being a " con-trolled company," since these topics are mentioned briefly in the next chapter of this book and are fully dealt with in existing books on estate duty.[39]

For present purposes it is sufficient to comment that if a settlor dies within five years after having settled shares in a " controlled company " which would have been valued on an " assets " basis had he retained them himself, the shares will still be valued on that basis.[40]   On the other hand, the burden of estate duty is alleviated, in respect of an assets valuation, by section 28 of the Finance Act, 1954.   This allows a reduction of 45 per cent. in that part of the estate duty on shares valued on the assets basis which is ascribable to those assets of the company which consist of machinery and plant, industrial hereditaments and agricultural land used for the business of husbandry carried on by the company.   And in some cases section 66 of the Finance Act, 1960, which abolishes " break-up " valuations for ordinary trading companies and provides that they shall always be valued on a " going concern " basis, may provide some relief.

Moreover, even after five years, if a settlor is himself the first-named trustee[41] and has the right to vote in respect of settled shares—and,

---

[38]   See " Valuation of Minority Shareholdings in Private Companies for Estate Duty Purposes," by Mr. W. B. S. Walker [1958] B.T.R. 16.
[39]   See Dymond, 12th ed., Chap. 12; Hanson, 10th ed., pp. 861 *et seq.*; Green, 4th ed., Chap. 8.   The principles applicable to " market " valuation are explained by Danck-werts J. in *Re Holt* [1953] 1 W.L.R. 1488.   See also *McNamee* v. *Rev. Comm.* [1954] Ir.R. 214.   Under s. 30 (1) of the Finance Act, 1954, " arm's length " sales within three years may provide the basis of valuation, rather than the value of the company's assets.
[40]   *Cf. Re Hall* [1956] A.C. 491.
[41]   *i.e.*, first named on the company's register.

possibly, if he is a trustee other than the first named—notwithstanding that the settled shares may not "pass" on his death, his voting rights may affect the valuation of any shares in the company which the settlor himself retains apart from the settlement: see *Barclays Bank Ltd. v. I. R. C.* [1961] A.C. 509 (*Shipside's* case). (This is a point to be borne in mind in selecting the trustees.) Whenever shares in a family company are settled, especially if one of the objects of the settlement is to take control out of the hands of the settlor, most painstaking scrutiny must be made of the whole transaction, including a review of the company's memorandum and articles. It is not practical to do more in this chapter than to utter a special warning: each case requires individual consideration.

Anomalies of the present law

It was stated in the first edition of this book that the question of estate duty on gifts and settlements merited the further consideration of the legislature. It has since received that consideration, and the result can scarcely be commended. No real attempt has been made to deal with the absurdity of the situation which has arisen because a tax intended to be a tax on inheritance, a death duty, is made to do service as a tax on gifts. Notwithstanding the reductions introduced by section 64 of the Finance Act, 1960, in the event of a donor dying in the third, fourth or fifth year after the gift, estate duty on gifts may still be fairly described as erratic and arbitrary. Thus, if a millionaire gives a small cottage to a former servant, the State will confiscate eighty per cent. of the value of the gift if the millionaire dies one and a half years later; if he dies five and a half years later, the gift is undisturbed. Had the gift been of a small farm, not a cottage, somewhat less than half of it would have been in danger of confiscation. It is possible to multiply examples of this nature, which demonstrate the erratic quality of estate duty as it applies to gifts. The question merits the further consideration of the legislature. Apart from detailed amendments of such complexity that hard-pressed legislators must be forgiven if they themselves appear only partially aware of what it is they are enacting, it seems unlikely that the law will be reformed in the near future. Until reform takes place, while it may still be impolite to look a gift-horse in the mouth, the wise donee will certainly ascertain whether or not his benefactor is long in the tooth.

Tax: Assessment of the settlor

In practice a person who makes a settlement of property in favour of his children or grandchildren usually hopes to make substantial savings of income tax and surtax, as well as reducing the burden of estate duty. It therefore becomes necessary to explain in some detail the provisions of the Income Tax Act, 1952, which deal with settlements, and which aim at making the settlor assessable to tax even on income which he has settled on some other person. These provisions apply most strictly to settlements made on children of the settlor, and therefore, although there are also several provisions in the Act aimed at all settlements, it will be convenient to discuss primarily the effect of the Act on settlements in favour of a child or children of the settlor.

" Child " is a wide term for present purposes and includes a stepchild, an adopted child and an illegitimate child.[42] It is presumed that " adopted " means adopted by an Adoption Order made under the Adoption Act, 1950, or otherwise made by a court having jurisdiction: therefore it does not include a child merely looked after by the settlor under an informal agreement.

Most of the provisions in question are found in Part XVIII of the Income Tax Act, 1952, as amended. That Part contains three distinct sets of provisions and a successful settlement on children must satisfy all three. They are set out in sections 397 to 403 (as amended by section 20 of the Finance Act, 1958), " Settlements on Children Generally "; sections 404 to 411 (as amended by sections 21 and 22 of the Finance Act, 1958), " Revocable Settlements, Settlements where Settlor retains an Interest, etc. "; and section 415, " Surtax Liability of Settlors in certain Cases not otherwise dealt with in Part XVIII." Each of these sets of provisions constitutes a formidable barrier. Each must therefore be dealt with in turn.

(i) *Settlements on children of the settlor*

The provisions made by sections 397 to 403, inclusive, of the Act were first introduced by the Finance Act, 1936. They have now been amended, and thereby made more simple and reasonable, by section 20 of the Finance Act, 1958, which is retrospective in its effect. The general policy of the enactments is that the income of a settlement made in favour of a child of the settlor is to be treated, during the unmarried minority of the child, as income of the settlor; income which is, however, accumulated during such minority is in certain circumstances not so treated. The practical upshot is that a parent will save no income tax or surtax by settling capital on his child and using the income of that capital for the benefit of the child. In order to effect a saving of tax, the income, or part of it, must be accumulated.

The restrictions imposed on settlements on children by the enactments in question only apply where, in the year of assessment in question, the settlor is chargeable to tax as a resident in the United Kingdom.[43]

The governing rule is that, during the life of the settlor, any income under the settlement paid to or for the benefit of a child of the settlor in any year of assessment shall, if at the time of payment the child was both an infant and unmarried, be treated for all the purposes of the

---

[42] Income Tax Act, 1952, s. 403; and *cf. I. R. C.* v. *Russell* (1955) 36 Tax Cas. 83.
[43] s. 397 (4).

Income Tax Acts as the income of the settlor for that year, and not as the income of the child or of any other person.[44]

Any person reading section 397 of the Income Tax Act out of its context might readily assume that this means simply that income accumulated instead of being paid for the maintenance, education and benefit of the infant is excluded from the section, and is assessed as the income of the infant, not of the settlor. This, however, is not so. The following two sections extend the net wider, so as to include in the settlor's income in certain circumstances even income which is accumulated. The draftsman is bound therefore to frame his settlement so as to avoid these two sections as well.

The two sections in question, sections 398 and 399 of the Income Tax Act, 1952, as amended by section 20 of the Finance Act, 1958, are of some complexity. One of the things which they provide is that income which is accumulated during the unmarried minority of the beneficiary is deemed to be income of the settlor, unless the settlement is " irrevocable." The draftsman must therefore ensure, not only that the income may be accumulated during the unmarried minority of the beneficiary, but also that the settlement is " irrevocable." This is not the straightforward task it might seem to be, since the word " irrevocable " is endowed with an artificial meaning.

Section 398 refers to section 397 and in particular to the words in that section " Where . . . any income is paid to or for the benefit of a child of the settlor in any year of assessment, the income shall . . . be treated . . . as the income of the settlor. . . ." Section 398 (1) (a) provides that the income which shall be deemed to be paid to or for the benefit of a child of the settlor (and which will therefore be treated as the settlor's income) shall include income which, by virtue or in consequence of a settlement to which the chapter (*i.e.*, sections 397 to 403) applies, is so dealt with that it, or assets representing it, will or may become payable or applicable to or for the benefit of the child in the future (whether on the fulfilment of a condition or the happening of a contingency or as the result of the exercise of a power or discretion conferred on any person or otherwise). Prima facie the effect of this paragraph is to make all income arising under the settlement, whether it is accumulated or not, chargeable to tax as income of the settlor; moreover, the following paragraph, 398 (1) (b), extends the scope of the preceding paragraph so as to include a settlement on a class of children as well as a settlement on a single child; this is done by providing that, in the absence of any express apportionment, accumulated income is to be allocated in equal shares to each of the settlor's children who are potential beneficiaries under the settlement.

The wide effect of section 398 (1) is, however, immediately cut down by the provisions of section 398 (2).

[44] Income Tax Act, 1952, s. 397 (1), as amended by Finance Act, 1958, s. 20 (2).

By virtue of section 398 (2) (a), the provisions of section 398 (1) shall not apply to the income of an " irrevocable " settlement, unless and except to the extent that that income consists of (or represents directly or indirectly) sums paid by the settlor which are allowable as deductions in computing his total income, *i.e.*, sums paid under a covenant as opposed to income derived from settled investments. The main effect of these complex sections therefore is, in simple terms, that an " irrevocable " settlement of capital will enable the settlor to succeed in his object of reducing his liability to tax provided always that the income arising during the infancy of the child is accumulated.[45]

What then is an " irrevocable " settlement? For this it is necessary to turn to section 399 of the Income Tax Act, 1952, as amended by section 20 (5) of the Finance Act, 1958. The word is not defined by those sections, or, indeed, by any other enactment; section 399 does, however, describe three types of settlement which are not deemed to be irrevocable, and, as amended by section 20, a further three types of settlement which are not deemed to be revocable. The draftsman has therefore to avoid the first three obstacles and to try to achieve a settlement of the second type which will be deemed not to be revocable.

While, in order to advise in any particular circumstances, the actual wording of section 399 as amended must be carefully considered, the complicated provisions of the section may be summarised quite shortly. It gives an artificial meaning to the word " irrevocable " by compressing it from three directions. First, if any part of the income or assets representing income arising under or comprised in the settlement can in any circumstance whatsoever be applied to or for the benefit of the settlor, or, during the life of the settlor, the spouse of the settlor, during the lifetime of any child who is a beneficiary under the settlement, the settlement is not irrevocable. Secondly, it is not irrevocable if it can be determined by the act or on the default of any person.[46] Thirdly, it is not irrevocable if it provides for the payment of any penalty by the settlor in the event of his failing to comply with its provisions.

On the other hand, the proviso to section 399, as amended, gives three different circumstances which are expressly stated as not in themselves making a settlement revocable. The first is where, although there is in the settlement a possibility that income may be applied for the benefit of the settlor or his wife or her husband, that possibility can only arise on the bankruptcy of the child or on an assignment or a charge on the income being executed by the child. The second circumstance is

---

[45] For a case on s. 398 (2) before the 1958 amendments, see *I. R. C.* v. *Jamieson* [1963] 3 W.L.R. 156.

[46] It must now be taken as established that an unlimited power of advancement is a power to determine the settlement: see *I. R. C.* v. *Kenmare* [1958] A.C. 267; 37 Tax Cas. 383; *cf. I. R. C.* v. *Saunders* [1958] A.C. 285; 37 Tax Cas. 416, both of which cases dealt with the provisions contained in s. 404 of the Income Tax Act, 1952. It must be noticed, however, that the wording of s. 399 refers to the determination of the settlement, whereas s. 404 is more stringent, since it refers to the determination of the settlement or any provision thereof.

where, although the settlement may be determined, it can only be so determined so as to benefit persons other than the wife or husband of the settlor.[46a] Thirdly, protective trusts under section 33 of the Trustee Act, 1925, are not in themselves sufficient to make a settlement revocable in the relevant sense; this applies, however, only where the period for which income is directed to be held on protective trusts for the benefit of the child is not less than the life of the child.

In addition to the statutory provisions which have just been summarised, the settlement must be irrevocable according to the general principles of law concerning the meaning of the word "irrevocable."

(ii) *Revocable settlements, settlements with interest reserved, etc.*

From the complex provisions of sections 397 to 403 of the Act a number of fairly simple rules for the guidance of settlors wishing to benefit their infant children may be extracted. It is better, however, to defer consideration of these until discussion of actual precedents and to pass for the moment to sections 404 to 411 of the Act. These sections re-enact the provisions originally found in section 38 of the Finance Act, 1938, and are headed "Revocable Settlements, Settlements where Settlor retains an Interest, etc." They have been extended in scope by sections 21 and 22 of the Finance Act, 1958.

Section 404 (2) of the Act,[47] as amended by section 21 (2) of the Finance Act, 1958, provides that the income arising under certain revocable settlements is to be treated for the purposes of the Act as the income of the settlor and not as the income of any other person. A revocable settlement is within the category affected by this provision if its terms are such that two conditions are satisfied: first, that any person has or may have power to revoke or otherwise to determine the settlement or any provision thereof or to diminish the property comprised in it or to diminish the amount of any payments which are or may be payable under the settlement or any provision thereof to any person other than the settlor and his spouse; and secondly, that on the exercise of that power the settlor or his or her wife or husband will become entitled to the whole or any part of the property then comprised in the settlement or of the income arising from the whole or any part of that property.[48] Where the power of revocation extends only to a part of the property comprised in the settlement, it is only the income arising from that part which is to be deemed to be the income of the settlor.

It was formerly possible to avoid section 404 (2), which applied to revocable settlements, by providing a power to appoint all but £100 of the settled funds to the wife of the settlor.[49] But since section 21 of

---

[46a] See Finance Act, 1958, s. 20 (5). Previously a power to appoint to, for example, a nephew would have rendered the settlement revocable.

[47] s. 404 (1) also deals with settlements, but only, in effect, settlements of income; that is, of covenants to make annual payments. Such covenants are dealt with elsewhere in this book, pp. 1 *et seq.*

[48] Income Tax Act, 1952, s. 404 (2) (*a*) (*b*); Finance Act, 1958, s. 21 (2) (*a*) (*b*).

[49] *I. R. C.* v. *Saunders* [1958] A.C. 285; 37 Tax Cas. 416.

the Finance Act, 1958, extends the range of section 404 (2) to include
" diminishable " settlements, that possibility no longer exists.

Settlements under which the settlor retains an interest are covered by
section 405 of the Act. By subsection (1), so long as the settlor retains
an interest in any income arising under a settlement, or in the property
comprised in a settlement, any income so arising during the life of the
settlor in any year of assessment shall, to the extent to which it is not
distributed, be treated for all the purposes of the Act as the income
of the settlor for that year and not as the income of any other person.
In other words, if the income of a settlement in which the settlor retains
an interest in the relevant sense is accumulated, it is to be treated,
for income tax and surtax purposes, as income of the settlor. This
applies only where the settlor " has an interest " in the settlement, and
subsection (2) of section 405 goes on to say that the settlor shall be
deemed to have an interest, if any income or property which may at
any time arise under or be comprised in the settlement may become
payable to or applicable for the benefit of the settlor, or the settlor's
wife or husband, in any circumstances whatsoever.[50] It is considered
that the possibility that the settlor may acquire any part of the settled
funds by reason of a gift *inter vivos* or a testamentary disposition in his
favour on the part of a beneficiary, or by reason of his being one of the
persons entitled to share in the estate of a beneficiary in the event of
the beneficiary dying intestate, does not constitute an interest in the
settlement: see *Walker's Trustees* v. *I. R. C.* (1955) 34 A.T.C. 135.

Settlements which contain a discretionary power for the benefit of
the settlor or any spouse of the settlor are covered by section 22 of the
Finance Act, 1958. Section 22 provides that if there is a discretionary
power contained in the settlement under which the whole or any part
of the income or property which may at any time arise under or be
comprised in the settlement may be paid or applied to or for the benefit
of the settlor or any spouse of the settlor, the income arising under the
settlement shall be treated as the income of the settlor for tax purposes.
The section covers a discretionary power even if the consent of some
person is required for its exercise. And the mere possibility of income
or property being paid or applied for the benefit of the settlor or the
settlor's spouse brings section 22 into operation. It is not necessary that
there should have been an actual payment or application. By subsection (3), however, the income of the settlement will not be treated as
the income of the settlor, if the income or the property is only payable
or applicable to or for the settlor or the spouse of the settlor under the

---

[50] In *I. R. C.* v. *Bernstein* [1961] Ch. 399; 39 Tax Cas. 391 it was held that a trust
for accumulation under the terms of a settlement was inconsistent with the statutory
power of advancement and, therefore, the power of advancement was not applicable
so that no advancement could be made in favour of the settlor's wife, a beneficiary
under the settlement. In these circumstances the Revenue's claim to charge the
settlor to surtax under the provisions of s. 405 of the I. T. A., 1952, in respect of
income arising under the settlement, failed.

discretionary power in any of the events mentioned in the proviso to section 405 of the Income Tax Act, 1952.

As a result of these enactments and also the similar provision found in section 415 of the Act, it is sometimes suggested that an effective settlement must be framed so as to exclude the settlor and his wife from even the remotest possibility of acquiring any kind of beneficial interest in the property settled. It will be noticed, however,[51] that a precedent is given in this book in which the settlor retains a considerable potential interest in the property—and it is advisable in the circumstances contemplated in that precedent that he should do so, since the only other beneficiary contemplated is an infant whose interest is made contingent upon his attaining the age of twenty-one, and it would therefore have been risking a considerable loss of capital to have settled the property so that, in the event of the infant son dying under twenty-one, the settled fund would have passed to some other person.

In fact, the settlor or his wife may still retain an interest or the chance of benefiting under a discretionary power provided that strict regard is had to three rules, two laid down by the proviso to subsection (2) of section 405 which by subsection (3) of section 22 of the Finance Act, 1958, is made to apply to section 22 (1) and the third the result of judicial interpretation. First, the settlor shall not be deemed to have an interest, so long as the income or property can only become payable or applicable to him or his wife in one of the following four events:

(i) the bankruptcy of some beneficiary under the settlement;

(ii) any assignment or charge of any part of the settled property by a beneficiary;

(iii) in case of a marriage settlement, the death of both parties to the marriage and of all the children of the marriage; and

(iv) the death under the age of twenty-five or some lower age of some person who would be beneficially entitled to that income or property on attaining that age.

The second circumstance, in which the settlor shall not be deemed to have an interest, is contained in paragraph (b) to the proviso to section 405 (2) and will often overlap the first circumstance already referred to; it is wider, however, in that it extends, for example, to a settlement where the vesting of the capital in the beneficiary is postponed until the beneficiary has attained an age greater than twenty-five years. The effect of the enactment is that the settlor shall not be deemed to have an interest, so long as some beneficiary is alive and under the age of twenty-five during whose life no interest under the settlement can become payable to the settlor, or applicable for his benefit, except in the event of that beneficiary becoming bankrupt or assigning or charging his interest.

[51] At p. 123, *post.*

The third rule, now established by a decision of the House of Lords,[52] is that, even if the settlement reserves some possible benefit for the wife of the settlor, it is not to be considered to be caught by the section if the settlement is so framed that the benefit cannot arise until after the settlor's death—if it is, in fact, a benefit to the widow, not to the wife, of the settlor. It may be mentioned here that no interest is retained by reason only of the fact that under the investment clause in the settlement the trustees have power to invest trust money in the shares of companies in which the settlor is financially interested.[53]

(iii) *Special surtax provisions*

The foregoing are, in outline, the conditions which must be satisfied in order to insure that for the purposes of income tax the income of the settlement is not deemed to be income of the settlor. The provisions described apply to both income tax and surtax. It now becomes necessary to consider the provisions which were first introduced in section 28 of the Finance Act, 1946, and are now re-enacted as section 415 of the Income Tax Act, 1952, and which are confined in their effect to the surtax liability of the settlor.

Section 415 proceeds by the familiar method of enacting that, for the purposes of surtax, income arising under a settlement shall be treated as the income of the settlor and not of any other person: this provision is to apply to all income under any settlement, unless it can be brought under one or more of the five exceptions set out in section 415 (1).

One of the five exceptions may be dismissed shortly since it only excepts income which is by some other provision of the Act treated as income of the settlor. The other four are as follows:

(1) Where the income is payable to an individual (other than the settlor or a person in his service or a person accustomed to act as his solicitor or agent) for his own use;

(2) Where the income is applicable for the benefit of an individual (other than the settlor or a person in his service or a person accustomed to act as his solicitor or agent) named in that behalf in the settlement, or of two such individuals so named;

(3) Where the income is applicable for the benefit of a child or children of an individual named in that behalf in the settlement (provided, however, that neither that individual nor the child

---

[52] *Vestey's Executors* v. *I. R. C.* [1949] 1 All E.R. 1108, 1117, 1121, 1134; 31 Tax Cas. 1.

[53] Indeed, in *Vestey's Executors* v. *I. R. C.*, *supra*, there was a wide power to invest in stocks, shares or loans, but only at the direction in writing of certain " authorised persons," who were defined by the settlement to be the settlors during their joint lives and the survivor during his life and after his death four named persons, members of the family of the settlors. It was held by the House of Lords that the right thus conferred on the authorised person was a fiduciary right, to be exercised for the benefit of the beneficiaries; accordingly the right was not an " interest " within s. 38 of the Finance Act, 1938, now s. 405 of the Income Tax Act, 1952.

or children are persons in the service of the settlor or persons accustomed to act as his solicitor or agent)[54]; and

(4) Where the income is income of property of which the settlor has " divested himself absolutely " by the settlement.

Now an infant settlement may be drafted so as to come under paragraph (2), above. This could, it is conceived, only extend to a settlement on a named infant where the infant has a vested interest, so as to exclude the settlor or any other person from the possibility of receiving the income in any event, and such a settlement is seldom found in practice.

What it comes to, therefore, with regard to section 415 is that the settlor must " divest himself absolutely " of the property from which the income arises under the settlement, in order to avoid liability for surtax in respect of the income arising. Subsection (2) of section 415 lays it down that the settlor shall not be deemed for the purposes of the section to have divested himself absolutely of any property, if that property, or any income therefrom, or any property directly or indirectly representing proceeds of that property or income from it may become payable to the settlor or applicable for his benefit in any circumstances whatsoever. No reference is made to the settlor's wife.

Were the matter to rest there, almost every settlement would be caught by the section. Fortunately the proviso supplies a list of exceptions, described, rather less fortunately, as cases where the settlor " shall not be deemed not to have divested himself absolutely of any property." If no income or property can become payable to or for the benefit of the settlor except in any of the following circumstances, then so far as section 415 is concerned, the income of the settlement is not deemed to be income of the settlor. The first two circumstances are the bankruptcy of the beneficiary under the settlement, and an assignment of or charge on the property or income being made by the beneficiary: thirdly (although this is hardly applicable to a settlement on an infant since it is expressly confined to marriage settlements), the death of both parties to the marriage and of all or any of the children of the marriage; lastly, the death under the age of twenty-five or some lower age of some person who would be beneficially entitled to the property or income on attaining that age.

It will be observed that the circumstances referred to bear a close resemblance to those described in section 405 of the Income Tax Act, 1952, which deals with an interest retained by the settlor. As a general rule, a settlement drafted so as to escape the phrasing of section 405 will automatically succeed in escaping section 415, except where reliance is to be placed on proviso (b) to subsection (2) of section 405.

---

[54] If the income is applicable for the benefit of a child or children of the settlor, the question arises whether s. 397 does not apply so as to make the income the settlor's income. Where a child of a person in the service of the settlor is named in the settlement or the income is payable to him for his own use, it would seem that either of the first two exceptions applied.

(iv) *Summary of rules*

It may be useful at this stage to set out a number of rules of thumb which may be found helpful in practice.

(1) A settlor should be asked when he acquired the property to be settled so that, if necessary, a joint election may be made by the settlor and the trustees to avoid any charge to tax on the settlor under Case VII of Schedule D.

(2) An infant beneficiary's interest in income should vest on the beneficiary attaining twenty-one or earlier marriage. Vesting of an interest in capital may be postponed until a later age.

(3) Where the beneficiary is a child of the settlor, there should be a trust to accumulate the income arising from the trust fund during the child's unmarried minority, but the retention of a power to maintain is unobjectionable.

(4) If a reversion is retained for the settlor on the failure of the trusts in favour of the infant, it must not be possible for income or capital to become payable to the settlor except on the beneficiary's death under twenty-five or some lower age, or his bankruptcy, or on the assignment of his interest by the beneficiary. For example a gift over to the settlor in the event of failure of issue, or after a protective trust, should be avoided.

(5) If a power to make and declare new trusts is required, it should normally be vested in the trustees and should be drawn so as to exclude the settlor or any spouse of the settlor as an object of the power.

(6) If the beneficiaries are a class of existing and future infant children of a named person, care should be taken to close the class at the earliest convenient date.

(7) Accumulations may be directed for up to two years. Otherwise care should be taken that one of the periods other than the life of the settlor or a period fixed by reference to his life, *e.g.*, twenty-one years after his death, has been chosen as the period during which income is to be accumulated.

(v) *Loans to the settlor*

Care must be taken, once the settlement has been executed, that no part of the settled funds or of the income thereof is paid or transferred to the settlor or to any wife of the settlor. This is necessary owing to the very stringent provisions of section 408 of the Income Tax Act, 1952, which provides that any capital sum paid directly or indirectly in any relevant year of assessment by the trustees of a settlement to the settlor shall be treated as income of the settlor for that year, to the extent to which the amount of that sum falls within the amount of income available up to the end of that year. Furthermore, any excess is carried forward to the next year, and so on. Although aimed at evasion devices, section 408 penalises many quite innocent transactions. It extends to loans and repayments of loans, and to sums paid to the settlor's wife or husband. Where shares in a family company are settled, it may even catch repayment of loans made by the settlor to the company (see section 411 (4) of the Income Tax Act, 1952).[55] For example, a settlor may settle shares in a family company (being a company to which section 245 of the Income Tax Act, 1952, is applicable, and the income of which would, if a surtax direction under section 245 were made, be apportioned in part to the trustees of the settlement) at a time when there is a balance of remuneration due to him from the company which appears in the company's balance sheet as " director's loan account." If the so-called loan is repaid by the company, the repayment may amount to the payment of a " capital sum " by a " body corporate connected with the settlement " within the meaning of section 408 (3). If this is a correct view, to the extent to which income arising under the settlement has been accumulated, the repayment of money by the company to the settlor will attract tax. It has been the practice of the Estate Duty Office to treat director's loan accounts as " debentures " for the purpose of applying section 55 of the Finance Act, 1940. It is a moot point whether undrawn remuneration is accurately described as " a loan."

It is sometimes advisable to forbid loans to the settlor or his wife by an express clause in the settlement.

For estate duty purposes a debt incurred by a settlor by reason of a loan to him by the trustees of his settlement out of the settled fund may be wholly or partly disallowed as a deduction from the estate of the settlor on his death under the provisions of section 31 of the Finance Act, 1939.

Tax: Assessment of infant beneficiaries

Assuming that a settlement may be drafted which, in addition to reducing the burden of estate duty on the death of the settlor more than five years after the settlement, also insures that the income which arises is not treated for tax purposes as income of the settlor—that is to say, which avoids liability under Part XVIII of the Income Tax Act, 1952—consideration must be given to the further question: what tax is payable on the income of the trust fund? For unless some lower rate of tax or extra relief or allowance is applicable by reason of the settlement, no saving of income tax will have been achieved.

As regards the trustees who are in receipt of the income of the trust, they are liable to be assessed to tax at the standard rate on all income coming into their hands, other than that which has been taxed at source. In practice, a return form (usually Form 1) is issued automatically every year soon after April 5 to the trustees of every trust known to

---

[55] In *Potts' Executors* v. *I. R. C.* [1951] A.C. 443; 32 Tax Cas. 211, it was held that sums debited to a current account between the settlor and a company connected with the settlement within s. 411 (4), were not capital sums paid directly or indirectly to the settlor within s. 408.

the Inspector of Taxes. On this must be declared the untaxed income (normally on the preceding year basis), unless a "nil" return is made. In addition, the trustees are required to make a return of the total taxed income of the trust (Form R. 59) and to show particulars of charges (e.g., annuities), administration expenses, and the division of the income among the beneficiaries. If a beneficiary is entitled to receive untaxed income direct, the trustees are absolved from their liability to be assessed (see section 367 of the Income Tax Act, 1952).

The trustees deduct tax at the standard rate on paying income to the beneficiaries and give a certificate of the tax deducted (Form R. 185E). The beneficiary includes his share of income on his personal return as income taxed at source, and will be entitled to claim repayment of tax from his own Inspector of Taxes if he is entitled to a balance of personal reliefs.

(i) Loss of child allowance

An infant as an individual is entitled to the same reliefs and allowances to which an adult taxpayer is entitled. Sums paid under a trust for the maintenance of an infant, although not paid into his hand, become his income for tax purposes, unless deemed to be income of the settlor under one or other of the provisions discussed above.[56]

If, therefore, a settlement has been executed (such as a settlement on an infant by his grandparent or uncle) under which income may be applied for the infant's maintenance, and so become the income of the infant for tax purposes, a claim for personal and reduced rate reliefs may be made on the infant's behalf and a refund of tax may be obtained. Prima facie, therefore, the amount refunded will be the amount of income tax saved by the settlement. There may, however, be a loss to be set off against this: this is the reduction in the " child allowance " enjoyed by the child's parent under section 212 of the Income Tax Act, 1952, which will result if the child's own income exceeds £115.[57] To compute the net saving of tax which may be effected by a settlement where income is to be used for a child's maintenance, a calculation must be made of the amount of the gross income of the child and the tax saved on it must be set off against the reduction in the child allowance which the parents will suffer.

This can best be explained by examples, using the rates and reliefs expected to be in force in 1964–65.

EXAMPLE 1:
Under a settlement made by his grandfather, an infant, who has no other income, is entitled, contingently upon his attaining twenty-one, to a fund which produces an income, after tax is deducted (at the standard rate), of £49.

---

56 *Drummond* v. *Collins* [1915] A.C. 1011; 6 Tax Cas. 525; *Johnstone* v. *Chamberlain* (1933) 17 Tax Cas. 706.
57 Formerly, if the income of the child exceeded £100 in any year of assessment, the parents lost the whole child allowance. This anomaly was corrected as respects the year 1964–65 and all subsequent years by s. 13 of the Finance Act, 1963, which belatedly adopted the recommendation in the majority report of the Royal Commission on Taxation (Second Report: Cmd. 9105, para. 183).

If the whole of this sum is paid to maintain the infant, a claim can be made for a repayment of tax, since the infant is entitled to a personal allowance of £200. The infant is therefore entitled to have refunded the whole of the tax already deducted, a sum of £31, making an actual income received for the infant under the settlement of £80.

The infant's parents are entitled to claim, against their own income, the " child allowance " of £165, £140, or £115, [58] notwithstanding the income of the child.

The result is that the infant is benefited, without any loss to the parents, and at minimum cost to the grandfather.

EXAMPLE 2 :

Under a similar settlement an infant having no other income is entitled to a fund producing a net income of £98.

Here the infant can, as in the first example, reclaim the tax deducted, a sum of £62, making an actual income received for the infant under the settlement of £160.

The infant's parents lose the first £45 (the difference between £160 and £115) of the child allowance.[59-60]

The result is that the infant is benefited at minimum cost to the grandfather, but at a cost of part of the parent's child allowance, which will cost them as much as £17 8s. 9d. (£45 at standard rate) if the parent pays tax at the standard rate, and more if the parent pays surtax.

EXAMPLE 3 :

Under a similar settlement an infant having no other income is entitled to a fund producing a net income of £196.

The child cannot claim back the whole tax deducted, as on the gross income (£326) he is liable to pay £9 15s. 6d. tax. He will therefore claim back £116 4s. 6d., making an actual income received for the infant of £312 4s. 6d.

The result is that the infant is benefited at minimum cost to the grandfather but the parents will lose the whole of the child relief, i.e., the income tax and surtax on £165, £140, or £115.

It will be observed from these examples that whereas, before the year 1964–65, the loss by the parents of child relief could, as was pointed out in earlier editions of this book, result in the covenant causing a reduction in the aggregate net income of the child and its parents, that disadvantage no longer exists. It is no longer necessary so to arrange matters that the child's income does not exceed £100 a year. Calculations intended to produce an exact figure representing the most advantageous amount to be covenanted would seem to be no longer possible.

(ii) *Reliefs on accumulated income*

Under many settlements the income is accumulated until the infant reaches the age of twenty-one; indeed, accumulation is necessary if tax is to be saved where the infant beneficiary is a child of the settlor. In such a case the trustees will pay tax at the standard rate, either by deduction at source or by direct assessment, and will add the net income to capital. If the beneficiary has a vested interest in the income— although this is not usual in practice—the income may be his income,

[58] See s. 212 (1), Income Tax Act, 1952, as amended by s. 12 of the Finance Act, 1963.
[59-60] See s. 212 (4), Income Tax Act, 1952, as amended by s. 13 of the Finance Act, 1963.

even though accumulated, and a claim should be made each year for the
personal allowance of the infant,[61] since otherwise the claims will be
out of date after the six-year limit: Income Tax Act, 1952, section 507.

In the more usual type of settlement, however, where the infant has
an interest contingent on attaining twenty-one or some later age, and
income is accumulated, no reliefs or allowances can be claimed during
the infancy (except on any sums actually expended for the child's
maintenance), since the income accumulated is not the infant's income.
For the same reason no surtax is payable. Nevertheless, it is
provided by section 228 of the Income Tax Act, 1952, that where
income is accumulated " for the benefit of any person contingently on
his attaining some specified age or marrying," the reliefs or balance
of relief in respect of all years when the beneficiary's interest was only
contingent can be reclaimed as if the accumulated income had been
the income of the beneficiary during the period of the accumulation
and the appropriate refund will be made when the beneficiary attains
a vested interest provided a claim is made within six years of the end
of the year of assessment in which the contingency happens.

Section 228 is strictly applied and its application in particular cases
may give rise to difficulties.

If, for example, the interest of the infant beneficiary is made to
vest " on his attaining twenty-one, if he is then resident in England,"
no reliefs or allowances may be claimed under section 228. The reason
for this is that the words " contingently on his attaining some specified
age or marrying " are to be construed strictly, and if any other contingency is introduced the section is not satisfied.[62] Thus where
a trust fund was held for the children who should attain twenty-one
of a named woman, so that all the children born to the woman at any
time should participate in the fund, it was held that, since the class
would not close until the death of the woman, the claim under
section 228 made by her two children, who both attained twenty-one
in her lifetime, failed.[63]

The beneficiary must have the income " accumulated for his benefit,"
but the " benefit " for the purpose of section 228 does not mean that
the claimant must be entitled to the accumulated income, as such, on
the happening of the contingency. It is sufficient if he has a life interest
in the accumulations.[64] And this is so even if the life interest is

---

61 *Gascoigne* v. *I. R. C.* [1927] 1 K.B. 594; 13 Tax Cas. 573; *Edwardes-Jones* v.
   Down (1936) 20 Tax Cas. 279; *Stanley* v. *I. R. C.* [1944] K.B. 255, 259; 26 Tax Cas.
   12. See *post*, p. 114.
62 See *Stoneley* v. *Ambrose* (1925) 9 Tax Cas. 389; *Dain* v. *Miller* (1934) 18 Tax Cas.
   478.
63 *I. R. C.* v. *Bone* (1927) 13 Tax Cas. 20.
64 If income is accumulated and added to capital held for the child contingently upon
   attaining twenty-five, it is submitted that in the normal case, where the income is
   payable to the child between twenty-one and twenty-five, the claim should be made
   on attaining twenty-one and not postponed until twenty-five.

constituted under protective trusts.[65] It was held that where the trusts were so drafted that the infant (a daughter) had a life interest only, with a power of appointing a life interest to a husband and remainder to her issue with a gift over to a stranger, the section was satisfied, primarily because there was a life interest in the settled accumulation of income but secondly because such trusts for daughters are for their benefit.[66] On the other hand, a mere discretionary trust, or a life interest which the trustees may reduce in amount so as to benefit some other person will take the trust outside the section.[67] A trust subject to a power of appointment, which is in fact not exercised, may be within the section.[68]

In a case where the settlor wishes to benefit a class of children including one or more existing children and also future children the benefit of section 228 may be obtained, provided the class of future children is made to close before or at the time that the eldest reaches twenty-one or otherwise attains a vested interest. If this happens, the eldest child may argue, on attaining a vested interest, that the accumulations which have been made for him have, in view of the closing of the class, been made for his benefit contingently only on his attaining twenty-one, or whatever age is chosen, or his marrying. As far as the present practice goes, this argument is believed to be accepted, but the authorities are not decisive.[69]

An infant settlement should not be drafted which makes the beneficiary's interest vest on a given date, or after a given time, since this will not satisfy the terms of section 228.[70]

Where it is desired to provide for a class of future children of a named person, the proper course is to provide expressly that the class is to close on a certain date, as for example, the attainment by the firstborn child of his majority. It is not considered advisable to rely on the well-known rule in *Andrews* v. *Partington* (1791) 3 Bro.C.C. 60 (as applied in *Re Bleckley* [1951] Ch. 740), according to which, where a gift is settled on a class of children some of whom are not in existence at the date of the gift, and the share of each child is made contingent on the attainment of a specified age or marrying, the class closes when the first child fulfils the contingency.

The precise ambit of section 228 has never yet been considered by the House of Lords. The existing position may be thus summarised: if an infant's settlement is made on a named infant or infants, contingent on the attaining by each of a specified age or marriage, this will be

---

[65] *Lynch* v. *Davies* [1962] T.R. 319.
[66] *Dale* v. *Mitcalfe* [1928] 1 K.B. 383; 13 Tax Cas. 41.
[67] *Dain* v. *Miller, supra*; *I. R. C.* v. *Maude-Roxby* (1950) 31 Tax Cas. 388.
[68] *Chamberlain* v. *Haig-Thomas* (1933) 17 Tax Cas. 595.
[69] As to the method of dealing with accumulations under such a trust, see *Re King* [1928] 1 Ch. 330.
[70] *White* v. *Whitcher* [1928] 1 K.B. 453; 13 Tax Cas. 202.

certain of coming expressly within the section. Where future children
are included, or more complex trusts are engrafted, there is bound to
be some risk that the application of section 228 will be disputed.

One further point requires particular mention. No matter whether
the interest which vests in the beneficiary is an absolute interest in
capital or only a life interest in income, the claim which is made for a
refund under section 228 is a claim personal to the beneficiary. Consequently, the beneficiary is absolutely entitled to the tax refunded, even
though the income itself in respect of which the refund is made has
been capitalised: *Re Fulford* [1930] 1 Ch. 71.

Section 228 of the Income Tax Act, 1952, only extends to settlements
which have avoided the snares and traps set by Part XVIII of the Act;
that is to say, settlements the income of which is not deemed to be the
income of the settlor.

(iii) *Surtax*

Surtax will be payable on income received by an infant beneficiary
under a settlement if his total aggregate income from all sources including
the settlement exceeds £2,000.

It is usual, in drafting a settlement, to give an infant beneficiary an
interest, either in capital or in income, contingently on his attaining his
majority. It is clear that in such circumstances a beneficiary is assessable, during his minority, on so much of the income as is paid for his
benefit and is not deemed (under any of the statutory provisions) to be
the income of the settlor. Income which is accumulated is not part of his
total income for tax purposes.

Where the settlement gives the infant a vested interest, the same rule
applies as regards income paid or applied for his benefit. But with
regard to accumulated income a distinction must be made. Settlements
to which section 31 of the Trustee Act, 1925, applies, either by implication or express incorporation, or which have provisions similar to those
contained in section 31, are to be distinguished from other settlements.[71]
By subsection (2) (i) of section 31 it is provided that, even where the
infant has a vested interest, the accumulated income is to be set aside,
and is to be payable to him only upon his majority or earlier marriage.
It has been decided in *Stanley* v. *I. R. C.* [1944] K.B. 255; 26 Tax
Cas. 12 that where an infant has a vested life interest to which section
31 applies, the income which is accumulated is not part of the infant's
total income for surtax purposes.

With regard to an infant who has a vested interest in capital it is
sometimes suggested that the decision in *Gascoigne* v. *I. R. C.* [1927] 1
K.B. 594; 13 Tax Cas. 573, 587, is authority for the view that the income
forms part of his total income even if it is accumulated. That decision is
not, strictly speaking, applicable to interests affected by section 31 of the

[71] *Per* Lord Greene in *Stanley* v. *I. R. C.* [1944] K.B. 255, 260; 26 Tax Cas. 12.

Trustee Act, 1925. But where the infant has a fully vested interest in capital, section 31 (2) (ii) gives him the accumulations in any event, so that his right to them is vested, but payment only is deferred. Thus, the principle established by the *Gascoigne* case does extend to such interests.

An infant may be assessed direct, both to income tax and surtax: see *R.* v. *Newmarket Income Tax Commissioners, ex p. Huxley* [1916] 1 K.B. 788; 7 Tax Cas. 49. The parent or guardian of an infant may also be assessed to income tax as the representative of an incapacitated person under section 363 of the Income Tax Act, 1952. It is the usual practice for the parent or guardian to be repaid any tax reliefs due, but for the infant to be assessed direct on earnings, *e.g.,* as a sole trader or a partner, but more commonly the infant suffers deduction of tax under P.A.Y.E. on his remuneration from an employment.

For surtax, the minor is only assessable personally, and it was held in *I. R. C.* v. *The Countess of Longford* [1928] A.C. 252; 13 Tax Cas. 573, 616, that there is no power to assess the guardian of the infant or the trustee administering a fund in which the minor has an interest.

Capital Gains Tax

Until 1962 the transfer of assets to trustees of a family settlement did not of itself normally give rise to any tax questions. Now, as a consequence of the provisions contained in Chapter II of the Finance Act, 1962, relating to short-term capital gains, it is necessary to consider whether the voluntary transfer of any particular asset to trustees to be held by them upon the trusts of the settlement will give rise to a charge to tax under Case VII of Schedule D on the settlor.

The charge under Case VII is made on any gain arising on the disposal of chargeable assets within the appropriate chargeable period. Chargeable assets include all forms of property (whether situated in the United Kingdom or not) including options, debts and incorporeal property generally; but tangible movable property (other than commodities, currency and certain trade assets) is excluded.[72] The chargeable period in the case of land is three years and in other cases (except the special case of the disposal of shares in a land-owning company[73]) is six months.[74]

Generally, the acquisition and disposal of an asset by way of gift is treated, for Case VII purposes, as being made for a consideration equal to the market value.[75] And if a settlor acquires an asset and disposes of it by way of gift to trustees of a settlement within the relevant chargeable period, he will, prima facie, be chargeable under Case VII on the gain he would have made if he had sold the asset at market value.[76]

---

[72] Finance Act, 1962, s. 11 (1) (2).
[73] *Ibid.,* s. 14 (6).
[74] *Ibid.,* s. 10 (2).
[75] *Ibid.,* s. 12 (3) (a).
[76] *Ibid.,* Ninth Schedule, para. 4 (1).

However, in such a case, the settlor and the trustees may jointly elect that the settlor shall not be chargeable and that the trustees shall be treated for Case VII purposes as if the settlor's acquisition of the asset in question was the trustees' acquisition.[77] In order that the trustees in turn may avoid any Case VII charge they will have to ensure that they retain the asset for a period extending beyond the appropriate chargeable period (calculated, of course, from the date of the settlor's acquisition, where a joint election has been made). Trustees of settled property[78] are treated as a single and continuing body of persons for the purposes of Case VII.[79]

Where, apart from a joint election, the settlor would not be chargeable under Case VII of Schedule D, the trustees may make an election on their own.[80] The consequence of such an election will be that the settlor's acquisition of the asset will be treated for Case VII purposes as if it was the acquisition of the trustees.

Stamp duty

Where a settlement of any property is voluntary it is, subject to certain exceptions, liable as a voluntary disposition *inter vivos* under section 74 (1) of the Finance (1909-10) Act, 1910.[81] The rate is now 10s. in respect of every £50 of the value of the property taken under the voluntary disposition: Finance Act, 1963, s. 55. The stamp duty on a voluntary disposition *inter vivos* is the same as that which would be chargeable if the instrument were a conveyance or transfer on sale, with the substitution in each case of the value of the property conveyed or transferred for the amount or value of the consideration for the sale.

Accordingly, as most settlements are voluntary dispositions of property or investments already vested in the settlor, the usual stamp duty payable on a settlement, whether of land or investments, is at the rate of 10s. for every £50 of the value of the property settled. Where, however, the settlor is in course of buying property or investments which he intends to settle forthwith, it is not necessary to pay, in addition to the stamp on the sale (10s. per £50) a further stamp at the same rate, as on a voluntary disposition of the same amount. The conveyance may be completed by transfer direct by the vendor to the trustees, in which event it is considered that the settlement will bear a 10s. stamp in place of the *ad valorem* duty.

It is provided also that, in every case of a voluntary conveyance or transfer *inter vivos*, the stamp duty must be adjudicated.[82] In practice,

---

[77] *Ibid.*, Ninth Schedule, para. 3 (2) (3).
[78] *Ibid.*, s. 16 (1).
[79] *Ibid.*, s. 12 (6).
[80] *Ibid.*, Ninth Schedule, para. 3 (3).
[81] Settlement duty, formerly payable in certain circumstances where voluntary disposition duty was not payable, was abolished by Finance Act, 1962, s. 30.
[82] Stamp Act, 1891, s. 74 (2).

a settlement is usually effected by more than one document, so that stamps are required both for the settlement itself and for the document or documents which transfer the legal title in the property transferred to the trustees. The practice is to have adjudicated both the settlement and the document or documents of transfer.

It is sometimes said that stamp duty as on a voluntary disposition *inter vivos* can be avoided, by the settlor simply executing a Declaration of Trust, constituting himself settlor, so that he transfers nothing. This is quite wrong. If a document in fact transfers a beneficial interest to a person other than the donor or settlor it constitutes a voluntary disposition of that interest, no matter what the parties choose to call the document.

Which document is stamped

The question arises, which should bear the *ad valorem* stamp : the settlement or the transfer. As a general rule, where ordinary marketable securities or land form the whole of the settled property and duty is payable at £1 per cent., it makes little difference to the total amount payable whether the *ad valorem* stamp is put on the settlement or on the transfer. Technically, it should go on whichever is last executed, and, since the settlement is usually executed after the transfer, albeit on the same day, it seems that the settlement should in strictness bear the stamp. There are two cases which illustrate the point. In *Albert Martin* v. *I. R. C.* (1930) 15 A.T.C. 631, the facts, in so far as they concern the point now under discussion, were that the transfer preceded the settlement, although both bore the same date. The transfer was liable to a 10s. stamp as a conveyance which did not carry the beneficial interest (*i.e.*, " a conveyance or transfer of any kind not hereinbefore described "); the settlement was liable to bear *ad valorem* duty as a " voluntary disposition " on the value of the benefit conferred on the beneficiaries other than the settlor—an amount in the circumstances substantially less than the value of the property settled. On the other hand, in *Ansell* v. *I. R. C.* [1929] 1 K.B. 608, where marketable securities were voluntarily settled, together with other property which for the present illustration need not be described, the settlement preceded the transfer of the securities. The settlement was stamped, in respect of the securities, with an *ad valorem* stamp under the Finance (1909–10) Act, 1910, as a voluntary conveyance, and the transfer bore only a deed stamp. The court approved this method of stamping.

The practice, where the documents are executed and presented for stamping simultaneously, is to put the *ad valorem* stamp, where it is at the rate of 10s. per £50, on the transfer, and to use only a 10s. stamp for the settlement. Where the settlement is executed and presented for stamping before the transfers of property are executed, the exact legal position is not clear. The Stamp Office may be prepared to agree that, as the settlement does not effect a voluntary disposition, since the trusts are imperfectly constituted until the trust property is transferred to the trustees, a deed stamp of 10s. only is payable, and that the transfers will then bear voluntary disposition duty.

Where a settlement is made of land under the Settled Land Act, 1925, it is expressly provided that the vesting deed shall be stamped with a deed stamp only, and that any *ad valorem* stamp which is required shall be borne by the trust instrument.[83]

Lower rates of stamp duty

If the settlor is himself to be the trustee of the settlement and executes a declaration of trust instead of a settlement, the declaration will, in itself, be a transfer *inter vivos* of the equitable interest, so as to incur voluntary disposition duty.

(i) *Oral settlements*

A settlement may be created without executing a written settlement at all. Where personalty is settled by the person who has both the legal and the beneficial title to it, no writing is necessary to create equitable interests in that personalty; and where there is no document there is nothing to stamp, by virtue of the well-established rule that it is the document which is stamped, not the transaction. In consequence, where a settlement is genuinely made by an oral declaration of trust, by a beneficial owner who has the legal title, no liability to stamp duty arises: thus, for example, a settlor could announce the terms of settlement before witnesses, constituting himself the sole trustee. In practice this will not usually be a satisfactory method of constituting a settlement, however desirable it may appear in theory. The settlor would normally have to read out the declaration from some draft prepared beforehand, and it would be arguable that this draft really constituted the settlement, the reading being merely a colourable device. It would be different if a genuine settlement had previously been executed, and all the settlor subsequently wished to do was to subject further property to the same trusts by making a verbal declaration. From this last case is to be distinguished the case where the property to be settled is owned by the settlor in equity only, the legal title being vested in others. The question then is whether in order to dispose of his equitable interest by declaring trusts the settlor is obliged to use writing because of the provisions in section 53 (1) (c) of the Law of Property Act, 1925, or whether an oral declaration suffices. The decision of the House of Lords in *Grey* v. *I. R. C.* [1960] A.C. 1 establishes that writing is necessary. It would not be any more effective as a means of saving stamp duty to follow a verbal declaration with a deed reciting the declaration at length and appointing new trustees in lieu of the settlor.

---

[83] Settled Land Act, 1925, s. 4 (3).

This could be treated as one transaction, the declaration and the deed together constituting a transfer *inter vivos*.[84]

The most cogent objection to the adoption of devices of this kind for saving stamp duty is that the validity of the settlement itself may be impugned and the saving of tax or estate duty intended to be effected may be frustrated.

(ii) *Settlements of exempted property*

One way of economising on stamp duty is to settle investments which are exempt from duty, that is to say, " Government or parliamentary stocks or bonds." These will be exempt from the duty under the Finance (1909-10) Act, 1910.

A similar rule applies where what is settled is assigned to the trustees without any document of transfer, chattels, for example, or bearer bonds.

(iii) *Bonus shares*

Where the settlor owns shares in respect of which a bonus issue is made, he may renounce the bonus shares in favour of the trustees, by completing the Form of Renunciation which is usually appended to an allotment letter. If this Form is so worded that it does not name the persons in whose favour the renunciation is made, it causes the allotment letter to become a negotiable instrument the title to which passes by delivery. If the settlement recites that the renunciation is about to take place, and is in fact executed before the renunciation takes place, the settlement will not constitute a voluntary disposition, and thus will not require to be stamped *ad valorem*. The delivery of the allotment letter will be a voluntary disposition but as this is effected by an act—delivery —and not by a document, no stamp is required. The practice was once widespread, of first setting up a settlement with a trust fund consisting of a small sum of money, and then adding bonus shares to the settlement by a complicated procedure, involving an allotment letter, renunciation thereof, an oral declaration by the settlor, and a written declaration by some bystander. The abolition of settlement duty by the Finance Act, 1962, has rendered this elaborate procedure unnecessary.

(iv) *Marriage settlements*

A settlement made in consideration of marriage is not (except as provided by section 64 of the Finance Act, 1963) " a conveyance or transfer operating as a voluntary disposition *inter vivos*," and consequently, being outside of section 74 of the Finance (1909-10) Act, 1910, only the fixed stamp of 10s. is required. In view of this provision and the exemption from estate duty enjoyed by gifts in consideration of marriage,[85] the marriage of a child is an advantageous occasion upon which to execute a settlement.

---

[84] See *Oughtred* v. *I. R. C.* [1958] 2 All E.R. 443; and *cf. Cohen and Moore* v. *I. R. C.* [1933] 2 K.B. 126.

[85] Finance (1909-10) Act, 1910, s. 59 (2), as amended by the Finance Act, 1963, s. 53. See *post*, Chap. 5.

(v) *Mortgages*

Caution must be exercised where the property to be settled consists of money invested in mortgages of land. A voluntary transfer *inter vivos* of a mortgage is caught by the 1910 Act, and so carries *ad valorem* duty at 10s. per £50.[86] This is so, even though the Stamp Act, 1891, as amended, gives the present rate of 1s. per £100 on transfers of a mortgage.[87] A saving of stamp duty is possible, if, instead of settling the mortgage, a sum of money is first settled. Provided that the settlement is executed before the money is paid by the settlor to the trustees, the settlement will not require any *ad valorem* stamp. The trustees may then lend the money on a fresh mortgage, incurring thereby further liability at the rate of 2s. 6d. per £100 advanced. Or, alternatively, the trustees could purchase the mortgage from the settlor with the money he has settled, and take a transfer of the mortgage which, since it is not a " voluntary transfer *inter vivos*," is not caught by the Finance Act, 1910, and so, instead of bearing duty at the rate of 10s. per £50, is liable under the heading " Transfer, assignment, disposition or assignation of any mortgage, etc." to *ad valorem* duty at the rate of only 1s. per £100.

(vi) *Sums of money*

It is not always convenient to settle a sum of money, but, where this is done, provided that the settlement is executed before the money is paid by the settlor to the trustees, no *ad valorem* duty is payable. The extent to which stamp duty will be saved will depend upon the nature of the investments in which the settled fund is to be invested. When the intended investments are ordinary stock, *ad valorem* duty will usually be payable on the transfer of the stock to the trustees. It is further submitted that, where a settlement has been executed for a sum of money, the settlor may subsequently, by an entirely separate transaction, orally declare that further property which is vested in himself is to be held on the trusts of the settlement, and that, in consequence, no *ad valorem* stamp duty is payable.

The adoption of this method is, however, subject to the caveat entered above, that it should not be allowed to jeopardise the saving of tax or estate duty which the settlement is designed to achieve.

(vii) *Colonial stock*

Where the property settled is Colonial stock to which the Colonial Stock Act, 1877, applies, or is Canadian Government stock inscribed in books kept in the United Kingdom, liability under the 1910 Act arises, but the rate applicable is only 10s. per £100.

Certificates of value

The rate of £1 per cent., which (subject to relief for smaller transactions) now applies to conveyances on sale, and thus to settlements

---

[86] *Martin* v. *I. R. C.* (1930) 15 A.T.C. 631.
[87] This and other rates were doubled by s. 52 of the Finance Act, 1947.

which are also voluntary dispositions *inter vivos,* has been arrived at by degrees over the years. The rate laid down in the Stamp Act, 1891, was generally 5s. per £50. This was doubled by section 73 of the Finance (1909-10) Act, 1910, redoubled by sections 52 *et seq.* of the Finance Act, 1947, and reduced by section 55 of the Finance Act, 1963. The rates are now laid down by section 55 of the Finance Act, 1963. But where conveyances or transfers contain a certificate of value, and the amount or value of the consideration or, in case of a voluntary disposition, the value of the property conveyed or transferred, does not exceed certain specified sums, the rates are lower.[88] These reduced rates do not, however, apply to transfers of stock or marketable securities.[89] As a result, settlements of stock or marketable securities, however small, bear the flat rate of 10s. for every £50, without any relief.

Where a " certificate of value " is included in a settlement, other than a settlement of stock or marketable securities, and the value of the property is not more than £4,500, no stamp duty is chargeable under the heading "Voluntary disposition *inter vivos*": see section 55 (4) of the Finance Act, 1963. Where the value of the property is more than £4,500 but not more than £6,000, the rate chargeable is 5s. per £50; and in any other case the rate chargeable is 10s. per £50.[90] Where stock or marketable securities are settled, however small the amount involved, a certificate of value is not appropriate.

Stamp duty on revocable settlements

It is sometimes suggested that a considerable economy may be made in stamp duty by including in a settlement an overriding power of revocation. Since, however, such a power, while it exists, will in most cases undo any saving of tax which the settlement might have achieved, and may in many cases, even after it has ceased to exist, undo any potential saving of estate duty, it may be that the economy in stamp duty effected by such a power will be regarded as too dearly bought.

It is settled that, in assessing the *ad valorem* duty on a settlement operating as a voluntary conveyance *inter vivos,* account must be taken of any power of revocation in the settlement, as affecting the value of the interests transferred: *Stanyforth* v. *I. R. C.* [1930] A.C. 339.[90a] In consequence, if the settlor reserves an overriding power to restore the property to himself, the value of the property conveyed—so runs the argument—cannot be very great, and the stamp duty payable must be negligible. It is understood that this argument is normally accepted by the Stamp Office, except where it appears that a release of the power has

---

88 See now Finance Act, 1963, s. 55 (4).
89 See now Finance Act, 1963, s. 55 (2).
90 Finance Act, 1963, s. 55 (1).
90a *Cf. Morgan* v. *I. R. C.* [1963] Ch. 438 and see note by Mr. J. G. Monroe in [1963] B.T.R. 150.

already been executed, or the decision has already been taken to release the power, at the time the settlement is presented for stamping. It is therefore imperative, if a revocable settlement is executed, to delay until after the settlement and all the transfers of property to the trustees have been stamped and adjudicated, any question as to the exercise or release of the power of revocation.

On the death of a settlor who has such a power at the date of his death, the whole of the property settled is deemed to pass under section 2 (1) (c) of the Finance Act, 1894. It is, however, often suggested that this liability may be escaped if, some time after executing the settlement, the settlor releases his power of revocation and survives the release by five years. This view is based on section 59 (3) of the Finance (1909–10) Act, 1910.

It is to be observed that property settled subject to a power of revocation may be deemed to pass under one or both of two distinct provisions. Section 2 (1) (c) of the Finance Act, 1894, incorporates section 38 of the Customs and Inland Revenue Act, 1881, and section 11 of the Customs and Inland Revenue Act, 1889. Section 38 (2) (c) of the 1881 Act brings into account " any property passing under any past or future voluntary settlement . . . whereby the settlor may have reserved to himself the right by the exercise of any power to restore to himself or to reclaim the absolute interest in such property." Section 11 of the 1889 Act refers to " . . . property taken under any gift, whenever made, of which property bona fide possession and enjoyment shall not have been assumed by the donee immediately upon the gift and thenceforward retained, to the entire exclusion of the donor, or of any benefit to him by contract or otherwise." Now a power of revocation will almost invariably bring the settlement within the latter provision, and, if it gives power to restore the absolute interest to the settlor, within the former provision as well.

Section 59 (3) of the Finance (1909–10) Act, 1910, it is true, provides that a subsequent release of a power of revocation shall have the effect of starting the five-year period; but it is expressed to apply to the latter of the above two enactments only. It does not deal with property passing under a settlement whereby the settlor may have reserved to himself power to reclaim an absolute interest in the property. It is arguable, therefore, that property comprised in a settlement which reserves a power of revocation is deemed to pass on the settlor's death, even if he survives the release of the power by five years, by virtue of section 38 (2) (c) of the 1881 Act. This argument is somewhat tenuous, since it is not easy to reconcile with the definition of " settlement " in the Finance Act, 1894,[91] but until it has been pronounced upon by the

---

[91] See Finance Act, 1894, s. 22 (1) (i); Settled Land Act, 1925, ss. 1 (1), 117 (1) (xxiv), 119 (2); Interpretation Act, 1889, s. 38. It can be said that both the original settlement and the release of the power of revocation together constitute the settlement under which the property passes.

courts, it leaves it insufficiently clear that the release of such a power will remove the potential liability for estate duty on the settlor's death at whatever date it may occur.

For the above reasons, it is possible that an absolute power of revocation, even if subsequently released, may cause the property over which it operates to be deemed to pass on death, even if the settlor survives the release of the power by five years. It must be admitted that at present the practice of the Revenue is not to press a claim for estate duty where an absolute power of revocation has been released more than five years before death. There is no guarantee that this practice will continue.

A power to revoke and declare new trusts in favour of a defined class of which the settlor is not a member is not caught by the former of the two enactments referred to above, and its employment is, therefore, a factor to be considered in drafting a settlement, but only where such a power is genuinely required for its own sake. Its inclusion will not reduce the amount of stamp duty payable.

Quite apart from the objection set out above to the adoption of a power of revocation as a means of saving stamp duty, it cannot be said to be certain that the device will itself be effective. The Revenue could argue that the release attracted a full *ad valorem* stamp or that the settlement and release must together be treated as one transaction for the purposes of stamp duty.[92]

PRECEDENT No. 15

Settlement on an Infant (whether a Son of the Settlor or not) Providing for the Fund to Vest Absolutely on his Attaining the Age of Twenty-one or marrying. Variation where Vesting is to be Postponed to the Age of Twenty-five. Widest Range of Investment

In this precedent the settlor settles a fund for the benefit of an infant, who may be a child of the settlor, so that the infant becomes absolutely entitled to the capital settled upon attaining his majority or marrying while still an infant. Alternative clauses are provided which postpone to twenty-five the age at which capital vests in the child. This has no advantage or disadvantage as respects tax and estate duty: but for family reasons the settlor may prefer not to give capital at the early age of twenty-one years.

The estate duty advantage to be gained from a settlement in this form is that if the settlor survives the settlement by five years no duty will be payable on his death.

If the beneficiary is a child of the settlor, the advantage as regards

---

92 *Cf. Oughtred* v. *I. R. C.* [1958] 2 All E.R. 443 and *Cohen and Moore* v. *I. R. C.* [1933] 2 K.B. 126.

tax is that, provided the whole income arising under the settlement is accumulated during such time as the beneficiary is an infant and unmarried, it suffers standard rate income tax, but is not caught by section 397 of the Income Tax Act, 1952, as amended by section 20 of the Finance Act, 1958, so as to be deemed to be income of the settlor for tax purposes. If the beneficiary is not a child of the settlor, the income may be used for the maintenance, education and benefit of the beneficiary until he reaches the age of twenty-one years or marries, without being deemed for tax purposes to be income of the settlor.

Parties.   THIS SETTLEMENT is made on the —— day of —— 19— BETWEEN —— of —— in the County of —— (hereinafter called " the Settlor ") of the one part and —— of —— in the County of —— and —— of —— in the County of —— (hereinafter called " the Trustees ") of the other part;

WHEREAS:

Recitals.   (A) The Settlor wishes to make provision for his son/nephew —— (hereinafter called " the Beneficiary ") who was born on the —— day of —— 19— and accordingly to create such trusts as hereinafter appear;

(B) The Settlor has caused to be transferred into the joint names of the Trustees the investments mentioned in the Schedule hereto;

Witnesseth.   NOW for effectuating the said desire and in consideration of the natural love and affection of the Settlor for the Beneficiary THIS DEED WITNESSETH as follows:

Trust to sell and convert.   1. THE Trustees shall stand possessed of the investments specified in the Schedule hereto Upon Trust that the Trustees shall either permit the same to remain as invested or shall at their discretion sell call in or convert into money all or any of the said investments and shall at the like discretion invest the money arising thereby in the names or under the control of the Trustees in any of the investments hereinafter authorised with power from time to time at the like discretion to change such investments for others of a like nature.

In exercising their power to convert investments trustees must bear in mind the provisions relating to short-term capital gains contained in

Chapter II of the Finance Act, 1962.[93] For example, any gain realised on the sale of shares acquired within the preceding six months will attract a charge to tax in the hands of the trustees under Case VII of Schedule D. And if the shares disposed of are shares in a landowning company as defined in section 14 (6) of the Finance Act, 1962, a charge to tax might be made under Case VII notwithstanding that the trustees have held the shares for more than six months.[94]

Trust for beneficiary.
    2. THE Trustees shall stand possessed of the investments specified in the Schedule hereto and the investments for the time being representing the same (hereinafter called " the Trust Fund ") upon the following trusts :

Maintenance.
    (1) Until the Beneficiary attains the age of Twenty-one years or marries before attaining that age Upon Trust to pay or apply the whole or such part if any as they may think fit of the income of the Trust Fund for or towards the maintenance education or benefit of the Beneficiary and so that they may either themselves apply the same or may pay the same to the parents or either parent or the guardians or guardian of the Beneficiary for such purposes as aforesaid without themselves seeing to the application thereof And to accumulate the surplus if any of such income not so paid or applied at compound interest by investing the same and the resultant income thereof in any of the investments hereinafter authorised And to hold the same as an accretion to the Trust Fund with power to apply the accumulations of any preceding year or years or any part thereof as if the same were income of the current year ;

    If the beneficiary is a child of the settlor, any income paid or applied under this clause to or for the benefit of the beneficiary while he is under twenty-one years of age and unmarried will be treated as the income of the settlor for tax purposes by virtue of section 397 of the Income Tax Act, 1952, as amended by section 20 of the Finance Act, 1958. On the other hand, if the beneficiary is not the child of the settlor, income applied for the maintenance, education or benefit of the beneficiary will be the income of the beneficiary, not the settlor, for tax purposes. In such a case the trustees should normally bear it in mind that, if in any year of assessment an infant has an income exceeding £115 a year, his parent will lose all or part of the child allowance.

    Therefore it will almost always be beneficial to accumulate income

[93] See p. 115, *supra.*
[94] Finance Act, 1962, s. 14 (1) (2).

if the beneficiary is a child of the settlor. It must be remembered that the rule imposed by section 397 as amended may not be circumvented by accumulating income for a few years and then advancing the sums accumulated in the form of capital: the money advanced would be deemed to be the income of the settlor in the year of assessment in the course of which it was advanced: see Income Tax Act, 1952, s. 398 (2) (b).

Even if the beneficiary is not a child of the settlor it may be beneficial to accumulate part at least of the income. Income accumulated, whether or not the beneficiary is the child of the settlor, bears income tax at the standard rate, but not surtax. Moreover, the possibility of a claim under section 228 of the Income Tax Act, 1952, must be borne in mind. In such a case where the beneficiary is not the child of the settlor, or in a case where the settlor being the beneficiary's parent is dead, the situation may occur where it is desired to resort to income which arose in past years and has been duly accumulated, and to use it for the purpose of maintaining or advancing the beneficiary in the present year. The question has to be considered, whether the application of past accumulations for this purpose may cause the sum applied to be income of the beneficiary in the year of assessment during which the application is made. It is sometimes suggested that the principle to be applied in answering this question is to have regard to the purpose for which the accumulations are to be applied. If that purpose is of an income nature—for example, maintenance, or payment of current school fees—it is argued that the accumulations so applied must be treated as income of the beneficiary and reliance is placed on the comment of Lord Greene M.R. in *Cunard's Trustees* v. *I. R. C.* (1946) 27 Tax Cas. 122: *cf. Milne's Executors* v. *I. R. C.* (1956) 37 Tax Cas. 10. On the other hand if the purpose is of a capital nature—for example the purchase of articles or of a share in a business—it is conceded that the accumulations do not lose their character as capital. It is submitted that to distinguish between applications of accumulated income for " income " and " capital " purposes in this way is fallacious. Apart from the provisions of section 398 (2) (b) referred to above income once accumulated is capital and cannot be reconverted to income by reference to the manner in which it is applied. The only payments out of capital which for tax purposes have the character of income are, it is submitted, recurrent annual payments in the nature of an annuity; these may be variable payments to supplement income to bring it to a specific figure or standard.

Income paid to the parent of a beneficiary under a clause in this form is clearly not paid for the parent's benefit, but for the benefit of the child. Section 22 of the Finance Act, 1958, is not, therefore, in point.

Twenty-one   (2) Upon the attainment by the Beneficiary of the
or marriage.   age of Twenty-one years or his earlier marriage Upon
Trust for the Beneficiary absolutely.

Formerly it was usual to postpone the vesting of capital to the age of twenty-two years, where the beneficiary was a child of the settlor. In view of the amendments to section 397 of the Income Tax Act, 1952, contained in section 20 of the Finance Act, 1958, this is no longer necessary or advisable.

On attaining twenty-one the beneficiary can submit a claim in respect of personal reliefs and allowances for the years during which income was accumulated under section 228 of the Income Tax Act, 1952. The sum recovered will belong to the beneficiary personally and will not, even when the trusts of the settlement continue to operate, be an addition to the settled capital.[95]

It follows from this provision that during the infancy of the beneficiary the trustees should, if this is possible, keep a record of the income of the beneficiary in addition to the income accumulated for him under the settlement, and of his personal allowances and any reduced-rate reliefs enjoyed, in order to facilitate the calculation of the repayment due under section 228.

The following variation may be used where it is desired to postpone the age at which the beneficiary is to take the capital to twenty-five years. It is important not to substitute an age greater than twenty-five years without ensuring that some person other than the settlor or any spouse of the settlor is named as the ultimate beneficiary under clause 3 of the settlement.

Income at twenty-one or marriage.

(2) From and after the attainment by the Beneficiary of the age of Twenty-one years or his earlier marriage Upon Trust to pay the income of the Trust Fund to the Beneficiary until he dies or attains the age of Twenty-five years; and

Twenty-five.

(3) Upon the attainment by the Beneficiary of the age of Twenty-five years Upon Trust for the Beneficiary absolutely; but

Death under twenty-five.

(4) In the event of the Beneficiary dying under the age of Twenty-five years leaving a child or children Upon Trust for such of the children of the Beneficiary as shall attain the age of Twenty-one years and if more than one in equal shares absolutely.

Trust in default.

3. SUBJECT to the foregoing trusts the Trust Fund and the income and the accumulations if any of the income thereof or so much thereof as shall not have become vested or been paid or applied under any of the trusts or powers affecting the same shall be held In Trust for the Settlor absolutely.

---

[95] Re Fulford [1930] 1 Ch. 71.

An ultimate resulting trust in favour of the settlor is unobjectionable from the point of view of estate duty.[96] Nor will it result in accumulated income being treated as the settlor's income under section 405 of the Income Tax Act, 1952, since proviso (a) (iv) to subsection (2) of that section contains an express saving where the fund can only revert to the settlor on the death of a beneficiary under the age of twenty-five or some lower age. Proviso (d) to subsection (2) of section 415 similarly excludes any adverse application of that section.

The point has been mooted whether in a settlement in the present form the power of advancement under section 32 of the Trustee Act, 1925, could be exercised in favour of the settlor being the person entitled to the trust fund in the event of the failure of the prior trusts declared by the settlement. This being a power exercisable at the discretion of the trustees under which property comprised in the settlement might be applied for the benefit of the settlor, it is suggested that the income arising from the property which could be so applied should be treated as the income of the settlor for tax purposes in accordance with the provisions of section 22 of the Finance Act, 1958, dealing with the exercise of discretionary powers in favour of a settlor. If valid, the point would also enable a claim to be made under section 405 of the Income Tax Act, 1952, in respect of accumulated income. The Revenue are not known to have taken the point under either section. It is submitted that there are at least two reasons why the point would not be valid.

First, it cannot, it is suggested, be said of a person in the position of the settlor that he has a presumptive or vested share or interest in the trust property within the meaning of proviso (a) to subsection (1) of section 32 of the Trustee Act, 1925. Secondly, section 32 is to be read subject to the provisions of section 69 (2) of the Trustee Act, 1925, which provides that powers conferred by the Act are to apply if and so long only as a contrary intention is not expressed in the settlement.[97] It is arguable that the trusts of a settlement in the present form are such that a contrary intention is clear, namely, that nothing should be paid to the settlor whether under the power of advancement or otherwise unless the trusts in favour of the beneficiary have failed. The settlor is simply the "long stop." The trust in his favour only states expressly what the law would otherwise imply. Those who have doubts as to the effectiveness of these arguments may prefer to include an express clause excluding any application of the trust fund in the settlor's favour otherwise than under the "long stop" trust. Such a clause might be in the following form:

Exclusion of settlor.   SAVE as is hereinbefore expressly provided the Trust Fund and the income thereof shall at all times be possessed and enjoyed to the entire exclusion of the Settlor

---

[96] See *Cmmr. of Stamp Duties for New South Wales* v. *Perpetual Trustee Co., Ltd.* [1943] A.C. 425 and *St. Aubyn* v. *Att.-Gen.* [1952] A.C. 15 at p. 49.
[97] See *I. R. C.* v. *Bernstein* [1961] Ch. 399; 39 Tax Cas. 391.

and of any benefit to him by contract or otherwise and no part thereof shall be paid or lent to or applied for the benefit of the Settlor or any wife of the Settlor in any circumstances whatsoever.

The draftsman may prefer to include the above clause at the end of the settlement, and to consider adopting the slightly different form to be found in the following precedent.

Investment.   4. MONEY to be invested under the trusts hereof may be applied or invested in the purchase of or at interest upon the security of such stocks funds shares securities or other investments or property of whatsoever nature and wherever situate (including the purchase or improvement of a freehold or leasehold dwelling-house situate in the United Kingdom or elsewhere for use as a residence) and whether involving liabilities or not or upon such personal credit with or without security as the Trustees in their absolute discretion shall think fit and to the intent that the Trustees shall have the same powers in all respects as if they were absolute owners beneficially entitled.

This clause gives to the trustees the widest powers of investment normally conferred upon the trustees of a simple settlement, such as the present. Other clauses will be found in some of the precedents which follow. Under modern conditions a settlor's best protection would seem to lie in the quality of the persons he selects as trustees rather than in the restrictions he places upon their powers of investment. The express reference to a dwelling-house to be used as a residence is included to meet any objection based on *Re Power* [1947] Ch. 572.

Money should not be invested in loans to the settlor without considering the tax position in the light of section 408 of the Income Tax Act, 1952 (which also applies where the loan is made to the spouse of the settlor), and the possibility that the loan may not be deductible for estate duty purposes: Finance Act, 1939, s. 31.

Moreover, there may be an argument that if money is lent to a settlor he will not for estate duty purposes have been excluded from possession and enjoyment since the date of the settlement: see *Chick* v. *Commissioner of Stamp Duties* [1958] A.C. 435. For tax purposes a loan at a commercial rate of interest is not an application for the borrower's benefit within the meaning of section 405 of the Income Tax

Act, 1952: see *Vestey's Executors* v. *I. R. C.* [1949] 1 All E.R. 1108;
31 Tax Cas. 1.

Trustee
indemnity.   5. THE Trustees (which term for the purposes of this
clause includes any of them or any person or body corporate appointed to be a Trustee of this Settlement but
does not include the Settlor or any spouse of the Settlor
or any Trustee charging remuneration) shall not be
liable for the consequences of any error or forgetfulness
whether of law or of fact on the part of any of the
Trustees or their legal or other advisers or generally for
any breach of duty or trust whatsoever unless it shall
be proved to have been committed given or omitted in
personal conscious bad faith by the Trustee charged to
be so liable And accordingly all persons claiming any
beneficial interest in over or upon the property subject
to this Settlement shall be deemed to take with notice
of and subject to the protection hereby conferred on
the Trustees.

Trustee
charging
clause.   6. ANY Trustee other than the Settlor or any spouse
of the Settlor being a solicitor or other person engaged
in any profession business or trade shall be entitled to
be paid all usual professional business and trade charges
for business transacted time expended and acts done by
him or any employee or partner of his in connection
with the trusts hereof including acts which a trustee not
being in any profession business or trade could have
done personally.

New trustees.   7. THE Settlor during his life shall have the power of
appointing any new Trustee or Trustees hereof.

Where the settlor either is a trustee or has the power of appointing
himself to be a trustee, and there are the usual charging and indemnity
clauses, it could perhaps be argued that he has reserved to himself a
benefit, for tax or estate duty purposes: see section 405 of the Income
Tax Act, 1952, and section 22 of the Finance Act, 1958, and *Oakes* v.
Commissioner of Stamp Duties [1954] A.C. 57.[98] It is therefore
prudent, where the settlor either is a trustee or can appoint himself
a trustee, either to exclude him expressly from the charging and
indemnity clauses, or to add an express provision excluding him from
any benefit under the settlement. The present practice of the Revenue

[98] See discussion at p. 78, *ante.*

appears to be not to claim that an ordinary charging clause or indemnity amounts to a benefit reserved.

IN WITNESS whereof the parties hereto have here-under set their hands and seals the day and year first above written.

SCHEDULE

[*The investments above referred to.*]

PRECEDENT No. 16

Settlement of Sum of Money on Infant (Whether a Son of the Settlor or not) Designed to Postpone the Time at which Actual Control of the Settled Property is Handed Over to the Beneficiary until he Attains Thirty-five Years of Age. Power to Purchase a Business for the Beneficiary

This precedent gives the beneficiary an interest in capital at the age of twenty-one or earlier marriage, but postpones the age at which he can call for capital to thirty-five years by including a power to resettle on his wife and children. In exercising the power to resettle the trustees should have regard to the tax position.

Normally, where property is settled upon a beneficiary, so as to give him an absolute interest, and the beneficiary at some later date wishes to pass the fund on to his own children, section 397 of the Income Tax Act, 1952, applies to the later transaction, so that no saving of tax is made by the beneficiary if he applies the income for the benefit of his children. This may be avoided by giving the trustees power to terminate the beneficiary's interest and reappoint the fund in favour of him, his spouse or issue.

The observations relating to the preceding precedent are for the most part also relevant to this precedent.

Parties.   THIS SETTLEMENT is made the —— day of —— 19— BETWEEN —— of —— (hereinafter called " the Settlor ") of the one part and —— of —— and —— of —— (hereinafter called " the Trustees " which expression where the context permits also includes the trustees for the time being of this settlement) of the other part;

Recitals.

(A) The Settlor desires to provide for his son/ nephew —— (hereinafter called "the Bene- ficiary") who was born on the —— day of —— 19— and accordingly to create such trusts as hereinafter appear ;

(B) The Settlor is about to pay to the Trustees the sum of £—— and it is apprehended that the Settlor may hereafter pay or transfer to the Trustees further sums or property to be held on the trusts hereinafter declared.

Formerly it was usual, where a large sum of cash was settled first to settle a modest sum, such as £100, and later to add the balance by paying a cheque to the trustees, accompanied by an oral declaration of trust in the form of a direction to the trustees to hold the additional sum upon the trusts of the existing settlement. This device was aimed at avoiding settlement stamp duty. That duty having been abolished by section 30 of the Finance Act, 1962, the device is no longer required.

If further sums or property are added to the settlement, it may be advisable to execute a short supplemental declaration: see Precedent No. 26, *post*. If additional investments, or property other than cash, are added to an existing settled fund *ad valorem* stamp duty will usually be attracted.

Witnesseth.

NOW in consideration of the premises THIS DEED WITNESSETH and it is hereby agreed and declared as follows :

Trust to sell and convert.

1. THE Trustees shall stand possessed of the said sum of —— pounds and of all further sums of money and property which may hereafter be paid or transferred to them to be held by them upon the trusts declared by this Deed Upon Trust that the Trustees shall in their dis- cretion sell or convert into money all or any the said property and shall at the like discretion invest the said sum of —— pounds and all such further sums as afore- said and the moneys arising from such sale and con- version in the names or under the control of the Trustees in any of the investments hereinafter authorised with power from time to time at the like discretion to change such investments for others of a like nature.

Trusts.

2. THE Trustees shall stand possessed of the said sum of —— pounds and such further sums and property and the investments for the time being representing the same (hereinafter called "the Trust Fund") upon the trusts hereinafter declared concerning the same.

Maintenance.

3. UNTIL the Beneficiary attains the age of twenty-one years or marries before attaining that age the Trustees shall have power to pay or apply the whole or such part if any as they think fit of the income of the Trust Fund for or towards the maintenance education or benefit of the Beneficiary and may either themselves apply the same or may pay the same to the parents or either parent or the guardians or guardian of the Beneficiary or (after the attainment by the Beneficiary of the age of seventeen years) to the Beneficiary himself for any of the purposes aforesaid without seeing to the application thereof And shall accumulate the surplus if any of such income at compound interest by investing the same and the resulting income thereof in any of the investments hereinafter authorised and shall hold the same as an accretion to and as part of the Trust Fund.

It will be observed that the above power of maintenance differs from that in the preceding Precedent, in that it gives the trustees power to get a good discharge by simply paying money to the beneficiary, once he is seventeen years of age. It may not always be advisable to allow the trustees to discharge their responsibility in this way.

Twenty-one or marriage.

4. IF the Beneficiary shall attain the age of twenty-one years or earlier marry the Trustees shall hold the Trust Fund upon trust for the Beneficiary absolutely.

It is considered that a claim under section 228 of the Income Tax Act, 1952, will be available to the beneficiary, even though his interest remains subject to defeasance under the power contained in clause 6 of this precedent: see *Chamberlain* v. *Haig-Thomas* (1933) 17 Tax Cas. 595.

Advancement.

5. THE Trustees may at any time or times but during the lifetime of the Settlor not without his consent in writing raise any part or parts or the whole of the Trust Fund and may pay or apply the same for the advancement or benefit of the Beneficiary freed from the trusts of this settlement in such manner as the Trustees think fit.

Power to
resettle
before bene-
ficiary is
thirty-five.

6. NOTWITHSTANDING the trust contained in clause 4 hereof the Trustees may at any time or times during the lifetime of the Beneficiary before he shall have attained the age of thirty-five years declare such trusts revocable or irrevocable in respect of the whole or any part or parts of the Trust Fund that shall not then have been paid or applied under the provisions of the last preceding clause hereof in favour of the Beneficiary and any wife widow child children (including adopted or legitimated children) or remoter issue of the Beneficiary and subject to such conditions limitations provisions for maintenance education support advancement and benefit protective and other discretionary trusts exercisable at the discretion of the Trustees or any other person or persons as the Trustees shall in their absolute discretion (but without offending the rule against perpetuities) think fit.

If the draftsman is of the view that a power in this form is in danger of causing forfeiture of the claim under section 228, referred to under clause 4 above, that danger may be removed by expressly restricting this power so that it applies to the original trust fund only and not to any accumulations; income will then have been accumulated for the benefit of the beneficiary contingently on his attaining some specified age within the meaning of the section without even the possibility of such accumulations going elsewhere.

The present power is intended to provide for the possibility of future children being born to the beneficiary. Were he to provide for such children by means of a settlement or even by means of releasing a life interest under an existing settlement, any payment of income for the benefit of such children during their infancy would be caught by section 397 of the Income Tax Act, 1952, and thus deemed for tax purposes to be income of the beneficiary.[99] The present clause is intended to avoid section 397; consequently it may be possible to use the income for the maintenance of future children of the beneficiary.

The question arises whether the consent of the beneficiary may be stated as a prerequisite to the exercise by the trustees of their power to resettle. It is considered that the Revenue would almost certainly claim—with a good chance of success—that by giving his consent the beneficiary was a " settlor " for the purposes of section 397 of the Income Tax Act, 1952. It would be preferable to give the beneficiary power to appoint trustees.

The above power may be adapted so as to allow the trustees to

[99] Cf. I. R. C. v. Buchanan [1958] Ch. 289; 37 Tax Cas. 365.

resettle for the benefit of persons other than the beneficiary and his wife, widow and issue: but under no circumstances should power be included to benefit the settlor or any spouse of the settlor: Income Tax Act, 1952, s. 405; Finance Act, 1958, ss. 21, 22.

The above power may also be adapted so that it may be exercised by the wife of the settlor during her life and thereafter by the trustees. It may also be adapted so that it may be exercised by the settlor during his life and thereafter by the trustees: but this introduces some slight risk that the five-year period may begin anew if the settlor exercises the power: see section 44 of the Finance Act, 1948, as amended by section 46 of the Finance Act, 1950.

On no account should the above power be limited to cease on the settlor's death: see section 2 (1) (a) of the Finance Act, 1894; *Parker* v. *Lord Advocate* [1960] A.C. 608 and the discussion thereof on page 88 above.

Wide investment clause including purchase of a business.

7 (1). MONEY to be invested under this settlement may be applied or invested within the following range that is to say in any investments of whatsoever nature or wheresoever (including the purchase of any rights interests or property whether movable or immovable and including the loan or deposit of money on any personal or other security and upon any terms) as freely as if the Trustees were absolutely and beneficially entitled to the money thus invested And section 32 of the Law of Property Act 1925 shall apply to any immovable property in England or Wales (but not elsewhere) so purchased and the Trustees shall have in respect thereof all the powers of disposition leasing mortgaging charging management repair building development equipment furnishing and improvement and other powers as if they were beneficial owners absolutely entitled (including full powers to stock farms and to carry on equip and finance any farming or other business in any part of the world) and may in that behalf (or in respect of any chattels for the time being held hereunder) make any outlay from the income or capital of the Trust Fund And the Trustees in their discretion may allow the Beneficiary (or any other person or persons for the time being prospectively or contingently entitled to any interest in the Trust Fund or any part thereof) to occupy have custody of or use any immovable property or chattels for the time being forming part of the Trust Fund on such terms or conditions

as to inventories repair replacement insurance outgoings or otherwise at all as the Trustees shall think fit And so that no Trustee shall be liable for any loss or damage which may occur to any property so forming part of the Trust Fund during or by reason of any such occupation custody or use except insofar as such loss or damage shall be occasioned by the conscious and wilful default or neglect of such Trustee.

(2) This power of investment shall include the purchase acquisition or effecting of any reversionary or deferred property or rights of any description or any life or life-endowment or sinking-fund or term or other policy or policies of insurance of whatsoever nature and at or subject to any premium or premiums whether single or payable periodically and with or subject to any options rights benefits conditions or provisions whatsoever And the Trustees shall have power to pay out of the income or capital of the Trust Fund as they in their discretion think fit all sums payable from time to time for premiums or otherwise for the effecting or maintenance of any such policy or policies or for the exercise or enjoyment of any option right or benefit thereunder And any surrender of any such policy or policies shall for all the purposes of this settlement be deemed to be a sale thereof.

In a case where there is a real possibility that the settlor may die within five years from the date of the settlement a policy on the life of the settlor will form part of the trust fund and the policy moneys will attract duty and be aggregable with the settlor's free estate on his death: see section 38 (8) and (10) of the Finance Act, 1957. If however, premiums on the policy are paid out of accumulated income and can be shown to have been so paid, the policy moneys will escape duty on the settlor's death within five years: see subsection (14) of section 38. It may, therefore, be advantageous to pay premiums exclusively out of accumulated income.

Indemnity.   8. IN the professed execution of the trusts and powers hereof no trustee shall be liable for any loss to the trust premises arising by reason of any improper investment made in good faith or for the negligence or fraud of any agent employed by him or by any other trustee hereof although the employment of such agent was not strictly necessary or expedient or by reason of any mistake or omission made in good faith by any trustee hereof or by reason of any other matter or thing except wilful fraud or wrongdoing on the part of the trustee who is sought to be made liable.

Charging.

9. ANY Trustee being a solicitor accountant or other person engaged in any profession business or trade shall be entitled to be paid all usual professional or business or trade charges for business transacted time expended and acts done by him or any employee or partner of his in connection with the trusts hereof including acts which a trustee not being in any profession business or trade could have done personally.

New trustees.

10. THE Settlor during his lifetime and after his death the Beneficiary shall have the power of appointing any new trustee or trustees hereof provided that neither the Settlor nor any wife of the Settlor shall be a trustee hereof.

Trustees may retire.

11. IF any of the Trustees shall at any time desire to withdraw and be discharged from the trusts hereof he may do so by notice in writing signed by himself and given to the Settlor and after his death to the Beneficiary and upon giving such notice the Trustee so doing shall cease to be a trustee of this settlement to all intents and purposes except as to the acts and deeds necessary for the proper vesting of the trust property in the continuing or new trustees or trustee or otherwise as the case may require which acts and deeds shall be done and executed at the expense of the Trust Fund.

Exclusion of Settlor.

12. NOTWITHSTANDING anything to the contrary hereinbefore expressed or implied no discretion or power conferred upon the Trustees or any other person by this Deed or by any rule of law or arising in consequence of the exercise of any power conferred upon the Trustees by this Deed shall be exercised and nothing in this Deed shall operate so as to cause or permit any part of the capital or income of the Trust Fund to be or become lent or payable to or applicable directly or indirectly for the benefit of the Settlor or any person for the time being the spouse of the Settlor except in the event of the death of the Beneficiary an infant and unmarried.

IN WITNESS, etc.

PRECEDENT No. 17

Settlement of Investments upon an Infant (other than a child of a Settlor Resident in the United Kingdom) under which the Beneficiary has an immediate vested interest in capital

This precedent gives the beneficiary an immediate vested interest in the settled capital. During the minority of the beneficiary the trustees have the like powers as to maintenance, education and advancement as if the interest of the infant were contingent upon his attaining his majority, with a like duty to accumulate unapplied income.

But under this form of settlement the whole income as it arises should be treated for income tax and surtax purposes as income of the beneficiary, whether or not it is accumulated: see *Gascoigne* v. *I. R. C.* [1927] 1 K.B. 594; 13 Tax Cas. 573, 587; and contrast *Stanley* v. *I. R. C.* [1944] K.B. 255; 26 Tax Cas. 12, which are discussed above at page 114.

If the beneficiary is the infant child of the settlor, this form of settlement will not effect any saving of tax, whether or not the income is accumulated, since the whole income will be caught by section 397 of the Income Tax Act, 1952. A possible exception would be where the parent was not resident in the United Kingdom but wished to provide for his child's education and maintenance in the United Kingdom; in such a case section 397 would not operate: see subsection (4). If the beneficiary is not the infant son of the settlor, then, even if the income is accumulated, the infant will be entitled to reclaim from the Revenue in each year a sum representing his personal allowance and reduced rate relief, and conversely will, if his income exceeds £2,000 a year, be liable to pay surtax. On the other hand, section 228 of the Income Tax Act, 1952, will have no application. It follows that in particular cases this type of settlement may be useful, since, even if the income is accumulated, the infant will enjoy the tax reliefs immediately, and will not have to wait until attaining his majority. Against this advantage must be weighed any surtax liability of the infant, the fact that his parents may lose the whole or part of the child relief even though the income is accumulated for the infant, and the possibility of estate duty being payable if the infant dies under the age of twenty-one years.

Parties.   THIS SETTLEMENT is made the —— day of —— 19— BETWEEN —— of —— (hereinafter called " the Settlor ") of the one part and —— of —— and —— of —— (hereinafter called "the Trustees" which expression shall where the context permits also include the Trustees for the time being of this Settlement) of the other part;

Beneficiary.

WHEREAS the Settlor wishing to make provision for —— (hereinafter called " the Beneficiary ") who was born on the —— day of —— 19— has by a transfer bearing the same date as this Settlement transferred to the Trustees —— shares in —— Limited ;

Witnesseth.

NOW THIS DEED WITNESSETH as follows :

Trust to sell and convert.

1. THE Trustees shall stand possessed of the recited shares upon trust that the Trustees shall with the consent of the Settlor during his life and thereafter in their discretion sell or convert into money all or any the said shares and shall with the like consent and at the like discretion invest the proceeds arising from such sale or conversion in the names or under the control of the Trustees in any of the investments hereinafter authorised with power from time to time with the like consent and at the like discretion to change such investments for others of a like nature.

Under this clause the trustees must obtain the settlor's consent before they vary the settled investments. This will not give the settlor an interest in the settlement such as will produce any adverse tax result: see *Vestey's Executors* v. *I. R. C.* [1949] 1 All E.R. 1108; 31 Tax Cas. 1.

Beneficiary absolutely entitled.

2. THE Trustees shall stand possessed of the recited shares and the investments for the time being representing the same (hereinafter called " the Trust Fund ") in trust for the Beneficiary absolutely.

Maintenance.

3. UNTIL the Beneficiary attains the age of twenty-one years the Trustees shall have power to pay or apply the whole or such part or parts if any as they think fit of the income of the Trust Fund for or towards the maintenance education or benefit of the Beneficiary and may either themselves apply the same or may pay the same to the parents or either parent or the guardians or guardian of the Beneficiary or (after the attainment by the Beneficiary of the age of seventeen years) to the Beneficiary himself for any of the purposes aforesaid without seeing to the application thereof And shall accumulate the surplus if any of such income not so paid or applied at compound interest by investing the same and the resultant income thereof in any of the investments hereinafter authorised and shall hold the same as an accretion to and part of the Trust Fund.

Investment: wide range.

4. MONEY to be invested under the trusts hereof may at the discretion of the Trustees be applied or invested in any manner following namely :—

Wide range of investments.

(a) In or upon any of the public stocks or funds or Government securities of the United Kingdom of Great Britain and Northern Ireland or any British State (by which expression is meant any Kingdom Realm Dominion Commonwealth Union Dependency or Colony forming part of the British Commonwealth of Nations or any province or State having a separate local legislature and forming part thereof), or any foreign Government or State or any securities the interest on which shall be guaranteed by Parliament;

(b) Upon mortgage of freehold or leasehold property in the United Kingdom, such leaseholds having not less than twenty years to run at the time of such investment being made;

(c) On mortgage of leaseholds having any term of years to run together with a sinking fund policy at an annual premium securing the payment on or before the expiration of the term of a sum not less than 20 per cent. larger than the sum lent;

(d) On the security of any interest for a life or lives or determinable on a life or lives or any other event in real or personal immovable or movable property in the United Kingdom or any British State or any foreign country together with a policy or policies of assurance on such life or lives or against such event;

(e) On the security of any reversionary interest whether vested or contingent in any real or personal property together in the case of a contingent reversion with a policy of insurance covering the contingent risk;

(f) In the purchase or upon the security of any real or immovable property in any part of the world;

(g) In or upon the bonds debentures debenture stock mortgages obligations or securities or the guaranteed preferred or ordinary stock or shares or ordinary preferred or deferred or other stock or shares of any company or any public municipal or local body or authority in any part of the world.

5. [*Trustee indemnity, see p.* 136.]

6. [*Trustee charging clause, see p.* 137.]

7. THE Settlor during his life shall have the power of appointing any new trustee or trustees hereof but so that neither the Settlor nor any wife of the Settlor shall be so appointed.

IN WITNESS, ETC.

PRECEDENT No. 18

Settlement on Existing Sons and Daughters of the Settlor With Settled Shares, Giving Sons Life Interests and Daughters Protected Interests. Power to Re-settle Shares and to Release Protected Life Interests. Narrow Range of Investments

The income would normally be accumulated during the respective minorities of the beneficiaries. As each beneficiary attained twenty-one years of age or married, he or she would be entitled to claim from the Revenue authorities a sum representing his or her personal reliefs on the income of his or her share during the years in which income was accumulated: see the Income Tax Act, 1952, s. 228; *Lynch* v. *Davies* [1962] T.R. 319. These repayments would belong to each life tenant absolutely, and would not be subject to the trusts affecting his or her share of the trust fund: *Re Fulford* [1930] 1 Ch. 71; see *ante*, p. 112.

Stamp duty at the rate of £1 per cent. (voluntary disposition duty) will be payable in respect of so much of the settled funds as consists of investments other than bearer bonds or similar assets (*e.g.*, allotment letters) or investments, such as Government Securities, exempt from stamp duty.

Parties.   THIS SETTLEMENT is made the —— day of —— 19— BETWEEN —— of, etc. (hereinafter called " the Settlor ") of the one part and —— of, etc. and —— of, etc. (hereinafter called " the Trustees ") of the other part;

WHEREAS :

Four
children.

(A) The Settlor has four children namely his sons —— and —— and his daughters —— and —— (hereinafter called collectively " the Beneficiaries ") who were born on the —— day of —— the —— day of —— the —— day of—— and the —— day of —— respectively ;

(B) The Settlor desires to make provision for the Beneficiaries by creating such trusts as hereinafter appear ;

Investments
settled.

(C) The Settlor is about to pay or transfer into the joint names of the Trustees the money and investments specified in the Schedule hereto and it is apprehended that the Settlor may hereafter pay or transfer or cause to be paid and transferred to the Trustees further money or investments to be held upon the trusts hereof ;

Witnesseth.

NOW for effectuating the said desire and in consideration of the natural love and affection of the Settlor for the Beneficiaries THIS DEED WITNESSETH as follows :

Trust to sell
and convert.

1. THE Trustees shall stand possessed of the Trust Fund (which term shall wherever it occurs in this Deed mean the money and investments specified in the Schedule hereto and all other if any the money and investments which may hereafter be paid or transferred to the Trustees as aforesaid and the investments for the time being representing the same respectively) Upon Trust to permit the same to remain as invested or in their discretion to sell call in or convert into money the whole or any part thereof and invest the money arising thereby in the names or under the control of the Trustees in any of investments hereby authorised with power from time to time at the like discretion to vary such investments for others of a like nature.

Beneficiaries
at twenty-
one.

2. THE Trustees shall stand possessed of the Trust Fund Upon trust for such of the Beneficiaries as attain the age of twenty-one years or marry before attaining that age and if more than one in equal shares.

Trusts of
each share.

3. NOTWITHSTANDING the trust aforesaid the share of each Beneficiary shall be retained by or under the control of the Trustees and held upon the following trusts :

Sons: life interests.

(1) The Trustees shall stand possessed of the share of each of the Beneficiaries —— and —— and the accumulations if any of the income made during his minority Upon Trust to pay the income thereof to him during his life;

Daughters: protective trusts.

(2) The Trustees shall stand possessed of the share of each of the Beneficiaries —— and —— and the accumulations if any of income made during her minority Upon protective trusts for her benefit during her life;

Issue of each beneficiary.

(3) From and after the death of each of the Beneficiaries the share of such Beneficiary and the accruals thereto shall be held as to capital and income In Trust for the children or remoter issue (ascertained on the footing that adopted or legitimated children are the children of their adopted or legitimated parents or parent as the case may be) of such Beneficiary or for such one or more of them and at such ages or times and in such shares if more than one and for such interests and upon such trusts for their benefit and with such provisions for their maintenance advancement education or benefit and generally in such manner as the Beneficiary shall from time to time by deed or deeds revocable or irrevocable or by will or codicil appoint And in default of and subject to any such appointment In Trust for all or any the child or children of the Beneficiary who being male shall attain the age of twenty-one years or being female shall attain that age or marry under that age and if more than one in equal shares;

Hotchpot.

(4) No child of any Beneficiary who or whose issue takes any part of the share of such Beneficiary under any appointment by such Beneficiary shall in the absence of any direction by such Beneficiary to the contrary take any share in the unappointed part except upon bringing the share or shares appointed to him or her or to his or her issue into hotchpot and accounting for the same accordingly;

Cross-remainders.

(5) If the trusts hereinbefore declared concerning the share of any Beneficiary shall fail then subject to the trusts and powers hereinbefore declared in favour of such Beneficiary and his or her issue the original share of such Beneficiary and also any share or shares accruing under this provision and all accumulations (if any) of income

or so much thereof respectively as shall not have become vested or been paid or applied under any trust or power affecting the same shall be held In Trust for such of the others of the Beneficiaries (other than any Beneficiary or Beneficiaries the trusts for whom and whose issue have also at the time of such failure already failed or determined otherwise than by the absolute payment or transfer of a share) as attain the age of twenty-one years or marry under that age and if more than one in equal shares Provided that every further share accruing to any Beneficiary under this provision shall be retained and held by the Trustees upon and subject to such of the trusts and powers hereby declared concerning the original share of that Beneficiary as shall be then subsisting or capable of taking effect and as one fund for all purposes including any hotchpot provision with such original share.

Maintenance and advancement.   4. SECTION 31 (relating to maintenance and accumulation) and section 32 (relating to advancement) of the Trustee Act, 1925, shall apply hereto with the following variations :—

(a) Section 31 shall have effect as if the words " the Trustees think fit " were substituted in subsection (1) (i) for the words " may in all the circumstances be reasonable " and as if the proviso at the end of subsection (1) commencing with the words " Provided that in deciding " and ending with the words " the income of each fund shall be so paid or applied " were omitted;

(b) Section 32 shall have effect as if the words " one half of " were omitted from proviso (a) to subsection (1) thereof.

Ultimate gift over.   5. SUBJECT to the trusts and powers hereinbefore contained the Trust Fund and the income thereof and all statutory accumulations (if any) of income or so much thereof respectively as shall not have become vested or been paid or applied under any trust or power affecting the same shall be held In Trust for —— absolutely Provided that in no circumstances whatsoever shall any income arising under or property comprised in this settlement be payable to or applicable for the benefit of the Settlor or any wife of the Settlor.

It is considered that the provisions of section 415 of the Income Tax Act, 1952, make it necessary to exclude the settlor. In view of the protective trusts included in this Settlement, it is considered that section 405 of the Income Tax Act, 1952, and section 22 of the Finance Act, 1958, will apply unless both the settlor and the settlor's wife are excluded.

If in any case it is particularly desired to provide that the settlor or his wife shall take the fund in the event of the prior trusts failing, it is suggested that the protective trusts should be set out in full so that the forfeiture thereunder operates only in the event of the beneficiary " becoming bankrupt or assigning or charging his interest," these being the words used in section 405 (2) (b) of the Income Tax Act, 1952 : see also proviso (a) to that subsection and section 415 (2) (a) and (b) of the Income Tax Act, 1952.

Power to resettle.   6. AFTER any Beneficiary shall have attained a vested interest in the income of a share or the whole of the Trust Fund the Trustees shall have power at any time or from time to time in the lifetime [and with the consent in writing] of such Beneficiary by deed to appoint and declare that such share or part of a share shall be held on such trusts for the benefit of such Beneficiary or the wife or husband or children or remoter issue of such Beneficiary and in such shares and at such times and with and subject to such conditions limitations and provisions for forfeiture and such powers and discretions exercisable by such person or persons and such provisions for maintenance and otherwise as the Trustees in their absolute discretion [and subject only to the consent of such Beneficiary] shall think fit And so that the trusts and powers declared by this settlement shall subsist only so far as not varied by the trusts so declared.

If the words in square brackets are employed, there may be some risk that the Revenue may seek to establish that the beneficiary in question is a " Settlor " as defined by section 403 of the Income Tax Act, 1952, with the result that any income applied during the lifetime of the beneficiary for the maintenance of his infant children will for tax purposes be treated as income of the beneficiary.

Since section 399, proviso (ii), of the Income Tax Act, 1952, has now been amended by section 20 (4) of the Finance Act, 1958, it is considered that the above power may be extended by including in the class of possible beneficiaries any persons other than the settlor or any wife of the settlor. Previously such a widely drawn class of beneficiaries would never have given rise to a charge to tax on the settlor on the footing that the settlement was not irrevocable within the meaning of section 399 : see *I. R. C.* v. *Jamieson* [1963] 3 W.L.R. 156.

146   FAMILY SETTLEMENTS

Power to
release
protected
interest.

7. NOTWITHSTANDING the protective trusts herein-before declared either of the Beneficiaries —— or —— may during her lifetime by deed declared to be made in exercise of the power hereby conferred on her surrender unto the Trustees her protected life interest in the whole or any part or parts of the share original or accrued of such Beneficiary and thereupon the Trustees shall stand possessed of such share or part or parts of such share upon the trusts in this deed declared concerning the same upon the footing that such protective life interest has terminated without any forfeiture.

It may also be advisable to add a power for the trustees in their absolute discretion to release the forfeiture in respect of any particular act, or generally. It is not advisable to settle property on protective trusts without providing some means by which the life tenant can dispose of her interest so as to accelerate the interests of the reversioners. The surrender of her life interest by the life tenant will be a settlement within the meaning of section 403 of the Income Tax Act, 1952, so that any income which becomes payable to the infant unmarried children under the " settlement " will be treated as the income of the life tenant for tax purposes: see *I. R. C.* v. *Buchanan* [1958] Ch. 289; 37 Tax Cas. 365.

Investment:
narrow
range.

8. TRUST moneys may be invested in or upon any of the public stocks or funds or Government securities of the United Kingdom of Great Britain and Northern Ireland the Realm of Canada the Commonwealth of Australia any Australian State or the Dominion of New Zealand or any securities the interest on which is or shall be guaranteed by Parliament or upon freehold or leasehold securities in England or Wales (such leaseholds having not less than 60 years to run at the time of making such investment) or in or upon the debentures or debenture or secured loan stock of any railway canal dock harbour gas water or other public utility company incorporated by special Act of the Parliament of the United Kingdom or of any British State or by Royal Charter or in or upon the guaranteed or preference stock or shares of any such company as aforesaid which shall have paid dividends on its ordinary capital at the rate of at least 3 per cent. per annum for at least three years prior to the date of making such investment or in or upon the stocks bonds debentures or securities of any municipality

county or district council or other local authority situate
in the United Kingdom or in or upon any other stocks
funds or securities for the time being authorised by law
for the investment of trust funds but nevertheless not in
any stocks funds bonds shares or securities transferable
by mere delivery or by delivery and endorsement.

The above is the narrowest range of investment which is in practice
advisable. In the majority of cases, a much wider range should be
adopted in the interests of the beneficiaries, since it is usually sound
policy to have part of the trust fund invested in ordinary shares of
substantial commercial undertakings.

Power to
purchase
land.
9. (i) TRUST moneys may at the discretion of the
Trustees be invested or laid out in the purchase of land
in any part of the United Kingdom of any tenure including leaseholds held for a term of which not less than 60
years shall be unexpired at the time of purchase and
whether by way of investment or for the residence of any
one or more of the Beneficiaries and his or her spouse
issue and dependants.

(ii) The property so purchased may be subject to any
improvement charges of any sort or nature restrictive
covenants restrictions easements profits à prendre
tenancies rentcharges or other incumbrances or liabilities
affecting the property and the opinion of counsel that
the title may be accepted shall conclusively protect the
Trustees acting thereon.

(iii) All such property shall be assured to the Trustees
for the estate purchased by them Upon trust at their discretion to sell the same and to hold the proceeds of such
sale after payment of the costs thereof upon the same
trusts and subject to the same powers and provisions
(including the power in this present clause contained) as
the money so laid out would have been subject to had it
not been so laid out.

Apportion-
ment.
10. IN the execution of any of the trusts or powers
hereof the Trustees
(i) may (without prejudice to any jurisdiction of the
court) decide what money represents income and what
represents capital ;
(ii) may in reference to any property or the proceeds
of any property from time to time subject to the trusts

hereof or any share therein and as between the persons interested exercise the powers of appropriation and other incidental powers conferred on personal representatives by section forty-one of the Administration of Estates Act, 1925, without any of the consents made requisite by that section; [and every decision allotment apportionment setting apart and valuation made in exercise of the said powers shall be as binding upon all persons then or thereafter to be beneficially interested in the premises as if the same had been duly made by a court of competent jurisdiction].

The strictures made in *Re Wynn* [1952] Ch. 271 on clauses which oust the court's jurisdiction may well apply to the words in square brackets. Their effect must be open to question: see below at p. 155.

Trustee indemnity.

11. IN the professed execution of the trusts and powers hereof no trustee shall be liable for any loss to the trust premises arising by reason of any improper investment made in good faith or for the negligence or fraud of any agent employed by him or by any other trustee hereof although the employment of such agent was not strictly necessary or expedient or by reason of any mistake or omission made in good faith by any trustee hereof or by reason of any other matter or thing except wilful and individual fraud or wrongdoing on the part of the trustee who is sought to be made liable.

Charging.

12. ANY Trustee being a solicitor or other person engaged in any profession business or trade shall be entitled to be paid all usual professional business and trade charges for business transacted time expended and acts done by him or any employee or partner of his in connection with the trusts hereof including acts which a trustee not being in any profession business or trade could have done personally.

As neither the settlor nor his wife may be appointed a trustee of the settlement because of the provisions in clause 13, there is no need to exclude the settlor or his wife from any entitlement under the trustee charging clause.

New trustees.

13. THE Settlor during his lifetime and after his death his present wife during her lifetime or until she remarries shall have the power of appointing new trustees but so

that neither the Settlor nor any wife of the Settlor shall
be appointed a trustee hereof.

IN WITNESS, ETC.

THE SCHEDULE

PRECEDENT No. 19

Settlement of Investments on Existing and Future Children of the Settlor Giving an Interest in Capital on Reaching the Age of Twenty-one Years or Earlier Marriage. Provision for Settlor's Widow

It often happens that a settlor wishes to set aside a substantial block
of assets immediately, and yet is unwilling to settle them on his existing
children, thereby depriving his future children, if any, of a fair share in
the income enjoyed by their elder brothers and sisters. A settlement on
a class not yet closed may provide the solution. The following precedent
may be adapted to the individual wishes of each settlor, but considerable
circumspection is required in each case. To avoid unnecessary complexity, it is often useful to group together at the beginning of the
operative part of the deed all the phrases requiring definition, and later
to group together the powers conferred on the trustees.

Parties.

THIS SETTLEMENT is made the —— day of ——
19— BETWEEN —— of —— in the County of —— (hereinafter called " the Settlor ") of the one part and —— of
—— in the County of —— and —— of —— in the County
of —— (hereinafter called " the Original Trustees ") of
the other part.

WHEREAS :

Existing
children.

(A) The Settlor was married on the —— day of ——
19— to —— and there are at the date hereof two
children of the said marriage and no more namely
—— who was born on the —— day of ——
19— and —— who was born on the —— day of
—— 19— ;

Future
children.

(B) The Settlor wishes to provide for his said two
children and for future children hereafter to be
born to him by his said wife and to create such
trusts as hereinafter appear ;

Irrevocable.

(C) The Settlor desires that this Settlement shall be irrevocable immediately upon the execution thereof;

Funds settled.

(D) The Settlor is about to pay or transfer into the joint names or control of the Trustees the money and investments specified in the Schedule hereto and it is apprehended that the Settlor may hereafter pay or transfer or cause to be paid or transferred further money or investments to be held on the trusts hereof;

NOW in consideration of the premises THIS DEED WITNESSETH as follows :—

Definitions:

1. IN this Settlement the following terms shall where the context so admits have the following meanings:

Trustees.

(a) " the Trustees " means the Original Trustees or other the Trustees or Trustee for the time being of this Settlement;

Trust fund.

(b) " the Trust Fund " means

    (i) the money and investments specified in the Schedule hereto;

    (ii) all money and investments paid or transferred to and accepted by the Trustees as additions to the Trust Fund; and

    (iii) the investments and property from time to time representing such money investments and additions or any part or parts thereof;

Beneficiaries.

(c) "the Beneficiaries" means the said —— and —— and all the children of the Settlor hereafter born to him by his said wife —— before the —— day of —— one thousand nine hundred and ——;

It is advisable to enter here the date upon which the elder of the existing children will attain the age of twenty-one years.

It is sometimes argued that the date to be inserted should be not later than two years after the execution of the settlement. The reasoning upon which this argument is based is that, until the death of the settlor, the interest of each beneficiary is defeasible, by reason of the fact that the settlor may have further children, so reducing the share which each child may expect to obtain upon reaching the age of twenty-one years. The death of the settlor removes this possibility of defeasance. Therefore there is a beneficial interest arising on his death within the meaning of section 2 (1) (d) of the Finance Act, 1894. This benefit is valued, having regard to section 28 of the Finance Act, 1934, so that the whole fund, including any accumulations of income added to capital during the settlor's life, will pass for the purposes of estate duty. Therefore, prima facie, all future children should be excluded. There is, however, little harm in including those born within two years, since in any event the whole fund will pass for estate duty purposes if the settlor fails to survive the five year period, subject to relief under section 64 of the Finance Act, 1960, if he lives for more than two but less than five years. Such is the argument, and it calls in aid the decision of the House of Lords in *Adamson* v. *Attorney-General* [1933] A.C. 257. It is submitted that this argument cannot be sustained.

The *Adamson* case decided that there is a passing under section 2 (1) (d) where an interest under a settlement, which during the settlor's life-time was subject to be defeated either by the exercise by the settlor of a power of appointment reserved to him during his life or by the death of the beneficiary entitled to the interest, becomes absolute and indefeasible on the settlor's death. The present case is quite different. There is no power of appointment reserved to the settlor during his life. Nor is it accurate to say that the death of the settlor removes a possibility of defeasance : it admittedly closes the class of beneficiaries, but all it does thereby is to define the quantum of each child's expectancy, which remains, after the death as before it, a future contingent interest.

On the other hand, it may be prudent to insert a date not later than the date upon which the eldest child will reach the age of twenty-one years. If a later date were inserted, the interest of the eldest child upon attaining that age would be a vested interest liable to be divested in the event of further children being born and attaining the age of twenty-one years : it could thus be argued that the *Adamson* case applied, with the result that, in the event of the settlor dying after the first child had attained the age of twenty-one years but before the date inserted, a part of the settled fund would pass under section 2 (1) (d). It is doubtful whether the Estate Duty Office would claim duty. Moreover any claim made could be met—with what degree of success it is not certain—with the argument that very little duty is payable. The reason for this is that the beneficiary's interest before the death is vested in possession, liable to be partially defeated, and all that the death does is to remove the liability to such partial defeasance. Section 28 of the Finance Act, 1934, does not apply, since it is limited to " interests in expectancy " not to interests vested in possession. The value of the " beneficial interest " arising on the death is thus likely to be very small.

Moreover, were a date to be taken later than such twenty-first birth-day, it would be open to the Revenue to argue that the eldest child was outside the ambit of section 228 of the Income Tax Act, 1952, and could not consequently claim his personal reliefs in respect of income accumu-lated during his minority (see *I. R. C.* v. *Bone*, 1927 S.C. 698, 13 Tax

Cas. 20; *Dale* v. *Mitcalfe* [1928] 1 K.B. 383, 13 Tax Cas. 41; see also *ante*, p. 112). While this argument has not yet been pronounced upon by the courts, and, in view of section 31 of the Trustee Act, 1925, and *Re King* [1928] Ch. 330, is not necessarily conclusive, it constitutes a factor to be taken into account.

This precedent may be adapted to the case where it is desired to postpone the vesting of capital to the attainment of the age of twenty-five or some other age greater than twenty-one. Where this is done a definition should be included here of a " perpetuity day," as in the following precedent.

Trusts for beneficiaries.   2. (1) THE Trustees shall stand possessed of the Trust Fund upon Trust for such of the Beneficiaries as shall attain the age of twenty-one years or marry before attaining that age in equal shares absolutely.

Maintenance.   (2) The trust aforesaid shall carry the intermediate income and the provisions of section 31 of the Trustee Act, 1925, shall apply to this Settlement accordingly subject nevertheless to the following variations :

(i) the words " may in all the circumstances be reasonable " shall be omitted from paragraph (i) of subsection (1) thereof and there shall be substituted the words " the trustees shall in their absolute discretion think fit " and

(ii) the proviso at the end of subsection (1) thereof shall be omitted.

It is usually advisable to vary the strict terms of section 31 of the Trustee Act, 1925. Moreover, the section does not, in terms, apply to a contingent class gift. Awkward questions may arise where one member of the class has attained a vested interest, but it is not yet certain how great his interest is, by reason of the possible future diminution or enlargement of the class of beneficiaries. Generally, the trustees should deal with the income as it arises by referring only to existing beneficiaries; the rules are set out in *Re King* [1928] Ch. 330.

Gift in default.   (3) Subject to the trusts hereinbefore declared and to the powers hereby or by law vested in the Trustees and to each and any exercise of such powers the Trustees shall hold the Trust Fund and the income thereof in trust for —— absolutely.

It is considered that the person named here may be the settlor or any wife of the settlor and that the settlement would not thereby be caught by section 405 or 415 of the Income Tax Act, 1952, or section 22 of the Finance Act, 1958.

3. DURING the period commencing upon the execution of this Settlement and terminating upon the last of
the following events to happen namely the death of the
said —— (the wife of the Settlor) and the attainment of
the age of forty years by or earlier death under the age
of forty years of the last surviving Beneficiary of the
Beneficiaries now living the Trustees being at least
two in number shall have power by deed or deeds
revocable or irrevocable to declare such trusts (together
with such conditions limitations provisions for maintenance education advancement benefit protective trusts
and discretionary trusts to be carried out at the discretion of the Trustees or any other person or persons) for
the benefit of any widow of the Settlor or any issue of
the Settlor whether now living or born hereafter and of
whatever generation and the spouses widows or widowers
of any such issue and in respect of the whole or any part
or parts of the income or capital of the Trust Fund as
the Trustees shall in their absolute discretion think fit
AND the trusts hereinbefore in this Deed declared shall
take effect subject to the terms of any such deed
    PROVIDED that—
    (1) The power hereby conferred on the Trustees shall
not be exercised so as to benefit whether directly or
indirectly either the Settlor or any wife of the Settlor
and
    (2) The said power may at any time or times be
wholly or partially released as if vested in the Trustees
otherwise than in a fiduciary capacity.

The above power is intended to illustrate what may be achieved, if
desired, in the way of providing for future resettlement: it is, however,
apprehended that in most cases the settlor would prefer that his children
should take their interests without the possibility of defeasance, and
accordingly that this power would be omitted or greatly curtailed.

It will be observed that the widow of the settlor may be named as a
possible object of any resettlement. It is considered that this would not
have any adverse tax consequences under section 404 of the Income Tax
Act, 1952, or section 22 of the Finance Act, 1958, since the person
referred to is the widow, not the wife, of the settlor. Moreover, the fact
that it is the death of the settlor which enables the widow to qualify as
an object of the power does not cause any part of the trust fund to pass
on his death for estate duty purposes, since as the object of a discretionary power she has nothing that could be termed an " interest " or

" benefit " in the trust fund, more particularly as the power is not " in the nature of a trust ": see *post*, p. 186.

Additional powers :

4. THE Trustees shall have the following additional powers exercisable at their sole discretion :

investment;

(a) Power to invest any money in such manner and in such part of the world as the Trustees may think fit and (in particular) in the making of loans at interest with or without security;

purchase of land;

(b) Power to purchase lands or buildings in any part of the world although the purchase is not made for the production of income;

(c) Power to sell lease mortgage charge license or otherwise deal with any land comprised in the Trust Fund as if the Trustees were a sole beneficial owner;

(d) Power to vary or transpose any investments into or for any other or others of any nature hereinbefore authorised and to vary the terms of or property comprised in any security;

(e) Power in relation to land outside England to cause or allow the same to be and remain vested in any nominee of or trustee for the Trustees and to exercise over or in relation to such land all such powers as are by law conferred on trustees holding land in England on trust for sale and to do and take all such acts and proceedings (if any) as may be proper to enable such powers or any of them to be so exercised;

(f) Power to apply any money not being income in the erection alteration improvement or structural repair of any building on or the execution of any other work on or the acquisition of any right for the benefit of any land held on the same trusts as the moneys applied thereon or therefor under this power;

residence;

(g) Power to permit any person entitled to any interest in the Trust Fund whether in possession or not and whether vested or contingent to reside in any dwelling-house or occupy any land or building which or the proceeds of sale of which may for the time being be subject to the trusts hereof upon such conditions as to payment of rent rates taxes and other outgoings and as to repair and decoration and generally upon such terms as the Trustees in their discretion think fit;

determine doubts.

(h) Power to determine as they shall consider just all questions and matters of doubt arising in the administration of the trusts of this Settlement and so that every such determination whether made upon a question actually raised or implied in the acts or proceedings of the Trustees shall so far as the law may permit be conclusive and that none of the Trustees and no person having formerly been one of the Trustees and no estate of any deceased Trustee shall be liable for or for the consequences of any act done or omitted to be done or any payment made or omitted to be made in pursuance of any such determination as aforesaid notwithstanding that such determination shall subsequently be held to have been wrongly made.

It has been decided in *Re Wynn* [1952] Ch. 271, that a provision which makes the determination of a trustee in a matter of doubt binding on the beneficiaries is void. Any determination by the trustees in accordance with the terms of the above clause is, however, only conclusive " so far as the law may permit." It is contemplated that determinations made by the trustees may subsequently be held to be wrong. As there is, therefore, no attempt to oust the jurisdiction of the court, it is considered that a power to determine doubts in the above form is not one which would be held to be void by the trustees. Nor is it thought that such a clause would be open to criticism as misleading the trustees and beneficiaries as to their true position and rights. It is, however, uncertain how far, if at all, the decision in *Re Wynn* invalidates an indemnity conferred on a trustee who acts upon a determination made by himself or some other trustee. It is considered that a clause in the terms set out above may usefully be included, notwithstanding the decision in *Re Wynn*.

Trustee indemnity.

5. (1) Every discretion or power hereby conferred on the Trustees shall be an absolute and uncontrolled discretion or power and no Trustee shall be held liable for any loss or damage occurring as a result of his concurring or refusing or failing to concur in an exercise or proposed exercise of such discretion or power.

(2) In the professed execution of the trusts and powers hereof no Trustee (other than a Trustee charging remuneration for so acting) shall be liable for any loss to the Trust Fund arising by reason of any improper investment made in good faith or for the negligence or fraud of any agent employed by him or by any other Trustee hereof although the employment of such agent was not strictly necessary or expedient or by reason of any mistake or omission made in good faith by any Trustee hereof or by reason of any other matter or thing except wilful and individual fraud or wrongdoing on the part of the Trustee who is sought to be made liable.

Corporate trustee.

6. (1) A trust corporation may at any time be appointed to be a Trustee or the sole Trustee of these presents.

(2) Where any trust corporation (other than the Public Trustee) is appointed as aforesaid it may charge and deduct such reasonable remuneration and charges as shall be agreed in writing prior to or upon such appointment between the person or persons making such appointment of the one part and the trust corporation of the other part.

The court has power, where there is no provision in the settlement, to appoint a trust corporation to act as trustee, and to fix remuneration (see Trustee Act, 1925, s. 42). The court is generally unwilling to do so unless it has proved impossible to find individuals willing to act as trustees. Accordingly, a clause such as this is often advisable. Care should be taken that the trustee indemnity clause does not confer too great a licence on a paid trustee. Similar clauses are to be found on pages 211 and 218, *post*.

Charging.

7. ANY Trustee (other than the Settlor or any person who is for the time being the wife of the Settlor) being a solicitor or other person engaged in any profession business or trade shall be entitled to be paid all usual professional business and trade charges for business transacted time expended and acts done by him or any employee or partner of his in connection with the trusts hereof including acts which a trustee not being in any profession business or trade could have done personally.

Director trustees.

8. ANY Trustee hereof (except the Settlor or any person who is for the time being the wife of the Settlor) may act as an officer or employee of any company shares

or debentures of which form part of the Trust Fund or as an officer or employee of any subsidiary company of any such company and may retain for himself any remuneration which he may receive as such officer or employee notwithstanding that any votes or other rights attached to any such shares or debentures may have been instrumental either alone or in conjunction with other matters or by reason of their non-exercise in procuring or continuing for him his position as such officer or employee or that his qualification for any such position may be constituted in part or in whole by the holding of any such shares or debentures.

The above clause is advisable where shares in a family company are settled. Without it, trustees would normally be bound to account to the beneficiaries for fees gained by acting as director, where the trust property provides the director's qualification holding.

New trustees.   9. THE power of appointing new Trustees hereof shall be vested in the Settlor during his life.

Exclusion of settlor.   10. SAVE as hereinbefore expressly provided :—

(1) No part of the Trust Fund or the income thereof shall in any circumstances whatsoever be lent to the Settlor or any person for the time being the wife of the Settlor ; and

(2) No power or discretion hereby vested in the Trustees or in any other person shall be capable of being exercised in such a manner as to benefit either directly or indirectly the Settlor or any person for the time being the wife of the Settlor But so that the Trustees shall not be concerned to see or inquire what use is made by any person in whose favour any such power or discretion as aforesaid is exercised of any money or property taken by such person under such exercise.

The first part of the above clause is not necessary, but is useful by way of warning, that a loan to the settlor, even if made on proper commercial terms, may be caught by section 408 of the Income Tax Act, 1952, so that the amount of the loan will be deemed to be income of the settlor. (See *Potts' Executors* v. *I. R. C.* [1951] A.C. 443; 32 Tax Cas. 211; *ante*, p. 108.)

The second part of the above clause or some similar provision is often inserted out of abundance of caution, to ensure that sections 405 and 415 of the Income Tax Act, 1952, and section 22 of the Finance Act, 1958, do not apply to the settlement.

It must be observed however that it may be desirable to include in this settlement an ultimate gift over to the settlor or his wife, and the above clause does not prevent such a gift from taking effect.

IN WITNESS, etc.

SCHEDULE

PRECEDENT No. 20

Settlement of Investments and Leaseholds on Existing and Future Children of the Settlor Giving a Wide Power of Appointment to the Trustees and Subject thereto in Shares Vesting on the Attainment of the Age of Thirty-five. Sons to Receive Greater Shares than Daughters

The following precedent is similar to the foregoing, but includes leasehold land among its investments, and provides that no child is to be able to claim the capital until the age of thirty-five, or at an earlier marriage with the settlor's consent. Here, again, great care must be exercised in adapting this precedent to particular circumstances. Reference should also be made to the notes on the last preceding settlement.

Parties.

THIS SETTLEMENT is made the —— day of —— 19— BETWEEN —— of —— (hereinafter called " the Settlor ") of the one part and —— of —— and —— of —— (hereinafter called " the Original Trustees ") of the other part ;

WHEREAS :

Existing children.

(A) The Settlor has at the present time —— children, namely —— —— and —— who were born on the —— day of —— etc. respectively ;

Irrevocable.

(B) The Settlor wishes to make such irrevocable settlement for the benefit of his children whether born before or after the date hereof as is hereinafter contained ;

Funds transferred.

(C) The Settlor has transferred into the joint names or control of the Original Trustees the investments particulars of which are contained in the First Schedule hereto to be held by them upon the trusts and with and subject to the powers and provisions hereinafter declared and contained concerning the same ;

Leaseholds
transferred.

(D) By an Assignment bearing equal date herewith
but executed immediately before this Deed and
made between the same parties and in the same
order as this Deed certain leasehold properties
situate at —— in the County of —— (short
details of which properties and their respective
leases are contained in the Second Schedule
hereto) were assigned unto the Original Trustees
for the residue of the terms granted by the said
leases and at the rent and subject to the covenants by the lessee and the conditions by and in
the said leases reserved and contained Upon
Trust to sell the said properties and to stand
possessed of the net moneys to arise from any
such sale after payment of costs and also of the
net rents and profits of the premises until sale
after payment of the rent reserved by and all
outgoings payable under the said leases Upon
the trusts declared concerning the same by this
Deed and with and subject to the powers and
provisions hereinafter declared and contained
concerning the same ;

The assignment should vest the leaseholds in the trustees upon trust
for sale, confer upon them the powers of management contained in
clause 6 (4) of this precedent and contain a power of appointing new
trustees similar to that in clause 10 of this precedent. In the event of a
new trustee being appointed, two separate appointments should be
executed, one of the assignment, the other of the settlement.

Witnesseth.

NOW in consideration of the premises THIS DEED
WITNESSETH as follows :

Definitions :

1. IN this Settlement unless the context otherwise
requires :

Trustees.

(a) " The Trustees " means the Original Trustees and
other the trustees or trustee for the time being of
this settlement ;

Trust fund.

(b) " The Trust Fund " means
(i) the moneys and investments specified in
the First Schedule hereto and the leasehold
properties specified in the Second Schedule
hereto and the proceeds of sale thereof,

   (ii) all moneys investments and properties paid
    or transferred to and accepted by the
    Trustees as additions to the Trust Fund,
    and

   (iii) the investments and property from time to
    time representing such moneys investments
    properties and additions or any part or
    parts thereof respectively;

Beneficiaries. (c) " The Beneficiaries " means the said —— and
    (*naming the existing children*) and all the
    children of the Settlor hereafter born to him
    by any wife before the expiration of twenty-one
    years from the date of execution of this Deed
    [or before the first of the said —— and ——
    (*naming the existing children*) to attain the age
    of thirty-five years attains that age whichever
    period be the shorter] ;

 This class of beneficiaries may be compared with the class in the
preceding precedent. A shorter period than twenty-one years may usefully be substituted. The words in square brackets should be used if
appropriate according to the ages of the existing children.

Perpetuity (d) " The Perpetuity Day " means the day on which
day.   expires the period of twenty-one years calculated
    from and after the death of the last survivor of
    such of the descendants of His late Majesty King
    George the Fifth as are living at the date of
    execution of this Deed;

Children (e) " children " and " issue " are to be construed on
and issue.   the footing that adopted and legitimated children
    are the children of their adoptive and legitimated
    parents or parent respectively.

Overriding 2. THE Trustees shall stand possessed of the Trust
power to Fund and the income thereof upon such trusts for the
appoint. benefit of the Beneficiaries their respective spouses
    widows widowers and issue of whatever generation
    or any one or more of them exclusive of the other or
    others in such shares and proportions and subject to such
    terms and limitations and with and subject to such pro-
    visions for maintenance education or advancement or for
    accumulation of income during minority or for the pur-
    pose of raising a portion or portions or for forfeiture in

the event of bankruptcy or otherwise and with such discretionary trusts and powers exercisable by such persons
as the Trustees being at least two in number shall from
time to time by Deed or Deeds revocable or irrevocable
executed before the Perpetuity Day but without infringing the rule against perpetuities appoint.

Beneficiaries
at thirty-five.
    3. IN default of and until and subject to any and
every appointment as aforesaid the Trustees shall stand
possessed of the Trust Fund and the income thereof for
such of the Beneficiaries as shall be living on the
Perpetuity Day or before the Perpetuity Day attain the
age of thirty-five years and if more than one in equal
shares but nevertheless so that the share of each
Beneficiary being a son of the Settlor shall be twice as
great as the share of a Beneficiary being a daughter of
the Settlor.

Since future children are members of the class of beneficiaries, and
it is desired to postpone vesting beyond the age of twenty-one, care is
required to avoid any adverse operation of the perpetuity rule. Accordingly the gift must be expressed to vest not later than the perpetuity
day.

Children of
beneficiaries.
    4. IF any of the Beneficiaries shall die before the
Perpetuity Day under the age of thirty-five years leaving
a child or children him or her surviving the Trustees
shall stand possessed of the share of the Trust Fund
which such Beneficiary would have taken had he or she
attained the age of thirty-five years before the Perpetuity
Day upon trust for any such child or children who shall
be living on the Perpetuity Day or shall earlier attain
the age of twenty-one years or marry and if more than
one in equal shares absolutely.

Gift in
default.
    5. SUBJECT as aforesaid and subject to every exercise
of the powers hereby or by law conferred on the Trustees
the Trustees shall stand possessed of the Trust Fund
and the income thereof upon trust for —— absolutely.

The name to be inserted here may be that of one of the beneficiaries,
but should not be that of the settlor or the wife of the settlor.

Additional
powers :
    6. THE Trustees shall until the Perpetuity Day and
during such further period if any that the law may allow
have the following additional powers :

investment;   (1) Power to invest any money falling to be invested under the trusts hereof in the purchase of or at interest upon the security of (*etc. as the investment clauses on pp.* 129, 135, *ante*).

(2) Power to sell any investment or property for the time being forming part of the Trust Fund or to change the same for others hereby authorised;

(3) Power in making or varying any investments under the power herein contained to purchase from or sell to any individual Trustee any authorised investment or property forming part of the Trust Fund provided that such purchase or sale shall be made at the full market price of such investment or property as ascertained at the expense of such individual Trustee by means of an independent professional valuation made under the supervision of the Trustees other than such individual Trustee;

manage   (4) Power in addition to the powers of management
land;   conferred by law upon trustees holding land upon trust for sale to sell exchange convey lease mortgage charge agree to let license and otherwise conduct the management of any land held subject to the trusts hereof as if they were the absolute owners of such land;

improving   (5) Power to apply any money for the time being
land;   forming part of the Trust Fund in improving or developing any land held subject to the trusts hereof or erecting extending improving or rebuilding any buildings upon such land;

reside;   (6) [*Power to allow Beneficiaries to reside, see ante, p.* 154.]

unauthorised   (7) Power without obtaining any order of the court to
transactions;   effect any of the transactions referred to in section 64 of the Settled Land Act 1925 and section 57 of the Trustee Act 1925 at the discretion of the Trustees and without the leave of the court or the necessity of asking the opinion of the court Provided that this power shall only be exercised where the transaction to be effected is in the opinion of the Trustees expedient in the interests of all or some or any one of the Beneficiaries;

appropria-   (8) Power in relation to any investments of property
tion;   or money from time to time forming part of the Trust Fund and as between the Beneficiaries and all persons

beneficially interested therein to exercise the powers of appropriation and other incidental powers conferred on personal representatives by section 41 of the Administration of Estates Act 1925 without any of the consents made requisite by that Act.

Other powers should be added if they may be required by the trustees. See the powers in Precedent No. 24, *post.*

Indemnity.   7. [*Trustee indemnity, see ante, pp. 148, 155.*]

Trust corporation.   8. [*Power to appoint a trust corporation, see ante, p. 156, post, p. 218.*]

Charging.   9. [*Professional charging clause, see ante, p. 130.*]

New trustees.   10. THE power of appointing new Trustees hereof shall be vested in the Settlor during his life but the Settlor or any wife of the Settlor shall in no circumstances be appointed a Trustee hereof.

Exclusion from benefit.   11. THE Trust Fund and the income thereof shall be possessed and enjoyed by the person or persons beneficially entitled thereto by virtue of this Settlement to the entire exclusion of the Settlor and of any benefit to him by contract or otherwise and no part of the Trust Fund or the income thereof shall be paid to or applied for the benefit of the Settlor or any wife of the Settlor in any circumstances whatsoever.

IN WITNESS, ETC.

THE FIRST SCHEDULE

[*Details of the investments settled*]

THE SECOND SCHEDULE

[*Details of the land settled*]

PRECEDENT NO. 21

Settlement of Money on Existing and Future Grandchildren of the Settlor Giving an Interest in Capital on Reaching the Age of Twenty-one Years. Wide Powers to Apply Income for the Maintenance of Beneficiaries and to Advance Capital. Overriding Power to Appoint Shares among Beneficiaries

The following is a form of settlement which may frequently be employed with advantage. It may be adapted so as to benefit any class of infants, other than children of the settlor.

The precedent contemplates that the income of the trust fund will be wholly paid out for the beneficiaries' education and maintenance as it arises. Any payments so made will be regarded as income of the beneficiary, who will be able to reclaim from the Revenue so much of his personal reliefs as has not been set off against other income of the beneficiary. As has been explained earlier in this chapter, care is required in gauging the amount to be applied to each beneficiary in each year of assessment, in order that the beneficiary's parent should not lose any part of his child allowance without making a compensatory gain in the reliefs enjoyed by the child (see *ante*, p. 110).

It may in practice be desirable to accumulate the income of a beneficiary's share rather than expend the income as it arises. If this is done, the beneficiary will be unable to claim his personal reliefs against the income so accumulated. It is submitted, however, that on his attaining the age of twenty-one he will be able to make a claim under section 228 of the Income Tax Act, 1952, since the trusts give him an interest contingent on attaining twenty-one in default of appointment and of any exercise by the trustees of their various discretions (see *Chamberlain* v. *Haig-Thomas* (1933) 17 Tax Cas. 595; *ante*, p. 112).

Parties.   THIS SETTLEMENT is made the —— day of —— 19— BETWEEN —— of —— (hereinafter called " the Settlor ") of the one part and —— of —— and —— of —— (hereinafter called " the Original Trustees ") of the other part ;

Recitals.   WHEREAS :

Existing grand-children.

(A) —— (hereinafter called " the Son ") who is a son of the Settlor was married to his present wife —— on the —— day of —— 19— and there are now living two children of the said marriage (hereinafter called " the Existing Children ") namely —— who was born on the —— day of —— 19— and —— who was born on the —— day of —— 19— ;

Future grand-children.

(B) The Settlor wishes to declare such trusts for the benefit of the Existing Children and any children who may hereafter be born to the Son by his said wife as are hereinafter contained ;

Sum settled.

(C) With a view to the settlement intended hereby to be made the Settlor has paid to the Trustees the sum of £—— and it is apprehended that the Settlor may hereafter cause to be paid or transferred to the Original Trustees further money or investments to be held on the trusts hereof ;

Witnesseth.

NOW THIS DEED WITNESSETH and it is hereby declared as follows :

Definitions :

1. IN this settlement the following terms shall unless the context otherwise requires have the following meanings :

Trustees.

(a) " the Trustees " shall mean the Original Trustees or other the trustees or trustee for the time being of this settlement ;

Trust fund.

(b) " the Trust Fund " shall mean :

(i) the said sum of —— ;

(ii) all moneys and investments paid or transferred to and accepted by the Trustees as additions to the Trust Fund ; and

(iii) the investments and property from time to time representing such sum and additions or any part or parts thereof ;

Beneficiaries.

(c) " the Beneficiaries " shall mean the Existing Children and all the children of the Son who shall be born to him by his said wife before the expiration of twenty-one years from the date of this Deed or before either of the Existing Children shall attain the age of twenty-one years (whichever first occurs) ;

Perpetuity day.

(d) " the Perpetuity Day " shall mean the day on which expires the period of twenty-one years calculated from and after the death of the last survivor of such of the descendants of His late Majesty King George the Fifth as are living at the date hereof.

2. THE Trustees shall stand possessed of the Trust Fund and the income thereof on the following trusts :

Shares as trustees appoint.

(1) Upon such trusts for the benefit of the class consisting of the Beneficiaries and their wives husbands widows widowers children and adopted and legitimated children or any one or more of the members of the said class exclusive of the other or others in such shares and proportions and subject to such terms and provisions and with such provisions for maintenance education advancement and benefit and such protective and discretionary trusts (the same to be exercised at the discretion of the Trustees or any other person or

persons) as the Trustees shall from time to time by deed or deeds revocable or irrevocable executed before the Perpetuity Day but without infringing the rule against perpetuities appoint Provided always that the Trustees shall be at liberty at any time wholly or partially to release the said power of appointment or to contract not to exercise the same in all respects as if such power was a power conferred upon the Trustees in their capacity as individuals and not as trustees;

Maintenance and advancement.

(2) In default of and subject to any such appointment the Trustees may until the Perpetuity Day pay or apply all or any part of the income of the Trust Fund to or for or towards the maintenance education advancement or benefit of all or such one or more exclusive of the other or others of the Beneficiaries for the time being living in such proportions and manner as the Trustees shall in their absolute and uncontrolled discretion from time to time think fit Provided always that the Trustees shall be at liberty at any time wholly or partially to release their discretionary power hereunder or to contract not to exercise the same in all respects as if such discretionary power was a power of appointment conferred upon the Trustees in their capacity as individuals and not as trustees;

It is considered that the trustees may exercise this power by actually paying out income for the benefit of beneficiaries, e.g., by paying school bills, medical expenses, costs of board and lodging at university, etc., or by paying moneys to the parents of any beneficiary, or by paying premiums on a suitable policy (see clause 4 (2), post) or by allocating a sum of income to a beneficiary, so that he becomes the owner thereof although incapable of giving a valid receipt, and retaining such income and carrying it to a separate account: see Re Vestey's Settlement [1951] Ch. 209.

It is advisable for the trustees to keep a careful record in a minute-book or by notes in the accounts, of each exercise of their discretion.

Beneficiaries at twenty-one.

(3) Subject to the trusts and powers aforesaid the Trust Fund shall be held in trust for the Beneficiaries who attain the age of twenty-one years or earlier marry and if more than one in equal shares absolutely and so that this trust shall for the purposes of section 31 of the Trustee Act, 1925, carry the intermediate income of the Trust Fund and accordingly the provisions of that section (as hereinafter varied) shall apply.

Variation of
section 31.

3. SECTION 31 of the Trustee Act, 1925, shall apply to these presents as if :

(i) the words " may in all the circumstances be reasonable " had been omitted from paragraph 1 of subsection (1) thereof and in substitution there had been inserted the words " the trustees may in their absolute discretion think fit " and as if the proviso at the end of subsection (1) had been omitted therefrom ; and

(ii) the Trustees were thereby authorised at any time during the infancy of any of the Beneficiaries on whose account accumulations of income may have been made to apply those accumulations or any part thereof as if they were income arising in the current year and applicable as well for the benefit of any other or others of the Beneficiaries as for the benefit of that Beneficiary on whose account the accumulations were made.

Advance-
ment.

4. THE Trustees shall have the following additional powers exercisable until the Perpetuity Day and during such further period if any that the law may allow :

(1) at any time or times in their absolute discretion to raise the whole or any part or parts of the then expectant presumptive or vested share of any of the Beneficiaries in the Trust Fund under the Trusts hereinbefore declared and to pay or apply the same for his or her advancement maintenance education or benefit in such manner as the Trustees shall think fit.

(2) Power to deal with any income applicable for the maintenance advancement or benefit of any of the Beneficiaries under any of the provisions of this Deed by paying or transferring the same to his or her parent or guardian for the benefit of such Beneficiary without being further answerable for the proper application thereof or by paying or contributing towards the payment of the premiums or costs of any policy of insurance by the terms of which any sum or sums of money may in any contingency be payable to or applicable for the maintenance education or benefit of such Beneficiary.

It should be noted that a payment to the parent which is applied by him in paying a premium on a policy on his life will only constitute payment for the child's benefit if the policy is effectively held for the child's absolute benefit.

Such further powers may be added as may be required: see *post*, p. 209.

Gift in default.

5. SUBJECT to the trusts hereinbefore declared and to the powers conferred on the Trustees by this Deed and to each and any exercise thereof the Trustees shall stand possessed of the Trust Fund and the income thereof in trust for the Son absolutely.

Investment.

6. TRUST moneys may be invested or laid out in the purchase of or at interest upon the security of such stocks funds shares securities or other investments or property (real or personal) of whatsoever nature and wheresoever situate and whether involving liability or not and whether producing income or not as the Trustees shall in their absolute discretion think fit including the purchase with or without vacant possession of any real or leasehold property as a residence for any person for the time being interested in the income of such moneys and the purchase of chattels for the use of such person or persons to the intent that subject as aforesaid the Trustees shall have the same full and unrestricted powers of investing and transposing investments and laying out moneys in all respects as if they were absolutely entitled thereto beneficially.

Charging.

7. ANY of the Trustees (excluding the Settlor and any wife of the Settlor) being a solicitor accountant or other person engaged in any profession or business shall be entitled to charge and be paid all usual professional and other charges for business transacted time spent and acts done by him or any partner of his in connection with the trusts hereof including acts which a trustee not being in any profession or business could have done personally.

Indemnity.

8. IN the professed execution of the trusts and powers hereof no trustee shall be liable for any loss to the trust premises arising by reason of any improper investment made in good faith or for the negligence or fraud of any agent employed by him or by any other trustee hereof although the employment of such agent was not strictly necessary or expedient or by reason of any mistake or omission made in good faith by any

trustee hereof or by reason of any other matter or thing except wilful and individual fraud or wrongdoing on the part of the trustee who is sought to be made liable.

New trustees.   9. THE Son during his life shall have power to appoint a new trustee or trustees hereof.

IN WITNESS, ETC.

THE SCHEDULE

PRECEDENT No. 22

Settlement for the Benefit of a Child, with Provision for His or Her Children Present and Future [1]

Stamp *ad valorem*. This precedent is designed to meet the case of an elderly person of means with children who are married and have started families and can best be helped by a provision of funds for the maintenance and education of their families, so that moneys for these purposes need not wholly come out of the taxed income of the married children or bear estate duty on their deaths.

The real primary objects of the settlement are the married children so that clause 3 enables the trusts to be altered as occasion may require— *e.g.*, to give a life interest to a surviving spouse—and clause 4 enables funds to be taken out of settlement without stamped deeds.

The definition of " the closing date " can be so used as to rule out children born after the beneficiary attains a specified age (say fifty, in the case of a lady) or after a grandchild attains twenty-one. If the beneficiary is male, the closing date should be fixed by reference not to his death but to the first anniversary of his death.

Existing infant children may die under twenty-one and the beneficiary be left childless, at least for a time : in this case, the income must go back to the beneficiary until the birth of another child. But if desired, the trust can be terminated under clause 3.

It is suggested that it is usually better not to have as trustees the settlor, or the beneficiary, or the spouse of the beneficiary. In this connection, section 46 (1) of the Finance Act, 1950, should be borne in mind.

Parties.   THIS SETTLEMENT made the —— day of —— 19—
BETWEEN A B of, etc. (hereinafter called " the Settlor ")
of the one part and X of, etc., and Y of, etc. (hereinafter

---

[1] This precedent is taken from a draft prepared by the late Mr. A. H. Withers of counsel, which first appeared in *The Conveyancer and Property Lawyer*.

Witnesseth. called "the Original Trustees"), of the other part WITNESSETH and it is hereby agreed and declared as follows :—

Irrevocable. 1. THIS settlement is made by the Settlor by way of absolute and irrevocable settlement and in consideration of his natural love and affection for his child hereinafter named and for divers other good causes and considerations.

Definition. 2. IN this settlement the following expressions have the following meanings, that is to say :—

(a) THE TRUSTEES means the Original Trustees or other the trustees or trustee from time to time of this settlement.

(b) THE TRUST FUND means and includes (1) the sum of £—— already paid by the Settlor to the Original Trustees for the purposes of this settlement; (2) all moneys and investments hereafter paid or transferred by any person or persons to and accepted by the Trustees as additions to the trust fund; and (3) the investments and property from time to time representing the aforesaid sum moneys and investments or any part or parts thereof.

(c) THE BENEFICIARY means P of, etc., who is a child of the Settlor [and was born on the —— day of —— 19—].

(d) THE CLOSING DATE means whichever of the following dates comes first namely (1) [the first anniversary of] the day of the death of the Beneficiary; [(2) the date on which the Beneficiary attains the age of —— years] and (3) the date on which the age of twenty-one years is attained by that child of the Beneficiary who first attains that age.

Overriding powers of appointment. 3. THE Trustees shall hold the Trust Fund and the income thereof UPON TRUST for such person or persons (whether or not being or including the Beneficiary) for such purposes and with and subject to such powers and provisions and generally in such manner in all respects as the Beneficiary and either (1) any two other persons (being Trustees of this settlement) or (2) any trust corporation within the meaning of the Trustee Act, 1925 (being a Trustee or the sole Trustee of this settlement) shall by any deed or deeds revocable or irrevocable jointly appoint and in default of and until and subject to any such appointment UPON the trusts and with and subject to the powers and provisions hereinafter declared and contained

PROVIDED ALWAYS that each Trustee shall have an absolute discretion to join or abstain from joining in any such appointment as aforesaid without incurring any responsibility in that behalf and that each trustee in considering whether to join or abstain from joining in any such appointment as aforesaid is hereby authorised and requested (but in no sense required) to consider what in all the circumstances of the case is most for the benefit of the Beneficiary and to give effect to all reasonable requests of the Beneficiary and to ignore entirely the interests of all other persons interested in any manner under the trusts of these presents.

Power to appoint to beneficiary.

4. SUBJECT as hereinbefore declared the trustees may at any time or times during the life and with the consent in writing of the Beneficiary as to all or any part or parts of the Trust Fund transfer or raise and pay or appropriate the same to the Beneficiary for the absolute use and benefit of the Beneficiary or raise and pay or apply the same for the advancement or otherwise for the benefit of the Beneficiary as the trustees shall think fit.

Trusts in favour of beneficiary and his children.

5. SUBJECT as hereinbefore declared the trustees shall as from the date hereof hold the Trust Fund and the income thereof on the trusts following that is to say :

(a) All income of the Trust Fund accruing whilst the Closing Date has not arrived and there is not actually living a child (previously born) of the Beneficiary shall belong to the Beneficiary absolutely.

(b) Subject as aforesaid the Trust Fund and the income thereof as from the date of this deed shall be held in trust for such child or children of the Beneficiary as (1) is or are now living or shall be born before the closing date and (2) attain the age of twenty-one years and if more than one in equal shares.

AND to this trust sections 31 and 32 of the Trustee Act, 1925, shall apply save that the proviso to section 31 (1) and the proviso (a) to section 32 (1) shall not apply.

(c) Subject as aforesaid the Trust Fund and the income thereof as from the date of this deed shall be held in trust for the Beneficiary absolutely.

Investment.   6. DURING the life and with the consent of the Beneficiary the Trustees may invest any money in such manner and in such part of the world as the Trustees may think fit and (in particular) in the making of loans at interest with or without security.

New trustees.   7. THE power of appointing a new trustee or new trustees shall be vested in the Beneficiary during the life of the Beneficiary but so that neither the Settlor nor any wife of the Settlor shall be appointed a trustee hereof.

Professional charging clause.   8. ANY trustee (other than the Settlor and the woman for the time being the wife of the Settlor) for the time being hereunder being a solicitor or other person engaged in any profession or business shall be entitled to charge and be paid all usual professional or other charges for business done by him or his firm in the premises before the expiration of twenty-one years from the death of the Beneficiary whether in the ordinary course of his profession or business or not and although not of the nature requiring the employment of a solicitor or other professional person.

Settlor excluded from all benefit.   9. THE foregoing provisions of this deed shall take effect subject as follows that is to say :

PROVIDED ALWAYS that under no circumstances shall any benefit whatsoever be taken under this deed by the Settlor or by any woman to whom he has or shall have been married and (in particular) no power or discretion created or conferred by this deed or by any appointment made hereunder shall be exercisable in favour of the Settlor or any such woman.

[10. *Statement as to value if appropriate.*]

IN WITNESS, ETC.

PRECEDENT No. 23

Settlement by a Father on His Eldest Child with Provision for the Accumulation of Income for Twenty-one Years to Provide Portions for Younger Children. Intended to Save Surtax and Esate Duty

Stamp *ad valorem.* This settlement is intended to meet the case of a settlor who has substantial capital of which he wishes to divest himself with a view to saving surtax and estate duty should he live five years but who does not wish to give immediate and absolute interests to his adult children, feeling that there is no reason why they should inherit immediately what, apart from the desire of the settlor to save estate duty, they would not take until his death. It is impractical to direct accumulations for twenty-one years *simpliciter*, since should the testator die before the expiration of the period, the accumulations would cease under section 164 (1) of the Law of Property Act, 1925, and on his death estate duty would become payable even if he had lived more than five years from the date of the settlement : *Adamson* v. *Att.-Gen.* [1933] A.C. 257. This settlement provides for accumulations for twenty-one years by use of the provisions of section 164 (2). It is only appropriate to the case where a settlor has two or more children since it is based on the power under section 164 (2) (ii) of the Law of Property Act, 1925, to accumulate income indefinitely (provided the perpetuity period is not exceeded) for the purpose of raising portions for any child, children or remoter issue of the settlor. For the trust for accumulations to be within the exception in section 164 (2) it is essential that the sum raised as portions should be held on separate trusts for different persons to those taking the capital of the fund the income of which is accumulated. See *Re Bourne's Settlement Trusts* [1946] 1 All E.R. 411.

This settlement is based on the following assumptions : (1) That the settlor has sufficient assets at his disposal outside the settlement to enable him to make provision by his will for his wife and for any other persons for whom he wishes to provide. (2) That the settlor does not want the income accumulated for younger children to be available for their maintenance or benefit but has other resources available for that purpose. (3) That the settlor is prepared for the benefit of the settlement to be limited to younger children born within twenty-one years from its date, when the trust to accumulate income for portions will cease and the trust fund will vest in the adult children. In these days a trust for twenty-one years, with further trusts of the shares of children who at the expiration of that period are not of an age to take vested interests, is generally as long a trust as it is expedient to create. However, if the settlor wishes all after-born children to share in the portions fund, the trusts can be amended or the form of settlement in *The Conveyancer and Property Lawyer*, Vol. 13 (N.S.), p. 565, can be used with the necessary modifications.[2]

Parties.   **THIS SETTLEMENT** is made the —— day of—— 19— BETWEEN A of, etc. (hereinafter called " the Settlor ") of the one part and B of, etc., and C of, etc. (hereinafter called " the Original Trustees ") of the other part.

[2] The authors desire to express their thanks to Miss B. A. Bicknell of counsel for permission to reprint this Precedent, which first appeared in *The Conveyancer and Property Lawyer.*

Recitals.

WHEREAS :

(1) The Settlor being absolutely entitled to the moneys and investments specified in the Schedule hereto and being desirous of settling the same in manner hereinafter appearing has paid or transferred or is about to pay or transfer the same to the Original Trustees.

(2) The Settlor has four children and no more namely D E F G who are all under the age of twenty-one years.

(3) The Settlor is desirous of making provision for his said children and any after-born children of his and their issue in manner hereinafter appearing.

Witnesseth.

NOW THIS DEED WITNESSETH that in consideration of his natural love and affection for his said children and for divers other good causes and considerations the Settlor declares and IT IS HEREBY AGREED AND DECLARED as follows :

Irrevocable.

1. This Settlement is irrevocable.

Definitions.

2. In this Settlement the following expressions have the following meanings :

Trustees.

(A) " The Trustees " means the Original Trustees or the survivor of them or other the trustee or trustees for the time being of this Settlement and (notwithstanding any context) a sole trustee may act for all the purposes of this Settlement.

Trust fund.

(B) " The trust fund " means and includes (1) the moneys and investments specified in the Schedule hereto ; (2) all moneys and investments paid or transferred to and accepted by the Trustees as additions to the trust fund ; (3) the investments and property from time to time representing the said moneys investments and additions or any part or parts thereof respectively.

Date of distribution.

(C) " The date of distribution " means the —— day of —— 19—.

The date of distribution will be the expiration of twenty-one years from the date of the deed. This date can be postponed for a further period. It must fall, however, within the trust period as defined in clause 2 (D), which is the latest date permissible under the perpetuity rule.

Trust period.

(D) " The trust period " means the period which expires at the end of twenty-one years after the death of the last survivor of such of the following persons as have been born before and are living at the date of this

Settlement namely the descendants of the Settlor's father and the descendants of His late Majesty King George the Fifth.

Eldest child.

(E) " The Eldest Child " means the eldest child of the Settlor living at the date of distribution or who being then dead has left issue then living.

Younger children.

(F) " The Younger Children " means any child of the Settlor born before the date of distribution other than the Eldest Child.

Accumulation.

3. THE Trustees shall accumulate the income of the trust fund accruing before the date of distribution or before the determination of the trust period whichever first happens at compound interest by investing the same and the resulting income thereof in any investments in which capital money is hereby or by statute authorised to be invested.

Trusts of accumulations (portions fund): younger children.

4. FROM and after the date of distribution the Trustees shall stand possessed of the investments representing the accumulations directed by clause 3 hereof (hereinafter called " the portions fund ") upon the following trusts that is to say :

(i) In trust for all such one or more to the exclusion of the others or other of the Younger Children and their issue at such age or time or respective ages or times if more than one in such shares and with such trusts for their respective benefit and such provisions for their respective advancement maintenance and education at the discretion of the Trustees or of any other person or persons as the Settlor shall by any deed revocable or irrevocable appoint.

It can be argued that any exercise of this special power is a "disposition" within section 44 (1) of the Finance Act, 1940, as extended by section 46 (1) of the Finance Act, 1950, so that estate duty is payable as on a gift in the event of the settlor dying within five years from the date of the exercise of the power. However it is understood that the present practice of the Estate Duty Office is not to rely on this argument.

(ii) In default of and subject to any such appointment upon trust to divide the portions fund into as many equal shares as there shall be Younger Children who or some issue of whom shall be then living on the date of distribution and to appropriate one of such shares to each of such Younger Children who or some issue of whom shall be then living.

PROVIDED ALWAYS that any share appointed to a child of the Settlor or to his or her issue under the foregoing power shall in the division of the unappointed part of the portions fund be brought into hotchpot by and as against the share of the portions fund appropriated to such child.

(iii) The share of the portions fund which is hereinbefore directed to be appropriated to any of the Younger Children shall be held on the following trusts and with and subject to the following powers wherein such share and all additions thereto are referred to as the Settled Share and that one of the Younger Children to whom such share is appropriated is hereinafter referred to as " the Younger Child " that is to say :

(A) So long as the Younger Child is alive and under the age of twenty-one years the Trustees may at their discretion pay all or any part of the income of the Settled Share to the Younger Child (notwithstanding infancy) for his or her own absolute use and benefit or pay or apply all or any part of the income for or towards the maintenance education or benefit of the Younger Child in such manner as the Trustees may think fit and shall accumulate the surplus (if any) of the income by appropriating the same to the Younger Child and investing the same in augmentation of the Settled Share but so long as the Younger Child is alive and under the age of twenty-one years the Trustees may at any time or times if they think fit apply such accumulations or any part thereof as if the same were income of the Settled Share arising in the then current year.

Any income paid to the child during infancy will be treated as the settlor's income for income tax purposes.

(B) Subject as hereinafter declared the Trustees shall hold the income of the Settled Share upon trust for the Younger Child until he or she dies or attains the age of twenty-five years or the trust period expires whichever shall first happen and subject thereto shall hold the

Settled Share in trust for the Younger Child absolutely if he or she is alive at the expiration of the trust period or attains the age of twenty-five years before such expiration and subject as aforesaid upon trust for all or any the children or child of the Younger Child who shall be living at the expiration of the trust period or shall before such expiration attain the age of twenty-one years or marry and if more than one as tenants in common in equal shares absolutely.

(C) Subject as hereinbefore declared the Settled Share and the income thereof shall be held on the same trusts as would have been applicable thereto if the Younger Child had died unmarried before the date of distribution.

(iv) Subject as hereinbefore declared the Trustees shall stand possessed of the portions fund upon the trusts hereinafter declared of the trust fund.

Trusts of trust fund: eldest child.

5. FROM and after the date of distribution the Trustees shall stand possessed of the capital and income of the trust fund upon the following trusts that is to say :

(i) Upon trust for the Eldest Child living at the date of distribution who shall attain the age of twenty-one years or marry under that age absolutely.

(ii) Subject as aforesaid upon trust for all or any the children or child of the Eldest Child who shall be living at the expiration of the trust period or who shall before such expiration attain the age of twenty-one years or marry and if more than one as tenants in common in equal shares.

(iii) Subject as hereinbefore declared the Trustees shall stand possessed of the trust fund upon trust for X absolutely.

Powers of trustees.

6. THE Trustees shall have the following powers namely :

(1) Power to allow the investments specified in the Schedule hereto and all investments transferred to and accepted by the Trustees as additions to the trust property as and when the same respectively shall be received in possession by the Trustees or any of them or any part or parts thereof respectively to remain in the actual state

of investment thereof so long as the Trustees may think fit.

(2) Power at any time or times with the consent in writing of the Settlor during his lifetime and after his death at the discretion of the Trustees to sell call in or convert into money the aforesaid investments or any of them or any part thereof respectively.

(3) Power with such consent or at such discretion as aforesaid to invest the moneys produced by such sale calling in or conversion or any other capital moneys which may be received by the Trustees in respect of the trust fund (when the same respectively shall have been received by the Trustees) in the names of the Trustees in any manner hereinafter mentioned that is to say :

(i) In any of the public stocks or funds or government securities of the United Kingdom.

(ii) In the purchase (whether for income occupation or other purposes) of land in England or Wales being either freehold or held for a term of which not less than fifty years shall be unexpired at the date of purchase all lands so purchased to be held by the Trustees upon trust to sell the same with such consent or at such discretion as aforesaid and with full power to postpone conversion.

(iii) In or upon the stocks funds shares debentures mortgages or securities of any corporation body or company municipal county local commercial or of any other description incorporated or registered in the United Kingdom.

(iv) Upon the security of any interest for a life or lives or determinable on a life or lives or any other event in real or personal immovable or movable property wheresoever situate or arising together with a policy or policies of assurance on such life or lives or against such event.

(v) Upon loan to or deposit with any building society in England or Wales.

(4) Power with such consent or at such discretion as aforesaid to vary or transpose any investments into or for any other or others of any nature hereinbefore authorised and to vary the terms of or property comprised in any security.

(5) Power during the trust period with such consent or at such discretion as aforesaid to apply any money (not being income) in the erection alteration improvement or structural repair of any buildings on any land held on the same trusts as the moneys applied therein under this power and (in particular) in the making of any works which though in the nature of improvements are not improvements authorised by the Settled Land Act, 1925.

Perpetuity period for powers.

7. EVERY discretion or power by this Settlement conferred on any person or on the Trustees and not expressly made exercisable only during a period allowed by law shall (notwithstanding anything to the contrary hereinbefore expressed or implied) only be exercisable during the trust period and during such further period if any (whether definite or indefinite) as in the case of the particular discretion or power in question the law may allow.

If the powers are not expressly limited to exercise during the perpetuity period, they may be held to be void as infringing the rule against perpetuities: *Re Allott* [1924] 2 Ch. 498.

New trustees.

8. THE power of appointing a new trustee or new trustees of these presents shall be vested in the Settlor during his life.

Charging clause.

9. ANY trustee (other than the Settlor and any woman for the time being the wife of the Settlor) for the time being hereunder being a solicitor or other person engaged in any profession or business shall be entitled to charge and be paid all usual professional or other charges for business done by him or his firm in the premises during the trust period whether in the ordinary course of his profession or business or not and although not of a nature requiring the employment of a solicitor or other professional person.

Remuneration of corporate trustee.

10. ANY corporation that is a trust corporation within the meaning of the Law of Property Act, 1925 (as amended in 1926) and is appointed to be a trustee of this settlement shall during the trust period have the powers rights and benefits as to remuneration or otherwise as at or prior to its appointment may be agreed in writing between such corporation and the person or persons

making such appointment or (in default of such agreement) in accordance with the corporation's published
terms and conditions as to acceptance of trusts current
at the date of its appointment.

IN WITNESS, ETC.

THE SCHEDULE

Schedule.   *[Particulars of the moneys and investments settled
by the above-written Deed.]*

CHAPTER 4

DISCRETIONARY TRUSTS

A MAN of property wishing to make provision for a wide class of persons which may include children, grandchildren, other relatives, friends, retired servants or employees, may find the prospect unattractive if bounty has to be met from taxed income. Outright gifts or family settlements of the type discussed in the last chapter may not be sufficiently flexible. Frequently a discretionary trust will provide both the degree of flexibility required and a ready means of reducing the incidence of income tax, surtax and estate duty. Indeed, the discretionary trust has been so successful as an instrument for mitigating the burden of tax and duty, that its inclusion among the avoidance devices likely to inspire future anti-avoidance legislation seems inevitable. Meanwhile, however, so long as the law remains unchanged, the would-be benefactor, if he is prepared to set aside a block of investments or other property and to surrender to trustees of his own choosing all decisions as to its management and ultimate destination, may discharge his obligations to the beneficiaries and effect a considerable saving in duty and tax. He must exclude himself, and during his lifetime his wife, from any benefit. In this way he can effectively alienate the income for tax purposes of the property and investments settled and may preserve the capital from the inroads of estate duty for a considerable period exceeding even the allotted span of three score years and ten.

If shares in a family company form part of the capital settled, they may thus be preserved intact for a long time. Moreover, it is possible to ensure that, during the settlor's lifetime, and even longer, no moneys are invested except in investments approved by the settlor. Consequently, the capital settled need not be lost to the family business, although the effect of executing the settlement may, if this is desired, cause the company to cease to be a " controlled company " for the purposes of sections 55 to 58 of the Finance Act, 1940, as amended by sections 29 to 31 of the Finance Act, 1954.

Requirements for a discretionary trust

There are certain requirements which must be observed if an effective discretionary trust is to be formed. A discretionary trust is not fundamentally different from the type of family settlement discussed in the previous chapter, and many of the points mentioned in that chapter have equal force when applied to discretionary trusts. Certain additional points, however, require to be mentioned.

(i) *Five-year period*

The trust should be formed at least five years before the settlor's death. If this is not done, the property settled will be deemed to pass on his death under section 2 (1) (c) of the Finance Act, 1894, and estate duty will be payable out of the property settled although the reductions in respect of the two, three and four year period, under section 64 of the Finance Act, 1960, are also obtainable. It should be observed, however, that it is a common practice to execute a settlement on discretionary trusts in respect of a small amount of property, and subsequently to transfer more property to the trustees from time to time to be held on the trusts declared in the settlement. Where this is done, it is not sufficient that the settlement was executed at least five years prior to death: each transfer of property, if it is to avoid estate duty entirely, must also be made at least five years before death and moreover the two, three and four year periods apply to each transfer.

(ii) *Discretion of trustees*

Another requirement is that the settlement must be drawn so as to give the trustees an absolute discretion. No beneficiary must be able to claim as of right any part of the funds settled, since otherwise a charge to estate duty will arise on his death. The capital should be preserved as long as possible and the beneficiaries entitled only to such sums of income as the trustees may allow. On the other hand, it is permissible to allow the trustees to appoint shares of capital to individual beneficiaries before the time for breaking up the trust has arrived. The trustees should bear in mind the possibility of estate duty becoming payable on the death of the appointee, when exercising this power.

(iii) *The perpetuity rule*

Another requirement arises out of the perpetuity rule. This is especially important because, to get the full benefit of discretionary trusts, the trustees should be given a discretion to apply the fund or its income for the benefit of a wide class of beneficiaries for the longest possible period. Now the perpetuity rule applies rather more strictly to discretionary trusts than to ordinary future trusts, because each exercise of the trustees' discretion is a fresh gift; consequently it is the exercise of the discretion which must be limited to a perpetuity period, and not only the trusts which may be created by the discretion. Thus if property is settled upon A for life, remainder to any widow he might leave for her life, with remainder over, the gift to the widow is valid. But were the property settled on A for life with remainder on discretionary trusts during the lifetime of any widow he might leave, the gift in favour of the widow would be void.[1] The best course, it is submitted, is to define a particular discretionary period and to limit the discretionary trusts to that period, with a gift over to take effect in default of exercise of the discretion. As will

---

[1] *Re Coleman* [1936] Ch. 528.

be seen from the precedents contained in this chapter, it is common practice to adopt as the measure of the discretionary period the lives of those members of the Royal Family living at the date of the settlement and the period of twenty or twenty-one years after the death of the last survivor.

(iv) *Trustee beneficiary*

Care should be taken to see either that no trustee is capable of being a member of the class of beneficiaries, or that some other safeguard is written into the settlement, or that the number of trustees is never reduced below two. For where a trustee is also a member of the discretionary class to whom capital may be appointed, and by reason of the death or retirement of the other trustees becomes the sole trustee, he may be " competent to dispose " of the whole property subject to the trust, so that the property is deemed to pass on his death.[2] This obstacle may be surmounted by refraining from appointing as trustees persons who are also objects of the trust, or by providing expressly in the trust deed that any person being a trustee is automatically disqualified as a beneficiary. It would also be possible to provide that a sole trustee should not be able to exercise any of the powers or discretions conferred on trustees,[3] or that a trustee who is also a beneficiary should be precluded from exercising or joining in exercising any discretion as to the beneficial application of income or capital.

(v) *Settlor or his wife as beneficiaries*

The trusts should be so drafted that neither the settlor nor any wife or husband of the settlor is capable of being a beneficiary.

As regards estate duty, there is no need to exclude the wife or husband of the settlor, but the settlor himself must be excluded, so as not to be an object of the discretion vested in the trustees, since if he were such an object, he would have reserved to himself an interest for life so as to make liability for estate duty arise on his death under section 2 (1) (c) of the Finance Act, 1894.[4]

For tax purposes, if either the settlor or his wife (but not the settlor's widow) is included as a possible beneficiary under a discretionary trust, the whole income arising under the trust is deemed to be that of the settlor, subject to certain exceptions, from the very inception of the settlement. This rule, which arises from section 22 of the Finance Act, 1958, is discussed more fully later in this chapter.

The class of beneficiaries

The essential characteristic of the usual type of discretionary trust is that it provides that, during a stated period, which terminates within

---

[2] *Re Penrose* [1933] Ch. 793.   [3] *Cf. Charlton* v. *Att.-Gen.* (1879) 4 App.Cas. 427.
[4] See the Customs and Inland Revenue Act, 1881, s. 38 (2) (c); *Att.-Gen.* v. *Hey-Wood* (1889) 19 Q.B.D. 326; *Att.-Gen.* v. *Farrell* [1931] 1 K.B. 81. While the point has never been decided, it is also arguable that the settlor is not excluded from the property taken under the gift, or from any benefit to him by contract or otherwise, within s. 11 (1) of the Customs and Inland Revenue Act, 1889.

the limits of the perpetuity rule, the trustees are to have a power—which they need never exercise—to dispose of capital among the members of the class of beneficiaries and subject to this, they must retain the capital and pay out the income as it arises among such one or more of the class of beneficiaries in such proportions as the trustees from time to time think fit. No single beneficiary has any enforceable interest to any part of the capital or income, until the trustees exercise their discretion in his favour. As a general rule it is important to ensure that the discretionary trust of income is in favour of a class of beneficiaries, the qualifications for membership of which remain the same as long as the discretionary trust lasts. If the trust is so drafted that on the death of any person a new group, fulfilling a new qualification, becomes entitled, there may be a " passing," under section 1 of the Finance Act, 1894, even though in fact largely the same persons constitute the two groups.[5]

Commonly, therefore, a discretionary trust will confer on the trustees a power to appoint capital in favour of any member of a group, for example, the issue and wives of issue of a named person, with a gift over of capital in default of such appointment to all the members of the class equally. There will at the same time be a discretionary trust of income of unappointed capital, to continue until a " break-up " day, or until the class of beneficiaries is reduced to one person. The object of such a trust is that no estate duty should become payable on the death of any member of the group, except the last and last but one to die, and the fund should be preserved intact for a long period.

One drawback is that, if the class of beneficiaries is allowed to diminish, for example, if there is a discretionary gift of income to six named persons during their lives, with a gift of capital over on the death of the survivor, liability to duty may arise on both of two events: the death of the last but one of the beneficiaries to die, and the death of the last. The reason for this is fairly obvious, since on the death of the last but one, the last survivor becomes entitled to the whole income, whereas previously he was entitled to nothing unless the trustees' discretion was exercised in his favour; on the death of the last survivor the whole fund passes to the person entitled to the capital under the settlement.

It is generally accepted that, to take the same example again, no liability to duty can arise on the death of the first four beneficiaries to die. This is understood to be the view accepted by the Estate Duty Office and it is submitted that it is correct, even though it has not been finally decided by the courts.[6] No express exemption is provided by statute,

[5] *Burrell and Kinnaird* v. *Att.-Gen.* [1937] A.C. 286.
[6] But see *Re Miller's Agreement* [1947] Ch. 615, in which it was stated by the Court that the mere chance of having a discretion exercised in his favour does not give a person any interest in property. Care is required to distinguish a rather different principle: that where trustees have a discretion to appoint shares between a number of ascertainable persons, but no discretion to withold the property entirely, those persons can, if all *sui juris*, together put an end to the trust: *Re Smith* [1928] Ch. 915. That does not mean that any one of the persons concerned has any interest in the fund which can properly be called a property right.

but the general view is that there can be no passing under section 1 or section 2 (1) (b) of the Finance Act, 1894, since it is impossible to point out the property which has passed, and until each separate exercise by the trustees of their discretion, no beneficiary is entitled to any interest at all.[7]

It is considered that no liability to estate duty arises on a settlor's death by reason of the fact that the settlor's consent is required for the exercise by the trustees of their discretion.[8]

Powers and trusts for a wide class

In the example referred to above income was settled on six named persons for their lives at the discretion of the trustees. In practice, however, powers and trusts of considerable complexity may be created so as to confer benefits on successive generations of beneficiaries. Here difficulty may arise, since it is a well-settled rule that the objects of a trust must be certain, that is to say, that the language employed must be certain and not vague and moreover that the trustees must at any time be able to ascertain definitely the persons who have vested interests in the capital and income of the trust property. A trust for a class of persons, even if drawn in language of sufficient certainty, fails unless all the persons having vested interests are ascertained or ascertainable.

On the other hand, where the trustees are not bound by a trust but have a power, whether to confer or to withhold a benefit, the requirement of certainty is far less stringent. Thus, for example, where a testator left residue to trustees upon trust to pay the income " to such person (other than herself) or persons or charitable institution or institutions in such shares and proportions " as X should from time to time during her lifetime direct in writing, with a gift over in default, it was held that there was a valid power.[9]

It is thus well established that a power, provided it is a power not coupled with any trust, does not require certainty of objects, in the sense that, although the language must show the settlor's intention with sufficient certainty, the trustee need not be able to ascertain all the possible objects of the power when he exercises his discretion: all that is necessary seems to be—to adopt the language used by Jenkins L.J. in the Court of Appeal in *I. R. C.* v. *Broadway Cottages Trust* [1955] Ch. 20 at p. 31—that " the qualification for membership of the unascertainable class is such as to make it possible to decide with certainty whether a given individual is or is not a member of it "; and see *Re Saxone Shoe Co., Ltd.'s Trust Deed* [1962] 1 W.L.R. 943. The same rule has been stated in slightly different language in *Re Gestetner*

---

[7] Until the decision of the House of Lords in *Public Trustee* v. *I. R. C.* [1960] A.C. 398, it was widely assumed that s. 2 (1) only applied where there was no " actual passing " under s. 1. It now appears that s. 2 (1) is an explanation of s. 1.

[8] See *Commissioner of Stamp Duties of N. S. W.* v. *Way* [1952] A.C. 95.

[9] *Re Park* [1932]' 1 Ch. 580; see also *Drake* v. *Att.-Gen.* (1843) 10 Cl. & F. 257; *Re Byron* [1891] 3 Ch. 474; *Re Jones* [1945] Ch. 105.

Settlement [1953] Ch. 672; *Re Coates* [1955] Ch. 495 and *Re Gresham's Settlement* [1956] 1 W.L.R. 573.

Although it is clear that the requirement as to certainty of objects is applied far less stringently to powers than to trusts, it does not follow that the difficulty is avoided by conferring powers on the trustees in place of express trusts. For if a power, or, what amounts to the same thing, a discretionary trust, is conferred on trustees without any gift over in default of exercise of the power or discretion, the trustees then have really no power to give or withhold; consequently they have a " power in the nature of a trust." Lord Eldon said on this topic [10]: " If the power be one which it is the duty of the party to execute (made his duty by the requisition of the will—put upon him as such by the testator, who has given him an interest extensive enough to discharge it), he is a trustee for the exercise of the power and not as having a discretion whether he will exercise it or not; and the court adopts the principle as to trusts, and will not permit his negligence, accident, or other circumstances to disappoint the interests of those for whose benefit he is called upon to execute it."

The practical upshot of the foregoing is that, where property is settled for the benefit of a wide class of persons not all of whom are always likely to be easily ascertainable, care should be taken that the trustees have only a power or discretionary trust in favour of that class, with a gift in default of exercise of the power or discretion in favour of a narrower class, all the members of which may be ascertained at any time. It is worth observing that in one case, namely, *Re Hooper's 1949 Settlement* (1955) 34 A.T.C. 3, the learned judge had before him evidence that the trustees, in whom was vested a power in the nature of a trust, could, by making inquiries and advertising, discover all the persons among whom they were bound to select recipients of the settlor's bounty. Accordingly the trust was held to be valid.

It may be useful to examine the facts of the decision in *Re Gestetner Settlement* [1953] Ch. 672, which well illustrate the points under discussion. The settlor desired to benefit a wide class including four named persons, any issue living or thereafter to be born who was a descendant of two named persons, any spouse, widow or widower of any such person, five charitable bodies, any former employee of the settlor or the widow or widower of such former employee, and any person for the time being the director or employee of certain named companies or the wife or husband or widow or widower of such person, or any director or employee of any company of which the said directors of the named companies were also directors. This is clearly a wide class, the membership of which could not easily be ascertained at any particular time. The settlor therefore defined the wide class, defined also a narrower class, namely, issue of the settlor, and defined a perpetuity

---

[10] *Brown* v. *Higgs* (1799) 4 Ves. 708; (1801) 8 Ves. 561.

period. He settled the capital of the trust fund upon trust for such of the wide class as the trustees should appoint, and in default of appointment upon trust for the narrow class. He then settled the income of the unappointed part of the trust fund, until the perpetuity day, upon discretionary trusts for the wide class, and subject to the exercise of such discretion upon trust for the narrow class. In short, he settled his property upon discretionary trusts and powers for a wide class, not all of whose members would be at all times ascertainable, with a gift in default to a narrower class all of whose members would at all times be ascertainable. It was held that the powers and trusts were valid.

Although the facts in *Re Gestetner* have been greatly simplified as stated, they are, it is hoped, sufficiently detailed to illustrate both the principles upon which a wide discretionary trust may be validly created and also the potentialities of this type of settlement.[11]

It may, however, be desirable in particular cases to make the objects of the trust as wide as possible. This may be so where the trust is created not for the benefit of a family, but in order to provide for old or poor members of a group, such as employees and ex-employees of a group of companies, and their dependants, which is not wide enough to make the trust charitable.[12] In such a case it may be desired to have a trust, in default of exercise of wide powers, so framed that a wide class of beneficiaries may benefit. As a rule of thumb the draftsman should restrict the class of trust beneficiaries—*i.e.*, those who take as the objects of a discretion in the nature of a trust—to existing persons whose names are known, classes of children, grandchildren or remoter issue of a named person, or persons who may in future come within the exact terms of a simple description, *e.g.*, the eldest son of X, the first daughter of Y to get married, the person entitled to the Earldom of Kew, the Vicar of the parish of Bray for the time being, the wife or widow of any child or grandchild of the settlor, and so forth. Broadly, the test for inclusion in the class of trust beneficiaries is: when the time comes to distribute income or capital among this class, will the trustees be able, without difficulty, to compile a list of all possible beneficiaries? The class of purely discretionary beneficiaries—*i.e.*, the objects of a discretion which need not be exercised—must be so defined that it is clear what is meant, so that the trustees can say whether a particular person is one of the class or not, even though they may not be able to compile a list of all members. Classes of dependants, former employees, and so forth,

---

[11] Reference should also be made to *Innes* v. *Harrison* [1954] 1 W.L.R. 668, in which a further provision that the trustees were to apply the trust income " at such time or times " as they might think fit for the benefit of the members of a vaguely defined class was held to be void as offending the rule against perpetuities.
[12] See *Oppenheim* v. *Tobacco Securities Trust Co., Ltd.* [1951] A.C. 297.

come under this heading.[13] But some classes are too vague even to satisfy this test: *e.g.*, members of the Jewish faith,[14] members of the Church of England,[15] such persons as were dependent on X for any of the ordinary necessaries of life, any poor relation of X. Moreover the uncertainty is not cured by using some such phrase as " such person as in the opinion of the trustees. . . ."[16]

Infant children of the settlor as beneficiaries

Where unmarried infant children of the settlor are included among the beneficiaries, any income paid or applied to or for the benefit of such children will be treated as the income of the settlor for tax purposes: see section 397 of the Income Tax Act, 1952, as amended by section 20 of the Finance Act, 1958. Income paid to beneficiaries who are not the infant children of the settlor is not caught by section 397 so as to be treated as the income of the settlor for tax purposes. If the income arising under the settlement is accumulated under an express direction to accumulate, it will not now, on account of the accumulation, be treated as the income of the settlor for tax purposes, provided that the settlor and any spouse of the settlor are excluded from the class of beneficiaries. Formerly the complex interpretation imposed upon the word " irrevocable " by section 399 of the Income Tax Act, 1952, meant that any income accumulated under such a settlement where infant children of the settlor and others were potential beneficiaries, would be deemed to be the income of the settlor for tax purposes: see sections 398 and 397 of the Income Tax Act, 1952. Section 399 of the Income Tax Act, 1952, together with sections 397 and 398, has been amended by section 20 of the Finance Act, 1958. In consequence, a settlement may be " irrevocable " within the meaning of section 399 of the Income Tax Act, 1952, even if beneficiaries other than the infant children are included in the discretionary class, provided that the settlor and the wife or husband of the settlor are excluded from the class of beneficiaries. The present rule, therefore, is that, where infant children of the settlor are included in a discretionary class together with other persons, the settlor and his spouse being excluded, any income which is paid to or applied for the benefit of the infant children of the settlor is deemed by virtue of section 397 of the Income Tax Act, 1952, to be income of the settlor for tax purposes; but income paid to or applied for the benefit of any other person is not caught by section 397, and, moreover, income which is accumulated under an express direction during the minority of any

---

[13] How far the draftsman may go is shown by the following authorities: *Re H. J. Ogden* [1933] Ch. 678; *Re Gestetner Settlement* [1953] Ch. 672; *I. R. C.* v. *Broadway Cottages Trust* [1955] Ch. 20; *Re Coates* [1955] Ch. 495; *Re Hooper's 1949 Settlement* (1955) 34 A.T.C. 3; *Re Gresham's Settlement* [1956] 1 W.L.R. 573; *Re Sayer* [1957] Ch. 423; *Re Eden* [1957] 1 W.L.R. 788.

[14] *Clayton* v. *Ramsden* [1943] A.C. 320.

[15] *Re Allen* [1953] Ch. 810.

[16] See *Re Coxen* [1948] Ch. 747, 761–762; *Re Jones* [1953] Ch. 125.

infant child of the settlor is not deemed to be income of the settlor for tax purposes.

The practical conclusion is that a settlement upon discretionary trusts may prove beneficial even where the class of beneficiaries includes the infant children of the settlor.

Normally a discretionary settlement is so worded that the income has to be paid to, or applied when received for the benefit of, one or more beneficiaries. The question arises, whether income can be applied for the benefit of an infant beneficiary if it is retained by the trustees for his benefit; and if so, and if that infant beneficiary is an unmarried child of the settlor, whether section 397 causes the income to be treated for tax purposes as income of the settlor. The answer to this question is rather complex. If the trust is to apply income " for the benefit of " the infant in question, it is considered, on the authority of *Re Vestey's Settlement* [1951] Ch. 209, that this trust may be performed by allocating income to the beneficiary and retaining it until he is able, upon attaining his majority, to give a valid receipt.[17] Income so dealt with is plainly caught by section 397 and is income of the settlor for tax purposes. It is considered that to allocate income to an infant beneficiary so that it is then held upon trust for him contingently upon attaining the age of twenty-one years is not possible, where the power is simply a power to apply it " for the benefit of " the infant.[18] If desired, the settlement may expressly authorise the trustees to allocate income to an infant so that it is then held upon trust for him contingently upon attaining the age of twenty-one years, and in the meantime is capitalised, and invested, and the income of the investments accumulated. Where this can be done, it is considered that the income so allocated is not part of the total income of the settlor, and even if the infant is a child of the settlor, is not caught by section 397. It is also considered that the accumulation and capitalisation in question are permitted by the " anti-accumulation " enactment, namely section 164 (1) of the Law of Property Act, 1925.

If income is allocated to an infant beneficiary, and is then retained by the trustees upon trust for the beneficiary contingently upon attaining the age of twenty-one years, there would seem to be no convincing reason why that income should not be the subject of a claim for repayment of tax under section 228 of the Income Tax Act, 1952.[19] The resultant income produced by the investment of the income so allocated is clearly income which satisfies the requirements of section 228.

---

[17] See *post*, pp. 194, 195.
[18] Notwithstanding the decision in *Pilkington* v. *I. R. C.* [1962] 3 W.L.R. 1051. Application for benefit of a beneficiary is not the same as advancement for his benefit.
[19] See *ante*, p. 112: see also *Dain* v. *Miller* (1934) 18 Tax Cas. 478; *I. R. C.* v. *Maude-Roxby*, 1950 S.C. 339; 31 Tax Cas. 388.

The settlor or his wife as beneficiaries : Income tax

Ever since section 22 of the Finance Act, 1958, became law, the position has been that, as a general rule both the settlor and the settlor's husband or wife must be excluded from the possibility of benefiting under the settlement as a result of the exercise of any discretion by the trustees or any other person. If they are not so excluded, the whole income of the settled funds is treated for tax purposes as income of the settlor. To this general rule there are certain exceptions, which are contained in the proviso to section 405 (2) of the Income Tax Act, 1952, and are imported into section 22 of the Finance Act, 1958, by subsection (3) thereof; but these exceptions are so narrow, and so inappropriate to a discretionary settlement, that it is not proposed to refer to them here. In practice the draftsman would be well advised to apply the general rule, that the wife of the settlor must be excluded as well as the settlor himself.

A settlement is caught by section 22 if its terms are such that any person has or may have the power immediately or in the future to pay or apply or secure the payment or application of any part of the income or capital of the settled funds to or for the benefit of the settlor or the wife or husband of the settlor. The question arises whether it is sufficient, in drafting a settlement, to exclude the wife of the settlor for the time being, or whether any woman who may in future become the wife of the settlor must also be excluded. To put the question somewhat differently, is it necessary to exclude from the discretionary class all persons who are not within the forbidden degree of consanguinity for marriage with the settlor ? [20] The enactment itself refers to " the wife or husband of the settlor," and not to " any person who may become the wife or husband of the settlor." It is therefore considered that in drafting a settlement regard must be had only to the existing wife or husband of the settlor, and to any wife or husband for the time being, and that it is not necessary to exclude any person who may in future conceivably become the settlor's wife or husband. It is considered that, in order for a settlement to be caught by section 22 as respects any particular sum of income, the wife or husband in question must have that status at the moment that the income comes into being. The fact that a beneficiary may possibly in future have that status is irrelevant. The exclusion, therefore, of " the spouse of the settlor for the time being " is considered to be adequate.[21]

A troublesome point arises with regard to the professional trustee charging clauses and director-trustee fee clauses which are often included in a modern settlement. It is considered that it would be open to the

---

[20] As to the prohibited degrees see Marriage Act, 1949, s. 76.
[21] In the absence of any such exclusion, the possibility of a payment being made to a beneficiary who could in certain circumstances, however remote, marry the settlor will be sufficient, as a matter of law, to cause ss. 21 and 22 to apply: cf. I. R. C. v. Tennant (1942) 24 Tax Cas. 215. See Law Society's Gazette, January 1959, p. 53.

Revenue to argue that the fact that the settlor or his wife could be appointed a trustee and thus enjoy the benefit of a trustee charging clause or directorship fee clause is sufficient to bring the settlement within section 22. It may be that the Revenue will shrink from the absurdities to which the logic of this argument leads. It is, however, considered that in practice the draftsman should take care that the settlor and his wife are excluded from the possibility of becoming trustees, or alternatively are excluded from the usual charging clauses, or that some other safeguard is written into the settlement.

In consequence of the decision of the House of Lords in *Vestey's Executors* v. *I. R. C.* [1949] 1 All E.R. 1108; 31 Tax Cas. 1, it may be assumed for practical purposes that references to " wife " or " husband " in Part XVIII of the Income Tax Act, 1952, or sections 20, 21 or 22 of the Finance Act, 1958, do not extend to " widow " or " widower." It follows that it is usually unobjectionable as regards income tax law to include the widow or widower of the settlor as a member of the discretionary class.

The settlor's wife as a beneficiary : Estate duty

As regards liability to estate duty on the settlor's death, the fact that his wife is a possible object of the discretion vested in the trustees does not give rise to any liability. This means that, provided he does not look for any saving of surtax, a settlor can settle a fund so that, subject to his surviving the statutory period, estate duty on his death and on the death of his wife is avoided, although the income is, during her lifetime available for her use. But often, in order to satisfy certain requirements of income tax law, referred to above, it is desired to benefit, not the wife of the settlor, but his widow. This gives rise to a troublesome point of law regarding estate duty.

It is settled law that where, on the settlor's death, one set of discretionary trusts terminates, and a new set commences, there is a passing of the settled fund for estate duty purposes; and this is so even if the two classes of beneficiaries are substantially the same. The rule laid down in *Burrell and Kinnaird* v. *Att.-Gen.* [1937] A.C. 286 at pp. 300–301 is that where there is a discretionary trust during A's lifetime for a group of persons fulfilling certain qualifications, followed on A's death by a similar discretionary trust for a group of persons fulfilling different qualifications, there is a passing of the whole trust fund, notwithstanding that one or more persons fulfilled both sets of qualifications. It could be argued that, where a discretionary trust is set up for a fixed period so as to benefit a class including a person described as " any widow left by X," the class must change on X's death. It is submitted, however, that this argument goes beyond the decision in *Burrell and Kinnaird* v. *Att.-Gen.* and is not supported by the general principle laid down in that case. For the rule is that it is the change in qualifications that causes the trust fund to pass, and not the fact that on X's death the class is either decreased or increased.

In practice the cautious draftsman may prefer to avoid the argument based on *Burrell and Kinnaird* v. *Att.-Gen.* This may be done if due regard is given to the distinction, which has been explained earlier in this chapter, between a discretion or power in the nature of a trust, and a purely collateral discretion. The distinction has already been drawn in relation to the rule as to certainty of objects: it is important in the present context, because the objects of a discretion in the nature of a trust have together—but not individually—an enforceable right to the capital or income, as the case may be, of the trust fund: see *Re Smith* [1928] Ch. 915; whereas the objects of a purely collateral discretion have no enforceable right, either individually or together, to any part of the trust fund, since the donee of the discretion is at liberty to exercise that discretion or refrain from exercising it at his will. In the *Burrell and Kinnaird* case the discretion was in the nature of a trust: the discretionary class thus had, as a class, an enforceable interest in the income of the settled fund.

It is possible to include the widow of the settlor as an object of a discretionary settlement so that she is a member of a class which benefits, if at all, only as a result of the exercise of a collateral discretion, and thus has no enforceable interest in any part of the trust fund, either individually or together with the other members of the discretionary class. Thus, for example, in Precedent No. 25, *post*, she could be one of the "Appointed Class," without being one of the "Beneficiaries." This would, it is submitted, render it reasonably certain that the trust fund does not pass under section 1 of the Finance Act, 1894, on the death of the settlor, by reason of a change in the beneficial objects of the trusts.

Separated wives

Where a husband and wife are separated, under a Court Order or by deed of separation or in such circumstances that the separation is likely to be permanent, they are, for many purposes of tax law, treated as two single persons: see section 361 of the Income Tax Act, 1952. But the rules relating to the taxation of the income of settlements made by either husband or wife make no distinction between spouses who are separated and those who are living together. In consequence of this anomalous rule it is often less advantageous for a husband to provide for his separated wife by a capital settlement which also provides for infant children of the marriage than to execute a deed of maintenance.

If the marriage ends, not merely in separation, but in divorce, the husband may provide for his ex-wife by a capital settlement without the income arising under such settlement being treated as his income for tax purposes. The references to "wife" in Part XVIII of the Income Tax Act, 1952, include a separated but do not extend to an ex-wife. This anomaly has no obvious justification. It would be simple to amend the law, so that a separated wife (within the intendment of section 361 of the Income Tax Act, 1952) is treated for the purposes of Part XVIII of the Act as if she were not the wife of the settlor.

Administration of discretionary trusts

The administration of a discretionary trust is likely to require more detailed attention from the trustees than a trust in the traditional form. It may be of assistance if a few points are briefly mentioned in this respect.

(i) Changing investments

Trustees of discretionary settlements, in common with trustees of all settled property, must bear in mind the effect of the provisions in Chapter II of the Finance Act, 1962, relating to the charge to tax under Case VII of Schedule D on short-term capital gains.[22] For example, any gain realised on the sale of real property acquired by the trustees within three years will attract a charge to tax on the trustees under these provisions.

(ii) Trustees' records

The trustees should exercise their discretion in respect of income within a reasonable time after the income arises. It is considered that they may exercise their discretion before the income arises, provided that they have a sufficiently clear idea of the amount and type of income likely to come into being. Thus the trustees could decide that the whole income of their fund arising in the following three years should be paid to a particular beneficiary. More often, however, trustees are likely to review the distribution of the trust income from time to time, and therefore it would normally be convenient to record a fresh exercise of discretion from time to time and at least once in every year of assessment. It follows that in addition to the usual trust accounts a record should be kept by way of minutes of the way in which the trustees exercise their discretion. Moreover, in dividing the income among possible beneficiaries, they may either simply allot it in shares, or alternatively they may allot particular dividends to particular beneficiaries. In a case where dividends are treated as having suffered deduction of tax at less than standard rate, by reason of double taxation relief, the trustees may find that the allotment of particular dividends to particular beneficiaries is the more advantageous method, since otherwise it might be difficult to determine in respect of any particular beneficiary what rate of income tax his income under the trust must be regarded as having suffered at source. It may be desired to determine this in order that the beneficiary may claim personal allowances and reduced rate relief.

[22] See p. 115, supra.

(iii) *Recovery of surtax*

When any surtax charged in respect of the income of a beneficiary under a discretionary settlement is not paid within six months of the date when it became due and payable, the Special Commissioners may, under the provisions of section 244 of the Income Tax Act, 1952, serve a notice on the trustees of the settlement requiring them to pay to the Commissioners any income or capital to which the beneficiary might become entitled on the exercise of the discretion of the trustees in his favour in satisfaction of the surtax remaining unpaid.

(iv) *Accumulation of income*

Trustees have no general power to accumulate income instead of allotting it to the beneficiaries. Section 164 of the Law of Property Act, 1925, limits the power to accumulate to four specific periods. Apart from this, under the general law, where income is allotted to an infant beneficiary, the trustees may either apply it for his benefit under section 31 of the Trustee Act, 1925,[23] or under some specific power, or alternatively are obliged to retain it, since until the infant attains the age of twenty-one he is unable to give a valid discharge to the trustees. It is considered that, as a general rule, where trustees exercise their discretion in favour of an infant and then retain the income pending the attainment by the infant of his majority, the income nevertheless is part of the total income of the infant for income tax and surtax purposes at the time when the discretion of the trustees is exercised in his favour. In this respect the decisions in *Gascoigne* v. *I. R. C.* [1927] 1 K.B. 594; 13 Tax Cas. 573 and *Stanley* v. *I. R. C.* [1944] K.B. 255; 26 Tax Cas. 12, which have been discussed above at p. 114 are relevant. If income is to be treated as the income of an infant beneficiary for tax purposes notwithstanding its retention by the trustees, there must be clear evidence that the income has been allotted to the infant so that it has become his absolute property and would pass as part of his estate in the event of his death.

Where the settlement directs or authorises the trustees to allocate income to an infant beneficiary, or to apply income for the benefit of an infant beneficiary, the trustees cannot deal with income otherwise than in such a way that it becomes part of the beneficiary's total income for tax purposes. This may be inconvenient. For example, the class of beneficiaries may be already well supplied with income, so that income allocated to an infant simply bears surtax, but really benefits nobody. Or again, the income allocated to an infant beneficiary may cause its parents to lose child relief. Where such circumstances are likely to arise, the draftsman should consider expressly conferring power on the trustees to allocate income in such a way that it is held upon " contingent trusts " for the benefit of an infant: the income is retained by the trustees, invested and capitalised, and is held upon trust for the infant contingently

---

[23] See *Re Vestey's Settlement, Lloyds Bank* v. *O'Meara* [1951] Ch. 209.

upon attaining twenty-one years of age. It is considered that such income does not form part of the total income of the infant, and, if the infant dies during minority, does not suffer estate duty on his death. Considerable ingenuity may need to be exercised to keep such contingent trusts within the letter of section 164 of the Law of Property Act, 1925, and within the perpetuity rule.

Where the beneficiary concerned is an adult the trustees have, as a general rule, no power to accumulate income. If the trustees should simply allot income to an adult beneficiary and then withhold it, it is considered that the income is nevertheless part of his total income for income tax and surtax purposes as soon as it is allotted to him: see *Hamilton-Russell's Executors* v. *I. R. C.*, 25 Tax Cas. 200. If the trustees do not allot the income for a particular period among the beneficiaries, but simply accumulate it on general account, it is considered that, as a general rule, the purported accumulation is invalid: in consequence, the trustees having failed to exercise their discretion, the income goes to those persons who under the settlement are entitled in default of the exercise by the trustees of their discretionary powers, and this may mean that the beneficiaries become entitled in equal shares.

(v) *The discretion of the trustees*

Discretions are conferred upon trustees by the use of phrases such as "in their discretion" or "in their absolute discretion" or "in their uncontrolled discretion." It is considered that there is little if any difference between these expressions: see *Re Bryant* [1894] 1 Ch. 324; the following rule as stated in *Costabadie* v. *Costabadie*, 6 Hare 410, is of general application with regard to the exercise of a discretion:

> "If the gift be subject to the discretion of another person, so long as that person exercises a sound and honest discretion, I am not aware of any principle or any authority upon which the court should deprive the party of that discretionary power, where a proper and honest discretion is exercised."

It is considered that the mere fact that subsequent events show that the discretion was after all wrongly exercised by the trustees does not undermine their position: *Re Schneider* (1906) 22 T.L.R. 223.

Of course, the trustees must exercise their discretion for the object for which it was conferred upon them, and not for some other object. They should not exercise a power of investing in the making of loans, by making a loan in order to accommodate the borrower. They should not appoint income to A because they wish to benefit B, to whom they have no power to appoint income, and they believe that A is likely to pay over the income to B.[24]

---

[24] See *Re Crawshay* [1948] Ch. 123; *Re Pauling's Settlement* [1962] 1 W.L.R. 86; *In Re Pilkington's Will Trusts* [1962] 3 W.L.R. 1051.

Unless the settlement permits the contrary, or is a settlement upon charitable trusts, the decision of the trustees as to the exercise of their discretion must be unanimous. If there is any likelihood that unanimity may not be obtainable, then it may be advisable to include in the settlement some clause permitting the decision of a majority of trustees to be binding upon an absent or dissenting minority.

Insurance by the trustees of the settlement

It has sometimes been suggested that the trustees of a settlement should be given express power to use the income of the settlement in paying the premiums of a policy of insurance upon the life of the settlor. The object of this is that, if the settlor should die within the five-year period, the trustees of the settlement have a sufficient sum of money, namely the policy moneys, with which to discharge the estate duty.

This question is dealt with more fully in Chapter 6. It suffices to observe here that if the premiums on a policy are paid out of capital, the policy moneys will themselves bear estate duty, unless the capital itself represents accumulated income. If the premiums on the policy are paid out of income, care is required to ensure that the policy moneys will not be distributable among the income beneficiaries.

Private companies

In practice discretionary trusts are often used, as are the more traditional types of settlement, in the re-organisation of the shareholdings in a family company with a view to reducing the burden of estate duty on the death of the person who is at once head of the family, majority shareholder, governing director, and general manager. It may be of assistance if an account is given, in barest outline, of the more important points that present themselves in planning the affairs of a family company.[25]

The greater part of the share capital of such a company is often vested in the head of the family, the other members having small shareholdings of no more than nominal amount or significance, while the board of directors consists of the same persons, or some of them, being in fact nominees of the head of the family without real power or knowledge of the workings of the company. The head of the family votes himself the powers of the whole board, thus becoming governing director and general manager, without however, in the normal case, having any written service contract. Dividends are rarely, if ever, declared. The profits made by the company are paid out in directors' fees and in paying the managing director for his services, and any surplus profits not so applied are retained in the company and invested either in fresh capital equipment, or in the purchase of investments.

---

[25] A full account of estate duty in connection with companies is given in Dymond's *Death Duties*, 13th ed., p. 349.

It is usually the case that the conditions just described have existed for many years: and a number of results follow from this. Thus it is commonly found that as a result partly of continually retaining profits, partly of the general rise in prices, the true value of the assets is out of proportion to the nominal share capital.

In addition, the company is often subject to potential liability for surtax. The Revenue have power under section 245 of the Income Tax Act, 1952, to make a " direction and apportionment " in respect of any trading company to which that section applies. As regards an investment company, a direction is to be made automatically in each year in respect of its investment income: see section 262 of the Income Tax Act, 1952; and the Special Commissioners have additional powers of apportionment in such a case: see section 260 of the Income Tax Act, 1952. There is for obvious reasons a tendency for private companies to seek to reduce the surtax paid by their shareholders by reducing the amount of the dividends and retaining the profits in the company. This would tend to increase the value of the shares. Moreover, it was at one time comparatively easy to arrange matters in such a way that the accumulated profits of past years could be returned to the shareholders as capital, thus avoiding surtax almost entirely. In order to prevent the wholesale avoidance of surtax, section 21 of the Finance Act, 1922, now section 245 of the Income Tax Act, 1952, was made law. By making a " direction and apportionment " under this section the Revenue may in effect collect from the company the surtax which would have been paid had the company distributed its profits when earned.

In addition, the company may be liable for profits tax. This is now payable by companies, but not by individuals or incorporated associations, and is payable at the rate of fifteen per cent. on the profits of the company, subject to abatement where the profits do not exceed £12,000 in any one chargeable accounting period. The profits upon which the tax is payable are computed in much the same way as income for income tax purposes, subject to certain important differences. For example, in the case of a director-controlled company, the amount of directors' remuneration that may be deducted is subject to defined limits, and the rules relating to annual payments within the meaning of sections 169 and 170 of the Income Tax Act, 1952, are modified.

Where a company suffers a surtax direction and apportionment under section 245 of the Income Tax Act, 1952, in respect of an accounting period, it is relieved from profits tax in respect of the corresponding chargeable accounting period. This is reasonable enough, because profits tax on corporations corresponds very roughly to surtax on individuals.[26]

---

[26] The word "roughly" should be emphasised. It is perfectly possible for the same profits to bear income tax at 7s. 9d. as well as profits tax at 3s. 0d., then, after distribution by way of dividend, to be "grossed up" and bear surtax at the rate of 10s. 0d.

If the taxpayer resorts to avoidance devices in order to reduce the burden of profits tax, the Revenue may seek to counteract their effect by employing the very wide powers conferred by section 32 of the Finance Act, 1951.

Estate duty on shares in controlled company

The foregoing description is typical of many private companies. When the chief shareholder dies it often happens that estate duty becomes payable at a very high rate; for reasons that will be explained shortly, a high and at first sight artificial rule of valuation is applicable. In order to pay this duty, money must be found from the company, unless the beneficiaries who had hoped to inherit and carry on the business are willing to sell it to some outsider and pay the duty out of the proceeds. It may be possible to change the share structure and sell part of the share capital to a company which specialises in saving private companies from being suffocated by estate duty. Apart from this possibility, a satisfactory solution is not always easy to find. The company may sell part of its capital assets; but if it then tries to place the moneys so realised into the hands of its shareholders who have to pay the duty, and is unable to do so by way of a capital profits dividend, it may find that a large part of such moneys are eaten away by surtax. A capitalisation, or bonus, issue of redeemable preference shares or short-dated debentures cannot be made to existing ordinary shareholders, in the hope of providing funds with which to pay the duty without first obtaining the consent of the Treasury under the Control of Borrowing Order, and considering the possibility of the Revenue making a surtax direction and apportionment and also invoking the " anti-avoidance " provisions of section 28 of the Finance Act, 1960. Formerly it was possible, without undue difficulty or expense, to effect a company reconstruction, whereby the existing company was wound up, the undertaking other than liquid assets vested in a new company, and the liquid assets distributed, as surplus assets on the winding up, among the shareholders of the existing company. Now, the Revenue view appears to be that in such a case the provisions of section 28 of the Finance Act, 1960, as amended by section 25 (5) of the Finance Act, 1962, apply and a charge to tax may be made on the assets distributed. But it would seem to be arguable that any tax advantage derived from such a reconstruction is derived exclusively from the liquidation of the existing company and not from any relevant transaction in securities or the combined effect of a transaction in securities and the liquidation of the existing company.

It is still possible for the executors to sell a suitable asset (for example, the freehold of the trade premises, if the deceased had retained it) to the company for cash. On the other hand a " cross-sale " of shares is almost certainly caught by section 28 of the Finance Act, 1960; this was the scheme whereby, if the estate owned shares in two family companies, the executors sold the shares in each company to the other company, for cash.

It is as part of a scheme to avoid such difficulties in advance, that a discretionary trust may often be of value. But before deciding the kind of scheme that may be employed, mention must be made of the valuation of shares for the purposes of estate duty.

(i) Market value

The value laid down by section 7 (5) of the Finance Act, 1894, is " the price which, in the opinion of the Commissioners, such property would fetch if sold in the open market at the time of the death of the deceased." The difficulty of applying this section to shares in a private company, whose articles contain restrictions on the sale of shares which cause them to have no " market value " in the normally accepted meaning of the phrase, has been considered, and solved, by the courts. The established rule is that one must assess the price that a willing purchaser would pay if he knew he would be duly registered as holder, but, once registered, would hold subject to the Articles of Association, so that his right of resale would be limited. In other words, the value of such shares is the price an outsider would have paid to stand in the deceased's shoes.[27] It is reasonable to suppose that an outsider would pay a substantial price to buy a majority shareholding. Thus, in order to obtain fifty-one per cent. of the votes in a general meeting and of the ordinary dividends, an outsider may in certain circumstances even be prepared to pay a price in excess of fifty-one per cent. of the value of the assets of the company. The corollary of this is that it might be argued, but it seems unlikely that the Revenue would agree, that the remaining forty-nine per cent. of the shares were worth much less than forty-nine per cent. of the assets of the company. The purchaser can look forward, probably, to dividends, but can hardly hope, without negotiation or intrigue, to enjoy the benefits of a directorship.

(ii) Assets value

Sections 55 to 58 of the Finance Act, 1940, introduced a new and complex method of valuation of shares, applicable to " controlled companies." Subsequent legislation has varied the rules and increased the complexity, and it is not proposed to give more than an outline of their practical operation. Where a " section fifty-five valuation " is applicable, the shares in question are valued without reference to the " market value," by assessing the total value of the assets of the company, including goodwill, as at the date of death, and, broadly speaking, dividing this total value among the shareholdings rateably. This method, if applied to a minority holding, normally produces a figure considerably

---

[27] See *I. R. C.* v. *Crossman, I. R. C.* v. *Mann* [1937] A.C. 26; *Re Holt, I. R. C.* v. *Holt* [1953] 1 W.L.R. 1488; see also *ante*, p. 97.

in excess of the " market value." However, when applied to a majority holding, it is likely to produce a figure rather less than the market value.

The Finance Act, 1954, has modified the provisions relating to " assets valuation," by providing that a reduction in the valuation has to be made in cases where the company owns agricultural land or industrial hereditaments used and occupied for the purposes of the company's business, or machinery and plant so used: see section 28 (2). The reduction is similar to that applicable to agricultural land passing on a death, namely forty-five per cent.; and it is made on the proportion of the shares, at their assets valuation, which is ascribable to such hereditaments, plant and machinery. Provision is also made for companies whose subsidiaries own or use such hereditaments, plant and machinery. It follows that, in a case where a large proportion of the assets of the company consists of industrial hereditaments and plant and machinery, the " assets value " of a majority holding is likely to be less than the " market value "; but in case of a small minority holding, the " market value " will probably still be lower than the " assets value."

(iii) *Section 46*

The enactments just referred to deal with the valuation of shares which pass, or are deemed to pass, on death. But by virtue of section 46 *et seq.* of the Finance Act, 1940, another, quite distinct, principle of liability may apply to a family company: the assets of the company may themselves be " deemed " to pass on the death of any person, whether a shareholder or not, who

(i) at any time made a transfer of property to the company, and

(ii) during the five years preceding his death, received any " benefits " from the company, or could have received " benefits " by the exercise of a power exercisable either by him or by some other person with his consent.

The enactments in question are of a complexity scarcely equalled by any other part of English statute law.[28] They are aimed at the device once commonly employed, whereby the owner of a company's share capital could give away or settle practically the whole of the shares (thereby ensuring that little passed on his death) and only retain a service contract, or a single master-share, which in fact gave him complete control of the company (thereby ensuring that during his lifetime he was not deprived of the enjoyment of the profits). These provisions afford a classic example of a law which, in order to catch evasion, imposes a heavy burden on innocent and guilty alike. Their harshness is tempered by the policy of the Revenue, who have announced that they will apply the statutory provisions " in a reasonable manner," [29] and in practice, it is understood, refrain from applying them except in cases where avoidance devices have been used. The decision, whether a

---

[28] See the remarks of Lord Simonds in *St. Aubyn* v. *Att.-Gen.* [1952] A.C. at p. 30.
[29] See *Law Society's Gazette*, July, 1944, p. 118.

particular transaction is an avoidance device or not, rests in the arbitrary discretion of the Revenue.

Controlled companies: Reduction of duties

Generally there are two main courses, either or both of which may be adopted when the head of the family company seeks to plan the payment of the duties arising on his own death. The first is to dispose of part of his shareholding; the second, to reduce the value of the shares.

In practice a discretionary trust in favour of members of the settlor's family, including several generations, or in favour of a group of employees, is often an appropriate course, since it avoids giving any one person an absolute interest in any part of the share capital. Where a group of employees is chosen, some care is required, to see that they are a class capable of being ascertained with certainty, or, if it is desired to benefit a wider and less definable body, that a second easily ascertainable class is added to the terms of the settlement.[30]

It was formerly thought to be possible to avoid estate duty by selling shares to trustworthy members of the seller's family, on condition that the buyer paid an annuity to the seller, for life, or paid the price by instalments—thus ensuring, in effect, that the seller enjoyed the dividends during his lifetime in the guise of an annuity or instalments of purchase-money. This device is now ruled out: see section 46 of the Finance Act, 1950, amending section 44 of the Finance Act, 1940.

Once it has been decided to set up a trust or trusts and to transfer to the trustees (of whom, for the reasons explained above at p. 77, the settlor should not be one) a part of the share capital, the further point arises, of how much of the capital the settlor should disencumber himself. This is linked to the question of the valuation of any shares retained and to voting control.

If the settlor retains " voting control," which means, broadly, that he has over fifty per cent. of the voting shares, or of the voting power on any question, the assets valuation will apply on his death in respect of the shares he retains. In computing what voting powers the settlor has, shares subject to a settlement made by him, of which he is a trustee and shares held by another as bare trustee for him, are added to the shares of which he is the beneficial owner [31]; but shares of which he is the holder, or a joint holder, as trustee of a settlement or will made by another person, are left out of account.[32]

As a general rule it is advantageous to surrender voting control. A number of points, however, must be considered which may in some cases make it more advantageous to retain control. Among these are the following:

---

[30] See *ante*, p. 185, and *post*, Precedent No. 25.

[31] See *Barclays Bank, Ltd.*, v. *I. R. C.* [1961] A.C. 509, and the cases therein cited; also Finance Act, 1940, ss. 55 (5), 58 (5).

[32] Finance Act, 1940, s. 55 (5).

(i) If the assets of the company include a high proportion of machinery and plant used for its business, or industrial hereditaments so used or occupied, the forty-five per cent. reduction introduced by the Finance Act, 1954, may considerably reduce the estate duty liability.

(ii) A similar reduction is applicable to agricultural land, but only if occupied by the company for its business of husbandry or forestry: land held as an investment does not enjoy the reduction: Finance Act, 1954, s. 28 (2) (b).

(iii) If the settlor owns the freehold of the industrial hereditaments and has leased them to the company, the reduction applies to his freehold interest: Finance Act, 1954, s. 28 (4).

(iv) If it is intended to sell the shares after the settlor's death to an outsider at a genuine commercial price, that price may be taken as the assets value: Finance Act, 1954, ss. 30 (1), 31 (4).

(v) Where there have been stock exchange dealings in shares of a company, those shares may be exempted from the assets valuation even though a person dies having a majority holding: Finance Act, 1940, s. 55 (4).

(vi) It may be possible so to arrange the share structure that a very small proportion of the shares has voting control, and yet, even when the assets valuation is applied, is not of an unduly high value. Where this is done, the risk of section 46 being invoked is increased.

When the settlor decides to give up voting control, consideration must next be given to sections 29 to 31 of the Finance Act, 1954. Perhaps the most important rule arising therefrom is that, even if voting control is given up, the retention of " powers equivalent to control " as defined in section 31—broadly, powers of controlling the board of directors in any way—may still cause the assets valuation to be applicable. It is curious that the retention of powers equivalent to control only has this effect in the three cases specified in section 29 (5) of the Finance Act, 1954: in the case most likely to arise in practice (in section 29 (5) (a)) the persons having control or powers equivalent to control *after* the death of the settlor come into consideration. It may sometimes be possible to avoid the assets valuation on a minority shareholding retained by a settlor, even where he retains during his lifetime the position of a governing director, in full command of the company's policy.

In considering a plan to reduce a settlor's shareholding and the value of the shares retained or settled, regard must be had to section 46 of the Finance Act, 1940. There is no method of avoiding or mitigating the effects of this section that can be stated as a general rule, although in individual cases where there is a strong probability of its application it may be possible to devise some alleviation to suit the particular facts. It may be advisable for a director who gives up control to take an appointment for his life under an agreement of the type of which precedents are given in Chapter 9.

Money owed by company to settlor

Where money is owed by the company to the settlor or his wife in such circumstances that it can be described as a " loan," it may be advisable, in view of the stringent terms of section 408 of the Income Tax Act, 1952, to ensure that the loan is discharged before the settlement is constituted. Otherwise, when the loan is repaid, the repayment may, to the extent that it does not exceed any income accumulated under the settlement, be deemed for the purposes of surtax to be income of the settlor. In order to avoid section 408, regard should be paid to the facts in *Potts' Executors* v. *I. R. C.* [1951] A.C. 443. If, by an oversight, a loan should happen to be repaid to the settlor, consideration should be given to the possibility of distributing all accumulated income before the end of the year of assessment.[33]

Exempt private companies

A point that may be overlooked in considering a plan which involves the setting up of a trust of shares in a family company is that, if it is a private company exempted from the necessity imposed by section 128 of the Companies Act, 1948, of filing a copy of its balance sheet and auditors' and directors' reports with its annual return, the terms of the trust may cause this exemption to be lost. Exemption is conferred by section 129 of the Act, and the Seventh Schedule. A trust, which is not a " family settlement disposing of the shares " as defined in the Seventh Schedule, paragraph 4, and is not " a scheme maintained for the benefit of employees of the company, including any director holding a salaried employment or office in the company " within paragraph 5, may cause this exemption to be lost. It was held by the Court of Appeal in *Re Prenn* [1961] 1 W.L.R. 569, that a family settlement does not " dispose of " shares if it is a settlement of cash, which the Trustees then invest in purchasing the shares.

Control and director control

There exists a considerable amount of confusion as to the meaning of " control " in relation to tax and death duties, and the words " control," " director control " and " decontrol " are frequently used without a very distinct notion of what is meant. It may therefore be helpful if a short explanation is given of different aspects of Revenue law in which the notion of control is important.

(i) *Estate duty*

As has been pointed out in this Chapter, section 55 of the Finance Act, 1940, causes shares in a company to be valued by reference to the assets

[33] See *ante*, p. 108.

of the company and not to the market value of the shares, where the deceased had control, that is a majority of votes at a general meeting. Moreover section 29 of the Finance Act, 1954, brings in the assets valuation where the deceased had certain wide powers of controlling the board of directors, which are sometimes given the name " quasi-control." The same section also brings in the assets valuation where the deceased had the beneficial interest in possession in one-half or more of the capital or distributed income of the company, although it is difficult to see what name could be invented to describe this concept.

It should perhaps be added that shares are not caught by the enactments just mentioned, or by section 46 of the Finance Act, 1940, unless the company is subject to " five man control," that is, is under the control of not more than five persons: see section 58 (1) of the Finance Act, 1940, which in effect imports into estate duty law the surtax conception of control mentioned hereunder.

(ii) Surtax

It is well known that section 245 of the Income Tax Act, 1952, gives the Revenue power to make a surtax direction and apportionment in respect of the income of certain types of company. Section 256 states what companies may be subject to section 245, namely " any company which is under the control of not more than five persons and which is not a subsidiary company or a company in which the public are substantially interested." The rest of the section explains the meaning of this definition.

(iii) Director control : profits tax

The legislation imposing the charge of profits tax makes use of the phrase " a company the directors whereof have a controlling interest therein." This phrase is not defined, and the courts have had no easy task to determine its meaning. Many of the authorities were reviewed by the Court of Appeal in S. Berendsen Limited v. I. R. C. [1958] Ch. 1. The concept is mainly of importance today because paragraphs 4 and 11 of the Fourth Schedule to the Finance Act, 1937, as subsequently amended, provide that in computing the profits for the purposes of the profits tax of a company the directors whereof have a controlling interest therein, no deduction may be made in respect of any interest, annuity or other annual payment paid to a controlling director other than a whole-time service director, and moreover only an arbitrary amount may be deducted in respect of directors' remuneration.

(iv) Retirement benefits

The provisions of the Income Tax Act, 1952, dealing with retirement benefits, namely sections 386 to 391 inclusive, use the concept of a company the directors whereof have a controlling interest therein, in order to define the further concept of a " controlling director." However, section 390 of the Income Tax Act, 1952, confers on the word " director " a wide meaning, which is different from the definition conferred upon the same word for profits tax purposes by paragraph 13 (b) of the Fourth Schedule to the Finance Act, 1937.

Thus, when the word " control " is used, it may mean that the company is subject to all or any one or more of at least four distinct types of control.

PRECEDENT No. 24

Settlement Upon Discretionary Trusts for the Benefit of Children, Grandchildren and Great-grandchildren of the Settlor. Trust to Last for Sixty Years, with Power to Determine it Sooner

This trust is intended to secure the property settled against any claim for estate duty for a period of sixty years. This form is suitable where the settlor has already a fairly large family of children and grand-children and is content to leave it to his trustees to apply the income where it is most needed.

If any child of the settlor is an infant, care should be taken that no income is paid to him or for his maintenance until after his twenty-first birthday, so long as the settlor is alive.

The form can be adapted for any case where it is intended to benefit a defined class of beneficiaries, but great care should be taken to ensure that the class is sufficiently well defined, otherwise the trusts as here drawn will be void for uncertainty.

Although it has been decided that all the members of a discretionary class have power to terminate the trust, if all adult and together absolutely entitled (see *Re Smith* [1928] Ch. 915), it is submitted that no one individual in the class has any property right which can pass on his death.

Parties.

THIS SETTLEMENT is made the —— day of —— 19— BETWEEN —— of —— (hereinafter called " the Settlor ") of the one part and —— of —— and —— of —— (hereinafter called " the Original Trustees ") of the other part ;

WHEREAS :

Provision for issue.

(A) The Settlor desires to make provision for his issue and accordingly to create such trusts as herein-after appear ;

(B) The Settlor has caused to be paid or transferred into the joint names or control of the Original Trustees the money and investments specified in the Schedule hereto and it is apprehended that the Settlor may hereafter cause to be so paid or transferred further money or investments to be held on the trusts hereof;

Witnesseth. NOW in consideration of the premises THIS DEED WITNESSETH as follows:

Definition: 1. IN this Settlement the following terms where the context admits have the following meanings:

Trustees. (1) " The Trustees " means the Original Trustees or other the trustees or trustee for the time being of this Settlement;

Trust fund. (2) " The Trust Fund " means

  (i) the money and investments specified in the Schedule hereto,

  (ii) all money and investments paid or transferred to and accepted by the Trustees as additions to the Trust Fund, and

  (iii) the investments and property from time to time representing such money investments and additions or any part or parts thereof;

Beneficiaries. (3) " The Beneficiaries " means all children grandchildren and great-grandchildren of the Settlor who are already in being or shall be born before the Vesting Day as hereinafter defined [and so that in determining whether or not a person is one of the Beneficiaries an adopted or legitimated person shall be treated as the child of his adoptive or legitimated parents as the case may be and of no other person],

Vesting day. (4) " The Vesting Day " means the day on which shall expire the period of sixty years from the execution of this Deed or the day on which shall expire the period of twenty years after the death of the survivor of those of the Beneficiaries who are in existence at the time of execution of this Deed whichever shall first occur.

If there is any considerable chance that the period of 20 years after the death of the survivor of the existing beneficiaries will end before the period of sixty years, thus causing the settled funds to pass for estate duty purposes, it would be advisable to substitute for the above clause a definition based on the lives of members of the Royal Family, as in the next following precedent.

Discretionary trust of income and capital.

2. (i) Until the Vesting Day the Trustees shall pay or apply the income of the Trust Fund within six months after such income arises and may in their absolute discretion from time to time pay or apply the whole or any part or parts of the capital of the Trust Fund to or for the benefit of all or such one or more of the Beneficiaries for the time being living in such shares if more than one and in such manner as the Trustees shall in their absolute discretion think fit.

(ii) Without prejudice to the generality of the foregoing the Trustees may apply capital for the benefit of any one or more of the Beneficiaries for the time being living and whether an infant or not by

(a) allocating or appropriating to such Beneficiary such sum or sums out of or investments forming part of the capital of the Trust Fund as the Trustees shall think fit either absolutely or contingently upon the attainment by him or her of a specified age or the happening of a specified event before the Vesting Day and so that the provisions of section 31 of the Trustee Act 1925 and the powers of the Trustees to invest and vary investments shall apply to any moneys or investments so allocated or appropriated

(b) settling the same on such trusts for the benefit of any such Beneficiary and any spouse of him or her and his or her widow or widower and his or her issue as the Trustees may think fit and so that any such settlement may confer on the Trustees thereof or on the person for whose benefit the same is made or on any other person such powers of appointment and otherwise in relation to the fund thereby settled and the income thereof as the Trustees may determine

(c) purchasing an annuity for the life of any of the Beneficiaries or any less period.

Trust of capital.

3. ON the Vesting Day the Trustees shall hold the Trust Fund or such part thereof as shall not have been paid transferred or applied under any trust or power herein contained upon trust for such of the Beneficiaries as are then living in such shares as the Trustees shall on or before the Vesting Day determine and in default of such determination in equal shares.

Gift in
default.

4. SUBJECT as aforesaid the Trustees shall stand possessed of the Trust Fund in trust for —— and —— absolutely.

The person or persons named here should not be the settlor or his wife. A charity may be named. As a general rule, care should be taken in adapting this precedent that there is a discretionary trust, as opposed to a power, of income and capital taking precedence over the ultimate gift in default. If the preceding provisions are not trusts, but mere powers, it is arguable that the whole Trust Fund passes on the death of the person named as entitled in default.

Investment.

5. MONEY to be invested under the trusts hereof may be applied or invested in the purchase of or at interest upon the security of such shares stocks funds securities land buildings chattels or other investments or property of whatsoever nature and wheresoever situate and whether involving liabilities or producing income or not or upon such personal credit with or without security as the Trustees shall in their absolute discretion think fit to the intent that the Trustees shall have the same powers in all respects as if they were absolute owners beneficially entitled [PROVIDED ALWAYS that during the lifetime of the Settlor the consent in writing of the Settlor shall first be obtained before any money may be applied or invested as aforesaid].

The proviso is intended to be used where property is settled which it would be undesirable to sell without special reason. The necessity for the consent of the settlor does not give him an interest for the purposes of section 405 of the Income Tax Act, 1952: *Vestey's Executors* v. *I. R. C.* [1949] 1 All E.R. 1108; 31 Tax Cas. 1.

Additional
powers:

6. THE Trustees shall until the Vesting Day and during such further period if any that the law may allow have the following additional powers:

to retain
investments;

(1) Power to allow the investments specified in the Schedule hereto and all investments at any time forming part of the Trust Fund to remain in the actual state of investment thereof so long as the Trustees may think fit and at any time or times [(but during the lifetime of the Settlor not without his consent in writing)] to sell call in or convert into money the aforesaid investments or any of them or any part thereof;

The words in square brackets are intended to be used in conjunction with the proviso to clause 5, above.

to vary
investments;
 (2) Power [(but during the lifetime of the Settlor not without his consent in writing)] to change or vary any investments for the time being forming part of the Trust Fund for others hereby or by law authorised ;

improvement
of land;
 (3) Power to apply any money for the time being forming part of the Trust Fund in improving or developing any land which or the proceeds of sale of which may for the time being be subject to the trusts hereof or erecting enlarging improving or rebuilding any buildings upon such land ;

residence;
 (4) Power to permit any beneficiary to reside in any dwelling-house occupy any land or have the custody and use of any chattels which or the proceeds of sale of which may for the time being be subject to the trusts hereof upon such conditions as to payment of rent rates taxes and other expenses and outgoings and as to insurance repair and decoration and for such period and generally upon such terms as the Trustees in their discretion shall think fit.

manage;
 (5) Power to sell lease demise let mortgage charge licence and generally manage and deal with any land of any tenure which or the proceeds of sale of which may at any time form part of the Trust Fund as if the Trustees were beneficial owners absolutely entitled ;

appropriate;
 (6) Power to appropriate any investment or property from time to time forming part of the Trust Fund in its actual state of investment in or towards the satisfaction of the beneficial interest of any person in the Trust Fund upon making such valuations as the Trustees may think fit and without the necessity of obtaining the consent of any person ;

pay to
parent;
 (7) Power to pay to the parents or either parent or any guardian of any infant any sum of income intended to be applied for the maintenance or education or benefit of that infant or any sum of capital intended to be applied for the advancement or benefit of that infant upon receiving from the said parents parent or guardian an undertaking so to apply the said sum of income or capital as aforesaid and so that the receipt of such parents parent or guardian shall be a complete discharge to the Trustees ;

borrow;
 (8) Power to borrow money on such terms and as to

interest repayment and otherwise as they may think fit and whether upon the security of the whole or any part or parts of the Trust Fund or upon personal security only and to use such money so borrowed in purchasing or subscribing for investments or property to be held as part of the Trust Fund or otherwise for any purpose for which capital moneys forming part of the Trust Fund may be used ;

majority
vote;

(9) **Power** to direct that during such period or periods if any as the Trustees may think fit the discretion relating to the distribution of income conferred upon the Trustees by Clause 2 hereof shall be properly exercisable by a majority of the Trustees for the time being hereof provided that the said majority so exercising any such discretion shall keep proper records thereof and shall without undue delay inform any minority of the Trustees not joining in such exercise of the manner in which the said majority have exercised the said discretion ;

insure
settlor;

(10) **Power** to effect any policy of insurance upon the life of the Settlor (and in particular a policy whereby a sum of money becomes payable in the event of the Settlor dying within 5 years of the date hereof) and to apply any part or parts of the capital or income of the Trust Fund or any accumulations of income of the Trust Fund in or towards the payment of any premium for the effecting or the maintaining of any such policy and power to borrow from any person including any one or more of themselves the moneys required for any such premium upon such terms as to repayment interest and otherwise as the Trustees in their absolute discretion think fit and to charge any part of the capital or income (including any future income) of the Trust Fund with the repayment of any moneys so borrowed ;

" educa-
tional "
policy.

(11) **Power** to deal with any income applicable for the maintenance education or benefit of any of the Beneficiaries under any of the provisions of this Deed by paying or contributing towards the payment of the premiums or costs of any policy of insurance by the terms of which any sum or sums of money may in any contingency be payable to or applicable for the maintenance education or benefit of such beneficiary.

Uncontrolled discretion.

7. EVERY discretion or power hereby conferred on the Trustees shall be an absolute and uncontrolled discretion or power and no Trustee shall be held liable for any loss or damage accruing as a result of his concurring or refusing or failing to concur in any exercise of any such discretion or power.

Trustee indemnity.

8. IN the professed execution of the trusts and powers hereof no Trustee being an individual shall be liable for any loss to the Trust Fund arising by reason of any improper investment made in good faith or for the negligence or fraud of any agent employed by him or by any other Trustee hereof although the employment of such agent was not strictly necessary or expedient or by reason of any mistake or omission made in good faith by any Trustee hereof [or by reason of any other matter or thing except wilful and individual fraud or wrongdoing on the part of the Trustee who is sought to be made so liable].

The words in square brackets are frequently found in clauses of this kind. It may, however, be open to question whether they do not go further than is required for the reasonable protection of a competent trustee.

Charging clause.

9. ANY Trustee being a solicitor or other person engaged in any profession or business shall be entitled to be paid all usual professional or proper charges for business transacted time expended and acts done by him or any partner of his in connection with the trusts hereof including acts which a trustee not being in any profession or business could have done personally.

Corporate trustee's charges.

10. ANY corporation that is a trust corporation within the meaning of the Law of Property Act, 1925, as amended in 1926, may be appointed to be a Trustee of this settlement or of any trust hereby created and upon such appointment shall have the powers rights and benefits as to remuneration or otherwise as at or prior to its appointment may be agreed in writing between such corporation and the person or persons making such appointment or in default of such agreement in accordance with the corporation's published terms and conditions as to acceptance of trusts current at the date of its appointment.

In practice, it may often be undesirable to appoint a trust corporation to be the sole trustee of a discretionary trust, since the duties require the personal attention of a family friend or a solicitor acquainted with the family's affairs. On the other hand, the appointment of a trust corporation may, in particular circumstances, be so advantageous, that it is as well to provide for its remuneration in the deed, thus avoiding the necessity of an application to the court. The next following precedent contains a rather wider power to appoint a corporate trustee.

Trustee's remuneration.   11. ANY Trustee other than a trust corporation or a sole Trustee shall be entitled to retain and be paid out of the annual income of the Trust Fund such sums as shall be determined by the Trustees as reasonable remuneration for acting as such Trustee but not exceeding in any year the sum of £100 or one —th part of the annual income of the Trust Fund or other the property in respect of which such Trustee so acts whichever be the smaller.

This clause should rarely be included unless there is property in the trust fund which requires considerable management. The payments made to each trustee may be regarded as earned income : see *Dale* v. *I. R. C.* [1954] A.C. 11; 34 Tax Cas. 468. On the death of any trustee entitled to remuneration, there will be no passing for estate duty purposes: *Public Trustee* v. *I. R. C. (Re Arnholz)* [1960] A.C. 398.

Settlor excluded.   12. NOTWITHSTANDING anything to the contrary hereinbefore expressed or implied no discretion or power by this Settlement conferred on the Trustees or any of them shall be exercised and no provision of this Settlement shall operate so as to cause any part of the income or capital of the Trust Fund to become payable to or applicable for the benefit of the Settlor or any wife of the Settlor.

A clause in these terms is intended to exclude the settlor and any wife of the settlor from the benefit of the trustee charging and remuneration clauses: this is considered to be advisable, in order to ensure that the income of the settled funds is not caught by section 22 of the Finance Act, 1958 and deemed to be the income of the settlor for tax purposes. Some such clause is also required to exclude any argument to the effect that the settlor could marry a member of the discretionary class where that class includes persons outside the prohibited degrees.

Irrevocable.   13. THE Settlement hereby created shall be irrevocable.

New trustees.   14. THE power of appointing new Trustees shall be vested in the Settlor during his life [but so that neither the Settlor nor any wife of the Settlor shall be appointed a Trustee hereof].

It is considered inadvisable for persons to be appointed as trustees who are also objects of the discretionary trust, since a trustee may become competent to dispose of the beneficial interest by being both sole trustee and an object of the discretion: see *Re Penrose* [1933] Ch. 793.

IN WITNESS, ETC.

THE SCHEDULE

PRECEDENT No. 25

Settlement upon Discretionary Trusts for a Wide Class Intended to Last for Eighty Years

This is a rather more complex settlement than the foregoing and is designed to benefit a very wide class of persons. Estate duty will not be payable on the death of the settlor, if he survives five years, and the usual reductions will be obtainable if he survives more than two, but less than five, years. The trustees have power to appoint shares in the capital at any time for the benefit of any of the class of beneficiaries, and in default of any such appointment may apply the annual income for the members of the class until the end of a specified period. No estate duty will be payable on the death of any beneficiary under the discretionary trust provided there are at least two surviving beneficiaries at the date of the death. The specified period during which the discretionary trust is to continue is to be at least thirty years but not more than eighty years.

Parties. **THIS SETTLEMENT** is made the —— day of —— 19— BETWEEN —— of —— (hereinafter called " the Settlor ") of the one part and —— of —— and —— of —— (hereinafter called " the Original Trustees ") of the other part ;
WHEREAS :

    (A) The Settlor desires to provide a fund to be applied for the benefit of the persons hereinafter described and accordingly to create such trusts as hereinafter appear ;

Sum settled. (B) The Settlor has caused to be vested in the joint names of the Original Trustees the investments mentioned in the Schedule hereto and it is apprehended that the Settlor may hereafter cause further money investments and property to be paid or transferred into the joint names or control of the Original Trustees ;

Witnesseth.   **NOW THIS DEED WITNESSETH** as follows:

Definition: 1. IN this Settlement the following terms where the context admits have the following meanings:

Trustees.   (1) " The Trustees " means the Original Trustees or other the trustees or trustee for the time being of this Settlement;

Trust fund.   (2) " The Trust Fund " means
(i) the investments mentioned in the Schedule hereto;
(ii) all moneys investments and property paid or transferred to and accepted by the Trustees as additions to the Trust Fund; and
(iii) the investments and property from time to time representing such investments and additions or any part or parts thereof;

Vesting day.   (3) " The Vesting Day " means the day on which shall expire the period of eighty years after the execution of this Settlement or the period of twenty years after the death of the descendants of His late Majesty King George the Fifth living at the date hereof, whichever period shall first determine, or such earlier day as the Trustees may at any time not earlier than thirty years after the execution of this Settlement by Deed appoint to be the Vesting Day;

If the trust is allowed to carry on until the end of a perpetuity period fixed by reference to the death of the survivor of a class, it is considered that estate duty will be payable at the termination of that period. It is therefore advisable to give an alternative, either a period of years or a date to be fixed by the trustees, so that the discretionary trusts will terminate at a date having no reference to any death, thus preventing liability to estate duty from arising.

Beneficiaries.   (4) " The Beneficiaries " means the grandchildren and great-grandchildren of the Settlor and of —— who are already in being or shall be born before the Vesting Day;

Appointed class.   (5) " The Appointed Class " means:
(i) the Beneficiaries;
(ii) any wife, husband, widow, widower or child or other issue of any of the Beneficiaries;
(iii) the adopted or legitimated child or children of any of the Beneficiaries and the child or

children (including any adopted or legitimated child or children) of any such adopted
or legitimated child or children;

(iv) any person who shall have been a domestic
servant of any of the Beneficiaries for a continuous period exceeding five years;

(v) any person for the time being a partner or
former partner or employee or former
employee or the wife or husband or widow or
widower or child or other dependant of any
partner or former partner or employee or former employee of the firm of —— trading and
registered under the name of —— & Sons;

(vi) any person for the time being a director or
former director or the wife or husband or
widow or widower or the child of any
director or former director of the following
companies, namely —— Ltd., —— Ltd. and
—— Ltd., or of any company of which at
least one half of the issued share capital is
held by any one or more of the said
companies;

(vii) the following organisations and purposes, in
so far as they are charitable, namely ——,
——, —— and ——;

but shall nevertheless not include the Settlor or any per-
son who is or shall for the time being be the wife of the
Settlor or any person for the time being one of the
Trustees.

The appointed class may be drawn widely, since the members of it
benefit, if at all, as the objects of a power, not as the beneficiaries under
a trust, and it seems that, although the objects of a power must not be so
vaguely defined that the trustees are unable to choose from the class of
appointees with sufficient certainty, the same certainty is not required
as for a trust. Therefore the class of beneficiaries, who only benefit
if the trustees fail to exercise their powers of appointment, should be
so narrowly drawn that the trustees would at no time experience serious
difficulty in ascertaining all the members of the class.

It is considered that the word " dependant," which is often found in
settlements in practice, is not too uncertain: see *Re Sayer* [1957] Ch. 423;
Re Saxone Shoe Co., Ltd.'s Trust Deed [1962] 1 W.L.R. 943.

If brothers and sisters of the settlor and their children are to be
included in the definition of the beneficiaries or the appointed class, it is

convenient to refer to them as the lineal descendants of the settlor's father. But if this is done, care must be taken to exclude the settlor in terms.

Power to appoint.

2. THE Trustees shall stand possessed of the Trust Fund and the income thereof upon such trusts for the benefit of the members of the Appointed Class or any one or more of them exclusive of the other or others in such shares and proportions and subject to such terms and limitations and with and subject to such provisions for maintenance education or advancement or for accumulation of income during minority or for the purpose of raising a portion or portions or for forfeiture in the event of bankruptcy or otherwise and with such discretionary trusts and powers exercisable by such persons as the Trustees being at least two in number shall from time to time by Deed or Deeds revocable or irrevocable executed before the Vesting Day but without infringing the rule against perpetuities appoint.

It may be desired to make this overriding power even wider. It is considered that there is no legal objection to the creation of a power of appointment, exercisable by two trustees with the consent of the settlor during his life, in favour of a class consisting of all persons at any time in existence except, say, the settlor, any wife of the settlor or the trustees themselves. Such a power is open to objection on practical grounds, unless its exercise is limited to a short time. It is highly inadvisable to make it exercisable only during the settlor's lifetime, since it could be argued that section 2 (1) (d) of the Finance Act, 1894, applied so as to cause the whole fund to be deemed to pass on his death. There is no objection to a fixed period of twenty-one years.

Trusts of income.

3. (1) IN default of and subject to any such appointment as aforesaid the Trustees shall until the Vesting Day pay or apply the whole or such part if any as they shall think fit of the income of the Trust Fund within six months after it arises to or for the benefit of all or such one or more exclusive of the others or other of the Appointed Class in such proportions and manner as the Trustees in their absolute discretion shall think fit; and

(2) SUBJECT to the foregoing the Trustees shall until the Vesting Day deal with the income of the Trust Fund or so much thereof as shall not be paid or applied as aforesaid by paying or applying the same within six months after it arises to or for the benefit of such of the

Beneficiaries as shall be living for the time being in such shares as they shall in their absolute discretion think fit.

The question may arise, whether the trustees have power to deal with income at any time by determining to allot it to an infant beneficiary and then to retain and capitalise it for him contingently on his attaining the age of twenty-one. It is considered that they have no such power, unless it is expressly conferred upon them by the settlement or by an appointment executed in pursuance of a power conferred by the settlement: *cf. Re Vestey's Settlement, Lloyds Bank* v. *O'Meara* [1951] Ch. 209. The trustees may be able, however, to apply income for the benefit of an infant beneficiary in purchasing Savings Certificates or other appropriate investments to be held as the infant's absolute property.

Trusts of capital.   4. THE Trustees shall stand possessed of the Trust Fund on the Vesting Day (subject to any appointment made in exercise of such power as aforesaid) in trust as to income and capital for such members of the Appointed Class as shall then be living or any one or more of them and in such shares as the Trustees shall prior to or upon the vesting day determine and in default of such determination in trust for such of the Beneficiaries as shall then be living in equal shares absolutely.

Gift in default.   5. SUBJECT to the foregoing trusts the Trustees shall stand possessed of the Trust Fund and the income thereof in trust for such charitable purposes as the Trustees shall determine.

Specific individuals or charities can be named here. On no account must there be any possibility of the settlor or any wife, as distinct from a widow, of his taking an interest under, or in the event of the failure of, the trusts of the settlement. The possibility of being interested through some other person's estate is immaterial: *cf. Barr's Trustees* v. *I. R. C.*, 1943 S.C. 157; 25 Tax Cas. 72. The question, how far a wife or widow may receive a benefit under a discretionary trust, is discussed, *ante*, at pp. 190, 191.

The practice of referring the selection of an appropriate charity to the court, or of requiring the court's consent, should no longer be followed: *Re Hooker's Settlement* [1955] Ch. 55.

Investment.   6. [*Investment, see ante, p. 208.*]

Additional powers.   7. THE Trustees shall until the Vesting Day and during such further period if any as the law may allow have the following additional powers :

Add such powers as may be desired: see *ante*, p. 208.

8. [*Uncontrolled discretion, ante, p. 211.*]

9. [*Trustee indemnity, ante, p. 211.*]

10. [*Professional charging clause, ante, p. 211.*]

Corporate
trustee.

11. ANY body corporate (being either a trust corporation within the meaning of the Law of Property Act, 1925, as amended in 1926 or being a company with unlimited liability [or with capital of at least £100,000 unpaid on its shares] all of the shareholders of which are solicitors or chartered accountants and having power by its Memorandum of Association to undertake and carry out trusts) may be appointed to be a trustee of this settlement or of any trust hereby created and upon such appointment shall have the powers rights and benefits as to remuneration or otherwise as at or prior to its appointment may be agreed in writing between such body corporate and the person or persons making such appointment or in default of such agreement in accordance with the body corporate's published terms and conditions as to the acceptance and carrying out of trusts current at the date of its appointment.

Elsewhere in this book there are precedents of a clause permitting the appointment of a trust corporation with power to charge: see pages 156 and 211. The present clause however also permits the appointment of a company that is not a trust corporation. Some firms of chartered accountants have their own trust companies, with power to act as trustee and to charge remuneration. One obvious advantage, from the point of view of the firm of accountants, is that the work of administering the trust is thus more likely to " stay in the office " than if persons were appointed who might die or retire. From the point of view of the beneficiaries, the appointment of such a company obviates to some extent the necessity of appointing fresh trustees from time to time. It is considered that if such a company has limited liability and a small capital fully paid up, it offers insufficient protection to the beneficiaries; but a company having unlimited liability, and having as its shareholders the partners in a reputable firm of chartered accountants or solicitors would appear to give a substantial measure of protection to the beneficiaries. Similarly a company with a large unpaid capital but otherwise with limited liability may offer reasonable protection (although, so far as is known, no firm of accountants or solicitors has yet formed such a company).

12. [*Trustee's remuneration, ante, p. 212.*]

13. THE Trustees shall not be bound or required to interfere in the management or conduct of the business of any Company British or Foreign in any part of the

share capital or debentures or loan capital of which or of any subsidiary of which the Trustees shall hold or control the whole or a majority or any part of the shares carrying the control of the company or other the voting rights of the company but so long as there shall be no notice of any act of dishonesty or misappropriation of monies on the part of the Directors having the management of such Company the Trustees shall be at liberty to leave the conduct of its business (including the payment or non-payment of dividends other than cumulative preferential dividends) wholly to such directors And no beneficiary hereunder shall be entitled to require the distribution of any dividend by any company British or Foreign in which the trust fund or any part thereof may be invested or require the Trustees to exercise any powers they may have of compelling any such distribution.

Persons excluded.
14. NOTWITHSTANDING anything to the contrary hereinbefore expressed or implied no discretion or power by this Settlement conferred on any person or on the Trustees or any of them shall be exercised and no provision of this Settlement shall operate so as to cause any part of the income or capital of the Trust Fund to become payable or applicable for the benefit of the Settlor or any wife of the Settlor or for any person for the time being a trustee of this Settlement.

The settlor and any wife he may marry should be excluded, since otherwise there is the possibility that income of the trust fund will be deemed to be the income of the settlor by virtue of section 404 of the Income Tax Act, 1952, as amended by section 21 of the Finance Act, 1958, or section 405 of the Income Tax Act, 1952, or section 415 of the Income Tax Act, 1952, or section 22 of the Finance Act, 1958. It is considered advisable also to exclude the trustees, in order to avoid the possibility of a claim to estate duty on the death of a trustee, on the ground that he was " competent to dispose " of the whole of the fund. It was held in *Re Penrose* [1933] Ch. 793, that a person who has a limited power of appointment among a class of which he himself is a member is " competent to dispose " of the fund over which the power is exercisable, so that the whole fund is deemed to pass on his death under section 2 (1) (a) of the Finance Act, 1894.

Irrevocability.
15. THE Settlement hereby created shall be irrevocable.

New trustees.   16. THE power of appointing new Trustees shall be vested in the Settlor during his life [provided that the Settlor shall not be a Trustee hereof].

The words in square brackets are often used in practice as a safeguard to ensure that the settlor does not, by appointing himself a trustee, acquire " control " of the company in whose shares the Trust Fund is invested. In addition it avoids the risk of claim being made for estate duty under section 44 of the Finance Act, 1940, as amended by section 46 of the Finance Act, 1950, where the settlor is a trustee and the overriding power of appointment is exercised in favour of a relative of the settlor.

IN WITNESS, ETC.

THE SCHEDULE

PRECEDENT No. 26

Short Supplemental Deed for Use where Investments or Cash are Added to an Existing Settlement

Where an existing settlement mentions the possibility that later additions may be made to the Trust Fund, it is considered that in normal circumstances a further declaration of trust should be executed every time an addition to the Trust Fund is made. This declaration will require to be stamped in the same way as a settlement and thus adjudication is in most cases obligatory and in almost every case advisable. Since *ad valorem* stamp duty will not normally be payable where the shares added to the settlement are not yet registered but are represented by a renounceable allotment letter or bearer certificates, it is advisable to specify such shares.

Declaration.   THIS DECLARATION OF TRUST SUPPLEMENTAL to the Settlement [within] [hereinbefore contained] and made BETWEEN the [same parties as] [Settlor and the Present Trustees of] the said Settlement

Witnesseth.   WITNESSETH that the Settlor intends immediately upon the execution hereof to cause to be vested in the joint names or control of the Trustees to be held upon the trusts of the said Settlement as an addition to the Trust Fund the following assets :—

Cash.   (1) The sum of £—— cash.

Investments.   (2) —— registered stock units of 10s. each in —— Ltd.

Bonus or rights issue.   (3) An allotment letter entitling the holder [to —— shares of £1 each in —— Ltd.] [to subscribe for —— shares of £1 each at —— shillings a share].

Bearer security.   (4) £—— stock in —— Ltd., payable to bearer.

IN WITNESS, ETC.

PRECEDENT No. 27

Settlement of Investments Intended to Provide Subscriptions to a Number of Selected Charities in Accordance with the Settlor's Choice Over a Number of Years

Regular donors to charity may properly reduce the burden of income tax (but not surtax or estate duty) by executing " seven-year covenants." An alternative method of achieving the same result is by setting aside sufficient capital to produce the subscriptions and depriving the settlor of any possible interest therein. By this method it may be possible to reduce the burden of income tax, surtax and estate duty, while at the same time ensuring that, during the settlor's lifetime, the income is paid to the charities selected by the settlor at the time of executing the deed.

Estate duty is not payable on a gift made for public or charitable purposes, provided the gift was made without the retention of a benefit more than one year before the death of the donor: see section 59 (1) of the Finance (1909–10) Act, 1910. It is considered therefore that no estate duty will be payable on the settlor's death, if he survives the execution of the settlement by one year, on a proportion of the property settled representing the ratio between the value of the charitable gifts in the settlement and the whole of the settled fund.

Income tax and surtax will be saved, since the settlor has absolutely divested himself of the property settled, within the meaning of section 415 of the Income Tax Act, 1952. There will, however, be no saving of income tax in respect of income paid to a foreign charitable corporation carrying on its activities abroad: *Camille and Henry Dreyfus Foundation Inc.* v. *I. R. C.* [1954] Ch. 672; 36 Tax Cas. 126.

Section 447 of the Income Tax Act, 1952, confers exemption from income tax on many, but not all, types of income that is both applicable and applied for charitable purposes only. Such exemption extends to Schedule C income and to " any yearly interest or other annual payment " under Schedule D. The official practice is to regard the expression " annual payment " as including dividends on investments: see *R.* v. *Special Commissioners, ex p. Shaftesbury Homes* [1922] 2 K.B. 729; 8 Tax Cas. 371.

If any income suffers tax by deduction at source, the Trustees will either have to supply a form R. 185, duly completed, to each charity when they pay a sum of net income to that charity, or to agree with the Revenue that the Trustees may themselves reclaim the tax deducted, so that all payments that they make to charity are made " gross."

Parties.

THIS SETTLEMENT is made the —— day of —— 19— BETWEEN —— of —— (hereinafter called " the Settlor ") of the one part and —— of —— and —— of —— (hereinafter called " the Trustees " which expression where the context permits includes the trustee or trustees for the time being of these presents) of the other part :

Recital.

WHEREAS the Settlor is desirous of making such settlement as is hereinafter contained for the benefit of certain charities and of his grandchildren and has accordingly transferred into the joint names or control of the Trustees the investments mentioned in the First Schedule hereto ;

Witnesseth.

NOW THIS DEED WITNESSETH as follows :

Trust to convert.

1. THE Trustees shall stand possessed of the investments specified in the First Schedule hereto Upon Trust that the Trustees shall permit the same to remain as invested or shall with the consent of the Settlor during his life and after his death at the discretion of the Trustees sell call in or convert into money all or any of the said investments and shall with the like consent or at the like discretion invest the money arising thereby in the names or under the control of the Trustees in any of the investments hereby authorised with power from time to time with such consent or at such discretion as aforesaid to vary and exchange the same for others of a like nature.

2. THE Trustees shall stand possessed of the investments specified in the First Schedule hereto and the investments for the time being representing the same (hereinafter called " the Trust Fund ") and of the income thereof upon the trusts and subject to the powers and provisions following namely :

Power to pay income to selected charities.

(1) Upon trust during the period of —— years next following the date hereof [or until the earlier expiration of the period of twenty-one years from and after the death of the survivor of the descendants of His late Majesty King George the Fifth alive at the date of the execution of this Deed] to pay or apply the annual income of the Trust Fund as and when received to or for the charitable purposes of all or any one or more to the exclusion of the others or other of the bodies associations

and organisations whose names are set forth in the Second Schedule hereto in such shares and in such manner in all respects as the Trustees may in their absolute discretion think fit PROVIDED ALWAYS that

Payment to officer.

(a) the Trustees may make any such payment or application of income by paying the same to the person or officer named in the Second Schedule hereto opposite the name of such charitable body association or organisation as aforesaid and so that the receipt in writing of such person or officer shall be a good discharge to the Trustees without the necessity of seeing to the proper application of any sum so paid and

Wishes of settlor.

(b) in exercising their absolute discretion as aforesaid the Trustees may have regard to but shall not be in any way bound by the wishes of the Settlor as expressed to them from time to time in writing.

The draftsman should insert in the blank space on the first line of the above clause the number of years it is desired to keep the trust in being. This will usually be slightly longer than the expectation of life of the settlor. If the number so inserted is greater than twenty-one the words in square brackets should be included, since otherwise the clause may be bad for perpetuity. On no account should the clause be adapted so as to make the life of the settlor or of any other person the relevant period, since it would give rise to liability to estate duty on the termination of the life chosen.

Ultimate trust of capital.

(2) Subject as aforesaid Upon Trust as to both capital and income for such of the grandchildren of the Settlor (being children of ——— and ——— the children of the Settlor) as shall be living at the expiration of ——— years from the date hereof [or at the expiration of ——— years from the date hereof or the expiration of the period of twenty-one years from and after the death of the survivor of the descendants of His late Majesty King George the Fifth alive at the date of execution of this Deed whichever period shall first expire] and if more than one in such shares as the Trustees shall in their absolute discretion think fit And subject thereto upon trust for ——— absolutely.

This clause may require considerable adaptation to suit particular circumstances. The words in square brackets should be used if the period named in the preceding clause, which must be repeated in the appropriate blank space in this clause, exceeds twenty-one years. If desired, a charitable gift may be substituted for this clause. On no account must the settlor or any wife be given any benefit under the settlement, whether expressly or by reason of the fact that some part of the future income or of the capital of the trust fund is left undisposed of.

Trustee investments only.

3. TRUST moneys may with such consent or at such discretion as aforesaid be invested in or upon any investments in or upon which trust funds under the control of the High Court of Justice may for the time being be authorised by law to be invested but not in any other mode of investment.

This clause limits the powers of the trustees to invest outside the range of "trustee securities." It is inadvisable to employ this narrow range of investment, except for special reasons, in the usual family settlement. In choosing investments, the trustees should normally confine themselves to investments, the income whereof does not suffer tax by deduction at source, or which suffers such deduction at the full standard rate. If any income of the trust has suffered tax at less than the standard rate (e.g., dividends of a group of companies whose activities are largely carried on abroad), the trustees are able to reclaim from the Revenue only tax at the reduced rate. By investing in such a way as not to get the benefit of the full tax repayment, the trustees may be guilty of a breach of trust: Trustee Investments Act, 1961, s. 6 (1) (b). Units of a Unit Trust are in the wider range authorised by section 1 of the Trustee Investments Act, 1961.

Appropriation.

4. THE Trustees may appropriate any part of the Trust Fund in the actual condition or state of investment thereof at the time of such appropriation in or towards satisfaction of the share of any person in the Trust Fund as to the Trustees may seem just and reasonable according to the respective rights of the persons interested in the Trust Fund but without the necessity of obtaining any consents.

New trustees.

5. THE power of appointing new Trustees shall be vested in the Settlor during his life.

IN WITNESS, ETC.

Schedules.

THE FIRST SCHEDULE

[*Particulars of Investments*]

THE SECOND SCHEDULE

[*In the first column a list of Charities and in the second column a list of the officers authorised to give receipts and their addresses*]

CHAPTER 5

MARRIAGE SETTLEMENTS

THE marriage of the child of a man of property has for many hundreds of
years been regarded in England as a proper occasion upon which to
transfer part of the family fortune to the younger generation. Of recent
years the strict marriage settlement has suffered a decline in popularity
among all but the very rich, and has to some extent been replaced by the
out-and-out gift or by the settlement made on children while still in their
infancy. In fact, however, a marriage settlement, or marriage gift,
enjoys substantial advantages under the existing revenue law. Indeed,
if it is possible to piece together from the shapeless bulk of revenue legislation any general rules of policy, one such rule must be that marriage
gifts are to be encouraged.[1]

Estate duty

A gift or settlement prima facie becomes liable to estate duty on the
death of the settlor within five years by virtue of section 2 (1) (c) of the
Finance Act, 1894. But it is provided by section 59 (2) of the Finance
(1909–10) Act, 1910, that what may now be called " the five year rule "
shall not apply to gifts which are made in consideration of marriage.

The view was generally held for many years that the exemption provided by the Finance (1909–10) Act, 1910, applied only to gifts made in
favour of the persons " within the marriage consideration," namely the
husband, the wife, and the children and remoter issue of their marriage.
However this view was shown to be wrong by the decision of the House
of Lords in *Rennell* v. *I. R. C.* [1963] 2 W.L.R. 745, where it was held
that a settlement made on the occasion of the marriage of the child of
the settlor, the beneficiaries including persons not within the marriage
consideration, was nevertheless a settlement made in consideration of
marriage, with the result that the settled funds escaped estate duty on
the death of the settlor, even though he failed to survive the five-year
period.[2] As a result of that decision, sections 53 and 64 (dealing with
estate duty and stamp duty respectively) were included in the Finance

---

[1] Unfortunately, by the same type of reasoning, it is almost equally easy to demonstrate
that it is a principle of current revenue law that marriage itself should be discouraged
unless the wife goes out to work.

[2] In the *Rennell* case it was found as a fact that the original intention of the settlor
to make a marriage settlement was never abandoned by him and was not replaced by
an intention to make a family settlement on the occasion of the marriage. Lord
Cohen was not sure that if he had been the trial judge he would have arrived at the
same conclusion of fact: [1963] 2 W.L.R. at p. 760. Apart from s. 53 of the Finance
Act, 1963, it is unlikely that the decision in the *Rennell* case could have been
effectively used in practice in many cases because of the difficulty of producing
evidence to support the necessary finding of fact.

225

Act, 1963. The requirements that must be complied with in order to obtain exemption from estate duty are now in some ways more and in other ways less strict than they were thought to be prior to the decision of the House of Lords in the *Rennell* case.

While the Finance Act, 1963, lays it down clearly who may benefit under a settlement without causing the estate duty and stamp duty exemptions to be lost, the question, how to distinguish a gift made in consideration of marriage from any other type of gift, depends not on statute but on well established rules of common law. Virtually the only assistance given by statute in this respect is given by section 53 (2) of the Finance Act, 1963, which puts beyond doubt that a disposition made by either party to a marriage on or in contemplation of the marriage shall be treated for estate duty purposes as a gift, and not as a disposition for value.

Therefore, before explaining who are now within the " marriage consideration " it may be as well to indicate briefly the ambit of the term " in consideration of marriage."

The gift or settlement must be made before the particular marriage and in contemplation of it; or immediately after and in consideration of it (in practice this means on the day of the wedding); or at any time after the marriage but in pursuance of an agreement made prior to it. Thus a post-nuptial settlement is not made in consideration of the marriage. In practice, it is common for the parties to deal with the matter in two stages, to make an agreement before marriage (sometimes called " marriage articles "), and then at a date subsequent to the marriage to execute a settlement carrying into effect the trusts adumbrated in the articles. There is no special virtue in such an arrangement other than convenience. It retains, perhaps, a certain ritual significance for those who still consider that marriages are best arranged.

The exemption from the five year rule in favour of marriage gifts does not apply to all gifts made in consideration of marriage, but only to gifts *inter vivos* in respect of which liability would otherwise arise on the donor's death within five years under section 2 (1) (c) of the Finance Act, 1894. There is thus no exemption under this head where a settlor reserves to himself a life interest, or where a father having an interest for life in certain property releases it, upon his son's marriage, in order to accelerate the son's reversion, for in each of these cases there is liability apart from the liability in respect of *inter vivos* gifts imposed by section 2 (1) (c).

It is sometimes suggested that it is open to doubt how far the exemption extends to those transactions which are within the charge to duty contained in section 2 (1) (c). The relevant words of section 59 (2) of the Finance (1909–10) Act, 1910, are as follows:

" (2) So much of paragraph (c) of subsection (1) of section two of the Principal Act and this section as makes gifts *inter vivos* property which is deemed to pass on the death of the deceased, shall not apply to gifts which are made in consideration of marriage. . . ."

Section 2 (1) (c), incorporating section 38 (2) of the Customs and Inland Revenue Act, 1881, and section 11 of the Customs and Inland Revenue Act, 1889 (and as subsequently amended), extends the liability for duty to a number of types of property including the following: —

(1) Property taken as a *donatio mortis causa*;

(2) Property taken under a disposition purporting to operate as an immediate gift *inter vivos* not made bona fide five years before the death of the deceased;

(3) Property taken under any gift whenever made of which bona fide possession and enjoyment shall not have been assumed by the donee immediately upon the gift and thenceforward retained to the entire exclusion of the donor or of any benefit to him by contract or otherwise;

(4) Property accruing by survivorship;

(5) Property passing under a revocable settlement.

All of these types of property might possibly be described as "gifts *inter vivos*," and it is arguable that the marriage exemption therefore applies to them all. The better view, however, would seem to be that the exemption is limited to the second head above mentioned, since that head refers in terms to gifts *inter vivos*.

Persons within the marriage consideration

As stated above, section 59 (2) of the Finance (1909–10) Act, 1910, was interpreted by the House of Lords in *Rennell* v. *I. R. C.* [1963] 2 W.L.R. 745 as capable of including gifts on persons not within the "marriage consideration." The law as laid down in the *Rennell* decision continues to apply to any disposition made before April 4, 1963. However, any disposition made on or after that date is subject to section 53 of the Finance Act, 1963, subsection (1) of which is in the following terms:

" In the case of a person dying after the passing of this Act, a disposition purporting to operate as a gift *inter vivos* shall not be treated for the purposes of section 59 (2) of the Finance (1909–10) Act, 1910, as a gift made in consideration of marriage:

(a) in the case of an outright gift, if or in so far as it is a gift to a person other than a party to the marriage;

(b) in the case of any other disposition, if the persons who are or may become entitled to any benefit under the disposition include any person other than:

(i) the parties to the marriage, issue of the marriage, or a wife or husband of any such issue;

(ii) persons becoming entitled on the failure of trusts for any such issue under which trust property would (subject only to any power of appointment to a person falling within sub-paragraph (i) or (iii) of this paragraph) vest indefeasibly on

the attainment of a specified age or either on the attainment of
such an age or on some earlier event, or persons becoming
entitled (subject as aforesaid) on the failure of any limitation
in tail;

(iii) a subsequent wife or husband of a party to the marriage, or
any issue, or the wife or husband of any issue, of a subsequent marriage of either party;

(iv) persons becoming entitled under such trusts, subsisting under
the law of England or of Northern Ireland, as are specified in
section 33 (1) of the Trustee Act, 1925 (protective trusts), the
principal beneficiary being a person falling within sub-
paragraph (i) or (iii) of this subsection, or under such trusts
modified by the enlargement, as respects any period during
which there is no such issue as aforesaid in existence of the
class of potential beneficiaries specified in paragraph (ii) of
the said section 33 (1);

(v) persons becoming entitled under trusts subsisting under the
law of Scotland and corresponding with such trusts as are
mentioned in the foregoing sub-paragraph;

(vi) as respects a reasonable amount by way of remuneration, the
trustees of the settlement."

It is to be observed that the reference to " issue " includes persons
legitimated by a marriage or adopted by the parties to the marriage
jointly: see subsection (3) of section 53.

The law as it stands may be summarised as follows. An outright
gift obtains the exemption if it is a gift to either party to the marriage. A
gift by way of settlement gains the exemption only if the persons who
can possibly benefit under the settlement are limited to the classes
specified in section 53 (1) (b). If any person outside these classes is made
a beneficiary, it appears that exemption is lost for the entire gift, and not
merely to that part of the gift that constitutes bounty to persons not
specified in section 53 (1) (b). The result is to some extent capricious.
A settlement on discretionary trusts for the benefit of the husband, the
wife, their children and remoter issue, any illegitimate children that are
legitimated by the marriage, any subsequent husband or wife of either
party to the marriage and any issue of any subsequent marriage may
be a settlement that enjoys the exemption. But a settlement that
includes any children of a previous marriage may forfeit the exemption:
likewise a settlement which confers upon the husband or wife a power of
appointment in favour of a class other than the husband or wife and any
future spouse or issue of either of them, unless that power is limited to
take effect only in default of prior trusts in favour of issue of the
marriage.

Who may make the gift

It is clear that " gifts " between the parties to the marriage are within section 59 (2) of the Finance (1909–10) Act, 1910. There is, however, little direct authority to show in what circumstances a gift or settlement made by a third party comes within the section. In practice, it is understood, the Revenue authorities concede that gifts by the parent or grandparent of either party to the marriage may qualify and at least one case has been known where the gift of an aunt was admitted to be within the exemption. It is submitted that the section on its true construction extends to all gifts made by any person who by reason of any family or personal relationship has an interest in seeing the marriage established. This would appear to follow from the common law rule relating to marriage as valuable consideration. In *Shadwell* v. *Shadwell* (1860) 9 C.B.(N.S.) 159, an uncle was so delighted at the news of his nephew's engagement that he wrote to him promising to pay him £150 a year until his annual income derived from his profession of a Chancery Barrister should amount to 600 guineas. The Court of Common Pleas held, by a majority, that this promise was given for valuable consideration. " The marriage," said Chief Justice Erle, " primarily affects the parties thereto; but in a secondary degree it may be an object of interest to a near relative and in that sense a benefit to him."

It is submitted that the rule as stated by Chief Justice Erle should be slightly modified, and that it extends not only to near relatives, but to any person who has a genuine interest in seeing the marriage established: such may be employers, god-parents, or personal friends. Once it is admitted that consideration may consist of the benefit derived from seeing a party married, the true test for applying the rule should be the existence of the benefit, not the nature of the relationship between the donor and the married couple. Apart from *Shadwell* v. *Shadwell*, however, judicial comment on this topic has not been plentiful and it cannot therefore be certain what the outcome of litigation in any particular case is likely to be.

Death before the settlement is finally constituted

As stated above, a marriage settlement is often executed after marriage in performance of an agreement made prior to the marriage. This is a matter of convenience, where the exact trusts, or the identity of the property to be settled, cannot be agreed before the marriage is solemnised. There is thus no objection to a pre-nuptial agreement, setting out the trusts and then stating that investments, as yet unascertained, to the value of such-and-such an amount, are to be settled.

It is not, however, the case that estate duty may be avoided by agreeing to settle property and then in fact failing to do so. If the settlor dies before the settlement is finally constituted, so that there is no trust or lien in existence at his death, but only a contract creating a

debt, the rule is that this debt is not deductible in determining the value
of the deceased's estate for estate duty purposes: section 7 (1) (a) of the
Finance Act, 1894; and see *Lord Advocate* v. *Alexander's Trustees* (1905)
42 S.L.R. 307. On the other hand, an agreement, made in consideration
of marriage, to settle specified property actually owned by the settlor
may create a trust or lien of that property forthwith, so that exemption
will be gained if the settlor dies before transferring the property to the
trustees. And if property is transferred or settled pursuant to an ante-
nuptial agreement entered into many years previously, the transferor's or
settlor's death within five years of the actual transfer of the property will
not give rise to a claim. The genuineness of the agreement and that it
was made in consideration of the marriage must, of course, be clearly
established.

Tax on marriage settlements

In the case of marriage settlements or gifts, as with other settlements
or gifts, it is now necessary to consider whether the making of the gift
will give rise to a charge to tax on the settlor or donor under the provisions in the Finance Act, 1962, relating to short-term capital gains.
When the gift would establish a chargeable disposal for the purposes of
these provisions, the settlor and trustees or the donor and donee may
jointly elect that the settlor or donor shall not be subject to a charge to
tax under Case VII of Schedule D and that, for Case VII purposes, the
trustees or donee shall be treated as if the acquisition of the asset in
question by the settlor or donor was their acquisition.[3]

The traditional form of marriage settlement confers life interests on
the husband and wife—usually giving to each a first life interest in the
fund settled by his or her side of the family—and then provides a power
of appointment among the issue, with a gift over among the children of
the marriage in equal shares in default of appointment.

The traditional form is often unsuitable for modern requirements.
For example, if under a settlement in traditional form the ultimate gift
over in default of children of the marriage is to nephews and nieces of the
husband and wife, it may happen that it becomes certain that the
marriage is unlikely to produce children, and yet, since the law does not
presume a woman to be past the age of child-bearing until a fairly late
age,[4] it is not possible for the husband and wife to agree with their
nephews and nieces to put an end to the settlement and divide the capital
between them. Or again, where the parents of the spouses, or of one of
them, makes the settlement, giving life interests to each spouse in turn,
it may well happen that as soon as children are born, the spouses will
find themselves paying a high rate of income tax and surtax on the
settled income, and yet using the whole income for the purpose of maintaining and educating the children.

[3] See Finance Act, 1962. Ninth Schedule, paragraph 3 (2) and (3).
[4] See *post*, p. 285.

This second example will repay closer examination. As has been stated previously, a child may have an income in respect of which he is liable to pay income tax and surtax.[5] As a general rule, however, it is not possible for a parent to settle an income on his own infant child, unless the whole income (in excess of five pounds a year) is to be accumulated. Section 397 of the Income Tax Act, 1952, as amended, has the effect of causing such income if not accumulated to be treated as the income of the parent for the purposes of tax. On the other hand, a grandparent may effectively settle income on his grandchildren so that it is treated as their income, with the advantages as regards personal reliefs and allowances that may be thereby enjoyed.

The view was at one time held that it might be advantageous to let the grandparent settle on the parent for life, and subject thereto to the children, and then, as each child is born, let the parent release part of his life interest, thereby accelerating the reversion of the child, and enabling the income to be applied for the maintenance and education of the child. This view is not now tenable. The rule must now, since the decision in *I. R. C.* v. *Buchanan* [1958] Ch. 289; 37 Tax Cas. 365, be accepted as established that a parent who releases his life interest so as to benefit his own children as remaindermen is himself a " settlor " within the meaning of section 403 of the Income Tax Act, 1952: in consequence, the income of the settled fund after the release is, to the extent to which it is used for the maintenance or education of the children of the life tenant, deemed to be income of the life tenant for tax purposes. There is clearly a measure of rough justice in treating income which becomes payable to the remainderman by reason of the life tenant's surrender of his interest as having been provided by the life tenant.

It may, however, be observed that if the father of the bride has made a marriage settlement and subsequently his daughter releases her life interest in favour of her infant child, there are two " settlors." Consequently the provisions of section 401 apply and it is only income " originating " from the infant's parent which can be treated as the parent's income under section 397. Having regard to the manner in which income " originating " from a settlor is defined, it is submitted that no income can be attributed to the life tenant who has released her interest. This argument was accepted by the Special Commissioners in *I. R. C.* v. *Buchanan* [1958] Ch. 289, did not form part of the reasoning of the learned judge in the High Court and was dismissed in a word by the Court of Appeal on the grounds that a testator (the trust arose under a will in that case) could not be a " settlor."

A possible solution, it is suggested, is for a marriage settlement to provide that the children are to receive incomes of their own as soon as they are born. Where only a modest sum is settled, it may be convenient to provide that the whole of the income of the settled fund is

to go to the children of the marriage as soon as a child is born. The child
or children would, through their parents or the trustees, make a claim
each year for repayment to them of so much of the tax deducted at
source as represented his or their reliefs and allowances; and the child's
parent would not be liable to include the income of the fund in his total
income for surtax purposes.

Where a more substantial sum is settled, it may be advisable to
provide that a fraction of the income is to be diverted to each child.
Such a form of settlement could, it is suggested, in certain circumstances
confer greater financial benefits on the parties to the marriage than a
settlement in traditional form. In other cases a discretionary settlement
for the benefit of the parties to a marriage and their children might
offer the greatest advantage. Again, the traditional form of settlement
could be employed, giving life interests to the husband and wife with
remainder to the issue, but providing, however, that, during such time as
there are in existence infant children of the marriage, the trustees are
to have an overriding discretion to apply any part of the income of the
settled funds for their benefit.

It is considered that, having regard to the definition of the word
" settlor " in section 403 of the Income Tax Act, 1952, a person who
agrees to marry in consideration, or partly in consideration, of his
prospective father-in-law providing a settlement for the benefit of the
future children of the marriage, is clearly not a settlor.

Stamp duty

A gift or settlement made in consideration of marriage is not a voluntary disposition *inter vivos* for the purposes of section 74 (1) of the
Finance (1909-10) Act, 1910, and therefore the rates introduced by that
Act (which have since varied so that they now stand at 10s. for every
£50 of the value of the property comprised in the gift or settlement) do
not apply. Until the decision in *Rennell* v. *I. R. C.* [1963] 2 W.L.R.
745, it was not certain to what extent a gift could be said to be made in
consideration of marriage if it benefited persons other than persons
" within the marriage consideration," that is, the husband, the wife and
the future children and remoter issue of the marriage.

The *Rennell* decision is no longer law, and the position is now established by section 64 of the Finance Act, 1963. This lays it down that
marriage shall not be deemed to be the consideration for a conveyance
or transfer " except in so far as the conveyance or transfer is a disposition
such as, in the case of a person dying after the passing of this Act, would
be treated for estate duty purposes as a gift made in consideration of
marriage."

The reference to estate duty directs the reader's attention to section
53 of the Finance Act, 1963, which has been dealt with earlier in this
chapter. That section lists the classes of persons who are for estate duty
purposes deemed to be within the marriage consideration. The use of the

phrase " except in so far as " seems to indicate that partial exemption may be obtainable. If this is correct, the position, so far as concerns stamp duty, is that the assets settled must be valued, and notionally divided into two parts, one part representing the value of the interests taken by persons within the marriage consideration for the purposes of section 53, the other part the value of the interests of other persons. It is only the first of these two elements that obtains exemption from stamp duty.

PRECEDENT No. 28

Short Form of Marriage Articles in Consideration of the Marriage of the Son of the Settlor

It may sometimes happen that a settlor makes up his mind to create a settlement upon the occasion of the marriage of a child, without leaving a sufficient period of time before the marriage in which to settle the exact form of the trust, or even to come to a final decision as to which property is to be put into the settlement.

In such circumstances a document along the lines of the following precedent may prove useful. However, it is emphasised that such a document should never be allowed to become a substitute for a proper marriage settlement. If the alternative in clauses 1 and 4 of the precedent is adopted of simply stating the value of the investments intended to be settled, without specifying them, it must not be forgotten, that until the covenant has been performed by the settlor selecting investments and transferring them to the trustees, no saving of estate duty may be obtained in the event of the settlor's death. On the other hand, once the covenant has been performed, the settled fund is taken out of charge to estate duty on the death of the settlor, even though he may not survive the five-year period.

Parties.   **THESE MARRIAGE ARTICLES** are made the —— day of —— BETWEEN —— of —— (hereinafter called " the Settlor ") of the first part —— of —— (hereinafter called " the Husband ") of the second part —— of —— (hereinafter called " the Wife ") of the third part and —— of —— and —— of —— (hereinafter called " the Trustees ") of the fourth part;

Intended. Marriage.   WHEREAS a Marriage is intended shortly to be solemnised between the Husband (who is the son of the Settlor) and the Wife;

Witnesseth.   Now in consideration of the said marriage THIS DEED WITNESSETH and it is agreed as follows:

Settlement.   **1.** The Settlor shall settle [the investments and property mentioned in the Schedule hereto] [investments and property having a value at the time of the transfer hereinafter mentioned of not less than —— pounds].

Transfer.   **2.** The said investments and property shall be transferred into the joint names or control of the Trustees before or within six months after solemnisation of the said marriage.

Terms of Settlement.   **3.** Before or within six months after solemnisation of the said marriage the Trustees shall cause to be prepared a Settlement or Settlements relating to the said investments and property and containing the following provisions :

(1) Such trusts and such powers and discretions exercisable by such person or persons and such conditions limitations and provisions for accumulation maintenance advancement forfeiture and defeasance as the Trustees shall in their absolute discretion (but during the lifetime of the Settlor not without his consent in writing) think fit : provided that no persons other than the Husband the Wife and the children and remoter issue of the said marriage and the other persons mentioned in section 53 (1) (b) of the Finance Act 1963 shall be included as objects of any such trust power or discretion ;

(2) Such full and wide powers of investment improvement of trust property effecting of insurance selling leasing mortgaging and managing trust property appropriation borrowing and such indemnities and professional charging clauses as the Trustees shall reasonably require ;

(3) A provision giving power of appointing trustees to the Settlor during his life and thereafter to the Husband during his life.

(4) A provision excluding the Settlor and any spouse of the Settlor from benefiting under the Settlement.

Power to accept property.   **4.** [The Trustees may in their absolute discretion accept other property which they consider to be of equal value in place of any investment or property hereby agreed to be settled.] [The Trustees may in their absolute discretion accept any property upon such valuation as they may think fit in satisfaction of the obligation of the Settlor to make the Settlement hereinbefore mentioned.]

Original Trustees.   5. The Trustees shall be the original trustees of the said Settlement and the expression " the Trustees " shall therein be defined as meaning the Trustees for the time being hereof.

Time for marriage.   6. These Articles shall be void unless the said intended marriage takes place within three months of the date hereof.

IN WITNESS, ETC.

THE SCHEDULE

[*List of Investments.*]

PRECEDENT NO. 29

Settlement Made in Consideration of the Marriage of the Daughter of the Settlor

This precedent is intended for the situation where, before the marriage takes place, the wife's father settles a modest fund of investments with a view to providing ultimately for the children of the marriage but so that until any child is born the income of the settled fund will be payable to the wife.

Until a child is born, the income will be that of the wife, and the husband will be assessed to income tax and, if appropriate, surtax in respect of it. As soon as a child is born, the income will be diverted to the child, so that the trustees may accumulate income or may apply it for the child's maintenance: in either case, the income will be that of the child, not of the husband and wife, for tax purposes.

The Deed should be stamped 10s.

Parties.   THIS DEED OF MARRIAGE SETTLEMENT is made the —— day of —— 19— BETWEEN —— of —— (hereinafter called " the Settlor ") of the first part —— of —— (hereinafter called " the Husband ") of the second part —— of —— (hereinafter called " the Wife ") of the third part and —— of —— and —— of —— (hereinafter called " the Trustees " which expression where the context admits shall include the survivor of them or other the trustees or trustee for the time being of these presents) of the fourth part;
WHEREAS :

Intended marriage.

Agreement for Settlement.

Witnesseth.

Trusts until marriage.

Trust for sale.

Overriding power of appointment.

(A) A marriage is intended shortly to be solemnised between the Husband and the Wife who is the daughter of the Settlor;

(B) The Settlor has agreed with the Husband and the Wife that in consideration of the said marriage duly taking place he will make provision for the Husband and the Wife and the issue that may be borne to them and has in pursuance of the said agreement caused to be transferred into the joint names of the Trustees the investments mentioned in the Schedule hereto;

NOW in pursuance of the said Agreement and in consideration of the said intended marriage THIS DEED WITNESSETH and it is hereby declared as follows:

1. THE Settlor hereby directs the Trustees that the Trustees shall stand possessed of the investments specified in the Schedule hereto Upon Trust for the Settlor until the said intended marriage and after the solemnisation thereof Upon the trusts and subject to the powers and provisions hereinafter declared concerning the same.

2. THE Trustees shall stand possessed of the investments specified in the Schedule hereto Upon Trust that the Trustees may either allow the same or any part or parts thereof to remain as actually invested so long as the Trustees shall think fit or may at any time or times with the consent of the Settlor during his lifetime and after his death with the consent of the Husband during his lifetime and thereafter at the discretion of the Trustees sell call in or convert into money the same or any part thereof and shall with the like consents or at the like discretion invest the moneys produced thereby and any other capital moneys which may be received by the Trustees in respect of the trust premises in the names or under the control of the Trustees in or upon any investments hereby authorised with power with such consents or at such discretion as aforesaid to vary or transpose any investments for others of any nature hereby authorised.

3. THE Trustees shall stand possessed of the said investments and the money and investments for the time being representing the same (hereinafter called "the Trust Fund") Upon Trust for such one or more or all of the children who may be borne by the Wife to the

Husband and at such age or time or respective ages or times if more than one and in such shares and with such trusts for their respective benefit and such provisions for their respective advancement and maintenance and education at the discretion of the Trustees or of any other person or persons as the Husband and Wife during their joint lives and the survivor of them during his or her life shall within twenty-one years of the execution hereof appoint.

4. In default of and until and subject to any such appointment as aforesaid the Trustees shall stand possessed of the Trust Fund Upon the Trusts following namely :

Income to wife.
(1) The income of the Trust Fund accruing before the Closing Date (which expression where it occurs herein has the meaning hereinafter assigned to it) shall so long as there is not actually living any child borne by the Wife to the Husband be paid to the Wife ;

Income and capital to children.
(2) Subject thereto the Trust Fund and the income thereof shall be held in trust for such child or children borne hereafter by the Wife to the Husband before the Closing Date as shall attain the age of twenty-one years and if more than one in equal shares And to this trust section 31 of the Trustee Act 1925 shall apply save that the proviso to section 31 (1) shall not apply ;

(3) Subject thereto the Trust Fund shall be held In Trust for the Wife absolutely.

The foregoing two clauses may be modified to suit individual circumstances. Thus the income may be given to the husband and wife equally, rather than to the wife alone, or provision may be made for the husband in the event of the wife predeceasing him. Where a very large sum is settled, it would be advisable, perhaps, to provide that, as each child is born, part only of the Trust Fund should be allotted to that child, the rest still being held upon trust for the husband and wife. It must be emphasised that, as it stands, the precedent does not provide for the husband and wife once their children have grown up. There would be no objection to adapting this precedent, so that, although each child enjoys the benefit of the income until his majority, or until the April 6 after the date on which he attains his majority, the income or capital thereafter reverts to the husband or wife as the case may be.

Investment.
5. Money to be invested under the trusts hereof may be applied or invested in the purchase of or at interest

upon the security of such shares stocks funds securities land or other investments or property of whatever nature and wheresoever situate and whether involving liabilities or not or upon such personal credit with or without security as the Trustees shall in their absolute discretion think fit and to the intent that the Trustees shall have the same powers in all respects as if they were absolute owners beneficially entitled.

Trustee indemnity.

6. THE Trustees (which term for the purpose of this clause includes any of them or any person or body corporate appointed to be a trustee of this Settlement but does not include any Trustee charging remuneration) shall not be liable for the consequences of any error or forgetfulness whether of law or fact on the part of any of the Trustees or their legal or other advisers or generally for any breach of duty or trust whatsoever unless it shall be proved to have been committed given or omitted in personal conscious bad faith by the Trustee charged to be so liable

And accordingly all persons claiming any beneficial interest in over or upon the property subject to this Settlement shall be deemed to take with notice of and subject to the protection hereby conferred on the Trustees.

Trustee charging.

7. ANY Trustee being a solicitor accountant or other person engaged in any profession or business shall be entitled to be paid all usual professional or proper charges for business transacted time expended and acts done by him or any partner of his in connection with the trusts hereof including acts which a Trustee not being in any profession or business could have done personally.

New Trustees.

8. THE power of appointing new Trustees hereof shall be vested in the Settlor during his life and after his death shall be vested in the Husband and the Wife jointly during their joint lives and in the survivor of them during his or her life but neither the Settlor nor any person for the time being the Wife of the Settlor shall in any circumstances be appointed a trustee hereof.

Closing date.

9. THE expression " the Closing Date " wherever it occurs in this Settlement means the day upon which the

age of twenty-one years is attained by that child hereafter borne by the Wife to the Husband who first attains
that age or the day on which the wife attains the age of
fifty years or the first anniversary of the death of the
Husband whichever day first occurs.

IN WITNESS, ETC.

THE SCHEDULE

[List of Investments.]

PRECEDENT No. 30

Settlement Made in Consideration of the Marriage of the Daughter of the Settlor

This precedent is intended for the situation where a substantial sum
of investments is settled by the wife's father, who wishes to retain the
traditional form of marriage settlement whereby the wife's fund is settled
upon the wife for life, with power to appoint a life interest to the
husband if he survives her, and so that the capital is settled upon the
children of the marriage, subject to powers of appointment in favour
of children and remoter issue.

The trustees have very wide overriding powers, which are contained
in clause 3. During a stated period, taken in this precedent as 20 years,
the trustees have a power to resettle the whole Trust Fund for the
benefit of the wife and the issue of the marriage: during the life
of the settlor his consent is a prerequisite to the exercise of this power.
As soon as children are born to the marriage the trustees have a discretionary power relating to the income of the settled fund: they can,
during such time as any child of the marriage is living and an infant,
pay or apply income for the benefit of that child without the consent of
the wife or husband. It is reasonably clear that any income so applied
by the trustees is income of the child in question (see *Drummond* v.
Collins [1915] A.C. 1011), and is not income of the husband or wife.
Were the consent of the husband or wife made a prerequisite to the
exercise by the trustees of this power, it is considered that they would
become settlors within the meaning of section 403 of the Income Tax
Act, 1952, so that the income applied for the benefit of the children
would be treated as income of the wife or husband for tax purposes.

It will be observed that the situation contemplated is that the settlement is made after the marriage, in performance of an antenuptial
agreement.

Parties.

THIS DEED OF MARRIAGE SETTLEMENT is made the —— day of —— 19— BETWEEN —— of —— (hereinafter called " the Settlor ") of the first part —— of —— (hereinafter called " the Husband ") of the second part —— of —— (hereinafter called " the Wife ") of the third part and —— of —— and —— of —— (hereinafter called " the Trustees " which expression where the context admits shall include the survivor of them or other the trustees or trustee for the time being of these presents) of the fourth part;

Recitals:

Marriage.

WHEREAS :

(A) The Husband and Wife were married on the —— day of —— and previous to such marriage the Settlor who is the Father of the Wife agreed with the Husband and the Wife that in consideration of such marriage taking place he would make such Settlement as is hereinafter contained;

Transfer.

(B) The Settlor has accordingly transferred into the joint names or control of the Trustees the investments mentioned in the Schedule;

Witnesseth.

NOW in pursuance of the said Agreement **THIS DEED WITNESSETH** and it is hereby declared as follows :

Retain or sell.

1. THE Trustees shall stand possessed of the investments specified in the Schedule hereto Upon Trust that the Trustees may either allow the same or any part or parts thereof respectively to remain as actually invested so long as the Trustees think fit or may at any time or times with the consent of the Settlor during his life and after his death at the discretion of the Trustees sell call in or convert into money the same or any part thereof and shall with the like consent or at the like discretion invest the moneys produced thereby and also all capital moneys which may be received in respect of the said investments in the names or under the control of the Trustees in or upon any investments hereby authorised with power with such consent or at such discretion as aforesaid to vary or transpose any investments for or into others of any nature hereby authorised.

Primary trusts:

2. THE Trustees shall stand possessed of the said investments and the money and investments for the time being representing the same (hereinafter called " the

Trust Fund ") subject to each and every exercise of the powers and discretions conferred upon the Trustees by Clause 3 hereof upon the following Trusts namely :

Wife's life interest.

(1) Upon trust to pay the income thereof to the Wife during her life and

Income to Husband.

(2) After her death upon trust to pay to the Husband such part or parts or the whole of the income thereof during his life or during such lesser period as the Wife may [by deed or deeds revocable or irrevocable or] by will or codicil appoint and

Issue.

(3) Subject thereto upon trust as to the capital and income thereof for all or such one or more exclusively of the others or other of the children child or remoter issue of the Husband and Wife at such age or time or respective ages or times if more than one in such shares and with such trusts for their respective benefit and such provisions for their respective advancement maintenance and education at the discretion of the Trustees or of any other person or persons as the Wife shall by any deed or deeds revocable or irrevocable or by will or codicil appoint and in default of and subject to any such appointment

Children.

(4) Upon trust for all or any the children or child of the Husband and Wife who being male attain the age of twenty-one years or being female attain that age or marry and if more than one in equal shares and

Wife.

(5) Subject to the foregoing trusts and powers Upon Trust for the Wife absolutely.

Powers and discretions.

3. NOTWITHSTANDING the trusts and powers hereinbefore contained the Trustees shall have the following overriding powers and discretions namely :

Power to apply income for children.

(1) During such time as there shall be living an infant child or infant children of the Husband and Wife and whether or not the Husband or Wife shall then be living the Trustees shall have power to deal with the whole or any part or parts of the income of the Trust Fund as it comes into their hands by paying or applying the same to or for the benefit of all or any one or more of such child or children of the Husband and Wife in such shares and in such manner as the Trustees in their absolute discretion from time to time think fit and

Power to declare new trusts

(2) During the period of twenty years from and after the execution of this Deed the Trustees being at least two in number shall have power by deed or deeds revocable or irrevocable [but during the life of the Settlor not without his consent in writing] at any time or times to appoint and declare such trusts in respect of any part or parts of the Trust Fund or the income thereof for or for the benefit of any one or more of the following namely the Wife the Husband and the children or remoter issue of the Husband and Wife with such provisions for maintenance education or advancement or for forfeiture in the event of bankruptcy or otherwise and subject to such gifts over conditions limitations and such powers and discretions exerciseable by such person or persons whether or not being the Trustees and generally in such manner as the Trustees in their absolute discretion shall think fit;

PROVIDED ALWAYS THAT:

Power to release.

(a) the Trustees may at any time or times by deed or deeds either wholly or partially release any of the powers conferred upon them by this Clause as if the same were conferred upon them beneficially and not in any fiduciary capacity and

Exclusion of settlor and his wife.

(b) none of the powers conferred upon the Trustees by this Clause shall be exercised so as to benefit either directly or indirectly either the Settlor or any person for the time being the wife of the Settlor.

Investment.

4. MONEY to be invested (*etc., copy or adapt the investment clauses from pages 146, 237*).

Trustee indemnity.

5. THE Trustees (*etc., see the trustee indemnity on page 238*).

Charging.

6. ANY Trustee (*etc., see page 238*).

New trustees.

7. THE power of appointing new Trustees hereof shall be exercised by the Settlor during his life [and after his death by the Wife during her life] [and after her death by the Husband during his life] but the Settlor shall in no circumstances be appointed a Trustee hereof.

IN WITNESS, ETC.

THE SCHEDULE

[*List of Investments.*]

PRECEDENT No. 31

Deed of Gift made after a Marriage whereby in Performance of an Ante-nuptial Agreement a Third Party Transfers to the Husband and Wife a House to be Held by Them as Joint Tenants

The situation visualised is that a relative of the husband or wife, wishing to provide them with a house, was unable to find sufficient ready money, or a suitable house, before the marriage was solemnised, and therefore made a mere verbal or written agreement to transfer into their joint names property of a named value. A suitable house now having been found and purchased by the donor, who has taken a conveyance into his own name, he conveys it into the names of the husband and wife. An alternative method of completing the gift would be for the vendor to convey direct to the husband and wife.

It is considered that no estate duty will be payable on the death of the donor in respect of the subject-matter of the gift even though he may die within the five-year period : see *ante*, p. 225.

Stamp duty of 10s. is payable on the deed.

Parties.

THIS DEED OF GIFT is made the —— day of —— 19— BETWEEN —— of —— (hereinafter called " the Donor ") of the one part and —— of —— and —— of —— (hereinafter called " the Husband " and " the Wife " respectively) of the other part :

WHEREAS :

Antecedent agreement.

(A) The Husband and the Wife were married on the —— day of —— and on or about the —— day of —— 19— in contemplation of such marriage the Donor agreed [in writing] [orally] with the Husband and the Wife to convey or transfer to the Husband and the Wife as joint tenants as soon as he could conveniently do so after the said marriage and in any event within one year thereof investments land or other property to the value of £—— ;

Agreement to convey.

(B) The house and land mentioned in the Schedule hereto are of the value of £—— as the parties hereto hereby acknowledge and the parties hereto have agreed that the Donor shall convey the same to the Husband and Wife in full performance of the agreement hereinbefore recited ;

Witnesseth.

NOW THIS DEED WITNESSETH and it is agreed and declared as follows :

Conveys.   1. THE Donor as Settlor hereby conveys unto the Husband and Wife the property mentioned in the Schedule hereto To HOLD unto the Husband and Wife in fee simple as joint tenants.

Joint tenancy.   2. THE Husband and Wife shall stand possessed of the said property upon trust to sell the same with power at their discretion to postpone any such sale and shall stand possessed of the net proceeds of sale after payment of expenses and of the net rents and profits until sale after payment of rates taxes repairs and other expenses and outgoings In Trust for the Husband and Wife as joint tenants beneficially.

IN WITNESS, ETC.

THE SCHEDULE

[Description of house and land.]

Since this deed will form a document of title to the house and land, but will be unlikely ever to form a root of title, the most convenient description would normally be by reference to some earlier conveyance.

CHAPTER 6

INSURANCE POLICIES

THE existing law provides extensive exemptions and reliefs from the burden of income tax and estate duty, where policies of insurance have been effected.[1] Indeed the present position is such that this form of saving may be said to receive preferential treatment under the tax and estate duty code. The relevant rules are technical and all but capricious in operation. The purpose of this chapter is to state some of the ways in which the advantages may be obtained and the more obvious pitfalls avoided.

Income tax

Section 219 of the Income Tax Act, 1952, provides relief from income tax, but not from surtax,[2] in respect of premiums paid by the taxpayer on certain types of policy. Subsection (3) indicates the type of policy in respect of which relief may be claimed. Generally, the policy must be one securing a capital sum on death, whether or not in conjunction with any other benefit. The life assured may be that of the taxpayer or his wife. Subsection (4) also provides relief where the premium is paid by a wife in respect of an insurance on her life or that of her husband. The reliefs are available even though the policy has been assigned or charged or made subject to a trust. Thus the reliefs are available even where the policy in question has been made subject to a trust, under the Married Women's Property Act, 1882, or otherwise, with a view to reducing the burden of estate duty.

Broadly, in the case of insurance made after 1916, the relief is given from income tax at the standard rate on two-fifths of the amount of the premium, but sections 219 and 226 of the Income Tax Act, 1952, qualify the relief by reference to the total income of the claimant and the capital value of the sum assured under the policy in question. In the case of insurance made before 1916 the terms of the reliefs are governed by the provisions in sections 225 and 226 of the Income Tax Act, 1952.

One of the ways in which an insurance policy could be employed as an instrument of tax avoidance was at one time to pay the first premium on a policy, and then to borrow each subsequent premium from the insurance company, charging the policy with repayment thereof. Thus, in case of a " with profits " policy, the assured would be able to gain considerable surtax relief in respect of the interest on the borrowed

---

[1] See *Income Distribution and Social Change* by Richard M. Titmuss at Appendix E.
[2] See Finance Act, 1957, s. 14.

premiums, while at the same time building up a substantial asset in the policy at no cost to himself beyond the initial premium. Now, however, borrowings against policies are subject to the stringent provisions of sections 241 and 481 of the Income Tax Act, 1952.[3]

Estate duty: gifts of policies

Where the holder of a fully paid up policy gives away or settles the policy, liability to estate duty under section 2 (1) (c) of the Finance Act, 1894 (imposing estate duty upon gifts *inter vivos*), as modified by section 64 of the Finance Act, 1960 (providing relief where the donor dies more than two years but less than five years after making the gift), is likely to arise on his death in the same way as if the gift were of any other kind of property. The question may arise after five years, whether there is a passing on the donor's death under section 2 (1) (d) of the Finance Act, 1894. This enactment brings into charge to duty " any . . . interest . . . provided by the deceased . . . to the extent of the beneficial interest accruing or arising . . . on the death of the deceased."

It is established by the decisions of the House of Lords in *D'Avigdor-Goldsmid* v. *I. R. C.* [1953] A.C. 347 and *Westminster Bank* v. *I. R. C.*, *Wrightson* v. *I. R. C.* [1958] A.C. 210, that no liability arises under section 2 (1) (d) merely by reason of the fact that policy moneys become payable on the death of the life assured. A policy of insurance is the same chose in action before, as after, the death of the life assured. Neither its increase in value upon that death nor the fact that moneys become payable thereunder upon that death are benefits accruing, or arising within the meaning of section 2 (1) (d). On the other hand, the circumstances of a particular case may bring in section 2 (1) (d): as where the identity of the person entitled to the policy moneys cannot be ascertained until the death of the life assured. For example, when the policy is written in favour of the wife of the assured if she survives the assured and, subject thereto, for the children of the assured. In such circumstances the identity of the person who becomes entitled to the policy moneys is only established at the date of the death of the life assured.

In many cases where a policy is the subject-matter of gift, it is not yet fully paid up, and the donor goes on paying premiums after making the gift, although he is under no obligation to do so. A curious point arises here. Where a man pays a premium on a policy which is not his property—for example a policy which he has given or settled—there is no general presumption that he intends to make a gift of the premium. Unless the beneficial owners of the policy are persons in whose favour the presumption of advancement operates—for example the wife or children of the donor—or unless there is some evidence of an intention to

---

[3] Contrast *I. R. C.* v. *Wesleyan and General Assurance Society* (1948) 30 Tax Cas. 11, and see generally an article by William Phillips in [1961] B.T.R. 351, where this topic is fully discussed.

make a gift of the premium, payment of the premium may create a lien on the policy in favour of the donor: see *Re Smith* [1937] 3 All E.R. 472. Therefore in some circumstances it may be advisable for the donor to address a short memorandum to the donee or trustees to whom the policy has been transferred, stating that no future payment of premiums is to give rise to any lien unless otherwise expressly declared in writing at the time of payment.

Where a donor intends to make provision for a donee by means of a policy which has still to be effected, he should not enter into any covenant that he will do all things to procure the issue of the policy, at least when the policy is a single premium policy. The Estate Duty Office have been known to take the point that entering into such a covenant is itself a disposition on the part of the donor within the meaning of section 45 (1) of the Finance Act, 1940. By reason of the provisions in section 18 (1) and (2) of the Finance Act, 1957, the property in question for estate duty purposes might then be traced into the policies. And this property, so the argument runs, would be aggregated with other property passing: see section 45 (3) of the Finance Act, 1940, and section 38 (10) of the Finance Act, 1957.

Section 34 of the Finance Act, 1959

This section has greatly simplified the law relating to estate duty on gifts of policies that are not fully paid up at the time of the gift. The section does not affect any liability that may arise under section 2 (1) (d) of the Finance Act, 1894. It does, however, in most cases reduce what would otherwise have been the amount of liability to duty under section 2 (1) (c) of the Finance Act, 1894. The charge under section 2 (1) (c) extended to money received under a policy of assurance when the policy was kept up by a donor for the benefit of a donee by virtue of the provisions in section 11 of the Customs and Inland Revenue Act, 1889, which are incorporated in section 2 (1) (c).

At the risk of over-simplification, the position may be stated as follows. Every payment of a premium by way of gift is treated as a gift of a slice of the benefits under the policy. The slice is computed by comparing the amount of the premium in question with the aggregate amount of all the premiums paid in respect of the policy. It is not possible to ascribe to the earlier premiums any additional share of the benefits under the policy, notwithstanding that the earlier premiums would have been accumulating in the hands of the insurance company longer than the later premiums, and thus contributing more to the benefits received under the policy.

To see how these rules work in practice, one may take the example of a man who has insured his own life for £20,000, and has paid fourteen annual premiums. He transfers the policy to his wife by way of absolute gift, and goes on paying the premiums. He dies six years after making the gift, having paid six premiums since the date of the gift.

One first must ascertain how many premiums were paid in the five-year period preceding death. Assume that a premium was paid in each year of the five. Then the slice of the policy ascribable to the earlier premiums, *i.e.*, fifteen-twentieths, or £15,000, is free of estate duty. The balance, namely £5,000, is liable to bear estate duty. Each of the five premiums paid within the five-year period is thus represented by £1,000. It is necessary, however, to ascertain which premiums were paid within two, three and four years of the death, in order to apply section 64 of the Finance Act, 1960, and to determine what slice of each sum of £1,000 is deemed to pass and thus bear duty.

If, when proposing to make the gift of the policy to his wife in the above example, the deceased had desired to reduce the liability to estate duty, he might have considered the following possibilities:

(1) He could have given the policy to his wife, and allowed her to pay the further premiums, giving her sufficient cash to do so. The whole of the policy moneys would thus have avoided estate duty. Admittedly the gifts of cash would be prima facie liable for duty, but they might well be exempt as part of normal and reasonable expenditure under section 59 (2) of the Finance (1909–10) Act, 1910; moreover, they would almost certainly amount to much less than £5,000.

(2) He could have converted the existing policy into a fully paid up policy and effected a fresh policy under the Married Women's Property Act, 1882. This would have the advantage of separate aggregation.

(3) He could have surrendered the existing policy, using the moneys to pay the first premium on a fresh policy effected under the Married Women's Property Act, 1882. Alternatively, he could in some other way have converted the existing policy into a policy under the Act in such a way that he did not have an interest in the fresh policy.

(4) Had the gift of the policy been made in consideration of his marriage, he could have covenanted with his wife to keep up the policy. Consequently the whole of the policy moneys would have been exempt from estate duty on his death under section 59 (2) of the Finance (1909–10) Act, 1910.

In each of the above cases income tax relief under section 219 of the Income Tax Act, 1952, could still be obtained.

Policies as separate estates: non-aggregation

Very often a policy of insurance is effected with a view to reducing the estate duty payable by ensuring that, even if the policy moneys pass on the death of the assured, they bear duty at a rate which is ascertained by treating the policy moneys, or some beneficial interest in them, as an estate by itself, not to be aggregated with the other property passing. Such separate aggregation may further reduce the duty payable since the aggregate value of the other assets passing on the death may then be such that a lower rate of duty will be payable in respect of them also.

In order to achieve this result the provisions contained in the proviso to section 4 of the Finance Act, 1894, must be satisfied. As subsequently amended by section 12 (1) of the Finance Act, 1900, these are as follows:

" Provided that any property so passing, in which the deceased never had an interest, shall not be aggregated with any other property but shall be an estate by itself, and the estate duty shall be levied at the proper graduated rate on the principal value thereof."

The problem, therefore, is to effect a policy in such a way that the life assured never has an interest in the policy, although he pays all the premiums necessary to effect it and keep it up. The usual solution to this problem is to create by way of trust a gift to which the policy is subject from the moment of its inception, and under which the life assured, namely, the donor or settlor, has no beneficial interest of whatever kind.

It might be suggested that, if a gift is charged with estate duty under section 2 (1) (c) of the Finance Act, 1894, by reason of the donor dying within the five-year period, the gift must of necessity be property in which the donor had an interest, so that in consequence there can be no separate aggregation. This view gains some support from a dictum of Lord Macintosh in the Court of Session in *Potter* v. *I. R. C.* (1958) 37 A.T.C. 58 at p. 65, and at first sight it seems plausible. How can a man be said not to have had any interest in property when he was the man who made a gift of it ? It is considered, however, that this view is incorrect. So far as is known, it is not taken by the Estate Duty Office. Moreover, section 33 (2) of the Finance Act, 1954, and section 34 of the Finance Act, 1959, both of which deal with estate duty on policies of insurance, are more readily reconcilable with the contrary view.

The true situation, it is submitted, is that it is possible for a gift to be made of property in which the donor never had an interest. Suppose a man wishes to give his wife a present, and tells her to choose a brooch. She goes to the shop, accompanied by her husband, and chooses a brooch, the husband standing by silently—or at any rate without saying anything that indicates to the shop assistant that it is he and not his wife who intends to pay for the brooch. The shop assistant thus sells the brooch to the wife. The ownership of the brooch passes directly from the vendors to the wife, so that the husband at no time has any interest therein. All that the husband does is to sign a cheque for the purchase price and hand it to the shop assistant. He has thus made a gift of a brooch in which he himself never had an interest.

Similarly, if a husband takes out a policy of insurance on his own life, and makes an effective declaration of trust of the policy in favour of his wife, either before or at the same time as taking out the policy, he has made a gift of the policy in favour of his wife, but has never had an interest in the subject-matter of the gift. Section 34 (2) of the Finance

Act, 1959, provides that where a premium is paid by way of gift, the payment is to be treated as a gift " of rights under the policy ": thus this enactment does not change the existing legal position whereby the donor paying the premium has no interest in the subject-matter of the gift, which is not the premium but the beneficial interest in the policy.

If in a particular case the decision is taken to effect a policy which is to be a separate estate on the death of the assured, a number of intricate points of law must be kept in mind.

(i) *The policy must be subject to a trust*

The situation under consideration is that a man of property wishes to insure his life for a substantial sum of money, in order that the cash may be made available on his death to the person or persons upon whom the burden of estate duty is likely to fall. In order to ensure that he never has an interest in the policy, the assured must create a trust as mentioned above. Where the person whom it is desired to benefit is the spouse or child of the assured, it is possible to create the trust by simply causing the policy to be issued with a memorandum endorsed thereon stating that the policy is effected for the benefit of the wife or children of the assured in accordance with section 11 of the Married Women's Property Act, 1882.

Section 11 of the Married Women's Property Act, 1882, does not in itself cause any saving of estate duty. It does nothing more than allow a trust to be created with economy of language. The most important part of the section simply provides that a policy of assurance effected by a man on his own life, and expressed to be for the benefit of his wife or of his children or of his wife and children or any of them, or by any woman on her own life, and expressed to be for the benefit of her husband, or of her children, or of her husband and children or any of them, shall create a trust in favour of the objects therein named, and the moneys payable under any such policy shall not, so long as any object of the trust remains unperformed, form part of the estate of the insured. Thus, where a policy is effected under section 11 of the Act, an immediate equitable interest is created in favour of the objects named: see *Cousins* v. *Sun Life Assurance Society* [1933] Ch. 126.

Although in practice resort is usually had to a policy under the Married Women's Property Act, it is possible to achieve a similar result by means of a carefully worded nomination policy, or by means of a policy effected at the same time as or immediately after the execution of a settlement, whereby the insured creates trusts in respect of his entire interest in the policy. In practice, the better course is to draft a formal declaration of trust, since if an attempt is made to draft a nomination policy, there is a risk that instead of creating a trust (as in *Re Webb* [1941] Ch. 225) the words used will be construed as an attempt to create a *jus quaesitum tertio*, an attempt which is bound to be ineffectual under English law, though not under Scots law: see *Re Engelbach's Estate* [1924] 2 Ch. 348; *Re Sinclair's Life Policy* [1938] Ch. 799.

(ii) *The settlor must have no interest in the policy*

Thus a policy which provides for payment to the wife of the assured if she survives him, but otherwise to the assured, will not form a separate estate for estate duty purposes: *Sharp's Trustees* v. *Lord Advocate*, 1951 S.C. 81; *Att.-Gen.* v. *Pearson* [1924] 2 K.B. 375. Further, even though the policy will produce no income until the death of the assured, it should be made plain that the beneficiaries, or one of them, takes a vested interest in the policy immediately upon the execution thereof. Even the remotest resulting trust in favour of the settlor must be excluded. Thus a policy expressed to be for the benefit of such of the five children of the settlor as may be living one year hence will not be separately aggregable, even if all the children are surviving after one year, and at the death of the settlor, because during that year the settlor had a remote contingent interest.

In drafting the trusts care is required to ensure that the settlor may not take any part of the policy moneys by reason of a professional charging clause, or any similar provision.

If the trusts to which the policy is subject create numerous contingent interests, and then finally state that if those interests all fail the policy is to be held upon trust for the personal representatives of the assured as part of his estate, it is considered that the assured has not been excluded from all interest. It was, however, decided by the House of Lords in *Walker* v. *I. R. C.* (1955) 34 A.T.C. 135, a Scottish appeal, that the possibility of inheriting the moneys as a person entitled to succeed on intestacy to the estate of the person who or whose estate was expressed to be entitled beneficially to the policy is not such an interest.

Even where the assured does not have an interest in the policy at the time of execution, there is often a risk that he will acquire such an interest subsequently. Thus, if he effects a policy under the Married Women's Property Act, 1882, in favour of his four children in equal shares, and one of his children dies an infant intestate in the lifetime of the assured, so that the assured inherits the estate of that infant, the assured will acquire an interest under the policy. In such a case the only practical thing to do may be to convert the policy into a fully paid up policy and effect a fresh policy. Where large sums are at stake it may be prudent when a policy is effected for the beneficiaries to make wills, if they are of age, directing that any interest under the policy shall, in the event of their dying in the lifetime of the assured, accrue to the other beneficiaries, or alternatively so to draft the trusts of the policy as to cause the beneficial interest of any child to accrue on his premature death to the others.

(iii) *Finance Act, 1959, s. 34*

As stated earlier in this chapter, section 34 of the Finance Act, 1959, combined with enactments incorporated into section 2 (1) (c) of the Finance Act, 1894, brings into charge to duty on the death of the assured a slice of the policy moneys, which is calculated by comparing the premiums paid in the five years preceding his death with the total premiums paid. Thus, where a man effects a policy subject to a trust, so that he has no interest therein, he may make a considerable saving of duty by reason of separate aggregation if he dies within five years; and in addition may hope that if he survives the five-year period the burden of duty will be gradually reduced. If the policy eventually becomes fully paid up, and he survives the payment of the last premium by the five-year period, he may hope that the entire policy moneys are taken out of charge to duty.

(iv) *Finance Act, 1894, s. 2 (1) (d)*

A policy of insurance is a chose in action, namely, a contract between the insurers and the assured. The benefit of the chose in action continues after the death of the assured, and it is still the same chose in action, although it is one of the terms of the contract—indeed the main term— that a sum or sums of money become payable by reason of the death. As stated above, the decisions in *D'Avigdor-Goldsmid* v. *I. R. C.* [1953] A.C. 347 and *Westminster Bank* v. *I. R. C.*, *Wrightson* v. *I. R. C.* [1958] A.C. 210 establish that there is no beneficial interest accruing or arising on the death of the assured merely by reason of the fact that the policy moneys thereupon become payable.

However, the terms of the trust to which the policy is made subject in any particular case may themselves bring in liability under section 2 (1) (d). Thus, if the trusts are " in favour of the person who shall be the widow of the assured, but if there is no such person then the children of the assured," it is plain that during the lifetime of the assured neither his wife nor his children have an absolute interest in the policy, while on his death either his wife or his children will gain such an absolute interest: the identity of the person entitled to the policy moneys is not established until the death of the assured. In such a case liability under section 2 (1) (d) will exist.[4]

Even where such a liability exists there can, nevertheless, still be separate aggregation because the assured will never have had an interest under the policy.

Cases may arise where the settlor is anxious that the absolute vesting of the policy should not take place before his death. Such a case may be where under his will he leaves his whole estate to his wife if she survives him but not otherwise, and he desires that the policy should be in similar

---

[4] The liability imposed by s. 2 (1) (d) was, after the decision in *Adamson* v. *Att.-Gen.* [1933] A.C. 257, extended to the full value of the beneficial interests which accrued or arose on the death by s. 28 of the Finance Act, 1934.

terms. In such a case it is necessary to balance with some care the desirability of carrying out the exact terms of the settlor's intention, which will give rise to a section 2 (1) (d) claim, against the benefit which may be gained by escaping section 2 (1) (d) and incurring only the liability under section 34 of the Finance Act, 1959. In this respect it must be borne in mind that the liability under section 34 is further diminished in most cases by section 64 of the Finance Act, 1960, which allows a reduction of duty in case of gifts made within the five-year period, but more than two years before the death of the donor. The relief afforded by section 64 does not apply to claims made under section 2 (1) (d).

(v) *Aggregation of separate policies*

Until 1954 it was, at least in theory, possible for a man enjoying a high income to effect a series of small policies, so that each one, being property in which he " never had an interest," was treated as an estate by himself, so that estate duty on each policy could thus be wholly avoided. Section 33 (2) of the Finance Act, 1954, puts a limit on the benefit to be derived from this course. Although reference must be made to the wording of the section in order to determine how to deal with any individual case, it is possible to state, in general terms, that there are now two distinct categories into which interests under policies fall for purposes of aggregation. Classification into one or the other of these is made by reference, not to the policy, but to the interests of the persons beneficially entitled to the policy moneys. The two categories are as follows:

(1) Any interest in a policy to which a person is absolutely and indefeasibly entitled on the deceased's death is aggregated with all other such interests to which that person is then entitled.

(2) Any other interest in any policy bears a duty at a rate determined by aggregating all the policy moneys passing on the deceased's death in which he never had an interest.

In practice the first category is likely to be the more common. The distinction between the two, for which it is hard to perceive any justification, may perhaps be illustrated by a simple example.

Suppose that T had effected two policies under the Married Women's Property Act, 1882:

(i) The moneys were to be payable to his widow absolutely.

(ii) The moneys were to be held in trust for his widow for life, then for such of his two children as might reach the age of 25, and, failing that, for the widow absolutely.

On T's death one child was aged 26, the other 22.

The widow is absolutely and indefeasibly entitled to the whole of the benefit of the first policy and to a life interest in the moneys payable under the second policy. Aggregation is therefore made of these two interests (the life interest being valued for this purpose) to determine the rate of duty on each interest.

The elder child is absolutely and indefeasibly entitled to an interest in the second policy, and this interest is separately aggregated, that is to say, it bears duty at a rate appropriate to the value of the interest.

The younger child is not absolutely entitled to any interest, since he has not yet attained twenty-five; his interest accordingly bears duty at a rate ascertained by aggregating both policies.

Conversion of existing policies

As stated earlier in this chapter, a gift of an existing policy has certain advantages. However, if it is desired to obtain advantages even in the event of the assured dying within five years, a gift of the policy will not serve. One possible course is to convert the existing policy into a fully paid up policy, and then to effect a fresh policy. In practice, however, this is rarely feasible, since the assured is not able to obtain such attractive terms as before. Some insurance companies advise conversion of an existing policy into a policy written under the Married Women's Property Act, 1882. The object is to ensure that the new policy is property in which the assured never has any interest. It is considered however that considerable circumspection is necessary if this course is to be adopted.

A policy is a contract. If the parties to a contract simply amend some of the terms thereof, it is arguable that nevertheless it is the same contract. Therefore if the assured merely agrees with the insurers to amend some terms of the policy, and at the same time declares a trust in respect of the amended policy, the better view would appear to be that the assured has had an interest in the amended policy. In consequence, it will not enjoy separate aggregation. On the other hand, if a fresh policy is effected under which moneys are not payable to the former assured at all, so that he has no right even in contract to sue for those moneys, the new policy would appear to be an entirely different contract from the old, in that the parties are different. Therefore, if the old policy is surrendered, the surrender being the consideration for the issue of an entirely fresh policy to two persons as trustees of a contemporaneous settlement executed by the assured, it is considered that (although there seems to be no reported decision on the point), the new policy is property in which the assured never had an interest.

Annuity and policy combined

As appears from the foregoing parts of this chapter, a life policy combined with a gift or settlement thereof can be used to effect a double saving of estate duty: the policy may be aggregated as a separate estate, and thus cause duty to be payable at a reduced rate, and in addition estate duty may be avoided on that slice of the policy moneys that is ascribable to the premiums paid more than five years before death, with appropriate reductions in respect of premiums paid more than two but less than five years before death.

However, it may be that, by reason of age or poor health, the settlor is unable to obtain life insurance on acceptable terms. Moreover, it may not be practical or convenient for the settlor to undertake the regular burden of paying the future premiums on the policy. Indeed, the settlor may be unable to accept without hardship any reduction in his future income. In such a case, consideration should be given to the possibility of the settlor effecting a life insurance and at the same time buying a life annuity from the same insurance company. In some circumstances an insurance office may be willing to provide the annuity and the policy without evidence of health. Even where this is not possible, the life office may offer advantageous terms, on the ground that it is in effect insuring itself against having to pay up under the policy.[5]

The annuity would enjoy the tax relief under section 27 of the Finance Act, 1956. The effect may indeed be that the settlor increases his spendable income, even after paying the future premiums on the life policy. Thus it is possible to prepare a scheme whereby the individual settlor increases his future income, and yet both reduces the prospective burden of estate duty and increases the net estate which his family may expect to inherit on his death.

Many insurance brokers are able to prepare a scheme to suit an individual case, showing the exact amount of saving to be achieved. The advantages of the scheme may be readily appreciated, but the disadvantages are perhaps less apparent. One disadvantage is that future inflation could seriously undermine the expected benefits. Again, a substantial fortune is tied up in one or more insurance policies, so that the beneficiaries are kept out of their money until the death of the settlor; whereas if the settlor simply made a gift of part of his fortune, the beneficiaries would obtain immediate enjoyment of the income. Again, the increased spendable income may be brought about simply by reason of existing high rates of tax. Consequently, if rates of tax are later reduced, the advantage is similarly reduced. Thus a settlor having both earned and unearned income, who effected a policy and annuity at a time when surtax was imposed upon all incomes exceeding £2,000 a year, may now find that the benefit looked for is smaller than it was, because earned income enjoys relief from surtax, and this could exempt the first £5,000 of the settlor's income from all surtax liability. As a general rule, the effecting of a policy coupled with an annuity offers greater savings of estate duty in the case of an old settlor than in the case of a young or middle-aged settlor.

---

[5] See Professor G. S. A. Wheatcroft in [1960] B.T.R. 400, where the advantages of an annuity and policy are discussed and illustrated. In practice the insurance office may rely on the " eighty per cent." rule: a rule of thumb that, if the sum insured is no more than 80 per cent. of the sum invested in purchasing the annuity, no medical evidence will be required.

Insurance against estate duty

Generally, it is possible to insure the risk of a settlor dying within the five-year period at a comparatively small cost. Moreover, since section 64 of the Finance Act, 1960, became law, many life offices will readily insure the life of a settlor so that a stated sum of cash becomes payable in the event of his dying within two years, with payment of the same sum reduced by fifteen per cent., thirty per cent., and sixty per cent. respectively, in the event of the death of the settlor within the third, fourth or fifth year after effecting the policy.

Thus, if a settlor makes a gift of £10,000, and it is expected that on his death the rate of estate duty will be fifty per cent., it would be appropriate to effect a policy whereby the following sums become payable:

On death within two years: £5,000.
On death within the third year: £4,250.
On death within the fourth year: £3,500.
On death within the fifth year: £2,000.

The problem presents itself, how to effect such a policy so that it provides cash for the payment of estate duty, and thus in effect make the gift a gift free of estate duty, and yet ensure that the policy moneys themselves pay little or no estate duty, and do not increase the rate of estate duty payable on other property. To this problem there is no easy solution. A number of cases require separate treatment.

(i) *Absolute gifts*

Where a donor makes an absolute gift to an adult donee, the simplest and best course is for the donee to effect the insurance policy in his own name and for his own benefit. The donee will pay the premium or premiums out of his own moneys, and thus will take the insurance moneys, in the event of the settlor dying within the five-year period, as his property without any estate duty liability.

(ii) *Settled gifts*

Where the gift consists of settled property which is vested in trustees, a complex situation has to be dealt with. One course that should not be adopted, except possibly in exceptional circumstances and when the trustees have the appropriate power, is for the trustees simply to invest any part of the capital of the settled funds in paying the premiums on a policy of insurance on the life of the settlor. The danger here is that any policy moneys that become payable, will, by virtue of section 38 (8) of the Finance Act, 1957, be chargeable to estate duty on the settlor's death; and, because the settled fund has in most cases to be valued as at the date of death, the policy moneys may increase the total value of the property passing to such an extent as to cause a higher rate of duty to become payable.

If it is possible in the particular circumstances, the safest course is usually for the trustees of the settlement to have, and to exercise, a power whereby they accumulate sufficient income in the first one or two years of settlement as a general accrual to the capital of the settled fund, to enable them to invest that accumulated income in paying the premiums on a policy. It follows that the best policy is one whereby only one or two annual premiums are payable. It is considered that where this course is adopted the policy moneys do not bear estate duty on the death of the settlor. The accumulations themselves are expressly taken out of charge to estate duty by section 38 (14) of the Finance Act, 1957. It follows that the policy moneys, which can be traced as representing the accumulations, are also taken out of charge to estate duty.

It may be thought from the foregoing that every settlement should contain a power or a direction to accumulate income for one or two years, and effect a policy. The problem is not as simple as that. Such a power may cause estate duty liability to arise, not only under the gift provisions, but also under section 1 of the Finance Act, 1894, under the principle in *Re Hodson's Settlement, Brooks* v. *Attorney-General* [1939] Ch. 343. In such a case the exemptions conferred on accumulations by section 38 (14) of the Finance Act, 1957, may not be available. Generally, therefore, the device of causing premiums to be paid out of accumulated income can be used freely in a case where under the settlement income is to be accumulated for the benefit of infant beneficiaries; but should be used with considerable circumspection in other cases, where the only permitted accumulation period is the life of the settlor.

In the normal case, a settlement simply does not produce sufficient income to pay the first premium on a policy, until some months after it has been established. Plainly in such a case it is better to have a policy in existence from the moment when the settlement is established. Something must, therefore, be patched up until accumulated income is available to pay the premium. One possibility is for the trustees, having determined that the first year's income is to be accumulated, to pay the premium themselves or borrow cash in order to pay the premium, with a view to repaying themselves or the lender as soon as income is available. This course could give rise to difficult problems if one of the trustees dies within the five-year period. The situation is rather too involved, and too dependent upon the facts of the individual case, to merit further treatment in this work.

In case of a discretionary settlement, the settlement could simply contain power to employ income in paying the premiums. While the situation is not clear, it is considered that the better view is that the policy moneys are taken free of estate duty, and do not increase the liability of the other assets.

(iii) *Insurance by the settlor*

In addition to making a settlement, the settlor may effect an insurance on his own life, coupled with a trust either expressly written into the insurance or effected under the Married Women's Property Act, 1882. The trusts relating to the policy should be identical to those relating to the gift. The object is to ensure that the policy moneys are separately aggregated, and that the residue thereof after payment of estate duty thereon is available to discharge the estate duty on the settled funds.

(iv) *Release of life interest*

Where a gift consists of the release by a life tenant of his life interest, or where a life tenant releases his life interest in part of the fund in consideration of the assignment to him by the remaindermen of their reversionary interest in the remaining part of the fund, it may be advisable to effect insurance against the life tenant dying within five years. Indeed, if an application is made to the court under the Variation of Trusts Act, 1958, in order to make effective arrangement whereby a trust fund is divided between a life tenant and the remaindermen, the court may require that insurance is effected against the possibility of the life tenant dying within the five-year period. Having regard to section 38 (12), proviso, of the Finance Act, 1957, it will usually be preferable for the trustees or the remaindermen to effect the policy, paying the premiums out of the capital of the fund released by the life tenant. Since the settlement comes to an end in respect of this fund, the fund is valued as at the date when the settlement comes to an end, namely the date of the release of the life interest; and if the policy is effected the following day, or even the following minute, it is not brought into charge to estate duty. If, however, the release of life interest does not bring the settlement to an end, it may be better for the life tenant himself to effect insurance coupled with a trust, in order to gain the benefit of separate aggregation.

(v) *Insurance by a discretionary beneficiary*

Where a discretionary trust is set up, the simplest course may appear to be to arrange for one or more of the discretionary beneficiaries to insure the life of the settlor, the idea being that if the settlor should die within five years they will simply use the moneys to pay the estate duty. This may work in practice, but it is open to a number of objections. Thus, there is no obligation on the beneficiaries to use the insurance moneys in this way. If they do so, they will themselves be making gifts, and in all probability these will be gifts from which they themselves have not been excluded. Thus, there will be a further estate duty problem on their deaths.

In many discretionary settlements, the settled assets consist largely of shares in a family company. In such a case the practical answer may be for one or more of the beneficiaries to insure the life of the settlor, so that if he dies within five years they receive substantial sums of cash free of duty. The settlement trustees will, however, be faced with heavy estate duty liability. In order to meet this, the trustees could sell part of the other assets comprised in the trust fund to the individuals who have received the large sums of cash. Thus, the trustees will have cash for the payment of the duty, and the individual members of the family will hold the shares or other assets. Provided the price paid by the trustees is carefully worked out, there need be no liability to estate duty on the deaths of the individuals who buy the shares or other assets, since they would have given no more than proper consideration for the shares.

PRECEDENT No. 32

Declaration of Trust by way of Absolute Gift of a Policy about to be Effected by the Donor

Declaration.

THIS DECLARATION OF TRUST made the —— day of —— by me —— of

Witnesseth.

WITNESSETH that I hold the policy of insurance upon my life which I am about to effect with the —— Insurance Co Limited at an annual premium of £—— payable during my life or until I reach the age of —— years whereby a sum of £—— will become payable to my personal representatives upon my death Upon Trust for

Trust.

—— of —— who is my —— for his own use and benefit absolutely

No lien.

And I declare that if I shall pay any further premium in respect of the said policy no lien or charge shall thereby be created it being my intention that the more beneficial interest in the said policy shall be held upon trust for the said .

IN WITNESS, etc.

The above represents the simplest form of declaration of trust, where the person effecting the policy desires to make a gift thereof to a person who is neither his spouse nor his child, and is thus outside the ambit of section 11 of the Married Women's Property Act, 1882.

This form should not be used where the beneficiary is an infant, since in such case provisions for trustees and powers of investment would be required.

The advantage of executing a declaration of trust before effecting the policy, over first effecting the policy and then making a gift thereof, is, broadly, that whatever slice of the policy moneys is chargeable to estate duty on the death of the life assured will obtain the benefit of separate aggregation under the provisions of section 33 (1) of the Finance Act, 1954.

The settlor must, of course, realise that the beneficiary can at any time call for a transfer of the policy. The settlor is under no obligation to go on paying the premiums.

——————

PRECEDENT No. 33

Trust Deed settling a Policy about to be Effected by the Settlor

Parties.

THIS TRUST DEED is made the —— day of —— 19— BETWEEN —— of —— (hereinafter called " the Settlor ") of the one part and —— of —— and —— of —— (hereinafter together called " the Trustees " which expression where the context admits includes the trustee or trustees for the time being hereof) of the other part ; WHEREAS :

Policy.

(A) The Settlor is about to effect with the —— Insurance Company Limited at an annual premium of £—— payable until the Settlor dies or reaches the age of —— years a policy of insurance whereby the sum of £—— will become payable to the Trustees upon his death ;

Memorandum.

(B) It is intended that a memorandum of the number of the said policy shall be indorsed on this Deed ;

Trusts.

(C) The Settlor desires to declare such irrevocable trusts binding on himself and the Trustees in respect of the policy and the moneys payable thereunder and the whole benefit thereof as are hereinafter contained so that the Settlor shall have no interest in or benefit from the said policy under any circumstances whatsoever ;

Witnesseth.

NOW THIS DEED WITNESSETH AND IT IS HEREBY DECLARED as follows :

Trusts of Policy.

1. The said policy and all moneys to become payable thereunder or under any substituted policy or policies including bonuses and moneys received on the sale or surrender of the same and accumulations of income from any such moneys and the whole benefit of the said policy and the investments from time to time representing the same (hereinafter called " the Trust Fund ") and the income thereof shall be held upon the following trusts namely :

Powers to appoint.

(1) Upon such trusts and in such shares and with and subject to such powers conditions and limitations in

favour of any one or more of them namely —— and ——
(who are the infant grandchildren of the Settlor) as the
Settlor may at any time by deed or deeds revocable or
irrevocable executed [during his lifetime] [during the
period of two/five years from the date hereof] appoint
and in default of and subject to each such appointment

Grandchild-
ren.
(2) Upon trust for such of them the said grandchildren of the Settlor as may be living at the death of
the Settlor and if more than one then in equal shares
but if none of them shall be living at the death of the
Settlor then

(3) Upon trust for the last survivor of the said grandchildren for his own benefit absolutely.

No lien.
2. The Settlor hereby declares that if he shall pay
any further premium in respect of the said policy he
shall not thereby acquire any lien or charge in or over
the Trust Fund.

Powers:
3. The Trustees shall from and after the issue of the
recited policy have the following powers in addition to
any powers conferred upon them by law namely :

Sell *etc.*
(1) All the powers of an absolute owner as respects
the recited policy or any policy forming part of the Trust
Fund including the power to exercise any option afforded
by the said policy or any policy as aforesaid or to sell or
realise any such policy or to convert the same into a fully
paid up policy or into any other form of assurance

Borrow,
(2) Power to borrow money on the security of the
said policy or any such policy as aforesaid in order to
pay any overdue or future premium or any other sum
necessary for keeping on foot or restoring the same

Chargeable,
(3) Power to mortgage surrender or otherwise deal
with the said policy or any such policy as aforesaid in
such manner as the Trustees shall consider most beneficial to the persons beneficially interested under the
trusts hereinbefore declared

Invest,
(4) Power to invest the moneys payable under and
the proceeds of sale of the said policy and any such
policy as aforesaid and any other money requiring to be
invested under the trusts hereof in or upon any investment of whatsoever nature and wheresoever situate
including the shares stocks debentures or other securities
of any limited company whether public or private

registered in Great Britain and including the purchase of freehold or leasehold land either as an investment or for residential purposes and the purchase of any property whatsoever and wheresoever including any loan or deposit of money on personal or other security and upon any terms or conditions whatsoever as if the Trustees were the absolute beneficial owners thereof and so that the Trustees shall not be liable for any loss which may occur at any time in connection with or in consequence of any investments made under the powers hereby conferred upon them

Appropriate, (5) Power to appropriate any part of the Trust Fund in its actual state of investment and after making such valuation as the trustees shall think fit in or towards the satisfaction of the interest of any person beneficially interested in the Trust Fund or the income thereof but without the necessity of obtaining the consent of that or of any other person.

Charging. 4. Any Trustee for the time being hereof being a person engaged in any profession or business shall be entitled to charge and be paid all usual professional or other charges for business done by him or his firm in relation to the trusts hereof and also his reasonable charges in relation to disbursements or for other work or business done and all times spend by him or his firm in connection with matters arising in the premises including matters which might or should have been attended to in person by a Trustee not being in any profession or business.

New Trustees. 5. The Settlor shall during his life have power of appointing new trustees hereof provided that the Settlor shall not appoint himself to be a trustee hereof.

Settlor excluded. 6. Notwithstanding anything to the contrary hereinbefore expressed or implied no part of the Trust Fund or of the income thereof shall under any circumstances be paid or lent to or applied for the benefit of the Settlor and no power hereinbefore contained shall be exercised and no provision of this Deed shall operate either directly or indirectly for the benefit of the Settlor.

IN WITNESS, ETC.

MEMORANDUM

On the —— day of —— the said —— Insurance Company Limited issued to the Trustees Policy No. —— which is accordingly held upon the trusts of the above-mentioned Deed.

(To be signed by the Trustees and Settlor)

Where the beneficiaries are adult many of the powers included in this precedent will be superfluous and may be omitted.

The trusts contained in clause 1 are intended as no more than an illustration, and in particular cases it may be desirable to include trusts of a more complex nature. It is necessary to bear in mind that liability to estate duty may arise, not only under the provisions relating to gifts in section 2 (1) (c) of the Finance Act, 1894, as amended by section 34 of the Finance Act, 1959, but also under section 2 (1) (d) of the Finance Act, 1894, on the beneficial interest accruing or arising on the death of the settlor. No matter under which paragraph liability arises, the policy will be a separate estate and thus enjoy separate aggregation, and a lower rate of estate duty: see Finance Act, 1894, s. 4, proviso; Finance Act, 1954, s. 33 (1).

However, liability under section 2 (1) (c) begins to diminish two years after the payment of the first premium, and disappears entirely five years after the payment of the last premium; whereas liability under section 2 (1) (d) where it exists, will usually not diminish. Where the settlor retains a power of appointment, as in clause 1 (1) of the above precedent, or where the beneficial interests are made contingent upon the beneficiaries surviving the settlor, there may be liability under section 2 (1) (d). As a rule of thumb therefore the following broad principles may be stated:

(1) Unless there are particular reasons to the contrary, the trusts should be so worded that the beneficiaries take interests which are immediately vested or become vested before the death of the settlor.

(2) If the settlor desires to retain a power of appointment, there is usually no disadvantage if such a power is retained for two years only. If the settlor dies during this period the liability under section 2 (1) (c) is as great as that under section 2 (1) (d). However, a power retained for a longer period may be retained at the cost of increased estate duty liability.

(3) There must under no circumstances be any resulting trust to the settlor. In order to meet the possible argument that the trust is not completely constituted the settlor must, as well as the trustees, be bound by the trusts.

CHAPTER 7

VARIATION OF EXISTING SETTLEMENTS

NORMALLY the object of varying an existing settlement is either to reduce the estate duty which is likely to be payable on the death of a person who is entitled to some interest in the income of the settled fund, or to remedy some defect in the settlement as a result of which more income tax and surtax is being paid on the income of the settled funds than would be paid on that income under the settlement as varied. In this chapter it is the first situation which is primarily under consideration. Since each settlement of necessity requires individual consideration, it is not possible to cover the whole of the topic save in general terms. Therefore it is proposed in this chapter to deal first with the most common methods of varying a settlement which are resorted to in practice, and then to deal with other subsidiary matters which occasionally arise. The methods to be discussed are the following:—

- (a) The surrender of the interest of a life-tenant in possession to the remainderman.
- (b) The surrender of a reversionary life interest to the remainderman.
- (c) The disclaimer of a life interest.
- (d) The release of an annuity.
- (e) The exercise by trustees of their power of advancement.
- (f) The division of the trust fund between the life-tenant and remainderman.
- (g) The sale of a reversion to the life-tenant.
- (h) Applications to the court.

The surrender of a life interest in possession to the remainderman

Where a life-tenant entitled in possession surrenders his life interest so that it merges with the interest of the remainderman, and survives the surrender by five years, the estate duty which would have been payable in respect of the property passing on the death of the life-tenant ceases to be payable, provided one or other of the following conditions, set out in section 43 (2) of the Finance Act, 1940, is satisfied:—

- (a) if bona fide possession and enjoyment of the property in which the interest subsisted was assumed immediately thereafter by the person becoming entitled by virtue of or upon the disposition or determination and thenceforward retained to the entire exclusion of the person who immediately before the disposition or determination had the interest and of any benefit to him by contract or otherwise; or

264

(b) in the case of a partial determination, if the conditions specified in the preceding paragraph were not satisfied by reason only of the retention or enjoyment by the deceased of possession of some part of the property, or of some benefit, by virtue of the provisions of the instrument under which he had the interest.

Generally, when the life-tenant releases his life interest or other limited interest, he does so voluntarily. But even if the life-tenant receives consideration for the release, the five-year period of survival is necessary since section 43 (1) of the Finance Act, 1940, applies where the limited interest has determined " whether for value or not "; moreover, section 3 (1) of the Finance Act, 1894 (which confers exemption where property passes by reason only of a bona fide purchase) does not apply since it is not solely by virtue of the purchase that the property " passes " on the life-tenant's death: *Att.-Gen.* v. *Llewelyn* [1935] 1 K.B. 94. If the parties desire it, the life interest may be sold, and not given, to the reversioner. But on the death of the life-tenant within five years the whole fund will pass as well as any part of the purchase price reflected in the free estate of the life-tenant. It is considered therefore that in almost every case, an actuarial division of assets is to be preferred.[1] It should be added that if a life interest is sold in consideration of an annuity to be paid by the reversioner, the annuity is a " benefit reserved by contract ": see *Att.-Gen.* v. *Worrall* [1895] 1 Q.B. 99.

If the death of the life-tenant occurs on or after July 31, 1957, the ascertainment of the assets which may be dutiable under section 43 of the Finance Act, 1940, will be regulated by section 38 (12) of the Finance Act, 1957. Section 38 (12) provides that where any property is deemed to pass on a death by virtue of section 43 of the Finance Act, 1940, then, for the purpose of duty chargeable on the death, the property in which the interest subsisted shall be taken to be the property comprised at the time of the death in the settlement under which the interest subsisted, except so far as that property neither is, nor represents, nor is derived from, property in which the interest subsisted immediately before the disposition or determination. The effect is that duty is charged on the trust funds as they exist at the death of the life-tenant, except any part of the trust funds to which the released life interest did not extend. The official view is that any addition to the trust funds by way, for example, of a bonus issue of shares will be part of the property passing. Others take the view that bonus shares do not represent and are not derived from the original shares to the holders of which they were issued.[2]

It not infrequently happens that when there is a disposition or determination of a life interest, the part of the trust funds to which the released life interest extends is taken out of the settlement altogether.

---

[1] See discussion at p. 273, *infra*.
[2] See, *e.g.*, Hanson's *Death Duties*, Sixth Cumulative Supplement, p. 106, and *cf.* discussion at p. 95, *supra*.

It may become the free and absolute property of the reversioner. The proviso to section 38 (12) of the Finance Act, 1957, defines the assets which are dutiable in this kind of case. The effect of the proviso is that the assets from which the life-tenant derived his income are traced down to the date at which they ceased to be settled and are for the purposes of estate duty valued at that date and not at the date of the life-tenant's death.

Where the disposition or determination of the life interest was effected or suffered before April 10, 1957, there is, in certain circumstances, an option for the accountable persons not to have the provisions of section 38 applied: see subsection (18) of section 38 of the Finance Act, 1957. If the option is exercised, the liability to duty will be ascertained according to the law in force before the Finance Act, 1957.

The disposition or determination of a life interest is a " relevant disposition or event " within the meaning of section 64 of the Finance Act, 1960: see subsection (2) (b) of section 64. Accordingly, the principal value of the property passing shall for estate duty purposes be reduced by 15 per cent. if the life-tenant survives the disposition or determination by two years, by 30 per cent. if he survives three years and by 60 per cent. if he survives four years: see subsection (1) of section 64.

Where the interests that are to take effect upon the death of the life-tenant are already vested, and only possession is postponed, so that one may presume the intention of the testator or settlor to have been to postpone possession of the remainder only to the extent that the life interest is valid and in existence, the release of the life interest accelerates those interests: and this may be so even though they are expressed to take effect " after the death of " the life-tenant: *Re Hodge* [1943] Ch. 300; *Re Taylor* [1957] 1 W.L.R. 1043; *Re Flower's Settlement Trusts* [1957] 1 W.L.R. 401 (a decision of the Court of Appeal). Thus if in a settlement a fund is settled upon trust for a wife during her life, with remainder to two named children, the release by the wife of her life interest will accelerate the interests of the children, and no difficulty is likely to arise. Furthermore, even if the interests in remainder are contingent, they may be so expressed that upon the surrender of the life interest they carry the income. Thus, if a fund is settled upon a wife for life, with remainder to such of the children of the marriage as shall attain the age of 21 years, although the children are not yet of the age of 21 years, the wife may release her life interest, and the income will then be applicable for the benefit of the children under section 31 of the Trustee Act, 1925. Indeed, cases may arise where a remainder which is at first sight only contingent is in fact so drafted that, if the life interest is terminated by reason of the surrender, the interests in remainder are accelerated, even though thereby the class of persons entitled may be changed: see *Re Davies* [1957] 1 W.L.R. 922; *Re Taylor* [1957] 1 W.L.R. 1043.

A class of case still remains however where it is clear that a release by the life-tenant of the life interest would not accelerate the interests limited to take effect after his death, but would simply leave a gap. The consequence might be that there would be a resulting trust for the settlor. A common case is where property is settled upon a wife for life, and after her death for such of her children as shall be living at her death. In this case, if the wife were to release her life interest, it would seem that the reversion could not be accelerated, since the persons entitled cannot be ascertained until the wife actually dies. In this class of case, therefore, there would be a resulting trust of income in favour of the settlor during the remainder of the wife's life: see *Re Flower's Settlement Trusts* [1957] 1 W.L.R. 401; *Re Young* [1959] 1 W.L.R. 457. The parties should, however, consider whether their purpose may not be partially achieved by resort to a power of advancement, if such a power is expressed or implied in the settlement. Alternatively, a possibility to be considered is for the life-tenant to assign his interest to the trustees upon trust to apply each sum of income as it arises in exactly the same way as it would fall to be applied under the trust instrument, if the life tenant had died immediately each sum of income arose. If this is done it can be argued that the destination of the income is the same both before and after the death of the life-tenant, so that on the death there is no " passing " for the purposes of section 1 of the Finance Act, 1894. A further possibility is an application to the court under the Variation of Trusts Act, 1958.

Where the life-tenant has a protective or discretionary life interest, it is usually impossible for the life tenant to execute an effective release of his life interest, even if other parties consent. In such a case the parties may consider resort to a power of advancement, or the making of an application to the court under the Variation of Trusts Act, 1958.

The surrender of a reversionary life interest

If a life-tenant in reversion surrenders his life interest so that it merges with the interest of the remainderman, section 43 (1) of the Finance Act, 1940, has no application, since it is restricted in its application to interests in possession. Therefore, where a reversionary life interest is surrendered, the settled fund is not chargeable with estate duty on the death of the reversionary life-tenant, whether or not he survives the five-year period, and whether or not he survives the prior life-tenant. There is however an argument, that the value of the reversionary life interest itself is chargeable to estate duty.

The argument is that, since the surrender is an extinguishment of a right at the expense of the life-tenant in reversion, it should be treated on his death within five years as a disposition made by him in favour of the remainderman so that the disposition will attract estate duty: see section 45 (2) of the Finance Act, 1940, and *cf. Re Stratton's Disclaimer* [1957] Ch. 132. Section 45 (2) makes the extinguishment of a right a disposition for the purposes of the enactments incorporated in section 2 (1) (c) of the Finance Act, 1894. It also extends the meaning of the expression " property " in relation to such a disposition to include the benefit conferred by the extinguishment of the right. This latter provision was necessary because *Attorney-General* v. *De Préville* [1900] 1 Q.B. 223 decided that a life interest was not " property " within the meaning of section 38 (2) (a) of the Customs and Inland Revenue Act, 1881, for property there meant property capable of devolution as part of the estate of a deceased and this could not include an interest limited to cease on his death. But so long as the value of the right extinguished, *i.e.*, the reversionary life interest, was to be ascertained on the date of the death of the " disponor," no effective claim could be made for estate duty under section 45 (2) of the Finance Act, 1940, because at the date of the death of the disponor the reversionary life interest had no value. However, the effect of subsections (3) and (16) of section 38 of the Finance Act, 1957, would appear to be that the value of an extinguished right is to be ascertained, not at the date of the death of the disponor, but at the date of the extinguishment. The donee of an interest in property which merges in another interest held by him in the same property is to be treated as divesting himself voluntarily of that interest. And where a donee voluntarily disposes of property comprised in a gift, the value at that date is the relevant value. In the case of a surrender of a reversionary life interest, therefore, it is argued that a claim for duty would arise on the death of the life-tenant within five years under section 45 (2) of the Finance Act, 1940. Even so, as the claim for duty would be on the value of the reversionary life interest at the date of surrender, and not on the capital of the settled fund, the resulting charge is, in most cases, unlikely to be onerous.

It is submitted that this argument takes insufficient account of section 38 (15) of the Finance Act, 1957; the effect of which is to cause the reversionary life interest to be of no value on the death of the reversionary life-tenant.[3]

In practice, the surrender of reversionary life interests may be advantageous where, for example, a fund is divided into several shares, each settled on a life-tenant with a system of cross-remainders in the event of the death of any life-tenant without issue. Suppose a fund of, say, £50,000, settled by will on the five children of the testator so that each has only a life interest with remainder to his issue, but so that if any child dies without issue, his share accrues to the shares of the surviving children. Let it further be supposed that all five children are over sixty years of age, but only one has issue, an adult son, who thus may count upon obtaining the whole £50,000 eventually. On the death of the first of the five children to die, one-fifth of the settled fund will

---

3 In *Dymond on Death Duties*, 13th ed., at pp. 208, 209, it is suggested that there is in fact no scope nor need for the operation of s. 38 of the Finance Act, 1957, because the meaning and intention of s. 45 (2) of the Finance Act, 1940, must be that the benefit should be quantified at the date of the extinguishment of the right and its value thereafter remains the same.

attract estate duty. On the death of the second, estate duty will be payable on one-fifth plus his accrued share in that fifth of the fund in which the first child had a life interest. So it will go on, and on the death of each of the five children a bigger share of the fund will attract estate duty. It could happen that the greater part of the £50,000 would disappear in estate duty.

In such a case a saving might be made if each of the five children surrendered his reversionary life interests in the shares of the other four. None of them would be giving up his or her present income. The loss of the possible increase in income on the death of a brother or sister would in the circumstances contemplated no doubt be acceptable: it could, if necessary, be compensated for, if the grandchild were to pay his uncles, aunts and parent for their surrenders by paying or agreeing to pay a capital sum or an annuity to them. If this capital sum or annuity represents no more than full consideration for the surrenders and is not charged on any property it is considered that the mere fact of its being paid or agreed to be paid will not give rise to any liability for estate duty.

The disclaimer of a life interest

Where a life interest in residue is bequeathed by will, and the life-tenant wishes to accelerate the interests of the remaindermen, he should *disclaim* the interest as soon as possible after the death, and, in any event, before accepting any income. If the life interest has never vested in possession, section 43 of the Finance Act, 1940, has no application to the disclaimer of it. It is therefore considered that, subject to any force that there may be in the argument mentioned above in relation to liability to estate duty on the value of a released reversionary life interest, no estate duty is payable on the death of the disclaiming life-tenant, even if he fails to survive the five-year period.[4]

By concession no duty is claimed in connection with the disclaimer by the surviving spouse of a person dying intestate of his or her rights under English law to a net sum charged upon the intestate's residuary estate: see No. 6 of the Estate Duty Extra-Statutory Concessions in Appendix IX of the 100th Report of the Commissioners of Inland Revenue, Cmnd. 341.

A disclaimer attracts less stamp duty than a deed of release.[5]

The release of an annuity

Where a life annuitant voluntarily releases his annuity, similar considerations apply as on a release of a life interest.

One method of saving the duty payable on the death of an annuitant under a will is for the trustees to purchase an annuity from an insurance company or from the Government, thereby releasing the trust fund;

[4] *Cf.* Dymond's *Death Duties*, 13th ed., p. 137.
[5] See *post*, p. 298.

they have, however, no power to do this unless it is expressly conferred on them by the will. Where the will confers this power and it is exercised, it is considered that no duty is payable in respect of the annuity on the annuitant's death, provided that the other constituents of the residuary estate or trust fund are freed from the charge.

No saving of duty will be made by releasing an annuity charged on property, in consideration of an annuity secured by the personal covenant of the persons entitled to the property so charged, because when this is done there is considered to be a "benefit by contract or otherwise" within the meaning of section 43 (2) of the Finance Act, 1940: *Att.-Gen.* v. *Worrall* [1895] 1 Q.B. 99. But there is a fine distinction here: if the annuitant does not release his annuity and accept another in its place, but retains his annuity and simply releases the property on which it was charged and accepts instead of the security of such property a covenant by the persons entitled thereto with the trustees to pay to them (the trustees) the annuity, such covenant not replacing the annuity, but being itself property held by the trustees upon which the annuity is charged, it seems probable that liability to estate duty is avoided on the annuitant's death: *Re Beit* [1952] Ch. 53, a decision of the Court of Appeal. (In that case the principle stated in *I. R. C.* v. *Duke of Westminster* [1936] A.C. 1; 19 Tax Cas. 490, as to the effect of the form, not the "substance," of the actual transactions, was followed.) The same result as in the *Beit* case would seem to follow if the annuitant releases the charge securing his annuity and accepts instead the security of an annuity purchased by the trustees in their own name from an insurance company or from the Government.

Advancements

It sometimes happens that a settlement contains an express power for the trustees to raise and apply capital for the advancement or benefit of any remainderman, and usually the consent of the life-tenant is a necessary prerequisite to the exercise of this power. In the case of settlements of personalty executed after 1925, the power of advancement set out in section 32 of the Trustee Act, 1925, is applicable, unless excluded by express words or necessary implication: see section 69 (2) of the Trustee Act, 1925, and cf. *Re Turner's Will Trusts* [1937] Ch. 15, and *I. R. C.* v. *Bernstein* [1961] Ch. 399, 39 Tax Cas. 391. This enables the trustees to advance up to one half of the prospective share of a beneficiary having a future or contingent interest in the capital of the trust fund for the advancement or benefit of that beneficiary.

A power of advancement may offer a means of saving estate duty in a case where the life interest cannot in practice be surrendered. Thus, if the fund is settled upon protective trusts for the benefit of a life-tenant under section 33 of the Trustee Act, 1925, so that the life interest cannot be surrendered, the trustees may exercise their statutory power of advancement, or any express power contained in the trust instrument, in favour of the remaindermen. It has been held that, where the life-tenant was entitled to a protected life interest in the statutory form, he did not cause a forfeiture of his life interest by giving his consent to an advancement: *Re Rees* [1954] Ch. 202. Where, however, the protective trust is drafted without reference to section 33, it depends upon its construction whether a consent to an advancement operates as a forfeiture.

An advancement may also be useful where, although it is possible in practice to surrender the life interest, for one reason or another a doubt is felt as to the wisdom of placing a large sum of capital at the immediate disposition of the remainderman. By resort to the power of advancement, it may be possible to settle the capital advanced.

Section 43 of the Finance Act, 1940, is treated as being applicable to advancements, where a prior life interest in the capital advanced is terminated. Moreover, the Revenue claim in practice that, where the consent of the life-tenant is required to the exercise of the power of advancement, the giving of that consent makes the life-tenant a settlor in respect of the income which he forgoes during the remainder of his lifetime in consequence of giving his consent to the advancement; as a result, section 397 of the Income Tax Act, 1952, will apply so as to make any such income which is paid to or for the benefit of an infant child of the life-tenant the income of the life-tenant for tax purposes.[6]

An advancement may have the additional advantage over a release of a life interest, that, if capital is simply transferred out of the settlement to the remainderman, the *ad valorem* stamp duty at the rate of £2 per cent. payable on the value of the life interest which is released is avoided.

It is considered that a power of advancement, where the words " advancement or benefit " are used, may authorise a variety of operations which would not usually be spoken of as " advancements " in the traditional interpretation of that word. Thus it has been held that in an appropriate case it may be for the benefit of a remainderman, although not for his advancement, if free capital is simply paid over to him: see *Re Powles* [1954] 1 W.L.R. 336; *Re Ropner* [1956] 1 W.L.R. 902; and compare *Re Vestey* [1951] Ch. 209. It has long since been decided that the word " benefit " is of wide import: see *Re Moxon's Will Trusts* [1958] 1 W.L.R. 165; and it may signify such things as the payment of accumulated debts, school bills and even housekeeping expenses: see *Lowther* v. *Bentinck* (1874) L.R. 19 Eq. 166; *Re Brittlebank* (1881) 30 W.R. 99.

A line of authorities of which *Roper-Cuzon* v. *Roper-Cuzon* (1871) L.R. 11 Eq. 452 is the earliest, establishes that a power conferred upon trustees to pay or apply any capital money subject to the trust for the advancement or benefit, in such manner as they may in their absolute discretion think fit, of any person having a future or contingent interest

6 *I. R. C.* v. *Buchanan* [1958] Ch. 289; 37 Tax Cas. 365.

in the capital subject to the trust, may properly be exercised by the trustees transferring capital funds, whether in the form of money or not, to a new settlement created for the benefit of the object of the power whom it is desired to benefit; and moreover that in a proper case this may be done even where the beneficiary has neither requested nor authorised the transaction. The authorities were reviewed by the House of Lords in *Pilkington* v. *I. R. C.* [1962] 3 W.L.R. 1051. It is now possible to state the following propositions:

(a) The trustees cannot under the guise of making an advancement create new trusts for no better reason than that they consider that they can devise better trusts than those which the settlor chose to declare: *Re Wills' Will Trusts* [1959] Ch. 1. On the other hand the trustees do not have to postpone the exercise of their power until some particular event happens or particular circumstances arise related to the personal needs of the beneficiary: *Pilkington* v. *I. R. C.* [1962] 3 W.L.R. 1051 at p. 1066. It is sufficient if the trustees consider that the beneficiary would be benefited by having the expectation of independent means without having to wait for the life-tenant to die (see *Pilkington* v. *I. R. C.*) or that it is desired to save estate duty (see *Re Collard's Will Trusts* [1961] Ch. 293).

(b) The power of advancement is not limited by the rule " *Delegatus non potest delegare.*" While the rule exists that trustees cannot delegate without authority, it must be accepted that the power of advancement is an authority to delegate: *Pilkington* v. *I. R. C.* [1962] 3 W.L.R. 1051 at p. 1065. In so far as the decision in *Re Wills' Will Trusts* [1959] Ch. 1 indicates the contrary, it must be taken to have been overruled by the *Pilkington* decision.

(c) The resettlement must not contravene the perpetuity rule, bearing in mind that the perpetuity period must be reckoned from the date of the original settlement, not the resettlement: *Pilkington* v. *I. R. C.* [1962] 3 W.L.R. 1051 at p. 1067.

(d) A power of advancement may be properly exercised, even where exercised in such a way that some person will gain a benefit in addition to the beneficiary, provided that the provision as a whole is for the benefit of the beneficiary. It is of course almost inevitable that, if a power of advancement is exercised by re-settling capital, some person other than the beneficiary in question may gain a benefit under the resettlement.

In exercising their power of advancement it is also necessary for trustees to take into consideration the application of the doctrine of fraud on a power. Trustees " must act with good faith and sincerity, and with an entire and single view to the real purpose and object of the power, and not for the purpose of accomplishing or carrying into effect any bye or sinister object " (sinister in the sense of being beyond the purpose and intent of the power): see *Duke of Portland* v. *Topham* (1864)

11 H.L.C. 32. In *Re Crawshay* [1948] Ch. 123 at pp. 134, 135 the Court of Appeal approved the following propositions:

" (i) One case of a fraud on a power is where the donee of a special power of appointment makes an appointment intended to benefit some person not an object of the power.

(ii) To establish a fraud on a power, it is not necessary to prove a bargain between the donee of the power and the appointee.

(iii) What the court looks to is the intention or purpose of the appointor in making the appointment.

(iv) Evidence is admissible as to the state of mind of the appointor, including statements by the appointor which go to show his or her state of mind at the material date. Such statements may be material though they are not contemporaneous with the date of the exercise of the power."

The risk of the application of the doctrine of fraud on a power is not simply academic. In *Re Pauling* [1962] 1 W.L.R. 86 a bank trustee with power to advance capital to certain beneficiaries was ordered to replace capital which it had advanced to those beneficiaries with the view to its being passed to a third party who was not an object of the power.

Partition of the trust fund between the life-tenant and remainderman

It may happen that the tenant for life under a settlement is unwilling to make a voluntary gift of his interest to the remainderman, but would be willing to agree to capital being handed over to the remainderman out of the trust fund, provided the life-tenant is compensated in some way. The discussion of this situation may be opened by stating that no estate duty will be saved if the life-tenant sells his interest to the remainderman in consideration for an annuity to be secured by the covenant of the remainderman. Since the decision in *Att.-Gen.* v. *Worrall* [1895] 1 Q.B. 99 it must be taken as established that the covenant is a " benefit reserved by contract " out of the life interest. Moreover, it makes no difference if the annuity is much smaller than the income of the trust fund.

The parties may find it advantageous to divide the capital of the trust fund between themselves on an actuarial basis. This may be effected by a Deed of Partition or Exchange, stamped with a 10s. stamp only. If this is done, it is considered that there has been an enlargement of the life interest of the life-tenant in that part of the fund which he takes, so that section 43 of the Finance Act, 1940, has no application to that part; furthermore, although there has been a " purchase " of the interest of the remainderman in this part of the fund within the meaning of section 28 (11) (a) of the Finance Act, 1958, so that, prima facie, subsection (1) of that section would impose a charge to duty, section 28 (4) in effect takes the transaction out of the scope of the section. In view of this, the trustees may release to the life-tenant the part of the fund allotted to him under the deed, and it bears estate duty on his death only so far as it forms part of his free estate. It is considered that the part of the fund taken by the remainderman is caught by section 43 of the Finance Act, 1940, so that estate duty in respect of it is only avoided if the life-tenant survives the date of the partition by the statutory five-year period. In the meantime the trustees are accountable for the duty.

It has been suggested that sometimes a sale by the life-tenant of his interest to the remainderman is advantageous. It is, however, considered that a partition must nearly always be preferable, since it is less expensive in stamp duty, and also gives rise to a more modest liability to estate duty under section 43 of the Finance Act, 1940, if the life-tenant dies within five years.

If the life-tenant, having received his share of the trust fund, uses it to purchase an annuity for himself, it is considered that this does not affect the estate duty problem. A factor not to be overlooked in considering whether a partition may be advantageous, is that the life-tenant will be able to purchase an annuity upon the favourable terms which result from section 27 of the Finance Act, 1956. As a general rule it would be inadvisable for the trustees to buy the annuity for the life-tenant. The Estate Duty Office might possibly contend that there has not been an actuarial division, but a release by the life-tenant of his life interest subject to a benefit reserved, with the consequence that estate duty will be payable on the death of the life-tenant in respect of the whole fund, even if the life-tenant survives the five-year period.

Care is required to see that the proportions in which the fund is split represent the fair value of the respective interests of the life-tenant and remainderman. If it should be found necessary to provide for equality money, additional stamp duty is likely to be payable. If there is an element of bounty on either side, there is the disadvantage that the death of the party giving the bounty will, if it occurs within the five-year period, cause additional estate duty to be payable.

Where the life-tenant and remainderman are separately advised, and arrive at the division of the fund by bargaining, it should in practice be a matter of no great difficulty to prove that there was no element of bounty on either side. Some difficulty may be encountered if the two parties are related, and employ the same solicitor. In such a case it is important to be able to show that a proper method was employed of valuing the respective interests of life-tenant and reversioner in the trust fund. An actuary may be employed for this purpose. It is, however, not indispensable to employ the services of an actuary in the valuation of the life interest and the reversion. Where an actuary is employed, it may make it more apparent that the division is genuine.

Although there is some difference of opinion among lawyers, accountants and actuaries as to the exact method of arriving at the values, it is fairly well settled that the better way is first of all to divide the fund into three parts, representing the life interest, the reversion and the estate duty payable on the death of the life-tenant: in assessing the amounts of these three parts, account needs to be taken of the expectation of life of the life-tenant, the income produced by the fund, the type of investment employed, and the probable amount of the estate duty payable on the life-tenant's death. It will be observed that simply valuing the life interest and the reversion and adding in the probable amount of estate duty need not in itself produce three figures that add up to the value of the whole fund. Of the three parts, one is clearly ascribable to the life-tenant, and one to the remainderman; and the third, representing estate duty liability, must be again divided, a proportion being added to the life-tenant's part, the balance to the remainderman's part. There are different views as to the proper method of this division: it is considered that it may properly be effected by division into two equal halves, or into shares corresponding to the life-tenant's part and the remainderman's part, or into shares agreed to after bargaining between the life-tenant and remainderman.

It may happen that the life-tenant has a special power of appointment among the remaindermen with a gift over to them in certain shares in default of appointment. Where this is so, it is reasonably clear that the life-tenant may validly release his power for the purpose of facilitating a partition of the fund: see Re Radcliffe [1892] 1 Ch. 227. Moreover, where he has already made a revocable appointment under the power, the life-tenant may validly revoke the appointment and release the power; Re Greaves [1954] Ch. 434. If, however, it is proposed that the life-tenant should exercise his power of appointment in order to facilitate a partition of the settled funds between himself and the appointee, care must be exercised to ensure that the appointment cannot be impugned by those entitled to the fund in default of appointment as being a " fraud " on the power. This means that the appointor must not be actuated by a desire to benefit himself or any person other than a possible object of the power. It is considered, on the authority of Re Merton [1953] 1 W.L.R. 1096 and Re Robertson's Will Trusts [1960] 1 W.L.R. 1050, that an appointment is not made in fraud of the power simply because the life-tenant making the appointment then proceeds to agree with the appointee on a division of the appointed fund, unless it is shown that the life-tenant is actuated by a desire to gain at the expense of the appointee. Thus, if a life-tenant takes only that part of a settled fund allocated to him by an actuary, it is considered that an appointment may validly be made.

The only shadow of doubt which exists in this point arises from the comments of Vaisey J. in Re Greaves, referred to above, to the effect that in Re Merton the appointment and the subsequent partition of the land were not part of the same transaction. Moreover, the Court of Appeal in Re Greaves apparently agreed with Vaisey J. that had the point arisen for decision in that case, the scheme which gave to the appointor " many thousands of pounds of capital through and by means of her execution of a fiduciary power " would not have been valid. This comment, clearly *obiter*, is obscure since the statement of the facts in the report reveals that on the subsequent division of the land the appointor, being the life-tenant, was to receive no more than the actuarial value of her life interest. It is submitted that, given a bona fide exercise by the appointor of the power of appointment in the interests of the appointees, it is of no consequence that the appointor is thereby put in a position to receive many thousands of pounds for his or her interest, being an interest worth many thousands of pounds. It is thought that trustees in any given case are entitled to be guided by what was said by Russell J. in *Robertson's Will Trusts*, referred to above, and to treat the comments made in *Re Greaves* as to the scheme there considered as explicable by reference to some factor not immediately apparent from the statement of the facts contained in the report.

The sale of a reversion to the life-tenant

The second edition of this book contained a section on the purchase of the reversion by the life-tenant as a method of avoiding estate duty on the death of the life-tenant, even if that death occurred within the five-year period. Section 28 of the Finance Act, 1958, an enactment of unusual complexity, provides that where a life-tenant purchases an interest in the settled fund expectant upon his interest, there shall be deemed to be included in the property passing on his death a sum of money equal to the amount or value of the purchase consideration. This applies only where the life-tenant dies within five years.

It is considered that this enactment makes purchase of the reversion unlikely to be advantageous except possibly in exceptional cases. It is, therefore, not proposed to deal with the topic in detail.

Applications to the court

So far, in considering what arrangements may be made between a life-tenant and remainderman, it has been assumed that the remainderman is an ascertainable person or class of persons *sui juris*. In practice, there may frequently be a class with one or more infant members, or a class of unborn persons.

Whereas persons who are *sui juris* may put an end to the trusts and negotiate any bargain or rearrangement, the sanction of the court is usually thought to be required on behalf of all persons who are not *sui juris*, *e.g.*, infants, incapacitated persons, and possible beneficiaries not yet born. In fact, the rule may well be that an infant who is able to understand what he is doing may be able to make a valid, though voidable, agreement. Be that as it may, cases often arise where no valid compromise is possible without an application to the High Court.

The Variation of Trusts Act, 1958, now makes it possible to effect an arrangement to vary existing trusts in a wide variety of circumstances.

So wide is the jurisdiction conferred on the court by this Act that the other jurisdiction of the court is unlikely to be invoked save in exceptional cases. It is proposed first to deal briefly with this other jurisdiction, and then to deal with the Variation of Trusts Act in rather more detail.

(i) *The inherent jurisdiction of the court*

The court may sanction a compromise on behalf of an infant in any case where there is a genuine dispute in which the infant is involved, and is not bound to reject a proposed compromise if its effect may be to reduce the possible liability of some of the parties to estate duty: see *Chapman* v. *Chapman* [1954] A.C. 429 at pp. 445, 457; *Re Lord Hylton's Settlement, Barclays Bank Ltd.* v. *Jolliffe* [1954] 1 W.L.R. 1055. The dispute may be only as to the true construction of the trust instrument, but unless there is some real dispute the court has no inherent jurisdiction to sanction any compromise: *Re Powell-Cotton's Settlement* [1956] 1 W.L.R. 23.

The court has also a jurisdiction, which is somewhat ill-defined, to vary trusts on what has been called " salvage " principles. This has been described by Lord Justice Romer, in delivering the judgment of the Court of Appeal in *Re New* [1901] 2 Ch. 534, in the following terms, which have also been quoted with approval in the House of Lords in the *Chapman* case:

> " But in the management of a trust estate, and especially where that estate consists of a business or shares in a mercantile company, it not infrequently happens that some peculiar state or circumstance arises for which provision is not expressly made by the trust instrument, and which renders it most desirable, and it may be even essential, for the benefit of the estate and in the interest of all the *cestuis que trust*, that certain acts should be done by the trustees which in ordinary circumstances they would have no power to do. In a case of this kind, which may reasonably be supposed to be one not foreseen or anticipated by the author of the trust, where the trustees are embarrassed by the emergency that has arisen and the duty cast upon them to do what is best for the estate, and the consent of all the beneficiaries cannot be obtained by reason of some of them not being *sui juris* or in existence, then it may be right for the court, and the court in a proper case would have jurisdiction, to sanction on behalf of all concerned such acts on behalf of the trustees as we have above referred to. . . .

> " . . . It is impossible, and no attempt ought to be made, to state or define all the circumstances under which, or the extent to which, the court will exercise the jurisdiction; but it need scarcely be said that the court will not be justified in sanctioning every act desired by trustees and beneficiaries merely because it may appear beneficial to the estate; and certainly the court will not be disposed to sanction

transactions of a speculative or risky character. But each case
brought before the court must be considered and dealt with according
to its special circumstances."

The court also has inherent jurisdiction to provide maintenance for
an infant beneficiary out of a fund in which he is interested, and possibly
also to order conversion of his estate from personalty to realty or vice
versa: see *Re Heyworth's Contingent Reversionary Interest* [1956]
Ch. 364. Section 53 of the Trustee Act, 1925, is also relevant in this
respect: see *Re Meux* [1958] Ch. 154.

(ii) *Section 57 of the Trustee Act, 1925*

It must now be accepted as established that the jurisdiction of the
court under section 57 extends only to the management or administration
of the trust property: the section suggests a practical step of an
administrative character capable of being effected by the trustees: see
Re Downshire's Settled Estates, Re Chapman's Settlement Trusts and
Re Blackwell's Settlement Trusts [1953] Ch. 218, at pp. 245 to 247. The
proposed transaction must concern the trust property itself, not the
interests of the beneficiaries therein. Thus this section overlaps the
Variation of Trusts Act, 1958. But, unlike the Act, the section does
not allow the court to re-write the beneficial trusts for the purpose of
allowing the beneficiaries to break open a settlement. On the other hand,
it was held in *Re Forster's Settlement* [1954] 1 W.L.R. 1450 that the
section conferred on the court power in the particular circumstances of
the case to sanction the purchase by the trustees of the interest of the
life-tenant, which had already been charged for the purpose of raising
capital on a number of occasions. Further, in *Re Cockerell's Settlement
Trusts* [1956] Ch. 372, the court authorised trustees to sell one of the
trusts' assets, although there was no power of sale in the trust
instrument. The asset in question was a reversionary interest, and the
sale of it effected a saving of estate duty.

(iii) *Section 64 of the Settled Land Act, 1925*

This section is rather more widely drawn than section 57 of the
Trustee Act, 1925, but only applies to land, whether held in strict settlement or upon trust for sale (see *Re Simmons' Settlement* [1956] Ch. 125).
The decision of the Court of Appeal in *Re Downshire* [1953] Ch. 218 at
pp. 259 to 260 still stands, in spite of the later House of Lords decision
in the *Chapman* case. The power conferred on the court by section 64 is
to authorise " any transaction affecting or concerning the settled land "
which would in the opinion of the court be for the benefit of the settled
land or any part thereof or the persons interested under the settlement.
The transactions in question are not limited to steps of an administrative
character.

(iv) *Section* 25 *of the Matrimonial Causes Act,* 1950

The Divorce Court has a very wide jurisdiction, after pronouncing a decree of divorce or nullity, to vary the beneficial trusts contained in any ante-nuptial or post-nuptial settlement made on the parties whose marriage is the subject of the decree. The decision in *Chapman* v. *Chapman* has no direct bearing on this wide jurisdiction: the court may override the wishes of the settlor and will not be deterred from exercising its power by reason of the fact that a saving of tax will result: *Thomson* v. *Thomson* [1954] P. 384.

Variation of Trusts Act, 1958

The full title of this Act is " an Act to extend the jurisdiction of Courts of Law to vary trusts in the interests of beneficiaries and sanction dealings with trust property." The Act applies to trusts of realty or personalty created before or after the passing of the Act under any will, settlement or other disposition. The court has jurisdiction if it thinks fit to approve any " arrangement " varying or revoking all or any of the trusts, or enlarging the powers of the trustees of managing or administering any of the property subject to the trusts. The approval of the court may be given on behalf of any infant beneficiary, any person who may become in future, but is not at present, the person answering a specified description or being a member of a specified class, or any person unborn. However, the court must be satisfied that the carrying out of the arrangement that is proposed would be for the benefit of the person on whose behalf the court is to approve the arrangement. The court also has jurisdiction to approve any arrangement on behalf of any person who has a discretionary interest under protective trusts, where the interest of the principal beneficiary has not failed or determined, even though the arrangement may not be for the benefit of that person.

The application must be made to the Chancery Division of the High Court under Order 55, rule 14A, of the Rules of the Supreme Court. The application should normally be by summons not *inter partes.*

The following examples illustrate the type of arrangement which may be brought before the court under the Act:

(a) A fund is settled upon a man for life with remainder to his children at the age of twenty-one years. He has one adult child and one infant child and the possibility of future children cannot be ruled out. He may apply to the court in order to approve a partition of the settled funds between himself and his existing and any future children. This is in practice a very common form of arrangement. If the life-tenant has a power of appointing an interest in income to his wife if she survives him, he may consider either exercising this power in order that his wife can join in the partition and take part of the capital, or alternatively expressly release the power or leave it to be released by implication by the arrangement, in which case his wife need not even be a party: *cf. Re Christie-Miller's Marriage Settlement* [1961] 1 W.L.R. 462. If the life-tenant has a power of appointment among his children and remoter issue, he may consider exercising this power prior to the arrangement, and if he does so not with a view to deriving any personal benefit or to benefiting any person outside the class of possible appointees, it is considered that he may make an appointment that cannot be impugned as a fraud on the power: *Re Robertson's Will Trusts* [1960] 1 W.L.R. 1050.

(b) In the case mentioned above, the life tenant may perhaps consider an arrangement whereby some small part of the settled funds, instead of being apportioned either to the life-tenant or to the remaindermen, is settled upon wide discretionary trusts for the benefit of the remaindermen and their future issue.

(c) A fund is settled upon protective trusts for the benefit of a spinster during her life, with remainder to such person or persons whomsoever that she may appoint by will, with remainder to her next-of-kin. The court may approve an arrangement whereby some small fraction of the settled funds is set aside upon trust for the benefit of the next-of-kin, perhaps with a provision for accumulation during the lifetime of the spinster, while the remaining part of the capital is released to the spinster. The persons who would be the next-of-kin of the spinster if she were to die at the date of issue of the summons should be made respondents to the application, but it would not be necessary to join other persons who might possibly become next-of-kin: *Re Suffert's Settlement* [1961] Ch. 1; *Re Moncrieff's Settlement Trusts* [1962] 1 W.L.R. 1344. Although it would not be necessary to make the arrangement beneficial for the persons who would be entitled under the discretionary trusts in the event of a forfeiture of the protective life interest, nevertheless it does not follow that the court would, without careful consideration, accede to the application: *Re Steed's Will Trusts* [1960] Ch. 407; *Re Burney's Settlement Trusts* [1961] 1 W.L.R. 545.

(d) A married woman now aged sixty years, the protective life-tenant of a settled fund, her adult and infant children being the remaindermen, desires to divide the funds between herself and her said children. She has already committed a forfeiture of her protective life interest. Here again the court would have regard to the reasons why the life interest was made protective, in accordance with the decisions in *Re Steed's Will Trusts* [1960] Ch. 407; *Re Burney's Settlement Trusts* [1961] 1 W.L.R. 545. The life-tenant's husband would no doubt agree to the proposed arrangement, but some provision would have to be made for any future husband and for any future issue of the life-tenant more remote than children that might be born during the life-tenant's lifetime. This could presumably be effected by settling some part of the trust fund for the benefit of a future husband, and a further part for the benefit of grandchildren and remoter issue. Discretionary trusts might well be found useful.

(e) A settlement does not allow funds to be invested in the purchase of a house as a residence for the life-tenant. In such a case it is considered that an application under the Variation of Trusts Act will be appropriate: see *Re Burney's Settlement Trusts* [1961] 1 W.L.R. 545. Apart from this, however, it is reasonably clear that, since the coming into force of the Trustee Investments Act, 1961, the court will not normally confer upon trustees wider powers of investment than those contained in the Act. If there are special circumstances justifying an extension of those powers, then it is possible that the court will make the necessary variation: see *Re Cooper's Settlement* [1962] Ch. 826; *Re Kolb's Will Trusts* [1962] Ch. 531.

(f) A fund is settled upon wide discretionary trusts, under which the present and any future wife of the settlor is a possible beneficiary. The effect of section 22 of the Finance Act, 1958, is that, no matter how the income of the fund is applied, it is treated for income tax and surtax purposes as if it were income of the settlor. The trusts could be varied by simply removing any reference to a wife of the settlor from the settlement, compensating the present wife by transferring part of the capital to her, and making provision for any future wife by setting aside a further part of the capital, the income thereof to be accumulated during the settlor's lifetime and held upon trust for his widow immediately upon his death. A somewhat similar arrangement was approved by the court in *Re Clitheroe's Settlement Trusts* [1959] 1 W.L.R. 1159.

(g) A settlement provides that during the lifetime of the principal beneficiary, who is a son of the settlor, the trustees shall apply for the benefit of the son such part if any of the income they may think fit, and shall accumulate the surplus as an addition to the capital. The direction for accumulation takes effect only during the lifetime of the settlor: Law of Property Act, 1925, s. 164 (1) (a). There is thus likely to be a passing on the death of the settlor even though he survives the five-year period: *Re Hodson's Settlement* [1939] Ch. 343. The court may approve an arrangement whereby, instead of being accumulated, the surplus income passes to those who are entitled after the death of the discretionary life-tenant.

(h) A fund is settled upon four brothers for their respective lives, with an elaborate system of cross-remainders, and a provision that on the death of the last survivor the capital is to be divided among a class of their issue. Such a form of settlement was surprisingly common a few years ago, and often ensures that the greater part of the fund is paid to the Crown by way of estate duty. A possible arrangement would be to get rid of the cross-remainders, and provide for discretionary trusts which terminate at a fixed date, perhaps December 31 after the date which would be the one-hundredth birthday of the youngest brother. On that day the capital could be distributed among the class of beneficiaries.

(i) All the beneficiaries under a settlement have emigrated to a country which has a law of trusts similar to the English law. The court

may approve an arrangement involving the English settlement on condition that the funds are transferred to an almost identical settlement in
the country to which the beneficiaries have emigrated: see *Re Seale's
Marriage Settlement* [1961] Ch. 574.

As stated above, the court has (except in the case of protective trusts)
no jurisdiction to approve any arrangement, unless it is shown to be for
the benefit of the person on whose behalf the approval of the court is
sought. It does not follow, however, that the court must approve an
arrangement simply because it is shown that the persons on whose behalf
the approval of the court is sought will get a somewhat larger benefit
under the arrangement than they are likely to get without the arrangement. The court will not normally exercise its jurisdiction unless it is
shown that the persons on whose behalf it is asked to give its approval
get a reasonably good bargain, that is, such a bargain as an adult person,
acting on proper advice, and without being unduly generous or obstinate,
would have obtained. The court will moreover have regard to the object
which the existing trusts were intended to achieve: *Re Steed's Will
Trusts* [1960] Ch. 407.

On the other hand, the arrangement need not be so engineered that
it is made reasonably certain that the persons on whose behalf the court
is to give its approval must benefit in all circumstances. Thus an
arrangement may still obtain approval even though it may in certain
unlikely contingencies prove less beneficial than the existing settlement:
Re Cohen's Will Trusts [1959] 1 W.L.R. 865. However, this principle
cannot be pressed too far. The court is unlikely to approve an arrangement on behalf of infants, where, for example, on the death of the life-
tenant within the five-year period, their inheritance is likely to be severely
depleted. In such a case it may be necessary to provide some additional
benefit to the children, either by way of insurance against the death of
the life-tenant within five years, or by giving them a substantially
increased share of capital.

As stated above, the procedure is by originating summons. It is the
practice for such summons to be heard in open court: *Re Rouse's Will
Trusts* [1959] 1 W.L.R. 372. As a general rule, it is considered undesirable for the trustees to be the applicants: *Re Druce's Settlement Trusts*
[1962] 1 W.L.R. 363. Normally, therefore, the application will be made
by the life-tenant or the other person or persons for the time being entitled
to the income of the settled funds. The trustees should be made respondents, or, if the applicants are themselves trustees, the independent
trustees should be made respondents, and if there are no independent
trustees it may be necessary to appoint some additional trustee for this
purpose. All the existing beneficiaries, adult and infant, should be
respondents, and if the existing settlement contains any charitable trust,
the Attorney-General should also be made a respondent: *Re Longman's
Settlement Trusts* [1962] 1 W.L.R. 455. In case of a class of beneficiaries,
those persons should be made respondents who are members of that class

at the date of issue of the summons: *Re Suffert's Settlement* [1961] Ch. 1; *Re Moncrieff's Settlement Trusts* [1962] 1 W.L.R. 1344. It is however considered that it is not necessary to join persons who are merely potential members of the class. It is considered not necessary to join persons who are interested only as the objects of a power which need never be exercised: *Re Christie-Miller's Marriage Settlement* [1961] 1 W.L.R. 462. In case of a respondent who is a mental defective, the Court of Protection should be notified as soon as the summons has been issued, and the practice direction laid down by the Court of Protection should be followed: [1960] 1 W.L.R. 17; see also *Re Sanderson's Settlement Trusts* [1961] 1 W.L.R. 36. As a general rule, where protective trusts are to be varied, it is probably not necessary to join as respondents all persons who may become interested under the protective trusts, provided that the interests have been guarded by the trustees: *Re Munro's Settlement Trusts* [1963] 1 W.L.R. 145. It is clear that, although the arrangement need not be beneficial to these persons, their interests cannot be entirely ignored: *Re Steed's Will Trusts* [1960] Ch. 407; *Re Burney's Settlement Trusts* [1961] 1 W.L.R. 545; *Re Munro's Settlement Trusts*, above. It does not follow, however, that they must in all cases be made respondents.

Formerly it was common for all the adult beneficiaries to execute a Deed of Family Arrangement, which contained a provision that it was to come into effect upon the approval of the court being obtained. However, that procedure was cumbersome, especially where the court suggested amendments to the scheme. The normal practice now is for the new trusts to be set out in a document called an " Arrangement " which is not executed by any party, and which derives its force from the fact that all parties agree to it at the hearing, either through their counsel, or by reason of the court exercising its statutory jurisdiction. Such an Arrangement can be set out in a Schedule to the originating summons, or, preferably, exhibited to an affidavit. There seems to be no authority whether the order of the court should be stamped, but the practice is not to submit the order of the court or any other document for stamping. In addition to approving the arrangement, the order normally directs that a memorandum be endorsed on the original settlement or probate: see *Re Joseph's Will Trusts* [1959] 1 W.L.R. 1019, although it is difficult to see why such a memorandum is more desirable in the case of an order of the court than in the case of any other document whereby the beneficiaries agree to vary their interests.

Where the Arrangement consists of a division of the trust fund between the life-tenant and others, the normal practice is for the life-tenant to pay the costs of all parties, and a provision to this effect can be included in the Arrangement. However, there is no objection to putting the provision for costs in the body of the order. However matters may be arranged, it is normal for the costs of negotiating the Arrangement prior to the issue of the summons to be included.

Partition with the approval of the court

It may be useful if mention is made of numerous points that may arise in practice in the kind of application to the court which is most common in practice, namely a partition of the settled funds between the life-tenant or life-tenants and the remaindermen. Let it be supposed that a considerable fund is settled upon protective trusts for the benefit of a married woman during her life, with power for her to appoint an interest in up to one half the income to any surviving husband, with further power for her to appoint the capital among her children and remoter issue, with a gift in default to her children at the age of twenty-one years in equal shares. The life-tenant is married and has several children, of whom one has attained the age of twenty-one years.

The first step will be to ascertain in general terms the type of arrangement that is likely to suit the circumstances of the case. Where a large fund is being considered, the type of arrangement set out in the precedent at the end of this chapter may be found suitable. This gives part of the capital to the life-tenant, part to the remaindermen, and settles the remaining part upon discretionary trusts for the benefit of the remaindermen and other issue of the life-tenant. There would appear to be no reason why the same solicitors should not act for all parties. Having ascertained the type of scheme required, the solicitors would make a rough calculation of the rate of estate duty on the death of the life-tenant. They would thus be able to work out what would be left for the remaindermen if the life-tenant died without obtaining the approval of the court to any variation. This may be referred to as " the net inheritance." An actuary may then be asked to advise, in general terms, and perhaps unofficially, how he would divide the settled funds between the following elements :

(a) Life interest.

(b) The reversionary life interest of the existing husband.

(c) Estate duty on the death of the life-tenant.

(d) The remaindermen.

The solicitors should then work out how much estate duty is likely to be payable if an amount equal to the " net inheritance " were allocated to the remaindermen, and the life-tenant were to die within five years. They should then obtain a quotation from insurance brokers of a single premium policy on the life of the life-tenant, which would provide a sum equal to the said estate duty liability.

The arrangement can then be drafted, presumably by counsel instructed on behalf of the life-tenant. At this stage only provisional figures and fractions can be inserted in the arrangement, to represent the amounts to be taken by the life-tenant and the remaindermen, the amount to be settled on discretionary trust, and the amount of insurance cover required.

At the same time a draft may be prepared of the affidavit intended to be sworn by the life-tenant in support of the summons. Normally this affidavit would exhibit the following documents:

(a) The existing settlement.

(b) The proposed arrangement.

(c) Instructions to the actuary and his report.

(d) A list of the investments and their values.

(e) A general statement of the assets likely to pass on the death of the life-tenant and the rate of estate duty likely to be payable.

(f) Medical certificates certifying that the life-tenant and (if he is also to benefit under the scheme) her husband have the normal expectation of life.

(g) A general statement of the other expectations of the children and remoter issue.

(h) A specimen of the type of insurance policy that can be obtained.

In addition the affidavit would give details of all parties, the reasons for making the application, the reason why the original settlement was made upon protective trusts, and any further points that may arise.

Armed with the draft arrangement and draft evidence the solicitors are able, on behalf of the life-tenant, to obtain a detailed report from the actuary and to obtain specimen policies, with quotations, and to prepare the other exhibits.

The various parties and their solicitors and counsel can then consider the proposed arrangement and finally agree the terms thereof and the shares in which the fund is to be divided. How difficult or protracted this negotiation may prove to be depends almost entirely upon the circumstances of the particular case. As a result of the negotiations, final figures may be entered in the arrangement, a draft originating summons prepared, as well as drafts of any further evidence. It should be remembered that if the settlor is still alive, he should be made a party, either as one of the applicants or one of the respondents, and should normally swear an affidavit stating the circumstance in which the settlement was created and what his attitude is to the proposed variation. In this respect see *Re Oakes' Settlement Trusts* [1959] 1 W.L.R. 502. The originating summons may then be issued, and thereafter the affidavits sworn. The hearing will normally be in open court.

Tenant for life past age of child-bearing

It is often assumed that there is a rule of law that a woman is deemed never to be past the age at which she is no longer capable of bearing children. In reliance on this rule it is also taken for granted that a life-tenant and remaindermen are, unless an order of the court is obtained, prevented from dividing the assets of the estate between themselves, where the life-tenant is a woman and the remaindermen are a class of her

children, since it is supposed that the possibility of future children being
born operates to prevent final ascertainment of all the beneficiaries.

In fact the rule above mentioned is probably confined in its operation
to the perpetuity rule, in the application of which a number of assumptions have to be made which run counter to normal experience.[7] The
court will in practice, in a suitable case, assume a woman is past child-
bearing. Thus in *Haynes* v. *Haynes* (1866) 35 L.J.Ch 303 there was a
settlement containing a gift to A for life, then to A's issue, and in default
of such issue to B. In fact, A was a spinster of 53 at the date of the
application to court. She and B agreed to divide the trust fund, which
was a fund in court, between themselves; and so applied for payment out.
The court made the order. A similar case, *Re Thornhill* [1904] W.N. 112,
was similarly decided in the Court of Appeal.[8] There would seem to be
no good reason why trustees should not act upon the same assumption.

Accountability of trustees

Where a life or other limited interest is disposed of or determines,
within the meaning of section 43 of the Finance Act, 1940, and estate duty
is payable under that section on the death of the life-tenant, the trustees
of the settlement are expressly made accountable for the duty; this means
the trustees at the death of the life-tenant, or if the settlement is by
then no longer in existence, the last trustees: Finance Act, 1950,
s. 44 (1).

Although, of course, the beneficiaries are also accountable, the rule
just stated means, as it stands, that the trustees cannot safely hand over
the whole of the trust fund to the beneficiaries after they have broken up
the trusts of the settlement. However, section 44 (3) of the Finance Act,
1950, provides for that situation: the trustees may obtain from the Commissioners of Inland Revenue a certificate of the amount which in the
opinion of the Commissioners may properly be treated as the prospective
amount of the duty. Upon such a certificate being given, the accountability of the trustees is limited to the amount certified.

If they succeed in obtaining a certificate, the trustees may discover
how much of the trust funds they should retain after the trusts have been
broken. The certificate does not, however, state the length of time that
the funds must be retained, and this is a matter for the legal advisers
of the trustees to decide. Under the existing law, the trustees will
normally be adequately protected if they retain the certified amount for
five years from the date when the settlement is broken.

Other transactions with existing settlements

An existing settlement which ties up property for several generations
in the inflexible manner customary a few generations ago may, in fact,

[7] See *Re Dawson* (1888) 39 Ch.D. 155; *Re Deloitte* [1926] Ch. 56.
[8] See also *Re White* [1901] 1 Ch. 570; *G.'s Trustees* v. *G.*, 1936 S.C. 837 at p. 859;
Re Westminster Bank Ltd. [1963] 1 W.L.R. 820.

simply preserve the property for the Revenue. Where family circumstances and lawyers have combined to tie up property in this manner, the work may have been done so efficiently that no rearrangement of the trusts is possible. The following transactions may assist in some cases.

(i) Sale of life interest

If a life-tenant or annuitant is paying a high rate of surtax, he may find it advantageous to sell his interest, or part of it, to an insurance company, or a company dealing in property of this nature, for a capital sum. The company, not being assessable to surtax, may be willing to pay a price greatly exceeding the net benefit derived by the life-tenant after payment of income tax and surtax.

(ii) Investment in agricultural land

The purchase of agricultural land by the trustees, provided they have power to do so, will cause the lower rates applicable to agricultural land to apply on the death of the life-tenant.[9] The Revenue concede the point that an interest under a trust for sale of land is an interest in land for this purpose.[10] Section 28 (2) (b) of the Finance Act, 1954, extends this relief to certain shares in controlled companies engaged in agriculture, as well as to industrial property: this is a useful widening of the rule, since many trusts contain a wide power to invest in company shares but do not permit the purchase of land.

(iii) Investment in timber

The purchase of timber may effect a saving of estate duty. Where an estate in respect of which estate duty is payable comprises land on which " timber, trees, or wood " are growing the value of the timber trees or wood is not taken into account for the purposes of estate duty unless and until they are sold: see section 61 (5) of the Finance (1909–10) Act, 1910. And when the timber is sold, the proceeds of sale are not aggregable for the purpose of determining the rate of duty either on the timber or on the rest of the estate: see section 9 of the Finance Act, 1912. If the timber is sold when felled or cut, estate duty is payable on the net moneys received after deducting all necessary outgoings since the death of the deceased. If the timber is sold growing, estate duty is payable on the value of the timber at the date of death. The deceased person with reference to whose death the duty is payable is the person on whose death the land was last actually chargeable with estate duty. The rate of duty is that appropriate to the estate of that person, excluding the timber.

---

[9] See Finance Act, 1925, s. 23. Agricultural land includes " pasture and woodland and also includes such cottages, farm buildings, farm-houses and mansion houses (together with the land occupied therewith) as are of a character appropriate to the property ": Finance Act, 1894, s. 22 (1) (g).

[10] Cf. Burdett Coutts v. I. R. C. [1960] 1 W.L.R. 1027.

(iv) *Investment in works of art*

Assuming the trustees have power to do so, the investment in works of art may avoid estate duty. Pictures, prints, books, manuscripts, works of art, scientific collections or other things not yielding income which appear to the Treasury to be of national, scientific, historic or artistic interest which are enjoyed in kind may be exempt from estate duty : see section 40 of the Finance Act, 1930.[11] In practice the Commissioners of Inland Revenue decide as to the qualification of objects for exemption and their decision is final. In the event of the sale of any object to which section 40 applies death duties become chargeable on the proceeds of sale in respect of the last death on which the objects passed, and at the rate attributable to that estate : there is no aggregation. However, death duties do not become chargeable if there is a sale by private treaty to the National Gallery, the British Museum or certain other bodies or institutions.[12]

(v) *The acquisition of a foreign domicile*

The acquisition of a foreign domicile by the life-tenant under a British settlement will not usually cause estate duty to cease to be payable on the settled property. Where, however, the property passing on the death of a life-tenant of foreign [13] domicile consists of securities which have been issued by the Government as tax-free securities under the provisions of section 22 (1) of the Finance (No. 2) Act, 1931, and section 60 (1) of the Finance Act, 1940, estate duty is not normally payable, even if the person becoming entitled on the death happens to be domiciled in Great Britain or Northern Ireland : Finance Act, 1951, s. 34. Similarly, where the property passing consists of immoveables situate outside Great Britain : *Philipson-Stow* v. *I. R. C.* [1961] A.C. 727; and possibly where it consists of moveables situate outside Great Britain : *Re Levick's Will Trusts* [1963] 1 W.L.R. 311.

If the beneficiaries are going to reside abroad so as to acquire a foreign domicile, the proper law of the settlement will remain British nonetheless,[14] and, therefore, estate duty will be payable on the life-tenant's death. It is considered that this liability may possibly be avoided if the settlement is terminated and a new settlement in identical terms is set up abroad. It may be possible to make an application to the court under the Variation of Trusts Act, 1958, for this purpose : *Re Seale's Marriage Settlement* [1961] Ch. 574.

(vi) *Improvement of settled land*

Where a tenant for life under an existing strict settlement of land carries out improvements on the settled estate, he may be able to recover

---

11 See also Finance Act, 1950, s. 48.
12 See Finance Act, 1921, s. 44, also proviso to s. 40 (2) Finance Act, 1930, Finance Act, 1956, s. 34 (2), and Finance Act, 1958, s. 31.
13 *i.e.*, outside Great Britain and Northern Ireland.
14 See Finance Act, 1949, s. 28 (2); *Marlborough (Duke of)* v. *Att.-Gen. (No. 1)* [1945] Ch. 78, 85; *Iveagh* v. *I. R. C.* [1954] Ch. 364, 370.

the costs of such improvements out of the capital moneys of the settlement: see Settled Land Act, 1925, s. 75 (2); *In re Duke of Northumberland* [1951] Ch. 202.[15] Further, any tax reliefs, for example maintenance relief under section 313 of the Income Tax Act, 1952, which may become due as a consequence of the expense incurred on such improvements, may be retained by the tenant for life, provided the expense is initially met by him: see *In re Pelly's Will Trusts* [1956] Ch. 81. What the position would be if the costs had been paid directly by the trustees of the settlement instead of being paid by way of recoupment to the tenant for life of the amounts expended by him has yet to be decided.

PRECEDENT No. 34

Release and Surrender whereby a Donee of a Power Releases the Fund from the Power and the Life-tenant and Life-tenant in Remainder Surrender their Interests in order to Benefit the Infant Children of the Life-tenant in Remainder

This precedent may be readily adapted to particular circumstances, where there is a life interest which it is desired to release. The release of the life interest operates as a voluntary disposition *inter vivos* and accordingly carries stamp duty at the rate of £1 per cent. on the value of the interest released (*I. R. C.* v. *Buchanan* [1958] Ch. 289; 37 Tax Cas. 365 and *Platt's Trustees* v. *I. R. C.* (1953) 32 A.T.C. 292) subject to the possibility of effecting a reduction by the use in appropriate cases of a certificate of value. In addition the release of the power requires a 10s. stamp. Adjudication is obligatory.

The authors are of the view that where both a life-tenant in possession and a life-tenant in remainder execute a release simultaneously, the life interest in remainder is, for the purposes of section 43 of the Finance Act, 1940, released *before* it becomes an interest in possession. Draftsmen who feel qualms about this and prefer to make a distinction between " before " and " at the same time as " may prefer to draft two separate releases.

Parties.　　THIS RELEASE AND SURRENDER is made the —— day of —— 19— BETWEEN —— of —— (hereinafter called " the First Life Tenant ") of the first part —— of —— (hereinafter called " the Second Life Tenant ") of the second part and —— of —— and —— of —— (hereinafter called " the Trustees ") of the third part; WHEREAS :

---

[15] See also *In re Sutherland Settlement Trusts* [1953] Ch. 792; *In re Lord Brougham and Vaux's Settled Estates* [1954] Ch. 24; and *In re Boston's Will Trusts* [1956] Ch. 395.

Trusts affecting trust fund.

(A) By his will made the —— day of ——, —— (hereinafter called " the Testator ") appointed the Trustees to be his executors and trustees and devised and bequeathed the residue of his estate unto the Trustees upon trust to sell the same and to stand possessed of the proceeds and the investments for the time being representing the same (hereinafter called " the Trust Fund ") upon trust to pay the income thereof to the First Life Tenant during her life and after her death to pay the income thereof to the Second Life Tenant during his life and subject thereto in trust for such of the issue (whether children or remoter issue) of the Second Life Tenant by any wife he might marry and in such manner as the Second Life Tenant should by Deed or Will or Codicil appoint and subject thereto and in default thereof in trust for such of the children of the Second Life Tenant as should attain the age of 21 and if more than one in equal shares and in default thereof upon certain trusts therein set out [or otherwise recite the settlement];

Death of testator, etc.

(B) The Testator died on the —— day of —— and probate of his said Will was on the —— day of —— granted to the Trustees out of the Principal Probate Registry;

Existing remainder-men.

(C) The Second Life Tenant has the following children, namely [recite their names and dates of birth];

Desire to release and surrender.

(D) The First Life Tenant and the Second Life Tenant desire to release and surrender their interests in the Trust Fund and the power of appointment of the Second Life Tenant in respect thereof for the purpose of accelerating the interests of the said children and of any future children of the Second Life Tenant;

Witnesseth.

NOW to give effect to the said desire THIS DEED WITNESSETH as follows :—

Release from power.

1. THE Second Life Tenant hereby releases the Trust Fund and all other if any the property now or which may hereafter become subject to the trusts contained in the

said Will from the power of appointment thereby conferred on him To the intent that the said power may be absolutely extinguished.

A donee of a power, whether exercisable by will or by deed, may, provided that the power is not exercisable in a fiduciary capacity, by deed release or contract not to exercise that power: Law of Property Act, 1925, s. 155.

The release or exercise of a power of appointment with a view to carrying out some transaction to avoid estate duty does not necessarily bring into operation the doctrine of fraud on a power: see *ante*, p. 275.

Surrender of life interests.   **2.** THE First Life Tenant and the Second Life Tenant hereby surrender and assign unto the Trustees ALL THAT the life interest of the First Life Tenant and ALL THAT the reversionary life interest of the Second Life Tenant in the Trust Fund To the intent that the said life interest and reversionary life interest shall forthwith be merged and extinguished in the capital of the Trust Fund and that the Trustees shall stand possessed of the Trust Fund upon the trusts declared by the said Will as if both the First Life Tenant and the Second Life Tenant were dead.

Certificate of value (where appropriate).   **3.** IT is hereby certified that the transactions hereby effected do not form part of a larger transaction or of a series of transactions in respect of which the value or aggregate value of the property conveyed or transferred exceeds the sum of [£3,500] [£4,500] [£5,250] [£6,000].

IN WITNESS, ETC.

This precedent may be adapted to meet various cases where it is desired to release a power of appointment and to accelerate the interests in default of appointment by surrendering a life interest. The effect for estate duty and income tax purposes will be as follows :—

(i) *Estate duty*

Estate duty will be payable on the death of the second life-tenant, unless he survives the transaction by five years. As he has assigned his interest before it became an interest in possession, no claim arises under section 43 of the Finance Act, 1940. But it would appear that the surrender is caught by section 45 (2) of the Finance Act, 1940. Therefore it is arguable that a claim for duty will probably arise on the death of the life-tenant within five years: see *ante*, p. 267.

Estate duty will be payable on the death of the first life-tenant, unless he survives the transaction by at least five years: see Finance

Act, 1940, s. 43. In view of the provisions of section 44 of the Finance Act, 1950, the trustees should, if the remaindermen's interests will vest within five years, obtain a certificate from the Commissioners of the amount which may be treated as the prospective amount of the duty payable on the first life-tenant's death, and thereby restrict their liability to the amount so certified; they will thereupon be able to distribute the remaining capital to the beneficiaries immediately or as soon as their interests vest. The rules for ascertaining the value of the life interest in these circumstances are now contained in section 38 (12) of the Finance Act, 1957.

(ii) *Income tax*

Where a parent settles property on his children, the effect of section 397 of the Income Tax Act, 1952, is that the income of the share of each child paid to or applied for him during his infancy, is deemed to be the income of the settlor for tax purposes. The general topic is more fully discussed elsewhere in this book.[16] The Revenue authorities take the view that a parent (being the life-tenant in possession) executing a surrender in favour of his children (being the expectant reversioners) is a " settlor " within the meaning of the section (see Income Tax Act, 1952, s. 403). And following the decision of the Court of Appeal in *I. R. C.* v. *Buchanan* [1958] Ch. 289; 37 Tax Cas. 365, this view would appear to be correct. Similarly in the case of a surrender of a life interest by a parent who has, as in the circumstances contemplated in the precedent, only a reversionary life interest, the parent is a " settlor " within the meaning of section 403 so that section 397 would apply. The claim for tax in the *Buchanan* case was limited to the period following the death of the life-tenant in possession. This involves the curious notion that the reversionary life-tenant having surrendered her life interest only became a " settlor " on the death of the life-tenant in possession who had released his life interest immediately after the release by the reversionary life-tenant of her life interest.

It was also argued in the *Buchanan* case that there were two " settlors " for the purposes of sections 401 and 403 of the Income Tax Act, 1952, namely the testator who provided the trust fund in the first place and the reversionary life-tenant who by releasing her life interest made income available for her infant children. This argument found favour with the Special Commissioners. Vaisey J. decided in favour of the taxpayer on other grounds. In the Court of Appeal only Lord Goddard C.J. referred to the argument, dismissing it as untenable on the footing that a testator could not be a settlor for the purposes of the section. It is respectfully submitted that the definitions of " settlement " and " settlor," which include any " trust " and any person who has provided funds for the purpose of the settlement respectively, are none

---

the less apt to include the trusts created by a will and the testator who provided the settled funds.

PRECEDENT No. 35

Appointment and Surrender whereby a Donee Exercises a Power of Appointment in Favour of his Existing Children and Releases the Fund so Appointed from his Life Interest, Retaining an Annuity

The stamp will require adjudication. In addition to a 10s. stamp on the appointment, *ad valorem* duty will be required on the value of the interest passing to the remaindermen as on a voluntary disposition *inter vivos*; see *Platt's Trustees* v. *I. R. C.* (1953) 32 A.T.C. 292. The normal rate of *ad valorem* duty is £1 per cent., but this may be reduced in appropriate cases where a certificate of value may be employed.

Parties. THIS APPOINTMENT AND SURRENDER is made the —— day of —— 19— BETWEEN —— of —— (hereinafter called " the Appointor ") of the one part and —— of —— and —— of —— (hereinafter called " the Trustees ") of the other part ;

WHEREAS :

Supplemental to principal deed. (A) This Deed is Supplemental to a Settlement (hereinafter called " the Principal Deed ") made the —— day of —— between —— of the 1st part, the Appointor of the 2nd part and the Trustees of the 3rd part ;

Principal deed. (B) By the Principal Deed the said —— directed that the Trustees should stand possessed of certain investments and moneys previously transferred into the names or control of the Trustees and the investments for the time being representing the same (therein and hereinafter called " the Trust Fund ") upon certain trusts namely upon trust to pay the income thereof to the Appointor during his lifetime and after the death of the Appointor in trust for such of the issue of the Appointor and in such shares and subject to such conditions and with such provisions as he should by Deed appoint and in default of such appointment upon the other trusts therein set out [*or otherwise set out the trusts in the Principal Deed, or so much of them as affects the present Deed*] ;

Remainder-
men.

(C) The Appointor has —— children and no more namely [*give names and dates of birth*];

Investments.

(D) The Trust Fund is now represented by the investments mentioned in the first and second parts of the Schedule hereto;

Desire to
appoint, etc.

(E) The Appointor desires to make such an irrevocable appointment in respect of the whole of the capital of the Trust Fund as is hereinafter contained and to release his life interest in a part of the Trust Fund in manner hereinafter appearing;

NOW to give effect to the said desire THIS DEED WITNESSETH as follows:

Appointment.

1. THE Appointor hereby irrevocably appoints that the Trustees shall (subject to the interest of the Appointor hereinafter referred to) stand possessed of the Trust Fund and all other if any the property now or which may become subject to the trusts of the Principal Deed in Trust for such of the said children of the Appointor namely —— and —— as shall attain the age of twenty-one years and if more than one in equal shares.

Surrender
reserving
an annuity.

2. THE Appointor hereby surrenders unto the Trustees ALL THAT the life interest of the Appointor in the Trust fund and all other if any the property now or which may become subject to the trusts of the Principal Deed EXCEPTING only the annual sum of —— pounds sterling out of that part of the Trust Fund represented by the investments specified in the second part of the Schedule hereto during the lifetime of the Appointor (the same to be a continuing charge on the income but not on the capital thereof) To the Intent that the said life interest other than the said annual sum shall forthwith be merged in the capital of the Trust Fund and that the Trustees shall stand henceforth possessed of the Trust Fund (but as to the income of the investments in the second part of the Schedule hereto subject to the payment to the Appointor of the said annual sum) upon the trusts hereinbefore appointed and free from the said life interest.

Certificate
of value
(where
appropriate).

3. IT is hereby certified that the transactions hereby effected do not form part of a larger transaction or of a series of transactions in respect of which the value or

aggregate value of the property conveyed or transferred exceeds the sum of [——] [——].

IN WITNESS, ETC.

SCHEDULE

[(1) *Investments released.*
(2) *Investments retained to secure the annuity.*]

This precedent is intended to meet the case where the life-tenant is prepared to surrender his life interest, but wishes to create and retain an annuity out of the fund.

Estate duty will be payable on the whole of the fund in which the interest subsisted if the life-tenant dies within five years: see Finance Act, 1957, s. 38 (12). It is now clear that the retention of an annuity out of the property released does not make estate duty payable except in respect of the " slice " upon which the annuity is charged, if the life-tenant dies after the five-year period: *St. Aubyn* v. *Att.-Gen.* [1952] A.C. 15. It is considered that liability to estate duty on the whole fund would continue after the five-year period, if the remainderman, being of age, convenanted to pay the annuity or if the annuity were charged on the whole of the fund.

As was stated with regard to the last precedent, if the appointor executes an appointment and release in favour of his own infant children, he is a " settlor " as defined by section 403 of the Income Tax Act, 1952, and consequently section 397 applies; any sums paid out for the benefit of an infant child will be treated for tax purposes as income of the appointor. It is therefore advisable to accumulate the income and to pay it to the child after he attains the age of twenty-one. Because of the amendment to section 397 of the Income Tax Act, 1952, contained in section 20 (2) of the Finance Act, 1958, it is not now necessary to wait until after the end of the year of assessment in which the child attains twenty-one before making the payment of accumulated income to him.

The converse of this precedent, by which the life-tenant would release so much of the fund as would produce an income of £x a year is not a practical proposition: there cannot be a merger of the annuity released with the reversion; on the death of the life-tenant the whole fund would pass and no estate duty would be saved.

PRECEDENT No. 36

Surrender of a Reversionary Life Interest in consideration of an Annuity to be paid to the Reversionary Life-tenant by the Remainderman

The advantages of this form of disposition are described above at page 267. In practice, where the settlement contains a complex system of cross-remainders, considerable variations to this precedent will be required. The precedent may be readily adapted to the situation where the remainderman pays a lump sum in place of the annuity.

Parties.

THIS DEED OF SURRENDER AND COVENANT is made the —— day of —— 19— BETWEEN —— of —— (hereinafter called " the Second Life Tenant ") of the first part —— of —— (hereinafter called " the Remainderman ") of the second part and —— of —— and —— of —— (hereinafter called " the Trustees ") of the third part;

WHEREAS :

Supplemental to principal deed.

(A) This deed is supplemental to a Settlement (hereinafter called " the Principal Deed ") made the —— day of —— 19— between —— of the first part —— of the second part and the Trustees of the third part and to an Appointment expressed to be supplemental to the Principal Deed and made the —— day of —— by the said —— in exercise of the power of appointment conferred upon him by the Principal Deed;

Trusts of released fund.

(B) By virtue of the Principal Deed and the recited Appointment and in the events which have happened the Trustees are possessed of certain investments and money and the investments for the time being representing the same (in the Principal Deed and hereinafter called " the Trust Fund ") upon certain trusts which so far as concerns one equal fourth part of the Trust Fund (hereinafter called " the Released Fund ") are the following namely: Upon Trust to pay the income thereof to —— (hereinafter called " the First Life Tenant ") during her lifetime and after her death upon trust to pay the said income to the Second Life Tenant during her lifetime if she shall survive the First Life Tenant and after the death of the survivor of the First Life Tenant and the Second Life Tenant Upon Trust as to capital and income for the Remainderman absolutely [*or otherwise set out the trusts affecting the Trust Fund so far as they are relevant*];

Agreement to surrender.

(C) The Second Life Tenant and the Remainderman have bargained and agreed that the Second Life Tenant shall surrender the life interest to which she is entitled in the income of the Released Fund contingently upon her surviving the First Life Tenant and that in consideration for her so doing the Remainderman shall covenant to pay her the annual sums hereinafter provided for;

NOW THIS DEED WITNESSETH as follows:

Surrender of reversionary life interest.

1. THE Second Life Tenant hereby surrenders and assigns unto the Trustees ALL THAT the reversionary life interest of the Second Life Tenant in the Released Fund to which the Second Life Tenant is entitled contingently upon her surviving the First Life Tenant to the intent that the said reversionary life interest shall forthwith be merged and extinguished in the capital of the Released Fund and that the Trustees shall stand possessed of the Released Fund subject only to the interest in the income thereof of the First Life Tenant Upon Trust for the Remainderman absolutely.

Covenant to pay annuity.

2. THE Remainderman hereby covenants with the Second Life Tenant so as to bind himself and his executors and administrators that from and after the death of the First Life Tenant he will pay to the Second Life Tenant during her lifetime such a monthly sum as after deduction of tax at the standard rate for the time being in force will leave the clear sum of £—— such sums to be payable on the first day of each calendar month and so that the last payment thereof shall not be apportionable.

IN WITNESS, ETC.

The release of a reversionary life interest is not caught by section 43 of the Finance Act, 1940.

Section 43 is restricted in its application to interests in possession. But since the surrender is an extinguishment of a right, it would appear that it should be treated as a disposition made by the life-tenant on his death within five years: see section 45 (2) of the Finance Act, 1940, and *cf. Re Stratton's Disclaimer* [1957] Ch. 132. The effect of section

38 (3) and (16) of the Finance Act, 1957, could be that the value of the extinguished right is to be ascertained at the date of the extinguishment. But on the basis that the claim for duty would be on the value of the reversionary life interest at the date of the surrender, and not on the capital of the settled fund, the claim is unlikely in most cases to be of any great value. See also section 38 (15) discussed at page 268, *ante*.

Precedent No. 37

Disclaimer of a Life Interest in Residue under a Will where the Life-tenant has not yet Entered into Possession of his Interest and Desires to Accelerate the Gift Over

Disclaimer.   THIS DISCLAIMER made the —— day of —— 19—
by —— of —— WITNESSETH that the said —— hereby
DISCLAIMS ALL THAT the life interest in the residue of the
estate of X Y deceased bequeathed to him by the will
dated the —— day of —— 19— of the Said X Y who died
on the —— day of —— 19—.
        IN WITNESS, ETC.

This disclaimer is intended to be used instead of a surrender, where the residue of an estate is settled. It should only be used if executed during the administration of the estate and in any event before the life-tenant enters into possession of his interest by accepting any income. Further, it must relate to the whole of an interest: a partial disclaimer is invalid. Normally a disclaimer of a life interest will accelerate the reversion, unless a contrary intention appears from the will: *Re Hodge* [1943] Ch. 300; *Re Davies* [1957] 1 W.L.R. 922 and the cases mentioned on page 266, *ante*.

Estate duty

It is clear that no estate duty will be payable on the life-tenant's death if he survives the disclaimer by more than five years.

If the life-tenant dies within five years liability to duty, if it exists, arises under section 43 or 45 (2) of the Finance Act, 1940. It seems reasonably clear that section 43 does not apply, since the wording of the section refers to a disposition or determination of the life interest, and a disclaimer is something quite different—it does not dispose of or determine the life interest, but prevents it ever coming into existence.

Section 43 only applies to a life interest in possession, and a life interest in residue cannot be said to be in possession until administration of the estate is complete. Section 45 would, however, appear to be applicable, so that the disclaimer is a " disposition ": *Re Stratton's Disclaimer* [1957] Ch. 132. Even so it is not certain that liability to estate duty will arise: see the discussion of subsections (3), (15) and (16) of section 38 of the Finance Act, 1957, *ante,* page 268.

A disclaimer of a legacy with a view to increasing the value of the residue is caught by section 45 of the Finance Act, 1940, so that estate duty is payable if the disclaiming legatee dies within five years: *Re Stratton's Disclaimer* [1957] Ch. 132, just as if the legatee had assigned the legacy by way of gift. Nevertheless it may, in some cases, be advantageous to execute a disclaimer in place of an assignment by way of gift, in order to gain other incidental advantages in relation to income tax and stamp duty.

Income tax

If a life-tenant surrenders his interest in favour of his own infant children, section 397 of the Income Tax Act, 1952, applies, and the income—if paid to or for the infant remaindermen's benefit—must be deemed to be income of the parent: *cf. I. R. C.* v. *Buchanan* [1958] Ch. 289; 37 Tax Cas. 365. Where the life-tenant, instead of surrendering, disclaims, it is submitted that section 397 cannot apply since a disclaiming beneficiary is not a " settlor " as defined by section 403. On this view income may safely be applied for the maintenance of the infant children of the disclaiming life-tenant, without such income being treated as income of the parent. But it cannot be said to be certain that the Revenue will accept this view without litigation.

Stamp duty

A deed stamp of 10s. is all that is required. This is in contrast to the *ad valorem* duty payable on the release of a life interest.

PRECEDENT No. 38

Partition of a Settled Fund between the Life-tenant and the Remainderman

It may happen that a life-tenant is unwilling to execute a voluntary release of his life interest, and it is also impracticable for the life-tenant to purchase the interest of the remainderman, perhaps because there are difficulties in raising the purchase price, or because the remainderman is interested in retaining in the family the assets constituting the trust fund, or because the burden of stamp duty is too heavy. In addition, if the life-tenant purchases the interest of the remainderman and dies within five years, duty will be payable both on the settled fund and on the purchase price: Finance Act, 1958, s. 28. In such a case a partition may prove useful.

The part of the settled funds taken by the remainderman will be liable for estate duty under section 43 of the Finance Act, 1940, if the life-tenant dies within five years of the partition. But it is considered that no duty may be claimed on the basis that there has been a disposition of a life interest which is to be treated as remaining in existence in the possession and enjoyment of the remainderman under the provisions in subsection (3) of section 38 of the Finance Act, 1957, because the disposition, being for full value in money's worth, does not attract duty.

The part taken by the life-tenant will not incur liability under section 43; it will bear estate duty only to the extent that it forms part of the free estate of the life-tenant at his death.

It is considered that a division in accordance with the advice of a qualified actuary is the most cautious course to adopt. But in practice any method of division may be used provided it represents a genuine bargain for full money's worth on either side, without any element of bounty.

Provided the partition represents a genuine bargain for full money's worth, the stamp will be only 10s.

Parties.   THIS DEED OF PARTITION is made the —— day of —— 19— BETWEEN —— of —— (hereinafter called " the Life Tenant ") of the first part —— of —— (hereinafter called " the Remainderman ") of the second part and —— of —— and —— of —— (hereinafter called " the Trustees ") of the third part ;

WHEREAS :

Settlement.   (A) The assets specified in the Schedule hereto and the money and property from time to time representing the same (hereinafter called " the Settled Funds ") constitute the trust fund which was set up by a Settlement made the —— day of —— 19— between A A of the first part B B of the second part and C C and D D of the third part [recite the general effect of the provisions thereof] ;

Trustees.   (B) The Trustees are the present trustees of the Settled Funds ;

Present trusts.   (C) By virtue of the terms of the recited Settlement and by virtue of the following deeds all of which were expressed to be supplemental to the said Settlement (namely) : [Here recite any supplemental deeds] and in the events which have happened the Settled Funds are now held by the Trustees Upon Trust to pay the income thereof to the Life Tenant during his life and after his death upon trust as to capital and income for the Remainderman absolutely;

Agreement to partition.

(D) The Life Tenant and the Remainderman have agreed to partition the Settled Funds between themselves and having caused proper valuations to be made of the assets constituting the same and acting in accordance with the opinion of a qualified Actuary instructed to value their respective interests in the Settled Funds have agreed to divide the Settled Funds and to make mutual exchanges of their interests therein without the payment of any equality money in manner hereinafter appearing;

NOW in pursuance of the said agreement THIS DEED WITNESSETH as follows:

Surrender of Life Interest in part.

1. THE Life Tenant hereby assigns and surrenders unto the Remainderman ALL THAT the interest of the Life Tenant in the income arising during his lifetime in so much of the Settled Funds as is represented by the assets specified in the First Part of the Schedule hereto TO HOLD unto the Remainderman To the Intent that the interest in the income thereof of the Life Tenant shall merge in the reversion expectant upon his death and the Remainderman shall henceforth be entitled to the said assets absolutely.

Assignment of reversion in part.

2. THE Remainderman hereby assigns and transfers unto the Life Tenant ALL THAT his interest expectant upon the death of the Life Tenant in so much of the Settled Funds as is represented by the assets specified in the Second Part of the Schedule hereto TO HOLD unto the Life Tenant To the Intent that the interest therein of the Life Tenant shall be enlarged and that he shall henceforth be entitled to the said assets absolutely.

IN WITNESS, ETC.

THE SCHEDULE above referred to.

FIRST PART.

[Here give a list of the assets comprised in the Settled Funds which are to go to the Remainderman]

SECOND PART.

[Here give a list of the assets comprised in the Settled
[Funds which are to go to the Life-Tenant]

PRECEDENT No. 39

Arrangement intended to be Submitted to the Court for Approval under the Variation of Trusts Act, 1958. Partition of a Settled Fund between a Life-Tenant and Infant and Unborn Remaindermen. Additional Benefit to Remaindermen by Discretionary Trusts

The situation contemplated is that a fund is settled upon the life-tenant for life with remainder to such of his children as being sons attain the age of twenty-one years or being daughters attain that age or earlier marry. The life-tenant has one or more infant children, and, while wishing to reduce the burden of estate duty on his death, is unwilling to do so by releasing his life interest voluntarily, and unable, since the remaindermen are not all adult and *sui juris*, to carry out a partition of the funds, as in Precedent No. 38 *ante*, without going to the court under the Variation of Trusts Act, 1958.

Briefly, the arrangement consists of a division of the settled funds between the life-tenant and the remaindermen on the footing that the life-tenant takes part absolutely, the remaindermen to take the greater part of the balance upon trusts which correspond closely to those in the settlement (see the First Schedule to the Arrangement) and the rest of the balance is settled upon discretionary trusts for the benefit of the remaindermen and their issue (see the Second Schedule to the Arrangement).

Generally, the settled funds should be divided so that:

(a) The funds in the First Schedule (in which are set out the trusts relating to the children's fund) are considerably greater than that part of the settled fund which the actuary, in dividing the fund between the life-tenant, the charge for estate duty, and the remaindermen, has allocated to remaindermen; and

(b) The funds in the First Schedule are little, if at all, less, than the " net inheritance," *i.e.*, than the amount to which the settled fund would be reduced if no arrangement were effected, the life-tenant died, and estate duty were paid; and

(c) The funds in the First and Second Schedules together are greater than the " net inheritance." The trusts relating to the discretionary fund are set out in the Second Schedule.

In practice, where the settled funds are comparatively modest in amount, a somewhat simpler arrangement than this would normally be advisable. The settled funds would simply be divided between the life-tenant and the remaindermen and the trusts in the First Schedule, and the Second Schedule would be omitted. However, where substantial trust funds are considered, the life-tenant may well form the view that he would not like his children to acquire the free dispcsal of their entire inheritance at the age of twenty-one years. If the original settlement confers upon the life-tenant a power of appointment among children and remoter issue, and he is not the settlor, then that power may be retained by him during his lifetime in respect of the children's fund. Otherwise, the funds may be divided on the footing that part only of that part of the funds which is allocated to the children is settled so that they have a vested interest at the age of twenty-one years, the balance being either settled upon the children for life with remainders over, the trustees having power to advance capital, or, as in this Precedent, settled upon discretionary trusts.

ARRANGEMENT

Revocation.

The trusts contained in a Settlement (hereinafter called " the Settlement ") dated the —— and made between —— of the one part and —— and —— of the other part are hereby revoked as respects the whole of the funds now held by the Trustees of the Settlement and in place thereof the said funds shall be held upon the following trusts namely :

Life Tenant.

(1) The Trustees of the Settlement shall hold —— parts of the capital and income of the said funds upon trust for —— (referred to in the Settlement as the Life Tenant) absolutely ;

Children's Fund.

(2) The Trustees of the Settlement shall hold —— parts of the said capital and income upon the trusts declared concerning the Children's Fund in the First Schedule to this Arrangement ;

Discretionary Fund.

(3) The Trustees of the Settlement shall hold the remaining —— parts of the said capital and income upon the trusts concerning the Discretionary Fund in the Second Schedule to this Arrangement ;

Appropriation.

(4) The Trustees of the Settlement shall so soon as may be practicable apportion the said funds between the parts thereof hereinbefore mentioned and for this purpose shall have power either to divide any investments forming part of the said funds rateably between the said parts or to appropriate any such investment or any part thereof to any of the said parts in such manner as the said Trustees shall in their discretion think fit and for this purpose the Trustees shall cause to be made all

proper valuations of the investments constituting the said funds;

As an alternative to the above clause, the Arrangement may be recast so that, instead of the trustees dividing the funds between the three parts, the investments are set out in a Schedule to the Arrangement, and in that Schedule are divided between the three parts.

Policies.   (5) The Trustees of the Settlement shall so soon as may be practicable use their best endeavours to effect with the —— Insurance Co. Ltd. or any other insurance office of repute two policies of insurance each at a single premium not exceeding £—— under which the following sums of money shall hereunder become payable to the Trustees :

EVENT	FIRST POLICY	SECOND POLICY
On the death of the said Life Tenant occurring during the two years commencing on the date upon which the approval of the court is obtained to this Arrangement :	£100,000	£20,000
On the said death occurring during the year commencing two years after the said date :	£85,000	£17,000
On the said death occurring during the year commencing three years after the said date :	£70,000	£14,000
On the said death occurring during the year commencing four years after the said date :	£40,000	£8,000

The said Trustees shall pay the premium in respect of the first of the said policies out of the capital of and shall hold the said policy upon the trusts relating to the Children's Fund. The said Trustees shall pay the premium in respect of the second of the said policies out of the capital of and shall hold the said policy upon the trusts relating to the Discretionary Fund.

The above figures are intended only to illustrate the type of " decreasing term " policy that is intended to be effected. The policy should be great enough to provide a sum of cash, equal, or almost equal to the amount of estate duty that is likely to be payable in respect of the children's fund or discretionary fund, as the case may be, in the event of the settlor failing to survive the five-year period.

A troublesome problem arises, to what extent it is possible to be certain that the policy moneys will not themselves bear estate duty. It is considered that where, under the Arrangement, the existing trusts of the settlement are revoked, the liability for estate duty in the event of the life-tenant dying within five years must be computed by reference to the assets comprised in the children's fund or discretionary fund, as the case may be, at the date of revocation, *i.e.*, at the date when the court approves the Arrangement; and in this respect see the proviso to subsection (8) of section 38 of the Finance Act, 1957. It follows that the policy moneys are not chargeable to estate duty on the death of the settlor, the policies not being assets of the settlement until after the settlement has been revoked. It is not absolutely certain that this view is correct, because it could be argued that even though the Arrangement revokes the settlement, if it replaces the trusts of the settlement by identical or similar trusts, the settlement has not come to an end within the meaning of the proviso to subsection (8), with the result that on the death of the life-tenant estate duty is chargeable on the assets in the fund on his death, including the insurance moneys. The argument perhaps gains some support from the circumstance that the court's jurisdiction under the Act is primarily to vary rather than to terminate trusts and settlements. If duty is payable on the policy moneys, the amount on which duty is payable is likely to be aggregable.

It is considered that the trusts affecting the policies ought to be so worded that the settlor cannot under any circumstances benefit.

The view is also sometimes expressed (and there is much to commend it) that the insurance policy should be effected not by the trustees but by the life-tenant out of his own moneys. If he is then excluded from all benefit, it is at least certain that some measure of separate aggregation will be obtained on his death. Moreover, although the policy effected by the life-tenant may have to be regarded as consideration for the purchase of the interests of the remaindermen, so that it is caught by section 28 of the Finance Act, 1958, nevertheless paragraph (b) of subsection (11) appears to lead to the result that in the event of the life-tenant dying within five years the policy is valued not as at his death but as at the date of the Arrangement. The value may, therefore, be no more and may even be less than the amount of the single premium paid.

First
Schedule.

THE FIRST SCHEDULE

TRUSTS RELATING TO THE CHILDREN'S FUND

It is intended that these trusts should be similar to, if not identical with, the trusts in the settlement taking effect after the death of the life-tenant. It is, however, not necessary to follow slavishly the wording of the settlement, if it can be made more lucid or simple, without substantially changing the beneficial interests.

306   VARIATION OF EXISTING SETTLEMENTS

If the settlement confers on the life-tenant a power of appointment among his children or his children and remoter issue, the question arises whether that power may or should be retained. One clear rule is that if the life-tenant is also the settlor the power must not be retained, at any rate for more than two years, because it may cause liability to estate duty to arise on the death of the settlor under section 2 (1) (d) of the Finance Act, 1894. Apart from that, no clear rule can be laid down for all cases. If the power is released, this may be regarded as conferring some additional benefit on the children, because the number of imponderables lying between them and their inheritance is reduced. In many cases a proper compromise may be, that the life-tenant retains the power, exercisable by deed only, either for a stated short period, or in respect of each child's interest until that child is, say, twenty-five years of age.

If upon any of the children attaining the age of twenty-one years, or being a daughter attaining that age or marrying, he or she demands to be paid out his or her share, the trustees must have regard to the possibility of future children being born, and also to estate duty liability if the life-tenant should not survive the five-year period; as to the latter posssibility, they may obtain a certificate under section 44 (3) of the Finance Act, 1950.

Definitions.   1. In this Schedule where the context admits:
" the Life Tenant " means the said ——— ;
" the Trustees " means the said ——— and ——— (who are the present Trustees of the above mentioned Settlement) and the survivor or survivors of them and other the trustees or trustee for the trusts hereinafter declared concerning the Children's Fund; and
" the Children's Fund " means that part of the capital and income of the funds hitherto held by the Trustees upon the trusts contained in the Settlement that by this Arrangement is directed to be held upon the trusts contained in this Schedule and the property from time to time representing the same.

Trusts.   2. The Trustees shall hold the Children's Fund upon the following trusts:
(1) Upon trust for all the children of the Life Tenant who being sons shall attain the age of twenty-one years or being daughters shall attain that age or marry under that age in equal shares and so that no child shall be excluded by reason of his or her not being born until after the date upon which the first or any child attains

the age of twenty-one years or being a daughter marries; and subject thereto

(2) Upon trust for the Life Tenant absolutely.

Powers. 3. The Trustees shall in the administration of the trusts hereof have the following powers in addition to the powers conferred upon them by law :

(1) Power to retain the investments for the time being forming part of the Children's Fund so long as the Trustees may think fit and at any time or times to sell call in or convert into money any of the said investments or any part thereof or to change or vary any of the said investments or any part thereof for others hereby or by law authorised.

(2) Power to invest any moneys requiring to be invested under the trusts hereof as follows :

[Normally the powers in the Settlement, brought up to date if need be].

(3) Power to appropriate any investment or property from time to time forming part of the Children's Fund in its actual state of investment in or towards the satisfaction of the beneficial interest of any person or persons in the Children's Fund upon making such valuations as the Trustees may think fit and without the necessity of obtaining the consent of any person.

4. [Trustee indemnity, ante p. 211]

5. [Professional charging clause, ante 211]

New Trustees. 6. The power of appointing new or additional Trustees of the Children's Fund shall be vested in the Life Tenant during his life.

THE SECOND SCHEDULE

TRUSTS RELATING TO THE DISCRETIONARY FUND

These trusts are intended to give some additional benefit to the remaindermen, so that it can fairly be said that they derive greater benefit if the Arrangement is put into effect than if it were not put into effect, and moreover have made with the life-tenant a bargain of the sort that might have been made had they been adults at arm's length. It is contemplated that discretionary trusts of this type would normally be constituted of much more than ten per cent. of the whole settled fund. Since discretionary trusts are often expensive to administer, it follows that discretionary trusts should not normally be brought into an Arrangement unless very substantial funds are being dealt with. The draftsmen may consider the alternative of increasing the Children's Fund and omitting a Discretionary Fund, or changing the Discretionary Fund so that each remainderman has some fixed share.

It is important that the beneficiaries under the Discretionary Fund are in effect the remaindermen and possibly their spouses and issue. The life-tenant is not to avail himself of the opportunity to bring in outsiders whom he may wish to benefit. It will be observed that, although the trustees have a complete discretion over income during the trust period, in addition to very wide powers of appointment, the ultimate trust of capital goes to a class that is not very different from the class of remaindermen under the existing settlement.

In this Schedule where the context admits:

" the Life Tenant " means the said —— ;

" the Trustees " means —— and —— (who are the present Trustees of the Settlement) and the survivor or survivors of them and other the trustees or trustee of the trusts hereinafter declared concerning the Discretionary Fund ;

" the Trust Period " means the period commencing upon the day upon which the approval of the Court is obtained to the Arrangement to which these trusts are Scheduled and terminating upon the expiration of the period of sixty years thereafter or upon the earlier expiration of the period of twenty years after the death of the last survivor of the descendants living of the said day of his late Majesty King George V ;

" the Beneficiaries " means the following persons (and so that the word " Beneficiary " shall be similarly construed) namely :

The existing children of the Life Tenant whose names and dates of birth are the following :

——

—— and

All children and remoter issue of the Life Tenant that may be born at any time during the Trust Period and ;

References to children and to remoter issue are to take effect on the footing that adopted children are the children of their adoptive parents or parent and of nobody else and that legitimated children are the children of their legitimated parents and of nobody else.

Trusts of

2. Subject to each and every exercise of the powers contained in the next following clause of this Schedule the Trustees shall hold the Discretionary Fund and the income thereof upon the following trusts :

Income.

(1) During the Trust Period the Trustees shall retain the capital of the Discretionary Fund and shall deal with the income thereof within a reasonable time and at all events within six months after it arises by allocating the same among the Beneficiaries for the time being living and if more than one in such proportions and such manner as the Trustees in their absolute discretion shall from time to time think fit ; and

Capital.

(2) At the end of the Trust Period the Trustees shall hold the capital and future income of the Discretionary Fund upon trust for such of the children of the Life Tenant whether now living or born at any time during the Trust Period as shall be living at the end of the Trust Period and if more than one in equal shares absolutely Provided that if any such child shall have died during the Trust Period leaving him or her surviving a child or children or remoter issue who shall be living at the end of the Trust Period such child or children or remoter issue shall take and if more than one in equal shares per stirpes that share in the Discretionary Fund which the child so dying would have taken if he or she had survived until the end of the Trust Period ; and

(3) Subject thereto the Trustees shall hold the capital and income of the Discretionary Fund upon trust for all the children of the Life Tenant who being sons shall attain the age of twenty-one years or being daughters shall attain that age or marry under that age in equal shares and so that no child shall be excluded by reason of his or her not being born until after the date upon which the first or any child attains the age of twenty-one years or being a daughter marries ; and

(4) Subject thereto the Trustees shall hold the capital and income of the Discretionary Fund upon trust for the Life Tenant absolutely.

Powers.

3. During the Trust Period the Trustees (being at least two individuals or being or including a trust

corporation) shall have the following powers exercisable in their absolute discretion namely:

Resettlement.

(1) Power by deed or deeds (whether or not reserving to the Trustees for the time being of the Discretionary Fund any power to revoke the same) at any time or times to appoint and declare such trusts in respect of the whole or any part or parts of the Discretionary Fund or the income thereof for the benefit of any one or more of the Beneficiaries and their respective spouses widows and widowers with and subject to such conditions limitations gifts over provisions for the raising of a portion or portions and powers of appointment and other powers and discretions (including but not limited to protective trusts) exercisable by such person or persons whether or not being themselves trustees and with such provisions and generally in such manner as the Trustees shall from time to time think fit;

Advancement.

(2) Power at any time or times during the Trust Period to raise or pay and transfer to or apply for or towards the education advancement or benefit of any one or more of the Beneficiaries so as to be free from the trusts hereof the whole or any part or parts of the capital of the Discretionary Fund:

Release.

Provided That the Trustee may at any time or times by deed or deeds either wholly or in part release either or both of the powers hereby conferred upon them in like manner as if the same powers were conferred upon the Trustees otherwise than in a fiduciary capacity.

Trustees of allocated Income.

4. Where in the exercise of their discretion under sub-clause (4) of Clause 2 hereof the Trustees allocate any part of the income of the Discretionary Fund to any one of the Beneficiaries the Trustees shall if that Beneficiary shall be adult pay the same to that Beneficiary or as he shall direct and if that Beneficiary shall be an infant the Trustees shall have power to apply any part or parts or the whole of the said income so allocated for or towards the maintenance education or benefit of the infant in question; and any part of the said income so allocated to an infant but not so applied shall be retained by the Trustees and it and the resulting income thereof shall be invested in manner hereinafter authorised and shall be capitalised and held upon trust for the

infant in question contingently upon that infant attaining the age of twenty-one years or surviving until the end of the Trust Period and subject thereto shall become an addition to the capital of the Discretionary Fund : But so that the Trustees shall as respects the whole or any part or parts of the income so retained or the resulting income thereof have power to apply the same for or towards the maintenance education advancement or benefit of the said infant Beneficiary and the like powers in relation thereto as are conferred upon the Trustees in relation to the capital of the Discretionary Fund by sub-clause (1) of Clause 3 hereof.

Powers.   5. The Trustees shall in the administration of the trusts hereof have the following powers in addition to the powers conferred upon them by law :

[*add such powers as may be required*]

6. [*Trustee indemnity, ante p. 211*]

7. [*Professional charging clause, ante p. 211*]

New Trustees.   8. The power to appoint new Trustees hereof shall be exercised by the Life Tenant during his life but shall not be exercised in favour of the Life Tenant or any wife of the Life Tenant.

PRECEDENT No. 40

Instructions to Actuary

These instructions are intended to be used in conjunction with the foregoing precedent.

The following documents are enclosed :

Documents enclosed.   (1) A Settlement dated *etc.*

(2) A list of the assets now constituting the Trust Fund and their values as on the ——.

(3) A Statement of the income and the free estate and the other assets likely to pass on the death of the Life Tenant hereunder mentioned.

Proposed division.   We are instructing you on behalf of Mr. —— who is the Life Tenant in possession under the Settlement mentioned above to make certain valuations in order that an application may be made to the Court under the Variation of Trusts Act 1958 for the purpose of dividing up the Trust Fund by directing the Trustees to hold one fraction thereof upon trust for the Life Tenant absolutely, a further fraction thereof upon trust for his present wife absolutely, and the balance upon trusts corresponding to the trusts which under the Settlement are expressed to take effect upon the death of the Life Tenant subject to any interest in the income that he may appoint to any surviving wife.

The Life Tenant was born on the ———. His present wife ——— was born on the ———. They were married on the ———. The Life Tenant has ——— children only, all of whom are infants, namely : ——— and ———.

Upon his marriage to his said wife the Life Tenant, by deed retaining to himself a power of revocation, appointed to his said wife the whole income of the Trust Fund after his death until her remarriage. The power of revocation has never been exercised or released.

Under the existing law estate duty will be payable on the settled funds on the death of the Life Tenant but not on the death of his said wife. It is considered that the rate of estate duty is likely to be ——— per cent.

The Life Tenant and his said wife are both in good health and you are asked to assume that each has the normal expectation of life for a person of his or her age. The parties are happily married.

Valuations required.

Upon the assumption that the capital of the Trust Fund is to be divided between the Life Tenant his said wife and his existing and any future children, in fractions, without as yet allocating specific investments to any of these three parts, you are asked to report how you consider that the Trust Fund should be divided between the following four elements :

(1) The interest of the Life Tenant.

(2) The estate duty on his death.

(3) The reversionary interest of his said wife upon the footing that the power to revoke this interest is never exercised and

(4) The interests taking effect under the Settlement subject to the said interests of the Life Tenant and his said wife.

We consider that the shares in which the parties divide element (2) above, namely estate duty, is primarily a matter for bargaining between the parties, but if you have any views as to the basis upon which it would be proper to divide this element, we would be obliged if you would state them.

Insurance.   It is intended to give the Trustees power to effect an insurance policy on the life of the Life Tenant, which will provide cash, in the event of his dying within five years, sufficient to pay at least 80 per cent. of the estate duty liability of that part of the Fund that remains settled upon the trusts that under the Settlement are to take effect subject to the interests of himself and any wife. The premium is to be paid out of the funds so settled. The costs of the application to the Court of all parties will be paid by the Life Tenant.

In addition, you are asked to report what you consider to be the normal expectation of life of a man of the age of the Life Tenant enjoying good health and of a woman of the age of his said wife enjoying good health.

If you require further information, will you please ask for the same before making any report, as we are anxious that your report should not be made until after you have been satisfied that you have all the information you require.

CHAPTER 8

PARTNERSHIPS

A PARTNER formerly suffered a disadvantage in comparison with an employee, in that the Income Tax Act, 1952, made no special provision for pensions schemes for persons in business or practising as partners or on their own account.[1] This has to some extent been remedied now that the proposals in the report of the Committee on the Taxation Treatment of Provisions for Retirement [2] have, to a limited extent, been given statutory effect, but the position of the partner remains in many ways unenviable. In his younger days he may be obliged to find instalments of capital, in respect of which he will get no tax relief, in order to buy a share in the partnership, and later may find that in order to provide for his dependants he can accumulate capital only out of taxed income and that such capital may again be depleted by the estate duty payable on his death. It is therefore proposed in this chapter to examine some particular aspects of revenue and partnership law with a view to suggesting possible methods by which some alleviation of the heavy and often disproportionate burden of tax in such cases may be found. It is not easy to give precedents that will suit all the circumstances likely to be found in practice, but those set out at the end of this chapter may serve as a guide to the draftsman who wishes to incorporate some of the suggestions now put forward.

Earned and unearned income

Section 14 of the Finance Act, 1961, introduced considerable reliefs against surtax for earned income. Coupled with the relief against income tax allowed to earned income by section 211 of the Income Tax Act, 1952, as amended by section 12 of the Finance Act, 1957, the surtax relief has created a situation where considerable tax advantages may be gained by creating earned, as opposed to unearned, income. The definition of " earned income " is contained in section 525 of the Income Tax Act, 1952, and, so far as is relevant to the case of a partnership, earned income includes:

" any income which is charged under . . . Schedule D and is immediately derived by the individual from the carrying on or

[1] Pensions schemes are discussed in Chap. 9, *post.*
[2] Cmnd. 9063. The then Chancellor, Mr. R. A. Butler, indicated in his Budget Speech in the year 1954 that legislation was not likely to be introduced immediately because of the cost and that consideration of the report was required. His successor, Mr. Harold Macmillan, introduced legislation in the 1956 Finance Act which went some, but not all, of the way towards implementing the recommendations made in the report.

exercise by him of his trade, profession or vocation, either as an individual or, in the case of a partnership, as a partner personally acting therein."

Thus a sleeping partner is not entitled to earned income relief. It is, however, plain that the working partners enjoy earned income relief on their shares in the profits, whether actually drawn by them or not. Moreover, a " salary " payable to a partner is chargeable to tax under Schedule D and treated as a distribution of profits. If the terms of the partnership provide for interest on capital, then any interest payable to a working partner must be treated as a distribution of profits, is payable to him gross and not net, and · comes as earned income.

On the other hand, where, as frequently happens, one or more of the partners own the freehold or leasehold premises upon which the partnership business is carried on, and allow the partnership to occupy the premises at a rent, the Revenue take the view that the rent is not earned income. In such a case, it is suggested that the partners should consider reducing the rent to a low figure, and compensating the partners in question by either increasing their shares in profits or by providing that they should have " salaries." It is perhaps worth noting that the decision of the House of Lords in *Rye* v. *Rye* [1962] A.C. 496 establishes the proposition that two or more partners cannot create a valid lease in favour of themselves. The so-called lease can amount to nothing more than an agreement to allow the " leased " premises to be used for the purposes of the partnership business. It is considered that in such a case it is open to the partners to claim that any rent credited in the partnership account by the partners to themselves is not rent in the proper sense of the word at all, and is therefore a distribution of partnership profit, entitled to earned income relief.

There is nothing in section 525 to confer the status of " earned income " on a pension paid by the continuing partners to a retired partner. It is sometimes argued that a pension payable to the wife of a retired or deceased partner is included under the category of " earned income " by reason of subsections (1) (a) and (2) (b) of section 525. So far as is known, there is no published concession on the point, although it may be that individual inspectors of taxes may be prepared to concede that a widow is entitled to earned income relief.

Estate duty on the share of a partner

It is often possible, by careful drafting of the partnership deed, to reduce the estate duty which will be payable on the death of a partner. As a general rule, the share of a partner passes on his death to his executors as an asset of his estate, and his executors will frequently sell this share to the surviving partners.[3] The drawback of this arrangement is that estate duty becomes payable under section 1 of the Finance Act, 1894, on the share of the deceased partner, necessitating the payment by the executors of a substantial sum of money which may have to be raised within a short time.

(i) Option to purchase share

Even if the surviving partners are given an option in the deed of partnership to purchase the interest of the deceased partner at a price lower than its market value, estate duty may possibly be claimed on the full value of the partner's share, not on the amount of the price: see *Perpetual Executors and Trustees Association of Australia, Ltd.* v. *Commissioner of Taxes of the Commonwealth of Australia* [1954] A.C. 114; and *I. R. C.* v. *Crossman* [1937] A.C. 26. It is thought, however, that in some circumstances it may be possible to obtain exemption from estate duty on the excess of the value of the deceased partner's share over the option price, on the ground that the option was created for full consideration in money's worth.

(ii) Reduction of share in surplus assets

What passes on the death of a partner is an interest in the assets employed in the business the extent of which can only be ascertained by taking an account of the business, as on a winding-up or sale, and by valuing the deceased's share therein in the light of the partnership articles and the provisions of the Partnership Act, 1890, particularly sections 39 and 44. Although in the absence of authorities it is not possible to be dogmatic, some saving of estate duty may be made in an appropriate case, by separating the three distinct elements, capital, profits, and a right to surplus assets on a winding-up. There is no objection to varying the provisions of section 44 of the Partnership Act, 1890, so that the final surplus on a winding-up is not distributed among the partners in the proportions in which they are interested in profits, but in some other proportions. Thus it may be possible to provide that one partner has a large share in the profits but a small share in capital and no share in surplus assets on dissolution. Thus he will derive a large income from the business, but the value of his interest on a winding-up account will be small. The Revenue could argue that, although very little passed to his estate under section 1 of the Finance Act, 1894, there is alternative liability under section 2 (1) (b) by reason of the benefit arising to the other parties from the cesser of his interest in the profits. As against this, however, it could be contended that the benefit arising is reduced by the fact that the deceased and the goodwill attached to him is no longer available to

---

[3] The acquisition and disposal of the deceased partner's share by his executors will not give rise to any charge to tax under Case VII of Schedule D: see Finance Act, 1962, s. 12 (7).

contribute to the profit-making capacity of the firm. It could also be contended that, as the partnership deed constituted a commercial bargain, any passing under section 2 (1) (b) is a passing by reason only of a purchase for full consideration in money's worth, so that exemption from estate duty may be claimed under section 3 (1). No authorities give any direct assistance in gauging the strength of the above arguments.

(iii) *Accruer of goodwill*

One variation of the usual deed of partnership, designed to reduce the burden of duty, provides that on a partner's death or retirement his share in the partnership, or in some part of the assets of the partnership, passes by accrual to the surviving partners. This provision does not in itself save any duty (duty being payable either under section 1 of the Finance Act, 1894, on the footing that the share passes or under section 2 (1) (b) on the footing that there has been the cesser of an interest); in fact, it only renders the surviving partners the accountable persons instead of the executors, so that, in the absence of some express provision in the will for payment of duty, the partnership may be no better off. A provision for accruer to surviving partners has, however, the advantage that it opens the door to the operation of section 3 (1) of the Finance Act, 1894. Section 3 (1) is in the following terms :

" Estate duty shall not be payable in respect of property passing on the death of the deceased by reason only of a bona fide purchase from the person under whose disposition the property passes, nor in respect of the falling into possession of the reversion on any lease for lives, nor in respect of the determination of any annuity for lives, where such purchase was made or such lease or annuity granted for full consideration in money or money's worth paid to the vendor or grantor for his own use or benefit, or in the case of a lease for the use or benefit of any person for whom the grantor was a trustee."

Therefore, if articles of partnership provide that the share of any partner is to accrue on his death or retirement to the surviving partners, it may be possible to claim exemption from estate duty, provided that adequate consideration in money or money's worth is given to the partner in return for his share at his death.

For example, if two partners agree, as a commercial bargain with no element of bounty on either side, that either the whole or some part of the assets, such as a reserve fund, or the goodwill of a partnership, is to accrue to the survivor on the death of either, exemption from estate duty may be claimed in respect of such partnership assets on either partner's death. The same reasoning will apply if the accrual takes place on the retirement of a partner. Authority for these propositions is to be found in *Att.-Gen.* v. *Boden* [1912] 1 K.B. 539 (which illustrates how the assumption of an extra burden by a junior partner may be consideration in money's worth for the accrual of the senior partner's share) and *Att.-Gen.* v. *Ralli* (1936) 15 A.T.C. 523.[4] In the latter case, the partners carried on a very large financial business, for which it was necessary that substantial reserves should at all times be held. They agreed that on the death or retirement of a partner, his interest in the reserves should pass to the surviving partners. In fact, one of the partners retired a few days before his death. It was held that section 2 (1) (b) did not apply, and that section 3 (1) of the Finance Act, 1894, applied to whatever interest in the reserves was deemed to pass on his death under section 2 (1) (c), since the provisions for accruer contained in the partnership deed were " ordinary business terms entered into for business reasons." It would appear from that case that if partners agree as a matter of business to take nothing out of a partnership when they retire or die, considerable savings in estate duty may be effected.

Moreover, it is suggested that it may sometimes be found convenient in professional partnerships, instead of buying and selling shares of goodwill, to introduce new partners on their personal merits alone, without any premium or purchase of a share. The obvious disadvantage to a proposal of this kind is that a senior partner wishing to retire and to obtain some provision for his old age cannot sell his share. One solution would be to provide for a form of semi-retirement when the senior partner is not obliged to devote his whole energies to the affairs of the firm, and in consideration receives a smaller fraction of the profits. An alternative would be to introduce a system of retirement pensions payable by the continuing partners and secured by their covenants: such pensions could be made payable to the retired partner, or to his wife or, after his death, his widow, or to his other dependants. A third possible solution would be for the retired senior partner to become an employee of the firm, paid a salary or a salary and a small commission on profits in return for his acting as consultant when called upon to do so by the continuing partners. These solutions may not always be adequate. The parties could, as an alternative, consider reducing the value of goodwill to one year's purchase, or less.

Introduction of a son into partnership

Particular questions arise where a father decides to take his son into an existing business as partner, and foresees that the duty payable on his own death will seriously endanger the success of the business after his death, unless some diminution of the burden can be achieved. Although there is little authority on the points which arise, it may be of use to indicate certain items of importance.

(i) *Gift of a share in partnership*

A father may wish to benefit his son by taking him into partnership and giving him a share in the partnership assets and profits, or by

---

[4] See also *Re Thornley* (1928) 7 A.T.C. 178.

giving to a son who is already a partner an increased share in the assets
or profits. It is by no means easy to lay down general rules, since there
is a surprising scarcity of authority, but nevertheless the following
propositions may provide guidance in practice: —

(a) It is considered that the mere fact of taking a son into partnership by executing a deed of partnership whereby he acquires as a gift
a share in capital and profits does not amount to a gift of property in
respect of which it can be said either that the father has not been
excluded from possession and enjoyment or that a benefit has been
reserved. The father has admittedly some possession and enjoyment of
the assets used by the partnership; but these are not the subject-matter
of the gift. The interest of a partner in the assets of the firm is simply
the right to have them used for the firm in accordance with the terms
of the partnership. It is such an interest which the father has given to
the son.

(b) If the father makes a gift to the son of business assets, and thereupon he and the son form a partnership which makes use of those assets,
it cannot be said that the father has been excluded from possession and
enjoyment of the subject-matter of the gift: see *Chick* v. *Commissioner
of Stamp Duties* [1958] A.C. 435. Nevertheless, provided—as will
normally be the case—the father's possession and enjoyment in his
capacity as partner is obtained for full consideration in money's
worth, section 35 (2) of the Finance Act, 1959, will take the business
assets out of charge to duty, provided the father survives the five-year
period.

(c) If the father has already leased land (or, it seems, other assets)
to a partnership of which he and his son are members, the subsequent
gift to the son of the land subject to the lease cannot be said to be a
gift of property from the possession or enjoyment of which the father
has not been excluded: see *Munro* v. *Commissioner of Stamp Duties*
[1934] A.C. 61.

(d) If the father makes a gift of cash to the son, intending the
cash to be used by the son in buying from the father a share in a
partnership business, the subject-matter of the gift is regarded as being
the cash, provided at least that the son has dominion over the cash:
Potter v. *I. R. C.* (1958) 37 A.T.C. 58; see also Finance Act, 1957,
s. 38 (1).

(ii) *Succession to the father's share in the partnership*

Partnership articles between a father and son may provide that on
the father's death his share in the business, or in some major asset of
it, such as goodwill or a reserve fund, shall pass to the son automatically
and without any payment by the son. It is often possible to effect a
saving of estate duty on the father's death by providing in the articles
that the son shall give consideration for the share he hopes to inherit in
this way; if this consideration is given during the father's lifetime by

the son undertaking in the articles to shoulder the burden of the work
in the business, exemption from duty may be claimed under section 3 (1)
of the Finance Act, 1894. This is only possible if the whole arrangement
is a genuine business transaction, not a disguised act of bounty on the
father's part.

The distinction between business arrangements and acts of bounty is
difficult to draw, but some light is shed by the cases of *Att.-Gen.* v.
Boden [1912] 1 K.B. 539 [5] and *Re Clark* (1906) 40 Ir.L.T. 117. In
the *Boden* case, a father and his two sons carried on trade under terms
of partnership which provided that on the death of the father his whole
interest in the firm was to pass to the sons; for this they were to pay to
his estate the value of the interest, minus goodwill, and the goodwill
was to accrue to them without any payment at all. The father died
and estate duty was paid on the value of his interest without taking into
account the value of the goodwill. The Crown claimed a further payment of duty in respect of the goodwill which accrued to the sons. The
decision reached by the court was that the sons had given adequate
consideration for the goodwill in giving certain undertakings in the deed
of partnership; these undertakings were unusually stringent since the
deed contained the following terms : (1) neither son was to engage in
any other trade or business except with the father's consent; (2) both
sons were to give so much time and attention to the business as the
proper conduct of its affairs required; (3) the father was not bound to
give more time or attention to the business than he should think fit.
The court in effect held that these undertakings were sufficient consideration for the right to succeed to the goodwill on the father's death.

One may contrast that case with the decision of Palles C.B. in
Re Clark.[6] There the owner of a business had taken his two sons into
partnership, on the terms that each was to receive one-quarter of the
profits and that on the father's death they were to become jointly
entitled to the whole business. The owner retained certain powers of
charging capital sums on the business, and the sons undertook to give
their whole time to it. It was held that there was nothing in the nature
of substantial consideration in the sons' undertaking, and that therefore
the formation of the partnership was a gift, not a business arrangement.

The distinction between the two cases is apparently that in the *Boden*
case the sons took the whole burden of work off the father's shoulders,
and in return received only a share of goodwill on the father's death,
while in the *Clark* case the sons gave only the normal partnership undertakings and received the whole of the father's interest. It is considered

---

[5] *Boden's* case was commented upon in *Perpetual Executors and Trustees Association of Australia, Ltd.* v. *Commissioner of Taxes of the Commonwealth of Australia* [1954] A.C. 114 at p. 131. It is there stated that the learned judge in *Boden's* case held wrongly that there was a passing under s. 2 (1) (b) when in fact it was a passing under section 1. Whether this dictum is correct or not, it does not affect the judgment in *Boden's* case, which proceeded upon the ground that there was exemption by reason of a purchase under s. 3 (1) of the Finance Act, 1894.

[6] See also *Brown* v. *Att.-Gen.* (1898) 79 L.T. 572.

that the latter case is clearly on one side of the line, and that the *Boden* case is just on the other side.

It is thought that the Estate Duty Office will concede that a sale has taken place, where as a genuine bargain with his father, a son undertakes to take the whole burden of the business from his father's shoulders, and in return receives the goodwill of the whole business on the father's death, but may be unwilling to extend this principle generally to cases where the consideration for the son's undertaking is the passing of something other than goodwill, or where there is no genuine benefit to the father. As a matter of principle, however, there is no difference between an accrual of goodwill or of any other kind of business asset; the true test is whether there is a genuine commercial bargain or not.

If, taking the transaction as a whole, it is substantially an act of bounty and not in its nature a purchase, it appears that the whole of the property passing or deemed to pass on death is charged with duty.[7] An allowance or deduction may, however, be made in respect of any partial consideration that may have been given provided the sale was genuine and not a sham. It is considered that the principle in *Boden's* case is not vitiated by the provisions of section 44 of the Finance Act, 1940, as amended by section 46 of the Finance Act, 1950. The act of taking the son into partnership may be " a disposition made by the deceased in favour of a relative of his," but it is submitted that the undertaking on the part of the son to take the burden of the work may be " full consideration . . . in money's worth paid to him for his own use or benefit."

A rather similar situation to that arising in cases like the *Boden* case is met where the father agrees with the son as follows:

(a) Profits are to be shared so that the father gets, say, twice as much as the son.

(b) The son is to undertake the brunt of the work, as in the *Boden* case, while the father is under no obligation to do more than supervise.

(c) The father can expel the son for serious breach of any obligation under the partnership articles.

(d) If the partnership is dissolved by the court, or by the father expelling the son, or the son retiring, the firm is wound up so that surplus assets after repaying capital are distributed in the same shares as profits.

(e) If the partnership is dissolved by the father dying or retiring or becoming disabled, the surplus assets go to the son.

While the point has never been tested in the courts, it is considered that there is a chance that an arrangement along these lines may enable the surplus assets to be taken out of charge to estate duty on the father's death.

---

[7] See *Att.-Gen.* v. *Johnson* [1903] 1 K.B. 617.

(iii) *Providing a pension for the father*

If the father sells his share to the son for a capital sum payable by instalments, no special difficulty arises: the transaction will be deemed to be a gift, but allowance will be made, on the father's death, for the instalments actually paid: Finance Act, 1940, s. 44 (1), as amended by section 46 of the Finance Act, 1950. The instalments contemplated here are such as do not terminate on the father's death.

But it may be that the father, on retiring, wishes to sell his interest to his son in exchange for an annuity to himself for life, secured by the son's covenant. If this is done the transaction will be deemed to be a gift, since it comes within section 44 (1A) of the Finance Act, 1940 (as modified by section 40 of the Finance Act, 1944, and amended by section 46 of the Finance Act, 1950). The better course is therefore not to sell a share to a son or other " relative " in return for an annuity limited to cease on the vendor's death or on the death of any other person; but to make sure that the annuity to the vendor is one not ceasing on his death. In practice, it is not always easy to decide what period should be taken; a fixed term of years appears to be the solution, but the drawback here is that the Revenue may possibly claim that the annuity is in reality a series of instalments of capital, not income at all.[8]

Estate duty on partnership annuities

It is often convenient to provide for the payment of pensions to retired partners, or to the widows of deceased partners out of the profits of the partnership, or by the continuing partners personally by their joint and several covenant. Indeed, where the partners adopt articles which provide for goodwill or other assets to accrue to the continuing or surviving partners on the death of any one, in the manner suggested earlier in this chapter, it may become necessary to make some provision out of the partnership profits for retired partners and their dependants. It may be possible in some circumstances to provide the annuity in such a way that a saving of estate duty is effected.

(i) *Pension to retiring partner*

An annuity given by way of pension to a retired partner may be provided by insurance policies; if so, no question of estate duty need arise. Alternatively the annuity may be a fixed sum charged on the profits, or a fixed share of the profits. If so, there is prima facie a charge to duty on the death of the annuitant under section 2 (1) (b) of the Finance Act, 1894, since there is an interest ceasing on the death of the annuitant. This claim for duty may be avoided by securing the annuity by a personal covenant only. Where any of the continuing partners is a " relative "

---

[8] See p. 329, *post*, where this point is discussed.

of the retiring partner, some difficulty may be occasioned by section 44 (1) of the Finance Act, 1940, as amended.[9]

The provisions of the Finance Act, 1956, dealing with pensions for the self-employed, do not alter the existing position so far as pensions provided by the partnership deed are concerned, but add to the possible methods whereby a partner can make provision for his retirement. A partner may take advantage of the provisions contained in the Act to provide an additional pension out of his share of profits for himself over and above any pension which may be provided under the partnership agreement.

The provisions of the Act relating to pensions for self-employed persons are more fully discussed in the next chapter.

(ii) *Pension to widow of partner*

As a general rule, a partner should not, without carefully considering the estate duty position, confer upon his widow, otherwise than by will, an annuity charged on the partnership business or on any of the assets employed therein. The likelihood is that estate duty will be payable both on the death of the partner (under section 2 (1) (d) of the Finance Act, 1894) and on the death of his wife (under section 2 (1) (b)).

In this respect the decision in *Att.-Gen.* v. *Wendt* (1895) 73 L.T. 255 is of some assistance. That was a decision on section 38 of the Customs and Inland Revenue Act, 1881, and section 11 of the Customs and Inland Revenue Act, 1889, which are now incorporated into section 2 (1) (c) of the Finance Act, 1894, and is thus only indirectly an authority for the construction of section 2 (1) (d). The case arose out of a term in a partnership deed conferring on the widow of the senior partner, when he should die, an annuity of £700 out of the profits of the business. The court held that this in effect amounted to a gift by the senior partner to his wife, out of which he had reserved an interest: the interest reserved being the enjoyment of his share of the profits during his lifetime. Whether or not that case can still be regarded as authoritative, it is considered that it is clearly distinguishable from the case where the annuity given to the widow is not expressly charged on the profits of the business.

If the annuity is charged on the partnership assets, liability to duty may also arise on the death of the widow, since the annuity may be an " interest ceasing " on her death; here, since the widow's estate liable to duty is likely to be comparatively small (since whatever provision is made for her in her husband's will should, if the will is properly drawn, largely avoid estate duty on her death),[10] it is less likely that a high rate of duty will become payable.

If the widow's annuity is not charged on any part of the partnership assets, but is secured only by the personal covenants of the continuing partners, it is reasonably clear that no estate duty will be payable under

[9] See *ante*, p. 322.
[10] See *post*, Chap. 10.

section 2 (1) (b) of the Finance Act, 1894, on the death of the widow
by reason of the termination of the annuity.

Moreover, by securing the annuity by personal covenants only, it
may be possible to avoid or reduce any estate duty on the inception of
the annuity, *i.e.*, on the partner's death. Estate duty would be payable,
if at all, under section 2 (1) (c) of the Finance Act, 1894, on the ground
that the annuity is a gift made by the deceased in favour of his widow,
or under section 2 (1) (d), on the ground that the annuity is a benefit
arising on the death of the deceased. Liability under section 2 (1) (c)
—but not that under section 2 (1) (d)—would normally only arise where
the partner dies within five years of providing for payment of the
annuity.

One possible method of avoiding estate duty under sections 2 (1) (c)
and 2 (1) (d) is by ensuring that the widow has no legally enforceable
right to the annuity. In deciding whether to adopt this method or not,
one important consideration lies outside the strict province of the lawyer;
namely, whether, if the widow's pension is not enforceable, the surviving
partners are likely to fail to honour their obligation to pay it.

Apart from this, special attention must be paid to two decisions:
Re Miller's Agreement [1947] Ch. 615 and *Re J. Bibby & Sons, Ltd.,
Pensions Trust Deed* [1952] 2 All E.R. 483. In the former case a deed
of dissolution of partnership was in question. A retiring partner,
wishing to provide for his daughters after his death as well as for his own
retirement, transferred all his interest in the firm to the two continuing
partners in consideration of a capital sum and an annuity for his own
lifetime, and of a covenant to pay certain annuities to his three
daughters. The covenants were contained in a deed separate from the
deed of dissolution. By this deed, to which the partners were party,
but not the daughters, the continuing partners covenanted with the
retiring partner to pay to his daughters certain annuities to commence
on the death of the retiring partner and to continue for the respective
lives of the daughters, and to be paid exclusively out of income brought
into charge for income tax, and further charged " all their respective
interests in the profits and assets of the partnership firm with payment
of the said several annuities." The retiring partner died the following
year.

Upon the Revenue claiming estate duty under section 2 (1) (d)
of the Finance Act, 1894, the daughters, who were the accountable
parties for any duty that was payable, issued a summons to determine
the validity of the claim put forward by the Revenue. It was held that
no beneficial interest arose on the death of the retiring partner, since
the daughters had no right to sue on the covenants which he had made,
and that even the charge contained in the deed of covenant did not alter
this situation.

Although *Re Miller* has been criticised,[11] it is respectfully submitted that it is a correct decision and that it is consistent with the well-established principle that English law knows nothing of the *jus quaesitum tertio* (see *Dunlop Pneumatic Tyre Co., Ltd.* v. *Selfridge & Co., Ltd.* [1915] A.C. 847). Consequently a covenant by partners (whether included in the original partnership deed or made subsequently on dissolution) affords a method by which a partner can provide an income for his dependants with a possible saving of estate duty. At the same time, it must be emphasised that the covenant could not be enforced if the surviving partners failed in their undertaking. No doubt the executors of the deceased partner could sue on the covenant given by the surviving partners to the deceased partner and claim the full amount which the covenantors have failed to pay, but the person beneficially entitled to the covenant could not compel the executors to commence proceedings.[12]

In the second of the two cases above referred to, *Re Bibby*, the question in issue concerned the pensions fund of a substantial limited company. Under a trust deed the trustees were empowered to award pensions to retired employees of the company and the widows and children of retired employees, and although the scheme annexed to the deed was couched in terms which, taken alone, would suggest that a retired employee or his widow was entitled to a pension as a beneficiary under the trust deed, the body of the deed gave the trustees an absolute and uncontrolled discretion in the exercise of the powers conferred on them.

The court held that upon its true construction the deed put the fund at the discretion of the trustees, who were not bound to award a pension to any particular employee or widow. It followed that, if the trustees in fact exercised their discretion by awarding an annuity to the widow of an employee, to run from his death, there was no charge to estate duty under section 2 (1) (d), because the widow had no property, but a mere *spes* or hope of getting a pension if the trustees should award it to her; she was only one of a wide discretionary class of beneficiaries, and, although the class as a whole had rights in the fund, no individual had any right which would be enforceable by the individual or which could be termed property. In these circumstances the learned judge followed the decision in *Re Miller's Agreement* and held that the claim for estate duty failed. A subsidiary ground for the decision was that the

---

[11] By Denning L.J. in *Smith and Snipes Hall Farm, Ltd.* v. *River Douglas Catchment Board* [1949] 2 K.B. 500 at p. 517. See also *Drive Yourself Hire Co. (London), Ltd.* v. *Strutt* [1954] 1 Q.B. 250. The Revenue called in aid s. 56 of the Law of Property Act, 1925, according to which " a person may take an immediate or other interest in land or other property, or the benefit of any condition, right of entry, covenant or agreement over or respecting land or other property, although he may not be named as a party to the conveyance or other instrument." The court, however, followed the accepted interpretation of that enactment, and held that it did not give the daughters the right to sue on the covenant.

[12] See *Re Kay's Settlement* [1939] Ch. 329.

deceased employee was held not to have purchased or provided the annuity.

The principle could be applied to partnerships. If a partner is able to rely on the sense of duty of his fellow-partners, he may be content to leave it to their discretion to award his widow an annuity.

On the other hand it is possible so to draft annuity provisions in a partnership deed that the widows have enforceable rights to their annuities. If this is done, estate duty will be payable under section 2 (1) (c) of the Finance Act, 1894, in the event of the partner dying within five years, since the annuity is a gift made by him to his widow: even so it is considered that the annuity is property in which the partner never had an interest, and in consequence is separately aggregable for the purpose of determining the rate of duty payable.[13]

If the deceased dies after the five-year period, the question arises whether section 2 (1) (d) of the Finance Act, 1894, is applicable. That section applies where an interest has been provided by the deceased, to the extent that a beneficial interest accrues on his death. An annuity payable under a partnership deed must be accepted as " provided " by the partner to whose widow the annuity is to be payable. The better view, in the light of the decisions of the House of Lords in *D'Avigdor-Goldsmid* v. *I. R. C.* [1953] A.C. 347 and *Westminster Bank, Ltd.* v. *I. R. C., Wrightson* v. *I. R. C.* [1958] A.C. 210, is that, where the right to receive the annuity is vested in the wife of the partner before his death, the mere fact that it becomes payable upon his death does not constitute the accrual of a beneficial interest: consequently no duty is payable under section 2 (1) (d). Although the cases just mentioned concerned policies of assurance, the principle they establish must extend to annuities provided under a partnership deed.[14] In the absence of any authority dealing directly with such annuities it is not possible, however, to regard that question as settled beyond doubt.

It appears therefore that, if a widow's annuity is secured under enforceable covenants in a partnership deed executed more than five years before the death of a partner, estate duty may be avoided provided the widow's interest is vested before the partner's death. An annuity expressed to be payable to a named woman who happens to be the wife of a partner can be drafted in such a way as to be so vested. Where, however, it is desired to confer the annuity on " such person if any as shall be the widow of the partner," it is clear that, before the partner's death, no person has any vested right to the annuity: consequently, on the partner's death, liability to estate duty arises under section 2 (1) (d) of the Finance Act, 1894. Even so, the annuity will be one in which the deceased partner never had an interest, and thus will enjoy separate aggregation.

---

13 Notwithstanding the dicta of Lord Mackintosh in *Potter* v. *I. R. C.* (1958) 37 A.T.C. 58.

14 See [1953] A.C. 377–378, *per* Lord Asquith; [1958] A.C. 237–238, *per* Lord Keith of Avonholm.

A pension for the widow of a partner may also be provided in accordance with the provisions now contained in the Finance Act, 1956. This may be effected either by means of an insurance contract or by subscribing to a pension trust scheme of the type mentioned in the next chapter. Whether the pension is provided by means of an annuity under an insurance contract or under a pension trust scheme, the annuity will be treated for estate duty purposes as a life insurance within the meaning of section 33 (2) of the Finance Act, 1954, so as to be aggregable in accordance with the provisions of that section: see Finance Act, 1956, s. 35, and Finance Act, 1957, s. 39.

(iii) *Pension to retired partner and his widow*

It is often desired to provide in a partnership deed for a pension for the joint lives of a retired partner and his widow and the survivor of them. The danger is that estate duty may be payable under section 1 of the Finance Act, 1894, on the ground that the pension passes on the death of the partner (assuming he dies before his wife). This may usually be avoided if provision is made for two distinct pensions, one for the retired partner during his life, and another to commence at his death for his widow, during her life or widowhood. The cesser of the first pension would not give rise to estate duty liability if secured by covenant only. The commencement of the second pension on the death of the partner could give rise to liability under section 2 (1) (d).[15] This liability may be avoided by recourse to the principle in the *Miller* and *Bibby* cases,[16] or reduced by virtue of the fact that the pension is property in which the deceased never had an interest, and therefore separately aggregable.

Annuities for widows: taxation

It has already been shown that an annuity provided for a deceased partner's widow may be free of liability to estate duty on the partner's death. It is now proposed to show how such annuities are affected by taxation and to compare them in this respect with instalments paid on a sale of the partner's share.

Assuming for the purpose of illustration that the partnership articles provide for the payment of annuities which are clearly payments of income and not capital instalments, the partners liable to pay them are entitled or obliged, according to the circumstances, to deduct tax at the standard rate from the gross sum payable, under sections 169 and 170 of the Income Tax Act, 1952 (the old rules nineteen and twenty-one).[17]

---

[15] *Re Payton* [1951] Ch. 1081; *cf. Re Tapp* [1959] Ch. 443.   [16] See *ante*, p. 324.
[17] Three points must be noted: (i) If the partnership deed is so drafted that the annuitants have no enforceable right, the point may be taken that the payments in fact made are mere voluntary payments. This is easily remedied by the surviving partners executing covenants in favour of the annuitants, giving effect to the obligations assumed by the partners under the partnership deed; (ii) It is considered that, since there is valuable consideration for the annuity, s. 392 of the Income Tax Act, 1952 (imposing a "seven-year period") is not relevant; (iii) The annuitant must not be the partners' employee, solicitor or agent: see s. 415, Income Tax Act, 1952. Difficulty might, for example, arise if a retired partner in receipt of an annuity on occasions assisted his former partners.

The gross sums will be a charge deductible from the partners' incomes for the purposes of tax, so that, provided they are paying tax at the standard rate on their incomes, they will obtain the full benefit of this deduction for tax purposes, except insofar as the earned income relief, to which they are entitled, may be reduced: Income Tax Act, 1952, s. 221.

It was formerly the practice of the Revenue to set off partnership charges exclusively against partnership income. Thus, if the annuity was payable by the partnership, the gross amount would be charged at standard rate and any reliefs due to the individual partners, including earned income relief, would only be given on the net amount remaining of the amount assessed on the partnership.[18] If the partnership income was insufficient to meet the annuities in any year of assessment, any balance would be assessed under section 170 of the Income Tax Act, 1952, notwithstanding that the individual partners may have had other taxed income. It is understood that since May 1957, this practice has not been followed. The practice now adopted is more consistent with the law and is that where an individual partner has income other than his partnership income, the other income will be taken to cover his share of the partnership charges which are not covered by his partnership income. Provided, therefore, a partner has sufficient other income to cover his share of the partnership charges, no assessment under section 170 will be made on him. This new practice implements the recommendations of the Royal Commission on the Taxation of Profits and Income on this topic.[19]

EXAMPLE:

Partnership profits assessed	...	£3,200
Other partnership income ...	...	£200 (taxed at standard rate)
Gross annuities payable	...	£400
Two partners A ...	... ...	2/3 profits
B ...	... ...	1/3 profits

Assessment on partnership
Profits £3,200
Charges   200 (£200 charged at standard rate)
———
£3,000

Division A £2,000 less personal reliefs
         B £1,000 less personal reliefs

If the partnership had no other income, the whole of the annuities would be charged at standard rate before dividing the balance of the assessment, £2,800, between the partners (A = £1,867; B = £933).

Assuming a partnership loss, and no other partnership income, the annuities, £400, will be set off against the private income of A and B taxed at standard rate in appropriate proportions.

The widow or other annuitant will be entitled to reclaim tax in respect of her personal reliefs. If the widow or other annuitant has little

---

18 The assessment is made in one sum on the partnership but the tax may be claimed from each partner.
19 See the Report of the Royal Commission on Taxation (Cmd. 9474) in paragraphs 511, 512 and 513. See also *British Tax Encyclopedia*, § 6–121.

income other than the annuity, the repayment may amount to a substantial sum. Age relief, or marginal age relief, may be due if the widow has attained the age of sixty-five and " small income relief " if her total income does not exceed £450 with marginal relief up to £680. Unlike the widow of a director or employee, the widow of a partner does not appear to be entitled to earned income relief on her pension, although in individual cases an inspector may be willing to concede that the pension is given to the widow " in respect of the past services " of the deceased partner, and so entitled to be treated as earned income: Income Tax Act, 1952, s. 525 (1) (a).

It is not possible to give annuities expressed to be " free of tax," since this is prohibited by section 506 of the Income Tax Act, 1952.[20] The simplest course is to provide a fixed gross sum, so that although the recipient's net income will vary according to the rate of tax in force, a claim can be made for any repayments that may be due in respect of reliefs. If it should be desired to pay a tax-free annuity, the phrase used should be " such a sum as shall after deduction of tax at the standard rate for the time being in force leave the sum of £x."

Where the widow is not provided with an annuity, but with a sum representing her husband's share, paid by instalments, the tax situation is quite different, and is often less favourable. The instalments, being capital, are not taxable at all in the hands of the widow: *Foley* v. *Fletcher* (1858) 3 H. & N. 769. Correspondingly, they cannot be set off by the partners against their income brought into charge for tax. The widow is thus better off, the partners worse. Where the widow is of modest means and the surviving partners are comparatively well off, the payment of instalments of capital may mean that full advantage is not taken of the widow's reliefs and allowances, while the surviving partners obtain no tax relief in respect of the payments they have to make. On the other hand, in view of the substantial reliefs against income tax and surtax now granted to earned but not unearned income, a large pension payable to a widow having a substantial unearned income may be less favourable to the parties than payment of capital instalments: the situation could be brought about that the parties lose earned income relief without gaining any reduction in surtax liability, while the widow, having exhausted her reliefs by reference to her other income obtains no greater benefit than the net sum paid to her. Thus it is not possible to lay down a general rule that it is always advantageous to substitute annual payments for capital instalments.

Income or capital payments

Lastly a word must be said on the problem how to ensure that the payments provided for the widow in the partnership articles fall clearly on one side of the line or the other. Where the payments are expressed

[20] This is explained elsewhere in this book, p. 19, *ante*.

to be instalments of a specified capital sum, the matter is free from doubt; so also where the payments, however measured, are expressed to be instalments of the price to be paid in consideration of the deceased's share, and are to cease when a certain aggregate sum has been paid : see, e.g., *Ramsay* v. *I. R. C.* (1935) 20 Tax Cas. 79, where the price could fluctuate according to the aggregate of payments (of 25 per cent. of the net profits of the business for ten years). Thus, even if the total consideration is to be measured by reference to profits over a number of years, it may still be capital. On the other hand, an annuity of a fixed amount or of a share of profits, for life, is considered to be clearly an income payment.

This distinction was pointed out by the Lord President, Lord Normand, in *I. R. C.* v. *Hogarth* (1940) 23 Tax Cas. 491 at pp. 498 and 499. He said: " It is open to parties who are about to enter into an agreement of this kind either so to frame their agreement as to make that payment a capital payment although it may be measured by the fluctuating profits of the business in future years and although it may be paid by instalments, or, on the other hand, to make that payment an annual payment, and if they do the latter then any payment made will lead in appropriate circumstances to a claim for a relative deduction from assessment to surtax on those making the payment." Thus, an agreement to pay a proportion of the net profits of a business for *each* of three years was held to be a payment of an income nature. In contrast, in *I. R. C.* v. *Ledgard* (1937) 21 Tax Cas. 129, where the articles of partnership provided that the purchase money for the share of a deceased partner, in the absence of agreement, should be a sum equal to one-half of the share of profits for three years commencing from the date of death, the payment was held to be of capital. In that case, Lawrence J. said (at p. 135): " The fact that annual profits, which are of course, of an income character, are used as the measure of the sum does not affect the quality of the sum which is arrived at by that method."

A case near the borderline, which illustrates the distinction, is *Mackintosh* v. *I. R. C.* (1928) 14 Tax Cas. 15,[21] where Rowlatt J. decided that the payments were income. There it was provided that in the event of the death of a partner the survivors should continue to use the firm's name, trade marks and goodwill, paying to the executors of the deceased partner the sum of £500 quarterly for five years, " after which it may be enjoyed without further payment." The judgment lays stress on the point that the interest of the partner in goodwill, etc., was to accrue to the others without a valuation so that the annual payments to be made represented sums paid for the use of the outgoing partner's share of these assets.

The crucial test may be said to be whether or not any mention is made of a specific capital sum, either a named sum or a sum to be calculated by

---

21 See also *I. R. C.* v. *Ledgard* (1937) 21 Tax Cas. 129; and in contrast, *I. R. C.* v. *Hogarth*, 1941 S.C. 1; 23 Tax Cas. 491.

reference to a specified formula such as a fraction of the aggregate of the partnership profits for a number of years. Only where no such capital sum is specified nor can be inferred, will annual payments be truly income and not instalments of capital: see *I. R. C.* v. *Mallaby-Deeley* (1938) 23 Tax Cas. 153 at p. 169.

In this case it was decided that the payments under a deed of covenant, which made no express reference to a capital sum, were nevertheless of a capital, and not of an income nature. Therefore, the payments were inadmissible as deductions for surtax of the person making them. Sir Wilfrid Greene M.R. said: " The principle " [of the cases] " . . . must depend upon there being a real existing capital sum, not necessarily pre-existing but existing in the sense that it represents some kind of capital obligation. . . . If the method adopted of paying it is a payment by instalments, the character of those instalments is settled by the nature of the capital sum to which they are related. If there is no pre-existing capital sum, but the covenant is to pay a capital sum by instalments, the same result will follow." Thus, if a sum is agreed to be payable for a share of goodwill or other assets, the sum is of a capital nature and it will not be possible to transform it into payments of income simply by making the capital sum payable over a period under a deed of covenant.

Farming partnerships—agricultural relief

Where the estate in respect of which estate duty is payable consists of or contains " agricultural property," considerably reduced scales of duty apply to the agricultural property : Finance Act, 1925, s. 23 (1). For this purpose the term " agricultural property " is broadly defined and means " agricultural land, pasture and woodland, and also includes such cottages, farm buildings, farm houses, and mansion houses (together with the lands occupied therewith) as are of a character appropriate to the property " : Finance Act, 1894, s. 22 (1) (g).

A farming partnership will gain the benefit of agricultural relief on the death of a partner. Until recently, the practice of the Revenue was to make a distinction between cases in which a share " passed *in specie*," where agricultural relief was conceded, and cases, in practice the overwhelming majority, where there was no " passing *in specie* " and thus no relief. The distinction was rigidly enforced, despite its obvious lack of merit. It was shown by the decision of Buckley J. in *Burdett-Coutts* v. *I. R. C.* [1960] 1 W.L.R. 1027 to be wrong. Agricultural relief is obtainable, no matter what the terms of the partnership.

Another factor of which account may be taken in a proper case is that the market valuation of a farm with vacant possession is, on account of the difficulty of obtaining possession from a sitting tenant, usually substantially greater than the market valuation of a farm which has a sitting tenant protected by the Agricultural Holdings Act, 1948: and this is so, even if the tenant is paying the best rent reasonably obtainable. This factor is clearly important, as the principal value for estate duty purposes is, as respects free estate, the market value of the property at the death of the deceased. Therefore, where a farmer wishes to retain the control, and the greater part of the profits of his farm, during his life, the burden of duty may perhaps be relieved to some extent if he leases his land and other farming assets to a partnership, or possibly to a company, in which although other members of his family are interested, he has the majority interest and almost complete control.

Industrial partnerships

Section 28 (1) of the Finance Act, 1954, introduced a reduced rate of duty, similar to agricultural relief, payable on the passing of a business or interest in a business, in respect of property rated as "industrial hereditaments" used and occupied for the purposes of the business or in respect of machinery or plant so used.

PRECEDENT No. 41

Partnership Agreement in a simple form, where a Trader takes Two Sons into Partnership, Intending to Leave the Brunt of the Work to them, but to Retain a Substantial Share in the Capital and Profits until Death or Final Retirement. Provision to Ensure that on the Death or Retirement of the Father the Goodwill of the Business Passes to the Sons without payment

An individual who is solely entitled to a business may wish to retain control of the business until his death, but meanwhile to introduce his sons, or some younger person, who may take over the whole business on his death. This precedent is designed for such a situation. Provided a genuine bargain is reached, so that the duties undertaken by the sons, who bring in little or no capital, are adequate consideration for the benefits they receive, it is considered that no estate duty will be payable on the death of the father in respect of the share of the partnership assets which passes to the sons. It may be, however, that the Revenue will be unwilling to concede that estate duty is avoided, except on goodwill.

In the following precedent it is intended that each son should receive some small share in the capital of the business as soon as the deed is executed, and should also receive a substantial share in the net profits. The rest of the capital passes to the sons on the father's death.

The present form is also designed to show that a Partnership Agreement may be reduced to a very short form: indeed many laymen may prefer the shortest possible form and may not thereby be putting themselves into their lawyer's hands since the rules of any partnership so far as not expressed are to be found in the Partnership Act, 1890.

The present form will, of course, require adaptation for particular circumstances. Consequently the clauses which must be retained if liability for estate duty is to be reduced are indicated in the proper place.

Other clauses may be added. It will perhaps be convenient as a reminder to the draftsman to make a list of clauses which could be added if desired. These are found in the usual books of conveyancing precedents :

(1) Registration of firm under Registration of Business Names Act, 1916.

(2) Certificate of registration to be exhibited and names of partners to appear on letters.

(3) Conversion into limited partnership.

(4) One partner to receive a guaranteed minimum out of profits.

(5) Reserve fund to meet liabilities and a sinking fund policy where some of the property consists of leaseholds.

(6) Insurance against various liabilities.

(7) Partners to be just and faithful.

(8) View of majority to prevail on questions of management.

(9) No partner to give credit if forbidden, to release debts without consent or to guarantee payment of any debt.

(10) No partner to charge or deal with his share.

(11) No clerk or servant to be dismissed except by consent of a majority.

(12) No apprentice, pupil or trainee to be introduced except by consent of all partners.

(13) Power to introduce sons as partners.

(14) Power for any partner to determine partnership if no profits are made.

(15) Rent-free residence on premises of the firm.

(16) Expulsion of partner for breach of duty.

(17) Covenant not to compete in a certain area.

(18) Provision for annuities for deceased partner's widow.

(19) Power to advertise dissolution.

(20) Arbitration clause.

PARTNERSHIP AGREEMENT

Between A. A.

B. B.

C. C.

(hereinafter called " A," " B " and " C " respectively).

Name, etc.   1. BUSINESS of —— at —— under the registered name of —— in continuation of business carried on there by A.

Commencement.   2. COMMENCEMENT on —— 19—.

Duration Retirement.   3. DURATION to be lives of Partners and of survivors. Any Partner can by six months' written notice retire by dissolving the firm as regards himself only.

Death or compulsory retirement.   4. IN each of the undermentioned cases the firm shall be dissolved as regards the Partner in question (so that he shall be deemed to have retired) but not otherwise:

(1) permanent mental or physical incapacity (provided that this case shall not apply to A);

(2) conduct calculated to prejudicially affect the carrying on of the business;

(3) wilful or persistent breach of terms of partnership;

(4) death;

(5) bankruptcy.

In the absence of express agreement, a partnership is dissolved in accordance with sections 32 to 36 of the Partnership Act, 1890. This means, for example, that on the death or bankruptcy of one partner, the whole partnership is automatically dissolved, and that upon one partner becoming permanently incapable of performing his part of the partnership contract, any partner may apply to the court for an order for dissolution. These provisions are likely to prove inconvenient in almost any partnership, and particularly so where the senior partner wishes to make provision for himself during his lifetime, and to ensure the continuity of the firm after his death. Therefore the clause above, adapted to meet the requirements of each individual case, would normally be indispensable in the situation with which this precedent is intended to deal.

There is statutory authority for splitting the infinitive in paragraph (2): see Partnership Act, 1890, s. 35 (c).

Capital.   5. CAPITAL and assets are as stated in the agreed account in the Schedule hereto. Capital shall carry interest at —— per cent.

Profits.   6. PROFITS and losses to be shared [equally] [as follows :

A —— shares
B —— shares
C —— shares].

Accounts.   7. ACCOUNTS to be taken annually and the Auditor's certificate to be binding unless disputed within two months of being given.

Time and attention.   8. BOTH B and C shall be bound to give their full time and attention to the business and not to have any other business or employment. A shall give only such time and attention as he thinks fit and may have any other business or employment that does not compete with the firm.

Control.   9. ANY difference arising as to ordinary matters connected with the business may be decided by A alone if he so wishes.

Clause 9 above is in variation of section 24 (8) of the Partnership Act, 1890, which provides that any difference as to ordinary matters connected with the partnership business may be decided by a majority of the parties, but no change may be made in the nature of the partnership business without the consent of all existing partners.

Clauses 8 and 9, together with clause 4 (1), are designed to provide adequate consideration for A in return for the provisions of clause 10 below. Clause 10 provides for A's share, either in goodwill alone, or in the whole assets of the firm, to pass automatically and without payment to B and C on his death or otherwise ceasing to be a partner. It is considered that, provided the consideration provided by clauses 8, 9 and 4 (1) is adequate, that part of A's share which by reason of clause 10 passes without payment is exempt from estate duty: see Finance Act, 1894, s. 3 (1); Finance Act, 1940, s. 44 (1), as amended by Finance Act, 1950, s. 46; *Att.-Gen.* v. *Boden* [1912] 1 K.B. 539; *Att.-Gen.* v. *Ralli* (1936) 15 A.T.C. 523; *cf. Re Bateman* [1925] 2 K.B. 429; and see pages 320, 321, above.

Clause 10 may be used by omitting one or other of the parts in square brackets, or by adapting the second part in square brackets, either by providing a different method of valuation or by leaving out of account A's share in some additional or other asset than goodwill.

Death or
retirement
of A.
    10. UPON the partnership being dissolved as regards
A when both or either of B and C is a partner his whole
interest in the firm shall accrue [without any payment
whatever] to B and C equally and absolutely (or if only
one of them is then a Partner to that one alone) [who
shall pay to him or his estate in three equal annual
instalments (with interest at —— per cent. on the
unpaid balance) the value of his said interest, assets
being taken at book value and goodwill being left out of
account].

Death or
retirement
of B or C.
    11. IF the partnership is dissolved as regards either
B or C (whether or not A is then a Partner) then

    (1) his whole interest in the firm shall accrue to the
other (or if A is then a Partner to the other and A in
equal shares);

    (2) A shall make no payment but the other shall pay
to him or his estate in five equal annual instalments
(with interest at —— per cent. on the unpaid balance)
the proper value of the share in the said interest taken
by the other [all necessary valuations being made]
[assets being taken at book value and goodwill at one
year's purchase of his share in profits];

    (3) he shall not solicit customers and shall not carry
on or be in any way concerned in the business of ——
or any similar business within thirty miles of —— for ten
years.

Unless otherwise agreed, a partner's interest in a firm is measured
by taking a dissolution account, with all the requisite valuations, in
accordance with section 44 of the Partnership Act, 1890. If a partnership agreement provides an option for continuing partners to buy the
share of an outgoing partner, it is a common practice for a lower price
to be fixed than market price: this is often done by agreeing that assets
are to be taken at book value, or by " writing down " goodwill. This
practice does not in itself reduce the value for estate duty purposes of
the share of a deceased partner which passes on his death: see *Perpetual
Executors and Trustees Association of Australia, Ltd.* v. *Commissioner
of Taxes of the Commonwealth of Australia* [1954] A.C. 114. But where
there is a mutual agreement for automatic accrual of each partner's
share, a price lower than full market price being paid, it is considered
that the excess value of the share over the price passes by reason of a
sale only, and so is exempt from estate duty.

Arbitration.   12. DISPUTES shall be referred to a single Arbitrator under the Arbitration Act, 1950.

SCHEDULE

Statement of capital and assets.

_____

PRECEDENT NO. 42

Supplemental Deed of Partnership, where a Senior Partner, who wishes to be Relieved of the Burden of Work, Transfers part of his Share in the Capital and/or Profits to the Other Partners and Agrees that the Whole of the Goodwill shall Pass on his Death, in Return for the other Partners Taking the Burden of the Work and Agreeing to pay an Annuity to his Widow

It sometimes happens that a senior partner who enjoys the greater part of the profits of the partnership is reluctant to retire, and yet is unable to play a full part in the business, while the junior partners are increasingly loth to take a small share of profits and fear that on the death of the senior partner the payment of estate duty, even if the partners are not accountable, will necessitate the realisation of his share.   Each situation of course requires separate consideration, but there are a number of ways of modifying the partnership deed in order to reduce the burden of estate duty, and this precedent is an attempt to illustrate one such way. The senior partner is willing to accept a lower income, and in return to do less work, while not actually retiring, so that he is relatively better remunerated than before for the work he does.   By this means the share likely to pass on his death is reduced in value.   Furthermore, the senior partner in effect assigns to the others the reversion in his share of the goodwill of the business (it being supposed that the goodwill is a substantial asset), subject to a life interest reserved to himself.   The consideration for this, in addition to the shifting of the burden of work to the other partners, is an annuity payable to the senior partner's widow; it could alternatively be an annuity payable to the senior partner personally.   By this means it is intended that the passing of the goodwill on the death of the senior partner will be exempt from duty under section 3 (1) of the Finance Act, 1894: see _Att.-Gen._ v. _Ralli_ (1936) 15 A.T.C. 523.   On his death it is intended that the only duty payable in respect of partnership property will be that payable on the reduced slice of assets other than goodwill, which the senior partner retains.

This precedent should be used with the greatest caution where the partners are relatives within the meaning of section 44 of the Finance Act, 1940, as amended by section 46 of the Finance Act, 1950.   Reference should be made to the observations relating to the provision of a pension for a partner who goes into semi-retirement and leaves a son or other relative as full-time partner, *ante*, at p. 322.

Parties.

THIS SUPPLEMENTAL DEED OF PARTNER-SHIP is made the —— day of —— BETWEEN A.A. (hereinafter called " the Senior Partner ") of the first part, B.B. of the second part and C.C. of the third part (all of which parties are —— of —— in the County of —— and are hereinafter collectively called " the Partners ") :

WHEREAS :

Principal Deed.

(A) By a Partnership Deed (hereinafter called " the Principal Deed ") dated the —— day of —— and made between the Senior Partner and the said B.B. and C.C. (hereinafter called " the Junior Partners ") the Partners agreed to carry on the business and profession of —— in the shares following, namely, A.A., —— shares, B.B., —— shares and C.C., —— shares for the term of —— years, subject to the provisions contained in the Principal Deed and they have carried on the said business and profession accordingly up to the date hereof ;

Agreement.

(B) The Senior Partner has agreed with the Junior Partners :

    (i) to transfer to them part of his share in the [capital and] profits of the said business, and

    (ii) that on his death the whole of his share in the goodwill of the said business shall accrue to the Junior Partners ;

And In Consideration thereof the Junior Partners have agreed with the Senior Partner :

    (iii) to pay an annuity by way of pension to any widow of the Senior Partner who may survive him, and

    (iv) to permit the Senior Partner to take a less active part in the day-to-day running of the said business ;

(C) The Partners have further agreed that the share of the Senior Partner in the said business other than goodwill shall on his death be purchased by the Junior Partners if they so desire;

(D) It is intended that the Principal Deed shall continue to have effect as varied by these presents;

NOW in consideration of the premises THIS DEED WITNESSETH as follows:

Continued partnership.

1. THE Partners will remain Partners in the profession or business of —— in continuation of the business carried on by them for many years subject to the conditions and provisions of the Principal Deed as varied by this Deed.

Capital.

2. THE Capital of the firm, being the sum of £ —— , shall be deemed to belong to the Partners in the shares following, namely : as to —— parts to A.A. ; as to —— parts to B.B. ; and as to —— parts to C.C.

Profits.

3. THE Profits of the said business shall belong to the Partners in the shares following, namely : as to —— parts to A.A. ; as to —— parts to B.B. ; and as to —— parts to C.C. [or in the same shares as the Capital].

Time devoted to business.

4. (1) B.B. and C.C. shall devote the whole of their time to the partnership business and diligently employ themselves therein and promote the benefit and advantage thereof to the utmost of their power, but A.A. shall not be obliged to attend to the said business any further than he shall think proper and may either actively engage in the said business or abstain wholly or partially from any active part therein as he shall from time to time think fit : Provided that no Partner shall engage or be concerned or interested directly or indirectly in any other business;

(2) B.B. and C.C. shall in rotation attend at the partnership office on Saturday mornings to transact any formal business of the firm during office hours.

Holidays.

5. EACH Partner shall be entitled to take holidays in each year of not longer duration than the following, namely : A.A., so long as he shall think fit; B.B., —— weeks; C.C., —— weeks.

Share of senior partner on his death.

6. IN the event of the Senior Partner dying during the continuance of the partnership created by the Principal Deed and these presents leaving the Junior Partners or either of them him surviving as partners or partner, then in lieu of the provisions of clause —— of the Principal Deed (relating to the purchase by instalments of

the share of a deceased partner) the following shall have effect :

(i) The share of the Senior Partner in the partnership business including his capital therein and in the assets thereof (other than goodwill) shall as from the time of his death be purchased by and belong to such surviving partners or partner and if more than one in equal shares [or in shares proportionate to their then shares in the profits of the business] and they or he shall thereupon assume all the partnership debts and liabilities and the partnership shall be continued between the said partners if more than one under the provisions of the Principal Deed as varied by this Deed : Provided That if such surviving partners or partner shall within six months from the death of the Senior Partner give to his personal representatives notice in writing to wind up the partnership affairs, then the partnership affairs shall be wound up as if the partnership had, at the date of such death, determined by effluxion of time ;

(ii) The share of the Senior Partner in the goodwill of and attaching to the partnership business shall as and from the time of his death (and whether or not such notice in writing as aforesaid shall be given) accrue to such surviving partners or partner and if more than one in shares proportionate to their shares in the profits of the business at the time of such death but without the payment of any capital sum in respect thereof.

If desired, this clause may be adapted, so that the whole of the senior partner's share passes to the junior partners without payment, or at a payment which will decrease by an agreed amount each year that the senior partner survives; in either case, the following clause will also require amendment.

Value of senior partner's share.   7. (1) THE purchase-money for the share of the Senior Partner purchased under the foregoing clause hereof shall be the net value thereof after providing for the debts and liabilities of the firm on the day on which the purchase takes effect and in estimating such value the goodwill of the business shall be left out of account ;

(2) If the parties shall be unable to agree as to the value of the said share the same shall be ascertained by two independent valuers, one to be appointed by the

personal representatives of the Senior Partner and the other by the said surviving partners or partner or by an umpire to be appointed by the two valuers before they proceed to valuation and if the said personal representatives or surviving partners or partner shall fail to appoint a valuer for fourteen days after being called upon to do so or shall appoint a valuer who shall refuse or fail to act, then the valuer appointed by the other party shall make a final valuation alone which shall be binding;

(3) The purchase-money so ascertained as the value of the said share shall be paid by [six] equal annual instalments the first to be paid at the expiration of twelve months from the death of the Senior Partner and so that the instalments for the time being unpaid shall carry interest at the rate of —— per cent. per annum;

These instalments will not be liable to income tax or surtax in the hands of the executor of the will of the senior partner. On the other hand, being instalments of capital, they will not be deductible as an expense or as a charge on the income of the junior partners. Considerable amendment of this precedent is required in order to make the payments income and not capital.

(4) The said purchase-money may be apportioned between any of the items comprised in the said share as may be agreed.

Annuity to widow.

8. THE Junior Partners hereby jointly and severally covenant with the Senior Partner [(who hereby declares himself a trustee of the said covenant for his present wife or other the woman who shall survive him as his widow)] that in the event of the Senior Partner dying during the continuance of the partnership created by the Principal Deed and these presents they the Junior Partners or such one of them as shall immediately prior to such death remain a partner,

(i) will pay to any widow of the Senior Partner who shall survive him an annuity of £——, the same to continue to be paid during the lifetime of such widow or until she remarries or until the expiration of ten years from such death, whichever shall be the shortest period, and

(ii) will at all times after such death save harmless and keep indemnified the estate and effects of the Senior Partner against all debts and liabilities whatsoever of the said firm and from all proceedings costs claims and demands in respect thereof

    (iii) as between the Junior Partners any annuity payable to the widow of the Senior Partner as aforesaid shall be borne in the like shares in which they are entitled to profits for the time being.

The effect of sub-clause (iii) is that the surviving junior partner or partners who continue the business take over the obligation to pay the annuity. The surviving partner or partners may of course make such arrangements as are appropriate to mitigate the burden of the obligation on the introduction of new partners.

It is submitted that, if the words in square brackets are omitted, this annuity will not attract estate duty on the death of the senior partner under section 2 (1) (d) of the Finance Act, 1894: see *Re Miller's Agreement* [1947] Ch. 615, which is discussed *ante*, p. 324. The junior partners can in practice execute a covenant, soon after the senior partner's death, to pay the annuity. If this is not done, the annuity will remain unenforceable [22] and in the event of their deaths or bankruptcy, their personal representatives or trustee in bankruptcy might have a duty not to make any further payments, whether or not the junior partners execute such a covenant; however it is submitted that the payments made to the widow will be a charge on their respective incomes for tax purposes. The annuities, though unenforceable, will still be "annual payments" payable by virtue of the partnership agreement.

If the words in square brackets are included, estate duty will become payable on the senior partner's death in respect of the annuity. But it is considered that the annuity will be treated as an estate by itself, and not aggregated with the other assets passing on the death.

IN WITNESS, ETC.

—————————

PRECEDENT No. 43

Deed of Partnership between Members of a profession Superseding Existing Articles, Designed to Obviate the Sale of Shares in Goodwill to Future Incoming Partners and to Reduce Estate Duty on the Death of any Partner. Annuities for Retired Partners and for Widows and Dependants

It is hoped that this precedent will illustrate a structure of partnership which was not common until recently. The principal asset of the firm, namely goodwill, is in effect owned jointly by the existing partners, so that an outgoing partner receives nothing in respect of his interest in

—————————

[22] If it is desired to make the annuities enforceable, regard should be had to the discussion at p. 326, *ante*.

goodwill, and a new partner is not obliged to raise the money to buy a share. It is intended that, although on the death of any partner before retirement, there must be a passing of his share in goodwill to the other partners, full value will have been given for such a share, so that no estate duty in respect thereof will be payable on the partner's death: Finance Act, 1894, s. 3 (1). The disadvantage, that an outgoing partner has no goodwill that he can sell in order to provide for his old age, is largely counterbalanced by a system of annuities, and, in the long run, by the fact that new partners will tend to be chosen more for their ability than for the fortuitous consideration that they possess sufficient ready capital to purchase a share.

Where any of the partners are related to each other within the meaning of section 44 (2) of the Finance Act, 1940, it could perhaps be argued by the Revenue that the adoption of new partnership articles is a disposition within the meaning of section 44 of the Finance Act, 1940, as amended by section 46 of the Finance Act, 1950. This argument would carry some weight if there were great disparity of age between the related partners, for the true consideration for the surrender by the older partner of his share in the goodwill of the firm after his own death could be said to be, not simply the possibility of acquiring the share of another partner upon his prior death, but partly that possibility and partly the hope of obtaining retirement pensions for himself and perhaps his widow. It follows that where such circumstances exist, it may be advisable to draft the pensions so that they are payable for a fixed period not terminable upon death.

This precedent may be adapted to fit the case, where the partners wish that some payment, less than its full value, should be made to an outgoing partner or his personal representatives in consideration for the accrual of his share in goodwill, or other assets of the partnership, to the shares of continuing partners.

Parties. **THIS DEED OF PARTNERSHIP** is made the —— day of —— BETWEEN —— of —— (hereinafter called " A.A.") of the first part, —— of —— (hereinafter called " B.B.") of the second part, —— of —— (hereinafter called " C.C.") of the third part and —— of —— (hereinafter called " D.D.") of the fourth part:

Recitals. WHEREAS the parties hereto (hereinafter collectively called " the Partners ") have for many years been engaged in practice as —— and are desirous of entering into a fresh Deed of Partnership namely these presents to regulate the conditions under which the said business is carried on as from the date hereof;

NOW THIS DEED WITNESSETH and it is hereby agreed and declared as follows:

Name.   1. THE Partners and the survivors of them will
become and remain Partners in the profession or business
of —— in continuation of the business carried on by
them for many years and such business shall be carried
on under the style or firm name of ——.

Duration of   2. THE partnership shall continue [for the period of
partnership.
five years and thereafter] during such period as the
Partners or any two or more of them shall be living and
so that in the event of any Partner ceasing to be a
Partner by reason of his death or his retirement or
expulsion in accordance with the provisions of this Deed
the partnership shall not determine as regards the
surviving or continuing Partners.

Partners sometimes object to a clause in these terms because they
prefer not to be tied down for life. This objection is, however, often
based on a mistaken idea of the effect of the clause. In fact, if the
words in square brackets are omitted, any partner is at liberty to retire
at the end of each year of the partnership's existence; what he cannot
do is to determine the partnership so that it is wound up under the
Partnership Act, 1890. Therefore, in practice, the words in square
brackets would normally be advisable, so that some minimum period
is established during which no Partner may retire, except with the
consent of the other Partners.

Registration.   3. THE firm shall be registered under the Registration
of Business Names Act, 1916, in the manner and within
the time directed by that Act, and if at any time any
change is made or occurs in the particulars required to
be furnished for the purpose of such registration, a statement specifying the nature and date of such change and
signed by all the Partners for the time being shall forthwith be furnished to the Registrar in compliance with the
said Act,

Certificate of   4. THE certificate of registration of the firm shall be
registration.
kept exhibited in a conspicuous position upon the business premises in compliance with section 11 of the
Registration of Business Names Act, 1916, and the names
of the Partners shall in compliance with section 18 of
the same Act be written or printed on all letters of the
firm or on which the firm name appears.

Place of   5. THE business of the firm shall be carried on at
business.
——, or at such other place or places as the Partners
shall from time to time determine.

Lease of
office
premises.

6. A.A. and B.B. by whom the said leasehold premises are now held for the residue of the term of —— years from the —— day of —— granted by a lease dated the —— day of —— and made between —— of the one part and A.A. and B.B. of the other part at a rent of —— per annum shall stand possessed thereof in trust for the firm and shall be indemnified by the firm against such rent and the covenants and conditions contained in the said lease.

Capital.

7. THE following provisions relate to the capital of the firm :

(1) The capital of the partnership shall be the sum of —— Pounds which shall be taken as having been contributed by the Partners in the following amounts :

A.A. .... —— Pounds
B.B. .... —— Pounds
C.C. .... —— Pounds
D.D. .... —— Pounds.

Further
capital.

(2) If at any time hereafter it shall be determined by a majority of the Partners to increase the capital of the firm the additional capital shall unless otherwise agreed be advanced by the Partners in the same shares in which they shall for the time being be entitled to the profits of the firm.

Interest.

(3) Each Partner shall be entitled to interest at the rate of £— per cent. per annum on the amount of capital for the time being standing to his credit in the books of the firm and such interest shall be paid or credited before any division of profits is made.

Incidence of
outgoings.

8. THE outgoings expenses and losses incurred by the firm including the expenses of and incidental to attendances upon clients or otherwise incurred by any Partner on behalf of the firm and in the performance by any Partner of the duties of any office of profit or appointment held by him while a member of the firm shall in balancing the accounts of the firm be charged against revenue : Losses shall be borne and paid by the Partners in the shares in which they are entitled to the net profits.

Profits :

9. THE following provisions relate to the profits of the firm :

Shares.

(1) The Partners shall be entitled to the net profits of the said business in the shares following and the same

[shall be computed having regard to bills delivered to clients but otherwise disregarding work in progress] [shall be computed having regard to cash receipts only] [shall be computed in like manner as the profits of the said business have hitherto been computed for income tax purposes] and shall be divided between the Partners immediately after the settlement of the annual general account in each year:

A.A. .... —— parts;

B.B. .... —— parts;

C.C. .... —— parts;

D.D. .... —— parts.

Drawings.

(2) The Partners shall be at liberty by monthly drawings or otherwise to draw out of the said business in anticipation of their respective shares of profits and to be accounted for at the next yearly division of profits the following sums in any quarter of a year:

A.A., sums not exceeding £ —— ;

B.B., sums not exceeding £ —— ;

C.C., sums not exceeding £ —— ;

D.D., sums not exceeding £ —— .

(3) If in any year the amount so drawn out by any Partner shall on taking the general account be found to be in excess of his share of the net profits then immediately upon the taking and settling of such account the excess so drawn out shall be refunded without interest.

Profits from appointments, etc.

(4) All premiums which shall be received with articled clerks and all fees emoluments and benefits which shall be received or derived by any Partner while a member of the firm for services rendered or otherwise in respect of any office of profit or appointment held by him shall be treated and accounted for in the books of the firm as profits of the partnership.

Time devoted to business.

10. (1) EACH Partner shall at all times devote the whole of his time and attention to the partnership business and diligently and faithfully employ himself therein and carry on the same for the greatest advantage of the partnership.

(2) The following holidays shall be taken by each Partner: etc., etc. ——.

Just and faithful.

11. EACH Partner shall be just and faithful to the other Partners or Partner in all transactions relating to

the business of the partnership and shall give a true account of the same to them when and so often as the same shall be reasonably required, and shall upon every reasonable request inform the other Partners or Partner of all letters, accounts, writings and other things which shall come into his hands or knowledge concerning the business of the partnership.

Private debts to be paid.

12. EACH Partner shall punctually pay and discharge his present and future separate debts and engagements and shall at all times keep indemnified the other Partners or Partner and their or his representatives, and the property of the partnership, against the same and all actions, proceedings, costs, claims and demands in respect thereof.

Negative covenants.

13. No Partner shall except with the consent in writing of the other Partners :

(i) Carry on or be concerned or interested directly or indirectly in the profession and business of Solicitor except on account and for the benefit of the partnership nor engage in or undertake any other task, profession or business or become a director of any joint stock company;

(ii) Compound release or discharge any debt which shall be due or owing to the partnership without receiving the full amount thereof;

(iii) Become bail surety or security for any person or corporation or do or knowingly suffer anything whereby the property of the partnership may be seized, attached or taken in execution;

(iv) Assign or mortgage his share or interest in the partnership;

(v) Draw, accept or sign any bill of exchange or promissory note or contract any debt on account of the partnership or employ any of the moneys or effects thereof, or in any manner pledge the credit thereof, except in the usual and regular course of business;

(vi) Hire or, except in the case of gross misconduct, dismiss any clerk or employee of the firm or take any articled clerk or change the London agents of the firm;

(vii) Lend any money belonging to or give any credit on behalf of the firm in any case in which the other Partners shall have forbidden him to do so, or undertake any professional business of any kind on behalf of

any person or company after having been required by
the other Partners not to do so.

Other negative covenants should be added here to suit the requirements of particular partnerships.

Provision
for solicitor-
trustee.

14. IF any Partner shall be an executor or administrator or a trustee in any matter or business and shall not
be entitled, upon acting as solicitor in respect of the same
either by himself or by his firm, to be paid as such
solicitor out of the estate or otherwise, the other Partners
or any one or more of them may act as such solicitor on
their or his own account, and the Partner who is such
executor administrator or trustee shall not be entitled to
any share in the profit costs arising out of such business
or matter.

This clause is, of course, only intended to be adopted in the case of
a partnership of solicitors.

Bankers.

15. THE Bankers of the firm shall be —— —— or such
other bankers as the Partners shall from time to time
determine, and all moneys and securities belonging to the
firm shall be paid into and deposited with the said bank
to the credit of the firm account: All cheques on such
account shall be drawn in the firm name and may be so
drawn by any Partner.

Clients'
account.

16. ALL moneys and securities for money received by
the Partners or any of them on behalf of or as the property of a client or third person, except such of the same
as shall be required for the matter in hand on behalf of
such client or third person, shall forthwith be paid or
delivered to such client or third person or paid into or
deposited with the bank to an account separate and
distinct from any account relating to the property of the
firm.

Books of
account.

17. PROPER books of account shall be kept by the
Partners and entries made therein of all such matters,
transactions, and things as are usually entered in books
of account kept by persons engaged in concerns of a
similar nature, including particulars of all attendances
and professional business transacted by each Partner and
of all such names, times and places as may be necessary
or useful for the manifestation and conduct of the
partnership business.

Annual
account.

18. ON the —— day of ——, and on any subsequent anniversary thereof, a general account shall be taken of the assets and liabilities and all dealings and transactions of the partnership during the then preceding year and of all matters and things usually comprehended in accounts of a like nature, and in taking such account a just valuation shall be made of all things requiring valuation : Such accounts shall be entered in a book, which shall be signed by all the Partners, and when so signed shall be binding on them, save that if any manifest error shall be found therein and signified by any Partner to the other Partners within six calendar months after such signature the same shall be rectified.

Retirement.

19. ANY Partner may [at any time after five years from the execution of these presents] retire from the partnership on giving not less than six months' previous notice in writing, expiring on the said day on which a general account shall be taken, to the other Partners or Partner of his intention in that behalf, and at the expiration of such notice the partnership shall determine accordingly so far only as regards the Partner giving such notice.

The words in square brackets should only be used if a similar period is specified in clause 2, above.

In view of the provisions in this precedent which reduce the capital sums which a partner may expect to realise on his retirement by the sale of his share in the partnership, it may be thought that this form of partnership deed provides little inducement to an ageing partner to retire. If so, the next following clause may be used together with the variations indicated in square brackets so as to provide for compulsory retirement at the age of 70. Alternatively, provision could be made for employing retired partners for a fixed term as salaried consultants. This may necessitate some variation of the pension provisions.

Compulsory
retirement.

20. IF any Partner at any time during the continuance of the partnership shall [be living on the —— day of —— after he shall have attained the age of seventy years and not have been requested in writing by all the other Partners to continue to remain a member of the firm for such further period not exceeding seven years as shall be specified in the notice or shall still be a Partner at the termination of such further period or shall] become permanently incapacitated by mental or

physical illness ill-health accident or otherwise from attending to the business of the partnership and shall have received six months previously from [a majority of] the other Partners a notice in writing requesting him to retire then [and in any such case] the Partner in question shall be deemed to have retired [on the said —— day of —— or at the termination of the said further period or] upon expiry of the said notice [as the case may be].

The date to be inserted is that upon which a general account is directed by clause 18 to be taken. This is intended to avoid, where possible, the necessity of taking an account for the purpose of retirement during the course of a year of accounting.

Power to expel.

21. IF any Partner at any time during the continuance of the partnership shall commit or be guilty of any flagrant breach of any of the provisions or stipulations contained in clause 10, 11, 12 or 13 hereof or of any other flagrant breach of his duties as a Partner or shall fail to account for and pay over or refund any moneys for which he is accountable to the partnership within ten days after being required to do so in writing by any other Partner, [or shall act in any other respect contrary to the good faith which ought to be observed between Partners] or shall suffer his share of the partnership property to be charged for his separate debt, or shall become bankrupt or enter into any composition or arrangement with or for the benefit of his creditors [or shall become addicted to betting or gambling of any kind or to notorious intemperance or immorality or other scandalous conduct detrimental to the partnership business,] or shall absent himself from the said business for more than —— calendar months in any one year [or for more than —— consecutive days], then and in any such case the other Partners or Partner may by notice in writing expel such Partner as aforesaid and may publish a notice of dissolution of the partnership in the name of and against such Partner, whereupon the partnership shall immediately cease and determine accordingly as far only as regards such Partner, without prejudice to the remedies of the other Partners or Partner for any antecedent breach of any of the stipulations or agreements aforesaid : Provided that if any question shall

arise, whether a case has happened to authorise the exercise of this power, such question shall be referred to arbitration.

If it is desired to temper the harshness of the above clause, the words in square brackets, or some of them, could be omitted.

Outgoing Partner.

22. IN the event of any of the Partners ceasing to be a Partner by reason of his death or his retirement or expulsion in accordance with the provisions of this Deed the provisions contained in this clause shall have effect and so that references herein to " outgoing Partner " shall be taken as references to the Partner so ceasing to be a Partner and where appropriate shall include his personal representatives :

Account.

(1) An account similar to that prescribed in clause 18 hereof shall be taken up to the day upon which the outgoing Partner ceases to be a Partner from the foot of the last previous account and the assets of the firm other than goodwill shall be valued for the purposes of such account.

Interest and undrawn profits.

(2) The sum which upon taking the said account shall appear to be due to the outgoing Partner in respect of interest on capital and undrawn profits down to the date of his ceasing to be a Partner shall with all convenient speed but in any event within six months of his ceasing to be a Partner be paid to the outgoing Partner.

Goodwill.

(3) The share of the outgoing Partner in the goodwill and future profits of the partnership business shall accrue to the continuing Partners without the outgoing Partner or his estate or any person being entitled to any part of the said goodwill or future profits or to any payment in respect thereof.

Capital and assets.

(4) The share of the outgoing Partner in the capital and assets (including but not restricted to the lease above-mentioned and all office furniture books and papers) of the partnership business shall accrue to the continuing Partners who shall pay to the outgoing Partner a capital sum therefor in accordance with the provisions of this clause.

Instalments.

(5) The said capital sum shall be the value of the share of the outgoing Partner in the capital and assets as shown upon taking the said account and shall be

paid as to £— thereof to the outgoing Partner within six months of his ceasing to be a Partner and as to the balance thereof by not more than —— equal annual instalments together with interest at the rate of 5 per cent. per annum on the unpaid instalments from the date upon which the outgoing Partner ceases to be a Partner the first instalment with interest being paid one year after the said date.

Failure to pay instalments. (6) If any of the said annual instalments or interest or any part thereof respectively shall be in arrear and unpaid for thirty days after the time hereinbefore appointed for the payment thereof then the whole balance of the said capital sum then remaining unpaid shall forthwith become payable and shall carry interest at the rate of 5 per cent. per annum until paid.

Accruer of shares in goodwill. (7) The share of the outgoing Partner in goodwill and future profits and (unless otherwise expressly agreed in any particular case) the share of an outgoing Partner in capital and other assets of the partnership business shall accrue to the continuing Partners in the same shares in which at the time when the outgoing Partner ceases to be a Partner they shall be entitled to share in the profits of the firm.

(8) In addition to the foregoing there shall be paid to the outgoing Partner the following sums:

Unpaid bills. (i) a sum representing the fair value of his interest in all work in respect of which bills shall have been delivered to clients before the outgoing Partner ceased to be a Partner but shall not then have been paid and

Work in progress. (ii) a sum representing the fair value of his interest in all work either in progress or completed at the time the outgoing Partner ceased to be a Partner but in respect of which bills shall not previously have been delivered.

Auditor to ascertain sums. (9) Each of the said sums shall be ascertained by the auditor of the firm acting as an expert and not as an arbitrator and in ascertaining them he shall have regard to the expenses and outgoings charged or to be charged against them and to the income tax (if any) at the standard rate (but not surtax) payable by reference thereto and to any part thereof representing bad debts or in respect of which a reduced payment shall be accepted.

Payment of sums.   (10) The said sums shall be paid at such times and in such instalments as the auditor shall certify from time to time to be equitable in all the circumstances.

As appears from a perusal of paragraphs (3) and (4) of the above clause, the share of an outgoing partner accrues to the continuing partners: this is in contrast to the more traditional arrangement whereby the continuing partners have an option to purchase the share of an outgoing partner. It will also be noticed that goodwill passes without any payment whatever: this again is in contrast to the more traditional arrangement, under which goodwill is valued at so many years' purchase of the profits. The purpose of thus writing off goodwill is, as explained above at page 317, partly to reduce the estate duty that is payable on the death of a partner, and partly to ensure that the continuing partners and any new partner who might join the firm are not overburdened with the payment of excessive sums of capital. On the other hand, a retiring partner clearly forgoes a substantial asset. It is in order to provide some substitute for the additional capital which a retiring partner loses that the system of pensions demonstrated later in this precedent may be found useful.

As shown by the alternative words used in clause 9 (1) above, the partners may ascertain profits for the purpose of the annual account in one of three possible ways:

(i) on the cash basis, so that only payments, not earnings, are taken into account;

(ii) on the " bills delivered " basis, that is, having regard to earnings, and not to receipts, taking the delivery of the bill as being the date at which money is earned;

(iii) on the " work in progress " basis. This is the same as the " bills delivered " basis, except that an estimated sum is taken into account, representing the value of work which is in progress or has just been completed but in respect of which no bills have been delivered. In practice the estimate is far from easy to make, and the same figure tends to be adopted year after year.

Whichever basis is used, it does not follow that the Inspector of Taxes will accept it as a proper method of computing the profits for tax purposes, and some adjustment may be necessary. In particular, it is unlikely that any inspector will agree to a new partnership starting on the cash basis. When there is a change in a partnership and the business or profession is treated as newly set up from the date of the change, the Revenue practice appears to be to insist on the earnings basis being adopted instead of the cash basis. This will not affect a retired or deceased partner's liability to tax. However, any assessments for the period up to the retirement or death which have not become final may also be made on the earnings basis (instead of the cash basis) and a part of such assessments would be the liability of the retired or deceased partner. But there is no right to revise assessments which have become final: *Rankine* v. *I. R. C.* (1952) 32 Tax Cas. 520.

If either the " cash " basis or the " bills delivered " basis is adopted for the accounts as between the partners (whatever basis is taken for tax purposes), it follows that on a partner dying or otherwise ceasing to be a partner, the continuing partners benefit to some extent: if the " bills delivered " basis is taken, they benefit to the extent that work in progress does not require, when it is finally brought into account as a profit (*i.e.*, when a bill is delivered), to be shared with the dead or otherwise departed partner: if the " cash " basis is taken, they benefit to the extent that both work in progress and unpaid bills do not require to be so shared. Therefore the partners may well consider that some payment should be made to an outgoing partner, where the " cash " or " bills delivered " basis has been applicable, to compensate him for the benefit he has in effect given up to the continuing partners by the mere fact of ceasing to be a partner. The reckoning of what is a proper payment is likely to be complex in the extreme. Among the factors requiring to be taken into account is that income tax and surtax would have been paid by the outgoing partner on his share of the work in progress or unpaid bills. Moreover, the continuing partners pay income tax and surtax themselves on his share before they benefit from it. The tax position will vary, depending on whether the partners give a notice for the application of the continuing basis or not (as to which see clause 25, *post*). In all the circumstances the partners may come to the conclusion that they would prefer to allow the auditor of the firm to use his discretion in arriving at a just figure, without tying him down by complex provisions. It is with this in view that paragraphs (8), (9) and (10) in the above clause have been drafted.

Power of attorney, etc.

23. EACH Partner hereby irrevocably appoints every other Partner and the persons deriving title under the last surviving or continuing Partner and his or their substitute or substitutes to be his attorney or attorneys in the event of the partnership being dissolved as regards him only for the purpose of getting in and completing payment of any book or other debts of the firm and of giving notice to the clients of the firm of the change in the firm including the usual notice in the *London Gazette* and for the purposes aforesaid the attorney or attorneys in his name and on his behalf and as his act and deed or otherwise may sign seal deliver

execute or give any appointment of new trustees conveyance assignment receipt release covenant or other disposition notice advertisement or other instrument.

Not to compete.

24. No Partner retiring or being expelled shall within ten years thereafter carry on or be concerned or interested either directly or indirectly as principal agent director manager partner or otherwise in the profession or business of —— within a radius of —— miles from —— or solicit any person who while he was a Partner was a client of the firm.

Notice of application for continuing basis.

25. Upon the retirement expulsion or death of any Partner he or his personal representatives shall if so requested by the continuing or surviving Partners or Partner join with them or him in giving to Her Majesty's Inspector of Taxes a notice under subsection (3) of section 19 of the Finance Act, 1953, or any statutory replacement or modification thereof for the time being in force and the Partner so retiring or expelled or the personal representatives of such deceased Partner shall be indemnified by the continuing or surviving Partners or Partner against any income tax or surtax which may be payable by him or them as the result of giving such notice in excess of the income tax or surtax which would have been payable if no such notice had been given.

As regards any change in the constitution of a partnership which occurs on or after April 6, 1953, the present procedure is to assess the business or profession as though it had ceased at the date of change and a new one commenced at that date: see section 19 (1) of the Finance Act, 1953, as modified by section 34 of the Finance Act, 1960, and section 130 of the Income Tax Act, 1952, as to the cessation, and sections 128 and 129 as to the commencement provisions. As the result of a notice under this clause, applying section 19 (3) of the Finance Act, 1953, the business or profession will not be treated as ceasing, and commencing afresh, at the date of change, but the continuing basis will apply. This election can only be made if at least one person is a partner both before and after the change, and the notice must be signed by all the persons who were partners before and after the change and sent to the Inspector of Taxes within one year of that date. The result is that the trade or profession will be assessed throughout on the preceding year basis (Income Tax Act, 1952, s. 127, unless the trade or profession has begun within three years, in which case see section 129 (3), *ibid.*). The assessment for the year of assessment in which the change occurs will be apportioned between the old and the new partnerships (usually on a time basis, but exceptionally on a seasonal or other appropriate basis).

The disadvantage to a retiring partner (or the personal representatives of a deceased partner) in making an election under section 19 (3) of the Finance Act, 1953, is that in the event of a second change in the following year of assessment to which the cessation provisions are applicable an additional assessment might be made on the old partnership by reason of section 19 (4) (b). The latter subsection nullifies the effect of the decision in *Osler* v. *Hall & Co.* (1932) 17 Tax Cas. 68. This clause of the partnership articles indemnifies the retired partner, or the personal representatives of a deceased partner, against this risk of further liability to tax arising as the result of a subsequent change in the partnership.

It was formerly possible in many cases, particularly where the partners were assessed on the cash or bills-delivered basis, to make use of a discontinuance in order to take out of charge to tax the whole or a part of the moneys received after the discontinuance in respect of work completed before the discontinuance. Sections 32 to 35 inclusive of the Finance Act, 1960, bring such moneys into charge to tax.

Annuities to retired partners, etc. **26. (i)** From and after the date on which any Partner shall by reason of his death or retirement (but not by reason of his being expelled) cease to be a Partner the remaining Partners or Partner shall pay either or both of the following annuities as may in the circumstances be appropriate that is to say :

(a) an annuity equal to the specified amount as defined in subclause (ii) hereof commencing on the day following that upon which an outgoing Partner shall cease to be a Partner payable to such Partner during the remainder of his life or for a period of ten years whichever shall be the shorter period ; and

(b) an annuity equal to the specified amount as defined in subclause (ii) hereof commencing on the death of a Partner occurring either before or within ten years after his ceasing to be a Partner payable to his dependants as defined in subclause (iii) hereof during the remainder of a period of ten years from the date on which such Partner died or ceased to be a Partner whichever first occurred.

(ii) The specified amount referred to in the last preceding subclause hereof shall in any year be an amount equal to —— per cent. of the profits earned by the partnership in the preceding year and for the purposes of this subclause the profits earned by the partnership shall be calculated in like manner as the profits of the partnership are normally calculated for the purpose of the general account referred to in clause 18 hereof without any deduction being made for income tax payable in respect thereof.

The possible variations of this clause are infinite. In some cases future profits will provide a fair measure of what the retiring partner (or the family of a deceased partner) should receive. In other cases past profits may provide a fairer measure. In such cases a clause in the following form might be adopted :—

Amount of annuity.

" (ii) The specified amount referred to in the last preceding subclause hereof shall be an amount equal to —— per cent. of the average annual amount of the profits of the partnership (as calculated for the purpose of the general account referred to in clause 18 hereof and without any deduction being made for income tax payable in respect thereof) during the last five complete years preceding the date upon which such Partner dies or ceases to be a Partner or during such shorter period as the partnership shall have been in existence."

(iii) The dependants of a deceased Partner referred to in subclause (i) hereof shall be such person or persons other than himself or his personal representatives as the deceased Partner shall have nominated in writing before his ceasing to be a Partner and in default of such nomination shall be the widow and children of such Partner and the respective spouses widows, widowers, children and adopted children of any such children and any annuity payable to the dependants of a deceased Partner in accordance with the provisions of subclause (i) (b) hereof shall be paid or applied by the remaining Partners or Partner to or for the benefit of such dependants in such proportions and in such manner as the remaining Partners or Partner shall in their or his discretion think fit.

The annuities should be paid subject to deduction of tax at the standard rate by the remaining partners. The annuitant will be entitled to keep any refund he may obtain in respect of his personal allowances and reliefs.

It is considered that no liability to estate duty arises on the death of any annuitant, or on the death of a partner whose widow or dependants then become entitled to an annuity.

This clause is only intended to suggest one possible method of providing for former partners, and even as it stands it will require considerable amendment to fit particular circumstances. A possible variation would be to provide expressly for the payment of an annuity to a deceased or retired partner's widow and to include words of trust giving the widow thereby an enforceable right. The annuity might be liable for estate duty but it would not be aggregable with the deceased partner's free assets since it would be property in which the deceased never had an interest: see *ante*, p. 326.

Contribution
to the
annuities.
     27. THE annuities hereinbefore provided shall be paid less tax at the standard rate for the time being in force by the Partners who continue as Partners when the outgoing Partner ceases to be a Partner and out of their respective general funds of income and as a joint and several liability But so that they shall contribute thereto in the same shares in which they shall be from time to time entitled to share in the net profits of the partnership And any person thereafter being admitted a Partner of the firm shall be required to contribute to such annuities in such share as aforesaid and any Partner dying or retiring shall be indemnified by the continuing Partners against any claim made against him or his estate in connection with any such annuity.

Abatement
of annuities.
     28. IN any accounting year of the partnership in which the total of the annuities payable under the last two preceding clauses hereof shall exceed one —th part of the net profits of the partnership in the preceding accounting year the said annuities shall for that year only abate rateably so that they equal one —th part as aforesaid.

Dissolution.
     29. UPON dissolution of the partnership in any event not otherwise herein provided for, the affairs thereof shall be wound up and the assets and liabilities dealt with in manner provided by the Partnership Act, 1890, Provided that

     (1) the goodwill of the business shall not be sold but shall be divided between the Partners; and

     (2) annuities (vested or contingent) payable to any Partner who shall already have retired or to any widow or dependant of any Partner already then deceased shall cease to be payable and unless otherwise agreed shall be valued and the amounts at which they shall be so valued shall be payable to the persons entitled or

prospectively entitled to such annuities and shall rank and be treated as loans made to the firm by Partners.

Documents.   **30.** UPON the death retirement or expulsion of any of the Partners all deeds, drafts, letters and other papers relating to the business of the firm shall remain in the hands of or be delivered to the surviving or continuing Partners or Partner.

Serving of notice.   **31.** ANY notice hereby authorised or required to be given to the Partners or any of them shall be sufficiently given by leaving the same addressed to them or him at the office of the firm.

Arbitration.   **32.** IF during the continuance of the partnership or at any time afterwards any dispute, difference, or question shall arise between the Partners or any of them, or their or any of their representatives, touching the partnership or the accounts or transactions thereof or the dissolution or winding up thereof, or the construction, meaning or effect of this Deed or anything herein contained or the rights and liabilities of the Partners or their representatives under this Deed or otherwise in relation to the premises, then every such dispute, difference or question shall be referred to a sole arbitrator pursuant to the Arbitration Act, 1950, or any statutory modification or re-enactment thereof for the time being in force.

Mutual release.   **33.** THE Partners and each of them do hereby mutually release and discharge the others of them their executors and administrators, from all claims and demands, actions and proceedings whatsoever for or in respect of the covenants, agreements, and provisions contained in the Deed of Partnership dated the —— day of ——, which is intended to be wholly superseded by this Deed.

IN WITNESS, ETC.

——————

PRECEDENT No. 44

Assignment and Covenant where in consideration of an Annuity the Widow of a Deceased Partner sells to the Surviving Partners the Interest in the Partnership which has been bequeathed to her.

The situation visualised is that, under a professional partnership in traditional form, the share of a deceased partner has passed to his estate, the surviving partners having an option to purchase the share at its proper value, *i.e.*, on the footing of a winding-up account. The senior partner has died unexpectedly leaving the whole of his estate to his widow who is also sole executrix. The widow has little or no income apart from what she may obtain from the partnership, and the surviving partners, while enjoying the prospect of substantial incomes now that the senior partner has died, would not find it easy, after payment of income tax and surtax, to pay the capital to which the widow is entitled. The widow therefore agrees to forgo her rights in the partnership, in return for an assured income.

This precedent is unlikely to serve the situation, where the widow already enjoys an income sufficient to use up all or most of her personal and reduced rate reliefs and the surviving partners enjoy substantial earned income reliefs and pay little or no surtax. In such a case the widow would get little if any relief from the standard rate of tax deducted at source from the annual payments. On the other hand, the partners would lose earned income relief.

Parties.

THIS DEED OF ASSIGNMENT AND COVENANT

is made the —— day of —— 19— BETWEEN —— of etc. Widow (hereinafter called " the Widow ") of the one part and —— of etc. and —— of etc. (hereinafter called " the Partners ") of the other part

Recitals.

WHEREAS :

(A) The Widow is the widow sole executrix and residuary legatee of —— (hereinafter called " the Senior Partner ") who until his death on the —— 19— carried on the profession of —— in common with the Partners under Articles of Partnership dated the —— 19— ;

(B) The Continuing Partners have paid to the Widow the sum of £— in full satisfaction of the amount due to the Senior Partner at his death by way of undrawn profits and loans receipt of which sum is hereby acknowledged ;

(C) Under clause 20 of the said Articles the Partners have an option to purchase from the Widow the whole interest of the Senior Partner in the capital assets and goodwill of the said partnership at the price and upon the terms therein stated ;

(D) The parties hereto have agreed that in place of exercising the said option the Partners shall purchase from the widow the said interest of the Senior Partner for the annuity hereinafter secured and without the payment of any capital sum or sums ;

NOW in consideration of the said agreement **THIS DEED WITNESSETH** as follows :

Assignment of share in firm.

1. THE Widow hereby assigns and surrenders unto the Partners the whole interest in the capital goodwill future profits and other assets tangible and intangible of the partnership carried on by the Senior Partner and the Partners under the recited Articles of Partnership to which the Senior Partner was entitled at his death including all profits and interest on capital arising since his death To hold unto the Partners absolutely.

Partners to continue.

2. THE Partners shall continue in partnership together upon the terms of the recited Articles of Partnership or so much thereof as shall still be applicable upon the footing that they are entitled to share in capital in the following proportions namely :

and entitled to share in profits in the following proportions namely :

Annuity.

3. THE Partners hereby jointly and severally covenant with the Widow that they and each of them and their respective personal representatives will pay to the Widow out of the general funds of taxed income of themselves and their respective estates and failing such income out of untaxed income or capital the monthly sum of —— Pounds (£—) less tax such payments to commence on the 30th day of —— next and to continue during the lifetime of the Widow [or during the period of Twenty Years from the said 30th day of —— whichever shall be the shorter period] so that the last payment thereof shall not be apportionable.

Contributions to annuity.

4. THE Partners hereby agree with each other that they shall contribute to the said monthly sums in the same proportions in which they are from time to time entitled to share the profits of the said partnership and that they shall not take any other person or persons into partnership with themselves during the lifetime of the Widow except upon such person undertaking with each of the Partners or their personal representatives to contribute to the said monthly sums to an extent commensurate with his share in the profits of the said partnership from time to time.

It is considered that the continuing partners will be entitled to treat the monthly sums as annual payments charged against their incomes for the purposes of tax: see *ante*, p. 329. The question arises whether the payments should be set off primarily against partnership income, which is likely to entail loss of earned income relief, or whether they may be set off primarily against unearned income taxed at the full standard rate. As stated above, at p. 328, it is the practice of the Revenue to set off partnership charges against partnership income and only allow the excess of charges over income to be set off against the other income of the partner; so that there is likely to be a loss of earned income relief. It is not clear to what extent the Revenue would insist on applying that practice to the payments that fall to be made under the terms of this precedent. The draftsman who wishes to test the point should consider amending clause 3 above by inserting after the words " general funds of taxed income " the words " (but primarily out of unearned income)."

If either of the continuing partners is a relative of the widow within the meaning of section 44 of the Finance Act, 1940, that part of the deceased partner's share in the partnership which is assigned by the widow to him will be deemed to pass for the purposes of estate duty on the death of the widow, even if she survives the five-year period: see section 44 of the Finance Act, 1940, as modified by section 40 of the Finance Act, 1944, and amended by section 46 of the Finance Act, 1950. If it is desired to reduce this estate duty, it may be possible to do so by adapting the precedent, so that the annuity is payable for a fixed term of years, and not for the life of the widow.

As regards either of the continuing partners who is not a relative of the widow, it is considered that provided the assignment is given as a fair commercial bargain, and not by way of bounty, that part of the deceased partner's share which is assigned to such a partner is taken free of any liability for estate duty on the death of the widow, whether or not she survives the five-year period, since there has been no gift caught by section 2 (1) (c) of the Finance Act, 1894: see *Re Fitzwilliam's (Earl) Agreement, Peacock* v. *I. R. C.* [1950] Ch. 448.

Stamp duty will be chargeable on the above document as on a conveyance on sale, the consideration being computed by reckoning the total of the annual sums that will be paid over twelve years: Stamp Act, 1891, s. 56 (3). It follows that it is not possible to achieve any economy in stamp duty by expressing the annuity as a weekly or monthly sum rather than an annual sum. Additional stamp duty may be payable if one of the continuing partners assigns part of his share to the other, clause 2 being the document which effects such assignment.

CHAPTER 9

SERVICE AGREEMENTS AND PENSION SCHEMES

THE part played by pension arrangements as a method of providing additional remuneration for employees calls for little comment. In recent years the high level of taxation has given a new emphasis to this topic. The advantage which an employer may hope to derive from a pension arrangement by encouraging his employees to remain in his service throughout their working lives has long been recognised. Any scheme which enables more highly paid employees and staff to be given a substantial benefit in the form of a pension, the demands of the tax-gatherer notwithstanding, confers an additional advantage of great importance. But it is not only in the case of a highly paid employee that tax considerations are important. Unless due regard is had to a number of complex rules, the well-intentioned provision of a pension, or a gratuity, for a modestly paid employee may cause that employee to suffer an unnecessarily heavy burden of tax.

Tax considerations

It may be useful to the reader if a short summary is given of the main tax considerations which have to be taken into account when providing a pension for an employee. The fundamental rules do not differ greatly, whether the pension is to be paid by the employers themselves [1] or to be provided by means of insurance, or to be paid out of a fund in the hands of trustees, to which the employers propose to contribute.

(i) *Are the payments made by the employers a deductible expense?*

Payments made by employers, either in paying current pensions or in providing for pensions payable in future, are deductible in computing the taxable income of the employers only if two conditions are satisfied, namely, that the payment is made wholly and exclusively for the purposes of the trade; and that the payment is an income rather than a capital disbursement.

The payment of a pension to an ex-employee, even if there was no obligation upon the employers to pay it, may satisfy the test: see *Smith* v. *Incorporated Council of Law Reporting* [1914] 3 K.B. 674; 6 Tax Cas. 477. Indeed, even if the pension is commuted for a lump sum, it may still retain its character as an income disbursement: see *Anglo-Persian Oil Company Limited* v. *Dale* [1932] 1 K.B. 124; 16 Tax Cas.

---

[1] Problems which arise where the pension is to be paid by the employers themselves are discussed in an article by D. C. Potter in [1958] B.T.R. 362. The points dealt with therein must now be considered in the light of ss. 37 and 38 of the Finance Act, 1960.

253; and *Hancock* v. *General Reversionary and Investment Co., Ltd.* [1919] 1 K.B. 25; 7 Tax Cas. 358. On the other hand, the condition that the payment to provide a pension is made wholly and exclusively for the purposes of the trade will not be satisfied if it is not made with a view to earning profits or promoting the prosperity of the business, but as a means of spending profits. Thus if a small family company pays a pension to an ex-employee who is also a shareholder, it may be difficult to argue that the pension represents moneys laid out with a view to earning profits. The Revenue might argue that the expense was justified by reference to the advantage secured to the individual shareholder only and not by reference to commercial expediency: see *Samuel Dracup & Sons, Ltd.* v. *Dakin* (1957) 37 Tax Cas. 377. Similarly a payment is not deductible if it is made at a time when the employer is about to cease trade: see *Godden* v. *A. Wilson's Stores (Holdings), Ltd.* (1962) 40 T.C. 161.

Again, where a payment is made to set up a pensions trust, as opposed to maintaining its current solvency, it may fail to satisfy the second condition. The well-known words of Lord Cave in *British Insulated and Helsby Cables, Ltd.* v. *Atherton* [1926] A.C. 205; 10 Tax Cas. 155 are relevant in this respect:

" When an expenditure is made, not only once and for all, but with a view to bringing into existence an asset or an advantage for the enduring benefit of a trade, I think that there is very good reason (in the absence of special circumstances leading to an opposite conclusion) for treating such an expenditure as properly attributable, not to revenue, but to capital."

Where a pension scheme is approved under section 379 of the Income Tax Act, 1952, however, a single capital sum paid by an employer to the scheme may be spread over a period of years and allowed as a deduction in computing the profits of the employer in those years.

Another point which may require examination, where the employers are a company, is whether the payment of the proposed pension is expressly or impliedly permitted by the memorandum of association. Generally speaking, a company engaged in trade has implied power to pay pensions and gratuities to former employees where the payment is made bona fide to benefit and promote the prosperity of the company and is reasonably incidental to its business: see *Henderson* v. *Bank of Australasia* (1888) 40 Ch.D. 170. But a board of directors may not vote one of their own number a pension without the approval of the company in general meeting unless specifically authorised by the Articles of Association: see *Re Lee, Behrens and Co., Ltd.* [1932] 2 Ch. 46, and Article 87 of Table A, Companies Act, 1948. A company that has ceased trade has no implied power to use its assets, otherwise distributable among shareholders, in recompensing its employees for their past endeavours: *Parke* v. *Daily News* [1962] Ch. 927.

(ii) *Will the pension be taxable in the hands of the recipient?*

The answer to this question is—Yes. Indeed, it is provided by section 376 of the Income Tax Act, 1952, that even a pension paid voluntarily, so that the employers are at no time under any obligation to pay it, is taxed under Schedule E.[2] Moreover, even if the pension is provided by the employers purchasing it from an insurance company for a lump sum, it is taxed without the benefit of the exemption in respect of the " capital element " which is conferred upon pensions generally by section 27 of the Finance Act, 1956: see section 27 (8) (d).

Normally, a pension given in respect of past services will qualify under section 525 for earned income relief: this is so even if the pension is paid after the employee's death to some other person (s. 525 (1) (a)) or is a voluntary pension (s. 525 (2) (b)).

It has been suggested that, where a pension is voluntarily awarded to a retired employee, the pension itself—and not merely the separate payments of which it is constituted—may be chargeable to tax under the so-called " golden handshake provisions," namely, section 37 of the Finance Act, 1960. It is considered however that this suggestion cannot be substantiated, having regard to the words " not otherwise chargeable to income tax " in section 37 (1).

(iii) *Will a provision presently made for a future pension be treated as taxable emoluments?*

Provision can be made, either by the employers paying premiums on a policy intended to provide benefits for the employee on retirement, or by their contributing to a trust fund, or otherwise setting aside moneys out of profits, or simply agreeing with the employee to pay a pension when the proper time arrives.

Prior to the enactment of section 19 of the Finance Act, 1947 (now section 386 of the Income Tax Act, 1952), the law on this topic was not altogether clear. It would appear, from such decisions as *Smyth* v. *Stretton* (1904) 5 Tax Cas. 36 and *Edwards* v. *Roberts* (1935) 19 Tax Cas. 618, that provision for a future pension was to be treated as part of the current emoluments of the employee only if he acquired a present vested right, as opposed to a mere future contingent right, thereto.[3] Thus, for example, if employers pay the premiums on an endowment policy for the benefit of an employee, so that he gets the benefit of the policy in any event, and not subject to survival to any stated age or any other contingency, the premiums are treated as emoluments of the employee for tax purposes.[4]

---

[2] s. 376 of the I. T. A., 1952, re-enacts s. 17 of the F. A., 1932, which was passed to extend the scope of the charge under Schedule E so as to include a voluntary pension capable of being discontinued at the will of the payer. *Stedeford* v. *Beloe* [1932] A.C. 388; 16 Tax Cas. 505 had decided that such a pension was not within the scope of Schedule E.

[3] See also *Bell* v. *Gribble* (1903) 4 Tax Cas. 522; *Bruce* v. *Hatton* (1921) 8 Tax Cas. 180.

[4] The employee may get tax relief under s. 219 of the Income Tax Act, 1952. This type of provision is very common in practice, and often preferable to a superannuation scheme approved under s. 379 of the Income Tax Act, 1952.

The law has been made more strict by section 19 of the Finance Act, 1947 (now section 386 of the Income Tax Act, 1952). Subject to the exceptions specified in sections 386, 387 and 388, even "contingent" rights to a future pension are deemed to be emoluments presently taxable. The exceptions include approved superannuation schemes and approved retirement benefit schemes, which are dealt with later in this chapter.

It is considered that, where an employer is contemplating the award of a pension or gratuity to an employee about to retire, it is advisable, save perhaps in some exceptional circumstances, to defer the award of the pension or gratuity until after the retirement has taken place.

(iv) *If a fund is set up to provide pensions, will the income be exempt from tax?*

There is no general exemption from tax. But funds of an approved superannuation fund enjoy exemption, under section 379 (1) of the Income Tax Act, 1952. Where the scheme is operated by means of policies, not a fund, a similar exemption is conferred by section 24 of the Finance Act, 1956, on that part of the insurance company's business ascribable to those policies.[5]

(v) *Can a tax-free gratuity be paid to a retiring employee?*

A gratuity is taken free of tax only if it avoids a number of provisions aimed at bringing it into charge to tax.

Thus, a gratuity paid to an employee during service is normally part of the emoluments of his employment, chargeable to tax under Schedule E. This is so, even though payment of the gratuity is prompted by the approaching end of the employment.

A gratuity paid at or after the end of employment in performance of an obligation incurred by the employer during, and as part of the contract of, employment is chargeable to tax as part of the emoluments of employment: see *Dale* v. *De Soissons* [1950] W.N. 354; 32 Tax Cas. 118.

A gratuity paid to an employee after the end of his service and expressed to be by way of further remuneration for his past services, is probably chargeable to tax as part of the emoluments of employment: see *Allen* v. *Trehearne* [1937] 2 K.B. 568; 22 Tax Cas. 15; *Westminster Bank* v. *Barford* [1958] 1 W.L.R. 406; 38 Tax Cas. 68. This rule does not apply to a payment made as compensation for loss of office, or in general recognition of past loyal services.

A gratuity may be paid to an employee after he has retired by reason of injury or disability so as to be taken free of tax: Finance Act, 1960, s. 38 (1) (a). A payment made in return for a "restrictive covenant," even if the covenant is unenforceable at law, may be chargeable to surtax: Income Tax Act, 1952, s. 242.

---

[5] Retirement annuities under s. 22 of the Finance Act, 1956, enjoy comparable exemptions.

Any payment to an employee or ex-employee or his estate or any spouse, relative or dependant of his, and not otherwise chargeable to tax, may be caught by section 37 of the Finance Act, 1960, and thus brought into charge to tax. However, section 38 contains numerous exceptions to section 37, the best known being perhaps that applicable to sums totalling no more than £5,000.

Types of pension schemes

Two classes of pension schemes had, before 1956, received particular recognition by the legislature so far as tax is concerned: superannuation funds approved under section 379 of the Income Tax Act, 1952 [6]; and retirement benefit schemes approved under section 388 of the Income Tax Act, 1952,[7] to which the name " top hat " is sometimes applied. The expression " top hat " applied to such schemes—no doubt a nostalgic reference to the vanished headgear of those for whose benefit such schemes are frequently devised—is not a term of art. Strictly speaking, it probably only applies to schemes for the benefit of managing or executive directors and senior staff receiving salaries in excess of £2,000 a year. Since most of the schemes submitted for approval under section 388 are of this kind, the term " top hat " provides a useful compendious classification.

Section 22 of the Finance Act, 1956, introduced a third type of approved scheme, intended to benefit self-employed persons, " controlling " directors and others not able to enjoy the advantages of a superannuation or " top hat " scheme. It is proposed to deal with this type of scheme separately in a subsequent part of this chapter.

Superannuation funds approved under section 379 and retirement benefits schemes approved under section 388 have this feature in common: both derive the substantial tax advantages which they have to offer from concessions laid down by the legislature in apparently absolute terms, but in fact so framed that, for all practical purposes, the approval of particular schemes is left to the discretion of the specialist department of the Board of Inland Revenue which deals with all applications for approval of such funds and schemes. The departmental discretion is, however, exercised within well-defined limits and does not invite the criticism made of the Court of Chancery in the early days of its development that equity varied with the length of the Chancellor's foot.

It is also possible for pension schemes to be partially approved under the sections referred to, or to be operated without express approval but on the footing that contributors will obtain a measure of relief under section 219 of the Income Tax Act, 1952,[8] which provides for tax relief in respect of certain insurance premiums.

---

[6] Formerly s. 32 of the Finance Act, 1921.

[7] Formerly s. 21 of the Finance Act, 1947.

[8] Formerly s. 32 of the Income Tax Act, 1918, as amended by s. 20 of the Finance Act, 1932, and s. 29 of the Finance Act, 1948.

Schemes falling within this latter category are usually in form very similar to superannuation funds approved under section 379. Under section 219, assuming that the scheme provides for a lump sum payment on death or for a deferred annuity on retirement, two-fifths of the employee's contribution will obtain relief. This is the same relief as that to which an individual taxpayer is entitled in respect of premiums under policies providing for a capital sum on death effected on his own life or that of his wife. The relief is subject to a number of restrictions.

Relief under section 219 is given by way of relief against tax payable. In the case of a superannuation fund approved under section 379, relief is given by treating the employee's contribution as a deduction from his assessable income; this will reduce the income on which the employee's earned income relief will be calculated: *Frame* v. *Farrand* (1928) 13 Tax Cas. 861. Although, therefore, at first glance the relief afforded by a superannuation fund approved under section 379 appears to be more substantial than the relief obtained under a scheme falling within the scope of section 219, where lower paid employees are concerned, there may be little difference between the two.

Requirements of a superannuation fund

The condition which must be satisfied by a superannuation fund to qualify for approval under section 379 is that it must be shown to the satisfaction of the Commissioners of Inland Revenue that—

(a) the fund is a fund bona fide established under irrevocable trusts in connection with some trade or undertaking carried on in the United Kingdom by a person residing therein; and

(b) the fund has for its sole purpose the provision of annuities for all or any of the following persons in the events specified, that is to say, for persons employed in the trade or undertaking either on retirement at a specified age or on becoming incapacitated at some earlier age, or for the widows, children or dependants of persons who are or have been so employed, on the death of those persons; and

(c) the employer in the trade or undertaking is a contributor to the fund; and

(d) the fund is recognised by the employer and employed persons in the trade or undertaking.[9]

It is expressly provided that a fund may be approved at the discretion of the Revenue and subject to such special conditions as they may think proper to impose, notwithstanding that contributions may be returnable in certain circumstances, that the provision of annuities may not be the sole purpose of the fund (so long as it is the principal purpose) or that the trade or undertaking is partly carried on abroad.[10]

---

[9] Income Tax Act, 1952, s. 397 (3).
[10] *Ibid.*, proviso.

(i) *Trust deed*

The requirement that the fund shall be established under irrevocable trusts is satisfied in the normal case by the fund being constituted by a trust deed made between the company (or other employer) setting up the fund and the trustees of the fund. The rules of the fund are usually embodied in the deed or scheduled to it. A provision is commonly included in such a deed which enables the company (or other employer) to terminate its obligation to contribute to the fund. It may, however, be provided that in that event, or on the liquidation of the company or other event requiring the winding up of the fund, the fund as then constituted will be held upon trust for its existing members and their dependants entitled or prospectively entitled to pensions or other benefits. Power to amend the deed or rules under which the fund is established is usually included subject to some such qualification as that the primary purpose of the fund shall not be altered and that accrued benefits at the date of any amendment shall not be prejudiced. In the normal case, therefore, in this limited sense, the trusts of a fund may be said to be irrevocable.

(ii) *Recognition of the scheme*

Recognition of a fund by the employer is implied in cases where the employer is a contributor and has set up the fund; so also in the case of employees where the rules of the fund are available to all employees and all employees are voluntary or compulsory contributors. In the rules of many funds provision is made for the appointment of some trustees representing the employees. This, too, implies recognition of the fund. It is further sometimes claimed for such a provision that it gives employees confidence in a pension scheme to have a part in appointing the trustees. However this may work out in practice, as a matter of law it must be something of an illusion, since the law admits of no partiality in a trustee however appointed. In the case of a large fund it may well be found to be more convenient to appoint a corporate trustee. Over-detailed provision regarding the appointment of trustees may only result in the necessity of amending the rules.

(iii) *The discretion of the Revenue*

The conditions imposed by the Act for approval of superannuation funds are apparently absolute. Since, however, no fund in practice is ever likely to satisfy the strict letter of the statutory rules, the Revenue's discretion becomes the operative factor in almost every case. A number of practical rules of general application have been worked out of which the following are the most important. No pension payable out of an approved fund may exceed two-thirds of the salary to which the pensioner was entitled at the conclusion of his service, with a maximum, in the case of contributory funds, of £3,000. The " final salary " to which this rule is applied may be calculated on the average of the last three years of service or by some similar formula.

The employee's contribution must not normally exceed fifteen per cent. of the employee's salary. Not more than one-quarter of the contributions made on account of an employee must be attributed to any widow's pension payable out of the fund to the employee's widow. No capital sums may be paid to a member on retirement, whether by way of commutation of pension or otherwise; an exception to this rule is made in cases of serious ill health or where the pension payable would be trifling in amount. On the death of a member a capital payment equal to the actuarial reserve held on that member's account may be made. If a member leaves the employer's service before retirement age, he may receive back his own contributions to the fund but no part of any contributions to the fund made by the employer on his account; the employer's contributions may, however, be applied in providing a pension commencing at retirement age. If an employee ceases to be a member of an approved fund and his contributions are repaid to him, tax is payable at one-quarter of the standard rate on the sum so paid.[11] It is usual to include in the rules of such a fund a provision enabling the trustees to deduct any tax payable by them in respect of such a payment out of the sum payable to the member.

Other rules generally applied by the Commissioners of Inland Revenue in the exercise of their discretion under section 379 cover provisions for early and late retirement. Voluntary early retirement for members, other than those retiring on account of ill health, is normally allowed ten years or less before the normal retiring age, a usual retiring age being sixty-five. The rules of most funds provide for an appropriate reduction in the yearly amount of the pension payable in the event of early retirement. If retirement is postponed until after the normal retirement age has been attained, the usual rule is that the payment of a pension must be deferred until the actual date of retirement, with or without an increase in the yearly amount of the pension payable. But there are cases where an employee who remains in service beyond his normal retirement date draws both his wages and his pension. Where the payment of the pension is deferred in such circumstances the pension may be increased to its actuarial equivalent at the actual retirement date even if this exceeds £3,000 or the two-thirds limit.

A rule introduced since the National Insurance Act, 1959, became law, is that, if the Scheme is to enable its members to " contract out " of the State Scheme, it must assure the employee " equivalent pension benefits ": National Insurance Act, 1959, s. 7. This entails causing the Scheme to be certified by the Registrar of Non-Participating Employments, as well as approved by the Revenue.

The underlying principle which may be said to be the basis of approval of superannuation funds under section 379 is that if contributions to such a fund are to be made free of tax, by being admitted as

---

[11] See S.R. & O., 1921, No. 1699, Regulation No. 8.

deductions in computing the contributor's current tax liability, benefits must take the form of non-assignable non-commutable pensions. Consistently with this principle the rule referred to above is applied that on leaving a fund without qualifying for a pension a contributor may recover his own but not the employer's contributions; the latter he may only receive, if the rules of the fund so provide, as a deferred pension. If a contributor had an unquestionable right to recover his employer's contributions to the fund as well as his own, there would be no valid ground on which a claim for tax on the employee could be resisted in respect of contributions currently made to the fund by his employer on his behalf.[12]

(iv) *Tax advantages of a scheme*

If a fund is approved under section 379, all contributions to such fund, being ordinary annual contributions, are permissible deductions in computing the amount to be assessed on the employer under Case I or II of Schedule D [13] and on the employee under Schedule E [14] (usually dealt with under P.A.Y.E.). To the extent to which an employee's assessable remuneration is reduced by the amount of his ordinary annual contribution to the fund, he will, or may, receive less earned income relief, since this is calculated on the net amount. Otherwise the gift-horse is as good as it looks: the prospective pensioner can save for his old age out of income which has borne neither income tax nor surtax. The price to be paid is that subsequent benefits must take the form of a taxable pension.

The other substantial tax advantage offered by a fund approved under section 379 is that the investment income of the fund is exempt from tax by the express terms of the section.[15] Further, any short-term capital gain accruing to a person from his acquisition and disposal of investments and deposits held by him as part of a fund approved under section 379 is exempt from tax chargeable under Case VII of Schedule D.[16] Even in the case of unapproved funds the Revenue permit tax on investment income to be set off against the tax due on pensions paid from the fund so that the benefit of all tax borne is effectively passed on to the pensioners; and it appears that in practice some carry-forward of excess investment income is allowed so that the tax is set off against tax on pensions in future years. But to the extent to which the fund's income exceeds the outgoing pensions, the exemption enjoyed by an approved fund under section 379 confers a substantial advantage. Limited exemption is given to dividends and other income derived from the assets comprised in a superannuation fund which,

---

12 *Cf. Bell* v. *Gribble* [1903] 1 K.B. 517; 4 Tax Cas. 522; *Smyth* v. *Stretton* (1904) 20 T.L.R. 443; 5 Tax Cas. 36. (These cases were decided many years before there was provision for tax relief in respect of contributions to superannuation funds.)
13 Income Tax Act, 1952, s. 123.
14 Income Tax Act, 1952, s. 156, as amended by Finance Act, 1956, s. 10.
15 If the scheme is operated by means of policies of insurance, not a trust fund, a similar exemption applies to the insurance company: Finance Act, 1956, s. 24.
16 Finance Act, 1962, s. 15 (2).

because it is established for overseas employees working in a trade or under-taking carried on wholly or partly outside the United Kingdom, does not satisfy the provisions of section 379.[17]

(v) *Ordinary annual contribution*

The requirement that a contribution must be an " ordinary annual " contribution to qualify for deduction is primarily of importance when contributions are to be made to cover past service, as where, for example, the employees of a subsidiary company are admitted for the first time to a parent company's pension fund or where a new scheme is set up and some employees are credited with additional years of service representing past service.

A lump sum contribution which is neither ordinary nor annual will not be allowed to be wholly deducted for tax purposes in the year of payment. In the case of an employer's contribution it may be spread over a number of years by arrangement with the Revenue. Contributions by employees in respect of past service are less generously treated.[18] The point was raised in *Kneen* v. *Ashton* [1950] 1 All E.R. 982; 31 Tax Cas. 343. There Mr. Ashton, a railway employee, aged forty-eight, on promotion to a higher grade joined a railway superannuation fund approved under section 32 of the Finance Act, 1921 (the forerunner of section 379 of the Income Tax Act, 1952), and took advantage of a rule which enabled him to qualify for pension rights in respect of his past service on payment to the fund of " back contributions." By arrangement with the trustees of the fund the " back contributions " were to be paid by instalments over a period of six years.

Mr. Ashton claimed to deduct one of these instalments when computing his liability to tax under Schedule E in addition to the ordinary contribution payable by reference to his current service. The deduction claimed was disallowed on the grounds that the true nature of the payment described as " back contributions " was that it represented the purchase price of the right to be deemed to have been a member of the fund for a larger number of years than was in fact the case. Such a payment was not an " ordinary annual " contribution and payment by instalments could not alter the real character of the payments.[19]

A superannuation fund approved under section 379 may either be based on a group pension policy or may be based on a fund of investments held by the trustees of the fund. Most insurance companies which issue group policies have their own *pro forma* trust deeds and rules

---

[17] Finance Act, 1961, s. 21.

[18] It is understood that relief is normally allowed where a contribution is missed owing to sickness but it is made up during the same year of assessment.

[19] *Cf. I. R. C.* v. *Mallaby-Deeley* (1938) 55 T.L.R. 293; 23 Tax Cas. 153 on the relationship between the character of a payment for tax purposes and the way in which it is paid.

which may be adapted in any particular case to the employer's own requirements. In the case of a scheme based on its own fund of investments the trust deed and rules can best be prepared when the full details of the scheme are known and the actuarial basis of the fund has been calculated. Whether in any particular case a scheme based on an insurance policy is likely to be more effective than a scheme based on a fund of investments is a question on which the advice of an actuary should be sought.

Report of the Tucker Committee

Certain recommendations as to possible changes in the law affecting superannuation funds were made in the Report of the Committee on the Taxation Treatment of Provisions for Retirement (Cmd. 9063). The Committee's recommendations are based on the view that the governing principle for all schemes and funds should be that the build-up (*i.e.*, employers' and employees' contributions and the income from invested funds) of bona fide and reasonable schemes should be exempt from tax, and that all the benefits payable under such schemes should be subject to tax apart from a proportion taken as a lump sum within specified limits. All future schemes would require the specific approval of the Revenue before qualifying for the relief recommended by the Committee. Automatic approval would follow if certain conditions were satisfied and, in addition, the Revenue would have power to relax the rules in particular cases.

The principal conditions which the Committee suggested that a scheme should satisfy in order to secure automatic approval are that the employer is resident in the United Kingdom and carries on business wholly or partly in the United Kingdom; that the employer contributes at least one-third of the total cost of the scheme; that each employee is given a prescribed title to defined benefits, and that the terms of the scheme are made known to the employees concerned; that the diversion of the employee's own contributions to the scheme to any other purpose and their refund to him (except where circumstances arise which defeat the purpose of the scheme) are prohibited; that the refund of his own contributions to an employee before he has become entitled to any benefits is restricted to cases where the employee leaves the employment; that the benefits afforded by the scheme will accrue only on retirement at a specified age or on earlier incapacity or death; that the aggregate value of the benefits payable on retirement will not exceed the value of a pension equivalent to one-sixtieth of final remuneration (being the average remuneration over the last three years' service), multiplied by the number of years of service with the employer up to a maximum of forty with a marginal extension where the period of service exceeds forty years; that not less than three-quarters of the value of the benefits payable on retirement will be in the form of non-assignable and non-commutable pensions with certain fixed limits as to the amount which may be taken as a commuted lump sum; and that no period of service rendered by a person while he is a director, other than a whole-time service director, is to be taken into account for any of the purposes of the scheme.

If these conditions were satisfied, then according to the Committee's recommendations, the build-up of the scheme should be tax-free. The employer's regular annual contributions would be allowable as expenses for tax purposes and other contributions by the employer would also be allowed but might be required to be spread over a number of years. An employee's ordinary annual contribution would also qualify for relief, subject to a suggested limit equal to 15 per cent. of the employee's remuneration in any year with a right to carry forward the excess to later years should the necessary contribution exceed the prescribed limit.

The Committee also recommended that the investment income of all schemes should be exempt from tax, including that part of an insurance company's investment income which can be notionally appropriated to the policy or policies effected in connection with a particular scheme. This recommendation has been implemented by section 24 of the Finance Act, 1956.

Retirement benefit schemes

The legislation dealing with approved superannuation funds proceeds on the footing that certain positive tax advantages are to be available to such funds. The legislation dealing with retirement benefit schemes assumes that such schemes ought to be legislated against and achieves its positive effect by prescribing the limits within which schemes may operate without penalty: it does not give to the taxpayer any reliefs that he would, apart from the legislation, not enjoy, but removes advantages which existed under the general tax law.

Before the Finance Act, 1947,[20] which contained the provisions now found in sections 386–391 of the Income Tax Act, 1952, a company could agree with a director or employee to pay the premiums on a policy to mature on his retirement, or could set aside moneys or otherwise make provision for such retirement, in such a way that the director or employee was not assessed to tax on the benefit, namely, the right to a future pension, thus received. This is now completely changed. Moreover, an employer could, in assessing its own taxable profit, deduct reasonable payments made by way of paying such premiums, or otherwise providing pensions to ex-employees: see Smith v. Incorporated Council of Law Reporting [1914] 3 K.B. 674; 6 Tax Cas. 477; and cf. Mitchell v. Noble [1927] 1 K.B. 719; 11 Tax Cas. 372. This rule, which is still the law, is subject to the qualification that a lump sum payment made by an employer to set up a pensions or provident scheme may not be an admissible deduction: see Rowntree v. Curtis [1925] 1 K.B. 328; 8 Tax

---

[20] ss. 19 et seq.

Cas. 678; *British Insulated and Helsby Cables Ltd.* v. *Atherton* [1926] A.C. 205; 10 Tax Cas. 155.

(i) *The scope of section 386*

Section 386 of the Income Tax Act, 1952, is far-reaching. It provides that, where a company pays any sum (whether by way of contribution to an established pension fund or as a premium to provide a pension under a policy of insurance), with a view to the provision of any " retirement benefit " for any director or employee, then, subject to the exceptions listed in section 387, the sum so paid will be included in the director's or employee's taxable income for the year in which the payment is made. The section applies even where the retirement benefit is " contingent," that is, for example, where the director or employee does not qualify unless he serves a minimum period, or fulfils some other qualification.

The section also attacks pensions payable under the service agreement of a director or employee, where the company agrees to pay the pension but does not pay any premium or contribute to any fund for that purpose. It makes this attack by providing in subsection (2) that, in cases where there is no established pension fund to which contributions are made by the company, but an agreement or arrangement (a word of wide and uncertain import) is in force whereby the director or employee may receive a retirement benefit, he is to be currently liable to tax on the notional premium required each year to secure the particular benefit. This will involve an actuarial calculation and, in some cases—if, for example, no retirement age is specified under the " arrangement "—a certain amount of guess work.

Section 19 of the Finance Act, 1947 (the forerunner of section 386), was originally aimed at those who sought to alleviate the current burden of taxation by putting back into the bush one of the two ample birds they already had in the hand. When current remuneration is highly taxed, it is clearly advantageous to exchange a part of it for future pension benefits available when the remunerative office or employment comes to an end. It was formerly common for a company to employ its managerial staff under a contract giving both a salary and also a retirement pension, not necessarily with any idea of tax avoidance. As sometimes happens with snares, innocent prey may be trapped.

Two points regarding the liability under section 386 call for special mention. The first is the definition [21] of " retirement or other benefit," which is very wide and includes any payment, whether a pension, annual payment or a single lump sum, made in connection with a director's or employee's retirement or with a change in the nature of the service he performs for his employer, and whether made on, before or after retirement. This definition includes a pension payable to a widow of a retired employee, though not a pension payable only where the employee dies in

[21] Income Tax Act, 1952, s. 390 (1).

service. Secondly, the liability under the section is not expressly confined to schemes concerned with superannuation and retirement due to old age. For example, if, as part of a scheme for re-organising a company's affairs, an employee's contract of service is varied so that instead of continuing to be employed, say, as manager for another ten years at a salary of £x per annum, he is to serve for only four more years and then to retire or act in an advisory capacity only, when he will receive an allowance of £y per annum for the remainder of the ten years originally contracted for, during each of the four following years the employee would prima facie be liable to tax on £x plus the notional premium required to be paid for four years to produce a further £y for each of the next six years thereafter. He would also be liable to tax on the £y when he received it.

Where liability has been incurred under section 386 and the taxpayer can subsequently show that some event has happened by reason of which he has not received and can never receive the anticipated benefits by reference to which the original liability arose or any sum in substitution for such benefits, relief will be given by way of repayment of tax, or otherwise as may be appropriate.[22] No payment of a substituted lump sum in place of a prospective pension will avoid the liability under the section; nor is the substitution of a so-called " voluntary " payment for the original contractual payment which gave rise to the liability likely to be accepted as founding a claim for relief. Moreover, the company which makes an agreement for the provision of a retirement benefit for any director or employee is under a statutory obligation to forward the details to the Inspector of Taxes within three months.[23]

It has been suggested that section 386 imposes liability in respect of a pension awarded after retirement. The argument advanced by the Revenue is that a " director " or " employee " for the purposes of the section includes a past director or employee and that a pension presently payable is none the less a future retirement benefit in that some payments in respect of it will be made in the future. It is submitted that this argument entirely ignores the whole tenor of section 386, which imposes present liability in respect of benefits receivable on retirement in the future. Moreover, a pension is clearly a single benefit, so that once a pension has begun to be paid, it is a present and not a future benefit.

(ii) *Schemes excepted from section 386*

A scheme of retirement benefits must, if it is to be advantageous, come within one of the exceptions to section 386. Three exceptions are set out in section 387 (1), and of these one is now out of date and requires no further mention. Of the other two the first covers prospective benefits from a superannuation fund approved under section 379 or from a statutory superannuation fund; these are not within the scope of section

22 Income Tax Act, 1952, s. 387 (3).
23 Income Tax Act, 1952, s. 390 (5).

386 and no liability will be incurred in respect of contributions made by an employer to such funds. The second, which includes top hat schemes, covers any "excepted provident fund or staff assurance scheme." These expressions are defined in section 390 as follows:

" ' excepted provident fund or staff assurance scheme or other similar scheme ' means so much as relates to persons remunerated at a rate of two thousand pounds a year, or at a less rate, of any retirement benefits scheme as to which the following conditions are satisfied, that is to say—

(a) that the sums paid by the body corporate pursuant to the scheme in question in respect of any person for any period do not exceed ten per cent. of his remuneration for that period, and do not exceed one hundred pounds in the case of a period of a year or a correspondingly less or greater amount in the case of a shorter or longer period; and

(b) that no other retirement benefits scheme which relates to employees of the body corporate who are of the class to which the scheme in question relates, and who are remunerated as aforesaid, is subsisting for the time being, or, if there is any such other scheme subsisting, that it (so far as it relates to persons remunerated as aforesaid) and the scheme in question taken together satisfy the requirement specified in paragraph (a) of this definition."

It will be observed therefore that pensions for employees receiving no more than £2,000 a year can usually be provided under a scheme to which the provisions of section 386 will not apply.

Where a class of employee receiving more than £2,000 a year is to be provided for, or a scheme is to be set up involving unusually large payments by the employer, a further exemption to section 386, to be found in section 387 (2) (b) and section 388, becomes material. This exemption, which applies to "top hat schemes," only extends to retirement benefit schemes which are approved by the Revenue.

(iii) *Schemes approved under section* 388

As in the case of approved superannuation funds, approval is very largely a matter of the Revenue's discretion. An important requirement is that the main benefit provided by the scheme must be a pension for life on retirement. In addition there may be such provision for the payment of a widow's or dependant's pension as may be thought appropriate (see *post*, p. 386); if so, the widow's pension must usually be no larger in amount than her husband's pension.

Approval under section 388 is usually confined to pensions which do not exceed in amount one-sixtieth of the director's or employee's final salary for every year of his service with the company otherwise than as a controlling director.[24] In particular cases—if, for example, an employee is above the average age on joining the scheme—some relaxation may be allowed, subject to an overriding maximum of two-thirds of

[24] " Controlling director " is defined in s. 390 (1).

the director's or employee's final salary. Some provision for commuting pensions may be included in a scheme approved under section 388; but as a general rule not less than 75 per cent. of the benefits payable in respect of the employee under the particular scheme or any other scheme to which the employer contributes must be taken in the form of non-commutable, non-assignable pensions, on which, of course, tax will be payable.

(iv) *Controlling directors*

No scheme will be approved (subject to very limited exceptions) which benefits a " controlling director "—that is, a director owning more than five per cent. of the ordinary share capital of a company which is controlled by its directors by reason of their combined share-holdings.[25] A controlling director is for this purpose in the same position as a partner in a partnership firm: until the Finance Act, 1956, he could only provide for his retirement out of fully taxed income or with the limited tax relief allowed on premiums payable under life policies. Sections 22 and 23 of the Finance Act, 1956, provide a measure of tax relief.[26]

(v) *Payments to widows*

Since dead men pay no income tax, benefits payable on the death of a life-director to his widow or other dependants are outside the scope of section 386 [27] and a service agreement which merely provides for payments to a widow or dependants in the event of the death of a director or employee while in the company's service does not require to be approved under section 388.

(vi) *The name " top hat "*

As has been mentioned above, the commonest form of scheme approved under section 388 has acquired the name " top hat." The essence of a top hat scheme is the undertaking by a company to pay premiums to an insurance company under a policy to provide a pension at a specific age for one or more of its directors or employees. (In principle there is no reason why a company should not set up a funded " top hat " scheme but it is more common in practice to find such schemes operated with the assistance of an insurance company.)

The company's undertaking to pay the premiums must be in addition to any existing obligation to pay the director or employee a salary or other remuneration; the scheme should not involve the diversion of any part of the director's or employee's salary from his pocket to the insurance company, since in that event liability for tax on the whole of the director's or employee's contractual salary may be currently incurred

---

25 See s. 388 (1) (f).
26 These sections are discussed at p. 380, *infra.*
27 See s. 390 (1) where " retirement or other benefit " is defined.

quite apart from any potential liability under section 386.[28] For
example, if a director's or employee's salary was £5,000 and he agreed
to forgo £1,000 in return for the company paying a premium of £1,000,
he may find that his personal liability for tax on £5,000 persisted. The
director's or employee's salary is one thing: the provision of a pension
is something additional. No difficulty arises when a contract of service
is negotiated expressly on the terms that the employee will receive a
specified salary and the benefit of a top hat scheme: care must be
exercised where the employer is already contractually bound to pay a
specified salary and the intention is to substitute for part of the salary
the benefit of a scheme.

(vii) Establishing a " top hat " scheme

Frequently the only record or document establishing a top hat scheme
is a letter from the employing company to the director or employee
setting out the terms upon which the policy will be effected, the
premiums paid and the benefits provided. Such a letter is quite adequate
to meet the requirements of the Revenue for the purposes of approval
under section 388.

Circumstances may, however, arise in which the rights of the parties
created by such a letter are open to question. If, for example, a
company is to be wound up, the points which a liquidator may feel
bound to take regarding such an arrangement are very different from
the points which the company itself in the ordinary course of events
would ever be likely to take. In particular where under the particular
scheme provision is made for the payment of benefits to a widow or
dependants, various difficulties may arise as to the enforceability of
the beneficiary's rights or even as to the validity of the provisions
made.[29]

As an alternative to addressing a letter to the director or employee,
the company establishing a top hat scheme for one or more of its directors
or employees may execute a deed with trustees setting out the terms
and conditions upon which the scheme will be operated and the trusts
upon which the benefits to be provided will be held. Wide variations
are possible : an example both of a letter and of a trust deed establishing
a top hat scheme will be found in the precedents which follow.

It should be emphasised that there is no magic in operating such a
scheme by effecting a policy or policies of insurance. The employing
company may make what arrangements it will for providing pensions
and similar benefits; the provisions of section 386 will apply or not
as the case may be and the possibility of approval under section 388
will arise whatever method is adopted. It is for the employing company

---

[28] See *Smyth* v. *Stretton* (1904) 20 T.L.R. 443; 5 Tax Cas. 36.
[29] See as to the enforceability of a widow's rights, *Re Schebsman* [1944] Ch. 83; *Re
Miller's Agreement* [1947] Ch. 615; and *Re J. Bibby & Sons, Ltd., Pensions Trust
Deed* [1952] 2 All E.R. 483 (*sub nom. Davies* v. *I. R. C.*, 31 A.T.C. 355); also *ante*,
pp. 324 *et. seq.*

to decide by reference to commercial, not legal, considerations, what method offers the greatest advantages.

Pension schemes under the Finance Act, 1956

The Report of the Committee on the Taxation Treatment of Provisions for Retirement (Cmd. 9063) contained recommendations which would make available to all, and in particular to self-employed persons and controlling directors, the benefits enjoyed by individuals eligible for membership of superannuation funds and top hat schemes.

By a majority the members of the Committee supported the view that individuals not covered by schemes and not eligible to be included, should be entitled to belong to group schemes or to make individual arrangements (as by paying premiums under an individual policy of insurance effected for the purpose) which could be approved by the Revenue and, if approved, should give effect to the principle of taxing benefits but exempting build-up in the same way as existing approved schemes. Within certain prescribed limits, contributions would be available for full income tax and surtax relief. Benefits would be taxed as under schemes operated by employers and limits should be prescribed as to the amount of the contributions and of the pension which could be commuted and received in the form of a lump sum.

Partial effect was given to these recommendations in the Finance Act, 1956. Section 22 provides tax exemption in respect of a payment, made by an employee or self-employed person, either by way of a premium on an " approved annuity contract " or by way of contribution to an " approved trust scheme." Sections 22 and 23 contain detailed provisions restricting the amount of relief which may be obtained.

Subject to these provisions, which are illustrated by Precedent No. 51, *post*, the premium or contribution is allowed as a deduction from earnings or emoluments for tax purposes, with consequent saving of income tax and surtax, and loss of earned income relief. The benefit must, except in case of death, be taken as a taxable annuity of which no part may be commuted. The income of any approved trust scheme enjoys exemption from income tax, and there is corresponding relief under section 24 of the Finance Act, 1956, in respect of income from the investments of a company with whom an " approved annuity contract " is made. There is also exemption from any charge to tax under Case VII of Schedule D in respect of any gain made on the acquisition and disposal of such investments.[30]

Estate duty position [31]

Many of the considerations which apply to the liability for estate duty of annuities to partners, their widows and dependants (see *ante*, p. 322

---

[30] Finance Act, 1962, s. 15 (3).
[31] A useful summary of the practice of the Estate Duty Office with regard to estate duty on pension benefits will be found in Dymond's *Death Duties*, 13th ed. at pp. 337 *et seq.*

(Chap. 8)), are similarly applicable to employees' pensions under pension schemes. A purely gratuitous payment to the deceased's personal representatives is not liable to estate duty, and under this head a number of pensions are exempt from estate duty as being of an *ex gratia* nature.

The decision in *Re J. Bibby & Sons, Ltd., Pensions Trust Deed* [1952] 2 All E.R. 483, has already been mentioned (*ante*, p. 324, and see Chap. 8, *passim*). The effect of this decision is that in order for liability to estate duty to arise the right to the pension must be legally enforceable by an individual beneficiary. Secondly, if a scheme is non-contributory, the pension is not to be regarded as provided by the deceased employee. If a scheme is a contributory one, and the widow or other dependant has an enforceable right to a pension, estate duty may be payable under section 2 (1) (d) of the Finance Act, 1894.

How far claims under section 2 (1) (d) will continue to be effective once the implications of the decisions of the House of Lords in *D'Avigdor-Goldsmid* v. *I. R. C.* [1953] A.C. 347, *Westminster Bank, Ltd.* v. *I. R. C., Wrightson* v. *I. R. C.* [1958] A.C. 210, have been fully explored, may be open to question.

It is usually more advantageous if in the case of a pension to a widow (or other dependant) the contract or scheme provides for two separate pensions, one to the retired employee, and, after his death, a separate pension to his widow (or other dependant) and not one pension which is enjoyed in succession. The decision on this point is *Re Payton* [1951] Ch. 1081: see also *Re Tapp* [1959] Ch. 443, and compare *Re Weigall's Will Trusts* [1956] Ch. 424. In this case, the Austin Motor Co., Ltd., entered into a contract with an insurance company for the purpose of providing pension benefits to employees. An employee had an option (which was treated as exercised) to surrender the pension to which he was entitled for " a last survivor pension " which consisted of a smaller pension to himself and, if his wife survived him, to his wife for the rest of her life. It was held that as there were two separate interests, there was no passing on the husband's death and that estate duty was payable under section 2 (1) (d), and not section 1, of the Finance Act, 1894. As a consequence the benefit to the widow was exempt from aggregation with the rest of the deceased's estate because the deceased never had an interest in the property deemed to pass. But annuities for dependants provided under retirement annuity contracts or trust schemes approved under section 22 of the Finance Act, 1956, are to be treated as life policies in which the deceased had no interest and are to be aggregated as such in accordance with the provisions of section 33 (2) of the Finance Act, 1954: see Finance Act, 1956, s. 35, and Finance Act, 1957, s. 39.

State Pensions

The National Insurance Act, 1959, imposed upon the existing flat rate national insurance scheme a system of contributions graduated according to earnings with corresponding graduated additions to retirement pensions.[32] The graduated contributions first became payable in the week beginning 3rd April, 1961.[33] But it is possible to contract out of this system of graduated contributions, while continuing to pay flat rate contributions. Section 7 (1) of the 1959 Act provides that a person in a " non-participating employment " shall only pay flat rate contributions.

A non-participating employment is one where (a) the employee qualifies under a recognised superannuation scheme for retirement benefits by way of pension which are " equivalent pension benefits," that is, are on the whole as favourable as the right to benefit to be derived from graduated contributions under the National Insurance Act, 1959, and (b) there is in force a certificate [34] that the employment is to be treated as a non-participating employment.[35] The certificate is issued by the Registrar [36] of Non-Participating Employments, Ministry of Pensions and National Insurance, 17 Monck Street, Horseferry Road, London, S.W.1. An appeal may be made against a decision of the Registrar not to issue a certificate.[37] The Registrar has issued a leaflet about the arrangements for contracting out of the graduated pension scheme for the guidance of employers considering the question. He has also produced a suggested form of notice of intention to apply to contract out which has to be given to employees and other interested persons.

Section 8 of the 1959 Act sets out conditions which have to be satisfied before, in effect, a certificate will be issued by the Registrar; and these conditions have been subsequently expanded.[38] These conditions require that the pension scheme to which the employee who wishes to contract out belongs must provide, *inter alia,* that a pension will be available at the age of sixty-five years in the case of a man and sixty years in the case of a woman; that the pension will not be less than £2 6s. 2d. per annum for each year of service in the case of a man and £1 18s. 6d. in the case of a woman; that the pension will be payable for life and that it will be secured under a recognised superannuation scheme. A recognised superannuation scheme is established by Act of Parliament or other instrument having the force of law or is a scheme under which appropriate benefits are secured by irrevocable trust, contract of assurance or annuity contract satisfying such conditions as may be prescribed.[39]

---

[32] Graduated contributions are paid, accounted for and recovered in the same way as tax on Schedule E emoluments, that is to say, in accordance with (modified) P.A.Y.E. regulations: see the National Insurance (Collection of Graduated Contributions) Regulations S.I. 1960, No. 922.

[33] The National Insurance Act, 1959 (Commencement) (No. 2) Order, 1960 S.I. 1960 No. 1215 (C.10).

[34] National Insurance (Non-Participation—Certificates) Regulations, S.I. 1959, No. 1860.

[35] National Insurance Act, 1959, s. 7 (2).

[36] *Ibid.* s. 13.

[37] The National Insurance (Non-Participation—Appeals and References) Regulations, S.I. 1959, No. 2119.

[38] The National Insurance (Non-Participation—Assurance of Equivalent Pension Benefits) Regulations, S.I. 1960, No. 1103, as amended by S.I. 1961, No. 1378.

[39] National Insurance Act, 1959, s. 8 (4).

Most private pension schemes are recognised superannuation schemes and do provide benefits by way of pension which are on the whole at least as favourable as the benefits to be derived from graduated contributions under the National Insurance Act, 1959. Accordingly, most employers operating such pension schemes are likely to contract out of the graduated contributions system in the state pension scheme. And this has been the trend. In 1959 the Government thought that 2,500,000 employees would be contracted out. In fact, in April 1961, when the new system commenced, 4,250,000 were contracted out.[40]

With new pension schemes, and with existing pension schemes under which there are powers to vary the provisions of the schemes, such changes as may be required to satisfy the conditions for contracting out may be made. But there are existing pension schemes where there are no appropriate powers to vary the provisions of the schemes. In these cases the Chief Registrar of Friendly Societies has powers to make modifications in existing pension schemes in connection with the National Insurance Act, 1959.[41]

PRECEDENT No. 45

Service Agreement with Managing Director: Appointment for Life: Pension on Death During Service

This is a straightforward precedent of an agreement appointing an individual as managing director of a company for life. Such an agreement may be desirable, for example, where a majority shareholder in a private company makes over his shares to his children or the trustees of a trust for his children's benefit with a view to reducing estate duty on his death and wishes to protect himself against the possibility of the children biting the hand which has fed them (see pp. 196 to 203 ante). Although he has surrendered control of the family company, an agreement in some such form as this will give the head of the family a measure of protection during his life and will provide something for his widow on his death.

Both the managing director's salary and the widow's pension will rank as earned income for tax purposes.[42] If the company is one to which section 46 of the Finance Act, 1940, will apply on the managing director's death, remuneration under the agreement, if " reasonable," will not rank as a " benefit " for the purpose of calculating the benefits which the

---

[40] See " Contracting Out of State Pensions " by Mr. Arthur Seldon, The Times, January 23, 1963.

[41] National Insurance (Modification of Pension Schemes) Regulations, S.I. 1959, No. 1902.

[42] Income Tax Act, 1952, s. 525.

deceased enjoyed during the last five years of his life and the " slice " of the company's assets which is deemed to pass on his death.[43]

From the company's point of view both salary and pension will be deductible in computing the company's taxable profits. It should, however, be remembered that an excessive salary can be attacked by the Revenue as a distribution of profits and not really a payment made to earn the profits.[44] Only an expense incurred to earn the profits is admissible as a deduction in computing the company's profits for tax purposes.

As regards profits tax, consideration should be given to the question whether the managing director is a " whole time service director " within the meaning of the Finance Act, 1937, 4th Schedule, paragraph 13 (c). If he is not, regard must be had to the limits on the remuneration of directors imposed by paragraph 11, as amended by section 34 of the Finance Act, 1952, and to the definition of " director " in paragraph 13 (b).

Agreement. AN AGREEMENT made the —— day of —— 19— BETWEEN X Y Z Ltd. whose registered office is situate at —— (hereinafter called " the Company ") of the one part and A. B. of —— (hereinafter called " Mr. A. B.") of the other part :

Appointment of managing director. 1. MR. A. B. is hereby appointed managing director of the Company and as such managing director shall perform the duties assigned to him and exercise the powers vested in him from time to time by the directors of the Company.

Where practicable, the duties of the employee should be defined with a reasonable degree of certainty, otherwise difficulties could arise, if the employee began to neglect duties which were not specified in the contract, but which the employers wished him to undertake, and a question may arise whether the contract is sufficiently precise to be enforceable: see *Pocock* v. *A.D.A.C., Ltd.* [1952] 1 All E.R. 294. The suggestion sometimes made that it is as easy, and possibly more advantageous, to employ a man as a " consultant " rather than to pay him a pension may merit detailed examination in any particular case.

2. MR. A. B. shall hold the said office of managing director during the remainder of his life.

This clause must be read subject to section 184 of the Companies Act, 1948. That section, which was new in the 1948 Act, gives the Company

---

43 See Finance Act, 1940, ss. 46 (2), 47 and 51 (4).
44 *Copeman* v. *William Flood & Sons, Ltd.* [1941] 1 K.B. 202; 24 Tax Cas. 53; *Samuel Dracup & Sons, Ltd.* v. *Dakin* (1957) 37 Tax Cas. 377.

power, by an ordinary resolution of which special notice has been given in accordance with subsection (2), to remove any director, notwithstanding anything in its articles or in any agreement between it and him.

Section 184 does not deprive the director so removed of compensation or damages payable to him in respect of the termination of his appointment as director. In this respect the decisions in *Dale* v. *De Soissons* [1950] 2 All E.R. 460; 32 Tax Cas. 118, and *Henley* v. *Murray* [1950] 1 All E.R. 108; 31 Tax Cas. 351, should be observed: the principle arising therefrom is that it is usually better not to include in the agreement any provision that compensation will be paid if the agreement is terminated before it has run its course. If such compensation is provided for, the director will most probably be assessed to tax on the compensation as part of the emoluments of his employment.[45]

The damages payable would be assessed having regard, not to the loss of gross earnings suffered by the employee, but to loss of net earnings after payment of income tax and surtax: *British Transport Commission* v. *Gourley* [1956] A.C. 185. And, at any rate in a case where the damages amount to no more than £5,000, this basis of assessment would appear to be correct notwithstanding the provisions in section 37 of the Finance Act, 1960: see British Tax Encyclopedia, § 1–973. Where the damages amount to more than £5,000 so that the balance over £5,000 would attract a charge to tax under the provisions of section 37, it is suggested that the correct formula for assessing the amount to be paid is: such an amount as after the payment of tax under section 37 will leave the payee with an amount equal to his net earnings.

The question should be considered, whether the agreement should be submitted for approval to a General Meeting: Companies Act, 1948, Table A, reg. 87.

Whole time and attention.	3. Mr. A. B. shall unless prevented by ill-health throughout his tenure of the said office devote the whole of his time attention and abilities to the business of the Company and shall well and faithfully serve the Company and use his best endeavours to promote the Company's interests.
Salary and allowance.	4. (i) During his tenure of the said office Mr. A. B. shall be entitled to a fixed salary at the rate of —— pounds (£——) per annum or at such other rate as may from time to time be agreed between him and the Company (excluding any bonuses commissions or other similar payments) such salary to be payable by twelve equal monthly payments to be made on the last day of each calendar month.

---

[45] See " Compensation for Loss of Office " by H. H. Monroe [1956] B.T.R. 252.

(ii) In addition to the fixed salary payable as aforesaid Mr. A. B. shall be entitled to an allowance at the rate of —— pounds (£——) per annum towards the expenses necessarily incurred by him in connection with the business of the Company such allowance to be payable by twelve equal monthly payments to be made on the last day of each calendar month.

For the rules governing the liability to tax on directors' expense accounts see sections 160 to 168 of the Income Tax Act, 1952. By virtue of section 160, sums paid under the above clause towards expenses will be chargeable to tax as emoluments of the office of director, and the onus will be placed on the director of justifying moneys he has spent as expended " wholly exclusively and necessarily " in the performance of his duties: see Income Tax Act, 1952, Schedule 9, rule 7. In practice, the Inspector is likely to accept a reasonable sum as stated in clause 4 (ii), provided that it has been approved by the company's auditors.

Widow's pension.

5. THE Company hereby covenants with Mr. A. B. [and as a separate covenant with C. D. the present wife of Mr. A. B.] that in the event of his death occurring during his service as managing director of the Company under this Agreement the Company will pay to C. D. the present wife of Mr. A. B. (hereinafter called " the wife ") if she shall survive him a pension during the remainder of her life at the rate of —— pounds (£——) per [annum such pension to be payable by twelve equal monthly] [month] payments to be made on the last day of each month.

Since the pension payable under this agreement will only arise in the event of the managing director's death in the company's service, it will not rank as a retirement or other benefit within the meaning of section 390 (1) of the Income Tax Act, 1952, and so section 386 will not be applicable.

" Our law knows nothing of a *jus quaesitum tertio* arising by way of contract ": *per* Lord Haldane in *Dunlop* v. *Selfridge* [1915] A.C. 847 at p. 853. It follows, therefore, that a wife who is not a party to a contract between her husband and his employer can acquire no enforceable rights under that contract in the absence of express words creating a trust or constituting a covenant made by the employer with her: *cf. Re Schebsman* [1944] Ch. 83, *per* Lord Greene at p. 90.

In *Smith and Snipes Hall Farm, Ltd.* v. *River Douglas Catchment Board* [1949] 2 K.B. 500, Denning L.J. doubted this proposition as applied to a contract between an employer and an employee to pay a pension to the employee's widow. In *Dutton* v. *Poole* (1677) 2 Lev. 210, upon which Denning L.J. relied in the case cited, there are traces of an earlier principle regarding the enforcement of contracts for the benefit of interested third parties, namely that where consideration moves from a father, and the contract is for the benefit of his child, the natural love and affection between the father and child gives the child the right to sue as if the consideration had proceeded from himself. Although this principle may once have been applied in the common law courts it was (in spite of the observations of Denning L.J. in *Drive Yourself Hire Co. (London) Ltd.* v. *Strutt* [1954] 1 Q.B. 250 at p. 274) obsolete by the time of the decision in *Tweddle* v. *Atkinson* (1861) 1 B. & S. 393. Denning L.J.'s suggestion in the *River Douglas Catchment Board* case (*supra*) was no part of the decision in that case and was not endorsed by the other two members of the Court of Appeal. It is submitted that Lord Haldane's comment still states the law.

On this basis the words in square brackets in the second line of clause 5 may be used to give the widow an enforceable right to her pension.

It is considered that even if the widow is given an enforceable right to her pension estate duty will not (provided that she is named in the agreement) be payable under section 2 (1) (d) of the Finance Act, 1894, on the death of the managing director on the value of the widow's pension arising on his death: see *D'Avigdor-Goldsmid* v. *I. R. C.* [1953] A.C. 347; *Westminster Bank, Ltd.* v. *I. R. C., Wrightson* v. *I. R. C.* [1958] A.C. 210, which are discussed *ante*, at page 326. It is not certain that this view will be accepted by the Estate Duty Office, however. It is reasonably clear, nevertheless, that the pension will not be aggregable with the managing director's free estate. If the widow's claim to the pension could not be enforced there would be good grounds for resisting any claim for duty on the footing that the " interest " referred to in section 2 (1) (d) must be an enforceable interest: see *Re Miller's Agreement, Uniacke* v. *Att.-Gen.* [1947] Ch. 615, and *cf. Re J. Bibby & Sons, Ltd., Pensions Trust Deed, Davies* v. *I. R. C.* [1952] 2 All E.R. 483.

Where the choice is between possibly paying a small amount of estate duty and achieving a measure of security for the widow, or avoiding duty and leaving the widow without security, it seems probable that in most cases the former alternative should prevail.

A pension payable to the widow of a director in the above form qualifies for earned income relief: Income Tax Act, 1952, s. 525 (1) (a).

Testi-
monium.   IN WITNESS whereof the Common Seal of the Company has been hereunto affixed and Mr. A. B. has hereunto set his hand the day and year first above written.

The agreement will require to be stamped 10s. as a deed, and in addition a further stamp may be required representing 2s. 6d. per £5 on the amount of the annual sum payable to the widow as a pension.[46]   In practice, a rather fine distinction is sometimes drawn, and, if the pension is expressed to be payable only after the employee has served for a stated number of years, the agreement may require only the 10s. stamp.

PRECEDENT No. 46

Service Agreement for a Managing Director Providing a Pension on Retirement

This precedent provides a formal agreement for a managing director who wishes to have his position as to service and pension put into writing.   Since the agreement provides for the payment of a pension on retirement it must be approved by the Revenue under section 388 of the Income Tax Act, 1952, if the provisions of section 386 are to be avoided. The pension provision is in a form which is likely to be approved by the Revenue without difficulty provided that the managing director is not a " controlling director " within the definition in section 390 (1).

For the managing director to be a " controlling director " two factors must be present: first the company must be one which the directors control in the sense that between them they hold sufficient shares to obtain a voting majority, and secondly the managing director must own or be able to control more than five per cent. of the ordinary share capital of the company. If the managing director has at any time been a controlling director, the years during which he was such a director must be left out of account in computing the pension payable on his retirement.

If the pension provisions in the agreement are not approved by the Revenue the managing director will be liable to tax year by year while the agreement remains in force on an amount equal to the premium which would be required to be paid by the company to an insurance company to provide the managing director's pension. The agreement itself is silent as to how the pension will be provided: the company can either pay the pension out of current profits when the time comes or it can make some provision for the pension by way of insurance. The tax implications of any arrangement for providing the pension by insurance would require to be considered with some care.

Agreement.   THIS AGREEMENT is made the —— day of —— 19— BETWEEN X Y Z LTD. whose registered office is situate at —— (hereinafter called " the Company ") of the one part and A. B. of —— (hereinafter called " Mr. A. B.") of the other part;

[46] Finance Act, 1963, s. 57.

WHEREAS :

(A) Mr. A. B. is —— years of age and has for —— years or thereabouts been in the service of the Company and now holds the office of managing director (which office is hereinafter referred to as " the said office ") ; and

(B) The Company wishes to confirm the appointment of Mr. A. B. in the said office upon the terms and subject to the conditions hereinafter contained ;

NOW THIS AGREEMENT WITNESSETH as follows :—

Confirmation as managing director.

1. THE appointment of Mr. A. B. as managing director of the Company is hereby confirmed and as such managing director Mr. A. B. shall continue to perform the duties and exercise the powers which from time to time have been or may hereafter be assigned to or vested in him by the directors of the Company. Subject as hereinafter provided Mr. A. B. shall hold the said office until he shall attain the age of sixty-five years.

Duties of managing director.

2. MR. A. B. shall in the performance of his duties conform to all reasonable instructions that may be given to him from time to time by the directors of the Company and shall devote the whole of his time and attention (unless prevented by ill-health) to the performance of his duties in the said office and shall not without the written consent of the directors of the Company be engaged or concerned in the direction management or control of any business other than that of the Company.

Leave of absence.

3. MR. A. B. shall during his tenure of the said office be entitled to leave of absence for a period in each year not exceeding —— weeks. Any salary or commission payable to Mr. A. B. hereunder shall continue to be payable notwithstanding such leave of absence.

Salary.

4. THE Company shall pay to Mr. A. B. during his tenure of the said office a fixed salary at the rate of —— pounds (£——) per annum; such salary shall be paid to Mr. A. B. at such times and in such manner as shall from time to time be agreed between the Company and Mr. A. B.

Commission on profits.

5. IN addition to the said fixed salary the Company shall pay to Mr. A. B. during his tenure of the said office

a commission on the net profits of the Company to be
ascertained as hereinafter provided; such commission
shall be equal to —— per cent. of the net profits of the
Company and shall be paid to Mr. A. B. at such times
and in such manner as shall from time to time be agreed
between the Company and Mr. A. B.

Definition of profits. 6. THE net profits of the Company for each year
ending on the —— day of —— shall for the purposes of
the last preceding Clause hereof be the net trading profits
of the Company in such year after deducting:—

(a) all usual charges and expenses of the Company's
business including the fixed remuneration of directors
and salaries of employees and including the fixed salary
payable to Mr. A. B. under Clause 4 hereof;

(b) all taxes (other than income tax) paid or payable
by the Company in respect of or by reference to its
trading profits or other income or property; and

(c) all commissions or percentages of profits payable
to any director or employee of the Company other than
Mr. A. B.

The amount of the net profits of the Company for
each year ending on the —— day of —— shall be certified
in writing by the auditors for the time being of the Company and such certificate shall be binding on the Company and Mr. A. B. and the giving of such certificate
shall be a condition precedent to the right of Mr. A. B.
to receive any commission hereunder.

The adoption of a formula for fixing " net profits " for the purpose
of paying a commission is a fertile source of trouble. As a precaution
it seems prudent always to make the company's auditor, or other suitable
person, the final arbiter of the amount to be paid. It is also as well
to deal expressly with tax. For such guidance as the cases have to offer
on the point reference may be made to *Johnston* v. *Chestergate Hat
Manufacturing Co., Ltd.* [1915] 2 Ch. 338; *Edwards* v. *The Saunton
Hotel Co., Ltd.* [1943] 1 All E.R. 176, and *L. C., Ltd.* v. *G. B. Ollivant,
Ltd.* [1944] 1 All E.R. 510.

Cesser of office. 7. IF Mr. A. B.'s tenure of the said office shall cease
during the currency of any year ending on the —— day
of —— he or his personal representatives shall be entitled
to a rateable proportion of the fixed salary and commission which he would have received if he had lived and

been employed by the Company in accordance with the terms of this Agreement for the whole of such year.

Resignation.   8. AFTER the expiration of —— years from the date hereof Mr. A. B. shall be at liberty to resign the said office at any time after giving not less than —— months' notice in writing to the Company of his intention to resign.

Dismissal.   9. IF Mr. A. B. shall in the opinion of the directors of the Company fail for six consecutive months to perform his duties in the said office in accordance with the provisions of this Agreement the Company may by notice in writing terminate his tenure of the said office.

Pension.   10. (i) IN either of the events following that is to say :—

(a) if Mr. A. B. shall cease to hold the said office upon attaining the age of sixty-five years or

(b) if having attained the age of fifty-five years Mr. A. B. shall resign the said office in accordance with the provisions of Clause 8 hereof

the Company shall pay to Mr. A. B. during the remainder of his life a pension of an annual amount equal to one-sixtieth of Mr. A. B.'s final salary (as hereinafter defined) for each completed year of Mr. A. B.'s service with the Company since he attained the age of twenty-one years (not exceeding forty years in all) subject to a maximum amount of —— pounds (£——).

This formula fixes the managing director's pension by reference to his final salary and the length of his service with the company. It is a formula which is normally acceptable to the Revenue. The forty-year limit on service ensures that the pension will not exceed two-thirds of final salary, the permitted maximum. If desired, the pension payable can be expressed as a definite figure : it will then be necessary to satisfy the Revenue that the figure selected is unlikely to exceed two-thirds of final salary.

Final salary.   (ii) " Final salary " for the purposes of this Clause and the next succeeding Clause hereof means the average of the aggregate remuneration to which Mr. A. B. shall have been entitled by way of salary and commission under Clauses 4 and 5 hereof in each of the five years ending on the —— day of —— immediately preceding the date on which Mr. A. B. ceases to hold or resigns the said office.

For convenience in calculating the pension the company's annual accounting date should be inserted as the date on which the five-year period will end by reference to which " final salary " will be computed.

Option to take widow's pension.   (iii) Mr. A. B. shall have the option exercisable during the month preceding the date on which he first becomes entitled to a pension under paragraph (i) of this Clause by notice in writing to the Company to require that instead of paying the pension referred to in that paragraph (hereinafter called " the ordinary pension ") for the remainder of his life the Company shall pay a reduced pension (hereinafter called " the reduced pension ") to Mr. A. B. during the remainder of his life equal to such fraction of the ordinary pension as Mr. A. B. shall when exercising such option elect and a further pension (hereinafter called " the widow's pension ") commencing at the date of his death to his wife C. D. if she shall survive him during the remainder of her life the annual amount of the widow's pension to be determined by an actuary nominated by the Company for the purpose to the intent that the aggregate capital value of the reduced pension and the widow's pension shall be equal to the capital value of the ordinary pension;

Provided that the annual amount of the widow's pension shall not exceed the annual amount of the reduced pension.

This provision enables the managing director to provide a pension for his widow, if she survives him, by reducing his own pension. The advantage to be gained from providing a separate pension for the widow is that the managing director will not have had an interest in the widow's pension (see the proviso to section 4 of the Finance Act, 1894) and accordingly, even if estate duty should be payable on the value of the pension under section 2 (1) (d) of the Finance Act, 1894, the widow's pension will not be aggregable with the managing director's free estate: cf. Re Payton, decd., Payton v. I. R. C. [1951] Ch. 1081; Re Weigall's Will Trusts [1956] Ch. 424; Re Tapp [1959] Ch. 443. A separate pension for the widow is therefore preferable to any form of " joint and survivor " pension. Other aspects of a widow's pension are discussed, ante, at p. 386.

The provision of a pension for the widow here made is in a form usually acceptable to the Revenue. The total value of the pensions is subject to the same limits as would be apt for a single person for the managing director and the annual amount of the widow's pension cannot exceed the annual amount of the managing director's own pension.

(iv) Any pension payable under this Clause shall be paid to the person entitled thereto at such times and in such manner as shall from time to time be agreed between the Company and such person.

Widow's pension.

11. IF Mr. A. B. shall die during his tenure of the said office the Company shall pay a pension commencing at the date of his death to his wife C. D. if she shall survive him during the remainder of her life the annual amount of such pension being equal to one-third of one-sixtieth of Mr. A. B.'s final salary (as defined in paragraph (ii) of the last preceding Clause hereof) for each completed year of Mr. A. B.'s service with the Company since he attained the age of twenty-one years subject to a maximum amount of —— pounds (£——).

Pension to be inalienable.

12. MR. A. B. hereby covenants with the Company that he will not request the Company to commute and that he will not assign or alienate the pension rights conferred by this Agreement or any part thereof.

Pensions under retirement benefit schemes approved by the Revenue under section 388 of the Income Tax Act, 1952, must normally be non-commutable and non-assignable except that a provision may be included permitting up to 25 per cent. of the pension to be commuted. A proviso could, therefore, be added to this clause to the effect that on request the company will pay to the managing director after retirement a lump sum of an amount certified by an actuary to be equivalent in value to 25 per cent. of the total pension rights payable in respect of the managing director under this agreement, and that if such payment is made the annual pension payable to the managing director will be reduced by such an amount as the actuary shall declare to be appropriate. If a formula such as this is adopted and the option under clause 10 (iii) is exercised, the managing director will be able to commute more than 25 per cent. of his own pension leaving the widow's pension payable in full. The widow's pension must, however, still not exceed the reduced pension payable to the managing director.

Membership of Pension Fund.

13. So long as Mr. A. B. remains prospectively entitled to a pension under this Agreement he shall not be eligible for membership of any Pension Fund Superannuation Fund or other Retirement Benefits Scheme instituted or maintained by the Company for the benefit of any of its officers or employees.

This provision is necessary to ensure that the aggregate retirement benefits provided for the managing director by the company do not exceed the permissible limits for the purposes of approval under section 388 of the Income Tax Act, 1952.

Declaration of trust.

14. Mr. A. B. hereby declares himself to be a trustee for his wife C. D. of the benefit of the Company's undertaking herein contained to pay her a pension in certain events.

This provision gives the widow an enforceable right to her pension. Compare the alternative method of achieving the same end in clause 5 of Precedent 45, *ante*; and *cf. Lloyd's* v. *Harper* (1880) 16 Ch.D. 290.

Testimonium.

In witness whereof the Common Seal of the Company has been hereunto affixed and Mr. A. B. has hereunto set his hand the day and year first above written.

PRECEDENT No. 47

Form of Letter and Acknowledgment where a " Top Hat " Scheme is Effected for the Benefit of an Individual Executive

The essence of a " top hat " scheme is that a company pays the premiums on an endowment policy to provide a pension for one of its directors or executives. The scheme is approved under section 388 of the Income Tax Act, 1952, and the prospective pensioner suffers no immediate additional tax burden under section 386.

When a " top hat " scheme is set up the insurance company usually provides the company setting up the scheme with a letter or set of rules to send to each of the directors or executives whom it is intended to benefit under the scheme. This precedent shows a form of letter suitable for this purpose. Each insurance company usually adopts its own form. A letter such as that shown here is intended to satisfy the requirements of the Revenue so that the scheme may be approved under section 388. In practice it performs that limited task admirably. But other questions may arise. Does the letter constitute an enforceable contract between the company and its director or executive? Does the letter create a trust? Could a liquidator or receiver for debenture holders intercept the proceeds of a policy effected in accordance with the letter? To create an enforceable contract there must be consideration; but an undertaking by an employer to give an additional reward to an employee already contractually bound to serve him does not amount to a promise by the employer for which any consideration runs from the employee : see *Stilk* v. *Myrick* (1809) 2 Camp. 317, and contrast *Hartley* v. *Ponsonby*

(1857) 7 E. & B. 872. To create a trust, there must be clear words from which the intention to create a trust may be inferred: see, *e.g.*, *Vandepitte* v. *Preferred Accident Insurance Corporation of New York* [1933] A.C. 70.

One answer to any doubts which may be cast upon the effectiveness of a letter in this form may, of course, be the comment that since the whole scheme is an additional benefit voluntarily provided by the company, the director has no complaint if in the events which happen he receives less than he had hoped for. Provided that all parties are at one as to the basis on which the scheme has been set up this is a satisfactory answer, and the questions posed above need not be pressed. But if those questions are regarded as material, it is at least prudent to ensure that the form of letter adopted includes express words which enable definite answers to be given. An even better course is to adopt a legal form for the scheme such as that dealt with in Precedent No. 48. Where the director has no enforceable right to any benefits under the scheme it is clear that, in the event of his wrongful dismissal, he could not claim that the damages payable should include a sum in respect of his expectations under the scheme: see *Beach* v. *Reed Corrugated Cases, Ltd.* [1956] 1 W.L.R. 807 at pp. 816–817.

Dear ——,

Policy of insurance.
I write to inform you that the Company proposes to effect as from —— a policy of insurance on your life for an amount of £——. The policy will be an endowment policy maturing on ——.

The terms upon which the proceeds of this policy will be held are as follows :—

1. The policy will be effected on your life and will be held by the Company in trust for the purposes set out below.

Premiums.
2. The Company will pay all premiums under the policy.

Payment.
3. In the event of your death whilst in the service of the Company the sum assured under the policy will be payable to your legal personal representatives. Payment of the sum assured will be subject to the policy being then in force and to the terms set out in the policy as to special risks.

The sum assured, if payable to the deceased executive's personal representatives, will only attract estate duty under section 2 (1) (d) of the Finance Act, 1894, if the Revenue take the view that the policy was purchased or provided by the deceased. This in turn depends on the basis on which the scheme was negotiated and set up; if the provision of a pension by the company was voluntarily assumed as an addition to the company's contractual liability to pay an agreed salary, the sum assured will not under present practice be regarded as provided by the deceased executive but by the company and no duty will be payable. This is understood to represent the Revenue's present view as to the effect of the decision in *Re J. Bibby & Sons, Ltd., Pensions Trust Deed* [1952] 2 All E.R. 483; 31 A.T.C. 355.

Retirement pension.

4. (a) On retirement on or after the maturity date you will be entitled to the benefits arising under the policy. Subject to the provisions of paragraph (d) below these benefits will take the form of a pension payable to you during the remainder of your life. The pension so payable will not exceed two-thirds of the total remuneration receivable by you during the last year of your service with the Company.

(b) In the event of your remaining in the service of the Company after the maturity date no further premiums will be paid under the policy but payment of the benefits arising under the policy will be deferred until the date of your actual retirement from the Company's service and the benefits then payable will be appropriately increased.

(c) Should you retire from the Company's service with the consent of the Company within ten years before the maturity date, you will be entitled to receive a reduced pension payable from the date of your actual retirement during the remainder of your life.

(d) Provided that not less than three-quarters of the total benefits payable under the policy and under any other retirement benefits scheme of the Company in which you have an interest are taken in the form of a non-commutable and non-assignable pension, you may, with the consent of the Company, receive the balance of the benefits arising under the policy in the form of a lump-sum payment. In the event of your retirement from the Company's service occurring in exceptional circumstances of serious ill-health the Company may determine that the whole of the benefits arising under the policy shall be receivable by you in the form of a lump-sum payment.

The conditions contained in this paragraph represent the common form requirements of the Revenue for approval under section 388 of the Income Tax Act, 1952. If the individual executive is a member of any other pension scheme operated by the company his rights under such other scheme must be taken into account for the purpose of determining whether or not the individual policy provided for him and the terms upon which it is held are within the permitted limits.

Premature termination of service.

5. (a) In the event of your service with the Company being terminated before the maturity date by reason of ill-health or your dismissal for any cause other than fraud or misconduct, the policy will be assigned to you, in which case any premiums payable under the policy after the date of such assignment may be paid by you and the benefits arising under the policy will be subject to the like restrictions as to commutation and assignment as are contained in Clause 4 above and Clause 6 below.

(b) In the event of your service with the Company being terminated before the maturity date for any other reason (for example on your voluntary resignation) the disposition of the benefits arising under the policy will be at the discretion of the Company. In appropriate circumstances the Company may determine that the benefits arising under the policy shall be receivable by you in pension form at the maturity date. Any benefits which may at the discretion of the Company be determined to be payable will be subject to the like restrictions as are mentioned in paragraph (a) above.

It is regarded by the Revenue as an essential feature of an approved scheme that the employee shall not be able to join and leave the scheme as he will and receive the benefit of the company's contributions on his behalf every time he does so. Consequently in the event of an employee leaving the company's service otherwise than on account of ill-health or by reason of dismissal through no fault of the employee, it is usually provided that the payment of benefits is to be a matter for the company's discretion or, alternatively, that any benefit taken must be in the form of a pension commencing on the date which would have been the employee's date of retirement had he remained with the company. If this provision were omitted the company's contributions to the scheme might be regarded as part of the employee's current remuneration and taxed under Schedule E as such. And any pension subsequently paid might be regarded as income derived from an investment and not as earned income.

Benefits
inalienable.

6. (a) Except as provided above, the benefits under the policy cannot be commuted for a lump-sum payment.

(b) The benefits under the policy cannot be assigned, charged or alienated by you in any way.

Right to
discontinue.

7. The Company [incurs no binding obligation by reason of any of the terms of this letter and] reserves the right to discontinue payment of the premiums under the policy at any time, but such discontinuance will be without prejudice to any benefits previously purchased and such benefits will continue to be payable in accordance with the foregoing terms.

The words in square brackets may be desirable to ensure that the managing director is in no doubt as to what he is being offered, a moral assurance rather than a right.

Please complete the attached form of acknowledgment.

Yours faithfully,

Secretary.

To The Secretary,

—— Company Limited.

Acknowledg-
ment.

I acknowledge receipt of your letter of —— setting out the terms governing the policy of insurance which it is intended to effect on my life.

Signed

Date

PRECEDENT No. 48

Trust Deed and Rules for a " Top Hat " Scheme for Salaried Directors

If a " top hat " scheme is to be established for the benefit of a number of employees it will usually be found convenient formally to set up the scheme under a trust deed and rules similar to those set out in the following precedent. A single trust deed or a single set of rules without a trust deed can also be used for this purpose. The advantages of a formal scheme on this pattern over a series of letters to the individual employees concerned are considerable. Once the scheme has been approved in principle by the Revenue the approval of individual admissions to membership is comparatively simple. The rights of the parties under a scheme in this form are clearly set out and adequate provision is made for amending the scheme, winding up the company or terminating the company's liability to contribute. Trusts are clearly declared with consequent protection for widows and dependants who may be entitled to pensions in certain events under the scheme. Again most insurance companies have forms of their own for establishing schemes of this kind. Some of the forms commonly in use, however, may be found to leave unsolved some of the legal conundrums which can occur as soon as something out of the ordinary happens. It is thought that the following precedent may serve to draw attention to some of the points for which every well-drawn scheme should provide.

Parties.   THIS TRUST DEED is made the —— day of —— 19— BETWEEN The X Y Z Company Limited whose registered office is situate at —— (hereinafter called " the Company ") of the one part and A.B. of —— and C.D. of —— (hereinafter called " the present Trustees ") of the other part.

WHEREAS the Company wishes to establish a scheme for the purpose of securing pensions and other benefits for certain of the salaried directors and senior employees of the Company in accordance with the Rules hereinafter mentioned ;

NOW THIS DEED WITNESSETH as follows :—

Definitions.   1. IN this Deed unless the context otherwise requires :—

(a) " Members " means members of the Scheme admitted to membership in accordance with the Rules ;

(b) " Rules " means the Rules of the Scheme set out in the Schedule hereto and any additions thereto or variations thereof for the time being in force ;

(c) " Scheme " means the retirement benefits scheme constituted by the Trust Deed and the Rules ;

(d) " Trust Deed " means this Deed and any subsequent deeds made between the Company and the Trustees supplemental thereto ;

(e) " Trustees " means the present Trustees and every other the trustee or trustees for the time being hereof ;

and words importing the masculine shall include the feminine and words importing the singular shall include the plural.

Pensions scheme.   2. THE Company hereby establishes the Scheme and declares that the Scheme shall take effect and be administered in accordance with the provisions of the Trust Deed and the Rules.

Policies held on trust.   3. THE Trustees shall hold the policies referred to in the Rules and the benefits arising thereunder upon the trusts of the Scheme contained in the Trust Deed and the Rules.

Receipts and payments.   4. THE Trustees shall make all necessary arrangements for dealing with receipts and payments under the Scheme and may give vary and revoke instructions as to the custody and disposal of any policies and as to the giving of receipts and discharges for payments in connection with the Scheme.

Records and accounts.   5. THE Trustees shall keep a complete record of all matters essential for the working of the Scheme and shall keep proper accounts relating thereto.

Auditors, etc.   6. THE Trustees may with the consent of the Company appoint any persons to act respectively as auditor actuary or secretary of the Scheme and may with the like consent fix or vary the remuneration of such persons and terminate and vary such appointments.

Trustees acting as advised.   7. THE Trustees may act in relation to the Scheme on the advice or opinion of any lawyer actuary accountant or other professional person consulted by them and shall not be responsible for any loss occasioned by so acting.

Trustee indemnity.   8. No Trustee shall be liable to any person for any act error or omission as such Trustee except where the same is occasioned by his own gross negligence or wilful misconduct.

Expenses.   9. THE Company shall pay all expenses of and in connection with the administration of the Scheme including winding up.

Professional charging clause.   10. ANY of the Trustees being a solicitor or other person engaged in any profession or business shall be entitled to charge and be paid all usual professional or other charges for business done by him or his firm in relation to the trusts of the Trust Deed and the Rules and also his reasonable charges in addition to disbursements

for all other work and business done and all time spent
by him or his firm in connection with the administration
of the Scheme including matters which might or should
have been attended to in person by a Trustee not being
a solicitor or other professional person but which such
Trustee might reasonably require to be done by a solicitor
or other professional person.

Provision for the appointment of a corporate trustee can be quite
simply included in a scheme of this kind with an appropriate charging
clause: see *e.g.*, clause in Precedent No. 19 at p. 156.

New trustees.   11. THE power of appointing new Trustees shall be
vested in the Company.

It seems unnecessary in a scheme of this kind where the employer
is the only contributor to make elaborate provisions regarding the appointment of trustees representing the members.   It should not in any normal
case be difficult to find trustees who will have the confidence of all persons
concerned.

Variations of   12. THE Company and the Trustees may from time to
the scheme.
time before the termination of the Scheme by deed
supplemental to the Trust Deed make any amendments
or additions to the Trust Deed or the Rules PROVIDED
that no such amendment or addition shall :—

(a) vary the main object of the Scheme namely the
provision of pensions and annuities for life for
salaried directors and senior employees of the
Company on retirement at a specified age;

(b) extend the duration of the Scheme beyond the
limit permitted by law;

(c) vary the rights of any person or persons in respect
of benefits payable or prospectively payable under
the Scheme by reason of the past membership of
any retired member; or

(d) take effect unless Either such amendment or addition does not in the opinion of the Trustees substantially diminish the total value of the benefits
prospectively payable under the Scheme by reason of the present membership of any Member or
Members Or the amendment or addition is
approved in writing by every Member by reason

of whose membership any benefits are prospectively payable under the Scheme which will or may be diminished by such amendment or addition.

The limits imposed by this clause on the power to amend the scheme are intended to satisfy the Revenue that the scheme is one under which the main benefit afforded to members is the provision of a pension or annuity for life within the meaning of section 387 (2) of the Income Tax Act, 1952, and to safeguard the accrued rights of members and past members.

13. THE Scheme shall terminate upon the happening of the first of the following events to occur namely :—

> (i) the expiration of three months after the giving of notice in writing of such termination by the Company to the Trustees; or

Where the scheme as a whole represents an addition provided by the company to its employees' contractual remuneration it may be considered desirable to include some such provision as this enabling the company to terminate its obligation to contribute under the scheme.

> (ii) the expiration of a period of twenty years after the death of the last survivor of the lineal descendants living at the date hereof of His late Majesty King George V.

A perpetuity clause such as this is normally found in every deed setting up a superannuation fund or pension scheme. It seems possible that this may be an example of the maxim *communis error facit jus.* There are two aspects of the law as to perpetuities: first the vesting of interests created by a deed must not be indefinitely postponed, and secondly property must not be tied up so as to become inalienable. Under most superannuation funds and pension schemes interests are only created when a member joins the fund or scheme and at latest any interest which that member has vests on his death. Moreover provision is usually made for the termination of the fund or scheme by the company in certain circumstances. In principle, therefore, it does seem possible that some, if not most, superannuation funds and schemes are not within the scope of the rule against perpetuities at all.

Why then is a perpetuity clause such as this usually found? In 1924 the Telegraph Construction and Maintenance Company, Limited, applied to the court to determine whether a fund established by the company offended against the perpetuity rule. That case is reported in Vol. 56 of the *Journal of the Institute of Actuaries* and apparently nowhere else. From that report it appears that the fund in question was rather more akin to a benevolent fund than a pension fund and that all parties to the summons were agreed that the trusts of that particular fund did offend against the rule and the only question canvassed was whether or not the fund was charitable. Had the fund been held to be charitable the rule would not have applied to make the trusts invalid. That decision, however, namely that the particular fund in question was not charitable, appears to have been regarded ever since as authority for the view that the perpetuity rule applies to superannuation funds and pension schemes. Until an occasion arises for the point to be debated in the House of Lords it seems probable that this view, right or wrong, will prevail.

Meanwhile Parliament has provided what was intended to be a short and effective way round the difficulties created by the perpetuity rule. Following the publication of the " Report of the Departmental Committee on the effect of the Rule of Law against Perpetuities in its application to certain Superannuation Funds and Funds with analogous purposes " in 1927 (Cmd. 2918), the Superannuation and Other Trust Funds (Validation) Act, 1927, was passed. That Act provides that the perpetuity rule shall not apply and shall be deemed never to have applied to the trusts of any fund registered under the Act with the Registrar of Friendly Societies. Registration involves compliance with further regulations and the sending of annual returns and accounts. In the result perpetuity clauses continue to appear in deeds setting up funds and schemes and the provisions of the Act are largely kept in reserve to deal with those cases where the need for a perpetuity clause may have been overlooked and doubts arise as to the validity of the trusts of the fund or scheme.

14. ON the termination of the Scheme the following provisions shall have effect for the purpose of winding up :

Winding up.

(a) the Trustees shall assign any policy then held by them which shall have been effected under the Rules on the life of any Member then living and in the Company's service to such Member absolutely free of all the trusts of the Scheme but subject to the terms and conditions upon which the same was originally issued ; and

(b) the Trustees shall continue to pay and apply in accordance with the Rules all annuities and other benefits payable or applicable under the Scheme by reason of the past membership of any retired Member who has before such termination ceased to be in the Company's service PROVIDED that if

> any annuity or other benefit shall then be pro-
> spectively payable or applicable under the Scheme
> to or for the benefit of more than one person as
> the Trustees may in their discretion determine
> the Trustees shall forthwith hold such annuity or
> other benefit upon trust for all the persons pro-
> spectively interested therein who shall then be
> living in equal shares absolutely.

This clause provides that when the scheme is wound up all interests are to vest at once and all discretions exercisable by the trustees are to be exercised at once. This ensures compliance with the perpetuity rule.

Reconstruc-
tion of
company.
> 15. IF the Company shall be wound up for the pur-
> pose of reconstruction or amalgamation with any other
> company the Trustees may make such arrangements as
> they shall in their discretion think fit for the continuance
> of the Scheme in conjunction with such reconstructed or
> amalgamated company as if such last-mentioned com-
> pany were the Company and the Trust Deed and the
> Rules shall thereafter take effect in all respects as if such
> company had been a party to the Trust Deed instead of
> the Company.

A clause such as this enables a scheme to be transferred to a new company on a reconstruction of the old company without reference to the members.

> IN WITNESS whereof these presents have been entered
> into the day and year first above written.

THE SCHEDULE

RULES OF THE X Y Z COMPANY LIMITED SALARIED DIRECTORS PENSION SCHEME

1. *The Scheme*

The Scheme shall be called " THE X Y Z COMPANY LIMITED SALARIED DIRECTORS PENSION SCHEME " and shall come into force as from the —— day of —— 19—.

2. *Definitions*

In these Rules unless the context otherwise requires:

(a) the "Company" means The X Y Z Company Limited or any other company which may pursuant to Clause 15 of the Trust Deed take the place of the X Y Z Company Limited under the Trust Deed and the Rules;

(b) the "commencing date" means the —— day of —— 19—;

(c) "eligible director" means any salaried director of the Company;

(d) the "Insurer" means the —— Company Limited or any other insurance company with which the Trustees may in accordance with the Rules effect any policies to provide the benefits payable under the Scheme;

(e) "member" means an eligible director or senior employee of the Company admitted to membership of the Scheme in accordance with Rule 3;

(f) the "pension date" in relation to any member means the date on which such member attains the age of sixty-five years;

(g) "remuneration" in relation to a member means the yearly salary payable to such member by the Company but does not include any director's fees so payable;

(h) the "Rules" means these Rules and any additions thereto or variations thereof for the time being in force;

(i) "service" means whole time service as a salaried director of the Company or otherwise as a salaried employee of the Company;

(j) the "Scheme" means the retirement benefits scheme constituted by the Trust Deed and the Rules;

(k) "sum assured" means in respect of any member the sum payable under any policy effected on the life of such member in accordance with the Rules;

(l) the "Trust Deed" means the deed dated the —— day of —— 19— and made between the Company of the one part and —— and —— of the other part and any deeds supplemental thereto;

(m) the " Trustees " means the Trustees for the
time being appointed under the Trust Deed;
and words importing the masculine shall include the
feminine and words importing the singular shall include
the plural.

3. *Admission to Membership*

As from the commencing date or any anniversary
thereof the following persons may be admitted to
membership of the Scheme namely :—

(a) such eligible directors as the Company shall in its
absolute discretion determine; and

(b) such other senior employees of the Company or
class of such employees as the Company may
with the consent of the Insurer and the approval
of the Commissioners of Inland Revenue agree to
admit :

PROVIDED that the admission of such employees to membership of the Scheme may be
made subject to such special terms and conditions
as may be agreed when such employees are
admitted.

4. *Insurance to provide Benefits*

(a) When each member joins the Scheme the Trustees
shall effect with the Insurer a policy on the life of
such member and in the names of the Trustees
for a sum assured of such an amount payable
at the pension date or earlier death of such
member as the Company in its discretion but
subject to the provisions of paragraph (d) of this
Rule shall determine.

(b) Every such policy shall contain a provision whereby the sum assured may be exchanged at the
pension date in whole or in part for an annuity
payable during the remainder of the life of the
member and such other provisions as shall in the
opinion of the Trustees be necessary for providing
in respect of the member on whose life the same
is effected the benefits to be provided under the
Scheme.

(c) At the discretion of the Company the sum assured
in respect of any member may be increased on

any anniversary of the commencing date by such an amount as the Company in its discretion but subject to the provisions of paragraph (d) of this Rule shall determine but so that the same shall not be increased after the member has attained the age of fifty-five years.

(d) The sum assured under the policy effected on the life of a member when such member joins the Scheme shall be such that the yearly amount of the pension to be thereby provided at the pension date in accordance with the provision referred to in paragraph (b) of this Clause shall not exceed an amount equal to two-thirds of the member's remuneration at the date when the policy is effected and the like limit shall apply to the sum assured if increased pursuant to the provisions of paragraph (c) of this Clause with the substitution of the date when such increase is effected for the date when the policy is effected.

The purpose of this paragraph is to keep the pensions and benefits to be provided under the scheme within the limits normally approved by the Revenue under section 388, that is a maximum pension equal to two-thirds of the member's final salary.

(e) The Company shall so long as a member shall remain in the Company's service pay to the Insurer the premiums from time to time payable under the policy effected on the member's life.

This records the company's undertaking to pay the premiums to provide members' pensions. A possible variant of this provision would be a rule which allowed the company to discontinue the payment of premiums in any individual case at its discretion. Under the scheme as set out in the precedent the company can at any time terminate its liability in respect of the scheme as a whole by giving notice under clause 13 of the trust deed.

5. Pension Benefit

(a) If a member retires from the Company's service at the pension date the Trustees shall subject as hereinafter provided apply the sum assured in respect of such member in the provision of an annuity on the life of the member and shall hold such annuity upon trust to pay the same to the member during the remainder of his life.

(b) At the option of the member (such option to be exercised by the member within one month before the pension date by giving notice in writing to the Trustees) the Trustees shall apply such part only as the member shall request of the sum assured in respect of the member in the provision of an annuity on the life of the member in accordance with the provisions of paragraph (a) of this Rule and shall apply the balance of the sum assured in the provision of an annuity on the life of the member's wife and shall hold such annuity upon trust to pay the same from and after the member's death to the member's wife during the remainder of her life :

PROVIDED that the yearly amount of any annuity provided on the life of the member's wife shall not exceed the yearly amount of the annuity provided on the life of the member.

This provision enables the member to give up part of his own pension for a pension on the life of his wife commencing at his death. Such a pension, it is thought, would be purchased or provided by the member who would have given up part of his own pension to obtain it, and would consequently attract estate duty on the member's death under section 2 (1) (d) of the Finance Act, 1894. The pension would not, however, be regarded as aggregable with the member's free estate: *cf. Re Payton, Payton* v. *I. R. C.* [1951] Ch. 1081; *Re Weigall* [1956] Ch. 424; *Re Tapp* [1959] Ch. 443. In view of the decisions in *D'Avigdor-Goldsmid* v. *I. R. C.* [1953] A.C. 347, and *Westminster Bank, Ltd.* v. *I. R. C., Wrightson* v. *I. R. C.* [1958] A.C. 210, it may be that if the wife is named when the option is exercised, her interest will arise at that point or, at the latest, one month before the pension date so that on her husband's death no benefit will arise and consequently section 2 (1) (d) will not apply.

6. *Retirement after the Pension Date*

If a member remains in the Company's service after the pension date the Trustees shall arrange with the Insurer that the sum assured in respect of such member shall be payable on his retiring from or dying in the service and shall be increased (but without payment of any further premium) by such amount as may be agreed between the Trustees and the Insurer and Rule 5 shall apply on the member's retirement from the service in like manner as if he had retired from the service on the pension date with the exception only that references therein to the sum assured shall be read and construed as if they were references to the sum assured as increased under this Rule.

7. *Early Retirement*

If a member retires from the service either within ten years before the pension date or on account of ill-health (unless on such retirement the member by written notice to the Trustees elects to be treated for the purposes of the Rules as if he had ceased to be in the service in circumstances to which paragraph (a) of Rule 10 would apply) the Trustees shall surrender the policy effected on the life of such member and shall apply the surrender value thereof in like manner as if the surrender value were the sum assured and the member had retired at the pension date and Rule 5 shall apply with the exception only that references therein to the sum assured shall be read and construed as if they were references to the surrender value realised in accordance with the provisions of this Rule :

PROVIDED that if the yearly amount of the annuity which could be provided on the member's life is in the opinion of the Trustees trivial or the member is in serious ill-health the Trustees may at the written request of the member pay to the member all or any part of the surrender value and the foregoing provisions of this Rule shall apply only to the balance (if any) of the surrender value.

8. *Commutation*

(a) Any annuity provided in pursuance of the provisions of any of the last three preceding Rules shall be non-commutable except that if a member so requests (which request shall be made to the Trustees in writing within one month before the member's retirement from the service) the member may commute a proportion not exceeding the maximum permitted proportion specified in paragraph (b) of this Rule of the yearly pension benefits which would otherwise be provided for or on

account of such member under the Scheme and in
that event the provisions of paragraph (c) of this
Rule shall take effect.

(b) The maximum permitted proportion of the yearly
pension benefits to be provided for or on account
of a member under the Scheme which a member
may commute in accordance with the provisions
of paragraph (a) of this Rule shall be such that
not less than three-quarters in value of the benefits provided for or on account of the member
under the Scheme shall be payable or applicable
in the form of one or more non-commutable pensions or annuities.

(c) If a member shall commute a proportion of the
yearly pension benefits which would otherwise be
provided for or on account of such member under
the Scheme in accordance with the provisions of
paragraph (a) of this Rule the Trustees shall
apply such part of the sum assured in respect of
the member (or of the surrender value of the
policy effected on the life of the member as the
case may be) as may be necessary to provide
the yearly pension benefits not so commuted in
the provision of such benefits in accordance with
the Rules and shall hold the balance of the sum
assured (or the surrender value) upon trust for
the member absolutely.

The effect of this rule is that a member may take up to one-quarter
of the sum assured as a lump sum cash payment. If, however, he is
entitled to benefits under any other scheme established by the company,
his rights under that scheme must be taken into account in determining
what proportion of his pension rights may be commuted under this
scheme. Where a member has exercised the option to provide a widow's
pension, it is intended that the pension to be commuted shall be the
member's own pension.

9. *Death in Service*

If a member dies while in the Company's service the
Trustees shall hold the sum assured in respect of such
member upon trust to pay or apply the same as the
Trustees shall in their absolute discretion think fit to or
for the maintenance or support or otherwise for the benefit of all or any to the exclusion of the other or others of

the widow children and more remote issue of the member and the persons who if the member had died intestate would have been entitled in distribution to his estate.

There are two possible grounds for arguing that no estate duty will be payable on the death benefit provided under this rule: (a) because the sum assured is not purchased or provided by the deceased member so as to come within the provisions of section 2 (1) (d) of the Finance Act, 1894; see *Re J. Bibby & Sons, Ltd., Pensions Trust Deed* [1952] 2 All E.R. 483; 31 A.T.C. 355, and the Notes to the last Precedent [47]; and (b) because no one member of the group of beneficiaries prospectively entitled to benefit under this rule has an enforceable right to any fraction of the total sum payable, see and *cf. Re Miller's Agreement, Uniacke* v. *Att.-Gen.* [1947] Ch. 615, and *Bibby's* case, *supra.*

It occurs to the authors that the point might be taken that the group of beneficiaries together, being all the persons entitled under the discretionary trust, could combine to enforce payment by the trustees so that the interest arising on the member's death might be said to be an enforceable interest and therefore not within the scope of *Miller's* case, *supra.* It is understood, however, that it is not the present practice of the Revenue to take this point where the sum payable under a fund or scheme such as this is payable at the trustees' discretion to one or more members of a group. (The right of the members of a discretionary group under a trust to enforce payment is illustrated in *Re Smith* [1928] Ch. 915.)

10. *Leaving the Service before Pension Date*

(a) If a member ceases to be in the Company's service before the pension date otherwise than by reason of his death voluntary resignation or dismissal for fraud or misconduct or by reason of his retirement in circumstances to which Rule 7 applies (unless on such retirement he elects to be treated for the purposes of the Rules as if he had ceased to be in the service in circumstances to which this paragraph applies) he shall be entitled to the benefits specified in paragraph (c) of this Rule.

(b) If a member ceases to be in the Company's service before the pension date by reason of his voluntary resignation or dismissal for fraud or misconduct he shall be entitled to the benefits specified in paragraph (c) of this Rule to such

[47] *Ante,* p. 395.

extent only and upon such special terms and conditions as the Trustees with the approval of the Company shall determine.

(c) The benefits referred to in the preceding paragraphs of this Rule are the following benefits, namely :

(i) the right to have the policy effected on the life of the member converted to a paid-up policy and assigned to the member such paid-up policy to provide a sum payable at the pension date or earlier death bearing the same proportion to the sum assured in respect of the member before such conversion as the number of premiums paid bears to the total number of premiums paid and prospectively payable under the policy and to be subject to the like conditions (so far as appropriate) as to the application of the sum payable under the policy in the provision of annuities as are contained in Rule 5 and to the like conditions as to the commutation of such annuities or a part thereof as are contained in Rule 8 ; and

(ii) the right to pay premiums to the Insurer to secure an additional policy of insurance on the life of the member for a sum assured payable at the pension date or earlier death equal to the sum assured in respect of the member under the Scheme less the amount to be provided under the paid-up policy referred to in the preceding sub-paragraph such additional policy to be issued without production of evidence of health and at the same premium as was payable under the original policy on the member's life effected under the Scheme and to be subject to any special terms and conditions which applied to such original policy.

If a member of his own volition retires from the company's service before qualifying for a pension, he is not as of right to be entitled to the benefit of any contributions by the company on his account. Where, however, he is forced to retire by reason, for example, of ill-health or redundancy, he is to be permitted to receive the pension already purchased for him at pension age and (on the assumption that the insurance company concerned agrees to such a provision) he may himself continue to pay premiums on a policy at the same advantageous rates as he would in effect have received under the scheme.

11. *Evidence of Health*

Each member may be required to produce evidence of health satisfactory to the Insurer on his admission to membership of the Scheme and on any increase of the sum assured in respect of such member.

12. *Company's failure to pay Premiums*

If the Company shall for any reason fail to pay any premium under any policy effected on the life of a member the Trustees shall be at liberty to enter into such arrangements with the Insurer regarding such policy (not being such as to affect the approval of the Scheme under section 388 of the Income Tax Act, 1952, or any statutory modification thereof for the time being in force) as they shall in the circumstances think appropriate and so that without prejudice to the generality of this Rule such arrangements may include all or any of the following provisions, namely :

(a) a provision that the policy shall be treated in whole or in part as a paid-up policy ;

(b) a provision that all or any of the premiums payable under the policy may be deducted from the sum assured under the policy or from the surrender value thereof ; and

(c) a provision that all or any of the premiums payable under the policy shall be paid by the member together with such provision regarding the benefits to arise under the policy as the Trustees may consider appropriate.

A rule in this form will be of particular importance where the company under the scheme has power to cease paying premiums in individual cases.

13. *Policies to be held for the Company*

Subject as hereinbefore provided any policy effected under the Scheme and any annuities provided in accordance with the Rules shall be held upon trust for the Company.

PRECEDENT No. 49

Provision of a Pension for a Retired Employee with Benefits for his Dependants

The situation contemplated is that an employee has retired, for whom no provision has been made by way of pension scheme. However, the company employing him is willing to provide a pension and benefits for his wife and dependants, and moreover, although it does so voluntarily, is willing to bind itself to continue to provide the pension and other benefits. Unless it so binds itself, the liquidator of the company might well consider himself obliged to discontinue payment of the pension and other benefits: see *Parke* v. *Daily News Limited* [1962] Ch. 927.

It is considered that all payments under this deed will rank as earned income: Income Tax Act, 1952, s. 525 (1).

It is considered that, although the payments under the deed are themselves income, the total benefit provided by the deed cannot be brought into charge to tax under the " golden handshake " provisions, namely, section 37 of the Finance Act, 1960, because the benefits under the deed are " otherwise chargeable to income tax " within the meaning of section 37 (2) and moreover are probably not a " payment " within the meaning of section 37 (3).

The provision of the pension and the provision of the benefits for the wife and dependants are separate covenants and there will be no passing for estate duty purposes on the death of the employee.

All payments under the covenant are " annual payments," so that they must be paid net, under sections 169 and 170 of the Income Tax Act, 1952. However, having regard to the obvious convenience of treating the payments under Schedule E, P.A.Y.E., it is just possible that the local inspector of taxes may well agree that the pension should be treated during the lifetime of the employee as if it were a voluntary pension chargeable to tax under section 376 of the Income Tax Act, 1952, and Schedule E.

The amount of the provision made by this deed should not be greater than is proper having regard to the services rendered by the employee to the company. Moreover the company may well run into difficulty if the Revenue are able to show that the company is paying the pension and benefits as a way of distributing its profits and not for the purpose of earning future profits by demonstrating that its former employees are generously treated, and thus encouraging its existing and future employees: see *Dracup* v. *Dakin* (1957) 37 T.C. 377.

THIS DEED is made the —— day of —— between ——Limited whose registered office is at —— (hereinafter called " the Company ") of the first part —— of —— hereinafter called " the Employee ") of the second part and —— of —— and —— of —— (hereinafter together called " the Trustees " which expression shall where the context admits include the survivor of them and other the trustees or trustee of the covenant hereinafter made in favour of the Trustees) of the other part;

WHEREAS :

(A) The Employee served the Company faithfully and well from the —— day of —— 19— and retired from the service of the Company on the —— day of —— last;

(B) The Company desires to provide a pension for the Employee and the benefits hereinafter contained for his wife and dependants;

(C) This Deed has been approved by a resolution of the directors of the Company passed on the date hereof;

This deed should not be executed, and the company should not approve its terms until after the employee has ceased to be in the employment of the company. Otherwise it could be argued that the benefits hereunder constitute a future retirement benefit within the meaning of section 386 (2) of the Income Tax Act, 1952.

NOW THIS DEED WITNESSETH as follows:

1. The Company hereby covenants with the Employee that the Company will pay to the Employee during the remainder of his lifetime a monthly sum of £—— the first payment to be made on the first day of the month succeeding the month during which this Deed is executed and each subsequent payment to be made on the first day of each succeeding month and all payments to be made free of all deductions except income tax.

2. The Company hereby covenants with the Trustees that the Company will pay to the Trustees during the

period commencing upon the day upon which the Employee dies and terminating upon the day upon which expires the period of —— years thereafter from the date hereof or the day upon which —— who is the wife of the Employee (hereinafter called " the Wife ") dies (whichever period shall expire the later) a monthly sum of £—— the first payment to be made on the first day of the month following the month during which the Employee dies and subsequent payments to be made on the first day of each succeeding month and all payments to be made free of all deductions except income tax.

3. No apportionment shall take place of any of the sums hereinbefore covenanted to be paid.

4. The Trustees shall hold the sums hereinbefore covenanted to be paid to them to pay or apply the same within a reasonable time after the receipt thereof to or for or towards the maintenance support or benefit of all or any one or more to the exclusion of the other or others of the class consisting of the following persons namely :

The Wife,

[Name the other dependants]

and in such shares and such manner in all respects as the Trustees in their absolute discretion may from time to time think fit : so that the Trustees may have power to pay any sum to any parent or guardian of any member of the class hereinbefore mentioned for the time being an unmarried infant to be applied for the maintenance support or benefit of that infant without the Trustees themselves being responsible for the due application thereof and so that the receipt of such parent or guardian shall be a complete discharge to the Trustees.

5. The power of appointing new trustees of the covenants in favour of the Trustees hereinbefore contained shall be exercised by the Employee during his life.

6. [If required add a restrictive covenant.]

Where a sum not otherwise chargeable to tax is paid in consideration of the giving of a restrictive covenant, even a restrictive covenant that is not legally valid, the lump sum may be brought into charge to surtax under section 242 of the Income Tax Act, 1952. However, where the sums are otherwise charged to tax, section 242 has no application.

IN WITNESS, ETC.

Trust Deed and Rules for an Approved Superannuation Fund

This precedent illustrates the type of pension scheme for which approval can be obtained under section 379 of the Income Tax Act, 1952. The scheme is based on a fund of investments the income from which will be exempt from tax in the trustees' hands. Such schemes are, notionally at least, framed so as to be actuarially solvent on the footing that the members and the employer will contribute equally, or in fixed proportions, a regular sum calculated by reference to the remuneration receivable by the individual members. Usually the employer undertakes to make good whatever further sums are required to justify the initial actuarial optimism with which the scheme was started. The smaller the scheme, of course, the more likely the need to call on the employer for an increased contribution. Even actuaries must be hard pressed to achieve accuracy where the numbers of prospective members of a scheme are such that their average may well prove erratic. One solution to this problem is to base the scheme on a group insurance policy; the erratic average of the members is then merged in the "ideal" average of the insurance company. Whether this expedient will in the long run turn out more cheaply for the employer is a matter on which the advice of a competent independent actuary should be sought.

It is considered that, in a normal case, a trading company has power to establish a superannuation scheme for its employees, even though no power to do so is expressly conferred upon it by its memorandum of association: *Armour* v. *Liverpool Corporation* [1939] Ch. 422, 435; see also *Hutton* v. *West Cork Ry.* (1883) 23 Ch.D. 654; *Henderson* v. *Bank of Australasia* (1888) 40 Ch.D. 170.

It is assumed that application will be made for the members of the pension scheme to contract out of the graduated contribution system under the National Insurance Act, 1959.

THIS TRUST DEED is made the —— day of —— 19— BETWEEN X Y Z Limited whose registered office is situate at —— (hereinafter called "the Company") of the one part and A.B. of —— C.D. of —— and E.F. of —— (hereinafter called "the Present Trustees") of the other part

WHEREAS :

(A) The Company has determined to establish a pension fund for securing pensions on retirement and other benefits for certain of the employees of the Company

(B) The Company has requested the Present Trustees to act as trustees of the pension fund and the Present Trustees have consented so to act

NOW THIS DEED WITNESSETH and it is hereby agreed and declared as follows:—

Definitions.

1. IN this Deed the following expressions shall unless the context otherwise requires have the following meanings:—

"Actuary" means the Actuary or Actuaries appointed in accordance with Clause 11 hereof

"Auditor" means the Auditor or Auditors appointed in accordance with Clause 11 hereof

"Company" means X Y Z Ltd. or any corporation or company which shall for the time being be carrying on the business of X Y Z Ltd. and in succession thereto and shall have undertaken to perform the obligation of X Y Z Ltd. under the Trust Deed and the Rules.

"Fund" means the Pension Fund hereby established and all contributions paid to the Trustees under the Pension Scheme and all moneys investments and property for the time being representing the same or otherwise held by the Trustees upon the trusts hereby declared and the income thereof

"Members" means such persons as are for the time being members of the Pension Scheme in accordance with the Rules

"Pension Scheme" means the Pension Scheme established by the Trust Deed and the Rules

"Rules" means the Rules set out in the Schedule hereto and any alteration or modification thereof for the time being in force

"Trust Deed" means this Deed and any deed or deeds supplemental thereto

"Trustees" means the Present Trustees and all other the trustees or trustee for the time being hereof

And words importing the masculine gender shall include the feminine gender and words importing the singular shall include the plural.

Covenant by the Company.

2. THE Company hereby covenants with the Trustees to observe and perform such of the provisions of the Trust Deed and the Rules as are to be observed and performed by the Company.

This covenant is not as good as it looks. Under the Rules the company can determine its obligation to contribute to the fund and the pension scheme will come to an end. There is no reason in law why such an escape clause should be included for the company's benefit. The practical justification for such a clause is obvious.

Declaration of trust.

3. THE Trustees shall stand possessed of the Fund upon trust to apply the same in or towards providing the pensions and other benefits payable under the Rules.

Power to retain or vary investments.

4. THE Trustees may either retain as invested any investments or property for the time being forming part of the Fund or may sell the same if they shall think fit and shall invest in manner hereinafter provided the proceeds of any such sale and any money forming part of the Fund and not immediately required for the payment of pensions or other benefits with power to vary or transpose such investments for or into others of a like nature or to sell or realise the same as may be necessary for the payment of pensions or other benefits.

An agreeable moot point is the question whether section 164 of the Law of Property Act, 1925, applies to superannuation funds and pension schemes. That section limits the period during which the income of settled property may be accumulated. No period is mentioned in the section which can aptly be applied to a superannuation fund unless it be " the life of the grantor or settlor." But who is the settlor? The member or the company? And if the company, has the company a " life " for the purposes of section 164? Assuming the point to be well taken that section 164 applies but provides no possible period which can be adopted in the case of a superannuation fund, it must presumably follow that the trustees are acting in breach of trust if they accumulate the income of the fund, and therefore hold the accumulated income upon trust for the company and the members in appropriate proportions. Those trustees who find the suggestion convincing, that section 164 of the Law of Property Act, 1925, applies to render invalid the accumulation of income arising from property constituting a superannuation fund, may take comfort from the thought that they sin in good company; it is a well-established practice that the income from funds may be accumulated. No individual member would be likely to be able to show that he had suffered by reason of the trustees' breach of trust (if such it be). The point must await the attention of the liquidator of an insolvent company with a taste for litigating in the House of Lords and with nothing to lose but the creditors' money.

It was decided in *Re A. E. G. Unit Trust (Managers) Ltd. Deed* [1957] Ch. 415 that section 164 of the Law of Property Act, 1925, did not apply to accumulations of income made under a trust deed the object of which was to constitute a unit trust. Wynn-Parry J. thought that the transaction by which a person became a certificate holder in the unit trust involved a disposition of property by that person within the meaning of section 164. But he held that the section did not apply to every disposition of property, and that the disposition in that case was not within the ambit of the section. He tested the matter by reference to the permitted periods of accumulation set out in section 164, all of which he found to be inappropriate to describe a person who became a certificate holder in a unit trust. The judge reached a similar conclusion by considering whether the trust deed fell within the mischief which section 164 was designed to prevent. It may very well be that the accumulation of income under a superannuation fund or pension scheme is unobjectionable for the same reasons.

Authorised investments.

5. ANY moneys requiring to be invested hereunder shall be invested in or upon the security of such stocks shares debentures debenture stocks or other investments (including any policies of insurance annuity policies or annuity contracts) whatsoever and wheresoever situate and whether involving liability or not and whether or not authorised by law for the investment of trust funds or upon such personal credit with or without security as the Trustees shall in their absolute discretion think fit to the intent that the Trustees shall have the same full and unrestricted powers of investing and varying investments as if they were absolutely entitled to the Fund beneficially.

The power of investment can be cut down as required in any particular case. The power included here is in the widest possible form and would enable the trustees to purchase or subscribe for shares in the company itself. This may be a matter of importance when the directors of a small private company are anxious to establish a pension fund but have no available liquid resources, all surplus profits being required to finance the company's expansion. Under section 54 (1) (b) of the Companies Act, 1948, the company is authorised to provide funds for the purchase of its own shares where the shares are to be held by the trustees of a pension scheme for the benefit of the company's employees.

Power to borrow.

6. THE Trustees may whenever they think it desirable so to do raise or borrow any sum or sums of money and may secure the repayment of the same in such manner and upon such terms and conditions in all respects as the Trustees may think fit and in particular by charging or mortgaging all or any part of the Fund.

Power to retain cash balances.

7. THE Trustees may retain cash balances of such amount as they may think fit and shall not be chargeable in respect of any interest thereon or otherwise in respect thereof.

Power to appoint nominee.

8. THE Trustees shall have power to appoint any corporate body to act as their nominee for the purposes of this clause with power for the Trustees at any time or times in like manner to revoke or vary such appointment and any of the investments of the Fund may be made in the name of or transferred to the corporate body so appointed on the terms that the latter shall hold them for and on behalf of the Trustees and the Trustees may for this purpose enter into any agreement with such corporate body and may bind the Fund in respect of any indemnity to give effect thereto.

Appointment of trustees.

9. (i) Until the Company shall otherwise determine the number of Trustees shall not be fewer than three.

(ii) A corporation or company limited or unlimited may be appointed to be a Trustee hereof. A corporate Trustee may act through any of its directors or through an officer appointed for the purpose.

(iii) The power of appointing new Trustees shall be vested in the Company which may also remove from office any Trustee and may appoint a new Trustee either as an additional Trustee or in place of any Trustee who shall die or be removed or retire from office or become disqualified under the provisions hereinbefore contained or become incapable of acting. A new Trustee shall be appointed by Deed executed by the Company and the said new Trustee.

Many pension schemes provide for the appointment of trustees representing the employer and the members respectively. Provision can be made for the election by the members of trustees representing the members. Such provisions no doubt give confidence to the members and a sense of participating in the scheme. As a matter of law, however, they add nothing. The responsibility of the trustees will be the same however they may be elected or appointed.

Administration and management of pension scheme.

10. (i) The administration and management of the Pension Scheme shall be vested in the Trustees.

(ii) The Trustees shall meet at such times, not being less than once a year, and at such place as they shall decide, and shall make regulations for the conduct of their business, the summoning of meetings, the appointment of a chairman, the recording of resolutions, and all other matters in connection with their work. Two of the Trustees present at a meeting shall form a quorum. At all meetings of the Trustees all questions shall be decided by the votes of the Trustees present taken by a show of hands. In the case of an equality of votes the chairman of the meeting shall have a second or casting vote.

(iii) The Trustees shall exercise their powers and execute their duties under the Pension Scheme by resolutions passed at meetings of the Trustees provided that a resolution in writing shall if signed by all the Trustees be as effectual as if it had been passed at a meeting of the Trustees and may consist of one or more documents in similar form signed by one or more of the Trustees.

(iv) The Trustees may from time to time delegate any business to any two of their number.

(v) Any two of the Trustees may jointly give receipts and discharges for any moneys or other property payable transferable or deliverable to the Trustees or any of them and every such receipt or discharge shall be as valid and effectual as if it were a receipt or discharge signed by all the Trustees.

More, or less, elaborate provisions governing the administration of the pension scheme may be included. Any company's articles of association will usually provide the draftsman who leans towards elaboration with a happy hunting ground. The draftsman whose regulations are over-detailed should perhaps consider whether trustees are likely to be found who will observe them.

Appointment of auditor and actuary.   11. THE Trustees shall from time to time appoint an Auditor or Auditors and an Actuary or Actuaries upon such terms as to their tenures of office, duties and remuneration as the Trustees may think fit subject in the matter of remuneration to the consent of the Company.

The necessary professional qualifications of the auditor and the actuary can, if required, be mentioned in this clause. It is also a matter of choice whether the company's auditors or some other auditors act as auditors of the pension scheme.

Records and
accounts.

12. THE Trustees shall keep records of all matters relating to the Pension Scheme and shall keep accounts to show the position of and dealings with the Fund and the amounts contributed thereto. The said accounts shall be made up to the —— day of —— in each year and the Trustees shall cause the same to be audited annually by the Auditor who shall make and sign a report thereon which shall be open to inspection by any Member and by the Company.

Expenses of
administra-
tion.

13. THE Company shall pay all costs charges and expenses in connection with the establishment, administration and management of the Pension Scheme (other than expenses of investment).

Trustees may
act on
professional
advice.

14. THE Trustees may in relation to the Pension Scheme act on the advice or opinion of any lawyer, broker, actuary, accountant or other professional person and shall not be responsible for any loss occasioned by so acting.

Trustees'
interests.

15. No decision of or exercise of a power by the Trustees shall be invalidated or questioned on the ground that the Trustees or any of them had a direct or other personal interest in such decision or in the exercise of such power.

Trustees'
liability.

16. THE Trustees shall be entitled to all the indemnities conferred on trustees by law and no Trustee shall be liable for any acts or omissions not due to his own wilful neglect or default.

Actuarial
investigation.

17. THE Trustees shall cause the position of the Fund to be investigated by the Actuary at least once in every five years and the Trustees and the Company shall for that purpose furnish all necessary accounts and information to the Actuary. On each such occasion the Actuary shall make an actuarial valuation of the assets and liabilities of the Fund and shall report to the Trustees in writing on the financial position of the Fund. In the event of such report showing a deficiency in the Fund the Trustees shall determine what action (if any) shall be taken to restore the solvency of the Fund. In the event of such report showing a surplus in the Fund such surplus may at the option of the Trustees and with the advice of the Actuary be transferred to a reserve account or may be applied in increasing the benefits or prospective benefits of Members under the Pension Scheme.

It is provided in the rules that the company will contribute such sums as are required to preserve the solvency of the fund. The periodic actuarial investigation will ensure that the need for any additional contributions is known. Express provision could be made for the reduction of benefits in the event of an actuarial deficiency being found.

Duration of scheme.   18. THE Pension Scheme shall be wound up and the trusts thereof shall be determined in the events provided in the Rules and the Fund shall be applied in the manner provided by the Rules Provided that if not previously wound up the Pension Scheme shall be wound up and the trusts thereof shall be determined and the Pension Fund shall be distributed at such time and in such manner as shall ensure that such winding up determination and distribution shall occur before the determination of a period measured by the lifetime of the last survivor of the issue living at the date hereof of His late Majesty King George the Fifth and twenty years after the death of such survivor.

This clause is required to ensure that the fund will be wound up and all interests will vest within the period permitted by the rule against perpetuities. For the reasons discussed elsewhere (see p. 402) it may be open to doubt whether a pension scheme such as that here in question can offend against the rule. The alternative to including such a clause is to register the pension scheme under the Superannuation and Other Trust Funds (Validation) Act, 1927. This is done by applying in writing to the registrar with a letter signed by the trustees of the fund. The letter must give the address at which communications concerning the fund will be received by the secretary and be accompanied by two copies of the rules of the fund and a list of the names and addresses of the trustees of the fund.

Alteration of trust deed and rules.   19. THE Trustees may at any time and from time to time with the consent of the Company by Deed executed by the Trustees and the Company alter or modify any of the trusts powers or provisions of the Trust Deed or of the Rules provided that no such alteration or modification shall :—

(i) operate to effect a change of the main purpose of the Pension Scheme namely the provision of

> pensions for employees of the Company on retirement at a specified age;
>
> (ii) authorise the transfer or payment of any part of the Fund in any circumstances to the Company;
>
> (iii) take effect unless the Actuary shall certify that no pension payable to any Member or other person under the Pension Scheme at the date when such alteration or modification is made will be substantially prejudiced thereby;
>
> (iv) take effect unless the Actuary shall certify that the interests of any Member under the Pension Scheme in respect of contributions already received by the Trustees will not be substantially prejudiced thereby or the consent is obtained in writing of a two-thirds majority of those Members for the time being whose interests are certified by the Actuary to be affected by such alteration or modification.

To comply with the requirements of section 379 of the Income Tax Act, 1952, it must not be possible for alterations to be made to a scheme which would make it revocable or which would enable the fund built up without liability to tax to be distributed in a tax-free form to the members.

Winding up of company.   20. IF the Company shall be wound up for the purpose of reconstruction or amalgamation with any other company the Trustees may make such arrangements or enter into such agreements as they shall think fit for the continuance of the Pension Scheme in conjunction with such reconstructed or amalgamated company in like manner as if such company had originally been a party to this Deed.

IN WITNESS whereof the Company has caused its common seal to be hereunto affixed and the Trustees have hereunto set their hands and seals the day and year first above written.

THE SCHEDULE

Rules

Definitions

1. In these Rules the following expressions shall unless the context otherwise requires have the following meanings :—

" Dependant " has the same meaning in respect of a
member as in section 379 (3) of the Income Tax
Act, 1952.

" Eligible employee " means any male person in the
service of the Company being not less than
twenty-one years of age and holding a salaried
position on the staff of the Company and may
include a Director of the Company holding a full-
time salaried position.

" Equivalent pension benefits " means the benefit
by way of pension to be derived from graduated
contributions made in accordance with the provisions of the National Insurance Act, 1959, or any
statutory modification or re-enactment thereof
for the time being in force.

" Final salary " means in relation to any member the
average annual amount of such member's salary
during the last three years of his pensionable
service.

" Member " means an eligible employee who has
completed and submitted and in respect of whom
the Trustees have accepted an application for
membership of the Pension Scheme in such form
as the Trustees shall determine.

" Normal retirement age " means the age of sixty-
five years.

" Pensionable service " means service with the Company during which a member contributes to the
Fund in accordance with Rule 3 and such other
service as the Company may either generally or
in any individual case declare to be pensionable
service.

" Salary " means the fixed yearly salary receivable by
a member and does not include Directors' fees,
commissions or bonuses.

" Actuary "   " Company "   " Fund "   " Pension
Scheme " " Rules " " Trustees " and " Trust
Deed " have the meanings respectively assigned
thereto by Clause 1 of the Trust Deed.

The term " dependant " is used in section 379 (3) of the Income Tax
Act, 1952, and therefore must be presumed to have a definite meaning.

Those who demur at the presumption that Parliament is always certain may prefer a definition such as that contained in section 4 of the Workmen's Compensation Act, 1925. Another definition commonly found is:—

> " Dependant " means in relation to any person any other person who in the opinion of the Trustees is or was at the time of the death of such first-mentioned person dependent on such first-mentioned person for the provisions of all or any of the ordinary necessaries of life.

Membership

2. The Company shall require all persons entering its service on or after the —— day of —— 19— to apply for membership of the Pension Scheme and shall request all eligible employees in its service at that date to apply for such membership Provided that the Company may by giving written notice to the Trustees exclude any eligible employee from membership of the Pension Scheme and no application for membership submitted by such eligible employee shall be accepted by the Trustees. A person shall cease to be a member on ceasing to be in the service of the Company notwithstanding that he is hereinafter referred to as a member in relation to any benefit to which he may be entitled after leaving such service.

This rule contemplates that membership of the pension scheme will be a term of employment for all future employees. Whether a scheme is to be compulsory and what grades of employees are to be eligible for membership are matters to be settled according to the circumstances in each individual case.

Contributions

3. A member shall as from the date when he is admitted to membership of the Pension Scheme and until he shall cease to be in the service of the Company contribute to the Fund at the rate of five per cent. per annum of his salary for the time being.

4. The Company shall make all necessary arrangements for collecting the contributions of members (whether by way of deduction from their salaries or otherwise) and shall pay the same to the Trustees at such

time or times as may be agreed between the Company and the Trustees.

5. The Company shall contribute to the Fund in every year ending on the —— day of ——

(a) a sum equal to the aggregate amount of the member's contributions payable in that year and

(b) such further sum as shall be certified by the Actuary to be sufficient together with the existing assets of the Fund to provide the benefits payable under the Pension Scheme and to preserve the solvency of the Fund.

6. The Company's contributions shall be payable at such times and by such instalments as shall from time to time be agreed between the Company and the Trustees.

Benefits

7. All benefits under the Pension Scheme shall be payable in sterling at the registered office of the Company.

8. A member shall be entitled to whichever of the following benefits shall be appropriate according to the event which happens :—

(i) Pension on Retirement on the Normal Retirement Date.

A member who retires from the service of the Company on or after attaining normal retirement age having completed not less than ten years of pensionable service shall be entitled to a yearly pension commencing on the day following such retirement and payable during the remainder of his life by equal monthly instalments in advance the last instalment thereof not being apportionable. The amount of such yearly pension shall be one-sixtieth of the member's final salary in respect of each completed year of the member's pensionable service subject to a maximum of £3,000 or two-thirds of the member's final salary whichever shall be the less.

(ii) Pension on Retirement before the Normal Retirement Date.

A member who retires from the service of the Company within ten years before attaining normal retirement age having completed not less than ten years of pensionable service shall if such retirement is with the consent of the Company or on account of permanent ill-health (as to which the decision of the Company shall be final) be entitled to a yearly pension commencing on the day following such retirement and payable during the remainder of his life by equal monthly instalments in advance the last instalment thereof not being apportionable. The amount of such pension shall be such amount as shall be certified by the Actuary to be fair and reasonable having regard to the member's final salary and pensionable service.

(iii) Pension on Retirement after the Normal Retirement Date.

A member who retires from the service of the Company after attaining normal retirement age having completed not less than ten years of pensionable service shall be entitled to a yearly pension payable in the same manner and for the like period as if such pension were a normal retirement pension payable under paragraph (i) of this Rule. The amount of such late retirement pension shall be calculated in like manner and shall be subject to the like limits as such normal retirement pension subject to such increase as shall be certified by the Actuary to be fair and reasonable in the circumstances.

Provided always that any pension payable to a member under this Rule shall in any event be greater than the equivalent pension benefits of such member.

(iv) Benefit on Withdrawal.

A member who on ceasing otherwise than by reason of his death to be in the service of the Company is not entitled to a pension under the Pension Scheme shall be paid a sum equal to the amount of his own contributions to the Fund together with interest thereon at the rate of three per cent. per annum for every completed year from the date of payment to the date of his ceasing to be in such service.

If this clause is accepted by the Registrar of Non-Participating Employments and it takes effect in any particular case, it would appear that the Company would become liable to make a payment to the National Insurance Fund.[48]

(v) Benefit on Death.

On the death of a member while in the service of the Company there shall be paid to any dependant of the member nominated by him before his death or failing such nomination or if the dependant so nominated shall not then be living to such one or more of the member's dependants then living and in such proportions as the Trustees shall in their discretion determine a sum equal to the amount which would have been paid to the member under paragraph (iv) of this Rule if the member were alive and had ceased to be in the service of the Company on the date of his death not being then entitled to a pension together with a sum equal to the amount contributed to the Fund by the Company in respect of the member under Rule 5 (a)

Provided that if a member shall die leaving a widow him surviving but without having nominated a dependant for the purposes of this Rule he shall be deemed to have nominated his widow.

The benefits provided under this scheme are a normal retirement pension and early and late retirement pensions. On leaving the scheme a member is to receive back his own contributions in any event. Many schemes provide that pensions are to be payable for five years certain in any event or make some other provision which ensures that a member or his dependants will get some return even if the member's death occurs very shortly after his retirement.

The death benefit payable on a member's death in service is commonly made payable to a member's personal representatives. The advantage of making it payable to the member's dependants at the discretion of the trustees (always assuming that the trustees can in the circumstances appropriately exercise such a discretion) is that estate duty may be avoided on the benefit or, at least, the value of the benefit will not be aggregable with the member's free estate (see pp. 396, 411 above). Where the sums involved are likely to be quite small, it may be more convenient to provide that the death benefit shall be payable to a member's personal representatives.

48 National Insurance Act, 1959 s. 7 (3).

Dependants' Pensions

9. (i) A member may by notice in writing given to the Trustees at any time before he retires from the service of the Company elect to surrender part of the pension to which he may become entitled under the Pension Scheme for the purpose of providing a pension payable to a dependant nominated by him at the date of giving such notice so long as the part of the pension retained by the member shall be greater than the equivalent pension benefits of such member. The dependant's pension shall commence one month after the last payment of the member's pension and shall be payable by equal monthly instalments in advance and shall continue during the remainder of the life of such nominated dependant the last instalment thereof not being apportionable.

(ii) The yearly amount of such dependant's pension shall be such as shall be certified by the Actuary to be just and reasonable having regard to the proportion of his pension surrendered by the member, to the member's age and the age of the nominated dependant but so that the yearly amount of such dependant's pension shall not exceed the pension payable to the member following such surrender.

(iii) Any such notice as aforesaid may be revoked by a member at any time and shall be deemed to have been revoked if the nominated dependant shall die before the member retires from the service of the Company.

(iv) If any estate duty shall be payable by the Trustees on the death of a member in respect of a dependant's pension payable under this Rule the Trustees may to the extent that the amount of such duty shall not be paid to the Trustees by the legal personal representatives of the member or by the person entitled to such pension recover as they shall think fit the whole or any part of such duty either by way of deduction from any instalment of the pension so payable or by reducing each instalment of such pension by an amount to be determined by the Actuary which bears to such instalment the same proportion as such duty or such part thereof (as the case may be) bears to the capital value of such pension or partly in one way and partly in another.

A pension payable to a member's dependant under this rule is an interest provided by the member for the purposes of section 2 (1) (d) of the Finance Act, 1894. Estate duty will therefore be payable in respect of the actuarial value of the pension but this value will not be aggregable with the member's free estate.

Commutation

10. The Trustees may in exceptional circumstances of ill-health or incapacity or if the amount of a pension would be trivial commute any pension or part of a pension payable under the Pension Scheme by the payment of a lump sum the amount whereof shall be determined by the Actuary.

Assignment

11. No member or other person entitled to a pension under the Pension Scheme may assign or charge his interest under the Pension Scheme or any part thereof and the interest of any person under the Pension Scheme who contravenes this Rule shall forthwith cease and determine.

On the footing that the employment of the member is a non-participating employment for the purposes of the National Insurance Act, 1959, one consequence of a rule of this kind taking effect is that the company would be likely to become liable to make a payment to the National Insurance Fund.[49]

To obtain approval of a scheme all pensions must be non-commutable and non-assignable. The intention is that having had the benefit of making tax-free contributions to the scheme, a member shall only receive his benefits from the scheme in a taxable form. The Tucker Committee has recommended that limited commutation should be permitted as in the case of " Top Hat " schemes.

Dismissal

12. Nothing in the Pension Scheme shall fetter the right of the Company to dismiss any employee or to reduce any employee's salary. The benefit to which a member might claim to be entitled under the Pension Scheme shall not be used as a ground for increasing damages in any action brought by such member against the Company.

Claims

13. A person whether a member or person claiming through or under a member shall not have any claim

---

49 National Insurance Act, 1959, s. 7 (3).

right or interest upon to or in respect of the Fund or any contributions thereto or any interest therein or any claim upon or against the Trustees or the Company except under and in accordance with the provisions of the Trust Deed and the Rules.

Disability

14. If any person entitled to a benefit under the Pension Scheme shall in the opinion of the Trustees be incapable by reason of physical or mental infirmity of dealing with his affairs the Trustees may if they think fit pay or apply any benefit to which such person is entitled to any relative or dependant of such person or to any person or persons on his behalf without being bound to see to the application thereof and a receipt given by the person or persons so paid shall be a complete discharge to the Trustees for such payment.

Income Tax

15. Where a member's contributions are repaid to him or where a lump sum is paid in commutation or in lieu of pension the Trustees may deduct therefrom a sum not exceeding the amount of any income tax payable by them in consequence of such repayment or payment.

Tax is payable at one-quarter of the standard rate on any contributions repaid to a member under a pension scheme approved under section 379. This represents the rate of tax which, taking into account earned income relief and other allowances, the member might have paid on his contributions had they not in fact been allowed as a deduction for tax purposes.

Termination of Company's Liability

16. The Company may terminate its liability to contribute to the Fund by six months' notice in writing to the Trustees expiring at any time or by immediate notice in writing to the Trustees in the event of the Company being wound up and thereupon the liability of members to contribute to the Fund shall also cease.

Winding up of Pension Scheme

17. (i) The Pension Scheme shall be wound up in either of the following events namely

    (a) if the Company shall terminate its liability to contribute to the Fund as provided in Rule 16;

(b) on the expiration of the period referred to in Clause 18 of the Trust Deed.

(ii) On the winding up of the Pension Scheme the Fund shall be realised and the net proceeds thereof after payment of all proper costs charges and expenses shall be applied :—

(a) in the purchase from the Government or an insurance office of repute of non-commutable and non-assignable annuities of the same amount and duration as the pensions payable or which may become payable to such persons as are then entitled to pensions under the Pension Scheme such members as have attained normal retirement age and such persons as may on the death of any such persons or members become so entitled ;

(b) in the purchase in like manner of similar annuities whether immediate or deferred for members then prospectively entitled to pensions or other benefits under the Pension Scheme such annuities to be of such amounts and payable on such terms as shall be determined by the Actuary to be just and reasonable having regard to such members' prospective interests ;

(c) in the payment to the Company of any balance which may remain.

Any such annuity as aforesaid shall be purchased in the name of the person for whose benefit it is payable and the Trustees may in exceptional cases of serious ill-health or incapacity or where the amount of the annuity would be trivial pay to the person entitled the amount which would otherwise be applied in purchasing an annuity.

Copies of Rules

18. Each member shall on admission to membership of the Pension Scheme receive a copy of the Rules.

Alteration of Rules

19. The Rules may be altered or modified from time to time in the manner provided by the Trust Deed.

PRECEDENT No. 51

Trust Deed establishing a Funded Pension Scheme under section 22 of the Finance Act, 1956, for Persons of a Particular Occupation

The object of the following precedent is to illustrate a simple type of trust scheme which it is hoped will comply with the requirements of the Finance Act, 1956, and will stand a reasonable chance of obtaining the approval of the Revenue.

Section 22 (5) of the Act requires that a trust scheme must, in order to qualify, be administered in the United Kingdom, and must be established there under irrevocable trusts by a body of persons comprising or representing a substantial proportion of the individuals engaged or connected with a particular occupation. This sounds at first as if the body administering any particular trade or profession is bound to undertake a complex administration if it wishes to set up a scheme. It may be questioned whether this is necessarily the case. It is suggested that all that is required from the professional body is a Trust Deed setting up the scheme, and a certain minimum of supervision. The whole running of the scheme can in practice be left to a bank or some other corporate trustee or trustees who will charge remuneration for acting. There seems to be no reason why a bank or any other trust corporation should not in fact prepare its own form of Trust Deed, and make it available to the various professional bodies who might wish to set up identical schemes, which can thus be administered with the minimum of administrative complication.

The type of trust scheme here considered is one which provides no element of insurance, but is purely a method of saving against old age, death or incapacity. This greatly simplifies matters and reduces the cost of administration. In essence the scheme is simple and is fundamentally different from the group retirement benefit schemes set up under other legislation. The member pays so much each year to the Trustees. The Trustees invest the moneys and accumulate the income, keeping a separate account of each member's fund. When the member reaches the age of 70 or some age between 60 and 70 (he need not retire from work), or becomes incapable of carrying on work, the Trustees realise the investments which they are holding for such member and apply the moneys in buying a life annuity for him. The Trustees do not themselves pay any annuities: indeed, they cannot, since they hold, not one trust fund, but a group of individual trust funds. They carry no assurance risk and need to make no actuarial calculations.

There are various detailed requirements which appear from the precedent which follows, or may be gathered from the Act, and it is not proposed to set them out here in full. Briefly, the expected advantages of the scheme are as follows: —

(1) The member gets full relief from income tax and surtax on the contributions he pays (although such contributions must not exceed the narrow limits set out in the Act).

(2) The "build-up" is also tax-free: that is, the contributions are invested at compound interest free of tax. And any gain made on the acquisition and disposal of investments is not subject to short-term capital gains tax.

(3) The Trustees are not bound to invest in fixed-interest securities. It is thus possible to build a hedge against inflation. This may in practice prove to be one of the most attractive features of this type of scheme.

(4) The member can always see what he has got saved at any particular time. The experience and facilities available to the Trustees, assuming that one is a corporate trustee, will ensure that the member's savings are held in a well-balanced portfolio.

(5) The member is not obliged to contribute a fixed amount in each year. He can obtain the full tax relief in each year if he wishes. On the other hand, he may omit to make any contribution at all in any particular year. There is nothing in the Act to suggest that the member must commit himself to a particular contribution in every year.

(6) A scheme in this form requires less complex administration than a scheme which tries to copy a funded superannuation scheme.

(7) Even old or ageing persons may become members with advantage.

A possible disadvantage of a scheme in this form may be that a member will have to make separate provision, presumably by insurance policies, to cover more fully the event of his premature death or disability. A policy giving short-term pure life cover may be appropriate. A group policy of this kind might perhaps be combined with a scheme as outlined above.

In addition, the member may not take any part of his accumulated fund as a capital sum. This feature is common to all pension schemes, except that most Top Hat schemes permit commutation up to one quarter of a member's interest. The Tucker Committee recommended that power to commute up to one quarter of a member's pension rights should be given to members of superannuation funds and to the self-employed. This recommendation has not yet been followed: until it is, the "top hatted" form a privileged class.

It must be emphasised that this precedent is simply intended to suggest a line of approach. It is possible that the Revenue will, in practice, make stringent requirements in individual cases, which will necessitate amendments that will reduce the benefits conferred by the type of scheme contemplated. The question may possibly arise in particular cases, whether a restriction imposed by the Revenue is within the terms of the Act.

Trust Deed.　　**THIS TRUST DEED** is made the —— day of ——
BY THE —— TRUST COMPANY LIMITED whose registered
office is situate at —— and which is a Trust Corporation
AA of —— Incorporated Tinker and BB of —— Incorporated Tinker :

Resolution
establishing
scheme.　　WHEREAS at a General Meeting of the Incorporated
Society of Tinkers held at Tinkers Hall in the City of
London on the —— day of —— 1956 it was duly resolved
that a Trust Scheme should be established in conformity
with the provisions of Part III of the Finance Act, 1956,
for the purpose of providing retirement benefits for members of the said Incorporated Society AND it was further
resolved that the parties hereto should be authorised to
execute this Deed of which a draft was presented to and
approved by the said General Meeting :

Section 22 (5) of the Finance Act, 1956, requires that the scheme
is established under irrevocable trusts by a " body of persons comprising or representing a substantial proportion of the individuals "
engaged in a particular occupation (or one or other of a group of occupations). Many professions and trades have satisfactory professional bodies
who will no doubt explore the possibilities of a trust scheme. Even
where there is no such body, it appears to be possible within the terms
of the Act for individuals to co-operate in order to set up their own
scheme. It may even be that all the tradesmen of a particular town
could co-operate in the same scheme. In the last resort, much may
depend on whether the Banks and other Trust Corporations decide that
the administration of such schemes is work which they are willing to
undertake. It is suggested that perhaps a Bank could act as custodian
trustee, while the management could be entrusted to a Unit Trust
Management Company.

The requirement of irrevocability is best satisfied not by making the
Trust Deed itself irrevocable but by making it clear that each member
will be unable to recover from the Trustees any sums he has once
paid to them otherwise than in accordance with the provisions of the
scheme.

The two individual trustees are intended to have the task of general
supervision only, and to act without remuneration.

Witnesseth.　　**NOW THIS DEED WITNESSETH** and it is hereby
declared as follows :—

Definitions.　　1. THIS Deed is to be interpreted according to the law
of England and in conformity with the Income Tax Acts

and moreover the following expressions herein where the context permits have the following meanings :—

(i) " The Trust Company " means the above-mentioned the —— Trust Company Limited;

(ii) " The Trustees " means the Trust Company and the above mentioned AA and BB or other the trustees or trustee for the time being of this Deed;

(iii) " Tinker " means any person being a member of the Incorporated Society of Tinkers;

(iv) " Qualifying Tinker " means a Tinker resident in Great Britain who carries on or is employed in the trade of Tinker in Great Britain;

(v) " the Scheme " means the retirement benefit scheme established by this Deed;

(vi) " Year " means year of assessment;

(vii) " Member " means a person admitted to membership in accordance with the provisions of clause 3 of this Deed;

(viii) " Relevant Earnings " and " Net Relevant Earnings " have the meanings assigned to them by the Finance Act, 1956;

(ix) " Permitted Contribution " of any Member in respect of any year means the amount of money which by virtue of section 23 of and the Third Schedule to the Finance Act, 1956, qualifies to be deducted or set off against the relevant earnings of such Member for the year in question (that is to say, the sum of £750 or one-tenth of the net relevant earnings of such Member whichever is less as provided by the said section 23 or such other sum as is provided for by the said Third Schedule);

This definition must be read in conjunction with clause 4 (5) below. Section 23 (1) and (2) of the Act gives the impression that a member of a retirement benefit scheme may subscribe any sum not exceeding £750 in any year, whether or not it represents 10 per cent. of his net relevant earnings: thus a man with net relevant earnings of £750 may subscribe the whole, and although he will get only £75 allowed as relief against tax, the balance will be carried forward to future years, and meanwhile the income of the £750 will be accumulated free of tax.

(x) " Closing Day " means in respect of any Member the day expiring twenty-one years after his death ;

(xi) " the Society " means the Incorporated Society of Tinkers ;

(xii) " Dependant " of a Member means a person who immediately prior to the death of such Member is either wholly or to a substantial extent dependent on the Member within the meaning which such expression bears in section 61 of the Clergy Pensions Measure, 1948.

In view of the decisions in *Re Sayer* [1957] Ch. 423 and *Re Saxone Shoe Co. Ltd.'s Trust Deed* [1962] 1 W.L.R. 943, it is probably unnecessary to define the word " dependant," particularly as the word is used in section 22 of the Finance Act, 1956. The cautious draftsman may, however, prefer to use a definition. See also *ante*, p. 427.

Law of England.
2. THE Scheme shall take effect upon the execution of this Deed and shall be administered in and in accordance with the law of England.

Membership.
3. IN consideration of its appointment as trustee the Trust Company hereby declares that any Tinker shall be entitled if at the time he is a Qualifying Tinker and subject to the approval of the Trustees which shall not be unreasonably withheld and upon payment to the Trust Company of an initial fee of Five Pounds to become a Member of the Scheme.

It is considered that this clause has no binding legal effect but is merely explanatory. It is intended that the fee of five pounds should form part of the remuneration of the Trust Company.

The following clauses, namely clauses 4 to 9, contain the essence of the trust scheme, while the later clauses, from 10 onwards, contain administrative provisions.

Payments into the scheme.
4. THE following provisions shall regulate payments by Members :—

Amount payable.
(1) Each Member shall be entitled in respect of any year during the whole or any part of which he is a Qualifying Tinker to pay to the Trustees a sum which (together with all other sums paid by him or on his behalf in respect of that year and qualifying for relief

under Part III of the Finance Act, 1956) does not exceed the Permitted Contribution of such Member.

No obligation   (2) A Member shall not be obliged to make any payment other than the initial fee but shall endeavour to make some reasonable payment in each year unless unavoidably prevented.

Until death or retirement.   (3) A Member shall be entitled to make such payments as aforesaid in each year up to and including the year in which he dies or retires from the Scheme.

Time for payment.   (4) So far as possible each Member shall make his payments for each year in one instalment during the months of May or June.

It is considered that self-employed persons would be able to ascertain the amount of their Relevant Earnings at the beginning of each year of assessment, and that some clause such as the above may be administratively convenient.

Certificate.   (5) Each payment shall (unless the Trustees dispense with this requirement generally or in any individual case) be accompanied by a Certificate signed by the Member in such form as the Trustees shall reasonably require stating that the payment does not (together with all other sums if any paid by the Member or on his behalf and qualifying for relief under Part III of the Finance Act, 1956, in respect of the year in respect of which the payment is tendered) exceed his Permitted Contribution

Members quitting the profession.   (6) Any Member who ceases to be a Qualifying Tinker may nevertheless continue to make payments in accordance with this Deed in respect of any year in which he has Relevant Earnings from any trade profession vocation office or employment carried on by him.

As the above clause shows, a member is not bound to make any payments at all, although the initial subscription is included expressly in order to discourage those who do not seriously intend to contribute regularly.

The certificate mentioned in sub-clause (5) is designed to avoid the possibility of any member deliberately paying more than his permitted contribution. Accidental overpayments could be made returnable, or could be carried forward to subsequent years under section 23 (2) of the Act. A troublesome problem may well arise in practice, where a member makes an overpayment which is invested by the Trust Company, since it appears from the Act that the future income would be free of tax. It may be that the Revenue will require special clauses regarding overpayments to be included, before giving approval to a trust scheme. On the other hand it is possible that the Revenue will not object to the amount of a Member's Contribution, provided it does not exceed £750, on the ground that the eventual annuity will be subject to tax. If so, clause 4 (5) could be omitted.

Although no provision is made in this precedent for suspension of a member, it may be that a clause providing for suspension (though not, in view of clause 9, for expulsion), would be appropriate in particular cases.

Trustees to invest and accumulate.
5. THE Trustees shall stand possessed of the payments made by each Member Upon Trust to invest the same in any of the investments hereinafter mentioned (with power to sell exchange or vary any such investments for others of a like nature) and to accumulate the income of such investments at compound interest and invest the same as aforesaid (with power as aforesaid) and hold the same as an accretion to the capital thereof during the lifetime of the Member or until he retires from membership.

It appears from the Act that the build-up of the fund can be free of tax. Unless this is restricted in any way by regulations made under the Act or by the manner in which the Revenue exercise their discretion to approve schemes, it represents one of the most advantageous aspects of a trust scheme. The man with 30 years of professional life before him and present Net Relevant Earnings of £1,000, may ponder what sum £100, invested in equities 30 years ago and accumulated tax-free would by now have produced, and compare this with the possibilities of deferred-annuity insurance.

Member's fund.
6. THE Trustees shall stand possessed of the said payments made by each Member and the said accumulations and the investments property and money for the time being representing the same (hereinafter called "the Member's Fund") Upon the following trusts:

Annuity on retirement.
(1) In the event of the Member retiring from membership Upon Trust to apply the Member's Fund in the purchase from the Government or from the Trust Company or from some reputable company incorporated in Great Britain and dealing in annuities of such one of the annuities or sets of annuities mentioned in clause 7 hereof as the Member shall in the year prior to or in the month following his retirement from membership in writing nominate and (in default of nomination) of an annuity payable to the Member during his life; and

Return on death.   (2) In the event of the Member dying before retirement from membership upon such trusts as the Member shall by Will or codicil declare concerning the same and in default thereof Upon Trust to pay the same to the personal representatives of the Member as part of his estate.

It is the above clause combined with clause 9 that makes the scheme irrevocable so as to satisfy the requirement of the Act. It is considered that the rule in *Saunders* v. *Vautier* (1841) 4 Beav. 115, does not apply so as to enable any Member to demand at any time that, in lieu of the trusts set out above, his fund should be paid over to him. Were that rule to be applicable, the Revenue might withhold their approval of the scheme, on the ground that it was in fact revocable.

Annuities.   7. THE annuities and sets of annuities hereinbefore referred to in respect of any Member are the following (all being incapable of assignment commutation or surrender) :—

(1) An annuity payable to the Member during his life; or

(2) An annuity payable to the Member during his life together with an annuity of no greater amount payable after his death to any spouse of the Member who shall survive him during her life or during her widowhood; or

(3) An annuity payable to the Member during his life together with an annuity of no greater amount or any number of annuities which together are of no greater amount payable after his death to any dependant or dependants of the Member during his or her or their life or lives;

PROVIDED THAT any such annuity may in lieu of being an annuity for life or lives be an annuity for life or for ten years certain.

This clause may admit of some elaboration, but it is submitted that in view of the wording of section 22 (2) of the Act, its provisions should not require to be extensively amended. Annuities for the dependants of a deceased member provided under a trust scheme approved under section 22 are treated as life policies in which the deceased never had an interest and are to be aggregated as such in accordance with the provisions of section 33 (2) of the Finance Act, 1954: see Finance Act, 1957, s. 39.

Recipient of annuity.   8. EVERY such annuity as aforesaid shall be payable to the person or persons entitled to the same or if the Member so elects before death or retirement to Trustees appointed by the Member to be held upon trust to pay or apply the same to or for the benefit of the person or persons entitled thereto and subject to such powers directions restrictions and conditions as the Member may appoint.

Retirement.

9. A MEMBER shall retire from membership of the Scheme on the first of the following events to happen but shall not otherwise so retire under any circumstances whatsoever :—

(1) Upon attaining the age of 70 years;

(2) Upon serving notice of retirement on the Trustees at any time after attaining the age of 60 years;

(3) Upon serving notice of retirement on the Trustees at any time after becoming incapable through infirmity of mind or body of carrying on his occupation or any occupation of a similar nature for which he is trained or fitted.

This clause is intended to reflect the provisions of paragraphs (2) (b) and (3) (b) of section 22 of the Act. If in any particular occupation it is customary for persons to retire at an earlier age than 60, provision may be made for retirement from the scheme to take place before 60, at some age in the fifties; (section 22 (3) (c)).

Investment.

10. MONEY to be invested for the purposes of the Scheme may be invested or applied in any of the following ways namely :—

(1) In or upon any stocks funds or securities for the time being authorised by law for the investment of trust funds;

(2) Upon freehold or leasehold securities in England or Wales (such leaseholds having not less than 60 years to run at the time of making such investment);

(3) In the purchase or upon the security of any real or immovable property in any part of the world;

(4) In or upon the stocks funds shares debentures mortgages or securities of any corporation body or company municipal county local commercial or of any other description incorporated or registered in the United Kingdom in respect of which permission has been granted at the date of investment for dealings on the London Stock Exchange;

(5) In the purchase of units in any Unit Trust Scheme

authorised for the purposes of the Prevention of Fraud (Investments) Act, 1958.

This clause is capable of considerable amendment. The Act has no restriction on the type of investment that may be bought, but it is considered that in practice the Revenue might well refuse their approval to a scheme which allows investment in private companies or in loans to individuals.

It may conceivably be possible to allow individual members a measure of choice with regard to the type of investments in which their payments are to be invested.

In practice, it is considered that shares in a Unit Trust Scheme authorised under the Prevention of Fraud (Investments) Act, 1958, may offer the readiest solution to the Trust Company or other trustees if they are unwilling to venture into the choice of investments themselves. This would be particularly true if the professional, mercantile or other body setting up the scheme considered that it could dispense with the help of a paid trustee for the administration of the scheme but was chary of venturing into the mysteries of investment policy. Investment in a Unit Trust Scheme might also solve the problem of allocating the investments purchased in each year among the members who make payments in that year. The possibility may be considered of a Unit Trust Scheme or an Investment Company being established specially for the purposes of a pension scheme. Another possibility which deserves consideration is that of appointing two corporate trustees, namely a Bank, to act as custodian trustee, and a Unit Trust Management Company, to carry out the whole administration of the scheme. If this is done, there seems to be no reason why the expenses of running the scheme should be any greater than those already occasioned by investment in units of a Unit Trust.

The remaining clauses of this precedent are for the most part administrative and may require extensive modification to suit individual cases.

Retain cash.　　11. THE Trustees may retain cash balances of such reasonable amount as they may think fit and shall not be chargeable in respect of any interest thereon or otherwise in respect thereof.

Administration.　　12. THE administration and management of the Scheme shall (subject to the provisions of this Deed) be vested in the Trustees. The Trustees shall meet at such times being not less than once a year and at such places as they shall decide and shall make such regulations (not being inconsistent with this Deed) for the conduct of their business and the administration and management of the Scheme as they shall think fit. The decision of a majority of the Trustees shall bind a dissenting or non-voting or absent minority. The Trustees other than the

Trust Company shall have power to delegate to the Trust Company all matters other than those affecting the general policy of the Scheme.

Advice.

13. THE Trustees may in relation to these presents act on the advice or opinion of any lawyer broker actuary accountant or other professional person obtained by the Trustees and shall not be responsible for any loss occasioned by so acting.

Power to determine questions.

14. THE Trustees shall have full power to determine whether or not any person is entitled from time to time to any annuity or other payment or benefit in accordance with the Scheme and in deciding any question of fact they shall be at liberty to act upon such evidence or presumption as they shall in their discretion think sufficient although the same be not legal evidence or legal presumption. The Trustees shall also have power conclusively to determine questions and matters of doubt arising on or in connection with the Scheme or the annuities or other payments or benefits thereunder.

Records accounts and audit.

15. THE Trust Company shall keep a complete record of all matters necessary for the working of the Scheme and shall also keep accounts to show both generally and as regards each Member the position of the funds comprised in the Scheme and the amounts contributed thereto. The said accounts shall be made up to the 31st day of March in each year and the Trust Company shall cause the same to be audited annually by an Auditor appointed by the Trustees who shall have access to all books papers vouchers accounts and documents relating to the Scheme and shall make and sign a report on such accounts which report together with a general Balance Sheet of the Scheme shall be open to inspection by any Member and by the Society at such place or places as the Trustees shall from time to time determine.

Custody of records.

16. THE Trust Company shall have sole custody of all records vouchers accounts letters share and stock certificates documents of title and other papers relating to the Scheme and the Trustees other than the Trust Company shall have access thereto at all reasonable times, and each Member shall have access to so much thereof as concerns that Member's Fund but otherwise all matters relating to the Scheme and to each Member's Fund shall be confidential.

Payments.   **17.** ALL payments in connection with the Scheme shall be made to or by the Trust Company alone. All investments shall be made in the name of the Trust Company alone.

Additional powers.   **18.** THE Trustees shall have the following additional powers :—

Compromise.   (1) Power to settle compromise or submit to arbitration any claims matters or things relating to the Scheme or any Member's Fund in any manner ;

Variation of scheme.   (2) Power (with the consent of the Society) by Deed or Deeds to vary the trusts and provisions herein contained PROVIDED THAT (i) no such variation shall modify the main purpose of the Scheme or cause or be calculated to cause the Commissioners of Inland Revenue to withdraw their approval of the Scheme (ii) a copy of every such Deed shall be sent by post at his last known address to every member as soon as may be after its execution (iii) the provisions of every such Deed shall not apply to any Member who within six months after a copy shall have been sent to him serves notice on the Trustees requiring that the said Deed shall not apply to him.

Perpetuity.   **19.** THE trusts and powers herein shall apply in respect of each Member's Fund until the Closing Day of such Member.

The advisability of specifying some perpetuity period in a pensions scheme is a question upon which there is no settled view. It is considered that in a scheme such as the present, no trusts arise until a member joins, and each member creates a fresh trust so far as the perpetuity rule is concerned. Therefore, this clause, combined with clause 1 (x) defining " Closing Day," is all that is required.

Voluntary trustees.   **20.** THE Trustees other than the Trust Company shall receive no remuneration for so acting.

Remuneration.   **21.** THE Trust Company shall be entitled to the following remuneration :

(1) An initial fee of Five Pounds payable by each Member on being admitted to the Scheme ;

[etc. Complete the remuneration as agreed and deal also with administration expenses]

Trusts in default.   **22.** IN the event that any Member or wife or widow or dependant of a Member entitled or prospectively entitled to any interest in any Member's Fund or any annuity to be purchased out of any Member's Fund shall disappear or not be able to be found after searches or be unascertainable and in the event of any part of any Member's Fund falling to be disposed of on his death intestate as *bona vacantia* the said Member's Fund or such part or interest therein as aforesaid shall after the Trustees shall have obtained the opinion in writing of a barrister of at least ten years' standing practising at the Chancery Bar that further searches would be futile or impracticable, be held by the Trustees upon trust for the Tinkers Benevolent Fund or some other charity for the relief of poverty and distress among tinkers and their families and dependants as the Trustees shall in their discretion determine.

New trust corporation.
    23. IN the event of the Trust Company ceasing to be a trustee hereof the Society shall have power to appoint a Trust Corporation to act as trustee in its place and upon such terms as to remuneration as may at or prior to the time of such appointment be agreed in writing between the Society and the Trust Corporation so appointed.

New trustees.
    24. THE power of appointing a trustee or trustees of this Deed shall subject as aforesaid be exercised by the Society.

    IN WITNESS, ETC.

    THE SEAL, ETC.

CHAPTER 10

WILLS

THE drawing of a will for a person of property is nowadays properly considered as one part of tax planning in respect of his property. One reason is that the lay client who comes to have a fresh will drafted should be advised that, by disposing of his property, by means of gifts, settlement, covenants, etc., he may achieve his objects more economically than by the execution of a will. Another reason is that dispositions already made as part of tax planning may affect the size and nature of the gifts to be contained in the will. Thirdly, the drafting of the will itself should be done with a view to avoiding the worst burdens of tax and duty in respect of the estate, after the death of the testator: the testator should be concerned, not only with his own tax, but with tax payable in future by his beneficiaries.

It is not easy to draw precedents of wills intended to mitigate the burden of duty and tax, but it is hoped that the precedents contained in the present chapter, together with the notes thereon, will illustrate a number of points which often arise. The reader may find it useful if some of the more important considerations, which can scarcely be introduced as notes to actual precedents, are set out before the precedents themselves.

One additional tax consideration which now has to be borne in mind by personal representatives and legatees is the operation of the provisions in the Finance Act, 1962, relating to short-term capital gains. Under these provisions personal representatives are treated as a single and continuing body of persons but they are not chargeable to tax under Case VII of Schedule D in respect of an acquisition and disposal by reference to the vesting of the property of the deceased in them.[1] Similarly, a legatee is not generally chargeable to tax under Case VII in respect of the disposal of property acquired by him as legatee; but, where the property in question is shares in a land-owning company [2] or a company controlling a land-owning company, he will be liable to tax under Case VII on any gain made by him on the disposal of these shares if a charge to tax could otherwise be properly made under the provisions in section 14 of the Finance Act, 1962.

Burden of estate duty

It is not intended to set out the whole law relating to estate duty, but only to indicate in outline the persons who are accountable to the

[1] Finance Act, 1962, s. 12 (7).
[2] Finance Act, 1962, s. 14 (6).

448

Revenue for payment of the duty, and the incidence of the duty upon the various assets of the estate.

(i) *Accountability*

The person who is accountable is not necessarily the person who has to suffer the duty: he is simply the person to whom the Revenue looks for payment, and he usually passes on the burden to a person who also benefits by receiving part of the estate of the deceased. It seems natural that the executor should be accountable, and indeed it is enacted by section 8 (3) of the Finance Act, 1894, as modified by section 24 (2) of the Finance Act, 1962, that the executor or administrator is accountable for the duty in respect of all personal property situate in Great Britain and of all property, of whatever kind situate out of Great Britain, of which the deceased was competent to dispose at his death. Further, the personal representative is accountable for estate duty in respect of land in England and Wales which devolves upon him.[3] Further, a beneficiary to whom land in Great Britain passes or is deemed to pass on a death is accountable, as well as the personal representative.

In all other cases the accountable person is the beneficiary or trustee who takes the property or has it already vested in him, at the death. Thus there are many types of property, of which the deceased was not "competent to dispose," in respect of which the personal representatives of the deceased are not liable at all; examples of these are settled property which passes on the deceased's death, except property which devolves upon his personal representatives, *donationes mortis causa* and gifts made during his lifetime.

The foregoing shows, very briefly, who are accountable to the Revenue; the incidence of the burden of the duty as between the various types of property is determined according to different principles.

(ii) *The ultimate burden*

The fundamental distinction which determines the ultimate incidence of estate duty is between property which "passes to the executor as such" and property which does not "pass to the executor as such." This distinction originates from the Finance Act, 1894, which laid down no concise rules governing the incidence of the duty, but enacted, by section 9 (1), that " A rateable part of the estate duty on an estate, in proportion to the value of any property which does not pass to the executor as such shall be a first charge on the property in respect of which duty is leviable." What property therefore passed to an executor as executor in 1894? It is only by pursuing this question that the true meaning of the distinction becomes evident. For until the passing of the Land Transfer Act, 1897, realty did not automatically vest in the personal representative, but, unless the will expressly or impliedly devised

---

[3] Law of Property Act, 1925, s. 16 (1).

it to him as trustee or otherwise, devolved directly on the devisee or heir; consequently realty did not pass to the executor as such. The same was true of course of many other types of property such as gifts made by the deceased in his lifetime, settlements under which the deceased had an interest passing on his death, and so on. But personal property (including leaseholds) forming the free estate of the deceased, did in 1894 pass to the executor as executor. Thus there exists today an artificial distinction, based on a rule of law long since reversed, between free personalty (including leaseholds) on the one hand and all other types of property on the other.

The general rule is that the estate duty on property which passes to the executor as such is borne and paid, not by the beneficiary, but by the general estate of the testator, as a testamentary expense.[4] All other estate duty is, as stated above, a rateable charge upon the specific assets, so that the beneficiary must bear a rateable part of the estate duty.

The foregoing rule may be expressly altered by directions in the will of the testator; although he cannot prevent the duty on property not passing to the executor as such from being a charge on that property, he can direct that the charge be paid off out of other property forming part of his estate; equally he can direct that a rateable part of estate duty shall be borne by property which passes to the executor as such. In the case of a large estate, directions as to the incidence of estate duty can have far-reaching consequences, and in drawing a will of such an estate, it is important to consider whether such directions should be included. In practice, the commonest direction is the phrase "free of duty," sometimes tacked on regardless of its effect.

An example may illustrate how the duty is borne.

EXAMPLE:

A testator owns the following property, *inter alia*:
(1) A freehold house (in England).
(2) A row of leasehold houses (in England, let to subtenants).
(3) Investments in England.
(4) A life interest in a family settlement of realty, with a power of appointment.
(5) Furniture in the freehold house, a car and other chattels.
(6) A leasehold cottage (in England), owned jointly together with his wife.
(7) A freehold cottage and furniture in the Republic of Ireland.

If the total estate is valued at, say £60,000, it will probably bear estate duty at the rate of 35 per cent., that is, £21,000. This will be borne by the various assets in the following way, unless the will directs otherwise: The under-mentioned assets will bear a rateable part of the duty, that is to say, the beneficiaries will prima facie be answerable to the executor or the Revenue for 35 per cent. of the value of the individual asset:
(1) The freehold house.
(4) The interest in the settlement.

4 *Re Culverhouse* [1896] 2 Ch. 251; *Re Clemow* [1900] 2 Ch. 182, and *Re Buesst's Will Trusts* [1963] 1 All E.R. 280.

(6) The leasehold cottage (the wife would here be answerable).

(7) The cottage and the furniture in the Republic of Ireland.

The remaining assets will not prima facie bear their own burden of estate duty; it will be paid as a " testamentary expense." This means that it will be paid, like other debts and funeral and testamentary expenses, out of the assets in the order laid down by the Administration of Estates Act, 1925.[5] It is possible, in consequence, that property which is specifically bequeathed will escape the burden of estate duty altogether, while property which is given in a residuary gift will be entirely consumed by estate duty.

It will be appreciated from the above example that in order to draw a will for such a testator some thought should be given to the incidence of estate duty. A direction which may usefully be included in a will is one that a rateable part of the estate duty payable in respect of the estate shall be borne by the individual assets, whether or not such rateable part is by law made a charge on such assets.

" Free of duty " provisions

It is not always easy to discriminate between when the words " free of duty " should be used, and when they are redundant. Since the abolition of legacy duty and succession duty in 1949 they are likely to be less important than formerly, but may nevertheless be useful where it is desired to exonerate certain parts of the estate from estate duty at the expense of others.

Where property which does not " pass to the executor as such " within the meaning of section 9 (1) of the Finance Act, 1894—for example, a freehold house—is specifically devised by will, the words " free of duty " added to the gift will mean that the devisee takes the property exonerated from the burden of duty, which becomes a testamentary expense payable out of the general assets of the estate. Where, however, property passes to the executor as such, the words " free of duty " will usually have no effect at all, since the duty on such assets is a testamentary expense anyway, not paid out of the specific property.

The rule is clear enough, but in exceptional cases its application becomes complex. Where, for instance, the undisposed-of property and the residue are insufficient to pay the testamentary expenses, pecuniary legacies must begin to abate rateably, and once they have all been used up, specific devises and bequests begin to suffer. If this happens (and it is the aim of a well-drawn will to mitigate the possibility of it happening) there may be difficulties, since gifts " free of duty " are understood as being free both of the rateable part of duty otherwise falling to be borne by them and of the burden of duty which may, together with the other testamentary expenses, fall on specific gifts after the residue and the pecuniary legacies have been sacrificed.[6]

Rather than leave the incidence of duty to be decided by the general law, or exonerate only certain assets, it is sometimes advisable to include

[5] s. 34 (3) and First Schedule, Part II. See Williams on *Executors*, 14th ed., pp. 993 *et seq.*

[6] See *Re Ridley* [1950] Ch. 415.

in a will a positive direction to pay estate duty on the whole estate
out of particular assets.   Thus a direction that all debts and testamentary
expenses and all estate duty is to be paid out of residue will exonerate
realty from the burden it would otherwise bear.[7]   The advantage
of such a direction is that it may avoid the complex calculations which
sometimes have to be made, with a juggling of pecuniary legacies payable
out of realty and personalty in varying proportions, " free of duty "
provisions, wording which appears to vary the statutory order for abate-
ments of assets, and annuities which cannot be paid in full.[8]

Annuities

It was formerly common to make provision for dependants, other than
the residuary legatees, by bequeathing annuities to them for life.   Today,
in view of the high rates of income tax and surtax and the liability
to a claim for death duty on the death of an annuitant, great caution
should be exercised in advising a testator who desires to leave a number
of annuities.   Many of the points which arise in practice are fully
discussed in connection with the precedents of wills which appear later
in this chapter; it may be useful however if a number of points are
mentioned here.

(i) Taxation of an annuity

An annuity given by will is subject to income tax and surtax.   Moreover, as a result of sections 169 and 170 of the Income Tax Act, 1952,
the trustees who pay the annuity are entitled to deduct income tax at the
standard rate before paying the annuity (and under section 170 this
deduction is compulsory).   It is perhaps not generally understood that
income tax is payable and is deductible at source, even where the annuity
is paid out of capital moneys, and even where the amounts payable
vary from year to year, or are paid or refused entirely at the discretion
of the trustees.[9]   It follows that a direction to make up an annuity
out of capital to a fixed sum is one that should only be included in a
will after very careful consideration, since it involves paying income tax
to the Revenue on sums which originated as capital.   And if, pursuant
to a direction in a will, an annuity is purchased out of capital moneys,
no tax advantage will be derived under the relieving provisions contained in section 27 of the Finance Act, 1956: see section 27 (8) (c).

(ii) Annuity free of tax

A testator may wish to provide a tax-free sum for the annuitant.
Where an annuity is given clear of any " deduction," the word
" deduction " does not prima facie include income tax, because income
tax is not a deduction but a payment to be made by the recipient of

[7] Re Pimm [1904] 2 Ch. 345.
[8] See, for example, Re King [1942] Ch. 413; Re Anstead [1943] Ch. 161; Re Ridley,
supra.
[9] See post, p. 459.

the annuity.[10]   A testator who wishes to free an annuitant from paying income tax on the amount of the annuity, ought to use the words " free of income tax " or " without deduction of income tax "[11] and if he does not wish the words " income tax " to include surtax he ought to add " but not free from surtax."[12]

When an annuity is bequeathed " free of income tax," any repayment of tax recovered by the annuitant or due in respect of personal reliefs relating to the annuity must be handed over by the annuitant to the trustees.   That is to say, the annuitant is accountable to the trustees for such proportion of his reliefs in terms of tax as the amount of the annuity (grossed up at standard rate) bears to the total income of the annuitant for tax purposes.[13]   This is so even where the bequest is of " such a sum as will after deduction of tax payable in respect thereof leave in the hands of the annuitant the sum of £x."   If it is desired that the annuitant is not to be held accountable in respect of any reliefs, allowances or other repayments which he may claim, then the draftsman should show his intention specifically in the bequest, so that the phrase " free of income tax " is amended to some such phrase as " free of income tax at the standard rate."   Where such a phrase is employed, it greatly simplifies matters since the trustee is regarded as having deducted tax at standard rate from the gross amount of the annuity, and is not thereafter required to call upon the annuitant for any refund, even though the annuitant himself, being entitled to reliefs and allowances, may recover from the Revenue part of the tax borne by the trust fund.

It is possible that other words would achieve the same result, but the use of the formula " free of income tax at the standard rate " avoids ambiguity.   For example, in *Re Jones* [1933] Ch. 842, the phrase used was " such an annuity as after deducting income tax thereon at the current rate for the time being would amount to the clear yearly sum of £x free of duty," and it was held that the annuitant was entitled to retain the refund, as " current rate " implied the standard rate.   In contrast, in *Re Eves* [1939] 1 Ch. 969, where there was a bequest of a life annuity of £x " to be paid free of all duties and free of income tax at the current rate for the time being deductible at the source," it was decided that the words " at the current rate . . ." did not distinguish the case from *Re Pettit*; and in *Re Williams* [1945] 1 Ch. 320, where the phrase used was " free from income tax at the current rate for the time being deductible at source," it was also held that the annuitant must account to the trustees.   As was stated by Uthwatt J. (as he then was) in the latter case, the contrasting phrases are: " Such a sum as after deducting income tax leaves £x," (when *Re Pettit* does not apply) and " £x free of income tax," which means free of the annuitant's

---

[10] *Re Hooper* [1944] Ch. 171; *Re Batley, No. 1* [1951] Ch. 558 (on this point).
[11] *Re Williams* [1936] Ch. 509.
[12] *Re Reckitt* [1932] 2 Ch. 144.
[13] *Re Pettit* [1922] 2 Ch. 765; *Re Bates* [1946] Ch. 83; *Re Lyons* [1952] Ch. 129.   See also *ante*, p. 22, for an example of the calculation.

individual liability to income tax when the annuitant must hand back the refund or a proportionate part. Incidentally the form of order in this case shows that in the calculation there adopted the proportion is that of the grossed-up amount of the annuity compared with the total gross income for the purposes of income tax.

If all the persons interested in the trust fund are *sui juris* they may, of course, together agree to forgo any refund due under the decision in *Re Pettit*, a course sometimes adopted in practice.

(iii) *The annuitant's reliefs*

Since the decision in *Re Lyons* [1952] Ch. 129, the reliefs now taken into account are all the personal reliefs (including child allowance and life assurance), and also relief for trading losses under section 341 of the Income Tax Act, 1952, or section 15 (3) of the Finance Act, 1953. In practice, earned income relief and maintenance relief for property are left out of account. The reliefs should be calculated on the basis that the whole of the annuitant's income has borne tax at the standard rate. In calculating the total income, the earned income allowance and maintenance relief should be deducted from the appropriate sources of income. The annuity should be the amount grossed up at the standard rate for the year of the " tax free " annuity (*I. R. C.* v. *Cook* [1946] A.C. 1; 26 Tax Cas. 489).

The annuitant is allowed to deduct from his total income for surtax purposes the amount of the refund handed over to the trustees, grossed up at the standard rate, on the authority of *I. R. C.* v. *Duncanson* [1949] 2 All E.R. 846; 31 Tax Cas. 257. The trustees receiving a refund treat this as the net income of the trust fund, and if it is paid as income to a residuary legatee it will be treated as net income that has already suffered deduction of income tax at the standard rate.

(iv) *Estate duty on an annuity*

One of the most important considerations in deciding whether an annuity is a proper way of providing for a particular beneficiary is the estate duty that may be payable on the death of the annuitant. Duty is payable, if at all, under section 2 (1) (b) of the Finance Act, 1894, on the property charged with the annuity, as " property in which the deceased . . . had an interest ceasing on the death of the deceased," and is computed on the " slice " principle: that is to say the property on which the duty is payable is the sum which bears the same proportion to the value of the property out of which the annuity issues as the annuity bears to the annual income of the property. In other words, a gift of an annuity bears as great a burden of duty on the death of the annuitant (unless some such action as is later described is taken) as a gift of a life interest in specific property.[14] There was formerly a further

14 *Re Lambton's Marriage Settlement* [1952] Ch. 752; [1952] 2 All E.R. 201.

disadvantage arising out of a gift of an annuity, which produced serious results in cases where an annuity was charged upon a settled fund. The law in this respect was, however, changed by section 32 of the Finance Act, 1956.

(v) *Small annuities created inter vivos*

An important consideration, where a testator desires to provide an annuity arising on his own death, is the relief given to small annuities. In a proper case a testator may be able to bequeath an annuity by will, and so draft the bequest that he can, after executing the will, provide small annuities during his lifetime, which will operate to reduce the annuity in the will; the annuity in the will can then act as a supplement up to the amount stated therein of any annuity which the testator may provide while still alive.

By a small annuity is meant an annuity of less than £104 purchased by the donor while still alive. The exemption is somewhat curious in its operation. Section 15 (1) of the Finance Act, 1894, as amended by section 33 (1) of the Finance Act, 1935, runs as follows:

"Estate duty shall not be payable in respect of a single annuity not exceeding £52 purchased or provided by the deceased, either by himself alone or in concert or arrangement with any other person, for the life of himself and of some other person and the survivor of them, or to arise on his own death in favour of some other person; and if in any case there is more than one such annuity, the annuity first granted shall be alone entitled to the exemption under this section."

That seems simple enough, but section 33 (2) of the Finance Act, 1935, complicates matters:

"An annuity of less than £104 which would, but for the fact that it exceeds £52, be exempted from estate duty under the provisions of . . . section 15 (1), above . . . as amended by this section shall be chargeable with estate duty as if it were an annuity of twice the amount by which it exceeds £52 and as if the said provisions were not in force."

These exemptions apply only to annuities provided by the deceased in his lifetime and which therefore, since they arise on his death, bear estate duty under section 2 (1) (d) of the Finance Act, 1894; they do not apply to annuities left by will. The exemption applies whether or not the annuities were purchased within five years of death; it is available, where several annuities are provided for different beneficiaries, for the first annuity payable to each beneficiary.

The result seems to be as follows: an annuity of less than £52 is exempt; one of £60 is treated as if it were £16 (*i.e.*, twice the amount by which £60 exceeds £52); one of £100 is treated as if it were £96.

By providing annuities of £52 in favour of separate beneficiaries the full exemption may be gained in respect of each annuity.

By providing up to three small annuities in favour of the same person, a partial exemption may be gained. Thus, for example, suppose a person of means purchases three annuities in favour of a dependant, in the following order and of the following values:—

(1) £30;   (2) £100;   (3) £50.

For the purposes of estate duty on the death of the donor these are reckoned as follows:—

(1) nil;   (2) £100;   (3) £50.

Exemption is thus gained in respect of the smallest only, and very little is saved. But by providing the same annuities in a different order, a different result may be achieved, as follows:—

(1) £100;   (2) £50;   (3) £30.

These annuities, in this order, will rate for the purposes of estate duty as follows:—

(1) £96;   (2) nil;   (3) £30.

This gives a total value of £126 in place of the real value of £180.

(vi) *Annuities as separate estates*

The exemptions just mentioned apply to small annuities only. Mention must also be made of the exemption from aggregation which is considered to arise, as a result of section 4 of the Finance Act, 1894, in respect of any annuity, however large, provided by the deceased in his lifetime. This exemption applies since the annuity is " property in which the deceased never had an interest "; therefore, if the donor of the annuity creates it by charging it on his property, the exemption does not arise.

The advantage in purchasing an annuity is that this method of avoiding aggregation is probably effective even if death occurs within five years [15]; in this respect it is similar to the purchase of a policy under section 11 of the Married Women's Property Act, 1882.[16]

If the person providing the annuity does not die within five years it would appear that no estate duty is payable on his death in respect of the annuity, even though it then became payable. Section 2 (1) (c) of the Finance Act, 1894, is not applicable, the donor having survived the five-year period; section 2 (1) (d) is not applicable, since the annuity is a chose in action to which the annuitant is entitled before, as well as after, the donor's death; the fact that payments begin to be made is not a beneficial interest arising on the donor's death: see *D'Avigdor-Goldsmid* v. *I. R. C.* [1953] A.C. 347; *Westminster Bank* v. *I. R. C.*, *Wrightson* v. *I. R. C.* [1958] A.C. 210.[17]

An example will illustrate how the present exemption works.

[15] It is considered that s. 30 (2) of the Finance Act, 1939, does not cause annuities to be aggregable.
[16] See *ante*, p. 248. It has been argued by the Revenue by reference to the decision in *Potter* v. *I. R. C.*, 37 A.T.C. 58, that such policies are aggregable.
[17] *Ante*, p. 246.

EXAMPLE :

A dies leaving an estate of £50,000. In his will he gives an annuity of £2,000 to his wife. The estate will pay estate duty at 31 per cent., leaving only £34,500 to be distributed. This may well mean abatement of the annuity.

If, however, within five years of his death, A purchases from an insurance company an annuity of £2,000 for his wife, to arise on his death, the situation is different. A's estate will be depleted by the amount he paid in respect of the annuity, say, by £15,000. Suppose also that the value of the annuity at A's death is £20,000. The estate, being aggregated at £35,000, will pay duty at the rate of 21 per cent., a total of some £7,350, leaving £27,650 to be distributed. The annuity arising in favour of the wife (£20,000 value) will be separately aggregated, and thus bear duty at the rate of 12 per cent., which amounts to £2,400.

If A buys the annuity more than five years before his death, it would seem that it is not charged with estate duty at all.

There is no reported authority on the question, whether an annuity purchased by the deceased can be " property in which the deceased never had an interest." It is possible, therefore, that the Revenue may at some time refuse to grant exemption, with a view to obtaining a ruling from the court.

In order to gain the exemption, it is necessary that the deceased should have bought the annuity as a gift for the donee, and not simply have paid for an annuity bought by the donee. In other words, the deceased, not the donee, must have signed the proposal form. Furthermore, it is as well to avoid any argument by the Revenue to the effect that the purchase of an annuity by the deceased, even if the annuity is payable to a donee, confers on the donee no right of enforcing payment against the deceased or the person paying the annuity. In order to avoid this argument, the deceased should have made a short declaration of trust in favour of the donee. A few lines in a letter would suffice, such as : " This is to confirm that I am about to purchase an annuity for you of £——, of which I and my personal representatives are trustees for you."

Life interest bequeathed to widow

It is well known that an exemption from estate duty may be obtained by settling a life interest on the widow of the testator; if this is done, no estate duty is payable on the widow's death in respect of the settled property, provided duty has been paid in respect of that property on the husband's death. The manner in which this exemption arose is worth examining. Section 5 (4) of the Finance Act, 1894, provided that, once estate duty had been paid on any " settled property," no further estate duty should be payable in respect of that property, until the death of a person who was at the time of his death, or had been at any time during the continuance of the settlement, " competent to dispose " of such property. Settled property did not altogether escape, however, since an additional duty called the Settlement Estate Duty was payable out of such property. Now Settlement Estate Duty was abolished by section 14 of the Finance Act, 1914. The same Act also abolished the exemption

from estate duty which the Act of 1894 had conferred on " settled property "; at the same time, however, it expressly retained the exemption
in cases where estate duty on " settled property " had been paid upon
the death of one party to a marriage, so far as concerned the payment
of estate duty on the death of the other party to the marriage. It is this
provision which confers exemption today. There are, therefore, three
main requirements which must be fulfilled in order for the exemption to
arise; a few words should be said on each of them.

(i) *Estate duty must have been paid on the death of the spouse who
first dies, in this case the husband.* Thus no exemption may be obtained
where the provision for the widow is made by a settlement which avoids
estate duty on the husband's death.

(ii) *The widow must not be " competent to dispose " of the property
settled, either during her lifetime or at her death.* There are several
points arising out of this. A will might be drafted, intended to provide
for a widow and yet avoid estate duty on her death, which entirely
defeated the object it set out to achieve because it tried to give the
widow a number of instalments of capital (in the event of the income
being inadequate for her needs) by providing that the widow could demand
to have the income made up to a certain sum every year, and on
her so demanding the trustees were bound to comply. The effect might be
that the widow would be competent to dispose of almost the whole fund.
Another important point is that the widow is competent to dispose of the
settled fund if she has a general power of appointment in respect of it.
This is expressly provided by section 22 (2) (a) of the Finance Act, 1894,
which further provides that the expression " general power " includes
every power or authority enabling the donee or other holder thereof to dispose of property as he thinks fit, whether exercisable by instrument *inter
vivos*, or by will, or both. It is settled that the definition includes a
limited power which enables the donee to appoint to himself: *Re Penrose*
[1933] Ch. 793. The most cautious course is therefore to give the widow a
power limited to the issue of the marriage, or some other limited class of
which she cannot possibly be a member, so that she will not be competent
to dispose of the settled fund.

(iii) *The property in respect of which the exemption arises must be
" settled "; for this purpose the definition of " settlement " contained in
the Settled Land Act, 1882, was imported into the Finance Act, 1894, by
section 22 (1) (i).* Now, clearly, property settled on a widow for life with
remainders over is within the definition. Suppose, however, that a
testator does not give a life interest, but only an annuity; can there be
said to be a settlement, so that no estate duty is payable on the
annuitant's death? The answer to this question is that it is very probable, but not entirely certain, that the mere gift of an annuity of itself
makes a settlement, so as to exempt the fund out of which it is payable

from estate duty: see *Re White* [1938] Ch. 366, 376; [1939] Ch. 131; *cf. Re Waller* [1916] 1 Ch. 153, 158; *Armstrong* v. *Estate Duty Commissioners* [1937] A.C. 885, 894. On the other hand, it is clearly established that there is " settled property," where the will contains a direction to the trustees to set aside a fund to answer the annuity, and the trustees have done so: *Att.-Gen.* v. *Owen* [1899] 2 Q.B. 253; *Re Campbell* [1902] 1 K.B. 113. The same is true if there is no direction but only a power, and the power is in fact exercised: *Re Waller, supra.*

Where, therefore, a testator particularly desires to bequeath an annuity to his widow, it is as well to see that an express direction or power to appropriate a fund to answer the annuity is included in the will. The present practice of the Revenue is to treat any gift of an annuity as causing the estate to be " settled property," so as to give rise to the exemption.

Supplementing the widow's life interest

Since estate duty may be entirely avoided on the widow's death, a life interest or an annuity is generally the most convenient way of providing for her. The situation often arises, however, where the testator fears that the income of the life interest which he has bequeathed may be inadequate for his widow's needs, yet does not wish to leave her a large amount of capital which she may not require and yet which will bear a second burden of estate duty on her death. The most obvious solution— without reference to income tax liability—is to direct the trustees to make up the income of the estate out of capital in order to maintain a stated annual sum. Such a direction is in practice often found in wills.

As far as tax is concerned, a direction to supplement income out of capital to a stated amount is highly inadvisable. The life-tenant is assessed to income tax on the capital sums so paid, since in her hands they are income, not capital. To avoid this result, which seems unnecessarily generous to the Revenue, it was formerly the practice to give to trustees under the will a discretion to supplement the income from time to time if they thought fit, without placing any obligation upon them so to do. It was thought that since the life-tenant had no right to demand the payments out of capital, they could not be assessed as income. This view of the law was, however, upset by a series of decisions which show, first that recurring payments, even if made out of capital and of varying amounts,[18] may be assessed as income under Case III of Schedule D,[19] and secondly, that tax may still be charged even if the beneficiary has no right to be paid, but is forced to rely on the discretion of the trustees.[20]

It is clear therefore that any provision for supplementing income out of capital should be drafted with extreme care, if it is desired to

---

[18] *Moss Empires, Ltd.* v. *I. R. C.* [1937] A.C. 785; 21 Tax Cas. 264.
[19] See s. 123 of the Income Tax Act, 1952.
[20] *Lindus and Hortin* v. *I. R. C.* (1933) 17 Tax Cas. 442.

avoid the additional burden of income tax. What is not clear, however, is the exact dividing line between payments which are income and payments which are capital. In *Brodie* v. *I. R. C.*[21] the distinction was stated by Finlay J. as follows:

" If the capital belonged to the person receiving the sums—if he or she was beneficially entitled not only to the income but to the capital—then I should think that, when the payments were made, they ought to be regarded, and would be regarded, as payments out of capital, but where there is a right to the income, but the capital belongs to somebody else, then, if payments out of capital are made, and made in such a form that they come into the hands of the beneficiaries as income, it seems to me that they are income and not the less income because the source from which they came was—in the hands, not of the person receiving them, but in the hands of somebody else—capital."

It appears, therefore, that the draftsman must take care that the payments made out of capital to the widow are of the nature of capital in the hands of the widow; there must be no suggestion of keeping up a certain income, or style of living. This view of the law is reinforced by the decision of the Court of Appeal in *Cunard's Trustees* v. *I. R. C.*[22] There was in that case a gift in a will of the income of the testatrix's residuary estate to her sister, followed by the following clause:

" If in any year the income of my residuary estate should not be sufficient to enable my sister to live at The Grove in the same degree of comfort as she now lives there with me then I empower my trustees to apply such portion of the capital of my residuary estate by way of addition to the income as they in their absolute and uncontrolled discretion may think fit, moreover any capital so applied shall not be replaced out of the income of a subsequent year but shall be treated as an additional bequest to my sister." The court held that any payments of capital made to the sister under this provision were for the purposes of the Income Tax Acts annual payments, so as to be subject to income tax under Case III of Schedule D,[23] and consequently the trustees were correctly assessed on such sums under rule 21 of the All Schedules Rules[24]; Lord Greene M.R. said:

" That the payments were ' income ' in Miss McPheeters's hands is, in my opinion, beyond dispute, and the fact that they were made out of capital is irrelevant. The payments were to be made ' by way of addition to the income ' in order to enable Miss McPheeters to live in

---

21 (1933) 17 Tax Cas. 432, 439.
22 27 Tax Cas. 122; [1946] 1 All E.R. 159; and *cf. Milne's Executors* v. *I. R. C.*, 37 Tax Cas. 10.
23 See s. 123 of the Income Tax Act, 1952. Sched. D, Case III (a) charges to tax " any interest of money whether yearly or otherwise or any annuity or other annual payment whether such payment is payable within or out of the United Kingdom, either as a charge on any property of the person paying the same by virtue of any deed or will or otherwise or as a reservation out of it, or as a personal debt or obligation by virtue of any contract, or whether the same is received and payable half-yearly or at any shorter or more distant periods."
24 See now s. 170 of the Income Tax Act, 1952.

the same degree of comfort as before.   The testatrix was in fact providing for a defined standard of life for her sister, that provision being made in part out of income and in part (at the discretion of the trustees) out of capital.   The purpose was an income purpose and nothing else."

In order to avoid the effect of the *Cunard* case a number of provisions may be used, some of which appear in the precedents later in this chapter.   Thus a wide discretion may be given to the trustees to transfer capital to the widow whenever they see fit.   This may lay an unenviable burden on the trustees and so it may be preferable to set out a list of circumstances, on the happening of which they may exercise their discretion.   Again, it may carry out the testator's wishes to allow loans of capital to be made, repayable at death.

Wherever a will contains power to pay capital to the widow, as life-tenant, there is one point to be carefully considered: whether it is advisable to appoint the widow as executrix. It is arguable that if the widow ever becomes—even for a short time—sole personal representative, she will be " competent to dispose " of the capital by exercising the discretion, so that estate duty will be payable on her death.   It might accordingly be advisable to provide in the will that the power to advance capital shall not be exercisable if there is a sole trustee.

Payment of estate duty by widow

As stated above, if a testator settles his residuary estate upon his widow for life, exemption from estate duty may be enjoyed by the residuary estate on the widow's death.   Normally the residuary estate will itself be diminished by the estate duty payable on the testator's death in respect of the residuary estate and possibly in respect of other dispositions.   It was established in *Re Hall* [1942] Ch. 140 that even if the widow herself during the administration of the testator's estate, pays the estate duty chargeable on the residuary estate out of her own resources, thus in effect increasing the residuary estate by relieving it of the burden of estate duty, the exemption may still be enjoyed by the residuary estate on the death of the widow.   Provided that there is evidence that the widow did not thereby intend to create a charge in her own favour, there is no justification for denying the exemption to that part of the residuary estate that is equal to the estate duty discharged by the widow.

Where a widow voluntarily discharges the estate duty on a residuary estate of which she is the life-tenant, this must be a gift made by her in favour of the remaindermen.   However, while the point has never been decided by the courts, it would appear that it cannot be treated as a gift out of which the widow has retained a life interest.   All that she has done is to discharge an incumbrance on an estate in which she had a life interest.   The gift is subject to the normal rules imposing liability for estate duty should the widow die within the five-year period.   Nevertheless, by discharging the estate duty out of her free moneys, the widow probably suffers no loss of income, because had she not discharged the estate duty, the residuary estate, in which she has a life interest, would have been diminished proportionately.

It seems therefore that the practical effect of the widow discharging the estate duty is that she is able to make a gift of capital without suffering any loss of income: the effect is the same as if she were able to make a gift reserving a life interest and yet obtain the same estate duty advantages as if she had not reserved a life interest.

Property settled by will

Traditionally the British testator has tended to tie up his property for as long as possible, with life interests, protective trusts, powers of appointment and complex class gifts for unborn issue. Today the principal beneficiary under such a will is likely to be the Crown. In consequence a new set of rules, none of them hard and fast, must be observed. Many of these are illustrated in the precedents which follow, but many have been omitted here since they have already been dealt with in Chapters 2 and 3 in a different context.

The following rules of thumb may be of assistance to the draftsman:

(i) The principle of settling on the spouse for life may be extended to gifts which are usually made to the spouse absolutely, e.g., gifts of personal chattels.

(ii) The settlement should be as elastic as possible, and if it is to remain in existence for several generations it may be advisable to frame a discretionary trust.

(iii) If a protected life interest is given, there should be power to dispense with the forfeiture in certain circumstances.

(iv) A life interest with a gift over to the issue of the life-tenant is often being kind only to be cruel, since even if the life-tenant releases his life interest he cannot then gain any tax benefit by using the income to maintain his issue without paying substantial additional tax. It may be better, in order to benefit a person who already pays a high rate of tax, to bequeath an income to his children direct.

(v) Power to invest abroad should almost always be given to the trustees. It may in exceptional cases be advisable to give the trustees power to terminate the trusts absolutely and reconstitute them abroad.

(vi) Annuities should not be charged on a settled fund.

(vii) If property is settled free of duty, it is as well to make it clear that only duties payable on the death of the testator are included.

(viii) Express power to appropriate without the consent of the beneficiary should be given.

PRECEDENT No. 52

Will Leaving Residue to Widow for Her Life, Remainder to Issue as Widow Appoints, and in Default of Appointment to Children Equally. Power to Advance Capital to the Widow so that Such Payments shall not Incur Liability to Tax as Income of the Widow. Medium Range of Investments

I, A.B. of —— hereby revoke all testamentary dispositions heretofore by me made and declare this to be my last Will which I make this —— day of —— 19—.

Appointment of executors.
1. I APPOINT —— and —— (hereinafter called " my Trustees ") to be the executors and trustees of this my Will.

Chattels to wife.
2. I GIVE to my wife —— all articles and effects of personal domestic or household use ornament or consumption belonging to me.

Residue to be converted.
3. I GIVE all the real and personal estate not hereby or by any codicil hereto otherwise specifically disposed of and which I can dispose of by Will in any manner I think proper either as beneficially entitled thereto or under any general power unto my Trustees Upon Trust that my Trustees shall sell call in collect and convert into money the said real and personal property at such time or times and in such manner as they shall think fit with power to postpone such sale calling in or conversion of the whole or any part or parts of the said property during such period as they shall think proper and to retain the same or any part thereof in its actual form of investment without being responsible for loss And I direct that the income of such of the same premises as for the time being shall remain unsold shall as well during the first year after my death as afterwards be applied as if the same were income arising from investments hereinafter directed to be made or the proceeds of sale thereof and that no reversionary or other property not actually producing income shall be treated as producing income for the purposes of this my Will.

The practice is widespread of excluding not only the rules of equitable apportionment, as in the clause above, but also legal apportionment under the Apportionment Act, 1870, on the death of the testator. The result is that all income actually paid to the executors after the death is treated as income of the estate, and no part is treated as income of a period prior to the death and in consequence capital of the estate. This practice can result in tax disadvantages. Thus, if remuneration of the deceased, chargeable to tax under Schedule E, is paid to the executors, it may, if treated as income of the estate, suffer a second burden of income tax and surtax under the special provisions as to estates of deceased persons in course of administration contained in sections 418 to 424 (Part XIX) of the Income Tax Act, 1952.

Payment of debts and estate duty. **4. My Trustees** shall out of the moneys to arise from the sale calling in and conversion of or forming part of my said real and personal estate pay my funeral and testamentary expenses (including all estate duty leviable at my death in respect of my estate) and debts and the legacies given by this my Will or by any codicil hereto and the rule of equity known as the rule in *Allhusen* v. *Whittell* shall be disregarded.

Before paying the estate duty the trustees should, if the widow has free capital of her own and is well provided for, consider the possibility of her paying part of the estate duty out of her free capital: as to which, see *Re Hall* [1942] Ch. 140, and the comment on page 461, above.

Invest proceeds. **5. My Trustees** shall invest the residue of the said moneys in or upon any of the investments hereinafter authorised with power to vary or transpose such investments for or into others of a nature hereby authorised.

Life interest to wife. **6. My Trustees** shall pay the income of the investments above directed to be made or authorised to be retained and the investments for the time being representing the same (hereinafter called " the Trust Fund ") to my said wife during her life.

The gift of a life interest to the widow or widower of the testator is a well-known method of reducing the burden of estate duty. As a general rule, if property is settled on the spouse of the testator and estate duty is paid on the death of the testator in respect of that property, no further duty is payable on the death of the spouse. It appears, therefore, to be advisable, where it is convenient, to provide for a spouse by giving a life interest in as large a share of the estate as possible rather than by giving capital. An annuity of a fixed sum given to the spouse may have the same effect.

Gift of corpus to children, subject to appointment. **7. After** the death of my said wife my Trustees shall stand possessed of the Trust Fund and the future income thereof In Trust for all or any my children or remoter issue at such time and if more than one in such shares and with such provisions for maintenance education

advancement and such discretions and powers of appointment exercisable by such persons and with such gifts
over and generally in such manner as my wife shall by
deed or by will or codicil appoint And in default of
and subject to any such appointment In Trust for [all or
any my children or child who being male attain the age
of twenty-one years or being female attain that age or
marry and if more than one in equal shares] [such of my
children who shall be living at the death of my said wife
and if more than one in equal shares but so that if any
child of mine shall die in the lifetime of my said wife
leaving a child or children who shall attain the age of
twenty-one years or marry such child or children shall
take and if more than one in equal shares that share in
the Trust Fund that my child so dying would have taken
had he survived my wife].

Even though the widow has a limited power of appointment, no estate
duty will become payable on her death in respect of the residuary fund.
It is well settled that the exercise of a limited power by a will or deed
does not in itself give rise to liability for estate duty; this should not be
misunderstood, for usually, where there is a limited, or special, power
exercised by will, a claim for duty arises under a different head : because,
for example, the person exercising the power also enjoyed an interest
ceasing on his or her death. In the present circumstances, there is no
claim under any other head; consequently, the presence of a limited
power gives rise to no claim for duty.

Were the spouse given a general power, she would be " competent to
dispose " of the property subject to the power within the meaning of
section 22 (2) (a) of the Finance Act, 1894, and therefore a claim for
estate duty would lie. The reason for this is that the exemption conferred on property settled upon a spouse of the testator only applies
where the spouse was not either at the time of her death or at any time
during the subsistence of the settlement " competent to dispose " of the
property settled. It is well established that a person having a general
power of appointment over property is " competent to dispose " of the
property in question.

If the words in the first square brackets in clause 7 above are used,
the death of a child (after he has attained the age of twenty-one years)
during the widow's lifetime without bequeathing his share in the trust
fund to a person other than the widow would make the widow competent to dispose of a part of the trust fund equal to that child's share
in default of appointment. The words in the second square brackets
are intended to avoid this risk; but have the disadvantage that a
release by the widow of her life interest and power of appointment does
not cause an acceleration of the reversion.

Should the widow find after the testator's death that she enjoys an excessively large income and wishes to appoint or release the whole or part of the fund and then to release her life interest so as to accelerate the interests of the appointees or the children who are entitled in default of appointment, she should be advised concerning the income tax and surtax likely to be saved by such an appointment and release: see *ante*, p. 264. There would, of course, be no saving of estate duty, since none would be payable anyway in respect of her death.

Gift over to issue of brother.

8. SUBJECT to the foregoing trusts my Trustees shall stand possessed of the Trust Fund and the future income thereof In Trust for all or any the children or remoter issue of my brother —— as my said brother shall by deed or by will or codicil appoint And in default of and subject to any such appointment In Trust for all or any the children of my said brother who being male attain the age of twenty-one years or being female attain that age or marry and if more than one in equal shares and Subject thereto In Trust for —— absolutely.

Power to pay capital to wife.

9. (1) DURING the widowhood of my said wife my Trustees being at least two in number may from time to time notwithstanding the foregoing if in their uncontrolled opinion any of the events hereinafter specified has occurred pay transfer or apply such part or parts of the capital of the Trust Fund as they shall from time to time think fit (but not exceeding in the aggregate one moiety thereof) to or for the sole use or benefit of my said wife.

(2) The events above referred to are the following:

(a) the loss or serious damage by fire flood theft or otherwise at all of any dwelling house in which my wife shall at any time reside or of the furniture or contents thereof;

(b) the suffering by my wife or any child of mine maintained by my wife of any serious illness or injury or ailment of whatever nature necessitating any surgical operation or nursing or special treatment or drugs or period of convalescence;

(c) any great national emergency;

(d) the surrender by my wife of permanent residence in the United Kingdom;

(e) litigation to which my wife or any child of mine maintained by her may be a party;

(f) the interior or exterior repair or decoration of any dwelling house upon the purchase of the same as a residence for my wife or the laying out embellishment or stocking of the gardens and pleasure grounds enjoyed with any such dwelling house;

(g) any serious personal emergency or disaster in the private affairs of my wife.

The present provision is not guaranteed to avoid all question of assessment under Case III of Schedule D of the sums advanced, but it is submitted that it has a very good chance of so doing. The chances of success would be increased, if the list of emergencies were made shorter, since then the payments would be more likely to be large and irregular, and there would not be the " quality of recurrence " which is a vital circumstance in making the payments " annual payments " within the meaning of Case III of Schedule D: see *Moss Empires, Ltd.* v. *I. R. C.* [1937] A.C. 785, *per* Lord Maugham. Should the draftsman prefer not to make out such a list, he could give the trustees a wide power to advance capital whenever they thought fit, and leave it to the acumen of the trustees not to make regular payments, but to pay substantial sums at irregular intervals. It is submitted that as a matter of law sums paid under such a power would not be income and would not be taxable. The course suggested is designed to avoid argument and litigation.

Investment. 10. (1) MONEY liable to be invested under the trusts of this my Will may be invested in or on any of the following :

(i) Investments for the time being authorised as investments for trust money, or

(ii) Real or Leasehold securities whether by way of registered charge or otherwise in the United Kingdom or in any British Dominion Colony State or Dependency, or

(iii) The stock or securities of any British Dominion Colony State or Dependency or any province thereof or any foreign Government or State or of any municipal corporation or power gas electric light harbour or local authority in the United Kingdom or in any British Dominion Colony State or Dependency, or

(iv) The bonds mortgages debentures debenture stock or guaranteed or preference or ordinary stock or shares of any railway tramway canal water dock harbour electric light or power gas or other like company public or private incorporated in the United Kingdom or any British Dominion Colony State or Dependency under the Companies Acts or under any special Act of the Parliament of the United Kingdom or of any general or special Act of the Legislature of any British Dominion Colony State or Dependency or by Royal Charter and whether trading or otherwise carrying on business in Great Britain or any British Dominion Colony State or Dependency or elsewhere which shall have paid dividends on its ordinary stock or shares for at least three years prior to the date of investment, or

(v) The investment in shares of or by way of deposit with any permanent building society registered in the United Kingdom, or

(vi) The security of any life or contingent interest in any real or personal property together with an insurance on the life or other event.

(2) My Trustees in addition to the powers conferred on them by sections ten and eleven of the Trustee Act 1925 may make such arrangements generally on the reconstruction or winding up of any company as my Trustees may at their absolute discretion think fit.

(3) My Trustees may lend money on any security hereinbefore authorised in conjunction with money lent by any other persons by way of contributory loan and may accept the security in the names of my Trustees or in the name of any one of them together with other names or name or may permit the same to be taken exclusively in the names of other persons as may be deemed expedient.

By modern standards this is the narrowest range that can be advised, and, unless for a particular reason the testator prefers a cautious investment policy, it would be as well to substitute one of the wider clauses found elsewhere in this book, as, for example, on p. 476. Power to purchase land, including a residence for the beneficiaries, is included separately in the following clause.

Investment
in land.

11. (1) MY Trustees may instead of laying out all or any money held on the trusts of this my Will in the other investments hereinbefore authorised invest the same money in the purchase and paying the costs of the purchase of any buildings lands perpetual rentcharges or other real estate or chattels real in or arising in the United Kingdom or elsewhere at all and if in England or Wales being either freehold or leasehold for any term of years whereof not less than forty years is unexpired at the time of purchase and if elsewhere than in England or Wales of any tenure corresponding or equivalent to freehold tenure or in making improvements on any property so purchased.

(2) Property so purchased shall if situate in England or Wales be conveyed or assigned to my Trustees Upon Trust to sell the same with full power to postpone such sale and if situate elsewhere shall be conveyed or assigned to my Trustees either with or without any trust for sale or conversion as my Trustees shall think fit but nevertheless with power to sell the same.

(3) My Trustees shall stand possessed of any property so purchased and the proceeds of sale thereof and any other capital money arising under their statutory powers after payment of any costs incidental thereto and the net rents and profits until sale Upon the trusts and subject to the powers and provisions including this present power of purchasing land upon and subject to which the money laid out under this present power would have been held if the same had not been so laid out.

(4) With reference to any real estate including chattels real for the time being subject to the trusts of this my Will my Trustees may raise and pay out of the capital or income of the Trust Fund any money required to be paid on the exercise of the powers hereby or by statute conferred and in the opinion of my Trustees properly payable out of income or capital as the case may be.

(5) As regards any land or immovable property situate outside England or Wales the powers and indemnities given to my Trustees in regard to land in England by English law shall apply as if expressed in this my Will

and the net rents and profits thereof shall be applicable in like manner as if they arose from land in England.

Trustees of foreign land.

(6) In addition to the powers conferred by section twenty-three of the Trustee Act 1925 my Trustees may appoint any persons or corporations outside the jurisdiction of the English courts to act as trustees hereof in relation to any land or immovable property situate outside England and may pay to such trustees out of capital or income as the case may require any fees or other remuneration which may be customary in the country affected and make such arrangements generally with any such trustees as my Trustees may deem expedient without being responsible for any loss arising thereby.

Residence for beneficiaries.

(7) My Trustees may permit any person entitled to any interest in the Trust Fund whether in possession or not and whether vested or contingent to reside in any dwelling house which or the proceeds for sale of which may for the time being be subject to the trusts hereof upon such conditions as to payment of rent rates taxes and other expenses and outgoings and as to repair and decoration and generally upon such terms as my Trustees in their discretion shall think fit.

This clause contains only a restricted power to purchase leaseholds, and this is in keeping with the wishes of many testators. Should it be desired to allow the purchase of short-term leaseholds, a provision should be included empowering the trustees to take out a sinking-fund policy and pay the premiums out of the income of the leaseholds.

Appropriation.

12. THE power of appropriation conferred by the Administration of Estates Act 1925 shall be exercisable by my Trustees as well after as during the administration of my estate without any of the consents required by that Act.

Unless a clause of this nature is included in a will, appropriations in favour of legatees (other than residuary legatees) will incur stamp duty as on a conveyance on sale: see *Jopling* v. *I. R. C.* [1940] 2 K.B. 282.

Indemnity.

13. IN the professed execution of the trusts hereof no executor or trustee shall be liable for any loss to the trust premises arising by reason of any improper investment made in good faith or for the negligence or fraud of any agent employed by him or by any other executor or

trustee hereof although the employment of such agent was not strictly necessary or expedient or by reason of any mistake or omission made in good faith by any executor or trustee hereof or by reason of any other matter or thing except wilful and individual fraud or wrongdoing on the part of the executor or trustee who is sought to be made liable.

Professional charging clause.

14. ANY executor or trustee being a solicitor or other person engaged in any profession or business shall be entitled to be paid all usual professional or proper charges for business transacted time expended and acts done by him or by any partner of his in connection with the trusts hereof including acts which an executor or trustee not being in any profession or business could have done personally and in case of a deficiency of assets the said remuneration shall have priority over legacies and annuities hereby or by any codicil hereto bequeathed.

The draftsman should consider the inclusion, in addition to this clause, of a clause giving remuneration to the Trustees and a clause allowing them to retain directors' fees (see p. 477, *post*).

Power to appoint trustees.

15. MY wife during her widowhood [life] shall have power from time to time to appoint a new trustee or new trustees of this my Will.

IN WITNESS whereof I have hereunto set my hand the day and year first above written.

SIGNED etc.

PRECEDENT No. 53

Will. Gifts of Chattels and Pecuniary Legacies. Residue on Discretionary Trusts for the Testator's Family for as Long a Period as the Law Allows. Various Powers. Wide Power of Investment

I, A. B. of —— hereby revoke all testamentary dispositions heretofore by me made and declare this to be my last Will which I make this —— day of —— 19—.

Appointment of executors.

1. I APPOINT —— and —— (hereinafter called " my Trustees ") to be the executors and trustees of this my Will.

Chattels settled on wife and son.

2. (1) I BEQUEATH all my plate plated articles linen china glass books pictures prints furniture and other household effects unto my Trustees Upon Trust that my Trustees shall permit my wife to use and enjoy the same during her life and after her death shall hold the same In Trust for my son James absolutely.

(2) My Trustees shall not be bound to see to the preservation of the said articles or to their insurance nor be answerable for any loss or injury which may happen thereto during the life of my wife.

Estate duty having been paid on the death of the testator in respect of these chattels, no further duty will be payable thereon on the death of his widow. Although the trustees are given a wide indemnity, they should make an inventory of the chattels comprised in the bequest, both for their own protection and in order to facilitate the identification of the chattels so as to claim exemption from duty on the widow's death.

Personal chattels.

3. I BEQUEATH to my wife absolutely all my personal chattels as defined by the Administration of Estates Act 1925 with the exception of the articles bequeathed by the preceding paragraphs of this my Will or by any codicil hereto.

Pecuniary legacies.

4. I BEQUEATH the following pecuniary legacies free of duty :

(a) to A the sum of £ —— ;
(b) to B the sum of £ —— ; etc.

In most cases a pecuniary legacy will be free of duty automatically, since it is paid out of general personalty before realty is resorted to (see *Re Beaumont* [1950] Ch. 462; Williams on *Executors*, 13th ed., p. 980), and the estate duty on such personalty is a testamentary expense.

But if the pecuniary legacy, once the fund of personalty has been absorbed, becomes payable out of realty which bears its own estate duty, the legacy also bears its estate duty to the proportion that it is so payable: *Re Spencer Cooper* [1908] 1 Ch. 130; *Re Owers* [1941] Ch. 17; *Re Anstead* [1943] Ch. 161. For this reason it may be advisable to give some pecuniary legacies " free of duty," to make sure they are exonerated from such a burden; where, however, the testator gives his residuary realty and personalty in a mixed fund, out of which he directs payment of testamentary expenses, it is redundant to use the words " free of duty " with regard to a pecuniary legacy.

Where desired, the following words may be used instead of the words " free of duty ": " . . . and I direct that each such legacy shall be charged with a proportionate share of the estate duty if any payable in respect of my estate on my death.''

Residue:
trust for sale.

5. (1) I DEVISE and bequeath all the real and personal property whatsoever or wheresoever of or to which I shall be possessed or entitled at my death or over which I shall then have a general power of appointment or disposition by will except property otherwise disposed of by this my Will or any codicil hereto Unto my Trustees Upon the trusts and with and subject to the powers and provisions hereinafter declared of and concerning the same that is to say Upon trust that my Trustees shall sell call in collect and convert into money the said real and personal property at such time or times and in such manner as they shall think fit with power to postpone the sale calling in or conversion of the whole or any part or parts of the said property during such period as they shall think proper and to retain the same or any part thereof in its actual form of investment without being responsible for loss And I direct that the income of such part of the same premises as for the time being shall remain unsold shall as well during the first year after my death as afterwards be applied as if the same were income arising from investments hereinafter directed to be made of the proceeds of sale thereof and that no reversionary or other property not actually producing income shall be treated as producing income for the purposes of this my Will ;

Payment
of debts.

(2) My Trustees shall out of the moneys to arise from the sale calling in and conversion of or forming part of my said real and personal property pay my funeral and testamentary expenses and debts and the legacies given by this my Will or any codicil hereto and make provision for the payment of any annuities hereby or by any codicil hereto bequeathed by me and so that in relation to such payments the rule of equity known as the rule in *Allhusen* v. *Whittell* shall be disregarded ;

(3) My Trustees shall at their discretion invest the residue of the said moneys in or upon any of the investments hereby authorised with power to vary or transpose such investments for or into others of a nature hereby authorised.

6. (1) MY Trustees shall stand possessed of the residue of the said money and the investments and property for the time being representing the same (hereinafter called " the Trust Fund ") Upon Trust for such of the Beneficiaries hereinafter defined at such respective ages or times and in such shares and upon such trusts for the benefit of the Beneficiaries or any of them and upon such conditions and with such restrictions and in such manner as my Trustees [being at least two in number] may by Deed or Deeds revocable or irrevocable at any time or times before the Determining Day hereinafter defined (but without offending against the perpetuity rule) appoint ;

(2) In default of and subject to any such appointment as aforesaid my Trustees shall until the Determining Day pay or apply the annual income of the Trust Fund as it arises to or for the maintenance or support or otherwise for the benefit of all or any one or more exclusively of the other or others of the Beneficiaries for the time being in existence and ascertainable as my Trustees in their absolute discretion without being liable to account for the exercise of the same think fit Provided That until the expiration of the period of twenty-one years after my death my Trustees may in their discretion instead of paying or applying the annual income as aforesaid accumulate the same or any part thereof in the way of compound interest by investing the same and the resulting income thereof in the investments authorised by this my Will and shall hold such accumulations as part of the capital of the Trust Fund But so that however my Trustees may apply those accumulations or any part thereof as if they were income arising in the then current year ;

(3) In default of and subject to the powers and trusts aforesaid my Trustees shall until the Determining Day pay or apply the annual income of the Trust Fund to or for the benefit of such of the following persons as shall from time to time be living in such shares as they shall think fit namely my said wife my said sister ——, ——, ——, ——, ——, ——, ——, and my issue (whether children or remoter issue) and shall on and after the Determining Day stand possessed of the Trust Fund both

as to capital and income Upon Trust for such of the said persons as shall be then living in such shares as my Trustees shall in their absolute discretion think fit and subject thereto in equal shares absolutely;

Definitions.

(4) In this clause of my Will unless the context otherwise requires:

(a) " The Determining Day " means the day on which expires the period of twenty-one years after the death of the survivor of my said wife and the descendants of His late Majesty King George the Fifth living at my death [or the period of sixty years after my death whichever period shall first expire], and

(b) " The Beneficiaries " means my said wife my said sister ——, ——, ——, ——, ——, all the issue of myself or of my said sister who may be born before the Determining Day the spouse or widow or widower of any such issue and any child or children adopted by any such issue and the issue of any child or children so adopted and any of the following charities namely ——, ——, ——, ——, ——, but shall nevertheless not include any person being a Trustee of this my Will or in respect of the Trust Fund.

This clause is designed to create a discretionary trust for as long a period as possible in favour of a wide class, with a view to minimising the estate duty which may be payable on the deaths of the various beneficiaries. Such trusts are bound to give rise to difficulties of drafting and each case should be carefully considered on its own particular facts.

Generally, a discretionary trust in favour of a specified class is valid as long as the discretion is incapable of being exercised outside the perpetuity period: *Re Coleman* [1936] Ch. 528; where such a trust exists there cannot be any passing of any interest in the trust fund except on the death of the last but one and the last of the class to die, and on each of those deaths the whole fund passes. Furthermore, although as a general rule trustees under a discretionary trust have no power to retain any income in any year, but must pay the whole out to some or all of the beneficiaries, it is possible for the first twenty-one years after the death of the testator to direct accumulations of the whole or part of the income: Law of Property Act, 1925, s. 164 (1) (b).

It occasionally happens, however, that a testator wishes to stretch a discretionary trust so as to include a class of persons who are unascertainable at his death. Here it is important to remember that a trust in favour of uncertain objects is void (*cf. Re Astor* [1952] Ch. 534) while a mere power in favour of uncertain objects may be valid, provided it is not a " power coupled with a trust "; this proviso means that the power must allow the donee to exercise it in favour of a member of the class of beneficiaries or to refrain from exercising it at all: see *ante,* p. 185. For the purposes of drafting the safest way is to ensure that, after the power in favour of a wide, fluctuating class, there comes in default of appointment a trust in favour of a definite class. It is also as well to separate carefully the trusts of income and of capital, and to permit the trustees to appoint parts of the capital, if they see fit, before the end of the discretionary period. Further, a trustee should not be capable of becoming a beneficiary.

The method adopted in this precedent is to set out clauses as follows:

(1) An overriding power to appoint capital in favour of a wide, fluctuating class;

(2) a discretionary trust to accumulate income for twenty-one years;

(3) a discretionary trust to apply income in favour of the wide class for a long perpetuity period;

(4) a trust of income, in default of exercise of the discretion, for a defined class;

(5) a trust of capital at the end of the long perpetuity period, and in default of (1) above, in favour of the defined class.

There seems to be no reason why the wide class should not include charities, or even, as in *Re Gestetner Settlement* [1953] Ch. 672, persons who for the time being hold certain offices, such as directors of a family company.

Reference should also be made to the precedents of discretionary settlements, *ante,* pp. 205 and 213 and to the notes appended thereto.

Investment. **7.** Money liable to be invested under this my Will may be invested or applied in the purchase of or at interest upon the security of such stocks funds securities or other investments or property of whatsoever nature and wheresoever situate (including the purchase of any land or dwelling house of whatever tenure and whether situate in the United Kingdom or elsewhere for use as a residence and the improvement of any land or dwelling house so bought) and whether involving liabilities or not or upon such personal credit with or without security as my Trustees shall in their absolute discretion think fit and to the intent that my Trustees shall have the same powers in all respects as if they were absolute owners beneficially entitled.

Appropria-
tion.

8. MY Trustees may as well after as during the administration of my estate exercise the power of appropriation conferred by the Administration of Estates Act 1925 without obtaining any of the consents required by that Act.

9. ANY Executor or Trustee of this my Will being a solicitor or other person engaged in any profession or business shall be entitled to be paid all usual professional or proper charges for business transacted time expended and acts done by him or any partner of his in connexion with the trusts hereof including acts which any executor or trustee not being in any profession or business could have done personally.

Trustees
to retain
directorship
fees.

10. ANY Executor or Trustee of this my Will may act as an officer or employee of any company shares or debentures of which form part of the investments for the time being subject to any of the trusts and powers declared in this my Will or as an officer or employee of any subsidiary of any such company and may retain for himself any remuneration which he may receive as such officer or employee notwithstanding that any voting or other rights attached to any such shares or debentures may have been instrumental either alone or in conjunction with other matters or by reason of their non-exercise in procuring for him his position as such officer or employee or that his qualification for any such position may be constituted in part or in whole by the holding of any such shares or debentures.

This clause may sometimes be useful. Unless it is included, a trustee must account to the beneficiaries for fees of directorships which he obtains by virtue of the rights vested in him as the registered holder of the shares: *Re Gee* [1948] Ch. 284; *Re Llewellin* [1949] Ch. 225.

Remunera-
tion.

11. ANY Trustee acting as Trustee in respect of the Trust Fund shall be entitled to retain and be paid out of the annual income thereof as remuneration for acting as such Trustee the annual sum of £—— or one ——th part of the annual income of the property for the time being subject to the powers and trusts hereinbefore declared concerning the Trust Fund whichever shall be the lesser sum.

This provision is considered as a legacy from the testator, but at the same time may, as between the trustee and the Crown, be considered as " earned income," being " income arising in respect of any remuneration from any office or employment of profit," within the meaning of section 525 of the Income Tax Act, 1952: *Dale* v. *I. R. C.* [1954] A.C. 11; 34 Tax Cas. 468. On the death of any trustee, no estate duty will be payable in respect of the cesser of his interest in the income of the trust fund, because his interest was " only an interest as holder of an office " within the meaning of section 2 (1) (b) of the Finance Act, 1894: see *Public Trustee* v. *I. R. C.* (*Re Arnholz*) [1960] A.C. 398.

Indemnity.   **12.** [Indemnity, see *ante*, p. 470.]

New trustees.   **13.** My wife shall during her life have power to appoint a new trustee or new trustees of this my Will.

PRECEDENT NO. 54

Gift of Life Interest to Widow of Testator with Power to Maintain a Stated Income by Resort to Capital

It has been pointed out on page 459 that a power to make up the income of a fund to a stated annual sum by resort to capital has the effect of making the sums so paid liable to income tax, which the trustees will be obliged to deduct and account for under section 170 of the Income Tax Act, 1952. Consequently power to apply periodical sums of capital must be carefully worded. Precedent number 52 contains such a power designed to avoid the extra burden of tax, but refers only to emergencies. The following precedent is wider in scope, but it is admitted that the Revenue may possibly claim that the trustees should deduct tax; it is nevertheless the best that can be done where a fixed annual sum is aimed at, and any claim for tax should be resisted. It may be advisable to declare each payment to the tax inspector before the end of the year of assessment in which it is made and obtain his concurrence, that there is no obligation to deduct standard rate tax.

Life interest.   **1.** My Trustees shall stand possessed of the Trust Fund Upon Trust to pay the income thereof to my wife during her life and subject thereto, etc. . . . .

Power to pay capital.   **2.** Notwithstanding the trusts hereinbefore declared concerning the Trust Fund my Trustees may at any time or times in their uncontrolled discretion raise out of the capital of the Trust Fund and pay or transfer to my wife such capital sums or sum not exceeding in the aggregate the sum of £x as they shall think fit. Provided that the aggregate of the sums so paid or transferred in any financial year shall not exceed the difference between the income of my wife from the Trust Fund during the said financial year after deduction therefrom of income tax at the standard rate for the time being and the sum of £y.

It will be observed that no account is taken of reliefs and allowances to which the widow may be entitled. The reason for this is that if she has other income, it will be troublesome to assess the proportion of such reliefs and allowances properly ascribable to the life interest.

PRECEDENT No. 55

Gift of Life Interest to Widow of Testator with Power to Lend Capital

Life interest.
1. MY Trustees shall stand possessed of the Trust Fund Upon Trust to pay the income thereof to my wife during her life as long as she remains my widow and subject thereto, *etc., etc.*

Power to lend.
2. NOTWITHSTANDING the trusts hereinbefore declared concerning the Trust Fund my Trustees may if in any financial year during the life of my wife so long as she shall remain my widow the income of my wife from the Trust Fund after deduction of income tax at the standard rate for the time being in force shall be less than the sum of £x raise out of the capital of the Trust Fund and lend to my wife the difference between the said income after such deduction and the said sum of £x or such lesser sum as they shall see fit upon my wife undertaking in writing that such sums as may be thus paid to her shall be recoverable by my Trustees from her together with simple interest thereon at the rate of five per cent. per annum or such other rate as shall be agreed Provided that my wife shall not be obliged to repay any such moneys so lent or any interest thereon during her widowhood but may postpone repayment of the same until after her death or remarriage and Provided also that in assessing the sum which may in any financial year be lent to

> my wife in pursuance of this power the interest upon any
> moneys previously lent shall not be taken into account
> as income of the Trust Fund.

The above precedent is designed to reduce to a minimum the risk
of tax becoming payable on the sums of capital advanced to the widow,
and to reduce also the estate duty which may be payable on her death
on her full estate. It may be used in addition to the more usual
clause which gives an absolute discretion to the trustees to apply any
sums of capital for the benefit of the widow that they shall think fit.

PRECEDENT No. 56

Legacy of Investments for the Benefit of a Son of the Testator

Sometimes a testator finds it difficult to decide whether to give a
legacy to an adult child absolutely, or, particularly where the child is
married and has young children, to provide for these children. Sometimes the testator thinks it possible that the child will be otherwise well
provided for, so that any increase in his or her investment income would
increase the burden of taxation without conferring a comparable benefit.
Where this is so, provision for the infant children of the child may in
fact prove more beneficial to the child, especially if income is made
available for maintenance and education. On the other hand, it may
not be possible to plan ahead with sufficient certainty; and in any event,
the testator may wish to give his child a reasonable degree of control
over the legacy.

This precedent of a clause in a will is designed to give the son of the
testator something approaching complete control over the investments,
which are settled in such a way that the income may be used for the
maintenance and education of the son's infant children without being
deemed to be his income for tax purposes. When all the children are
adult, the son becomes absolutely entitled to the legacy, subject only
to a general power, or alternatively the children are entitled. If the son
should desire at any time to dispose of the legacy in any way, for
example by settling it on his children, he and one other trustee may
employ the general power in subclause (1) (a) for this purpose. If clause
(1) (c) is adapted so that the son takes the ultimate interest then in the
event of the power in clause (1) (a) being exercised it is considered that
the Revenue would be able to contend that it constitutes a gift of investments by the son within the meaning of section 38 (2) (a) of the Customs
and Inland Revenue Act, 1881 (see Finance Act, 1894, s. 22 (2) (b);
Att.-Gen. v. Farrell [1930] 1 K.B. 539; [1931] 1 K.B. 81), with resultant liability to estate duty in the event of the son dying within five

years of the power being exercised. But if clause (1) (c) is adapted for the benefit of the children, it is considered that the exercise of the power in clause (1) (a) is not a gift by him except of his reversionary interest (if any) in the legacy.

Legacy to trustees.

(1) I BEQUEATH all the shares in X. X. Ltd. to which I shall be entitled at my death unto my said son (hereinafter in this clause called " my son ") and A. B. upon trust to sell or retain the same with power to invest the proceeds of sale in any investments authorised by this my Will and to stand possessed of the same and the investments for the time being representing the same hereinafter called " my son's legacy " upon the following trusts namely :—

Power of appointment.

(a) upon such trusts in favour of such person or persons as my son and any one other person being at the time a trustee of my son's legacy shall by deed or deeds appoint and in default thereof and subject thereto

Discretionary trust.

(b) during such time as there shall be living one or more infant children of my son upon trust to pay or apply the income of my son's legacy to or towards the maintenance education advancement or benefit of all or any one or more of them my son and his said infant child or children in such manner as the trustees of my son's legacy for the time being shall think fit; and subject thereto

Trust for son or children.

(c) upon trust for [my son absolutely.] [such of the children of my son whenever born as shall during my lifetime or after my death attain the age of twenty-one years and if more than one in equal shares.]

" Children."

(2) IN this clause of my Will references to children of my son extend to children adopted by him either alone or jointly with another person under any order of any court having jurisdiction but do not include children born or so adopted after the age of twenty-one years shall have been attained by the first child of my son to attain that age.

New trustees.

(3) MY son shall have the power of appointing new trustees of my son's legacy.

PRECEDENT NO. 57

Various Annuities Bequeathed by Will

Where an annuity is left by will, the effects of estate duty and income tax require careful study, if unexpected results are to be avoided. The following precedent will, it is hoped, give some guidance on the points which require particular attention.

Annuity
liable to be
partially
adeemed.

1. I BEQUEATH to my daughter Jane if she shall survive me more than one year an annuity of £—— for her life the same to be considered as accruing from day to day but to be paid by equal half-yearly instalments in advance the first payment to be made at the end of one year after my death And I direct that if after the execution of this my Will and before my death I shall by any bond covenant agreement settlement purchase or gift other than by testamentary disposition provide for the payment of any annuity or of the income of any property or fund to my said daughter during her life or any lesser period the same shall operate (after deduction of any estate duty that may be payable thereout consequent upon my death) either wholly or proportionately as an ademption of the annuity hereby bequeathed.

Normally a gift of an annuity without express directions as to payment takes effect as from the death of the testator, although the first payment is not made until the end of the first year after death. To avoid the risk that the annuitant will die before receiving a penny of the annuity, and thus cause a further claim for estate duty, it is advisable to make the annuity contingent on survival of the annuitant for one year: if the annuitant dies before receiving any of the annuity, no estate duty will be payable; moreover, by the end of that year, it will probably have been possible for the trustees to make some provision to pay the annuity in such a way as to avoid the charge to estate duty on the annuitant's death: how this provision is made appears later, in paragraph 4 of this precedent.

It will be remembered that the liability for estate duty on the death of the annuitant arises under section 2 (1) (b) of the Finance Act, 1894, and that the rate of duty payable varies with the aggregate value of the annuitant's estate. Accordingly, if the person to whom the testator wishes to bequeath an annuity is likely to leave a substantial estate, the draftsman should seriously consider how to ensure that the least possible duty may be paid.

A separate question which arises on paragraph 1, above, is the provision of annuities by the testator during his lifetime. The testator is well advised, once he has decided to provide for a particular person by means of an annuity payable as from the testator's death, to purchase from a company dealing in such matters a small annuity, or a series of small annuities, for the person concerned, the idea being that the amount given by the will then represents a maximum to which the annuities given *inter vivos* are made up. Small savings of duty may be made in this way, and furthermore the saving may be made within any time before death: see *ante*, p. 455.

The testator should also consider the possible economy that may be effected by purchasing an annuity from a company during his lifetime, so that the annuity is a " separate estate " and thus not aggregated with the rest of the assets. This topic has already been dealt with on p. 456 in this chapter.

Settled
annuity.

 2. (1) I BEQUEATH to my sister Anne and to my said sister's daughter Elizabeth during their joint lives and the life of the survivor of them an annuity of £——;

 (2) The said annuity shall be considered as accruing from day to day but shall be paid by equal half-yearly instalments the first payment to be made at the end of six months from my death;

 (3) The payments of the said annuity shall be made to my said sister during her lifetime and after her death to her said daughter if she survives.

Where it is desired to settle an annuity, so as to be paid to B for life, then to A for life, care should be taken not to create two separate annuities each charged on the estate, but to create a single annuity to last from the testator's death for the lives of A and B and the survivor, and then to create life interests in favour of A and B respectively out of this continuing annuity. By adopting this latter course, the draftsman ensures that the estate duty which becomes payable on A's death is leviable under section 1 of the Finance Act, 1894, on the value of the annuity passing to B; if separate annuities are created there arises the heavier burden of duty on the " slice " principle under section 2 (1) (b): see *Re Duke of Norfolk* [1950] Ch. 467; *Re Tapp* [1959] Ch. 443. Where an annuity for joint lives and the life of the survivor is created by an instrument *inter vivos* different considerations apply: see *Re Payton* [1951] Ch. 1081, discussed *ante*, at p. 381.

Annuities:
free of
income tax;

 3. I BEQUEATH the following annuities:

 (a) to my former servant George during his lifetime an annuity of £—— free of income tax;

This gives George an annuity free both of income tax and surtax: see *Re Reckitt* [1932] 2 Ch. 144. The trustees will thus be obliged to pay the sum stated without deduction; they will be considered as having already deducted income tax at the standard rate. But if George is entitled to reliefs and allowances, he will probably be able to claim a refund of tax from the Revenue in respect of the annuity. It has been decided, however, that the annuitant is accountable to the trustees for that proportion that is attributable to the annuity of all reliefs and allowances to which he is entitled from time to time: *Re Pettit* [1922] 2 Ch. 765; *Re Lyons* [1952] Ch. 129. Moreover, the annuitant is bound to claim his refund and is in effect a trustee of his right to do so: *Re Kingcome* [1936] Ch. 566. Therefore an annuity of the present type will give rise to difficult calculations between the trustees and the annuitant.

A gift of " such an amount as will after the deduction of tax leave in the hands of the annuitant the sum of so much " will still make the annuitant liable to account: *Re Maclennan* [1939] Ch. 750.

free of income tax but not surtax;	(b) to my friend William during his lifetime an annuity of £—— free of income tax but not surtax;

This is the same as the preceding except that it is not free of surtax.

of a clear sum.	(c) to my aunt Mary during her lifetime an annuity of such sum as after deduction of income tax at the standard rate for the time being in force shall amount to £——.

This is generally the most advantageous way of giving a tax-free annuity. The trustees deduct tax at source on such a sum as will after such deduction leave the sum bequeathed; this is paid to the annuitant, who need not repay any part of the reliefs and allowances which she may be able to claim: *Re Jones* [1933] Ch. 842.

Payment of the annuities.	4. My Trustees shall have power to secure the proper payment of the annuities bequeathed by this my Will or by any codicil hereto by any of the methods following (or partly by one and partly by another) and so that my residuary estate shall until the payment is so secured be charged with each such annuity but after the payment is so secured shall be discharged therefrom;
	(a) My Trustees shall set apart and invest in their names or under their control in any of the investments by this my Will authorised with power to vary the same a sum the income whereof when invested shall be sufficient at the time of such

> investment to pay the said annuity and to pay the same accordingly with power to resort to the capital of the appropriated fund whenever the income shall be insufficient;
>
> (b) My Trustees shall obtain from —— or from —— or from the said —— and —— jointly and severally a covenant (and whether with or without such personal guarantees and sureties as my Trustees shall think fit) to pay to themselves the said annuity or any greater annuity with provision for reduction for prompt payment to the amount of the said annuity;
>
> (c) My Trustees shall purchase an annuity from the Government or from any public Company in the name of the annuitant to satisfy the annuity bequeathed.

These three methods of securing payment of the annuity are intended to give the trustees a wide scope, so as to secure payment in the way most advantageous.

(a) The first has the disadvantage that, if the income of the fund proves inadequate and recourse is therefore had to the capital, the payments of capital so made are considered as income and bear tax accordingly. Further, on the death of the annuitant, a charge for estate duty, for which the trustees are accountable, arises under section 2 (1) (b) of the Finance Act, 1894; in order to determine the rate of duty applicable, the " slice " of the capital set aside to secure the annuity which by its income produces the annuity is assessed and is aggregated with the other property of the annuitant.

(b) This gives the trustees power to purchase the annuity from the persons whose names are left blank, that is to say, the residuary beneficiary or beneficiaries under the will.

Where all the parties are *sui juris* and agree it is of course possible to exchange an annuity under the will for an annuity paid by a residuary legatee personally. The disadvantage to such a scheme arises from section 43 of the Finance Act, 1940; the surrender of the annuity is a determination thereof " by surrender, assurance, divesting, forfeiture or in any other manner," and so section 43 (1) (b) applies and the annuity is included in the property passing on the death of the annuitant to the same extent as if the surrender had never taken place; moreover, since the covenanted annuity is given in exchange for the surrender, there is a benefit reserved by contract, so that exemption does not arise even after five years.

Where, however, the annuity given by the will is left unchanged, but the property on which it is secured is changed, a different situation arises. The annuity does not determine under section 43, above. It becomes an annuity payable by the trustees, secured by a covenant given to the trustees by the residuary legatee. Since, therefore, when, on the death of the annuitant, a claim for duty arises, the property out of which the annuity was payable has itself disappeared, there is nothing which can be deemed to pass; consequently no claim, it is submitted, can arise. The principles here applied were laid down by the Court of Appeal in *Re Beit* [1952] Ch. 53.

It will be appreciated that recourse to this arrangement can only be possible where there is an adult residuary legatee absolutely entitled who will agree to the trustees making what is really an investment of the residue in his personal covenant. Where this is not so, paragraph 4 (b) should be omitted.

A rather simpler arrangement is for the testator to direct that the residuary legatee shall be obliged, before having the assets comprised in the residue transferred to him, to execute a covenant to secure an annuity to such and such a person. The annuitant thereby gets his annuity direct from the residuary legatee and not from the testator.

(c) This again is a convenient method of avoiding the loss caused by estate duty on the annuitant's death.

APPENDIX

THE Royal Commission on the Taxation of Profits and Income considered the problem of tax avoidance and made certain recommendations in their Final Report (Cmd. 9474). While questions of estate duty were not considered by the Commission, certain of their remarks and recommendations with regard to income tax and surtax may, it is felt, form a useful appendix to this book.

Chapter 6 of the Report deals with covenants, and the opening paragraphs are as follows:

COVENANTS AS TRANSFERS OF INCOME

144. The original system of income tax was constructed on the principle that annual payments made under covenant should be treated for tax purposes as the income of the recipient and not as the income of the payer. It seems natural enough to regard such payments as income of the recipient; but it is not so obvious that it is in accordance with correct principle to treat that fact as warranty for regarding the taxable income of the payer as reduced by an equivalent amount. For an income is taxed, generally speaking, without allowance for the fact that part of it is regularly paid over to this or that recipient or for this or that purpose, as rent or wages; and there is only a fine distinction between a charge on income, which is treated as reducing it, and an application of income, which is not. In some aspects it is important that the line should be drawn correctly.

145. According to the original conception, which is reflected in the provisions of the Income Tax Act of 1842, any annual payment, whether payable by virtue of a charge on the property of the payer or merely as a personal debt or obligation by virtue of a contract, was to be treated as income of the recipient and not as income of the payer, provided that it was payable " out of profits or gains brought into charge to tax." The machinery of deduction at source was employed, the whole of the income of the payer being assessed to tax in the first place without allowance for the annual payment but with a statutory right in him to recoup himself by deducting and retaining tax at the standard rate (as it became) when he made his payment. For the purposes of any reliefs or allowances due to the recipient deduction at the standard rate was merely provisional and he was entitled to claim an adjustment of tax from the Revenue according to his true marginal rate.

146. It has never been very clear precisely what constituted " annual payments . . . as a personal debt or obligation by virtue of any contract " for the purpose of this rule. It is fairly obvious that they did not include remuneration for services rendered, if only because the system required such payments to be taxed as income of the recipient by direct assessment and not by the process of deduction at source. Nor did they cover such payments as would enter into a computation of the profits of the recipient's trade, those profits again being taxable by direct assessment, under Case I of Schedule D. Moreover, the distinction between a charge on income and an application of income would have become almost meaningless if payments of this kind could have ranked as deductions from the income of the payer. Since we are not concerned to arrive at any precise definition of annual payment, it is enough to say that the kind of payment under contract which fell within the rule was of the nature of an annuity and that the class did not extend to payments in exchange for value received from the recipient. It is just because the payments in question arise from obligations voluntarily undertaken that they are habitually made in the form of covenants, a covenant being a promise made under seal. For the law treated a promise under the seal of a promisor as a binding obligation even if voluntarily

undertaken without value received in exchange, whereas a bare promise not so secured had no obligatory force.

Subsequently, the Report deals with existing limitations on the use of covenants and examines the possibility of further limitations. In this respect the following paragraphs are of interest:

LIMITATION OF TRANSFERS BY COVENANT

153. The remaining question is as to the adequacy of the present limiting conditions. We took the opportunity of asking the Board to survey the question for us and to make any further proposals that their experience of the matter suggested to be necessary. Their conclusion was that, although this sort of question had to be kept under constant review, it was not necessary at the present time to propose any further conditions.

154. We have decided, however, in the light of the information that they have given us, to recommend two measures, one of substance and one of procedure. In doing so, we recognise that in theory there is no limit to the number of qualifying conditions that could be laid down. There is no difficulty in thinking of possible lines of further restriction. For instance, covenants in favour of minor grandchildren or nephews and nieces might be excluded as well as covenants in favour of minor unmarried children, as at present: all relatives, even if adult, might be excluded: or arbitrary figures might be fixed to limit the amount of income that could qualify as a transfer under any one deed or all deeds by any one covenantor. But, if we proceed on the main assumption which we have accepted that the recognition of these instruments is not objectionable, it seems to us that the only limitations that ought to be imposed are those which experience may show to be required to prevent abuse of the system.

155. It appears that in recent years there has been an increasing tendency for covenantors to resort to the use of covenants for the purpose of discretionary trusts. Under this type of deed a covenant is made with trustees constituted for the purpose and the trustees are given the duty of distributing the annual payments that they receive among any one or more of a number of named beneficiaries and in such shares as they may decide. The trustees thus have full discretion to appropriate the money to one or more beneficiaries in one year and to others in another year and to vary the shares themselves from year to year. Sometimes the named beneficiaries are charities, sometimes named individuals; sometimes both classes are included. Presumably the main attraction of a covenant in this form is that the covenantor is able to keep an effective voice in the destination of the income each year as between one beneficiary and another, assuming that the trustees whom he has chosen are prepared to consult him as to the exercise of their discretion: in any event the settlor achieves a reduction of his taxable income without providing more than what may be in substance a series of isolated acts of benevolence towards persons or objects which vary from year to year.

156. We think that a disposition of this kind ought not to be allowed to rank for tax purposes. It achieves what is required for an effective transfer of income in the sense that the whole income is alienated from the covenantor for the requisite period, without any benefit or chance of benefit being retained for himself. But it fails to secure another thing which is, in our view, implicit in the idea of a genuine transfer of income when effected by annual payments under covenant, namely, that the income in question becomes the regular income of someone else for a commensurate period. Under these discretionary trusts there are no real transferees of the income except the trustees, who have no beneficial interest or ownership: the recipients of the payments have no individual title to the income for any definite period, they are mere objects of the trustees' discretion with no certainty that any one of them will have any particular share or even continuity of payment at all.

157. We recommend that a new statutory provision should be added to the code for the purpose of rendering covenants of this kind nugatory for tax purposes. Payments under such a deed should not be regarded as deductions from the income of the covenantor or as taxable income of the recipients. Care will have to be taken in

the drafting of any such provision to see that it does not go further than the mischief of the case requires. We do not desire, for instance, to interfere with the operation of a covenant in a marriage settlement in usual form under which the benefit of covenanted payments passes to different persons upon the event of death, remarriage, etc., or again, a covenant in a settlement which contains a life interest protected from alienation. Savings with a similar purpose are to be found in some of the existing statutory restrictions.[1]

158. The other recommendation that we wish to make relates to covenants for annual payments to relatives of the covenantor. At present the only control over these is the provision that disqualifies covenants in favour of an unmarried child under 21. Covenants in favour of adult children or other relatives were in use long before they attained any particular significance for the purposes of tax. Even under present conditions we see no public advantage in discouraging them. But at the same time the very circumstances of the family connection make it possible for abuses of the system to grow up and for covenants which satisfy all the legal requirements of a transfer of income to conceal private understandings by virtue of which the benefit of the income never really leaves, or is somehow returned to, the covenantor. Understandings of this kind are not recorded in writing—they do not need to be; nor are they discussed as bargains which would be capable of enforcement in a court of law—again there is no need for a legal sanction for a promise of which neither party even contemplates the failure.

159. We feel little doubt that a number of such understandings do exist and that they are no better than a fraud on the system. Obviously the Revenue authorities have little opportunity of detecting them or of analysing their exact status in law. It is unfortunate that the phrase "gentleman's agreement" seems to have obtained some currency in this connection. The essence of a gentleman's agreement is that the honour of the parties to it affords so certain a security for its strict fulfilment that it is unnecessary to inquire whether it is clothed in the form that would be requisite if a court of law were to be resorted to for its enforcement. It seems singularly inappropriate to find that this phrase is sometimes invoked to describe a family understanding which both parties fully intend to give effect to but which, to attain a tax advantage to which they are not properly entitled, they succeed in persuading themselves that they regard as "merely moral."

160. The extreme remedy for the danger of abuse in the field of covenants between members of a family would be to decline any recognition of them at all as transfers of income. We do not propose this, because we do not think that the circumstances justify it. While the danger of abuse is obvious and it is a reasonable certainty that some exists, the nature of the case makes it impossible to measure its extent : and, on the other hand, we have no doubt that in a great many cases a covenant of this kind in favour of an adult child or other relative constitutes a genuine provision for the covenantee and is as much a transfer of income as a covenant in favour of a stranger. To put such covenants under a special ban discriminates against the innocent in order to arrest what may be comparatively few guilty persons. What we recommend therefore is a procedural, not a substantive, change.

161. We think that every person who makes a claim for a deduction of annual payments from his total income for tax purposes on the ground that they are made under a covenant in favour of another individual should be required by statute, if that individual is a child, grandchild or other member of the covenantor's family, to produce formal declarations made by himself and by the recipient of the payments to the effect that there exists no agreement or understanding, whether or not regarded as having legal force, by virtue of which the benefit of any part of the payments is returned, directly or indirectly, to the covenantor or any other person designated by him. The declaration should be required to be made afresh for each year in which a claim is made. To require the production of such an affirmation each year is to place something of a burden on persons who make these covenants : but on the other hand we consider that, in view of the special circumstances, no less than this is required for the protection of the Revenue. "Family" is not a word of precise significance and some statutory definition will have to be adopted for the purpose of determining the range of the proposed requirement.

---

[1] See, for example, Income Tax Act, 1952, s. 405 (2) and s. 415 (2).

Tax avoidance is dealt with in Chapter 32, and upon the general question of what may be termed the ethics of tax avoidance the following paragraphs are of interest:

GENERAL CONSIDERATIONS

1015. Avoidance of tax is a problem that faces every tax system and is likely to continue to do so when rates of tax are high and the burden of tax is seen to have a major influence upon the affairs of business and upon every aspect of social and personal life. Not all systems attempt to solve the problem in the same way, nor is there necessarily any large measure of agreement as to what is involved in the idea of tax avoidance. But until some certainty is reached upon this question of definition, the question as to what sort of steps should be taken to prevent or correct it remains an aimless one. We propose therefore to begin by discussing the meaning of tax avoidance in so far as the phrase is used to denote something which a tax system should be concerned to control.

1016. It is usual to draw a distinction between tax avoidance and tax evasion. The latter denotes all those activities which are responsible for a person not paying the tax that the existing law charges upon his income. *Ex hypothesi* he is in the wrong, though his wrongdoing may range from the making of a deliberately fraudulent return to a mere failure to make his return or to pay his tax at the proper time. By tax avoidance, on the other hand, is understood some act by which a person so arranges his affairs that he is liable to pay less tax than he would have paid but for the arrangement. Thus the situation which he brings about is one in which he is legally in the right, except so far as some special rule may be introduced that puts him in the wrong.

1017. The treatment of tax avoidance in the United Kingdom would present much less difficulty if it were possible to assert as a matter of general principle that a man owes a duty not to alter the disposition of his affairs so as to reduce his existing liability to tax or, alternatively, for the purpose or for the main purpose or partly for the purpose of bringing this result about. But there is no such general principle, and we are satisfied that it neither could nor ought to be introduced. First, it is too wide to be maintainable. Suppose that a man, influenced by the high rate of taxation on his marginal income, distributes some of his investments among adult members of his family to whom he had been in the habit of paying allowances out of his taxed income. Suppose that another man, similarly influenced, sells some of his income-yielding investments in order to put the proceeds into National Savings Certificates. Is either a case in which the man ought to be treated for tax purposes as if his income was still what it was before the transaction? Secondly, there is no true equity to support such a general principle. Taken at any one moment of time the affairs of different taxpayers are arranged in the most various forms and the extent to which they respectively incur a burden of tax may vary correspondingly. There is no reason to assume that the situation of any one taxpayer at that moment is the fairest possible as between himself and others differently situated: and if there is not, it seems wrong to propound any principle that would have the effect of fixing each taxpayer in his situation, without allowing him any chance of so altering his arrangements as to reduce his liability to assessment.

1018. In fact the prevailing doctrine in this country tends in the opposite direction. To quote from a speech made in the House of Lords in a surtax appeal [2]: " Every man is entitled if he can to order his affairs so that the tax attaching under the appropriate Acts is less than it otherwise would be. If he succeeds in ordering them so as to secure this result, then, however unappreciative the Commissioners of Inland Revenue or his fellow tax-payers may be of his ingenuity, he cannot be compelled to pay an increased tax." This principle, well known, must not be understood as going beyond what it says. It does mean that the taxing authorities and the courts of law, if appealed to, must take the law and the legal consequences of transactions as they find them and that they have no mandate to impute to a man an income that he does not legally possess merely because he has dispossessed himself of it in order to save

---

[2] *Duke of Westminster* v. *C. I. R.* (1935) 19 T.C. 490 at p. 520, *per* Lord Tomlin.

tax. But it does not mean, on the other hand, that a man has any right violated or grievance inflicted if the statute law is so amended as to impute to him or to make it possible to impute to him for tax assessment an income larger than his legal one.[3] When these general principles are set against each other neither is seen to be of any assistance in identifying what are the special circumstances that justify such an imputation.

The Royal Commission made a number of recommendations, some of which have already received legislative recognition. The following extracts from the conclusions are some indication of what may be expected in some of the matters dealt with in this book:

SUMMARY OF RECOMMENDATIONS

1090. The principal recommendations we have made involving some change in the existing system may be briefly summarised as follows:—

Chapter 6—Covenants

(5) Covenants for the purpose of discretionary trusts should be rendered ineffective for tax purposes (para. 157).

(6) The maker of a covenant in favour of a child, grandchild or other member of his family should be required to produce each year formal declarations by himself and the beneficiary as to the absence of any agreement or understanding for the return, direct or indirect, of any part of the benefit (para. 161).

Chapter 7—Charities and charitable subscriptions

(7) A more restrictive definition of charity for tax purposes should be enacted (para. 175).

Chapter 32—Tax avoidance

(77) An expert body should be set up to examine whether any of the detailed provisions against tax avoidance are drawn too widely and whether they could be expressed with greater brevity and precision (para. 1029).

---

[3] See, for instance, the speech of Viscount Simon L.C. in *Latilla* v. *C. I. R.* (1943) 25 T.C. 107 at p. 117.

INDEX

ACCELERATION
of reversion, 266

ACCOUNTABILITY
of trustees, 286

ACCOUNTANT,
certificate by, 46

ACCUMULATION,
contingent trusts, 194
discretionary settlement, 194, 195
estate duty on, 90 *et seq.*
payments under covenant, 5 *et seq*
period allowed, 90, 194
policy of insurance, 93
portions, 172
power to, 194
reliefs on, 194
surtax avoided, 114, 194
two years, 91
will, in, 474

ACTUARIAL SPLIT
of trust fund, 273

ACTUARY,
employment of, 284, 311

ADDITION
to existing settlement, 220

ADMINISTRATION
of trusts, 193 *et seq.*

ADULT,
settlement upon, 169

ADULT CHILD,
covenant with, 32, 43

ADVANCEMENT,
or benefit, defined, 271
power of, 270
resettlement on, 272 *et seq.*

AGREEMENT,
separation, 54 *et seq.*

AGRICULTURAL LAND,
company owning, 202
estate duty, 200, 287
partnership farming, 331, 332

AGRICULTURAL PROPERTY
defined, 331

ALLOTMENT LETTER,
gift of, 119

ALLOWANCES,
covenant for maximum, 47, 50
lost by covenant, 17
lost by settlement, 110

ANNUAL PAYMENTS,
accumulated, 5
capital, distinguished, 12, 329
charitable income, 221
charity, to, 30
defined, 10 *et seq.*
fraction of income, 45
free of tax, 19, 452
surtax on, 15, 17

ANNUITY,
aggregation, 456
estate duty on, 380
free of tax, 19 *et seq.*, 452 *et seq.*
insurance and, 254
joint lives, 327, 483
partnership, 322 *et seq.*
sale of life interest for, 296
small, reliefs, 455
unenforceable, 324
will, in, 452 *et seq.*, 482 *et seq.*

APPLICATIONS TO COURT
to vary trusts, 276 *et seq.*

APPOINTMENT,
power exercised, 293

APPORTIONMENT,
surtax, 197

APPROPRIATION,
power of, 162, 209

ARREARS
of annual payment, 15

ART,
purchase of works of, 288

ASSETS VALUE,
estate duty, 98, 198, 199, 204

ASSIGNMENT
of share in firm, 359

ASSOCIATED OPERATIONS
benefit reserved, 86

BANK
as trustee, 76
fraud on power by, 273

BANKRUPTCY,
covenant until, 46

493

CONTROL OF BORROWING
redeemable shares, 198

COURT,
jurisdiction to vary trusts, 276 *et seq.*

COVENANT,
adult, with, 32
bankruptcy until, 46
capital asset bought by, 30, 359
charity, with, 30, 39
child of covenantor, 6, 28
discretionary, 5
employee, 29, 414
estate duty and, 25
extension of, 42
free of surtax, 24
free of tax, 19
grandchildren, for, 33
monthly sums, 26
payments accumulated, 5
pre-war, 24
revocable, 3
Royal Commission, 487 *et seq.*
servant, for, 29
seven years, 2
stamp on, 5 *et seq.*
substituted, 41

CROSS-REMAINDERS,
clause for, 143

DAMAGES
for dismissal, 385

DECONTROL
of controlled company, 201, 203

DEDUCTION OF TAX,
covenant, 13
failure to make, 18

DEED OF COVENANT,
form of, 1

DEED OF SEPARATION,
form of, 64

DEFEASANCE
removed, estate duty, 151

DEPENDANTS
defined, 426, 427, 439
pensions for, 431

DIMINISH,
power to, 103

DIRECTION,
surtax, 197

DIRECTOR,
beneficiary, 215
controlling, pension, 204, 378, 380
service agreement, 383, 388
trustee, 156

DIRECTOR CONTROL
of company, 203

DISAPPEARING TRICK,
disappeared, 94

DISCLAIMER OF LEGACY,
effects, 269, 298

DISCLAIMER OF LIFE INTEREST,
effects, 269
precedent, 298

DISCRETION,
exercise by majority, 210
exercise of, 195
objects of, 185

DISCRETIONARY COVENANT,
Finance Act, 1958...5
form of, 36 *et seq.*

DISCRETIONARY SETTLEMENT,
accumulation of income, 194
addition to, 220
administration of, 193 *et seq.*
charity, for, 221
children of settlor, 188
generally, 181 *et seq.*
income of, taxed as settlor's, 104
objects of, 183 *et seq.*
precedents of, 205 *et seq.*
records of, 193
requirements for, 181 *et seq.*
wife of settlor, 183, 190
will, in, 471 *et seq.*

DIVORCE,
maintenance on, 61 *et seq.*
variation of trusts on, 279

DOMICILE,
foreign, 288

DOUBTS,
trustees to determine, 155

DWELLING-HOUSE,
gift of, 84, 87
marriage gift, 243

EARNED INCOME
partnership, 314
relief lost, 15

EMOLUMENTS.
pension provision as, 365, 374

EMPLOYEES,
covenant with retired, 29, 414
gratuity to, 366
restrictive covenant, 366, 416
settlement for, 106, 213

EMPLOYMENT,
non-participating, 382

TIMBER,
  investment in, 287

TOP-HAT SCHEME,
  explanation, 375 *et seq.*
  letter to executive, 394
  rules of, 398

TRUST CORPORATION,
  charges of, 156
  use of, 76

TRUSTEE,
  accountable for estate duty, 286
  appointment of, 79
  assessment of, 109, 114
  bank as, 76
  beneficiary, 183
  company as, 76
  insurance by, 196, 257
  remove, power to, 80
  retirement of, 137
  selection of, 75
  settlor as, 77
  spouse of settlor as, 79

TUCKER COMMITTEE,
  report, 373 *et seq.*

UNCERTAINTY
  of objects, 187
  opinions of trustees, 188

UNENFORCEABLE PENSION
  partnership, 324
  service agreement, 386
  top-hat scheme, 408

VALUATION,
  assets, 97, 199
  evidence, required, 285
  market, 97, 198
  property passing, 94
  shares, 97 *et seq.*, 198, 199

VARIATION OF TRUSTS ACT,
  jurisdiction under, 279 *et seq.*
  parties to application, 282, 285
  protective trusts, 283

VESTED INTEREST
  given to infant, 138 *et seq.*

VOLUNTARY DISPOSITION,
  revocable stamp, 121
  stamp on, 116

WEEKLY SUM,
  covenant for, 26

WIDOW,
  annuity for, 323, 327
  estate duty, 191, 461
  life interest to, 457 *et seq.*
  loans to, 479
  object of discretion, 191
  partner's, annuity, 323
  paying estate duty, 461
  pension in service contract, 386, 393
  retirement benefit for, 378
  sale of share in firm, 359
  supplementary life interest, 459 *et seq.*
  wife not, 106

WIDOW'S PENSIONS,
  partnership, 323
  superannuation, 431
  top-hat, 392, 408
  unenforceable, 325, 387

WIFE,
  gift of house to, 87
  object of discretion, 183, 191
  separated, 192
  trustee, 79
  widow not, 106

WILLS,
  annuities in, 452 *et seq.*
  estate duty consideration, 448 *et seq.*
  settlements in, 471
  widow provided for, 457 *et seq.*

WOODLANDS,
  purchase of, 287

WORKS OF ART,
  investment in, 288

PRINTED IN GREAT BRITAIN

BY

THE EASTERN PRESS LTD.

OF LONDON AND READING